MODERN
POLITICAL SYSTEMS

7th Edition

MODERN POLITICAL SYSTEMS: EUROPE

ROY C. MACRIDIS *Editor*

PRENTICE HALL, ENGLEWOOD CLIFFS, NEW JERSEY 07632

Library of Congress Cataloging-in-Publication Data

Modern political systems: Europe / Roy C. Macridis, editor.—7th ed.
 p. cm.
 Includes bibliographic references.
 ISBN 0-13-595356-1
  1. Comparative government. 2. Europe—Politics and government.
I. Macridis, Roy C.
JF51.M6   1990
320.3′094—dc20   89-48658

Editorial/production supervision: *Edith Riker/Jeanne Sillay Jacobson*
Interior design: *Jeanne Sillay Jacobson*
Cover design: *Diane Saxe*
Manufacturing buyer: *Peter Havens*

Printed in the United States of America

10 9 8 7 6 5 4 3 2 1

ISBN 0-13-595356-1

PRENTICE-HALL INTERNATIONAL (UK) LIMITED, *London*
PRENTICE-HALL OF AUSTRALIA PTY. LIMITED, *Sydney*
PRENTICE-HALL CANADA INC., *Toronto*
PRENTICE-HALL HISPANOAMERICANA, S.A., *Mexico*
PRENTICE-HALL OF INDIA PRIVATE LIMITED, *New Delhi*
PRENTICE-HALL OF JAPAN, INC., *Tokyo*
SIMON & SCHUSTER ASIA PTE. LTD., *Singapore*
EDITORA PRENTICE-HALL DO BRASIL, LTDA., *Rio de Janeiro*

Contents

Preface

This seventh edition continues our efforts to translate recent developments in the field of comparative politics into a text adjusted to the needs and also the level and the background of the American undergraduate. It follows closely the overall plan of our previous editions. We have shortened the four major sections on Great Britain, France, the German Federal Republic, and the Soviet Union and expanded our coverage to include the Scandinavian and Mediterranean countries. There is also a special and revised section on the European Common Market.

All the authors in this volume have tried to adhere to the general view of politics we presented in previous editions—that the political system is a part of a larger system of social relations. We have therefore made a special effort to place politics and government institutions in their appropriate ideological, social, historical international, and economic settings.

For a book that began about thirty years ago, the infusion of young blood and new insights was an imperative. Professor Françoise de la Serre, a specialist on the European Common Market, assumed the sole responsibility for the section on the Common Market—its political and institutional developments in the light of the decisions made by the 12 members to fully integrate into a single market their economies by 1992. Professor Steven Burg, who contributed the section on Eastern Europe in the previous edition, is now the author of the section on the Soviet Union. Professor Thomas Lancaster is now the sole author of the Mediterranean section. Professor Dennis Kavanagh of the University of Nottingham and well known among American political scientists for his research and writing on British politics has written the section on Great Britain. Brent Smith has written the section on the German Federal Republic. I, therefore, while continuing to thank the old stalwarts—Professors Aspaturian, Finer and Karl W. Deutsch—extend here my most appreciative thanks to the newcomers.

Over a long period of time, Audrey Marshall of Prentice Hall has been of invaluable help to me in keeping some order in an undertaking where so many were involved and I wish to thank her warmly.

For this seventh edition, I am deeply grateful to Edie Riker of East End Publishing Services, Riverhead N.Y., for overseeing the entire production; to Sally Ann Bailey for copyediting; and to Jeanne Jacobson for production editing. They deserve a great deal of credit.

List of Contributors

STEVEN BURG is Associate Professor of Politics at Brandeis University. He has written numerous articles in professional journals on Soviet and East European politics and is the author of *Conflict and Cohesion in Socialist Yugoslavia* (Princeton University Press, Princeton, N.J., 1983).

FRANCIS G. CASTLES is Senior Research Fellow in Political Science at the Australian National University and was formerly Professor of Comparative Politics at the Open University in England. He has written books on Scandinavian political development and the growth of the welfare state in Australia and New Zealand. He is a leading figure in the area of comparative public policy research.

DENNIS KAVANAGH is Professor and Head of the Politics Department at the University of Nottingham, England. His most recent publications are *Thatcherism and British Politics* (Oxford University Press, 1987), *The British General Election of 1987* (Macmillan, 1988) and, with Peter Morris, *Consensus Politics From Attlee to Thatcher* (Blackwell, 1989).

THOMAS D. LANCASTER is Associate Professor in Political Science at Emory University. He is the author of a number of articles on Spain and the Mediterranean countries, co-editor of *Politics and Change in Spain* (Prager, 1985), and author of *Policy Stability and Democratic Change: Energy in Spain's Transition* (Pennsylvania State University Press, 1989).

ROY C. MACRIDIS is Professor of Politics at Brandeis University. He is the author of *French Politics in Transition—The Years After DeGaulle* (Winthrop, 1976); *Contemporary Ideologies* (Scott, Foresman and Co., 1988); *DeGaulle—Implacable Ally* (Harper Torch Paperbacks, 1968); Editor and Co-Author of *Foreign Policy in World Politics* (Prentice Hall, 1989), among many other publications and articles.

DIANE SAINSBURY is Assistant Director of the International Graduate School, University of Stockholm, where she teaches politics. She is the author of *Swedish Social Democratic Ideology and Electoral Politics 1944–1948* (1980), editor of *Democracy, State, and Justice* (1988), and guest editor of a special issue of the *European Journal of Political Research* on "Party Strategies and Party-Voter Linkages" (forthcoming).

FRANÇOISE DE LA SERRE is Senior Research Associate at the International Research Center of the National Foundation of Political Science, University of Paris, France. She has published many articles on the foreign policy of the European community and on European integration and political cooperation and the author of *La Grande Bretagne et la Communauté Européenne* (Paris, Presses Universitaires de France, 1987).

D. BRENT SMITH is Chief of the International and Interagency Affairs, NOAA/NESDIS—Harvard Ph.D., specializing in German Politics.

ROY C. MACRIDIS

1

Introduction

The subject of this text is European politics, with primary emphasis on the four major European nations: France, Great Britain, West Germany, and the Soviet Union. (Britain seems, at last, after joining the European Economic Community, to have become a part of Europe, but some may quibble about including the Soviet Union.) We also offer overviews of the Scandinavian countries; the European Economic Community (the "Common Market"—France, West Germany, Italy, Denmark, Belgium, Holland, Ireland, Britain, Luxembourg, Greece, and since January 1, 1986, Spain and Portugal); and countries in the Mediterranean area—Portugal, Spain, Italy, and Greece.

We hope to familiarize the beginning student with the respective historical backgrounds and political institutions of these countries. We also hope to initiate the student into a comparative study that seeks to identify similarities and differences and, if possible, explain them by presenting a common set of questions. What is the socioeconomic structure of a country? What are the relations between citizens and the elite? What are their respective political cultures? How do citizens make their demands known? How are the government structures set up, what functions do they perform, and how well?

The Soviet Union, Britain, France, and West Germany are by all standards "modern." So are the countries that comprise Scandinavia. The Mediterranean countries, on the other hand, have only recently been going through social, economic, and political modernization. We are, therefore, studying and comparing both highly developed systems and relatively underdeveloped even if modernizing ones.

Levels of modernization and also the rate of modernization have a direct impact upon political institutions and attitudes. In comparing the countries we shall discuss, we shall have to be particularly sensitive, therefore, to the relationship between socioeconomic forces and changes on the one hand

and political forms, attitudes, and institutions on the other.

THE ORGANIZING FRAMEWORK

Three basic "organizing ideas" provide a common framework for the study of the various political regimes we undertake in this volume: civil society, civic culture, and the state.

Civil Society

The term is commonly used to denote the array of groups and associations in the society—interest groups, educational associations, cultural associations, religious groups, and ethnic groups—and the manner in which they interact. How free are they? How do they make their demands known and how do they express their interests? How do they interact with governmental organizations and agencies? As societies modernize, interest groups and voluntary associations proliferate and assert themselves.

Civic Culture

The term "civic culture" is often used synonymously with "political tradition" or "political history." It is the set of values that shapes the attitude of the citizenry about their own role and about their relationship with the government. In their pioneer study, *Civic Culture*,[1] Almond and Verba identified three cultures—three types of relationships between individuals and their government: *a participant culture*, when the individuals freely interact with and participate in governmental decisions—through free elections, political parties, and lobbying; *a subject culture*, when individuals play little active role in governmental decisions but rather

submit to the government; and *a parochial culture*, when individuals are virtually separated from their government—they know little about it and have no positive attachments to it. In the modern or modernizing societies we are studying, including the Soviet Union and the Mediterranean, the civic culture is becoming increasingly participatory. The individuals and the associations and groups they form press increasingly for satisfaction of demands and for the development of institutional arrangements and mechanisms that will safeguard and legitimize their inputs. In all our discussions we pay particular attention to the evolving participatory mechanisms—groups, associations, and political parties.

The State

The state (and governments) is the ultimate repository of the decision-making authority. Its major task is to provide for the resolution of conflict, to regulate relationships through lawmaking, to preserve internal order (and provide defense from outside threats). The state is the ultimate authority that has the monopoly of force and can impose its decisions by force—if need be. But force has limits; generally speaking, governments must rely on consent rather than force and intimidation. This is the rule in the democratic states we study, but it is becoming increasingly so in one-party communist regimes, all of which have been undergoing a transformation in the direction of liberalization and participation.

The loose framework we suggest for the study of the individual countries consists then of three major concepts: civic culture, the civil society, and "government." Traditions and beliefs shape attitudes (behavior); associations and groups within the civil society press for the realization of demands; governments translate these demands into decisions. Figure 1–1 illustrates the dynamic relationship between civic culture, associations and groups, and governmental policy making.

---

[1] Gabriel Almond and Sidney Verba, *The Civic Culture* (Princeton, NJ: Princeton University Press, 1963).

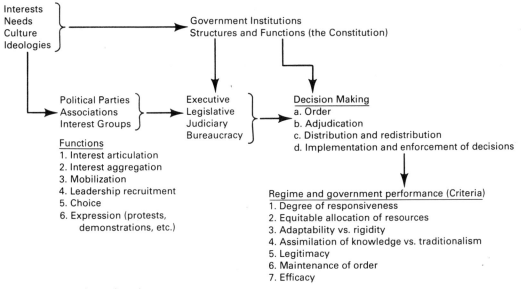

FIGURE 1-1 The Political System.

PLAN OF THIS BOOK

This text is not based on an overarching theory of politics but, rather, on a series of relevant categories for the study of politics suggested by theory. They are the categories into which we marshall and fit our data and suggest interrelationships that give us an idea of the dynamics of politics—governmental performance or not, stability or instability, change. We begin in each discussion with the civic culture, examining the source and the manifestations of values and beliefs about politics. We examine the "constitution" as the embodiment of the political values and practices for a political regime. A constitution sets forth the basic rules and procedures of governance. It is the embodiment, however tentative and fragmentary, of a desire on the part of a society to have some understanding about the rules under which government is organized and acts—about *what* government should do, and *how.* When agreement relates to *what,* we say that this is a *substantive* agreement. When we say that there is an agreement on *how,* we say that

there is a *procedural* agreement. A constitution usually involves both kinds of agreement. When a government has reached comprehensive and stable substantive and procedural agreements, we see this as a sign of a *consensual* society. When agreement appears to be fragile and is not widespread, we talk about *nonconsensus* or "a low level of consensus." If the conflict over the constitution is sharp, we speak of outright *dissensus.*

We then proceed to discuss the civil society—the organization of interests, levels of economic and social modernization, cultural and professional organizations, and political elites. We study the configurations of interests and the manner in which interests and associations interact with state agencies; the section on the Scandinavian countries contains an excellent review of what we call "corporatist" practices, that is, private interests and state agencies closely associated in decision making. We also investigate the degree, levels, and intensity of conflict among various interests—class, religious groups, ethnic groups—and the manner in which the state attempts to accommodate them.

We continue with the study of the governmental institutions and the political parties, looking at the structure of government for each country and the relationships among the major governmental structures—executive, legislative, judiciary, and civil service. We study semipresidential regimes, as in France, and parliamentary or cabinet systems, as in England and elsewhere on the continent, and examine the new and evolving governmental institutions in the Soviet Union. All along we pay particular attention to the political parties. Parties are the "links" or the "transmission belts" between the civil society and the governmental agencies. They translate demands into political platforms and, in so doing, structure and organize public opinion. Parties mobilize the electorate for political action and the realization of certain goals over others. The characteristics of the party system and the organization and ideology of major political parties is of critical importance, therefore, in gauging both conflicts and trends. In the same manner, the elections and election results—that we study in some detail—help us to gauge shifts and changes in public opinion over time and give us a profile of the political priorities in various countries.

In a last chapter for each of the countries we study, we give an assessment of governmental performance over time and discuss the prospects for the future. We discuss emerging conflicts, economic and social predicaments, and foreign policy issues: Will governments be able to surmount them and resolve them? What are the new party and ideological trends and how are they likely to affect performance? In this context, we discuss both the emergence of the Greens (the environmentalists) and the decline of the communist parties and the rise of socialist parties. But what kind of socialist parties are they? We also look into the emergence of new extremist right-wing parties and movements. Throughout we raise in our individual parts, but especially in Part VII, the prospects for the emergence of genuine European politics manifesting themselves through a European Parliament and a Euro-

pean executive: How integrative is the European movement and what influence will it have upon national governments?

Thus, our objectives are modest. All we hope to do is give the student a comprehensive view of politics in Europe and the Soviet Union. Political history and the organization of the society and of governmental structures are the landmarks that have guided us. They are also the tools that we have used to describe a variety of political manifestations as they differ from one country to another. They provide, at least tentatively, explanations for many of the differences we find. But we have not tried to build a "model" in terms of which we can presume to explain politics authoritatively. There is no such a comprehensive model as yet to organize our data, to link different phenomena, and to *explain* uniformities and differences.

EMERGING TRENDS AND PROBLEMS

What are the common trends we note and the problems facing most of the countries we study?

In the 1960s many students of Western Europe viewed modernization and development in evolutionary terms. Technology would continue to provide both the resources and means for the satisfaction of expanding human needs. There was no question that the state and its various agencies would continue to redistribute wealth to the poor and the handicapped in an equitable fashion. The problem did not appear socially divisive or explosive simply because it was taken for granted that the gross national product would keep growing, and hence that it would be easier to slice off large parts of the increments to provide for social services—leisure, health, retirement benefits, social and communal services, education, transportation, and so on. It was generally agreed that with the fundamental problem of economic necessity overcome, politics would become in Lenin's terms (though in an entirely different context) the "administration of things." Politics was to be the instrument for a rational and equitable distribution of goods and services—a technical problem.

In addition to economic growth, so widespread between 1950 and 1970, there were other signs that seemed to support the overall thesis of political stability. The political parties, it was also pointed out, were beginning to lose their sectarian and ideological character. Multiparty systems began to give place to large coalitions—two or three in number. Parties became increasingly comprehensive in their appeal; they came to be called "catch-all" parties, spreading their net far and wide to catch as many votes as possible from different groups, classes, regions, and interests. They became channels of compromise, where various heterogeneous groups sought and found accommodation. The catch-all party sought feasible solutions to existing problems. It would put an end to the instabilities of class or ideological politics and would surmount sharp social cleavages already blunted by the advent of prosperity. Like American parties, the Gaullists in France, the Christian Democrats and Social Democrats in Germany, even the Conservatives in Britain and the Communists in Italy seemed to move in the direction of catch-all parties.

Gradually a new consensus seemed to evolve. It crystallized around a number of beliefs: the inevitability of prosperity, the rational allocation and redistribution of the ever-growing wealth by experts, and the development of welfare programs to provide support by especially to equalize the living conditions of the citizenry. The "welfare state" received wide recognition, acceptance, and acclaim everywhere in Europe and even in the United States. Many equated this consensus with the emergence of a postindustrial society where, to put it bluntly, the problems of poverty and inequality would no longer plague the human condition. Abundance, peace, and domestic tranquility were just around the corner. An author summarized admirably these assumptions about European politics:

The argument in brief was this: that modernization and industrialization—and the economic growth, affluence, and widening opportunities for education they generated—were erasing the lines of cleavage that generated antisystem conflict within European societies. Radical movements and ideologies of both Left and Right fed on discontents that were drying up in contemporary societies. The inequalities of income, status, and power that had given rise to all-out challenges to the state in the past were diminishing. . . . Modernization and economic growth were making the working class affluent; the strength of working-class organizations compensated for the superior economic power of the capitalists. . . . Thus the very wide differentials of income, status, and power of European societies in the past would be progressively narrowed, and the distinctive class groupings of these societies would disappear.[2]

This view of European politics is no longer valid. Since the early 1970s a number of new trends—virtually all of them diametrically opposed to it—have been very much in evidence. I simply list some of them and touch briefly on each of them. Many are discussed in detail in the sections that follow.

1. Scarcity of resources, economic decline, and unemployment.
2. Growing inability of governments to cope with the rising demands and expectations of the citizens.
3. Problems in the redistribution of goods and the crisis in welfare politics.
4. Crisis of legitimacy and the rise of militant politics.
5. Demands for new forms of representation and participation.
6. Resurgence of ideological politics.
7. New pressures on the nation-states.

Growth of Scarcities

Since the early 1970s the economies of the West have experienced a halt in their economic growth that may well continue in

---

[2] Suzanne Berger, "Politics and Antipolitics in Western Europe," *Daedalus*, Vol. 108, no. 1 (1973), p. 28.

the 1990s. The pie is no longer getting bigger. Unemployment has reappeared and grown. Energy resources, despite ambitious plans to harness nuclear power, have fallen behind needs or have had to be met at ten times and more the original cost. The result has been the introduction of austerity programs that have ended the vision of abundance and profoundly disturbed those who took expansion and well-being for granted. Even faith in technology has begun to waver, now that it appears science has not delivered promised solutions and has begun to adversely affect the environment in which we live. Qualitative consideration has begun to undermine the hopes of quantitative benefits.

Rising Expectations

The terms *rising expectations* and *revolution of rising expectations* were first used to denote the attitudes of poor and ex-colonial peoples. The hope of attaining a standard of living even remotely comparable to those of European, American, or Soviet citizens injected a powerful revolutionary motive into their political orientations. But the term applies to the developed countries as well.

In the modern nations the optimistic picture of an ever-expanding economy has simply whetted demands and multiplied expectations. Since government is taken to be an instrument for the satisfaction of needs, these needs, expressed through interest groups or political parties, have simply pressed harder and harder upon those responsible for the allocations of goods and services. The more intense they have become, the harder it has been for governments to meet them. Suddenly, governments have come to appear unresponsive to the demands of their citizens.

Redistribution

The major crisis of democracies is the problem of redistribution. In essence, redistribution means taking goods from one person and giving them to somebody else. An income tax policy is redistributive if the monies collected from those who earn a salary or an income beyond a certain level are given to those who earn an income below a certain level. Goods can be redistributed in the form either of outright cash or, more often, services. A welfare state is one that institutionalizes a vast redistributive flow from the wealthier groups to the needier ones, one that channels goods and services directly or indirectly so as to produce at least a minimum degree of equality and common opportunities among all citizens.

It is when the national wealth ceases to expand, when economic growth stops, when inflation begins to jeopardize not only the gains of disadvantaged groups but also the solid advantages of the wealthier ones, that redistributive politics hit a snag. And it is on this snag that most of the countries we study find themselves caught today. Transfer of income from the wealthier to the poorer no longer yields enough to continue to provide the benefits already promised the poor. Group bargaining can at most maintain existing patterns of distribution. Emphasis on existing claims freezes expectations and demands at a given level. New groups and new claims cannot be heard. Gradually, the affection for and the involvement of citizens in their political system decline. With growing dissatisfaction, bargaining leads to confrontation and confrontation to violence.

Representation and Participation

Nineteenth-century political battles were fought over the extension of the franchise—the right to vote. The notion that certain groups or classes could represent the community by virtue of their superior education, wealth, or talents gave way to the realities of mass democracies. Only direct election in which all members of the community voted could give a truly representative quality to a legislature. Gradually the franchise was expanded both horizontally (to include everybody) and vertically (in the sense that representatives derived their powers *directly* from the people).

The 1960s and 1970s witnessed a strong reaction against the notion of representation that limits political participation only to elections, no matter how fair and inclusive. There is a growing demand by citizens for direct participation in all decisions that affect them. These demands are not limited to local and regional matters; they extend to *all* policies and decisions. Labor groups, consumers, students and teachers, artists, and doctors are to become directly involved in every decision that concerns their lives.

Demands for community control, functional representation, self-government in industry, workers' participation, industrial democracy (*autogestion* in France), and group consultations in Scandinavia—all question the adequacy of representative government. They are all demands for the direct participation of the individual—not as a citizen but as a doctor or worker or manager or consumer—in policy decisions. Citizens are calling for the creation of semi-autonomous bodies legislating for their locality or their profession in terms of their specific interests. They want control and power vested in these bodies at the expense of the national or local political organs. Such movements undermine the validity and the legitimacy of representative government as it has developed throughout Europe.

Crisis of Legitimacy and Militant Politics

A government should be able to govern. It should be able to make decisions on a variety of issues and it should be in a position to implement them within a framework of order and law. If not, a crisis is prevalent everywhere. The authority of the state is at stake; *people no longer accept it*. The crisis has given rise to new political forms of expression—demonstrations, violence, terrorism, formation of parapolitical organizations that want to assume power for themselves on behalf of their members and to bypass the political parties or the regular agencies of government. Revolutionary, subversive, and militant politics today are challenging assumptions about consensual political re-

gimes and inject a new dimension in democratic politics that is very difficult to assess. But crises begin to haunt single-party communist regimes in the Soviet Union and Eastern Europe—with the citizenry withdrawing consent from their government.

Resurgence of Ideological Politics and the Demise of the Catch-all Parties

Once more, with the French leading the way, there is a resurgence of ideology in the search of social justice and equality. The overall thrust is the very opposite of what we detected earlier. It is a movement away from the expert and back to the people and to what might be called expressive politics. The phenomenon is associated with single-issue groups (advocating one particular position or interest) and the effort to realize specific goals. It is a kind of "do it yourself" politics. In Britain, France, Spain, Greece, West Germany, and Italy, ideological politics, in which nationalism plays an important role, have resurfaced. They are likely to enhance existing cleavages along ethnic, religious and class lines and to undermine consensus, and governmental authority.

The Strains on the Nation-State: Internal and External

In the last two decades some nation-states have been facing the prospect of internal disintegration. In the United Kingdom, the Welsh and the Scots—to say nothing, of course, of the Irish—demand separation or autonomy. In Spain, the separatist movement among the Basques and the Catalans is gaining in intensity. In the most centralized and homogeneous democracy of all, France, there are separatist movements among the Corsicans, and also in Brittany and among the French Basques. Ethnic and separatist movements are beginning to undermine the authority of the Soviet Union. These separatist movements often put an additional strain upon the political system and feed into other conflicts and disagreements.

While the national states are struggling with severe internal stresses, the international community in which we now live is generating additional strains. From an economic and also a military viewpoint, national "independence" is something of an illusion. For most states—and this applies with particular force to Europe—interdependence is becoming a necessity for the procurement of labor; the rational utilization of energy; trade; defense; regional economic development; and overall relations with continents or large power units, such as the United States and the Soviet bloc. In Western Europe this is clearly shown by the efforts in the Common Market to coordinate and integrate the economies of 12 European countries.

As Charles Tilly points out, the nation-state is "losing its significance." There is a "devolution of power away from [it] both upward and downward—that is, in the direction of subnational and supranational units.[3] This adds to the crisis of the contemporary states—democratic or not.

BIBLIOGRAPHY

We list only some basic books dealing with comparative political analysis.

ALMOND, GABRIEL, and C. BINGHAM POWELL. *Comparative Politics: A Developmental Approach.* Boston: Little, Brown, 1966.

ALMOND, GABRIEL, and SIDNEY VERBA. *Civic Culture Revisited.* Boston: Little, Brown, 1978.

———. *The Civic Culture.* Princeton, NJ: Princeton University Press, 1963.

APTER, DAVID E. *Introduction to Political Analysis.* Boston: Little, Brown, 1977.

BEER, SAMUEL H. *Modern Political Development.* New York: Random House, 1974.

BERGER, SUZANNE, ed. *Organizing Interests in Western Europe.* Cambridge: Cambridge University Press, 1981.

BILL, JAMES A., and ROBERT L. HARGRAVE. *Comparative Politics, The Quest for Theory.* Lanham, MD: University Press of America, 1982.

BINDER, LEONARD, et al. *Crises and Sequences in Political Development.* Princeton, NJ: Princeton University Press, 1971.

BLACK, C. E. *The Dynamics of Modernization.* Princeton, NJ: Princeton University Press, 1966.

BLONDEL, JEAN. *Comparative Political Institutions.* New York: Praeger, 1973.

———. *Comparative Legislatures.* Englewood Cliffs, NJ: Prentice Hall, 1973.

———. *An Introduction to Comparative Government.* New York: Praeger, 1972.

BOGDANOR, V., and D. BUTLER. *Democracy and Elections, Electoral Systems and Their Political Consequences.* Cambridge: Cambridge University Press, 1983.

BUTLER, D., H. PENNIMAN, and A. RANNEY, eds. *Democracy at the Polls: A Comparative Study of Competitive National Elections.* Washington, DC: American Enterprises Institute, 1981.

CROZIER, MICHAEL, SAMUEL HUNTINGTON, and JOJI WATANUKI. *The Crisis of Democracy.* New York: New York University Press, 1975.

EASTON, DAVID. *Framework of Political Analysis.* Englewood Cliffs, NJ: Prentice Hall, 1965.

ECKSTEIN, HARRY. *The Evaluation of Political Performance: Problems and Dimensions.* Beverley Hills, CA: Sage, 1971.

FINER, SAMUEL. *Comparative Government.* Baltimore, MD: Penguin, 1970.

———, ed. *Five Constitutions—Contrasts and Comparisons.* Baltimore, MD: Penguin, 1979.

FRIEDRICH, CARL. *Constitutional Government and Democracy: Theory and Practice in Europe and America,* 4th ed. New York: Blaisdell, 1968.

GOLDTHORPE, JOHN, ed. *Order and Conflict in Contemporary Capitalism, Studies in the Political Economy of Western European Nations.* Oxford: Oxford University Press, 1984.

GREENSTEIN, FRED, and NELSON POLSBY, eds. *The Handbook of Political Science.* Reading, MA: Addison-Wesley, 1975. Especially vols. 5 and 7.

HEINDENHEIMER, ARNOLD, HUGH HECLO, and CAROLYN TEICH ADAMS. *Comparative Public Policy,* 2nd ed. New York: St. Martin's, 1983.

HOLT, ROBERT T. and JOHN E. TURNER. *The Methodology of Comparative Research.* New York: Free Press, 1970.

LaPALOMBARA, JOSEPH and MYRON WEINER. *Politics, Parties and Political Development.* Princeton, NJ: Princeton University Press, 1972.

LAWSON, KAY. *The Comparative Study of Political Parties.* New York: St. Martin's, 1975.

LINZ, JUAN, and ALFRED STEPAN, eds. *The Breakdown of Democratic Regimes.* Baltimore, MD: Johns Hopkins University Press, 1978.

---

[3] Charles Tilly, ed., *The Formation of National States in Western Europe* (Princeton, NJ: Princeton University Press, 1975), p. 638.

LIPSET, SEYMOUR MARTIN. *Political Man: The Social Bases of Politics*. Garden City, NY: Doubleday/Anchor, 1963.

MACRIDIS, ROY L. *Modern Political Regimes: Institutions and Patterns*. Boston: Little, Brown, 1986.

———. *Contemporary Political Ideologies*, 4th ed. Boston and Glenview, IL: Little-Brown and Scott, Foresman, 1986.

———, and BERNARD E. BROWN. *Comparative Politics: Notes and Readings*, 6th ed. Homewood, IL: Dorsey, 1986.

———. *The Study of Comparative Government*. Garden City, NY: Doubleday, 1956.

MOORE, BARRINGTON, JR. *The Social Origins of Democracy and Dictatorship: Lords and Peasants in the Making of the Modern World*. Boston: Beacon Press, 1966.

NORDLINGER, ERIC. *On the Autonomy of the Democratic State*. Cambridge, MA: Harvard University Press, 1981.

POWELL, BINGHAM. *Contemporary Democracies—Participation, Stability and Violence*. Cambridge, MA: Harvard University Press, 1983.

PRZEWORSKI, ADAMS, and HENRY TEUNE. *The Logic of Comparative Social Inquiry*. New York: John Wiley, 1970.

ROSE, RICHARD, ed. *Electoral Sociology: A Comparative Handbook*. New York: Free Press, 1974.

ROSE, RICHARD, and EZRA N. SULEIMAN, eds. *Presidents and Prime Ministers*. Washington, DC: American Enterprise Institute, 1980.

SARTORI, GIOVANNI. *Parties and Party Systems*. New York: Cambridge University Press, 1976.

———. *Theory*. Westport, CT: Greenwood, 1973.

TILLY, CHARLES, ed. *The Formation of Nation States in Western Europe*. Princeton, NJ: Princeton University Press, 1975.

PART II
GREAT BRITAIN: POLITICAL PATTERNS AND TRENDS

DENNIS KAVANAGH

1

Introduction

Britain's political system has often been admired and emulated by citizens of other states. As a long-established stable democracy, many observers have looked at the government of Britain for the secret of representative democracy.

Observers have often admired the *balance* in the political system. The country has long managed to combine effective government with assured civil liberties for its citizens and rights of political opposition. There has also been a mixture of medieval predemocratic institutions (like the monarchy and the House of Lords) and modern democratic practices. The political values have been blended into what two pioneering Americans have called a *civic culture*.[1] In such a culture, citizens have both a subject outlook (which respects government) and a partici-

pant one (which enables them to feel confident about their ability to influence government). Such an attitude is appropriate to the potentially contradictory requirements of modern democratic government.

Britain's political institutions and values are the product of history; they have evolved over centuries. In the twentieth century the population has not experienced such massive discontinuities as the collapse of the French regime in 1940 and 1958, the military defeat and division of Germany post-1945, or the 1917 revolution in Russia. Compared to many other states Britain's experience of political modernization has been relatively low cost.

THE UNCODIFIED CONSTITUTION

Britain lacks a constitution in the sense of possessing a formal written document that prescribes how the political system works

---

[1] G. Almond and S. Verba, *The Civic Culture* (Princeton, NJ: Princeton University Press, 1963).

and what the political and civil liberties of citizens are. But it certainly has a political constitution in the sense of agreed "rules of the game." Tradition—having done without one for so long—and the continuity of the English state from before a time when written constitutions were thought of, all help to explain its absence. There has been also a good deal of elite and popular satisfaction with the political system, at least when it was compared to the performance of other regimes that did have written constitutions. The rules of the game have evolved over the centuries, and there has been no equivalent to the constitutional convention which drew up the American constitution in 1787.

In fact, much of the British constitution is written in the form of *statute law*. Such laws include the Act of Union with Scotland (1707); the Parliament Act (1911), which, among other things, reduced the lifetime of Parliaments from seven to five years; the European Communities Act (1972) by which Britain joined the European Community; and various suffrage measures which have extended the vote to virtually all adults aged 18 or over. Another source is *common law,* custom, precedent, and judicial interpretations in the past which the courts follow today. There are also *conventions,* or informal rules of conduct, accepted by politicians and civil servants but not enforced by the courts. Much of the working of the political system depends on these understandings. They include such matters as the monarch's giving assent to bills that have passed by the two houses of Parliament, a government's duty to resign after losing a confidence vote in the House of Commons, and members of the cabinet supporting all government decisions or being expected to resign. It must be emphasized, however, that the force that conventions possess is dependent on their application: once they become generally ignored, they cease to be conventions.

MAIN FEATURES

Among the main principles of the British constitution four are worth noting:

1. *Constitutional Monarchy.* The struggle between Parliament and the crown for political supremacy in the mid-seventeenth century was resolved in favor of Parliament. After a civil war, the king, Charles I, was executed, and between 1649 and 1660 England did not have a monarch. The monarchy was restored in 1660, but Parliament's dominance was formally recognized in 1689. As Walter Bagehot noted in his famous *The English Constitution* (1867), the monarchy gradually became part of the "dignified" (or symbolic) constitution and the "efficient" (or actual) rulers were the cabinet and the prime minister. Today, Queen Elizabeth II still exercises a role in formally appointing the prime minister, opening and closing Parliament, giving her assent to legislation, and so on, but essentially she approves what has been decided elsewhere, usually by the cabinet. In the twentieth century, the role of the crown is largely symbolic; the monarch is the head of state and a symbol of national unity and continuity. The monarchy is more equipped to play this part as its political role has declined.

2. *The Supremacy of Parliament.* Parliamentary sovereignty means that an act of Parliament is not constrained by any higher law. The courts may interpret the statute, but they may not overturn it. In the absence of a written constitution, there is no judicial review by a body like the Supreme Court in the United States. One recent incursion on this sovereignty of Parliament stems from Britain's membership of the European Community (1972). Under the Treaty of Rome, which established the European Community, all member states accept that in the case of conflict between the treaty and domestic law, the former will have precedence. Only in this area can British courts set aside an act of Parliament.

3. *The Unitary State.* The writ of Parliament is supreme throughout the United Kingdom (Scotland, Wales, Northern Ireland, as well as England). Unlike the United States and West Germany there is no federal tier of government with its own powers. Local and regional authorities in Britain derive their powers from central government, and these may be withdrawn by the latter.

4. *The Flexible Constitution.* In large part the flexibility arises from the absence of a constitution that is written and thus difficult to amend. Above all, it arises from the supremacy of statute law. The classic illustration of this flexibil-

ity was during the two great wars of this century (1914–18 and 1939–45). General elections were due to be held, at the latest, by 1916 and 1940, respectively, but the Parliaments of the day simply extended their lives until the cessation of hostilities. In contrast the United States had to go ahead with its fixed calendar elections.

It is misleading to see the emergence of today's constitution as the outcome of a peaceful consensual process. The present settlement grew out of the bitter civil war of the seventeenth century, the threat of a revolution before the extension of the suffrage in the 1832 Reform Act, possible armed struggle over Irish Home Rule before 1914 and violence in Ireland after 1918. There were also bitter conflicts before 1914 over demands for votes for women and proposals to curb the powers of the hereditary House of Lords.

For most of the period there was general satisfaction with the country's political institutions and the lack of a written constitution. Indeed for much of this century, many felt a sense of political superiority to other West European states, largely because of the country's more secure history of constitutional government and its success in the two world wars.

Until about 1960 Britain's living standards and welfare services were still superior to those of most of her West European neighbors. But there was a growing awareness, at first among the opinion forming elites, that Britain's economy was falling behind that of other states. Between 1960 and 1972 Britain fell from seventh to fifteenth place in the league table of GNP per capita among OECD member states. Almost alone among West European states Britain did not experience an "economic miracle." This mood encouraged demands for reform. In the 1960s a number of royal commissions and inquiries sought to reform Britain's institutions. These included Parliament, the trade unions, universities, schools, the civil service, and even the constitution. Notwithstanding the reforms, the country's eco-

nomic performance continued to decline relative to many of her competitors.

During the 1970s further pressures for constitutional reform were felt. There was, for example, demand for devolution of decision making to an elected assembly in Scotland. Had the 1974 Labour government's attempts to set up such an assembly succeeded, some commentators wondered how a conflict between it and the Westminster Parliament might be resolved. Entry to the European Community in 1973 involved the incorporation of a large element of a written constitution into British law and expanded the power of British courts vis-à-vis the government. Moreover in 1975 the Labour government forced the introduction of a referendum over membership. This consultative exercise was not binding on Parliament, though it is difficult to imagine that Parliament (which had voted overwhelmingly for Britain to remain a member of the European Community) could defy the popular verdict of a referendum. Another pressure came from the Labour party's pledge in 1980 to abolish the House of Lords; if achieved this would have left Britain with a unicameral (single-chamber) form of government.

A number of commentators have expressed concern about the lack of formal checks and balances in the British constitution. It is worth restating the subordinate role played by the courts and local government, the weakness of the House of Lords and the absence of a Bill of Rights covering individual liberties. In a famous lecture in 1976 the prominent lawyer and Conservative politician, Lord Hailsham, argued that cabinet dominance over the Commons meant that the sovereignty of Parliament facilitated "an elective dictatorship" by the government.[2] He complained that the House of Commons was no longer an adequate defender of the citizens' liberties and suggested that a written constitution might be

---

[2] *The Dilemma of Democracy* (London: Collins, 1978), p. 6.

the best way of limiting the powers of Parliament. Lord Hailsham expressed his concern when there was a Labour government. Yet, today complaints about the power of government and calls for constitutional reform are more likely to come from the opposition parties.

At present there are few prospects of Britain adopting a written constitution. Busy governments are unlikely to be willing to sacrifice the necessary Parliamentary time to legislate on constitutional matters. Moreover, governments have little incentive to restrain their own powers and provide checks and balances that can be exploited by opposition parties. Similarly, the Conservative and Labour parties are unlikely to favor the introduction of a more proportional electoral system, as long as the present first-past-the-post system works to their advantage.

Major Events in Britain Since 1945

1945	ELECTION. Labour majority, 156. Clement Attlee prime minister.
1946–50	Nationalization: coal, cable and wireless, Bank of England, transportation, electricity, gas, steel.
	National Insurance and National Health Service Acts.
1947–48	Independence granted India, Pakistan, Burma, Ceylon.
1950	ELECTION. Labour majority, 5. Attlee prime minister.
1951	ELECTION. Conservative majority, 17. Winston Churchill prime minister.
1952	Death of King George VI. Accession of Queen Elizabeth II. Atom bomb tested. Steel denationalized.
1955	Churchill retires; Anthony Eden prime minister.
	ELECTION. Conservative majority, 58.
1957	Eden retires; Harold Macmillan prime minister.
	H-bomb tested. Britain adopts nuclear defence strategy.
	Foundation of the Campaign for Nuclear Disarmament (CND).
	Ghana granted independence.
	Britain refuses to join the EEC.
1959	Independence granted to Cyprus.
	ELECTION. Conservative majority, Macmillan prime minister.
1960/4	Independence granted to Nigeria, Sierra Leone, Tanganyika, Jamaica, Trinidad, Uganda, Kenya, Zambia, Zanzibar, Malawi, Malta.
1963	Harold Wilson becomes Labour leader.
	Macmillan retires; Lord Home prime minister.
	De Gaulle vetoes British entry to EEC.
1964	ELECTION. Labour majority, 6. Wilson prime minister.
1965	Independence granted to Gambia, Singapore, Malaysia, Botswana, Lesotho, Barbados, Guyana. Rhodesia's unilateral declaration of independence.
1966	ELECTION. Labour majority, 96. Wilson, prime minister.
1967	Wilson applies to join the EEC.
1968	De Gaulle again vetoes British entry to EEC.
	Race Relations Act, bans discrimination.
1970	ELECTION. Conservative majority, 30. Heath prime minister.
1973	Britain becomes a member of the EEC.
	Yom Kippur war; OPEC oil embargo; coal strike begins.
1974	(February) ELECTION. Labour minority of −24. Wilson remains prime minister.
	(October) ELECTION. Labour majority, 16. Wilson prime minister.
1975	Referendum votes 2 to 1 to remain within the EEC.
	Unions forced to accept "voluntary" pay restraint.
1976	Wilson retires; James Callaghan prime minister.
1979	Government defeated on "no confidence" vote by 311 to 310.
	ELECTION. Conservative majority, 44. Mrs. Margaret Thatcher prime minister.
	European Parliament elections: Conservatives, 60; Labour, 17; others, 4.
1980	Unemployment jumps to 2 million.
	Labour party votes in favor of withdrawing from EEC.
	Callaghan retires. Michael Foot becomes Labour leader.

1981	Social Democratic Party launched. "Alliance" formed between Labor groups and Liberals.
	Unemployment jumps to 2.5 million.
	Left-wing Labour wins control of Greater London Council.
1982	Unemployment jumps to 3 million.
	Argentina invades Falkland Islands.
	Argentina surrenders.
1983	ELECTION. Conservative majority, 144. Mrs. Thatcher, prime minister.
	Unemployment over 3 million.
	Coal strike begins (March).
	IRA blows up Brighton hotel at Conservative conference; narrow escape of Mrs. Thatcher.
	Kinnock becomes Labour Leader.
1985	Coal strike collapses (March).
	Inner-city riots; Tottenham (London), Handsworth (Birmingham).
1987	ELECTION. Conservative majority 100.
	Margaret Thatcher Prime Minister. Split in Alliance.
1988	Re-launch of new party Social and Liberal Democrats.
	Private sale of British Steel.
	Community Charge (poll tax) becomes law.
1989	Private sale of Electricity and Water industries.
	Unemployment falls to two million.
	Elections for European Parliament.
	Labour party policy moves in moderate direction. Accepts case for market economy.
June 1989	Euro ELECTIONS. Labour wins 47 seats out of 81. First election success over Conservatives since 1974.
July 1989	Government reshuffle. Mrs. Thatcher recruits four new Cabinet ministers to give "modern" look to Cabinet.

2

Context

Each political system is rooted in an environment or context that is shaped by factors such as geography, history, socioeconomic structure, and political culture. In the case of Britain, the environment has been extremely important. When her political institutions have been emulated by many newly independent African countries, and even the United States in the eighteenth century, they have operated very differently from those in the mother country. The environment has enabled British political institutions to take root in the country.

The United Kingdom consists of Great Britain, Scotland, Wales, England, and Northern Ireland. The island of Great Britain is separated from the European mainland by the 22-mile stretch of the English Channel. Historically, it has been detached from, but not uninterested in what happened on, the Continent. The natural frontiers provided by the sea and Britain's mastery of naval warfare preserved the country's

territorial independence for nearly a thousand years. The last successful foreign invasion was the Norman Conquest in 1066. Since then Spain, France, and, twice in this century, Germany have all made attempts to dominate the Continent and subjugate Britain. All failed.

The country's island position has been important for another reason. In the seventeenth and eighteenth centuries, rulers in many European states established large standing armies, partly to protect their borders and partly to suppress domestic rivals. The powerful armies were also useful for coercing the population and extracting taxation. In many European states at this time embryonic representative institutions were destroyed. But Britain, because of the security granted by the sea, had less need for a large standing army. Its location has thus been important in securing the civil liberties of the population.

Britain is 94,250 square miles in size: this

is small in relation to such West European states as France and Spain, let alone the United States and the Soviet Union. It is clearly not a superpower and, indeed, is smaller than a number of American states. But with a population in 1986 of 56.6 million (the fifteenth largest in the world), some international influence (it is one of the five permanent members of the United Nations Security Council), and one of the highest per capita incomes in the world, it is still an important medium-sized power.

SOCIETY

England dominates the United Kingdom. It has over 47 million of the 56.6 million total population (see Table 2–1). The capital city, London, is the seat of government, and the center of mass media, commerce, and business; with nearly 7 million inhabitants it is six times as large as the next most populous city, Birmingham. The populations outside England are distinctive in their national identities, religions, and party systems. For example, most people in Wales and Scotland think of themselves as Welsh and Scottish, respectively, and nationalist parties contest each parliamentary seat in those countries. Politics in northern Ireland is so different from that in the mainland that none of the main British parties bothers to contest seats in Ulster.

During the eighteenth and early nineteenth centuries Britain experienced an Industrial Revolution and became the "first industrial nation." At its peak, in the midnineteenth century, Britain supplied

half of the world's output of coal and iron and steel and about a third of the world's manufacturing goods. This economic strength made Britain for a time the foremost international power. Her overseas possessions in the British Empire provided a vast captive market for her manufactures. Industrialism had social and political consequences. The captains of industry exercised greater power and as people moved from the land to the towns so the population of the latter boomed.

More recently, in common with other postindustrial societies, there has been a sharp decline in manufacturing employment and, with it, in the size of the working class. Manufacturing employment has declined from just over 8 million in 1971 to 5.2 million in 1986, most of the fall occurring since 1979. There has been an expansion of jobs in the service sector and in self-employment, again most of the change occurring in the 1980s. There has also been a marked increase in unemployment. In 1979 the figure of 4.3 percent unemployment caused concern, but this had trebled by 1982. By the end of 1988 it had fallen to below 10 percent. Levels of unemployment and economic deprivation are greater in the northern regions—particularly Scotland and the northeast and northwest of Britain, areas that have traditionally depended on manufacturing. The burden of taxation on incomes as a proportion of earnings has fallen since 1979, in line with the Thatcher government's objective. But if we include insurance contributions (a social security tax) paid by all wage earners, then the level is about the same as in 1979. The biggest reductions have been for the relatively high earners.

Comparatively speaking, the British are socially homogeneous. Virtually everybody speaks English, some 96 percent of the population is white, and few are employed on the land. But down the centuries Britain has received immigrants, both welcome and unwelcome, from many different races— Angles, Saxons, Vikings, Normans, and in the nineteenth and twentieth centuries, Irish

TABLE 2–1 Population of United Kingdom, 1985 (in 000s)

Country	Population
England	47,112
Scotland	5,137
Wales	2,812
Northern Ireland	1,558
	56,618

Catholics and East Europeans. Since the mid-1950s there has been an influx of black immigrants particularly from India and new Commonwealth countries, such as Pakistan and the West Indies. Until 1962 citizens of Commonwealth countries had unrestricted rights of access to Britain. However, in that year the Commonwealth Immigrants Act restricted such entry and subsequent measures have reduced it to a trickle. In 1986 only 22,500 immigrants from the new Commonwealth were accepted for settlement. For the past two decades there have been strict limits on such immigration, triggered in part by public hostility in the past to the immigrants. Today the black population, nearly half of whom were born in Britain, amount to just over two and a half million or 4 percent of the population. The minorities have been concentrated in a number of cities, particularly parts of London, Birmingham, Leicester, and Bradford. In spite of antidiscrimination legislation there is much evidence that racial discrimination continues; for example, young blacks suffer rates of unemployment twice as high as those for young whites. In the 1980s there have been violent clashes between young blacks (and some whites) and the police in Birmingham, Bristol, and Liverpool.

In terms of religion Britain is hardly a melting pot. England has been predominantly Church of England, or Anglican, since Henry VIII's breach with Rome (1534) in the Reformation and his establishment of a national Church of England. Britain contained a substantial Catholic population until 1921, but it was based largely in Ireland. Indeed the withdrawal of that country from the United Kingdom in 1921 meant that Britain became overwhelmingly urban, industrialized, and Anglican. Some two-thirds of people admitting a religion today adhere to the Church of England or its sister Church of Scotland. Two other significant minorities are the nonconformists (about 16 percent) and Roman Catholics (about 13 percent). Britain is not a churchgoing country—less than one in five admit to attending church at least once a month—and churches are not much involved in politics, except when taking a public position on issues like abortion and pornography. More recently, the churches have crossed swords with government spokesmen by complaining that not enough is being done to combat deprivation in the inner cities, which suffer very high levels of unemployment.

The sense of Britain being politically different from most European countries was already evident in the seventeenth century. In this period absolute monarchy was the dominant form of government on the continent. The attempts by the Stuart kings in England to establish absolutist rule brought the country to a civil war (1640–49) in which the king, Charles I, was beheaded and Oliver Cromwell became a military dictator. Britain, before France, provided a revolutionary model; monarchical absolutism on the continental model was rejected. The monarchy was restored in 1660, and James II's renewed efforts to assert its predominance in 1688 were rebuffed. William of Orange from the Netherlands was invited to replace the deposed James II. In the constitutional settlement of 1688, sovereignty was vested in Parliament, and a "balanced" constitution (in the sense of a sharing of powers) was achieved between the two Houses of Parliament and the monarchy. In the Bill of Rights, which shortly followed, it was declared that the monarch could not raise money, make or suspend laws, or maintain a standing army, without the consent of Parliament.

But of course Parliament was hardly a representative body. The House of Lords consisted of the hereditary aristocracy, usually great landowners. The House of Commons was largely composed of the nominees of these magnates (who controlled many seats) or other wealthy figures. In 1832 the first step was taken to make the House of Commons a little more representative of the population. The Reform Act of that year extended the vote to some 7 percent of the adult population and granted seats to some growing towns. Further extensions of the suffrage in 1867, 1884, 1918, and 1928 (the last two to include women) made the electorate almost coextensive with the adult population (aged 21 or over). In 1970 the suffrage was extended again, to those aged 18 or over.

It was also in the nineteenth century that many of the important features of the British constitution were developed. These included the gradual extension of the suffrage, development of a professional and impartial civil service, emergence of cabinet and ministerial responsibility to the House of Commons, a limited, or figurehead, role for the monarchy, and supremacy of the House of Commons over the House of Lords. A person comparing the political systems in 1913 and 1988 would notice much greater continuity in the case of Britain than in any other European state.

Modern Britain, unlike many other states, has not known a political revolution. The evolutionary development since the seventeenth century and the gradual reform of the political institutions have permitted the continued existence of such medieval bodies as the monarchy and House of Lords, which have been swept aside in many other countries. In Britain the crown and the House of Lords gradually acquiesced to their loss of power and accepted a largely figurehead role. Today most of the monarch's powers have passed to the cabinet and prime minister and the House of Lords only has the power of delaying the passage of legislation by the House of Commons for one year but it does not have this power with regard to money bills. The British style has been one of adaptation rather than revolution, the pouring of old (predemocratic) wines into new (democratic) bottles.

POSTWAR BRITAIN

At the end of the nineteenth century it was clear that, with the rise of the United States and Germany, Britain's industrial preeminence was being lost. The continuous involvement in the great wars (1914–18 and 1939–45) left her economically exhausted. She had to sell many overseas assets to pay for the wars and lost many of her export markets. Since 1945 the country has suffered an abrupt relative economic decline, encouraging some economists to claim that Britain won the war but lost the peace. During the 1960s and 1970s annual British rates of economic growth were much lower than other West European states, indeed the lowest of all the 24 member states of OECD. The term "the British disease" is an all-purpose term to describe the country's low growth, and reputation for frequent strikes and poor workmanship. Yet it is worth noting that the postwar record of economic growth has been as good as any in the last hundred years. The trouble was that the performance was poor in comparison to that of other states.

1945 was perhaps the high point of British prestige in the twentieth century. In that year Britain was one of the "big three" victorious powers, along with the United States and the Soviet Union. She was ·of course much the weakest of the three in terms of military and economic strength, but her ability to withstand Hitler seemed a triumphant vindication of her political and social structures. With the postwar development of superpowers, however, Britain's international influence as a medium-sized state has declined. In this period Britain gradually abandoned her Empire, beginning with the Labour government granting of full independence to India and Pakistan in 1947. The process continued during the 1950s and 1960s, as many African states achieved independence. Today many of these ex-colonies are members of the British Commonwealth, an association of independent states of which the queen is head.

A mark of Britain's international decline and of the diminishing importance of the Empire was Britain's decision to apply for membership of the European Community in 1961. Earlier, Britain had resolutely stood aside from invitations to join the Community. Harold Macmillan was the first prime minister to turn to Europe in search of a new role for Britain. He was also impressed by the rapid rates of economic growth which the member states achieved and believed that entry would stimulate growth in Britain. The Conservative Prime Minister Heath signed the Treaty of Accession in January 1972 and entry was finally achieved in 1973. The 1974 Labour government insisted in renegotiating the terms of entry, and membership was confirmed by a 2-to-1 majority in a referendum in 1975.

In spite of her relative economic decline, Britain has enjoyed great political stability in the twentieth century. If political stability went hand in hand with economic strength in the nineteenth century, so it has continued at a time of relative economic weakness. In the course of the twentieth-century Spain, Portugal, Greece, France, Germany, and Italy have suffered either military dictatorships, fascism, internal collapse, or defeat in war. The continuity of Britain's political institutions is outstanding, and support for extremist parties, either of the left or right, has been minuscule.

In many other democracies civil liberties are set out in a written constitution or some other formal code. In Britain there is no bill of individual rights, for much the same reason as there is no written constitution. People have not overthrown a would-be dictatorial form of government for over three centuries. There are no statutory guarantees of freedoms of speech or assembly, for example. People are allowed to do broadly what they wish unless they break the law. For example, there is freedom of speech until it offends the laws against libel, slander, and racial discrimination. Similarly, freedoms of political association and demonstration are allowed until they infringe upon the law.

THE IRISH PROBLEM

The fusion of England with Scotland was accomplished in the Act of Union (1707), but Wales and Ireland had been subject to earlier military conquest by England and integration in the United Kingdom in 1536 and 1801, respectively. Since Ireland was predominantly Catholic, there was always concern among England's rulers that it might be a base for military operations against Protestant England, once Henry VIII broke with Rome. Ireland was never assimilated, and after strife throughout the nineteenth century, the Irish finally received their independence in 1921, but at a cost. The predominantly Protestant six northern counties refused to join the new state and, as Ulster or Northern Ireland, were allowed to remain a part of the United Kingdom, with their own parliament at Stormont.

Unfortunately Ulster's Protestant rulers did little to conciliate the Catholic minority, and troubles broke out in 1968. Growing increasingly impatient with the Protestant authorities, the British government finally suspended the Ulster Parliament in 1972, and since then the province has been under the direct rule of the British government. The Protestant or Unionist majority wishes to remain part of the United Kingdom while many Catholic nationalists want a "united" Ireland, in which Ulster merges with the Irish Republic. Both sides employ violence and have paramilitary troops. Successive British governments have said that they will accept Irish unity if and when the majority of the population wishes it. As long as there is a Unionist or Protestant majority a vote for such change is unlikely, but the government has of course raised a question mark about the long-term integration of Ulster in Britain. In 1985 the Irish and British governments signed an Anglo-Irish agreement that provided for consultation between the two governments and improved security arrangements. The Unionists want to have this scrapped on the grounds that it grants a role to a foreign government in Dublin to intervene in Ulster affairs. At present no solution is in sight. Ulster is a part of the United Kingdom governed without consent and consensus.

Dominated by religion and nationality, politics in Ulster is different from the rest of the United Kingdom. It differs in other respects. It has no form of elected local government. No main British party fights seats in Ulster at general elections. In elections to the European Parliament, it has a form of proportional representation. As part of its battle against terrorism in the province the Thatcher government has abolished the right to silence in courts for terrorist suspects, taken power to detain suspects for up to seven days, and has forbidden television channels to broadcast interviews with supporters of terrorism, including even elected politicians. Northern Ireland more than ever is a case of exceptionalism in British politics.

SOCIAL CLASS

Discussion of social class has been a major feature of analyses of British politics. In large part this has been because of the relative weakness of other social cleavages—race, language, and religion. For most of the postwar period commentators divided the electorate into two broad groupings, based on occupational class. The working class (60–66 percent) was so termed because its members were engaged in manual work; the middle class (about a third) was engaged in service and white-collar occupations. In recent years changes in patterns of employment have made the old two class model less useful. The decline of manufacturing industry, the growth of the service sector and self-employment, and the spread of affluence have all weakened the relevence of the old model. Britain is now a more bourgeois society; some two-thirds of homes are privately owned, including those of many workers.

Some analysts, impressed with the economic and political differences within social classes, claim that the more significant differences may be explained in regional terms, for example, north versus south. Others point to divisions between those employed in the public sector (largely dependent upon government expenditure) and the private sector, or those dependent on public services (for example, transport or housing) compared with those relying on private provision of these services. Researchers have recently provided a fivefold categorization of

TABLE 2-2 Social Class Divisions

Social Class	Percentage of Population
Salariat	27%
Routine nonmanuals	24
Petit bourgeois	8
Supervisors, technicians	7
Working class	34

Source: A. Heath, R. Jowell, and J. Curtice, *How Britian Votes* (Oxford: Pergamon, 1985).

social class in contemporary Britain (see Table 2-2). The two largest groups are the manual workers (down from 47 percent to 34 percent between 1964 and 1983) and a salariat of managers and professionals (up to 27 percent from 18 percent in those years). The manual working class has been reduced because the analysts have extracted the supervisors and the technicians as well as the self-employed.

EDUCATION

Over 80 percent of secondary school children (aged 11 to 16) are in comprehensive or nonselective schools. Some 10 percent attend a selective grammar or secondary modern school and 6 percent attend the fee-paying independent schools. This last group includes the prestigious and very expensive schools like Eton, Harrow, and Winchester. It is from these last schools that a large proportion of the elite, including Conservative MPs, senior civil servants, judges, and company directors come. It is worth noting, however, that Mrs. Thatcher is a grocer's daughter and went to her local grammar school before going to Oxford University. Britain's higher education system for long reflected elitist values. Until the 1960s only a tiny proportion of the 18-year to 21-year age group received a university education. The proportion has increased significantly in the last two decades, so that 15 percent now attend either polytechnics or universities. That figure is, however, still appreciably smaller than that in many other Western states.

3

The Role of Government—
Central and Local

The authority of central government in Britain has been firmly established since the late seventeenth century. With the exception of Ireland just before and after the 1914–18 war and, more recently, Ulster, the government's ability to make and enforce laws has not been seriously challenged. Yet the role of government has changed greatly in the twentieth century. Before 1914 most citizens could live their lives and have little contact with, or even awareness of, central government. The main activities of the state (in terms of employees and its spending) concerned defense, law and order, diplomacy, and finance. The oldest departments and, apart from the prime ministership, the most prestigious in British government—the Home Office, the Treasury, and Foreign Office—are those that deal with these functions.

As the electorate grew in the late nineteenth and early twentieth centuries, so more people increasingly looked to government to satisfy their housing, employment, education, and welfare needs. In turn, government has emerged as a big spender and big taxer. In 1900 there were 116,000 nonindustrial civil servants; today the figure is just under 600,000. Public expenditure was only 10 percent of GNP in 1900 compared to 43 percent in 1987.

During this century the composition of public spending has increasingly shifted away from defense to the welfare activities of social security, health, and education. Another stimulus to the expansion of government has been war. In the 1914–18 war government took control of industry and essential supplies and introduced food rationing and military conscription. During the 1939–45 war there were similar interventions by central government; total war meant that the community had to be mobilized for the struggle. After 1945 the state also assumed responsibility for managing the economy to provide for full employment and played a much larger role in housing, education, and welfare. It also took some key industries into state ownership.

PUBLIC CORPORATIONS

The most direct form of intervention in the economy is government ownership of an industry or firm. Before 1939 the state controlled a few activities, such as the British Broadcasting Corporation and the Central Electricity Board, which were managed as public corporations. The main feature of the public corporation is that each activity has its own management board and chairman, appointed by a government minister. The minister is responsible to Parliament for general policy but not for the day-to-day running of the corporation. This format was adopted as the best means of combining the principles of commercial freedom and public accountability. Between 1945 and 1951 when the Labour government took the coal, railway, steel, gas, and electricity industries into public ownership, each was run by a public corporation.

Since 1979 the Thatcher government has privatized (sold to the employees or the public) a number of these public corporations (see Table 6.1, page 56). Many of the industries were monopolies, and free market Conservatives objected that, since they were protected from competition or from commercial discipline, they were inefficient.

In addition, the ideology of the Thatcher wing of the Conservatives—many compared it to "Reaganism"—advocated sweeping liberal reforms in the direction of a free-market economy. We shall discuss this in more detail in Chapter 6.

PUBLIC SPENDING

Public expenditure is the sum total of money spent by central and local government, na-

tionalized industries, and public corporations. At present some 70 percent of the total is spend by central government, 25 percent by local authorities, and the rest by public corporations. In the financial year 1988–89 the total public spending bill was planned to be £156.8 billion, or 42.5 percent of national income. Within this total the big spenders were

Social security	£50 billion
Health	£21.8 billion
Education and Science	£21.9 billion
Defense	£19.2 billion

The overall amount of public spending and the figure for each department are arrived at by a process of bargaining between the relevant departments and the Treasury. The Treasury tries to get the cabinet to agree to a fixed total of public spending for the coming financial year. This is an important bargaining lever for the Treasury; if the aggregate figure of the departments' spending proposals exceeds what has already been agreed, then there follows a series of bilateral meetings between the Treasury and the departments to meet the original target. If disagreements remain then the issue is referred to a cabinet committee, called informally the Star Chamber. This committee largely consists of nonspending ministers and usually comes down on the side of the Treasury.

In the postwar period, government spending has steadily grown as a share of GNP. In all but a few years since 1957, the proportion has increased from year to year. In 1962–63, for instance, the proportion was 35 percent; by 1969–70 it rose to 40 percent, and in 1975–76 to 48.5 percent. When Mrs. Thatcher took over in 1979, the proportion was 43 percent. In spite of her determined efforts to cut that figure, it actually rose, until, by 1987–88, it fell back to 42.5 percent. One reason why the figure has grown is that in the 1960s and 1970s British governments spent money in anticipation of levels of economic growth that were rarely achieved. Lobbies for various interests and many departments also have an interest in expanding budgets. As the number of elderly people has increased and they live longer, so their demands for pensions and other services (notably health care) increase. In addition the large increase in unemployment between 1979 and 1983 imposed extra demands on the welfare budget. Such expenditure is virtually "out of control," without a change in government policy.

Richard Rose has calculated that some 30 percent of the population derive their primary incomes from government, as recipients of pensions, student grants, unemployment, sickness, or other benefits. Some 90 percent of families contain at least one beneficiary of the welfare state (for example, education or a pension), and some 28 percent of the work force are employed in the public sector by central and local government or by public corporations.

LOCAL GOVERNMENT

As noted in Chapter 1, Britain is a unitary political system, with sovereignty being centralized in Parliament. Such a system contrasts with the federalism of Germany or the United States in which the states have independent powers. Local authorities derive their powers from Parliament, which can alter or abolish them. Indeed in 1972 the government suspended the Stormont Parliament in Northern Ireland and in 1974 altered the boundaries of local government in Britain. In 1986 the Thatcher government abolished the Greater London Council and six other metropolitan county authorities.

Traditionally, there was something of a *partnership* between central and local government, involving give and take between the two tiers. Increasingly, however, the relationship has become one of *principal* and *agent*, in which the center makes policy decisions, with scant regard for local views, and expects local government to administer the policy.

In dealing with local authorities the central government has four important levers at its disposal. The first is its power to determine the structure of local government, already referred to. The second is powers of local government that can be granted and revoked at will by the center. If local authorities exceed or fail to carry out their statutory duties, the elected councillors—recognized as responsible for the policy—can be penalized and disqualified from office. Each year accountants examine local authority spending, and if they find unlawful expenditure, they can charge the local politicians responsible. Third, many of the policies which local authorities carry out are largely laid down by the center. For example, although the local authorities are responsible for building and running schools, appointing teachers, and controlling admissions, other matters such as the qualifications of teachers, school curriculum, and leaving age of students are under the control of Parliament. Even where policies are not laid down by parliamentary statute, central government departments send out circulars that contain policy advice.

Finally, there are financial powers. Around a half of local spending comes in the form of block grants from central government. The grants take account of the "needs" of areas (for example, numbers of old people, schoolchildren, and so on, who require services) and helps authorities throughout the country to provide services of approximately equal standard. In recent years the Thatcher government has increasingly laid down how the money is spent and also curbed the ability of local authorities to raise their own finance. For centuries, rates or (property taxes) were levied on each household and business. These two sources together provided some 30 percent of local government revenue. In 1981 the government tried to set a limit to the amount which some local authorities could increase their rates from one year to another. In 1988 the government passed a bill introducing a Community charge (poll tax) of about £200 to be paid by everybody aged 18 or over in the local community. The business rate is to be uniform throughout the country and set by central government.

Since 1945 the role and influence of local government in national life has declined substantially. It has lost its role in running hospitals and the gas, electricity, and water services to other agencies. The National Health Service, which provides "medicare" to the population, is administered through regional boards, members of which are appointed by local and central government. The same arrangement applies broadly to the administration of water, gas, and electricity. In each case, however, the boundaries of the regions are different, and there is no regional tier of government in Britain. Since its return to office in 1987, the Conservative government has further reduced the role of local authorities in education and housing (as discussed shortly). Yet is is worth noting that local authorities still employ some 10 percent of the work force, own about one-sixth of the housing stock, educate some 90 percent of school children, and account for about a quarter of all state spending.

A cardinal principle of public policy in Britain, and one that to some extent weakens local autonomy, is that people should receive similar benefits and similar entitlements regardless of where they live. Both parties, when in government, have been in favor of central direction. Labour governments, in support of redistribution to the less well-off, have traditionally looked to local authorities to promote a more equal provision of social services. They have, for example, insisted upon comprehensive or nonselective secondary education (after the age of 11) and encouraged the building by local councils of more houses for rent. Until 1979 the Conservatives favored more choice and regarded local authorities as a center of independence from central government.

Since 1979 central/local relations have changed radically. A more ideological Conservative government has been faced with a number of left-wing Labour authorities, particularly in London and the big cities of Sheffield, Liverpool, and Manchester. Some Conservatives saw these authorities as bastions of local socialism, a stronghold of public sector trade unions and wasteful spenders of public money. The government has wanted to control public spending and make a number of policy changes, particularly in education and housing, which have been resisted by the Labour authorities. The left-wing councils were determined to fight the "cuts" imposed by the Conservative governments. As they regularly exceeded government-decreed spending targets, so their central government grants were cut back further.

The Thatcher government has taken a number of measures to restructure the role of local authorities. It has taken more control over expenditure. It has insisted that local authority–owned houses should be offered for sale to tenants at a substantial discount. This policy has been enormously popular, and since 1979 more than a million tenants have bought their own properties. The government has also legislated to allow schools to "opt out" of local authority control. Finally, it has abolished the rating system which was the main source of independent local finance and replaced it with the European Community charge.

The local element in government in Britain has been substantially reduced in the past decade. Critics point to the low level of turnout in local elections, (about 40 percent), the predominance of national issues in the local campaigns, and what they regard as the needless "politicization" of issues. But with no regional level of government, no elected local government in Northern Ireland, no elected assemblies in Scotland or Wales, and a much diminished role for local government, Britain now has a political system that is perhaps the most centralized in the Western world.

4

Political Parties, Elections, and Pressure Groups

In a predominantly two-party system and in a largely consensual society political parties are almost bound to be coalitions. The Conservative and Labour parties have been good examples of catch-all parties, rejecting distinctive ideologies and sectional appeals and appealing to the nation as a whole.

The two-party system has had significant consequences for the conduct of British politics. Socially it has related to the class system (for there have been few other social cleavages to be expressed in politics); in Parliament, it has created the division between a coherent united government and a united opposition; and it has simplified the voters' choice at election time into voting for or against a government. The fact that the government is formed by members of the winning party also helps to promote cohesion in the cabinet.

Three features of the main British parties are worth noting. First, they are *program-matic*. At general elections parties present manifestos outlining the policies that they will pursue if elected to government. These are taken seriously by party leaders, and at election time local candidates are expected to support the policies. Although the winning party may claim to have a mandate, or support, for its policy—on the grounds that it won the election—in fact issues are only one factor in a voter's decision to support a political party. But compared with the personality and standing of the leaders and local candidates, the policies and perceived competence of the parties are more influential with the voters.

British parties are also *disciplined*. In voting in the House of Commons members are expected to vote in accord with the party line, and a politician who persistently breaks the party line can find himself or herself deprived of the party whip (i.e., effective membership in the party in Parliament). Although back-bench dissent has increased in recent years, British parties are still overwhelmingly united in voting.

Finally, the British parties are *centralized*. Although local parties nominate candidates, their choice is made from a list of candidates already approved by the party headquarters, or else the choice has to be ratified subsequently. Decisions about a party's policies, election strategies, and political tactics are decided at the center.

There have been several periods in this century when Britain has departed from the "norm" of two main parties and one-party majority government. Until 1918 four substantial parties were represented in the House of Commons. In addition to the dominant Liberal and Conservative parties there were some 30 Labour and 80 Irish Nationalist MPs. In the 1920s the declining Liberal party and rising Labour party vied to be the main alternative to the Conservatives. Between 1914 and 1945 there were also a number of minority or coalition governments; there were coalition governments for much of the war years, between 1916 and 1918 and 1940 and 1945. Thus only the period since 1945 deserves to be characterized by the labels of two-party competition and one-party government.

CONSERVATIVES

The Conservative party can trace its origins back to the seventeenth century and has had a continuous existence in its modern form for well over a century. The fact that it has been the normal party of government in the twentieth century has affected internal relationships within the party. Usually the party leader has been prime minister and its frontbench spokesmen ministers. It is not surprising, therefore, that the extra parliamentary elements have often deferred to the leadship. The party has also shown a remarkable ability to move from representing the landed interest in the first half of the nineteenth century to embrace the rising indus-

trial groups in the second half of that century, then the professional middle class, and, since 1918, a substantial minority of the working class. A secret of the Conservative party's electoral strength over the years has been its ability to so appeal to many social groupings. Its sheer durability is proof of its success.

It is difficult to characterize the party as an ideological one or to describe a distinct Conservative ideology. Yet there are values which many Conservatives hold dear. For example, they regard freedom of choice as crucial for the development of individual character. Hence the leaders' support for low levels of direct taxation (so that people can spend more of their money as they choose), indirect over direct taxation, free enterprise rather than state ownership of industries, home ownership, and some private provision of education and health care. In foreign affairs Conservatives have traditionally been associated with an assertive voice for British interests, a strong defense posture and support for the domestic forces of law and order. The party is pledged to retain nuclear weapons and Britain's membership of NATO.

Yet the party has also been adaptable, or opportunistic, in its defense of these values. For example, Conservatives had to give way over the reduction of the powers of the House of Lords in 1911, accept the moves to independence of many colonies after 1945, tolerate and even introduce measures of state ownership and state intervention in the economy, and live with a steady expansion of state provision of welfare.

A major factor in the electoral success of the Conservative party has been the ineptitude and divisions of the opposition parties. The Liberal party split in 1916, the Labour party has frequently been beset by internal divisions, and a number of Labour right-wingers split from it in 1981 to form the Social Democratic party. In the interwar years the party profited as the non-Conservative vote was divided between the declining Liberal and rising Labour parties. Something like this has again been happening in British politics in the 1980s, as the Alliance (Liberals and Social Democrats) and Labour parties competed for non-Conservative support.

The dominant strand in Conservative party philosophy has been the Tory or One-Nation tradition. As Samuel Beer has pointed out in his *British Politics in the Age of Collectivism* (1965), this view accepts a positive role for the state, particularly in providing welfare, achieving full employment, and taking care of the poor in society. Like the Labour party it has accepted a *collectivist* view of society. On the other hand, the neo-liberal element in the party prefers a smaller role for government, reduced state spending, and greater scope for the free market and individual choice.

There have been two key stages in the development of postwar Conservatism. After 1945 the Labour governments fashioned the main policies for the postwar era. As noted on page 23, it greatly expanded state ownership in major industries, established a national health service, and extended the welfare state. The Conservative party, under the influence of the "One-Nation" ideas, came to terms with these policies. The Conservative leaders in the 1950s and 1960s, Winston Churchill, Sir Antony Eden, and Harold Macmillan, believed that maintaining the postwar consensus was the best way to run the country and attract working class electoral support. In government in the 1950s, the party encouraged competition, greatly expanded home ownership, denationalized (or restored to private ownership) the steel industry, and abolished many of the Labour government's controls on prices. But there was a good deal of common ground with the Labour party (for example, no further denationalization and maintaining the welfare state). The strategy worked, and the party was continuously in government from 1951 to 1964, (see Table 4–1).

In February and October 1974 the party suffered two general election defeats and the "neo-liberals" in the Conservative party gradually achieved more influence. Under Mrs. Thatcher, who became leader of the

TABLE 4–1 Postwar Prime Ministers and their Terms, 1945–1979 to Date

Terms	Prime Ministers
August 1945	Clement Attlee
October 1951	Winston Churchill
April 1955	Antony Eden
January 1957	Harold Macmillan
October 1963	Alec Douglas Home
October 1964	Harold Wilson
June 1970	Edward Heath
March 1974	Harold Wilson
April 1976	James Callaghan
May 1979–	Margaret Thatcher

party in 1975 and prime minister in 1979, the party has won three successive general elections (1979, 1983, and 1987 (Table 4–2), and many Conservative policies have been designed to dismantle that postwar consensus.

CONSERVATIVE PARTY STRUCTURE

The structure of the Conservative party largely reflects the circumstances of its historical development. The party developed first as a grouping within Parliament and its leaders created the extraparliamentary organs to cater for a mass electorate in the late nineteenth century. In other words, the extra-parliamentary machinery was developed as a handmaiden of the parliamentary

TABLE 4–2 General Election Results, 1964–1987

Date of Election	Share of Vote Obtained by		Liberal Alliance (1983–1987)
	Conservative	Labour	
1964	43.4%	44.1%	11.2%
1966	41.9	48.1	8.5
1970	46.4	43.1	7.5
1974			
February	37.8	37.1	19.3
October	35.8	39.2	18.3
1979	43.9	37.0	13.8
1983	42.4	27.6	25.4
1987	42.2	30.8	22.6

leadership. The basic unit of the party is the local Conservative association in each constituency. This body raises funds, promotes the party's policies, and selects the candidate to fight in parliamentary elections. The National Union of Conservative Associations represents the local associations and organizes the party's five-day annual conference, which is attended by some 4,000 representatives. Although this body is addressed by the party leader and debates policy motions, it has no formal policy making role.

The party also has a Central Office, which is its professional bureaucracy. It is under the formal control of the party leader who appoints the chairmen of Central Office and Research Department and other senior officers. It consists of sections that supervise constituency organization, finance, policy research, and publicity, and the Research Department acts as a secretariat to the party in Parliament.

There is no doubt that power clearly lies with the party in Parliament and with the parliamentary leadership. If the leader is prime minister, he or she selects the cabinet and in opposition chooses his or her own "Shadow Cabinet" (unlike the Labour leader), appoints the chief whip, and has the greatest political control on policy. But the loyalty of Conservative MPs to the leader is not unlimited. They expect to have their views listened to, and, above all, they expect electoral success. Back-bench dissatisfaction has helped to remove a number of leaders: Balfour in 1911, Austen Chamberlain in 1922, Neville Chamberlain in 1940, Sir Alec Douglas Home in 1965, and Edward Heath in 1975.

The most important party function of Conservative MPs is to elect the leader of the party. Traditionally, when the party was in office, the leader "emerged." When a Conservative prime minister died or resigned, the party left it to the monarch to invite, after consultations with senior party figures, a prominent Conservative minister to form a government. In 1965 the party adopted a system of formal election by the MPs, and the rules were amended in 1975 to provide for an annual election. A candidate wins on the first ballot if he or she gets an absolute majority and a lead over the runner-up of more than 15 percent of those eligible to vote. If this condition is not satisfied, a second ballot is held a week later and new candidates may enter. To win on a second ballot a candidate must still have an absolute majority of votes. If a third ballot is required it is held among the three leading candidates and only a relative majority is required. In 1975 Mrs. Thatcher decided to challenge the incumbent, Mr. Heath, and she was elected on the second ballot. To date she has not been challenged in a leadership contest.

LABOUR

The Labour Representation Committee was established in 1900 and renamed the Labour party in 1906. It was established largely at the behest of the trade unions which supplied the bulk of membership and funds. The trade union leaders at that time were not particularly interested in socialist ideas, let alone Marxist ones. Their reasons for establishing a working class party were frankly sectional; they wanted to promote the interests of the trade unions, which at the time were being damaged by the decisions of the courts, and to get working men into Parliament. In the 1918 general election Labour profited from divisions among the Liberals and managed to become the second largest party in the House of Commons and, therefore, the official opposition.

In the same year Labour adopted socialism in its program *Labour and the New Social Order.* That document's famous Clause iv states that the object of the party is to "secure for the producers by hand or by brain the full fruits of their industry and the most equitable distribution thereof that may be possible upon the basis of the common ownership of the means of production and the best obtainable system of popular administration and control of each industry and service ...". The program talked of replacing capitalism, or production for profit, by a system of state ownership or nationalization of industries and services. Only in 1945, when Labour formed its first majority government, did it have the chance to enact much of this program.

LABOUR IDEOLOGY

Marxism has been only one element, and a rather insignificant one, in the values of the Labour party. Most early Labour MPs mentioned the Bible as a source of their ideas and inspiration. Many Labour leaders and MPs have accepted the criticisms of the economic failings and social divisiveness of capitalism, without believing in the inevitability of class conflict and political revolution. Very few have wanted to overthrow the British parliamentary system. Rather, they wished to capture political power and use the system for their own ends. The values of other groups, like nonconformists, the early Fabians, the trade unions, and the cooperators have contributed many elements to the party's ideology, notably its support for the "have-nots" social equality, and cooperation.

It is possible to discern a number of recurring elements in the party's ideology and objectives.

1. The public ownership (or nationalization) of the major industries. The early Fabians thought such steps essential to facilitate economic planning. After 1945 the coal, gas, electricity, railway, steel, and road transport industries were all taken into public ownership. This established the postwar mixed economy and gave the government more control over the economy.
2. The protection and enhancement of trade union activity by extending free collective bargaining and strengthening the negotiating rights of unions.
3. Redistribution to the less well-off through more progressive income taxes and the provision of state-financed welfare services. In 1947 the Labour government established the National Health Service, under which treatment was given free to all citizens who required it, and greatly expanded the welfare state.
4. The public provision (i.e., by state expenditure funded out of taxes) of social services, on the grounds that ability to pay should not determine one's entitlement to education and housing. In the 1987 general election Labour leaders said they would increase income taxes to pay for social programs.
5. An optimistic view of human nature and belief that state action to improve social and economic conditions will promote fraternity and social solidarity.

The Labour party has been prone to divide, at times bitterly, over the meaning of socialism, and there have been organized factions of the right and left. Those on the left of the party often attack the parliamentary leadership and Labour governments for not being "socialist" enough or betraying election promises. In particular, they have favored more egalitarian social and economic policies and sweeping measures of state economic intervention and state ownership of industry than those practiced by Labour ministers. The latter have often been accused by their left-wing critics of being mere "reformers." Those on the right-wing of the party have downgraded the importance of public ownership and sought to gain the confidence of industry and finance. They have regarded socialism as the promotion of greater equality, to be achieved through more spending on social programmes. Foreign policy and defense have also been recurring sources of division. On the whole the left is skeptical about the United States and NATO and has wanted Britain to give up her nuclear weapons and deny the United States bases in Britain for the use of nuclear weapons. The right has disagreed on all counts. It has also been more supportive of Britain's membership of the European Community, while the left has consistently opposed this on the grounds that its free competition policies limit socialist measures of economic intervention and planning.

For most of the postwar period the parliamentary party was led from the center-right. But during the 1970s the conference and NEC moved to the left. In more recent years, particularly after the exit of more than a score of right-wingers in 1981 and 1982, the left has gained in the parliamentary party. However, the left wing has now split into two groups, a "hard," almost Marxist group, centered around Tony Benn and Eric Heffer, and a "soft" left. The last two leaders, Mr. Foot (1980–83) and Mr. Kinnock, and most of the latter's leadership team, are from the second group.

The important position of the trade unions within the Labour party (discussed shortly) has been an undoubted source of organizational strength to the party. But ideologically it also presents problems. The trade unions firmly believe in free collective bargaining. As sectional bodies they wish to use their market or bargaining power to improve the conditions of members and to maintain or perhaps increase their wage differentials over other workers. It has proved difficult, however, to reconcile such a free market mentality with policies of greater economic equality and economic planning. Both the Wilson governments of 1964–70 and the Callaghan government of 1976–79 were involved in bitter confrontations with the trade unions.

LABOUR PARTY STRUCTURE

Individual members can join the Labour party through their constituency parties. In 1987 the individual membership figure was just over 300,000, a figure that has been in steady decline in the last three decades. In addition some 6 million members are indirect members, or affiliated through their trade unions. This membership (and the voting power that it confers) enables the trade unions to dominate two of the party's major policymaking institutions, the annual party Conference, and the National Executive Committee, which is elected at the Conference and runs the party between Conferences.

The unions command five-sixths of the votes at Conference and their votes elect 18 of the 29 members of the NEC. Conference decides the policy of the party though it is up to Labour MPs to decide when and how to implement it in Parliament. If a Conference resolution is carried by a two-thirds majority, it becomes part of the party's program. The party's manifesto for a general election is drawn up at a joint session of the Parliamentary leader and NEC. The National Executive Committee represents the different groups in the parties and consists of six groups:

1. Twelve of the 29 members are nominated and elected by the trade union membership.
2. Seven members are nominated and elected by the constituency parties.
3. Five women are nominated and elected by the entire Conference (which is trade union dominated).
4. The Socialist Associations and Cooperative Societies nominate and elect one representative.
5. The party treasurer is elected by the whole Conference (again, trade union dominated).
6. The Young Socialists are represented by their leader.

To these 27 members are added the parliamentary party's leader and deputy-leader, who sit ex officio. In 1981 the Labour party reformed its method of electing its leader and deputy-leader. Until then they were elected by Labour MPs. As part of its campaign to make the Parliamentary party more receptive to the party activists, the left sought to take the election away from MPs. Under the new system the leader and deputy-leader are elected by an electoral college in which the voting strength is allocated to the trade unions (40 percent), the constituency parties (30 percent), and the Labour MPs (30 percent). In theory, it is possible for a leader to be elected who has little support among Labour MPs.

The Labour leader is more beholden to groups outside of Parliament than is the

Conservative leader. In particular he or she has to maintain good relations with the leaders of big trade unions to make sure that both Conference and the NEC are manageable. In the 1970s the NEC came under the control of the left, and it proved extremely troublesome to Mr. Wilson and Mr. Callaghan when they were prime ministers. Under Neil Kinnock, the NEC has been more supportive of the leader. Similarly, the party organization is not under the control of the party leader but of the National Executive. Finally, in opposition, most of the Shadow Cabinet are elected by Labour MPs.

It is possible to read Labour's constitution in a way that suggests that the party's mass membership represented in Conference actually controls the party and decides policy. After all, the constitution formally vests party sovereignty in the Conference. Party leaders have down the years regularly pleaded with it not to "tie our hands" with inconvenient votes. Some observers have argued that the party's constitution is actually incompatible with the British constitution, in which Parliament is an independent body and MPs are not to be instructed by outside bodies. What would happen when Conference and the PLP were set on different courses? Whose will would prevail?

Until 1960 the dilemma did not arise because the parliamentary leadership usually got its way in Conference due to the support of the major trade unions. In 1960, however, the Conference narrowly voted for a unilateralist defense policy. The party leader, Hugh Gaitskell, with the support of the majority of Labour MPs, refused to accept the policy and pledged himself to reverse it. He managed to do it the next year. The autonomy of the parliamentary party seemed assured. In the late 1960s, however, some of the major trade unions moved to the left and a breach opened up between the Parliamentary leadership and the more left-wing Conference. That breach has never been fully healed. On the whole, Conference delegates have generally been to the left of the PLP and favored more radical socialist policies than the parliamentary leadership. Confer-

ences have often been embarrassing for the party leadership and presented the spectacle of a divided party to the public. Between 1974 and 1979 policies of the Labour government were regularly voted down and bitterly attacked in conference. Labour right-wingers were increasingly defensive after 1979 as the party adopted more left-wing policies and constitutional changes.

OTHER PARTIES

In March 1981 a number of Labour right-wingers broke away and formed the Social Democratic Party, which espoused many right-wing Labour policies. The leaders of the new party objected to changes in Labour party rules for electing the party leader and the reselection of MPs, and what they called "the drift towards extremism in the Labour party," particularly to unilateral nuclear disarmament and reversing Britain's membership of the European Community. Soon the party formed an electoral pact with the Liberal party and the two fought the 1983 and 1987 elections together as the "Alliance."

In the postwar period, the main third party has been the Liberal party. The Liberals were a party of government until 1918 and have supplied some of the country's outstanding prime ministers—Gladstone, Asquith, and Lloyd George. But the party's electoral support declined rapidly in the inter war years and after 1931 has had only a handful of MPs. Its electoral support gradually increased in the 1970s, and by 1979 it had 13 percent of the vote but still few seats. It has suffered from an electoral system that penalizes minor parties that spread their voting strength.

The SDP and Liberal parties formed an alliance for the 1983 and 1987 elections. In spite of gaining considerable electoral support, 25 percent and 23 percent, respectively, the new party gained few seats because of the electoral system. In 1983 the Alliance came within 200,000 votes of overtaking Labour as the second largest party in votes. Again, it suffered from the first-past-the-post electoral system. In 1988 the Liberals and a majority of the Social Democrats voted to merge in a new party, the Social and Liberal Democrats. It elected a new leader, Paddy Ashdown, to succeed the Liberal leader David Steel. The dissenting minority continues to call themselves the Social Democrats.

The non-English parts of the United Kingdom have their own distinctive party battles. In Wales the nationalist party (Plaid Cymru) defends Welsh culture and language. In Scotland the nationalists campaign for independence or separation for Scotland. In Wales and Scotland the nationalist parties enjoyed a rise in support in 1974 but it has not been sustained. In 1987 the Scottish Nationalists gained 14 percent of the Scottish vote, the Welsh Nationalists 8 percent of the Welsh vote. In Northern Ireland the Protestant Unionists are divided into two groups, Official Unionists and Democratic Unionists, and in 1987 these captured 12 of the 17 seats. The pro-united Ireland Sinn Fein party (which supports the terrorism of the IRA) gained 1 seat. The Social and Democratic and Labour party, which wants a united Ireland to come through peaceful and constitutional means, gained 3 seats.

IMPACT OF PARTIES

There has been a debate among students of British politics about whether the parties make a significant difference to government policies. Richard Rose has argued for a "consensus" model. He is impressed by the continuity of policy outcomes in many areas from the mid-1950s to 1983, particularly on the economy, regardless of changes of party control in government. On rates of inflation, unemployment, economic growth, living standards, and economic equality, the trends continued in the same direction, regardless of which party was in control. One may point to such forces for continuity as the civil service, external pressures, demands of pressure groups, and the "reality" of circumstances, all of which limits the influence of party ideology.

On the other hand, some observers (e.g., Finer, *Adversary Politics and Electoral Reform*) claim that Britain has adversary politics and point to abrupt discontinuities in policies when one party replaces another in office. When Labour replaced the Conservatives in 1974, there were abrupt reversals of policy over industrial relations, housing, education, and policies on incomes and the EEC. There was discontinuity again when the Conservatives returned to government in 1979 under Mrs. Thatcher. Her government scrapped the Labour government's incomes policy, consultation with the unions over economic policy, and plans for devolution of power for Scotland and Wales and commenced a program of selling off state-run enterprises. Her government's record is perhaps the best proof that parties can make a difference.

In fact, many of the most significant discontinuities in economic policy have occurred within the lifetimes of government rather than after changes of party. This applies to government decisions to seek entry to the European Community in 1961 and 1967, to virtually all incomes policies, and the U-turns in economic policy of the Heath government in 1972 and of the Wilson and Callaghan Labour governments in 1975–76.

ELECTIONS

To be entitled to vote in British elections a person must be aged 18 or over, a citizen of Britain or the Irish Republic, and have their name on the electoral register in a constituency. The register is compiled each year, but because of inaccuracies in registration, deaths, and movements of people, the actual register is out of date when it is published. The average official turnout figure in general elections of 75 percent is probably closer to 80 percent of those actually eligible to vote.

British election campaigns are rather short compared with the length of campaigns for the American presidency and Senate. Unless the government loses a key vote or a vote of confidence in the House of Commons (when general elections are virtually certain to follow), the prime minister is free to choose the date of the election within the five-year lifetime of the Parliament. Once the monarch dissolves Parliament (as requested by the prime minister), elections have to be held in less than a month.

The opportunity to name the date of the election is clearly an advantage to the government. The prime minister can take advantage of an upturn in the economy, divisions in the opposition parties, and evidence of increased support for the government in the opinion polls to choose the most helpful date for his party. Mrs. Thatcher's decisive victories in 1983 and 1987 certainly owed a lot to good timing. The government had been languishing in the opinion polls for much of 1981 and early 1982 (until the Falklands war) and for much of 1985 and 1986. Table 4–3 shows that in postwar elections governments have been as likely to lose ground (and elections) as to improve their position.

Britain is divided into 650 constituencies, each of which elects a member of Parliament. Every decade or so Boundary Commissions redraw constituency boundaries (or districts) so that electorates are approximately equal in size. The average size of a constituency electorate in 1987 was 66,000. Recent redistributions have shifted seats to the south of Britain and the suburbs and away from the north and inner cities to take account of population movements. In the process, the reallocation of seats have helped the Conservatives and penalized Labour.

Under the British first-past-the-post electoral system, the candidate with the most votes in the constituency wins. Because more seats are now fought by at least three candidates, more MPs are elected by a minority of votes in the constituencies. In 1983 and 1987 fewer than half of the 650 MPs had 50 percent or more of the vote in their constituencies.

The first-past-the-post majoritarian electoral system, in a predominantly two-party system, has usually helped one party to emerge with a majority of seats. Conversely, proportional electoral methods in multiparty systems help the emergence of coalition governments. The first are found largely in Anglo-American societies, the second in West European societies. Defenders of the British system point to its undoubted virtues. A predominantly two-party system facilitates meaningful electoral choice of a government. Only once in the postwar period (in February 1974) has an election failed to produce a party with a majority of seats. Voters are therefore able to hold the governing party accountable for its record at the subsequent election. This adds another dimension to the idea of responsible government.

But the first-past-the-post electoral system has also come under criticism in recent years. It has always worked against parties which spread their vote evenly. In 1983 and 1987 there was a new order of distortion when the Alliance gained only 3.5 percent of seats for 25 percent and 23 percent of the popular vote respectively. In the two elections the Conservatives were able to win landslide victories (61 percent and 57 percent of the seats in the House of Commons)

TABLE 4–3 Fate of Incumbents in British General Elections, 1950–1987

Election Year	Incumbent Party	Change in Vote (%)
1950	Labour	−2.2%
1951	Labour	+2.7
1955	Conservative	+1.7
1959	Conservative	−0.3
1964	Conservative	−6.0
1966	Labour	+3.8
1970	Labour	−4.9
1974		
February	Conservative	−8.6
October	Labour	+2.1
1979	Labour	−5.3
1983	Conservative	−1.5
1987	Conservative	−0.1

with only 42 percent of the popular vote. The system has also made the parties' parliamentary representation more regional. The more economically prosperous regions of Britain (the south and the Midlands) have cumulatively become more Conservative while the less prosperous north and Scotland have become more Labour. The electoral system works to "over-represent" the parties in these regions. In 1987, for example, the Conservatives gained 69 percent of the 516 seats in England with 46 percent of the vote; Labour gained 70 percent of the 71 seats in Scotland with 42 percent of the vote.

VOTING BEHAVIOR

After 1918, when most of the adult population first received the vote, social class became an important correlate of the voters' choice of party. In Britain a person's social class is usually determined on the basis of his or her occupation: manual or blue-collar workers are described as working class, white-collar workers as middle class. Class has been significant because of the relative weakness of such social divisions as race, language, and religion. But one famous judgment about class and voting—that "class is the basis of British politics; all else is embellishment and detail"—has been only partly true. Between a quarter and a third of the manual working class has regularly voted Conservative and helped it win most elections.

Occupational class has been losing its influence on voting in recent years. The rise of a large third party has obviously weakened the association between two classes and two parties. But class itself has also changed; it is no longer convincing to divide the electorate into a monolithic blue-collar or working class and a monolithic middle class. The decline of manufacturing employment and the growth of white-collar and service occupations has changed the balance between the classes. The working class is probably now less than half of the work force.

But the classes themselves are also in-creasingly differentiated. The middle class divides between those employed in the private sector and those employed in the public sector (for example, school teachers and administrators). Within-class differences are reflected in voting behavior. The Conservatives gained 65 percent of the vote in 1987 of middle class employed in the private sector but only 44 percent of those in the public sector. Labour's support is increasingly found in what is called the "old working class"—members of trade unions, those living in the north, workers in heavy industry, and nonhomeowners—and is a diminishing electoral group. The "new working class" as Ivor Crewe describes it, is increasingly home-owning, resides in south Britain, is car-owning, is not in a trade union, and is employed in the private sector. In 1983 and 1987 these workers decisively preferred the Conservatives over Labour (see Table 4–4).

Combined support for the two main parties has also been eroded in the postwar period. In general elections between 1945 and 1970 the average aggregate Labour and Conservative share of the vote was 90 percent. In the last five general elections that aggregate support has fallen to an average of 75 percent. There was great disappointment among Labour party supporters with the meager achievements of the Wilson government (1964–70) and Wilson-Callaghan government (1974–79) and among Conservatives with the Heath government (1970–74). One indicator of the weakening partisanship is the decline in the number of voters who call themselves "very" or "fairly" strong Labour or Conservative party identifiers. In 1964 82 percent did; by 1987 only 64 percent did (see Table 4–5).

Conservative support has held up well, notwithstanding the rise of support for the Alliance. Virtually all the decline in two-party electoral support has been at the expense of Labour. Between 1945 and 1970 two parties each had an average local support of some 45 percent of the electorate. The Conservatives' "base" now appears to be 40–42 percent, but Labour's is only about 35 percent. Indeed in virtually every election

TABLE 4-4 How the Working Class Voted (%)

	The New Working Class				The Traditional Working Class			
	Lives in South (40%)*	Owner-occupier (57%)*	Nonunion (66%)*	Works in Private Sector	Lives in Scotland/North	Council Tenant	Union Member	Works in Public Sector
Conservative	46	44	40	38	29	25	30	32
Labour	28	32	38	39	57	57	48	49
Liberal/SDP	26	24	22	23	15	18	22	19
Conservative/Labour Maj. 1987	Conservative +18	Conservative +12	Conservative +2	Labour +1	Labour +32	Labour +17	Labour +28	Labour +18
Conservative/Labour Maj. 1983	Conservative +16	Conservative +22	Conservative +6	Labour +1	Labour +38	Labour +17	Labour +10	Labour +21
Change from 1983	+4	+3	+7	+2	−1	−4	(−7)	(−2)

Source: I. Crewe, *Guardian,* 15 June 1987.

*Percentage of all manual workers.

TABLE 4–5 Decline in Party Identification, 1964–1987

	1964	1983	1987
% with a party identification	93	86	85
% identifying with Conservative	38	38	36
% identifying with Labour	43	32	31
	81	70	67
% Conservative identifiers only			
Very strong identifiers	48	34	32
Fairly strong identifiers	41	43	45
Not very strong identifiers	11	23	23
% Labour identifiers only			
Very strong identifiers	45	32	37
Fairly strong identifiers	43	39	41
Not very strong identifiers	12	29	22

Sources: British general election studies for 1964; BBC/Gallup Survey for 1983 and 1987.

between 1951 and 1983, Labour's share of the electorate declined. The exception was 1966. In the 1983 general election its share of the vote, at 27.6 percent, was its lowest since 1918 (when Labour was still a new party). The recovery in votes in 1987 was distinctly modest, to 31 percent.

The Labour party has been in electoral decline for some years. The old forces of social class, partisan loyalty, and collectivist values on which it relied have all been weakening. Some optimists make analogies with 1959 when the party had also lost its third successive general election. The party went on to win the next two general elections. But in 1959 the party was then only 5 percent behind the Conservatives in its share of the vote; now it is 11 percent. In addition, there is now a more substantial third party that can also collect anti-Conservative votes. We can, however, make too much of how social changes have eroded electoral support for the Labour party. Sociologists and political scientists acknowledge that the reduction in the size of the working class has caused a fall

in the Labour vote. Although they disagree on how much reduction in the size of the working class explains Labour's decline, they agree that the fall in votes has gone farther than would be expected on the basis of social trends alone. Other, more political, factors have played a role. In recent elections the party has been divided over defense and taxation and dogged by charges of political extremism. Its image, policies, and (particularly) the leadership of Mr. Foot in 1983 have all alienated voters.

By the time of the next general election, which is due in 1992 or earlier, it will have been more than 20 years since Labour last gained 40 percent of the vote in a general election (in the 1970 general election), and about a quarter of the electorate will have known only a Conservative government.

The Alliance gained much of its support from the unpopularity of the Labour and Conservative parties. No doubt this will be true of its successor, the Social and Liberal Democrats. Although the Alliance support lacked a distinctive social base (in the way that Conservatives may rely on the middle class and Labour on the working class) and on many issues has usually been "in between" the other parties, it has managed to attract support form the growing middle-class, well-educated public sector. After the 1987 general election Britain had two distinct two-party systems: a Conservative/Labour choice throughout much of the North of Britain and an Conservative/Alliance one in much of the south.

POLITICAL RECRUITMENT

The upper classes have dominated political leadership in Britain during the twentieth century. Between 1900 and 1964 over a third of the cabinet ministers were aristocrats (born or married into titled families). In large part this upper-class domination has been a consequence of the Conservatives being in office for such a large part of that period. In recent years MPs of all parties have been increasingly recruited from the managerial and professional occupations and from the ranks of former university graduates. But whereas Conservative MPs are drawn overwhelmingly from business (company directors and executives) and law (barristers and solicitors), Labour MPs are largely drawn from the ranks of teachers, lecturers, trade union organizers, and the welfare professions. There is also a difference in education. More than two-thirds of Conservative MPs have been educated at expensive public schools (in Britain, paradoxically, these are private fee-paying schools) and most of its university graduates come from Oxford and Cambridge universities. Labour MPs, by contrast, have usually attended grammar schools and "civic" (i.e, not Oxford or Cambridge) universities.

British politicians are increasingly "professional" in the sense that they are full time and pursue politics as a career. There is hardly any movement of senior people from other walks of life—such as business, civil service, universities, or commerce—into politics. Virtually all positions in the cabinet are filled by people who have been in the House of Commons for a long time (20 years or so, on average). This means that recruitment to government posts is dominated by people who have been socialized in Parliamentary rather than managerial skills.

Compared with their counterparts in the United States most British MPs are carpetbaggers; they will have had little prior connections with their constituencies when they are elected. There is no locality rule or even, in many seats, more than a mild preference for a candidate to have roots in the constituency. When a vacancy occurs the usual procedure for local parties is to seek nominations. A committee of the local party will then draw up a short list of about six persons and interview them. Candidates then address a larger meeting of the membership that ballots to choose the local party's official candidate.

Once an MP was elected he or she was, until recently, virtually assured of being the party's candidate until losing an election. But since 1981, local Labour parties that have a sitting Labour MP are required to hold a formal reselection not later than three years into the life of a Parliament. Since many Labour activists are left-wing, reselection is regarded as a device for forcing out right-wing MPs. At most, however, a score of Labour MPs were ousted for the 1983 and 1987 elections.

In common with politicians in most other national legislatures British MPs are overwhelmingly male, middle class, and middle aged (see Table 4–6). In spite of having a woman prime minister since 1979 and electing a record number of women MPs in 1987, only 6 percent of all MPs are women. The 1987 election was also notable for the return to the House of Commons of a record number of four Asian and Afro-Caribbean MPs—all Labour.

INTEREST GROUPS

Periodic general elections provide opportunities for people to choose a government and to give broad guidance to the rulers about matters of public policy. Elections, however, are crude instruments for reflecting popular preferences on policies. Voters cannot pick and choose between party programs. People also have specific interests, as parents, householders, pensioners, and workers, for example. They may also be con-

TABLE 4–6 Social Background of MPs, 1987

	Conservative (376)	Labour (229)	Alliance (22)
Median age	48	47	46
Education			
Public school	65%	14%	43%
University	70%	56%	75%
Oxbridge**	46%	26%	30%
Manual workers	1%	29%	0%

*Graduates of Oxford and Cambridge.

cerned about such matters as road safety, leisure opportunities, or nuclear weapons. Pressure groups exist to reflect the concerns of likeminded or similarly placed people, and are therefore an ancillary form of representation, alongside political parties. Moreover, they provide a *continuous* form of representation, compared to general elections, which are held every four years or so. Political parties are in the business of forming a government that will provide a coherent program of policies and defend it at the next general election. But parties and groups are often thrown together. In government parties are expected to have dealings with pressure groups, particularly in deciding the finer points of policy. Because spokespersons for pressure groups want to protect and promote their members' interests they are concerned with government policy in so far as it affects those interests.

There is a broad distinction between *interest* and *cause* groups. Most members of interest groups are motivated by shared economic interests, such as members of trade unions or business groups. Cause groups exist to promote an idea, such as nuclear disarmament, or the prohibition of cigarette smoking in public places. Ministers and civil servants often lack the information or expertise which is necessary to formulate policy and therefore they find pressure groups useful. Contacts with appropriate group spokespersons are helpful in working out policies that are practicable and acceptable. Approval from an affected group, or at least consulting with spokespersons, is also important for legitimizing policy. A minister lays himself open to criticism if his department has refused to have such discussions.

At times, relations may break down between the government and group. In 1970–71 the trade unions refused to consult with the Conservative government over its industrial relations legislation because the government was not prepared to negotiate on its central points. The failure to consult proved important in undermining the working of the eventual Industrial Relations Act (1971).

For the legislation to be effective trade unions had to register under a charter; most unions refused to register and the act was, in many respects, made inoperative.

Continuous contact with departments is a group's main goal. But groups may also try to influence the policy of the party. Business and finance are usually more sympathetic to the general economic policy of the Conservative party; the trade unions and the anti-poverty lobby are more sympathetic to Labour. Indeed, the trade unions are part and parcel of the Labour party (see page 31). But close identification between a party and a group has its problems for both. Although parties draw up programs to placate many groups, they also have to beware that to choose an identification or relationship with one group may alienate other voters. In recent years local Labour parties may have lost support as they have developed policies for particular groups like "the poor," the unemployed, blacks, women, gays, and lesbians.

A group's influence may depend on whether "its" party is in government. In a competitive two-party situation groups have to be prepared to deal even-handedly with any party in government. Perhaps the best example of close ties between a government and a group was the Social Contract between the trade unions and the 1974 Labour government. Under that, the trade unions promised restraint in wage settlements in return for a wide range of social and economic policies by the government. In particular, the Labour government promised to repeal legislation that the unions found offensive, provide new rights for the unions, increase spending on social welfare programs, and impose a system of price controls.

Groups may also approach members of Parliament. Although MPs are elected as members of political parties and are expected to support party programs they can still act on behalf of interests. MPs may belong to groups, or their constituencies may have clear economic interests, for example, being heavily dependent on coal-mining or defense contracts. They may ask questions in the House of Commons, speak to a brief from the group in debates, and table a motion that friendly MPs can sign. Groups also sponsor MPs. If the MP is paid a retainer by a group, then he or she is expected to declare his or her interest before speaking in Parliament on the issue. In the new Parliament, elected in June 1987, 139 of 229 Labour MPs were sponsored by the trade unions.

Groups may use other tactics to try and impress their views upon ministers. Spokespeople or sympathetic opinion formers may write newspaper articles or take part in broadcast discussions. Groups may also organize meetings and run advertisements to try and mold public opinion. In early 1988 the warnings of health unions about the underfunding of the health service were highlighted by mass media coverage of staff shortages, lack of beds, and young children being refused urgent operations. The adverse publicity was an important factor in pressuring the government to release extra funding. But threats by spokespeople to mobilize "our votes" for or against a party are not usually effective. Only a small proportion of voters are prepared to cast their ballot on the basis of a single issue. Despite the overwhelming public identification of trade union leaders with the Labour party, only 42 percent of union members voted Labour in 1987.

Groups may also mount public campaigns. A notable such case has been the Campaign for Nuclear Disarmament that wants Britain to relinquish her nuclear weapons and withdraw from NATO. The group has had no influence on the Conservative party, but since 1982 the Labour party has adopted a unilateralist defense policy. The effectiveness of sanctions or the withdrawal of cooperation by a group depends on its leverage over society. In the early 1970s the bargaining position of the coalminers was extremely powerful. Coal stocks were low, Middle East oil was extremely expensive, and the miners were able to hold out for high wage settlements. By the mid-1980s, however, the coal stocks were high,

the miners' union was divided, and the country had access to other cheap fuels. A yearlong strike by the miners in 1984–85 against pit closures failed. As a rule, resort to public appeals or use of sanctions is the sign that a group either lacks access to or influence in Whitehall.

No business group has a formal association with the Conservative party, though a number make financial contributions to it. At the end of the day, business and the Conservative party believe in free enterprise. The main advocate for the employers is the Confederation of British Industry (CBI), which was formed in 1965. Because the interests of its members are so diverse the CBI often finds it difficult to speak with a united voice on many issues. On the whole it welcomes the Thatcher government policies of tax cuts, privatization, curbs on public spending (though not for curbs on activities like road building and house building, which affects some of its member firms), and the reforms of the trade unions.

At present 40 percent of the work force is in trade unions (a decline from 55 percent in 1979), and most trade unions are affiliated to the Trade Union Congress, the body which speaks for trade unions. In the 1970s the term "corporatism" was often employed to describe the relations between government and the main producer interests. The Conservative government of Mr. Heath between 1972 and 1974 and the succeeding Labour governments tried to bargain with the unions and CBI over prices and incomes policies. Between 1974 and 1976 and TUC, for example, was virtually a partner of the Labour government.

Corporatism, however, was not really an appropriate term. The peak associations lack the authority over their own members to make "binding" deals with government. The TUC and CBI have little power to discipline their members. Since 1979 Mrs. Thatcher has set her face against such deals and has had little to do with the unions. A major difference from the 1970s has been the Thatcher government's determination not to have a formal incomes policy as part of its battle against inflation. During the 1960s and 1970s, the regular resort to incomes policy by government meant that trade unions had greater access to Whitehall. Since 1979 the unions have been weakened by the high levels of unemployment; they have lost over 3 million members. Moreover, the post-1979 legislation has further weakened the bargaining power of the unions.

5

Government and Parliament

In Britain the executive is not separate from the legislature; instead the cabinet emerges from Parliament, effectively from the House of Commons. Rather than the voters separately electing a president and a Congress, as in the United States, government ministers in Britain are drawn from and remain members of Parliament. Although there is no legal requirement that a minister be a member of either the House of Commons or Lords, such a qualification is regarded as essential because ministers are answerable to Parliament. As Walter Bagehot noted over a century ago in his *The English Constitution,* the British system *fuses* the legislature and the executive, whereas the American system *separates* them. The ruling party forms the government because it has most seats in the House of Commons and it remains the government as long as it retains a majority on key votes.

CABINET MINISTERS

The cabinet is the top tier of government. It consists of the heads of the major government departments and a few other nondepartmental ministers, such as the paymaster general or lord privy seal, who may carry out duties for the prime ministers, and the leaders of the House of Commons and House of Lords. There is something of a hierarchy within the cabinet, with the holders of the major offices like the Foreign Office, the Treasury, and the Home Office being more senior in status than ministers for education and science, Scotland, or Northern Ireland. Each departmental minister will also have under him junior ministers who help with departmental tasks and parliamentary private secretaries who help ministers with their parliamentary duties.

Although the size of the cabinet has

hardly altered in the twentieth century, that of the government has. In 1910 the size of the government was 42; under Mrs. Thatcher it has over 100 members. Yet the size of the cabinet in 1900 was 19, and in 1987 it was 22. In peacetime in the twentieth century, the size of the Cabinet has varied between 16 and 23. For most of the years of the great wars prime ministers operated with small (6 to 9) war cabinets. Many prime ministers have talked about their wish to have a small cabinet, in the interest of dispatching business more efficiently, but few have achieved it. A cabinet is more than just a decision-making body; it has to be large enough to include the heads of the major departments and represent members of different political wings in the parties. In addition lobbies for different interests, say, health or education, will be offended if "their" ministries are not included in the cabinet. A prime minister's decisions about the size of the cabinet has to balance the requirements of representativeness and efficiency.

Responsible Government

The conventions of ministerial and collective responsibility are at the heart of relations between the cabinet and the House of Commons. According to the convention of *collective responsibility,* cabinet ministers assume responsibility for all cabinet decisions, and a minister who refuses to accept such a decision, or speaks out against it, is expected to resign or face dismissal. Another aspect of the convention is that a government is expected to resign or seek a dissolution of Parliament if it is defeated on a major vote in the House of Commons. This is one way in which the House of Commons can hold the cabinet collectively responsible.

According to the convention of *ministerial responsibility* each minister is responsible to Parliament for the conduct of his department and the actions or inactions of his civil servants done in his name. The most notable resignation in recent years was that of the Foreign Secretary Lord Carrington, together with two other junior ministers in his department, in April 1982, following widespread criticism of government policy when Argentina captured the Falklands.

THE CABINET

A cabinet usually meets for three hours on Thursday mornings when Parliament is in session and on other occasions when the prime minister thinks it necessary. The cabinet has a number of important functions. It is the arena in which the most important decisions are taken: it plans the business of Parliament, it adjudicates in case of disputes between departments, it provides for oversight and coordination in the policies of government, and it provides political leadership for the party in Parliament.

Unlike its American namesake, the British cabinet is an important body. It consists of most of the political heavyweight figures in the ruling party, some of whom may have a following in the party. Mr. Attlee, the Labour prime minister (1945–1951), had to be sure of the support of such senior figures as Herbert Morrison, Sir Stafford Cripps, and Ernest Bevin. Mr. Macmillan (1957–1963) was similarly concerned about the reactions of R.A. Butler, his rival for the leadership. Mr. Callaghan (1976–79) often had precabinet discussions with such key ministers as the chancellor of the exchequer, Denis Healey, and the leader of the House, Michael Foot. Mrs. Thatcher appears to have relied less on senior ministers.

Although the cabinet consists of members of the same party, its decisions are not made in a political vacuum. "Spending" ministers (e.g., at education, health, or defense) are often battling with the Treasury (which usually wants to contain public spending). Ministers reflect different strands of opinion in the party. In the early years of Mrs. Thatcher's government, ministers who favored bigger public spending programs to tackle unemployment regularly clashed with ministers who attached priority to curbing inflation through strict control of public finance and the money supply, regardless of the effects on the economy.

Not surprisingly, much of the increasing workload of the cabinet in the postwar period has been delegated to cabinet committees. The prime minister alone decides which committees to set up and also appoints the members and terms of reference for each committee. The decisions from committees are then reported to the full cabinet. But effectively the committees make the decisions; were meetings of full Cabinet to overturn decisions of the committees, business would be difficult to dispatch. Some have argued that the committee system is a means by which the prime minister can bypass the whole cabinet and expand his or her own power.

The prime minister is more than *primus inter pares* (first among equals), as the textbooks used to describe the position. Apart from chairing the cabinet, he or she is the national leader, representing the country while abroad, speaking for the government in Parliament and broadcast interviews, and serving as the party leader. The last is important because it is the leadership of the party that makes him or her the prime minister.

The prime minister possesses three significant powers that distinguish him or her from cabinet colleagues. They are the rights to appoint and dismiss cabinet ministers; to seek a dissolution of Parliament (or terminate the government); and to summon, chair, and summarize cabinet meetings. These powers inhere in the office of the prime minister. But prime ministers can make different uses of the powers, and each is of course limited by political constraints.

The right to appoint to cabinet and other government posts is obviously an important resource for the prime minister. But it is exercised subject to some constraints. In the first place, government positions are limited to members of the House of Lords and House of Commons, mostly the latter. This is a consequence of the doctrines of collective and ministerial responsibility to Parliament. Richard Rose has presented a rule-of-thumb guide to the factors that influence a prime minister's appointments to cabinet.[1] First, a prime minister will certainly want to take account of a person's *political skill and administrative competence*. Second, he or she will wish to reward *loyalty*, as well as to try and "buy off" potential dissidents. Both Mr. Wilson and Mr. Callaghan were careful to include Tony Benn, a leading left-winger and dissenter from many government policies, in their Labour cabinets between 1974 and 1979. Inside the cabinet such persons can be constrained by collective responsibility; outside they may be damaging critics and a focus for opposition. Mrs. Thatcher's cabinet in 1979 included many who were skeptical of her economic policy but who were included because of their reported ability and political weight. On the other hand, she would not find a place for Mr. Heath whom she had displaced as party leader, on the grounds that he would oppose many of her policies. Finally, a prime minister will want the cabinet to *represent different strands in the party*. Traditionally, this has been important for the Labour party because it has long had well-defined left- and right-wing factions. In recent years, however, there have also been distinctive tendencies within the Conservative party.

The right of a prime minister to recommend a dissolution of Parliament to the monarch and thereby call a general election is certainly useful. The government can time its economic measures to have maximum electoral impact, for example, ensuring that levels of unemployment and inflation fall in the run-up to an election. In most election years in Britain there have been significant increases in real disposable incomes. The government can also make news. On the eve of the 1987 election, Mrs. Thatcher was

---

[1]"The Making of Cabinet Ministers," *British Journal of Political Science*, Vol. 1 (1971).

given a triumphant reception by Mr. Gorbachev in the Soviet Union. This dominated the mass media and confirmed her position as a major international statesperson.

In calling a general election, however, one must remember that a prime minister always has the most to lose—office itself. The prime minister can lose all, or the government may simply be returned to office. It is one of the loneliest decisions he or she can make. The responsibility cannot be shared. If the party loses, he or she will be widely blamed, while the position of rivals for the leadership may improve. The loss of office by Sir Alec Douglas Home in 1964, by Mr. Heath in 1974, and by Mr. Callaghan in 1979 effectively terminated their leaderships of their respective political parties, and Mr. Wilson's defeat in 1970 undermined his authority in the party. All except Mr. Callaghan called an election at a time entirely of their own choice. The record of postwar elections hardly supports the idea that incumbents are overwhelmingly favored. Of the 12 elections since 1945, the government has won 7 and lost 5, and the incumbent party has usually suffered a decline in its share of the vote compared to the previous election (see Table 5–1).

Not surprisingly, therefore, prime ministers are careful to consult with senior colleagues. Although the final decision is the prime minister's, being seen to consult in advance may help to spread some of the blame if the government loses.

The chairmanship of the cabinet also gives scope for prime ministerial direction to government. But a prime minister courts trouble if he or she refuses colleagues' requests to discuss an issue or persistently overrides the views of ministers. In 1981, as unemployment rose, cabinet critics of the government's economic policy forced Mrs. Thatcher to allow cabinet to discuss the economic strategy. In 1986 she managed to prevent Mr. Heseltine from arguing his case for a European-backed rescue operation for the Westland helicopter company (see page 45). In the event, a disgruntled Mr. Heseltine resigned and was soon followed by another cabinet minister, Leon Brittan, whose role in the affair was criticized by many Conservative MPs. Mrs. Thatcher could not have risked another resignation. Because a prime minister has to carry the cabinet, he or she often has to compromise.

British prime ministers travel light compared with the political leaders of many other countries. Mrs. Thatcher has a private office consisting of half a dozen civil servants as well as a press office. There is also a small (about six people) Policy Unit that helps with speech writing, advice on policies, and liaison with the party. Mrs. Thatcher has relied on her Policy Unit to a greater extent than previous prime ministers, using it to challenge the views of departments and push her own views. Some commentators have advocated the creation of a prime minister's department, on the grounds that a prime minister today increasingly has to

TABLE 5–1 Result of 1987 General Election

	Votes		Seats	
	Number	*Percentage*	*Number*	*Percentage*
Conservative	13,763,066	42.3%	375	57.0%
Labour	10,029,778	30.8	229	34.0
Alliance	7,341,290	22.6	22	3.5
Scottish Nationalists	416,873	1.5	2	0.3
Plaid Cymru	123,589	0.4	2	0.3
	32,536,137		650	

speak for the nation on so many issues. Such a department is, however, difficult to graft on to a cabinet system. Mrs. Thatcher herself has acknowledged that cabinet ministers are her chief advisers, and a powerful prime minister's department would almost certainly act as a barrier between prime ministers and senior colleagues.[2]

It is difficult to generalize about whether cabinet government has given way to prime ministerial government. Prime ministers differ in their energy, skills, and goals, and each prime minister is able to write a new page of political history. Two of the most dominant figures this century were Lloyd George and Winston Churchill, the successful war leaders. Both were dynamic men, impatient with bureaucratic delay, skeptical of party ties, and distrusted by many of their "safer" political colleagues. Yet at times of national crisis their skills and energy were widely seen as appropriate. Both were less successful as peacetime leaders. Mrs. Thatcher, for example, has seen her power in cabinet vary over time. Between 1979 and early 1982 as unemployment soared, the government was unpopular, and Mrs. Thatcher was seen as an electoral liability, so her cabinet was often argumentative and she lost battles. After the successful Falklands war, she became an electoral asset and was dominant in cabinet. In early 1986 the cabinet was divided over whether a British helicopter company should form a link with a British or European company, and two senior ministers resigned. Again, Mrs. Thatcher's authority in cabinet was weakened and her position was threatened. But as the economy revived and the party won another general election in 1987, so she was able to reassert herself.

More usually, prime ministers have been consolidators or modest reformers. They have been concerned to keep the party

united and to avoid troublesome issues. The Labour Premier Attlee (1945–51) once said, "The job of the Prime Minister in Cabinet is to get the general feeling—collect the voices. And then, when everything reasonable has been said, to get on with the job and say 'Well, I think the decision of the Cabinet is, this, that or the other. Any objections?' Usually there aren't!" Most prime ministers have seen their role as reflecting or speaking for a collective cabinet view. Even though she has lost a number of battles with her cabinet colleagues, Mrs. Thatcher has perhaps been the most commanding postwar prime minister. In contrast to most premiers, she believes in leading her cabinet from the front and boldly expresses her views even when she is in a minority. Over time she has used her power to appoint and to dismiss ministers to produce a more supportive cabinet. During 1981 she sacked a number of dissenters and appointed supporters. She has also been inclined to bypass the cabinet, relying on her Policy Unit and making decisions either in cabinet committees or in bilateral meetings between herself and departmental ministers. Her authority has also been enhanced by policy successes, particularly the recapture of the Falklands in 1982 and her two election successes in 1983 and 1987. She illustrates what can be achieved by a prime minister who is determined and energetic, has a clear strategy, and is lucky.

The cabinet can come into its own on particularly sensitive issues or on issues that cut across departments. In 1976 when the Labour government was negotiating the terms for a large loan from the international Monetary Fund, Mr. Callaghan, determined to avoid any resignations, held many cabinet sessions to agree on the terms. The same was true of Mr. Wilson's cabinet after the government's economic policies were seen to be failing between 1967 and 1969. As already noted, Mrs. Thatcher's position has at times been fragile and she has lost battles in cabinet. But most ministers are so busy with their own departmental matters that they have too little time to take an informed interest in

---

[2]See P. Hennessey, *Cabinet* (London: Blackwell, 1986), and R. Rose, "British Government: The Job at the Top," in R. Rose and E. Suleiman, eds., *Presidents and Prime Ministers* (Washington, DC: American Enterprise Institute, 1980).

other issues. They also have to shoulder constituency, parliamentary, and party duties. This gives an opportunity for prime ministerial direction.

THE CABINET OFFICE

Before World War I no minutes of cabinet meetings or formal records of decisions were kept. A Cabinet Secretarist was established in 1916 at the instigation of Lloyd George. The work of the Cabinet Office in relation to the cabinet and its committees is essentially threefold: to prepare the cabinet agenda, to record its proceedings and decisions, and to follow up and coordinate the decisions. It does the first by circulating relevant papers to minsters beforehand. The second is done by the cabinet secretary. Coordination is carried through by the Cabinet Office informing departments of cabinet decisions that affect them and then checking that appropriate action has been taken. Its record of the prime minister's summing-up of discussion on each item reflects the decisions of the cabinet and the government machine in Whitehall is expected to implement them. Each cabinet committee is similarly serviced and has its own secretariat, agenda, and minutes.

HOUSE OF COMMONS

A century ago the House of Commons enjoyed considerable power. Members of Parliament were relatively independent of party whips and debates on the floor of the House could switch votes. The Commons often made and unmade governments, initiated legislation, and controlled finance. But the rise of disciplined, mass programmatic parties has transformed parliamentary government into party government. Governments have increasingly controlled the timetable of Parliaments to push their legislation through. Today hardly any important decisions are taken on the floor of the House of Commons; rather they are settled among ministers, civil servants, and spokespersons of pressure groups. Virtually all the 650 MPs know that they are elected because of their party label.

The proceedings of the Parliament are controlled by a Speaker. He (there has been no female Speaker) is an MP elected by fellow members at the beginning of a new session of Parliament and usually reelected until he decides to retire. Once elected he is expected to be completely impartial.

Although the House of Commons is a legislature, *law initiation* is only a minor part of its duties. Legislation, control of the timetable, and finance are largely in the hands of the governing party. (The one exception is the opportunities that exist for private member's legislation). More important is the role of Parliament in *sustaining the government.* After all, the government owes its position to the fact that it is the majority party in the House of Commons and partly loyalty and discipline ensures that it usually gets its way in Parliament. Finally, the House is a *political arena* in which politicians can make their mark. As long as ministers are members of Parliament, so Parliamentary skills (debating ability, mastering a brief, and handling questions) are important for political leadership.

Because the outcome of votes is so largely predictable, some critics complain that debates are a waste of time. But parties are also concerned to "win the argument" in the debate, regardless of the vote. There are occasions when the assembled MPs can express their views to the nation. The lengthy debates on the annual budget or the government's legislative program each session provide opportunities for the parties to explain their rival philosophies and the cases for and against policies.

It is possible to exaggerate the passivity and timidity of government backbenchers in the House of Commons. It is not just a case of the government whips bullying the members to follow the leadership's line. Whips are really a two-way channel between the party leaders and the backbenchers. The government whips have to anticipate the reactions of critical backbenchers and often compromise to preserve a majority. The government at the end of the day is much more concerned with criticisms from its own side than those of the opposition parties. The former have to be kept on side; the disagreement of the latter is taken for granted. The Thatcher government has seen its normal majority in Parliamentary votes fall to very low levels in recent years as Conservative MPs have refused to support the government on controversial issues.

THE OPPOSITION

An important feature of a liberal democracy is the existence of a legitimate organized opposition. In Britain its importance is recognized in that the second largest party in the House of Commons is referred to as Her Majesty's Opposition. Such an institution is regarded as useful because it criticizes and presents an alternative to the government of the day. While being loyal to the crown and accepting the legitimacy of the government that has won the election, it also accepts laws which it dislikes, so long as these have been enacted in accordance with constitutional procedures. In each parliamentary session the opposition has some 20 parliamentary days when it can choose the topics of debate. In a debate in January 1988 a Conservative backbencher criticized opposing Labour members for doing little else but criticize the work of his government. Yet, in the words of a famous Conservative prime minister (Disraeli), the essential duty of the opposition "is to oppose."

The opposition is also a shadow or alternative government. It has a team of would-be ministers, including a leader, Shadow Cabinet, whips, and its own party program. In approximate proportion to its membership of the House of Commons it also appoints members to standing and select committees. If the opposition of the day can rarely defeat the government, then it can certainly modify legislation by amendment and, through criticisms, weaken the confidence of the government and undermine its support in the country.

As long as there is disciplined voting in the House, the government will get its legislation through and its position will be safe until the next election. Only when government supporters abstain or oppose in large enough numbers is there a chance of parliamentary defeat. There have been only two occasions this century when a government has lost a confidence vote and resigned, once in 1924 and again in 1979. On the latter occasion the Labour government was defeated on its proposals for devolution to assemblies in Scotland and Wales. Both cases were unusual because the government of the day was a minority government.

One means by which the House can oversee the executive is through the *select committees*. Whereas the standing committees examine the details of bills, select committees provide backbenchers with the opportunity to scrutinize government policy. The present system of committees was set up in 1979. There are 14 of them, and they oversee the major government departments. For example, the Agriculture Committee covers the work of the Ministry of Agriculture, Fisheries and Food, and the Energy Committee covers the Energy Department. The committees determine their own agenda, elect their own chairmen, and call and examine witnesses. Some of them have been extremely vigorous in questioning civil servants and ministers about policy, and they have produced numerous useful reports.

THE LEGISLATIVE PROCESS

To succeed, a bill must receive three readings in the House of Commons and House of Lords and be passed in identical form in both houses. It then goes on to receive the royal assent and becomes an act of Parliament. Each act begins with the words: "Be it enacted by the Queen's most excellent Majesty, by and with the advice and consent of the Lords Spiritual and Temporal, and Commons, in this present Parliament assembled, and by authority of the same".

The first step in the legislative cycle is for a bill to be introduced in the Commons to receive its *first reading*. This is something of a formality, with the title of the bill merely being read to the House. A few weeks later it is subject to a *second reading,* when its principles are debated on the floor of the House. The House is essentially asked if it approves of the bill as a whole before it is sent to committee. If the measure is supported it then goes to one of the *standing committees* of the House. The members of these committees are drawn in proportion to the strength of the parties in the House and they examine the bill in some detail. The amended bill is then debated in the House as a whole at what is called the *report stage,* and new clauses and further amendments may be added. Finally, the bill goes forward for its third and *final reading.* Once it is passed and then approved by the Lords, after a similar process, the royal assent is given and the bill becomes an act.

The great majority of bills (about 100) each session emanate from the government departments. Although the opposition has its rights, the government effectively controls the timetable of the House of Commons. While the final version of a bill will often be much amended compared to the original version, most of the amendments are actually made by the government.

There is also the possibility for a private member (a backbencher) to introduce a bill. Each session backbench members ballot for the right to introduce a bill on the first 20 Fridays of the session. The government is willing to give up a Friday, which is not a good day for parliamentary business. The House rises at 3 p.m. and most MPs go away for the weekend. Few such initiatives are carried through, without the help of the government. Issues dealing with matters of "conscience," for example, abolishing the death penalty or legalizing abortion have been successfully carried through by private members' bills.

HOUSE OF LORDS

The other two parts of the "Crown-in-Parliament" are the House of Lords and the monarchy. In Bagehot's terminology, they are now the "dignified" parts of the constitution. Until the Parliament Act (1911) the two Houses were co-equal. Today, however, the House of Lords are clearly subordinate to the House of Commons, because the latter is popularly elected. When people talk of "the will of Parliament" or of Britain as a representative democracy, it is the House of Commons that they have in mind. Until 1958 (when life peerages were first conferred), the House of Lords consisted overwhelmingly of hereditary peers (still largely the case) as well as a small number of bishops, archbishops, and law lords. Its powers were substantially reduced in the Parliament Acts of 1911 and 1949, and today it may not only delay a bill which has been passed by the House of Commons for a year. It retains an important judicial role. The House of Lords is the highest and final court of appeal in the land, although this role is confined to the dozen or so law lords who sit in the House.

The Lords do have time to scrutinize bills sent to it from the House of Commons, and sometimes the government introduces bills in the Lords. In contrast to the Commons, party discipline is more relaxed, there are a good number of cross-bench peers, and some of the life peers are people who have achieved distinction in many walks of life. This last quality may enhance the level of debate in the Lords. For much of the nineteenth century and until very recently, the House of Lords was the poodle of the Conservative party. The in-built Conservative majority in the chamber led it to reject controversial legislation of pre-1914 Liberal governments. In fact it has now become increasingly independent and has used its powers of amendment and delay to defeat the Conservative government over a hundred times since 1979.

There is widespread agreement that Britain needs a second chamber, so that all power does not lie with the majority party in the House of Commons. There is less agreement, however that the House of Lords, as presently constituted, is the ideal second chamber. By tradition, the Labour Party has been hostile; many in the party find it ludicrous that a predominantly hereditary body should have any power to revise or delay the bills of an elected House of Commons. The absence of agreement, however, about how the second chamber might be reformed has so far preserved it.

THE MONARCHY

In theory the monarch can still take many steps without consulting Parliament—including declaring war, signing treaties, granting pardons, or refusing the sign a bill that has been passed by both houses of Parliament. These are so-called *prerogative powers.* In practice the powers have gradually passed to the cabinet. The last time a monarch refused to sign a bill was in 1707. Yet the formal language of British government still has a royalist ring. For example, it is Her Majesty's Government, Her Majesty's Opposition, and the civil servants and armed forces are servants of the crown. But over a century ago the perceptive commentator Walter Bagehot wrote that Queen Victoria only possessed "the right to be consulted, the right to encourage and the right to warn." That remains the case today. The queen receives cabinet papers and advance copies of the cabinet agenda and has a weekly audience with the prime minister. Queen Elizabeth II has reigned since 1953, had eight prime ministers (including Churchill) serve under her, and clearly is a potentially well-informed person. As head of the British state the queen is popular and above party and is able to act as a unifying national symbol. Much of the respect and admiration for monarchy has derived from its past avoidance of political controversy. The monarch does this by acting on the advice of the prime minister of the day.

Yet if there was a deadlocked Parliament (i.e., no one party had a majority of seats in the House of Commons), the monarch might be drawn into controversy. In the absence of an obvious majority party leader, who would the monarch send for to form an administration? And if, in a multiparty situation, the prime minister of the day lost a majority and sought a dissolution, would the monarch be bound to grant him or her one—without trying to establish if somebody else might be able to form a government? In such situations the monarch and his or her advisers would have to make calculations about which person could best form an administration (including a possible coalition) that would have the support of a majority in the House of Commons. The decline of the two-party system in the 1970s and 1980s made these issues more pressing than they had once been.

THE CIVIL SERVICE

The head offices of the major government departments, such as the Foreign Office, Treasury, Home Office, and Education and Science, are situated close to the two houses of Parliament, in an area called Whitehall. At the head of each department is a minister, a political figure. But each department also contains a group of senior civil servants, the permanent secretary, deputy secretaries, assistant secretaries, and principals. These are the minister's main advisers on matters of policy, and he will probably see more of them than of his government colleagues. In theory, the minister is guided on policy by his party's values and program, and the civil servant's task is to advise and help implement and administer the policy. The reality is more complex.

Ministers are temporary, appointed and dismissed by the prime minister, and largely drawn from the ranks of elected politicians. The civil service is a career, appointments are permanent—though in exceptional circumstances (e.g., corruption), a civil servant may be discharged—and recruitment is by open competitive examination. Until 1969 the service in Britain was divided into three classes: clerical, executive, and administrative. The latter contained the crucial policy formulators and administrators, drawn exclusively from university graduates. Today the classes have been abolished though the senior members still play the crucial policy-making role.

The main tasks of senior civil servants may be briefly summarized. They are to brief the minister for debate and questions in Parliament, to help with speeches, to prepare legislation, to formulate policy proposals and make recommendations between different policy options, and to take decisions as the minister would wish on routine matters. Good civil servants know their minister's minds; it is often said that they are his eyes and ears.

Senior civil servants are engaged in a highly political role. But they must not be partisan. At the end of the day it is the minister who decides and it is he who is responsible (or answerable) to the House of Commons for the department's policy in general as well as crucial policy decisions. In the British system the doctrine of ministerial responsibility means that the minister gets the blame and the praise, however ill deserved.

The British civil service is based upon certain long-established principles. These are

1. *Anonymity.* Civil servants are expected to remain publicly silent on political and other controversial matters. It is ministers who speak in public for the department.
2. *Impartiality.* The civil servant as a servant of the crown is subject to limits on his or her political activities and freedom of expression. If civil servants wish to continue to serve governments of different political persuasions, then their impartiality must not be in doubt. Senior civil servants may not take part in national politics, apart from casting a vote in elections. Staff in lower grades may not stand for Parliament but are allowed to take part in local politics, subject to permission from their superiors.
3. *Permanence.* The principle of not being dismissed from post, without good cause, follows from the notion that civil servants serve the crown, not the government of the day.

These principles stand or fall together. Permanence depends upon impartiality, which in turn is helped by anonymity. The interlinking principles lie at the heart of the British idea of the bureaucracy as a *profession*.

In the 1960s some dissatisfaction was expressed with the civil service, largely on the grounds that it must have contributed to the mistakes of postwar British governments and the country's relative economic decline. A Committee of Enquiry into the civil service was established in 1965 (under Lord Fulton) to make suggestions for improvement. The committee reported in 1968 and repeated many of the conventional criticisms. It complained of the senior civil servants' narrow social background (too middle class), their exclusive education (most were from Oxford or Cambridge universities), and their "generalist" outlook (or lack of specialist skills). It recommended the recruitment of people with more "relevant" skills, including a greater number of graduates from the sciences and social sciences.

Fulton's recommendations were intended to make the civil service more "professional." Some reforms were made, notably, more training for the civil servants, the appointment of a limited number of political advisers for ministers, some of the classes were unified, and so on, but these did not amount to much. Little was done to bring in outsiders. The backgrounds of the recruits in the 1980s are broadly similar to those of Fulton years. They are still largely drawn from Oxford and Cambridge, graduates in the humanities (rather than social sciences or science), and male. Cynics said that the thrust of the report was frustrated because responsibility for implementing the reforms was left to the civil servants themselves.

Some of the criticisms of the civil servants are beside the point, and others appear designed to deflect blame from the failings of politicians. Yet there are some legitimate worries over the relations between civil servants and ministers. Some of the concerns are inherent in the nature of modern bureaucracy and government. For example, civil servants are permanent, while British cabinet ministers on average spend slightly less than two years in a department. At any time, inevitably, some ministers will be learning on the job and reliant on their officials. As issues have become so complex it is not surprising, therefore, that the balance of influence may favor civil servants. Yet it is the minister who remains exposed and politically accountable.

Critics also refer to the practice of senior officials and departments of serving on interdepartmental committees that "shadow" a cabinet committee. This is done to try and reconcile the different view points between departments so that there is less detail to bother the cabinet. Some ministers have complained that this exercise in "coordination" reduces their policy options and gives too much say to the civil servants. On the other hand, civil servants are interested in developing a coherent and coordinated government policy. After all, it is cabinet or collective government. Yet it is doubtful if a department prefers to have a "weak" minister, one that it can easily manipulate. An effective minister, one who is able to win his or her cabinet battles over policy or resources, increases the standing and morale of his or her department. An indecisive minister, or one who lacks a clear policy line, usually requires his or her officials to spend more time on "damage control" rather than policy-making.

It is also argued that at times there is outright obstruction and noncooperation by senior civil servants when they wish to frustrate a policy. This kind of criticism has come from right-wing Conservatives and the left wing of the Labour party. The Labour minister, Mr. Benn, claimed that he was obstructed when he was minister for industry and then for energy between 1974 and 1979. The problem, however, was that the then prime minister, Mr. Wilson, and most of the cabinet, disapproved of Mr. Benn's policies. As the message spread through Whitehall, so he became isolated. Civil servants have a problem when a radical minister is out of line with his or her government colleagues and will invariably back the latter.

Yet the record of Mrs. Thatcher's government has refuted the claims that the civil servants "run things." Mrs. Thatcher has not been an admirer of the civil service, or indeed much of the public sector. She is a free marketeer, admires wealth-creators and innovators, and wants to change things. Many on the right wing of the Conservative party have regarded the civil service as a self-serving and expanding bureaucracy, protected from the rigors of a competitive economy. But the civil service is by nature cautious, offering "balanced" judgments about policies, and does not "do" (i.e., create) anything. The civil service has had an interest in continuity in policy in many areas; abrupt chopping and changing makes it difficult for a "departmental view," or a body of accumulated wisdom about the best policy to emerge. It is not surprising that critics complain that the senior civil servants are "permanent politicians" and wedded to consensus politics. Not surprisingly, therefore, the old model of relations between civil servants and ministers has come under strain because of Mrs. Thatcher's radicalism and determination to change so many long-standing policies.

Mrs. Thatcher has certainly had an impact on the bureaucracy. She has sharply reduced the number of civil servants from over 730,000 in 1979 to just under 600,000 in 1987. She abolished the Civil Service Department in 1981 because she thought it was too generous in pay settlements for civil servants. She has also taken a close interest in high-level promotions, particularly at the level of permanent secretary and assistant permanent secretary. To date, more than 80 percent of such appointments have been made since 1979. She has been accused of promoting Thatcherites and therefore politicizing the service. In fact, she seems to have favored people who were willing to challenge the conventional Whitehall objections to change. Mrs. Thatcher has also relied on her Policy Unit to second-guess the views of civil servants in departments. Finally, the sheer number of policy discontinuities since 1979 show that the civil service can respond to a determined lead from the political arm of government.

There remain, however, some critics on the right or "free-market" wing of the Conservative party who regard the civil service as a drag to their plans for making greater cuts in public spending and reducing the size of the public sector. One former adviser of Mrs. Thatcher, Sir John Hoskyns, would go further. He has claimed that, for Mrs. Thatcher's revolution to advance further, many senior civil servants should be dismissed. Sir John regards them as "defeatist" and would appoint in their place people who believed more wholeheartedly in the government's program and were committed to implementing it. Such a policy would be a move in the direction of a more politicized civil service, for a government of another persuasion would probably want to bring in its own team of advisers. Clearly the old qualities of permanence, impartiality, and anonymity would be severely undermined.

On balance the civil service has served Britain well. It has attracted high-quality men and women. Their sense of duty and public service are widely admired abroad, and there have been remarkably few cases of civil servants being involved in cases of bribery or corruption.

6

The Thatcher Government

The Conservative government first elected in 1979, and reelected by large majorities in 1983 and 1987, has been one of the most remarkable in post-1945 Britain. There have been two formative periods since 1945. The Labour governments (1945–51) largely created the postwar consensus (see Chapter 2). Since 1979, much of that consensus has been energetically attacked and dismantled by Mrs. Thatcher's governments. Her rise was part of a more general reaction in Western Europe in the 1970s, against high taxes, inflation, trade union power, and the feeling that public spending was getting out of control.[1]

The Thatcher administration has been unlike most other postwar governments in two important respects. First, it is one of only two which have largely achieved their programs—the other being the 1945 Labour government. Second, it is the only one to have been both effective and have its electoral mandate renewed, as in the 1983 and 1987 general elections. Most other postwar governments have ended in failure, largely because of their lack of economic success, and between 1959 and 1979 no government was reelected after serving a near full term of office.

Mrs. Thatcher has established a number of landmarks. She is the first woman political leader of a western state, the longest-serving British prime minister this century, and the only party leader in over a century to win three successive general elections.

Another mark of her significance is that she has given her name to an "ism." We talk of Thatcherism but not of Churchillism, Heathism, or Wilsonism. Thatcherism is in part to do with her distinctive political style, particularly her no-nonsense, even abrasive

---

[1]On this, see D. Kavanagh, *Thatcherism and British Politics: The End of Consensus?* 2nd ed. (Oxford; Oxford University Press, 1989).

approach, and rejection of consensus politics as too often involving compromises and weakness. In a famous newspaper interview in 1981 she rejected, on grounds of political morality, consensus politics: "For me, consensus seems to be the process of abandoning all beliefs, principles, values and policies." It was "avoiding the very issues that have got to be solved merely to get people to come to an agreement on the way ahead." Thatcherism also reflects Mrs. Thatcher's beliefs in individual self-reliance, traditional moral values, the free market, and personal responsibility (or "standing on your own two feet"). Mrs. Thatcher is the first British prime minister not to have been an adult before or during World War II. Unlike most Tory leaders, she comes from a modest economic background; her father was a shopkeeper. Her "people" are such shopkeepers, those running small businesses, or those trying to purchase their own homes—the "improving" working class or petty *bourgeois.* Her ideas may echo those of Adam Smith, Friedman, or Hayek, but they owe more to her upbringing.

When she became party leader in February 1975 the Conservatives were in electoral decline. They had lost four of the five previous general elections and in October 1974 had suffered their lowest share of the vote in a general election in the twentieth century. This was a new and disturbing experience for a party that had long regarded itself as the national party of government. But there was also something of an ideological struggle in the party. The 1970–74 Conservative government, led by Mr. Heath, was a turning point for a number of Conservative free marketeers. The government had abandoned some of its original economic policies and quarreled with the trade unions. It reversed its policy of not rescuing troubled firms and adopted a statutory prices and incomes policy to combat inflation. Trade unions seemed to be almost as powerful as governments and the pressures making for much higher levels of public spending and for inflation seemed too strong to be resisted. Disruptive action by powerful unions

had helped to unseat the Conservative government in 1974 (and subsequently a Labour one in 1979). The party had lost its way.

One member of Heath's government, Sir Keith Joseph, who was a close ally of Mrs. Thatcher, played an important role in changing the climate of opinion that had supported the consensus. He argued that previous Conservative governments had assisted the "ratchetlike" progress of collectivism—increasing taxation, expanding public expenditure, intervening in and regulating industries, and undermining private enterprise and individual initiative. In the interest of policy continuity, they accepted the initiatives of Labour governments, but that party then took up further left-wing positions. The "middle ground" was moving away from the Conservative party. He also argued that governments were becoming overloaded with spending obligations. Keynesian economics had failed to find an answer to high inflation, and money supply had been neglected. He recommended that a future Conservative government should abandon the goal of full employment. If workers and employers set their prices and wages at too high a level, then they should be prepared to accept the consequences in terms of lost orders and lost jobs. Tax cuts, reduced public spending, less government regulation of economic activity, and strict limits on money supply became the new policy watchwords.

This intellectual critique from the political right of the consensus was helped by events and a general perception that it was failing. Keynesianism appeared to have no answer to inflation, the trade unions were able to defy governments, and miserable rates of economic growth frustrated demands for higher living standards and better public services. But a more resurgent left wing in the Labour party also wished to break with the consensus. It called for greater public ownership, increased economic planning, more public spending, and British withdrawal from the European Community. Mr. Benn told the 1979 Labour conference that the crisis of capitalism provided the opportunity for a future Labour government to abolish rather than save it. By 1979 influential figures in both Labour and Conservative parties proclaimed their desire to bury the postwar consensus. It was identified with decline.

The Thatcher government's major goal in 1979 was to promote what it called the enterprise economy. The program included

1. The extension of market principles in the economy. This involved a reduction of government regulations over economic activity and "privatization," or the withdrawal of the state from ownership or direction of many economic enterprises.
2. Trade union and industrial relations reforms, to strike a more acceptable balance between the two sides of industry.
3. Control of inflation through strict control of the money supply.
4. Restraint on public spending, in part to facilitate,
5. Income tax cuts, to provide incentives for work and to allow people to spend more of their money as they chose.

If one looks at the outcome, the record has on balance been pretty successful.

EXTENSION OF THE MARKET

Privatization has involved the sale of state-owned shares and assets to the work force or to investors, or transferring the functions of public bodies to the private sector.

For the most part it has meant the sale to investors of major state concerns like British Airways, British Gas, British Steel, and British Telecom; the sale of public housing to tenants, and the opening of some local authority services to private firms (Table 6–1). In 1989 the private sale of the nation's water supply and electricity industry are also planned. It is worth noting that in some of these privatizations (e.g., gas), there has been no increase in competition. Some 600,000 jobs and a third of the industrial sector have been shifted from the state to the private sec-

TABLE 6–1   Major Privatization of State-Owned Corporations, 1981–1987

Year	Corporation
1981	British Aerospace end 1985
1982	Britoil end 1985
1984	Jaguar cars
1984	British Telecom
1986	British Gas
1986	Trustees Savings Bank
1987	Rolls Royce
1987	British Airways
1988	British Steel
1989	Electricity Industry

tor. There has been a redrawing of the lines between the public and private sectors in the mixed economy. By 1990 the nation's telephone system, gas, electricity, water, steel, and the largest airline and airports will have moved to the private sector. The program amounts to the largest sell-off by the state since Henry VIII's dissolution of the monarchies in the Reformation.

TRADE UNIONS

Changes have been made in the law affecting picketing, union rule books, prestrike ballots, and election of union leaders. The legislation and rise in unemployment have certainly weakened the position of the trade unions. In major pieces of legislation the Conservative government has (1) made secondary picketing and sympathy strikes illegal, (2) made the achievement and maintenance of closed shops more difficult, (3) made trade unions legally responsible (and subject to heavy fines) for actions by their members and officers which breach the law, and (4) required unions to obtain a majority vote of members by secret ballot before industrial action can proceed. If trade unions break the law under (3) and (4), their funds are liable to seizure. Strikes by powerful groups of workers have been defeated. In 1980 a strike in the steel industry was defeated, as were strikes in the health and civil services in 1982. Since then, industrial action by the teachers and the miners have also been defeated. In 1984 the government decided to make trade union membership incompatible with work at the military intelligence center in Cheltenham. Compared with the 1970s the trade unions are more divided, they have fewer members, and their influence has declined. The government hardly consults with the unions on economic policy or employment training. One notable statistic is that the proportion of adults owning shares is 20 percent (up from 7 percent in 1979), almost the same figure who are members of trade unions!

INFLATION

This has been reduced to its lowest level for 18 years (although accompanied by the return of unemployment levels last seen in the 1930s) by 1987. Thatcher's government has been the first government since that of 1959 not to have introduced controls on prices or incomes.

ROLE OF GOVERNMENT

The public has been told in effect to look elsewhere than to the government for a solution to many problems. There has been a sharp reduction in the help available in state finance for housing and industry, and encouragement of private pensions and private home ownership, and a steady reduction in the real value of central government finance for local authorities and higher education. There has been a significant reduction in income tax, particularly on higher incomes. The top rate was reduced from over 80 percent to 60 percent in 1979 and then 40 percent in 1987. The standard rate (paid by the great majority) has been reduced from 33 percent in 1979 to 25 percent. The government has made no effort to "concert" its policies for economic growth or inflation with trade unions or employers. The "social contract" and corporatist styles of policymaking of the 1970s are dead. Yet there has also been a centralization of control in some

areas, notably schools, higher education, the health service, and many aspects of local government. Hence the paradox: the free market government has been ruthlessly interventionist and centralizing in chosen areas.

WELFARE

The government has tried to contain the rise in welfare spending by such means as increasing means-test provision, with the aim of concentrating more on the most needy (e.g., freezing student aid in higher education and child benefit or ending free school meals), replacing benefit grants with loans, and increasing charges for services (e.g., in health care).

LOCAL GOVERNMENT

Many measures have weakened local government *vis-à-vis* central government. Local authorities have suffered a significant reduction in their role in housing and education, and they have been subject to greater central control over raising local revenue and spending.

What is striking, and perhaps a mark of Mrs. Thatcher's radicalism, is that the government has been locked in combat not only with trade unions and local government but also with so many institutions that have for so long been regarded as part, along with the Tory party, of the British establishment. These include the senior ranks of the civil service, the universities, the Church of England, and the BBC.

Her right-wing critics say that she should have done more to reduce the role of the state in managing the economy and providing welfare. For all the protests about "cuts" in public spending, its share of GNP actually rose in the years after 1979 and fell back to the 1979 figure only in 1986. Within this greater total, there has been a reduction in real levels of state spending on housing and industry, a sharp increase in funds for defense, law and order, health, and social security (in large part because of higher unemployment). Others charge that the increase in unemployment (from 1.2 million in 1979 to 3 million by 1982) and loss of manufacturing capacity have been too heavy a cost.

Finally, it is worth noting the importance that Mrs. Thatcher has attached to restoring the authority of the state. The government pursued "strong" defense and law and order policies, spending much more on them than Labour would have done. This was notable, because most other spending programs at the time were being squeezed. The authority was also reflected in policies toward local government, trade unions (notably the miners, teachers, workers), and the broadcasting authorities. The government has been more interventionist than its predecessors in the running of schools and higher education. One author has claimed that the policies reflect a marriage of "the free economy and the authoritarian state." Mrs. Thatcher has been strongly pro-American and assertive of British interests in the European Community. At some political cost, the British government acceded to American requests to use British bases for their bombing raids on Libya in 1986.

The conservatives have enjoyed some luck since 1979. They have been a beneficiary of the electoral system, enjoying huge majorities in terms of seats (142 seats in 1983 and 100 in 1987) [see Table 5-1, page 45], in spite of having only 42 percent of the vote. They have also gained from the successful recapture of the Falklands in April 1982. Before this the prime minister and government has been languishing in the opinion polls. Finally, the government has profited from the divisions in 1981 within the Labour party and the split of the non-Conservative support in the electorate between Labour and the Alliance parties.

7

Prospects

The 1970s were a decade of constitutional uncertainty, continued relative economic decline, and political disorder. Conservative and Labour governments were voted out of office (in February 1974 and 1979, respectively) in the wake of industrial disruption. To add to persistent economic weakness, the government faced challenges to its political authority. Britain was a latter-day "sick man of Europe." The 1980s have been different in all these respects.

Many of the constitutional uncertainties have been removed. Britain's membership of the European Community was settled by the constitutional innovation of a referendum (1975). The Labour party said in 1983 that if it was elected it would begin a process of withdrawal. It has since accepted Britain's membership. In response to an upsurge in nationalism in Scotland, the 1974 Labour government agreed to devolution of decision making to an elected Scottish assembly, a proposal that was aborted when a referen-

dum of Scottish voters in 1979 failed to approve the measure by the requisite majority. There has been little pressure since. The electoral decline of the Labour party has, for the time being, removed the threat to the future of the House of Lords.

There is still some cross-party support for a bill of rights and for proportional electoral reform, but neither is likely to be achieved in the near future. Since 1987 a number of Labour-supporting commentators have favored proportional representation in the hope of gaining more seats for the alleged "anti-Thatcher" majority. The essential features of the old model—a unitary state, a sovereign Parliament, the two-party system, and the first-past-the-post electoral system were all under strain in the 1970s. Today such concerns are less pressing. In large part the pressures in the 1970s were a product of general dissatisfaction with the political system and its economic performance.

We have already observed that Britain has

had long-standing economic problems. After 1973 the onset of economic recession and lower economic growth posed problems for many Western states. In Britain the difficulties were exacerbated by the long-term economic uncompetiveness, slow economic growth, and restrictive practices in many sectors of the economy. On several indicators of economic performance, Britain performed worse than did most other OECD countries, and real living standards for the great majority of British people improved only slightly. Since 1982, however, British productivity and rates of economic growth have been among the best in Western Europe (though from a low baseline). The one black spot on the record has been unemployment, which soared from just over 1 million in 1979 to over 3 million in 1982. By December 1988, however, it had fallen continuously for 24 months.

In the 1970s British governments appeared to lack authority. The industrial relations policies of Mr. Heath's government (1970–74) were rendered ineffective by opposition from powerful trade unions. That government's statutory incomes policy—introduced as part of its battle against inflation—was broken by the coal miners in the winter of 1973–74. In frustration Mr. Heath called a general election and lost. The new Labour government virtually abandoned its anti-inflation policies in the face of strikes by trade unions in the 1979 winter of discontent and lost the general election of that year. Britain in these years seemed to provide a classic case of an ungovernable society in the grip of overly powerful trade unions. Some commentators expressed doubts that Britain's political institutions could cope with inflationary pressures, sectional rivalries, and the determination of particular groups to dislocate society. Whether it was a crisis of capitalism, as the left claimed, or a crisis of social democracy, as the right insisted, governments seemed unable to cope. In a farewell interview in 1976, President Gerald Ford warned Americans: "It would be tragic for this country if we went down

the same path and ended up with the same problems that Great Britain has."

Since 1979, however, the trade unions have been greatly weakened and inflation has been reduced. The authority of the Thatcher government was helped by its military success against Argentina in the Falklands in 1982 and Mrs. Thatcher's victory over the miners in their year-long strike between 1984–85. No longer is there talk of the weakness of British government or the overweening power of trade unions. The government has been jealous of its autonomy vis-à-vis such interests as local government, trade unions, public corporations, and the education and health lobbies. Mrs. Thatcher, perhaps like de Gaulle in France after 1958, has restored the authority of government.

The emergence of Conservative and Labour as the two major parties dates from 1918. In all subsequent general elections these parties have occupied the first two places in terms of popular votes and parliamentary seats. But since 1970 the gradual rise of the Liberal party and, more recently, its association with the new Social Democratic party in an alliance, posed the greatest threat to that system. During the 1980s the Alliance party sometimes outscored the other parties in opinion polls and by-election support, and there was much talk of the possible realignment of the party system.

Such a realignment could take one of two forms. First, the newly merged Social and Liberal Democratic party could replace Labour as the main rival to the Conservatives. It nearly overtook Labour in popular votes in 1983, but by 1987 Labour had increased its lead over the Alliance from 3 percent to 8 percent. The electoral system, as noted, is a major barrier to a new party's breakthrough in terms of seats in Parliament. A second possibility is that the party could gather a sufficiently large number of seats (say, 80 or more) to produce a multiparty Parliament and deny a clear majority to any one party. With a proportional electoral system, it could certainly do this; in the 1987 election the Alliance would have gained an extra 127 seats (149 instead of 22)! In turn, a multiparty Parliament and coalition government would probably lead to electoral reform and other changes in constitutional practice.

Yet in neither of the foregoing senses has there been a realignment. The 1987 election stopped the Alliance bandwagon. Much more damaging to it, however, was the bitter quarreling after the 1987 election between the leaders of the *two parties.* Much more than goodwill was lost amid accusations of bad faith and the refusal of David Owen and some dissenting Social Democrats to join the new party. Since 1987 support for the Alliance has declined sharply, and, in retrospect, the best time for a realignment may have passed.

Yet there has been an important change in the balance of advantage between the two major parties. The main loser in the last two decades has clearly been Labour. Its "normal" or basic vote now seems to be between 32 and 36 percent, compared to 40–45 percent in the 1960s. The Conservative party, with a base of some 40–44 percent—not much lower than it was in the 1960s—is able to gain landslide victories under the first-past-the-post system, as long as there is a significant third-party vote.

The 1987 election result seems to confirm the old adage that the Conservatives are the natural party of government in Britain. During the twentieth century the party has been in office, alone or in coalition, for more than two-thirds of the period. The postwar period has seen two lengthy periods of Conservative party rule between 1951 and 1964 and again since 1979.

Labour's third successive election defeat has encouraged doubts about whether it will ever form a government again. Social change, notably the spread of affluence and home ownership and the decline of the working class manufacturing and trade union membership are against it. But many of its policies and many aspects of its image have also alienated voters. The latest research suggests that perhaps a third of La-bour's electoral decline since 1964 is due to changes in the social structure, and two-thirds is due to policies and political factors. As noted on Chapter 4, the party relies heavily on social groups which are in numerical decline.

The postwar period to 1979 has often been characterized as one of postwar consensus, in policy terms. By consensus we do not mean agreement on policies. Political activity arises from disagreement over public affairs, and the Labour and Conservative parties hold different visions of their ideal societies. Rather, the term "consensus" refers to limited disagreements over policy (i.e., this is bargainable) and disputes over means rather than ends. Such policies as the pursuit of full employment, maintaining a mixed economy—with a significant role for state ownership of important enterprises and government management of the economy—conciliation of the trade unions or at least acceptance of their role as partners in economic management, were largely agreed between the political parties after 1950.

Yet all these policies had run their course by 1983. Of course, there were breaches in that consensus before 1979. The significance of Mrs. Thatcher, however, is that she was the first postwar party leader to want to attack the consensus, particularly in "rolling back the state." At present the government is engaged in substantially reducing the role of local government (called by critics the local "state") in education and housing and furthering its policies of weakening the trade unions and extending privatization. It is also working to remove what is perhaps the last significant domestic policy landmark of the postwar consensus, the virtual state monopoly of health care (in the National Health Service) and welfare.

It is too early to speak of the Thatcher governments' having forged a new *postcollectivist consensus.* This will only become evident if and when a successor government, particularly a non-Conservative one, continues the policies. So much of the new radicalism in the 1980s has depended on the commitment and energy of Mrs. Thatcher herself. The essential test of the emergence of a new policy consensus is passed when the initiating government's measures are largely accepted by the opposition. (It is worth noting, however, that a number of the policies—tax cuts, deregulation, and the encouragement of market forces—are found in some other countries.) By the 1950s in the United States the Republicans had come to terms with the New Deal (involving more active role for the federal government in the economy, help for the poor, and acceptance of American's greater role in world affairs). The British Conservatives in 1951 had to come to terms with the measures of the 1945 Labour government (particularly the extension of the welfare state and large measures of state ownership in industry). At present the Labour party still seems wedded to greater state intervention in the economy, restoring corporate-style bargaining between government and the major economic interests, abandoning Britain's nuclear weapons, and standing by a virtual state monopoly of the education and health services. But, compared to 1983, it now accepts Britain's membership of the European Community, lower rates of income tax, and the sale of council houses.

In the mid-1970s some of Mrs. Thatcher's supporters complained that previous Conservative governments had mistakenly pursued a so-called middle ground, a point midway between Labour and Conservative policies. They claimed that as each Labour government gave a turn of the screw, shifting the middle ground in a more socialist direction, this was accepted by a new Conservative government. Mrs. Thatcher has reversed the ratchet, and it is probable that her successors will find that the middle ground since 1979 has moved firmly to the right.

As the 1980s decade draws to a close, there are signs that the political agenda is accommodating new *postmaterialist* issues. The work force has changed, notably, with the decline in manufacturing employment, the growth of the service sector, of part-time and women workers, and of self-employment. Although the Green party attracted much less electoral support (less than 0.5 percent of the total vote in the 1987 election) than in some other West European states, all the parties now appear sensitive to environmental issues.

In fact, in the European Assembly election held in June of 1989, the "greens" surged to about 16% of the vote in England. Relations with the European Community are sure to become more significant. By the end of 1992 the EC will become a single internal market in which there will be free movement in goods, capital, and persons. Mrs. Thatcher and Britain are widely regarded as "bad" Europeans because of their resistance to many of the moves to integration, particularly on social reforms and membership in the European Monetary System. Pro-Europeans in Britain fear that just as Britain stayed aloof when the EC was created in 1957, so she may miss another opportunity after 1993.

BIBLIOGRAPHY

BELOFF, M. and G. PEELE. *The Government of the UK: Political Authority in a Changing Society.* London: Weidenfeld & Nicholson, 1980.

BIRCH, A. *Representative and Responsible Government.* London: Allen & Unwin, 1964.

BOGDANOR, V. *Multi-Party Politics and the Constitution.* Cambridge: Cambridge University Press, 1983.

BOGDANOR, V. *Devolution.* Oxford: Oxford University Press, 1979.

BUTLER, D. *Governing Without a Majority.* London: Collins, 1983.

BUTLER, D. *The Electoral System in Britain.* New York: Oxford University Press, 1968.

BUTLER, D. and D. KAVANAGH. *The British General Election of 1987.* London: Macmillan 1988.

COOK, C. and J. RAMSDEN. *Trends in British Politics Since 1945.* London: Macmillan, 1978.

CROUCH, C. *The Politics of Industrial Relations.* London: Fontana, 1979.

DE SMITH, S. A. *Constitutional and Administrative Law,* 2nd ed. London: Penguin, 1978.

DRUCKER, H. et al. *Developments in British Politics.* Macmillan, New York 1986.

FINER, S. E. *The Changing Party System.* Washington, DC: American Enterprise Institute, 1979.

———. *Adversary Politics and Electoral Reform.* London: A. Wigram, 1975.

FRY, G. *The Changing Civil Service,* London: Allen & Unwin, 1985.

GAMBLE, A. *Britain in Decline.* Macmillan, New York 1986.

GILMOUR, I. *Inside Right.* London: Quartet Books, 1978.

HEATH, A. R. JOWELL, and J. CURTICE. *How Britain Votes.* Oxford: Pergamon, 1985.

HECLO, H. and A. WILDAVSKY. *The Private Government of Public Money.* New York: Macmillan, 1981.

HENNESSEY, P. *Whitehall.* London: Gecker and Warsburg, 1989.

———. *Cabinet.* London: Blackwell, 1986.

——— and A. SELDON. *Ruling Performance.* London: Blackwell, 1987.

JOHNSTON, R. J. *The Geography of English Politics.* London: Croom Helm, 1985.

KAVANAGH, D.*Thatcherism and British Politics: The End of Consensus.* Oxford: Oxford University Press, 1987.

———. *British Politics: Continuities and Change.* Oxford: Oxford University Press, 1986.

KELLNER, P. and Lord CROWTHER-HUNT. *The Civil Servants.* London: Macdonald, 1980.

KING, A. *The Prime Minister,* 2nd ed. London: Macmillan, 1985.

MORAN, M. *Politics and Society in Britain.* London: Macmillan, 1985.

NORTON, P. *The Constitution in Flux.* Oxford: Martin Robertson, 1982.

NORTON, P. and A. AUGHEY. *Conservatives and Conservatism.* London: Temple Smith, 1985.

PUNNETT, R. M. *Front Bench Opposition.* London: Heinemann, 1978.

RIDDELL, P. *The Thatcher Government,* 2nd ed. Oxford: Blackwell, 1985.

ROSE, R. *Politics in England Today.* London: Faber, 1985.

———. *Do Parties Make a Difference?* 2nd ed. London: Macmillan, 1984.

———. *The Problem of Party Government.* London: Penguin, 1975.

ROSE, R. and I. MCALLISTER. *Voters Begin to Choose.* London: Sage, 1986.

STATIONERY OFFICE. *Social Trends.* London: HMSO, 1988.

TAYLOR, R. *The Fifth Estate: Britain's Unions in the 70s.* London: Routledge & Kegan Paul, 1978.

PART III
THE POLITICS OF FRANCE

Roy C. Macridis

1

Steadfast and Changing

France is a relatively small country—smaller in area than Texas—with approximately 56 million inhabitants. It is highly industrialized. Its progress since World War II in the production of nuclear energy, chemicals, airplanes, aluminum, telecommunications, and automobiles places France in almost the same industrial rank with West Germany. It has outstripped Britain and is exceeded only by the United States, the Federal Republic of Germany, and Japan. It is also a "wealthy" country—with per capita income at about $9,500 a year.[1]

Located in the western part of Europe and having both Atlantic and Mediterra-

nean coasts, France has been both a continental and a maritime power. Until World War II it had the second largest colonial empire, in Africa, the Middle East, and the Far East. More than 100 million people lived under the French flag, and the great majority remain linked to France by economic and cultural ties.

France has long been considered the crucible of what we loosely call Western civilization. Its name carries a special, even if not always a similar, message to every educated person in the world. It is the "oldest daughter" of the Roman Catholic church and the land where monarchy became associated with national greatness. But it is also the land of the revolution of 1789, in which all privileges were swept aside in the name of popular sovereignty, freedom, and equality and the Church was vilified. Napoleon spread the doctrine of the revolution and established his dominion over the greater part of Europe. France is a land of people who have

[1]Most of the data in Part III are from *Tableaux de 'Economie Française,* Institut National de la Statistique et des Etudes Economiques, 1987, Paris; and *Eurostat: Basic Statistics of the Community,* 25th ed., 1988, Luxembourg, Office of the Official Publications of the European Communities, Brussels, Belgium

constantly experimented with ideas, who take nothing for granted, especially in politics. No other nation has maintained its influence for so long and so profoundly affected our ideas and ways of life.

THE FRENCH POLITICAL CULTURE

The set of memories people have; the way they pattern their various personal relations; the ideas and values they hold about the political system; the roles they play and the manner in which they view themselves in the political system—all constitute their political culture.

The French political culture was traditionally viewed in terms of two fundamental traits which set it apart from the British political culture. One—often referred to as individualism—was the citizen's distrust of the state and its agencies, a general tendency to seek to be left alone. Individual concerns and aspirations were at odds with collective and state action. There was a contradiction between public and private life that impeded cooperative effort to bring about collective goods. The French, therefore, seemed to avoid associational activity based upon mutual effort and trust. They instead developed defensive attitudes and defensive mechanisms—the family, the trade unions, the village, the municipality, their deputies in Parliament—against state action. They "defended" themselves against something rather than working together for something. This mentality—born in a society where the peasantry, the individual artisans, craftsmen, and merchants, but also the liberal professionals and the intellectuals were the dominant social forces almost until World War II—is, however, being significantly changed.

The second trait may be called, for lack of a better term, "administrative jacobinism"— or simply *statism*. The creature of the French Revolution and more particularly the Napoleonic organization of the state, it puts reliance upon the state and its agencies to solve societal problems. The "state," suspect in terms of the doctrine of individualism, is considered as the sole instrumentality to provide service and resolve problems. In this sense, the French view themselves as "administered"—as subjects. Their inclination is to wait for the state, that they distrust, to respond to demands and needs. This *bureaucratic phenomenon*, as it has been called by one author, accounts for the remarkable pervasiveness of the French civil service and the citizens' reliance upon it to take the initiative in most social and economic matters— wages and salaries, education, economic growth, university organization and reorganization, and cultural activities. It also accounts for excessive red tape and ineffectiveness.

As is the case with "individualism," statism, too, is undergoing reconsideration today. Efforts to decentralize the state but also to inject new life and autonomy into the societal forces seem to be very much in evidence. Associational activity and effort is manifesting itself.

Because of its abstractness and propensity for ideological solutions—but also for a number of profound social and economic reasons—French political history displays a remarkable degree of discontinuity. In contrast with Britain, where we found regime stability and gradual change, France has experienced a high degree of instability and violent political change. Table 1–1 gives a bird's-eye view of the major political-regime changes in France since the revolution of 1789.

The constitutional changes have been associated—almost always—with major class and ideological cleavages: the aristocracy against the bourgeoisie, the middle classes against the workers, the propertied classes against the poor, the farmers against the landowners—all in various combinations, depending on the circumstances. Ideologies developed to justify and rationalize social and class conflicts: they became powerful incitements to action. Gradually they crystallized into institutionalized molds of thought, shaping motivation and political action. Conservatism, radicalism, socialism, communism, Bonapartism, and statism but *not* liber-

TABLE 1–1   The Instability of the French Political System

Republic	*Monarchy*	*"Bonapartism"*
The First Republic (1792–95), ended by military coup	L'Ancien Régime (to 1789), ended by revolution	Napoleonic dictatorship (1799–1814), ended by military defeat
The Second Republic (1848–51), ended by military coup	Constitutional monarchy (1789–91)	The Second Empire: Napoleon III (1851–70), ended by military defeat and revolutionary uprising
The Third Republic (1870–1940), ended by military defeat	The Bourbon Restoration (1814–30), ended by revolution	
The Fourth Republic (1946–58), ended by military uprising	The Orleanist "July Monarchy" (1830–48), ended by revolution	The Vichy régime: Marshal Pétain (1940–44), ended by military defeat of the Axis powers
The Fifth Republic (established 1958)		The Fifth Republic: some Bonapartist traits

alism, have been the most powerful ideological movements.

We might argue, then, that the political history of France has crystallized into behavior patterns that contrast sharply with British political patterns. The French political culture appears *fragmented* rather than consensual, *unstable* rather than gradualistic, and *ideological* rather than pragmatic, emphasizing revolution and violent change as opposed to compromise and agreement. Even today, despite the acceptance of the most recent constitution, the French continue to disagree sharply about the final ends of social and political life and about the means for accomplishing them.

A SOCIOECONOMIC PROFILE

Until a few decades ago the dominant characteristic of the French economy was relative underdevelopment. While industrialization advanced rapidly in Britain, Germany, Japan, and the United States, France's economy grew relatively slowly. In some decades it did not grow at all. Gross national income between 1870 and 1940 rose by about 80 percent, whereas that of Germany increased five times and that of Great Britain three and a half times. After a rise in economic production and investment between 1924 and 1931, net investment declined in the 1930s to a

point below zero—that is, France was living on capital, using factories and equipment without replacing them in full. The destruction of World War II, estimated at approximately 200 billion present-day dollars, was an additional blow. With industrial equipment destroyed or dilapidated and the transportation network paralyzed, the French economy was in a state of collapse at the end of the war.

The task facing the country in 1945 was twofold: to replace the industrial equipment that had been damaged or destroyed in the war and to eliminate the weak elements in the economy. This was the objective of the first Monnet Plan, for 1947–50 (eventually extended to 1952). Named after Jean Monnet, France's architect in economic planning and modernization, this plan had the following goals:

1. To ensure a rapid rise in the living conditions of the population.

2. To modernize and reequip the basic industries—coal mining, electric power, iron, cement, farm machinery, and transportation.

3. To bring agricultural methods and machinery up to date.

4. To devote the maximum resources possible to reconstruction.

5. To modernize and develop the export industries to ensure equilibrium in the balance of payments.

Since then economic planning has become a fixture of French national life. The "plan" sets forth the major parameters of economic growth sector by sector and often region by region for five-year periods.

State Controls

Several key economic activities were nationalized after 1944. Leaders of the left, and many Gaullists as well, believed that public ownership of certain industries was superior to private enterprise. By 1946 electricity, gas, and some automobile plants, notably Renault, had been nationalized, and the Bank of France and Air France (the most important airline) had come under state direction. A sizable part of the economic activity of France thus came under state ownership, which already included all rail transportation. Massive public subsidies, both for state-controlled activities and for private enterprises, were necessary after the war. An extensive program of social legislation was also adopted—old-age insurance, accident and unemployment compensation, maternity benefits, medical care (most of the patient's expenses for medical treatment, hospitalization, and drugs are paid by the national insurance fund), and family allowances that provide supplementary income to families with two children or more. Economic expan-sion was clearly discernible even before the advent of the Fifth Republic in 1958. France's economy began to grow at a rate comparable with that of West Germany.

France today is quite similar to other industrialized nations. Of its labor force of about 21 million, about 7–8 percent work in agriculture, 38 percent in industry, and 52 percent in the so-called tertiary occupations—merchandising, teaching, the professions, and other services (see Table 1–2). In 1988 the per capita income in France was sixth among the larger industrial nations.

SOCIAL CLASSES

The Workers. Of the some 21 million gainfully employed persons in France, a little over 6 million are considered industrial workers. Although it is difficult to generalize about such a large group of people, they do have certain common traits that put them in an identifiable socioeconomic category. In the first place, blue-collar workers are relatively poor and their standard of living has improved little, even in years of prosperity. A great many are immigrant workers from Tunisia, Morocco, Algeria, Portugal, Spain, and Italy. Unskilled workers average about $825.00 a month. The minimum wage is set at about $650.00 a month.

TABLE 1–2 Approximate Distribution of Working Population, 1986*

Occupation	Number (in thousands)	Percentage of Total
Farmers, agricultural workers, forestry	1,414	6.7%
Artisans, merchants, shopkeepers, "chefs d'entreprise" (with fifty and more salaried personnel)	1,763	8.2
Top managers and administrative personnel	2,074	9.6
Middle managerial, technical, public services	4,324	20.0
Salaried (civil services, public enterprises, household and personal services)	5,717	26.5
Workers	6,242	29.0
Total	21,534	100.0%
Salaried: 17,965 83.5%		
Self-employed: 3,569 16.5%		

Source: Adapted from *Tableaux de l'Economique Francaise, 1987.*

With modernization and the development of new advanced industries in chemicals, electronics, and nuclear energy, the working class has become diversified. White-collar workers earn two and three times the wage average. Within each occupation special skills create a wide range of wages and salaries—a range that separates one group of workers from another, creates relatively affluent categories of workers, and thereby undermines the vaunted "class solidarity" of the "proletariat."

The workers are divided into a number of trade union organizations: the Confédération Générale du Travail (General Confederation of Labor), or CGT, under the control of the Communist party; the Confédération Générale du Travail-Force Ouvrière (General Confederation of Labor-Working Force), or CGT-FO, which split from the communist-controlled CGT in 1947 and remains associated with the Socialist party; and the former Catholic trade union organizations, now called the Confédération Française Démocratique du Travail (French Confederation of Democratic Labor), or CFDT. In addition, there are a number of "independent" organizations.

It is always difficult to get reliable figures of trade union membership, but it is generally agreed that it has been going through a period of rapid decline. According to the most authoritative estimate of the European Trade Union Confederation, not more than 17 percent of the working force belongs to a union. The CGT, that boasted in 1946 a membership of over 5 million, is now down to less than 1 million. The CFDT has about 600,000 members; the CGT-FO about as many. The Catholic trade union—the CFTC (Confederation Française des Travailleurs Chretiens)—has maintained its membership at about 250,000. As for the white-collar and managerial personnel, its union—the CGC (Confederation Générale des Cadres)—has about 150,000–200,000 members. In all, out of a total of about 18 million of salaried personnel that includes workers, managerial, and clerical personnel, not more than 3 mil-lion belong to the respective unions open to them—a maximum of 17 percent .[2]

The Farmers. There are about 1.5 million farmers in France (individual owners, tenant farmers, sharecroppers, and agricultural workers), and they constitute about 8 percent of those gainfully employed. Half a million are agricultural workers who earn less than $500 a month. The rest own their land or lease it.

More than half a million farmers own such small holdings that they are unable to use modern techniques for increasing their productivity. As a result, until very recently the productivity of French agriculture was low compared with that of American, British, and Danish farmers. The authors of the Monnet Plan complained immediately after the Liberation that a French farmer produced only enough to feed 3 persons, whereas an American farmer could feed 16, a British farmer 7, and a Danish farmer 9.

There have been some dramatic changes, however, in the rural and agricultural regions of France since. Although about half the farmers left for urban centers since 1945, agricultural productivity increased rapidly, thanks to the use of tractors and fertilizers and also to the guaranteed market at relatively high prices provided by the Common Market. Cooperatives have sprung up everywhere, and efforts have been made to end the parceling of land. Today French agriculture provides about half the farm products of the European Economic Community. As a result, both living conditions and farm incomes have improved. There are fewer farmers, but they produce more and earn more than their fathers.

The ideologies that have had the most appeal for the farmers are radicalism and conservatism. The elements of radicalism—individualism and an antistate philosophy—are rooted in the thinking of many farmers. Conservatism, on the other hand, is particu-

[2]See *Le Monde*, Dossiers et Documents, no. 150 (December 1987), Paris.

larly prevalent in the areas where the Church remains influential.

The Middle Class. The term middle class covers many heterogeneous elements. Do we define it according to occupation? income? status? One French political scientist uses three criteria for categorizing French citizens: their job, their way of life and the manner in which they spend their income, and their income tax. On the basis of these criteria, the following groups belong to the French middle class: among the salaried are engineers, office personnel, the bulk of the civil servants, judges, teachers, professors, and noncommissioned officers; among the nonsalaried are members of the professions, small merchants, small businessmen, small entrepreneurs, and artisans. Together they are roughly estimated at 10 million people, or about 50 percent of those gainfully employed.

From the economic and social affinities that exist within the middle class, we might assume that it exhibits a common attitude in politics. But this is hardly the case in France, where the middle class has often changed political orientations and is today split into many different political loyalties. Indeed, the middle class supports virtually all political parties. In many instances middle-class groups have supported the Socialists and even the Communists. The bulk of middle-class votes, however, go today to the center groups and some to the Gaullists, though a good percentage may vote Socialist. All political parties in turn make a concerted effort to appeal to the various segments of this class.

Business Groups. Probably the most solidly organized professional group in France are the businessmen: industrialists, corporation managers, bankers, and merchants. Their strongest organization is the National Council of French Employers. Founded after World War I, it includes according to its own statement, almost 1 million firms employing about 5 million wage earners and salaried personnel. It also includes other business associations, of which the National Council of Small and Middle-Sized Businesses is one, and organizations representing particular industries, such as chemicals, steel, and shipbuilding.

The functions of the CNPF are (1) to establish a liaison between industry and commerce, (2) to represent business firms before the public authorities, (3) to undertake studies for the purpose of improving the economic and social conditions of the country, and (4) to provide information for its members. The council thus speaks on behalf of many powerful interests. Its "representative" character and huge size render it somewhat inflexible and immobile, and its highly diversified membership hinders achievement of a common attitude on particular issues.

French interest groups and lobbies are also directly active in the legislative process. Through their spokespeople they introduce bills and see to it that the proper amendments are inserted in pending legislation or that prejudicial amendments are blocked. Their influence with the executive branch and the bureaucracy has grown significantly ever since the constitution of the Fifth Republic was established. When a bill is passed, the interested lobby tries to prevent the release of any executive order that might be prejudicial to it or, conversely, attempts to see that the proper executive orders are issued. To do this, it often plants representatives in certain crucial administrative services—the ministries of public works, agriculture, veterans, finance, and industrial production. With the growing participation of the state in economic matters, "lobbying" at the ministerial level has greatly increased. Every interest attempts to "colonize" the government in a number of ways: by influencing administrators, by offering them important jobs in their own organizations, and by presenting them with facts and figures that appear to be convincing.

Intimate relationships between many interest groups and ministries have been gradually institutionalized into corporatist patterns thanks to which no decision is made without the consent of the interests involved and no decision is implemented without the active participation of the interest organization involved. When the French refer to "rigidities" in their economy, they have in mind these patterns resulting from cooperation between interests and political agencies that preserve obsolete economic structures and practices and impede free competition.

THE CHURCH

France is a predominantly Catholic nation (see Table 1–3). Yet of its some 48 million Catholics (the rest are either agnostic or belong to other denominations—Protestant, Jewish, and Moslem), not more than about 13 million can be classed as practicing believers. The great majority are only nominally Catholic. They observe only the basic sacraments prescribed by the church—baptism, communion, marriage, and extreme unction—and conform outwardly to some of the most important religious conventions. About 7 million "Catholics" are anticlerical and agnostic. Many densely populated urban centers, but also many rural areas in southern France, are virtually de-Christianized—without churches and priests. Much of the urban population, especially in the working-class districts is militantly atheistic. A close correlation exists between conservatism and attachment to the church and between communism and socialism and hostility to the church. The right, generally speaking, is religious; the left is overtly anticlerical and very often atheistic. The "progressive" Catholics are actively concerned with social and economic reform and are more interested in social action than in religious practice. Since World War II this group has been moving toward the left and has been responsible for establishing new reformist Catholic groups, parties, and trade unions. Many have joined the Socialist party, as have many Catholic voters.

THE MODERNIZATION OF FRANCE

The pace of the modernization accomplished in France in the last 30 years has been remarkable. Not only has the structure of the economy been rapidly modified, but the society has changed as well. It is a fully industrialized economy and a modern society—one in which significant sectors attain a level of technology unmatched by any other industrialized nation. Industrial production between 1945 and 1980 grew tenfold (making up for the sharp decline by World War II). In the years between 1958 to 1973 the gross national product rose at an annual rate of 5.5 percent—the highest, next to Japan. Between 1953 and 1984, 96.4 percent of households had acquired refrigerators (fewer than 5 percent had this in 1953), 91.2 percent acquired TV sets (as compared to 1.0 percent in 1953), 80 percent acquired telephones (9.3 percent in 1953), and 21 percent bought dishwashers as compared to 2 percent in 1968. The productivity of the French worker increased fourfold.

The Role of the State

While in West Germany and the United States the economy, and with it modernization and productivity, has remained largely in the hands of individual corporations operating in a free market, in France it is the state and its agencies that have played the

TABLE 1–3   Religion in France—A Profile

		Percentage (of the population)
Catholic		
Practice regularly (go to church every week or at least twice a month)	13	
Practice occasionally (go to church once in a while during great religious holidays.)	16	81
Non-practicing (go to church only occasionally—for the great ceremonies—baptism, marriage, funerals)	52	
Non-Catholic		7
(Protestant, Jewish, but primarily Moslem)		
Without religion		12

key role. The state has undertaken special projects, such as the Concorde plane and production of nuclear energy, and has made every effort to modernize and increase productivity in agriculture. In the last decade the state has assumed a commanding role in many sectors. It is the state that initiates new industrial projects, promotes economic and industrial activity, and in many instances directly manages a number of industrial firms.

The major instruments of state action have been the economic plan, fiscal policy, and direct action and investments through the nationalized industries. The plan continues to provide the major options for growth—sector by sector and sometimes industry by industry. The plan is the overall expression of the major targets of national economic activity. The ways in which it is implemented by the state and its highly trained civil servants are many. At least four are usually mentioned: (1) direct intervention by the ministries and their staff, (2) state subsidies and loans, (3) nationalization of industries and other forms of direct participation in economic activity, (4) state purchases.

The role of the state expanded significantly after the election in 1981 of a socialist president of the republic—François Mitterrand. His program comprised the nationalization not only of all the banks still in private hands (not more than 30 percent of the banking industry) but also of major industrial sectors—glass, piping, electronics, chemicals, pharmaceuticals, computers, steel, and aircraft. More than 35 percent of France's industrial production came under state control.

A Changing Class Structure

Economic and industrial modernization has modified French society. Communication among the French and among regions of France has increased rapidly, together with geographic mobility. The old distinct provincial centers have merged into common national attitudes and practices. Urbanization has brought a greater number of French people together: today only a small percentage live in hamlets of fewer than 2,000 people. France has become a mass society where people live alike, listen to the same radio and TV programs, consume the same products, and are closer to each other than ever before.

The rapid growth of the national income has benefited all groups. Workers' wages have increased rapidly: including the various social benefits, they more than tripled between 1955 and 1985. Technology has accounted for the growth of a body of white-collar workers and managerial personnel—the so-called *cadres*. Farmers have not only declined sharply in numbers but have changed their mode of life radically. Better communications now link the farm and the town. These "new" farmers have little in common with the mentality and the traditions of the peasantry that was the backbone of the country until World War II.

There is also a new elite: the old bourgeoisie, based on family wealth and status, has given way to one that consists of administrators, intellectuals, managers and technicians, and of course the political class that is recruited mostly from among them. It is a pragmatic and innovative elite concerned with the implementation of tasks, performance, economic growth, and material wealth rather than the continuation of traditions and the pursuit of ideologies. In short, it is a class of *technocrats*.

A NEW CONSENSUS . . . AND CRISIS

The portrait of France of a society ideologically divided and full of irreconcilable cleavages is fading.[3] Modernization is beginning to affect attitudes and behavior and to miti-

---

[3] I am indebted for this discussion to Alain Duhamel's excellent article "Le Consensus Français," in *L'Opinion Française en 1977*, Sofres, ed. (Paris: Presses de le Fondation Nationale des Sciences Politiques, 1978), pp. 87–101. Also see *L'Opinion* and *L'Etat de l'Opinion*, Sofres, 1987, 1988.

gate the conflicts of the past. The French are beginning to feel more at home with one another, with their political system, and with their society.

A number of surveys have indicated this. The majority of the French—over 60 percent—like their free society and prefer it by far to all others. For instance, only 5 percent would opt for the Soviet system or a "people's democracy"—even though some 20 percent voted for the French Communist party in the 1970s. If given a choice, 86 percent would choose the French nationality. The French remain attached to their nation and to its symbols, the "Marseillaise" and July 14. Two-thirds of them are unconcerned with the separatist movements that have emerged in Corsica, Brittany, and the Basque region. Virtually all political parties and movements are considered "patriotic." For instance, in 1977 only 21 percent mentioned the Communist party as "the least patriotic."

The antagonism that existed between the individual and the state is declining. Eighty-seven percent of the people believe it is desirable to be a good citizen. They value highly information about the political life of the country, compliance with rules, education for children, and the obligation to vote. Individual freedom, social security, freedom of the press, freedom of work, and a free economy are also cherished. The feeling of belonging to a class remains, and so does the perception of class conflict, but the notions of a class struggle and revolution are no longer taken seriously. Forty-seven percent believe that it is getting more difficult to rise socially; the same percentage believe that it is easier than before to receive a university education. Almost 60 percent believe that the social differences among the young are getting smaller.

With regard to class, a poll taken in the spring of 1983 revealed that 62 percent of the population believed that they belonged to one—35 percent declared themselves to be in the working class, while most others identified with the middle class. Furthermore, when asked which social class was gaining in importance, 42 percent declared that it was the middle class, 5 percent the bourgeoisie, and only 27 percent the working class. The rest had no opinion.[4] Thus the profile of French society is one of relative satisfaction, self-assurance, and a renewed sense of citizenship and community, with class cleavages diminishing in importance.

There are, however, clouds in the horizon, and some of them are quite ominous. We shall discuss them on concluding Chapter 5. One relates to the presence of many "immigrant workers" in France—about 4 million, of whom about half are from North Africa. In times of full employment, they were accepted in the factory and the workplace and were not viewed as a burden on the public services—mainly welfare and education. With unemployment in the 1980s running at about 10 percent—2.5 million—they began to be viewed with suspicion and outright hostility. Cultural differences between the North Africans and the French, including particularly religious differences, began to be exploited by right-wing leaders and boosted the ranks of the extreme-right-wing groups that advocated their exclusion from public services and their return to the countries of their origin. Jean-Marie Le Pen, the leader of the extreme right-wing—the National Front—gained about 10 percent of the votes in the European election of 1984 and again in the legislative election of 1986. In the presidential election of 1988, running as a candidate, he received 14.6 percent of the national vote. Was it a transient movement? Did it reflect a deep-set crisis of the traditions of democracy, equality, and fraternal solidarity to which the French are committed?

Another problem has been the economic crisis in the late 1970s and the 1980s. It challenged the remarkable 30 years of economic growth France had enjoyed after the end of World War II—referred to as the "Glorious Thirty." After 1977 unemployment began to rise—to become gradually "chronic"; infla-

---

[4]Sofres, *L'Opinion Française en 1984*, p. 159.

tion hovered in the early 1980s at around 10 percent a year; the public debt rose and so did the trade deficit. Economic growth came to a standstill, investment dropped precipitously with private investment shrinking down to almost zero—all this while welfare spending continued to rise.

Yet another serious problem is the aging of the French population. Many commentators fear that the earlier phase of a baby boom was giving place to what they called "papa boom"! A smaller working force would be forced to support a growing number of old and inactive. Many feared that the French were eating again into their capital. Many began to question the welfare state and the "Socialist state"—even among the Socialists. Many felt that unless drastic measures were taken to release individual talent and inventiveness by reducing the role of the state and the bureaucracy and allowing a degree of free enterprise and entrepreneurship, productivity and growth would come to a standstill and the society was doomed to a precipitous decline. Neither socialism nor Gaullism (in fact no political ideology or party) seemed to provide an answer.

As we shall see, the French voters in the elections of 1988 became confused and divided—over many of these issues: how to cope with the North African workers and their children; how to stop unemployment from growing—let alone create new jobs; how to reconcile welfare legislation with limited resources; how to invigorate the French economy through a return to market mechanisms—while preserving social and welfare services.

Major Events in France Since World War II

The Fourth Republic

August–December 1944	Liberation of the French territory.
September 1944	General de Gaulle assumes the government.
October 1945	A constituent assembly is elected.
January 21, 1946	De Gaulle resigns.
October 1946	Second draft of constitution is ratified in a referendum (yes, 53 percent; no, 47 percent).
November 10, 1946	Legislative elections A "tripartite" government is formed: Socialists-Communists and MRP.
April 1947	Communists are ousted from the government.
1949	France enters NATO.
June 17, 1951	Legislative elections The "Third Force" coalition (Socialists, Radicals, and MRP), excluding Gaullists and Communists, is founded to win a majority against Communists and Gaullists.

January 2, 1956	Legislative election
	  Communist, 25.9%
	  Socialist, 15.2%
	  Radical, 11.3%
	  Dissident Radicals, 3.9%
	  Ex-Gaullists, 1.2%
	  Moderate, 15.3%
	  Poujadists, 11.6%

May 13, 1958	Insurrection of French soldiers and settlers in Algeria and formation of committees of public safety.
June 1, 1958	General de Gaulle becomes prime minister and is authorized to prepare a new constitution.

Fifth Republic

September 28, 1958	Gaullist constitution overwhelmingly approved in referendum.
November 23, 1958	Legislative elections give overwhelming majority to all the parties supporting de Gaulle, but not the Communists who opposed him.
December 3, 1958	De Gaulle elected president.

Major Events in France Since World War II

October 1962	Amendment to the constitution allowing direct popular election of the President approved in referendum.
November 1962	Legislative elections give majority to Gaullists and their allies.
December 1965	De Gaulle is reelected on the second ballot as president of the republic for a second term.
March–April 1966	France withdraws from NATO, and all U.S. forces and installations leave France.
March 1967	Legislative elections give a narrow margin of victory to Gaullists and their allies.
May 1968	Uprising of students and workers.
June 1968	New legislative elections following dissolution of National Assembly give overwhelming victory to Gaullists and their allies. The Gaullist party alone has a majority.
April 1969	De Gaulle loses the referendum on decentralization and the reform of the Senate and resigns on April 28.
May–June 1969	New presidential elections. Georges Pompidou elected on second ballot against a disunited left and center.
April 1972	Referendum on Britain's entry into the Common Market is carried despite opposition of Communists, abstention of Socialists, and massive abstention of voters.
March 1973	Legislative elections. Gaullists and allies win a majority, despite decline in strength compared with 1968.
April 1974	Pompidou dies.
May 1974	Presidential elections. Giscard d'Estaing, leader of the Independent Republicans and long-time minister of finance in Gaullist cabinets, narrowly elected (50.8%).
August 1976	Prime Minister Chirac resigns and is replaced by Raymond Barre.
March 12–19, 1978	Legislative elections. "Center-right" consisting of Gaullists (RPR) and a new centrist formation (UDF) whose titular leader is President Giscard d'Estaing defeats left-wing coalition of Communists and Socialists and some leftist radicals. Despite internal rivalries and conflicts, the RPR-UDF majority supports the president.
April 26–May 10, 1981	Presidential election. François Mitterrand (Socialist) is narrowly elected on second ballot (51.7%).
June 14–21, 1981	The left wins in legislative elections. The Socialists alone gain an absolute majority in the National Assembly.
June 30, 1981	Formation of government with Pierre Mauroy as prime minister. Four Communists participate.

The Socialist Experiment (1981–86)

December 18, 1981	Nationalization of key industrial sections and virtually all banks adopted by National Assembly.
January 13, 1982	Thirty-nine hour workweek and five-week paid vacation decreed.
January 28, 1982	Decentralization law comes into effect.
June 9, 1982	Mitterrand announces "second" phase of socialist economic policy—the beginning of austerity measures and reduction in government expenditures.
June 16, 1984	European election. In France, the "opposition" parties (Gaullist, UDF, and others) receive 43%; the Socialists, 20.75%; the Communists, 11.20%; the extreme right (National Front), 10.95%.
July 17, 1984	The government of Pierre Mauroy resigns.
July 19, 1984	Laurent Fabius becomes the new prime minister. Key ministers (Education, Finance, Interior) change hands. The Communist party refuses to participate in the new government.
January 1985	Recurrence of violence in New Caledonia. Mitterrand visits the island.
April 1985	Electoral reform in favor of proportional representation is proposed by the government and subsequently enacted by the National Assembly.

Cohabitation (1986–87)

March 16, 1986	Legislative and regional elections: Center-right (RPR and UDF) and associated rightists win a slim majority. In the regional elections held for the first time, the center-right wins in 20 of the 22 regions and (sometimes with the help of the National Front) elects 20 of the presidencies of the regional councils.
March 20, 1986	Jacques Chirac (leader of the RPR) becomes the prime minister and forms a cabinet.

Major Events in France Since World War II

April 10, 1986	Chirac asks for a vote of confidence in the National Assembly. The vote is 292 for and 285 against.
May 20, 1986	Proposal to change the electoral law (from proportional representation used in the election of 1986 back to the majority system with two ballotings that had been used throughout the Fifth Republic). Motion of censure fails by five votes (284 votes of the 289 required to bring the government down).
July 14, 1986	President Mitterrand refuses to sign executive orders (*ordonnances*) to implement law authorizing the government to denationalize some 65 industrial units, insurances, and banks. (Many are denationalized, by individual legislative acts.)
October 4, 1986	President Mitterrand refuses to sign the new redistricting provided by the new electoral law. Subsequently, the redistricting is enacted by law.
March–April 1987	Privatization of three TV stations.
April 26, 1987	Jean-Marie Le Pen, leader of the National Front announces his candidacy for the presidential election scheduled for April–May 1988.
August 22, 1987	Uprisings and demonstrations continue in New Caledonia; repressive measures are taken against demonstrators.

	1988: A Socialist President Without a Majority
March 24, 1988	Presidential electoral campaign officially opens.
April 24, 1988	The first ballot returns indicate the continuation of the strength of the president and the weakening of Chirac—his major opponent—who fails to win 20% of the vote even though he comes in second.
April 28, 1988	Major televised debate between Mitterrand and Chirac.
May 8, 1988	Mitterrand wins the presidency with 54% of the vote.
May 9, 1988	Chirac resigns as prime minister.
May 11, 1988	Nomination of Michel Rocard as prime minister and negotiations for the formation of a cabinet.
May 14, 1988	Dissolution of the National Assembly by President Mitterrand and call for a new election scheduled for June 5 and June 12.
June 5, 1988	First balloting shows highest rate of abstention ever in the Fifth Republic—34.26%. The Socialists win 34.76% of the vote; the Communists, 11.32%. But the RPR and the UDF (UCR) receive about 39%, while the extreme right—the National Front—garners about 10%.
June 12, 1988	Second ballot. The Communists win 27 seats; the Socialists and their allies, 277; the center-right groups and their allies (UDR and RPR and independents rightists), 272; and the National Front, only 1. No party has the needed majority of 289.
June 15, 1988	President Mitterand asks Michel Rocard to form a second cabinet.
November 6, 1988	Referendum on the status of New Caledonia.
December 1–15, 1988	Widespread strikes and "social unrest."
March 1989	Municipal Elections. Gains by Socialists. Decline of Communists. Center-Right as Gaullists hold on to their positions and National Front maintains its voting strength.
June 1989	Election for European Parliament. Strong showing of the Environmentalist with 11% of the vote. Socialist show moderate gains.

2

The Fifth Republic:
The Institutions

The Constitution of the Fifth Republic originated with the enabling act of June 3, 1958. The National Assembly provided, by the requisite majority of three-fifths, that "the Constitution will be revised by the government formed on June 1, 1958"—that is, General de Gaulle's government. The "new" (but it is already over 30 years old!) constitution contained a number of ideas that had been developed by de Gaulle and many political leaders throughout the Third and Fourth republics.[1] Two major themes dominated the thinking of the framers: first, the reconstitution of the authority of the state under the leadership of a strong executive; second, the establishment of what came to be known as a "rationalized" parliament—a parliament with limited political and legislative powers.

---

[1]For a more detailed discussion of this constitution, see Roy Macridis and Bernard Brown, *The de Gaulle Republic: Quest for Unity* (Homewood, IL: Dorsey, 1960), Chap. 10.

THE LEGACY OF THE PAST

Every *new* constitution attempts to remedy past institutional arrangements that for one reason or another are held accountable for the malfunctionings of the political system. In attempting to set up a strong executive branch, a diminished parliament, and what they hoped would be a coherent and disciplined party system, the framers were addressing themselves to the evils of the past. Briefly, what were these evils?

Cabinet Instability

The constitution of October 1946 that ushered in the Fourth Republic was sharply criticized throughout its short life, even by those who had helped write it. It was portrayed as being dominated by lobbies, incapable of making needed decisions, and unresponsive to its leaders, who by and large were not commanding figures. The constitution vested supreme power in Parliament—notably in the lower house, the National Assembly. The prime minister and his cabinet governed as long as they had majority support in the National Assembly. The president of the Republic was elected by Parliament (the National Assembly and the Senate meeting together) and, like the British monarch, was only the titular head of state. Prime ministers came and went with disturbing frequency as the majorities shifted back and forth in the assembly. The 12 years of the Fourth Republic saw 20 cabinets form and dissolve, an average of about 1 every 8 months.

Party Multiplicity and Intraparty Divisions

In our discussion of Great Britain we saw a two-party system in which the parties are disciplined with one supporting the government on the basis of pledges formulated at election time and the other opposing it, hoping to replace it. In France, under the Fourth Republic, there were eight or ten parties, most of them without discipline, leadership, or platforms. In the legislature, a number of parliamentary groups, corresponding more or less to the political parties, formed weak coalitions behind a government that therefore was short-lived. The multiparty system led to a fragmented assembly, which in turn accounted for cabinet instability.

Because of their multiplicity and internal divisions, the parties in France could not perform two vital functions. They were not able to debate and clarify issues for the public. Members and leaders of the same party (except the Communists and possibly the Socialists) often advocated different things in different parts of the country, and their differences were not resolved in their party congresses. Second, under the Fourth Republic the parties could not provide for a stable government committed to certain policy objectives. After an election it was impossible to tell which combinations of political parties and parliamentary groups could provide temporary support for a prime minister

and which new combinations would bring about the prime minister's downfall.

The multiplicity of the parties led to a widening gap between the people and the government. The system did not give an opportunity to the people to choose their government and hold it accountable.

THE CONSTITUTION OF THE FIFTH REPUBLIC

It was to these major evils that General de Gaulle and his associates addressed themselves. A most important landmark was a speech made by de Gaulle at Bayeux on June 16, 1946, in which he outlined the ideas that were to serve as the foundations of the new constitution:

> The rivalry of the parties takes, in our country, a fundamental character, which leaves everything in doubt and which very often wrecks its superior interests. This is an obvious fact that . . . our institutions must take into consideration in order to preserve our respect for laws, the cohesion of governments, the efficiency of the administration and the prestige and authority of the State. The difficulties of the State result in the inevitable alienation of the citizen from his institutions. . . . All that is needed then is an occasion for the appearance of the menace of dictatorship.[2]

The crucial task of the powers of the constitution of the Fifth Republic was to create a strong and stable government but within the framework of the Republican tradition. The preamble solemnly declares the attachment of the French people to the Declaration of the Rights of Man of 1789 and to individual and social rights that were affirmed, after France's liberation, by the constitution of 1946. Article I proclaims that "France is a Republic, indivisible, secular, democratic, and social." It ensures the rights of all citizens and respect for all beliefs. Article 2 affirms that "all sovereignty stems from the

---

[2]The text of the Bayeux speech can be found in Charles de Gaulle, *Discours et Messages* (II, pp. 5–11, Editions Plon, Paris, 1970).

people." But this sovereignty is to be exercised not solely through the legislative assemblies, notably, the National Assembly, but also through referendums and through the president of the Republic.

The constitution established the familiar organs of a parliamentary system (Figure 2–1): a bicameral legislature consisting of the National Assembly (lower house) and the Senate (the upper house), a chief of state, a cabinet and a prime minister in charge of the direction of the policies of the government and responsible to the lower chamber (the National Assembly) with the right to censure and overthrow the prime minister and the cabinet. But in contrast with the Fourth Republic, it delegated broad powers to the chief of state (the president) and placed serious limitations on the legislature.

THE PRESIDENT OF THE REPUBLIC

The framers of the new constitution wished to give the president the prestige and prerogatives that would enable him to provide continuity for the state. To make the president the keystone of the Fifth Republic, both the symbol and the instrument of reinforced executive authority, the framers modified the manner in which he is elected and strengthened his powers.

The president was originally elected by an electoral college, which, in addition to the members of Parliament, included the municipal councilors, the general councilors, and the members of the assemblies and municipalities of overseas territories and republics. It was a restricted electoral college favoring rural municipalities and small towns and discriminating against the large urban centers. As a result, it was widely criticized as perpetuating the old political forces of the Fourth Republic.

In a message to Parliament on October 2, 1962, de Gaulle proposed to modify the constitution: "When my seven-year term is completed [in 1965] or if something happens that makes it impossible for me to continue my functions, I am convinced that a popular vote will be necessary in order to give . . . to those who will succeed me the possibility and the duty to assume the supreme task." His proposal was overwhelmingly accepted in a referendum and ever since 1962 the president has been elected by a direct popular vote.

Powers of the President

The constitution of the Fifth Republic maintains the political independence of the president, but gives him personal powers that he can exercise solely at his discretion:

1. The president designates the prime minister. Although the president presumably makes the designation with an eye to the relative strengths of the various parties in the National Assembly, it is a personal political act.
2. The president can dissolve the National Assembly at any time, on any issue, and for any reason solely at his discretion. There is only one limitation—he cannot dissolve it twice within the same year—and one formality—he must "consult" with the prime minister and the presidents of the two legislative assemblies.
3. When the institutions of the Republic, the independence of the nation, the integrity of its territory, or the execution of international engagements are menaced in a grave and immediate manner and the regular functioning of the public powers is interrupted, the president may take whatever measures are required by the circumstances (Article 16). Again, this is a personal and discretionary act that has been used only once. The president needs only to inform the nation by a message and to "consult" the constitutional Council. The National Assembly, however, convenes automatically and cannot be dissolved during the emergency period.
4. Finally, the president can bring certain issues before the people in a referendum:

The President of the Republic on the proposal of the government . . . or on joint resolution by the two legislative assemblies . . . *may* submit to a referendum any bill dealing with the organization of the public powers, the approval of an agreement of the Community or

Legislative

NATIONAL ASSEMBLY

577 members: 555 from metropolitan France and 22 from overseas territories and departments.

Mandate: Five years. Elected directly by equal and universal suffrage. Majority system (two ballots) in force since 1958 except in 1986 election.

Limited Legislative Powers: Legislates on civil rights, nationality, status and legal competence of persons, penal law and procedure, taxation, electoral system, organization of national defense, administration of local government units, education, employment, unions, social security, and economic programs. Authorizes declaration of war. Can initiate constitutional revision. Can delegate above powers to cabinet-votes organic laws. Can question cabinet one day a week. Meets in regular sessions for a total that does not exceed five months. Votes budget submitted by government.

(*All other matters fall within rule-making power.*) Can censure and overthrow prime minister and cabinet by absolute majority vote (289).

SENATE

317 members

Mandate: Nine years. Renewable by thirds every three years.

Elected indirectly by municipal and general councilors and members of National Assembly. Approximate size of electoral college: 110,000. Majority system, but proportional representation for seven departments with largest population.

Functions: Full legislative powers jointly with Assembly. Bills must be approved in identical terms by both houses unless prime minister, in case of discord, asks lower house to vote "definitive" text and thereby overrule Senate.

Executive

PRESIDENT OF THE REPUBLIC

Elected for seven-year term by direct popular election.

Personal Powers: Nominates prime minister; dissolves Assembly; refers bills to Constitutional Council for examination of constitutionality; calls referendums; must sign decrees with force of law; nominates three of the nine members of Constitutional Council; can send messages to legislature; invokes state of emergency and rules by decree; presides over regular meetings of cabinet members—Council of Ministers; He is not responsible to Parliament.

PRIME MINISTER AND CABINET

Prime minister proposes cabinet members to president for nomination; "conducts the policies of nation"; directs actions of government and is responsible for national defense; presides over cabinet meetings; proposes referendums; has law-initiating power. Refers bills to Constitutional Council. Prime minister is responsible before Assembly.

CIVIL SERVICE

Judiciary

THE ECONOMIC AND SOCIAL COUNCIL

Elected by professional organizations. Designated by government for five years as specified by "organic law." Composed of representatives of professional groups (approximately 195 members).

Gives "opinion" on bills referred to it by government. "Consulted" on overall government economic plans.

CONSTITUTIONAL COUNCIL

Composed of nine justices and all ex-presidents of Republic. President of the Republic, of Senate, and of National Assembly appoint three justices each.

Functions: Supervises presidential and legislative elections and declares returns. Supervises referendums and proclaims results. Examines and decides on contested legislative elections. On request of the prime minister or the presidents of the republic, the National Assembly, or Senate, or upon request of at least 60 Senators or 60 members of the National Assembly, examines and decides on constitutionality of pending bills, and treaties and on legislative competence of Assembly.

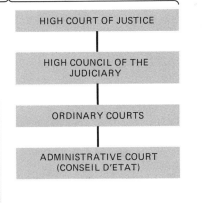

HIGH COURT OF JUSTICE

HIGH COUNCIL OF THE JUDICIARY

ORDINARY COURTS

ADMINISTRATIVE COURT (CONSEIL D'ETAT)

FIGURE 2–1   Major features of the constitution of the Fifth Republic.

the authorization to ratify a treaty, that without being contrary to the Constitution would affect the functioning of existing institutions (Article 11). (emphasis added)

Constitutional provisions to the contrary notwithstanding, the president claimed in October 1962 that this article empowered him to submit any amendments to the constitution directly to the people.

The constitution also vests explicitly in the president other powers that he can exercise at his discretion. He has the nominating power for all civil and military posts, and, unless otherwise provided by an organic law (a law that relates to the implementation of basic constitutional provisions that must be passed by absolute majority in both legislative houses), he signs all decrees and ordinances prepared by the Council of Ministers. He can raise questions of unconstitutionality on a bill or on a law before a special constitutional court—the Constitutional Council.

In terms of the *letter* of the Constitution the president, it should be noted, cannot veto a bill passed by the legislature. He has to sign it. He can only ask for what may be called a second deliberation that postpones enactment by 15 days—after which he has to sign. Again in terms of the *strict letter* of the constitution he cannot dismiss his prime minister—the latter simply resigns if he no longer has the president's confidence or for any other reason. Is the president obliged to sign executive orders *(ordonnances)* for the implementation of legislation passed by the national Assembly even when the assembly empowers the prime minister to issue them? The matter came up very forcefully in the years between 1986 and 1988 when the legislative majority was in the hands of the center-right parties with a Gaullist prime minister facing a Socialist president. Important issues such as denationalizations and electoral reform were enacted, empowering the prime minister and the cabinet to issue executive orders *(ordonnances)* to implement them. The president refused to sign them, and the prime minister was forced to go before the National Assembly to enact them in

the form of legislation. The National Assembly did, and the president had no alternative then but to sign the legislation enacted.

The president presides over the meetings of the council of ministers, receives ambassadors, and sends messages to Parliament. He negotiates and "ratifies" treaties and is kept informed of all negotiations leading to the conclusion of international agreements. He is commander-in-chief of the armed services and presides over the committee of national defense. He is the only person to decide on the use of nuclear weapons.

The President as Mediator (*Arbitre*)

The constitution explicitly charges the president with guaranteeing the functioning of the institutions of the government:

The President of the Republic shall see that the Constitution is respected. He shall ensure, by his arbitration, the regular functioning of the governmental authorities, as well as the continuance of the State.

He shall be the guarantor of national independence, of the integrity of the territory, and of respect for . . . treaties (Article 5).

Mediation is a personal act involving the exercise of judgment. As a mediator the president enjoys an *implicit* veto on almost every conceivable aspect of policy: in matters of war, foreign policy, the preservation of internal order, the functioning of governmental institutions, and the appointment of ministers. He is deeply involved in politics.

The President as "Guide"— As A Political Leader

DeGaulle, as president of the Republic between 1958 and 1969, gradually vested the presidency with broad leadership functions and his interpretation of his role was followed by his successors—Georges Pompidou (1969–74), Giscard d'Estaing (1974–78), and François Mitterrand (1981–). He claimed that "the President elected by the nation is the source and holder of the power of the state," the only person to "hold and to delegate the authority of the state." This ultimately meant that the office of the presidency became the seat of political power in France. The president concentrates in his hands the powers of the state. The office is the center of policymaking, not only in foreign affairs but also in domestic issues. Specialized presidential bureaus and offices virtually "duplicate" the ministries. They thrash out policy alternatives, and the minister—or even the prime minister—may be totally unaware of what is happening at the Elysée, the French White House. The prime minister and cabinet, who are responsible to Parliament and are technically in charge of determining and directing the policy of the nation, play a secondary role. De Gaulle's successors, Georges Pompidou and Valéry Giscard d'Estaing, maintained and in some instances even expanded presidential leadership and the broad interpretation of presidential powers. The Gaullist heritage was strengthened, and the Socialist president elected in May 1981 continued it.

The major elements of the theory and practice of presidential government in France are thus the following:

1. The president claims to incarnate the national sovereignty by virtue of his direct election by the whole nation. The president is responsible not only for broad policy guidelines but often for their execution.

2. The prime minister owes his authority and his position to the president and derives his powers not from the constitution or the confidence of the National Assembly, but from the president. He is the president's man. (In May 1972 Prime Minister Chaban-Delmas received an overwhelming vote of confidence in the National Assembly, only to be asked to resign from office within a few weeks by the president. The same happened to Prime Minister Michel Debrè (1962), to Prime Minister Georges Pompidou (1968), and also to the Socialist prime minister, Pierre Mauroy in 1984.

The presidents of the Fifth Republic have claimed to be above parties and to represent the national interest as mediators. In practice, however, they have not only identified with a party or a coalition of parties that provide a majority to the prime minister and the cabinet they designate, but have promoted the formation of such a "presidential" majority. At election time some, like de Gaulle, urged the voters to vote for the deputies who would support the president's policies. President Giscard d'Estaing, in a speech made prior to the legislative election of March 1978, made clear what the "good choice" for the French voters should be. It was a choice for the political parties that supported him and that he had worked hard to put together in a new coalition. As soon as he was elected president in 1981, Mitterrand dissolved the National Assembly and asked the electorate to give him a presidential majority to support him. They did—with the Socialist party gaining an absolute majority in the National Assembly.

The role of president has become that of a political leader. He is elected directly by the people, and he can test his policies and his leadership through a referendum, as de Gaulle did. However, it is difficult for the President to govern for long through a prime minister and a cabinet unless they agree with him and his policies. To have such a prime minister and cabinet, he must see that they are supported by a majority in the National Assembly. Such a majority has to be, therefore, a presidential majority. Inevitably, the president becomes a partisan political figure—urging, cajoling, influencing, at times compromising, and even playing "dirty politics"—in asserting his powers and popularity upon the National Assembly. If everything fails, he has the power of dissolution and the calling of new legislative elections—a threat that can be counted upon to produce discipline within the presidential majority in the National Assembly.

On the other hand, we must also understand clearly what the limits of presidential leadership are. If the president does not have a majority to support his prime minister and cabinet in the National Assembly, he will have to work with a prime minister and cabinet that may be opposed to his policies or be forced to dissolve or even to resign.

The political dominance of the presidency and the president suffered two blows recently. In the 1986 legislative election the Socialists and their allies were defeated, depriving President Mitterrand of majority support in the National Assembly. The legislative majority came into the hands of the center-right parties, forcing the president to designate their leader—Jacques Chirac—as prime minister. A period of "cohabitation" followed—with the president and the prime minister (supported by a majority in the National Assembly) representing rival party blocs. The second blow—even more severe—was what amounted to the president's defeat in the legislative elections of June 5–12, 1988. President Miterrand won an impressive victory and a reelection as president of the Republic in May 8, 1988. He then did what he had done in 1981—he dissolved the National Assembly and called for a presidential—that is, socialist—majority in the National Assembly. This time he came up short by a handful of deputies.

THE CABINET

In the language of the constitution, the cabinet, composed of the prime minister and his ministers, "determines and conducts the policy of the nation" and is "responsible before the Parliament." Special recognition is accorded the prime minister. He "directs" the action of the government and is "responsible" for national defense. He "assures the execution of the laws and exercises the rule-making power"—but on condition that all decrees and ordinances are signed by the president of the republic. He determines the composition of his cabinet, presides over its meetings, and directs the administrative services. He defends his policy before Parliament, answers questions addressed to him by members of Parliament, states the overall program of the government in special decla-

rations, and puts the question of confidence before the National Assembly. Thus, the 1958 constitution established a parliamentary government along with a strong presidency.

The functions of the cabinet were narrowly interpreted by de Gaulle. To begin with, it need not be composed of members of Parliament who simply resign their electoral mandate, as the constitution requires, to assume a cabinet post. Many cabinet members have come from the ranks of civil servants, technicians, professors, or intellectuals who had never been in Parliament. Significant areas were entrusted to technicians presumably able to implement the policies of the president. They became increasingly dependent upon the president, to whom they owed their position and by whom they could be removed.

During de Gaulle's nine-year presidency there were only three prime ministers. Under President Pompidou, cabinet stability was equally high: two prime ministers in just five years. Under Giscard d'Estaing's presidency (1974–81) there were two prime ministers in seven years. (see Table 2–1), and under Mitterrand's first presidency (1981–88), three. There was almost the same stability in some of the major ministries, but relative instability in the ministries of Education, Housing and Equipment, and Social Affairs. There were frequent reshufflings of the cabinet. Often the same individuals remained in the cabinet but changed posts. A hard core kept the key posts—Foreign Affairs, Defense, Interior, Finance, Justice. The leadership remained stable; changes were made in the periphery.

With the exception of some specific provisions, nothing in the constitution clearly demarcates cabinet functions and presidential functions. But one basic principle seems to have evolved from practice. If the president of the republic is interested in a given policy matter, he has the first and last word. If not, the prime minister and the cabinet have the freedom to make policy. Until now the trend has favored presidential initiative and lead-

TABLE 2-1   Governmental Stability, 1958–1988

Presidents	Prime Minister
De Gaulle December 1958– December 1965 December 1965– April 1969	Michel Debré January 1959–April 1962 Georges Pompidou April 1962–July 1968 Couve de Murville July 1968–June 1969
Pompidou June 1969–April 1974	Jacques Chaban-Delmas June 1969–July 1972 Pierre Messmer July 1972–August 1978
Giscard d'Estaing May 1974–May 1981	Jacques Chirac May 1974–August 1976 Raymond Barre August 1976–May 1981
François Mitterrand May 1981–May 1988	Pierre Mauroy May 1981–March 1984 Laurent Fabius July 1984–March 1986 Jacques Chirac March 1986–May 1988
May 1988–	Michel Rocard May 1988–

ership, but recent developments and electoral trends make it possible to envisage the president allowing more and more freedom of action and policymaking to a prime minister.

This is particularly the case when there is no clear presidential majority in the National Assembly. The president will have to accommodate his stance, to become adept in bringing about political agreements and coalitions, in seeking support from political groups other than the Socialist party, and in finding the means for rewarding friends and punishing enemies. He will have to do what the American president has been doing ever since the inception of the office and will have to develop the skills for doing it. In so doing, the Gaullist notion of the presidency as incarnating the majesty of the state above parties and factions will gradually yield to that of a skilled politician adept in compromise and susceptible to pressures and counterpressures that need accommodation. He will have, of course, powers that elude the

American president—that of dissolving the National Assembly and calling for an election, if and when compromise fails, and that of calling for a referendum on vital matters of state.

THE LEGISLATURE

The Parliament of the Fifth Republic is, as in the previous republics, bicameral. It consists of a National Assembly and a Senate—the lower and upper chambers, respectively. The National Assembly, elected for five years by universal suffrage, numbered 491 deputies in 1981. The number has been raised to 577 for the National Assembly elected March 16, 1986. The Senate, elected for nine years, consists today of 317 members. The Senate is elected indirectly by the municipal councilors, the department councilors, and the members of the National Assembly. One third of its membership is renewed every three years.

The two chambers have equal powers, except in three vitally important respects. First, the traditional prerogative of the lower chamber to first examine the budget is maintained. Second, the cabinet is responsible only to the National Assembly. The latter also has the last word on legislation. Article 45 of the constitution specifies that every bill "is examined successively in the two assemblies with a view to the adoption of an identical text." But if there is disagreement on the text of a bill, the prime minister *may* ask the National Assembly to rule "definitively." Many bills have been enacted into law over the head of the senate.

A Rationalized Parliament

The new constitution establishes a "rationalized" parliament, one whose powers are limited in the following ways:

1. Only two sessions of the two assemblies are allowed. The first begins in October and lasts for 80 days; the second begins in April and

cannot last more than 90 days—a maximum of 5 months and 20 days. Extraordinary sessions may take place at the request of the president or a majority of the members of the National Assembly "on a specific agenda." They are convened and closed by a decree of the president of the republic.

2. The Parliament can legislate only on matters defined in the constitution. The government (i.e., the prime minister and the cabinet) can legislate on all other matters by executive orders.

3. The government fixes the order of business of the legislature.

4. The president of the National Assembly is elected for the whole legislative term, an arrangement that avoids the annual elections that in the past placed him at the mercy of the various parliamentary groups. The Senate elects its president every three years.

5. The Parliament is no longer free to establish its own standing orders. Such orders must be found to be in accord with the constitution by the Constitutional Council before they become effective.

6. The number of parliamentary committees is reduced (only six are allowed), and their functions are carefully circumscribed.

7. The government bill, not the committees' amendments and counterproposals (as under the Fourth Republic), comes before the floor—unless the government accepts the amendment in advance.

8. The government has the right to reject all amendments and to demand a single vote on its own text containing only those amendments that it accepts—a procedure known as the "blocked" vote.

All these provisions are directed against "assembly government." By putting procedural rules into the constitution, the framers hoped to limit Parliament to the performance of its proper function of deliberation and to protect the executive from legislative encroachments. Many of the new rules reflect a genuine desire to correct some of the more flagrant abuses of the past and consistent with the strengthening of the executive in modern democracies. Others, however, are designed to weaken Parliament.

Relations Between Parliament and the Government

Four major provisions in the Constitution determine the nature of the relations between Parliament and the government. They concern (1) the incompatibility between a parliamentary mandate and a cabinet post, (2) the manner in which the responsibility of the cabinet before the Parliament comes into play, (3) the distinction between "legislation" and "rulemaking," and (4) the introduction of the "executive budget."

The Rule of Incompatibility. Article 23 of the Constitution is explicit: "The 'office' of a member of government is incompatible with the exercise of any parliamentary mandate." Thus, a member of Parliament who joins the cabinet must resign his seat for the balance of the legislative term. He is replaced in Parliament by his substitute *(suppléant)*—the person whose name appeared together with his on the electoral ballot. Despite the rule of incompatibility, however, cabinet members are allowed to sit in Parliament and defend their measures. They are not, of course, allowed to vote. If the cabinet "falls," or ministers resign, they find themselves without a parliamentary seat. However, their "substitute" may resign and force an election in the same electoral district, in which case the minister may run for reelection!

Responsibility of the Cabinet to the Legislature. The responsibility of the cabinet to the legislature comes into play in a specific and limited manner. After the prime minister has been nominated by the president of the republic, he presents his program before the National Assembly and asks it to express its confidence. If this program is accepted by the National Assembly, the cabinet is "invested"[3]; if defeated—and it can be defeated by

---

[3]However, there have been prime ministers who did not appear before the National Assembly to seek approval of their program, an indication that the prime minister and his cabinet ultimately derive their authority from presidential appointment.

a simple majority—the prime minister must submit his resignation to the president.

The National Assembly (but not the Senate) can bring down the prime minister and the cabinet. It has the right to introduce a motion of censure, which must be signed by one-tenth of its members, that is, 58 members. The motion is lost unless it is supported by an absolute majority of the members. In other words, blank ballots and abstentions count for the government. If the motion is carried by the requisite absolute majority (289 votes), the government must resign; if the motion is lost, then its signers cannot introduce another one in the same session.

The prime minister may also, after consultation with the cabinet, stake the life of his government on any general issue of policy or any legislative bill. This is equivalent to putting the "question of confidence." A specific bill on which the prime minister puts the question of confidence becomes law unless a motion of censure is introduced and voted according to the same conditions. If the motion is carried by an absolute majority, the bill does not become law and the government must resign. If the motion of censure is lost, the bill automatically becomes law and the government stays in office. In this manner bills *can* become laws unless there is an absolute majority against them and against the prime minister and his government.

Until 1988 this practice was used 36 times by the prime ministers—both Gaullists and Socialists. Twenty major bills were enacted in this manner. In 28 cases the National Assembly introduced a motion of censure, and it failed it every case. In fact, no motion of censure has been successful except once—in 1962!

Law and Rule Making. The constitution provides that "law is voted by Parliament." Members of Parliament and of the government can introduce bills and amendments. The scope of Parliament's lawmaking ability, however, is limited. It is defined in the Constitution (Article 34) to include regulations concerning civil rights and personal freedoms, crimes, taxation and currency, the electoral system, and nationalization of enterprises, as well as those dealing with national defense, local administration, education, property rights, civil and commercial obligations, and employment, unions, and social security. Everything else can be legislated by executive order.

The Budget. The Constitution establishes the "executive budget." This budget is submitted by the government to Parliament. Proposals stemming from members of Parliament "are not receivable if their adoption entails either a diminution of public resources or an increase in public expenditures" (Article 47). No bill entailing diminution of resources or additional expenditures is receivable at any time. If Parliament has not decided within seventy days after the introduction of the budget, then "the budget bill can be promulgated and put into effect by simple ordinance" (Article 47). Thus, the government may be able to bypass Parliament.

The Legislative Committees

Under the Fourth Republic, the legislative committees resembled those of the American Congress—they were numerous and powerful. They could decide the fate of virtually any bill by amending it, pigeonholing it, or failing to report it. Only the amended text of a bill could come from the committee to the floor of the legislative assembly. This situation has been drastically altered. Only six committees are allowed: foreign affairs; finance; national defense; constitutional laws, legislation, and general administration; production and trade; and cultural, social, and family affairs. Their composition ranges from 60 to 120 members, nominated to represent proportionately the political parties. They receive the bills, examine them, and are free to introduce amendments. But the government has the last word on bringing the bills before the floor and on accepting or rejecting amendments. Thus, the legislative process has been speeded up and improved. The government is no longer at the mercy of committees that were often inspired by parochial interests and, even more frequently, by political considerations.

The Senate

The Senate was conceived as the chamber whose detachment and wisdom would provide a balance against the National Assembly. Though deprived of the right to overthrow the cabinet, the Senate—whether displaying wisdom or not—turned out to be the most stubborn, if ineffective, opponent of the Gaullist majority in the years between 1958 and 1974. On numerous occasions involving major bills, the Senate refused to go along with the National Assembly. The conference committees between the National Assembly and the Senate failed to reach agreement, and the bills had to be voted two consecutive times by the National Assembly before they became law.

The Senate remains centrist—away from Gaullism or Socialism. The small towns and villages continue to play a dominant role in the election of senators. A strong centrist block has provided as much opposition to the Socialist majority in the National Assembly between 1981 and 1986 as it did to the Gaullists.

OTHER CONSTITUTIONAL ORGANS AND PROCEDURES

The 1958 constitution reestablished an Economic and Social Council. Representing the most important professional interests in France, this body has consultative and advisory powers regarding proposed economic and social legislation, particularly on measures related to economic planning.

As under the Fourth Republic, a High Court of Justice, whose members are elected by the National Assembly and the Senate, may try the president of the republic for high treason and the members of the government for criminal offenses committed in the exercise of their functions. A High Council of the Judiciary, presided over by the president of the republic, nominates judges to the higher judicial posts, is consulted about pardons by the president, and rules on disciplinary matters involving the judiciary. The same section of the constitution (Article 66) provides what amounts to be a writ of habeas corpus clause: "No one may be arbitrarily detained. The judicial authority, guardian of individual liberty, assures the respect of this principle under conditions provided by law."

The Constitutional Council

A striking innovation in the 1958 constitution was the Constitutional Council, composed of nine members who serve for a period of nine years. Three are nominated by the president of the republic, three by the president of the National Assembly, and three by the president of the Senate. They are renewed by a third every three years. In addition, all former presidents of the republic are members ex officio. A variety of powers was given to the Constitutional Council. It supervises presidential elections and referendums and proclaims the results; it judges the validity of all contested legislative elections, thereby avoiding long, bitter controversies in the legislative assemblies. It is the ultimate court of appeal on the interpretation of the constitution on a specified number of matters. All bills, including treaties, may be referred to it, before their promulgation, by the president of the republic, the prime minister, or one of the presidents of the two assemblies. The council's declaration of unconstitutionality suspends the promulgation of the bill or the application of the treaty. The council determines the constitutionality of the standing orders of the National Assembly and the Senate. It is the guardian of legislative-executive relations; it decides on all claims as to whether proposed legislation violates the constitution.

In 1974 an amendment to the Constitution allowed any 60 deputies or any 60 senators the same right of appeal reserved for the president of the Republic and the prime minister, the president of the National Assembly and the president of the Senate. This has accounted for a remarkable expansion of the number of cases brought before the council. Between 1958 and 1974, for instance, only some eight appeals on the constitutionality of legislative bills reached the council. Between 1974 and 1988 there have been 170—the rate growing from about 1 appeal per year to 13. In the course of this period of time, some 60 decisions invalidated pending legislation.

With the remarkable growth of the number of appeals came a broadening of the interpretation of "constitutionality" given by the council. At first it was limited to the strict letter of the 1958 Constitution. In two decisions, however, in 1970 and 1971 the council extended its jurisdiction to include the protection of the principles set forth in the Preamble of the Constitution—the Declaration of the Rights of Man of 1789—and the preamble to the Constitution of 1946 that includes basic social and economic rights and, finally, the "basic principles of the Republican tradition." A new body of law—the French call it "the body of constitutional principles" *(bloc de constitutionalité)*—has been acknowledged. It stands above legislation and must be protected against legislative encroachment. It comprises the Constitution itself, the preamble to the constitution, the basic republican constitutional proclamations of 1789 and 1946, as well as the basic principles of a republican (i.e., democratic) regime. The council feels free, therefore, upon appeal, to examine any ordinary legislative bill in terms of its conformity to these cardinal documents and principles.

The enlargement of the initiation of appeals (from the four high officers of the Republic to any 60 deputies and any 60 senators) coupled with the broadening of the interpretation of "the Constitution" have made, according to some, the Constitutional Council a "super-parliament"—able to intervene and prohibit the promulgation of a law that it finds incompatible with the Constitution. In fact, the Constitutional Council has invalidated pending legislation that infringed upon freedom of association, freedom of the press, and freedom from searches and seizures. It has given protection to foreigners and immigrants from administrative expulsion, prevented deprivation of property without adequate compensation, and favored equality of voting so that electoral districts would roughly correspond to the same population size. It has become the ultimate referee of the rights of the citizens—very often pushing its jurisdiction to protect individual claims and rights to matters of health care, employment, and housing. Many begin to compare the Constitutional Council with the U.S. Supreme Court as the ultimate arbiter in setting limitations upon the state. Many see in it a counterweight to the enormous powers the presidency acquired.

Amending the Constitution

Two ways to amend the Constitution are provided. An amendment proposed by the two legislative assemblies by simple majorities becomes effective only after it is approved in a referendum. A proposal stemming from the president of the republic and approved by the two chambers by simple majorities may go, at the president's discretion, either before the two chambers meeting jointly in a congress (in which case a three-fifths majority is required), or to the people in a referendum. In short, amendments that emanate from the government may go before either the joint congress or the people, whereas a proposal stemming from Parliament must always be submitted to the people in a referendum. In 1962 President de Gaulle invoked Article 11 to bypass Parliament and call directly a referendum to amend the Constitution.

A Note on Referendums

In addition to legislative and presidential elections—of which there were nine for the National Assembly and five for the presidency from 1958 to 1988—the Constitution provides for referendums, in which voters are asked to approve or disapprove major political reforms, including the text of the present Constitution on September 28, 1958 (see Table 2–2). There have been seven referendums in all—five under de Gaulle and one called by his successor Pompidou in 1972; the latest, on the status of New Caledonia, was held on November 6, 1988.

All referendums held under de Gaulle not only involved issues but engaged the personal responsibility of the president. De Gaulle made this responsibility explicit in every case, promising to resign if his measure was not endorsed. He thereby transformed a referendum into a plebiscite—a vote for or against the leader rather than for or against a policy measure. When his suggested constitutional reforms for decentralization and the modification of the composition and powers of the Senate failed to receive approval in the referendum of April 27, 1969, de Gaulle resigned.

The last two referendums, however, did not engage the responsibility of the president. The electorate was asked in April 1972 to approve Great Britain's entry into the Common Market, an approval that was taken for granted. Despite numerous abstentions, the treaty was approved by 67 percent of those voting. For Caledonia about 75 percent voted in favor of the continuation of the status quo—with the pledge to give the New Caledonians an option to vote for independence in 1998.

THE CHANGING ADMINISTRATIVE SYSTEM[4]

The administrative model that applied roughly until 1960 was centralizing and hierarchical. All powers stemmed from the center and were exercised by the government in Paris through its agents—the *préfets* and the mayors. They both represented the state—the Republic. In addition, the central government supervised all the officials of each territorial unit—departments or municipalities—for which representative assemblies were elected: the "general councils" for the department and the "municipal councils" for the municipality. The *préfet* in each department had disciplinary, initiating, and suspensive powers over the mayors and the municipal councils: he could revoke or sus-

[4]I wish to thank my colleague Professor Yves-Mény of the Institut d'Etudes Politique of the University of Paris for help on this section.

TABLE 2–2   Three Crucial Referendums under de Gaulle

	*Sept. 28, 1958**	*Oct. 28, 1962[†]*	*April 27, 1969[‡]*
Registered voters	26,603,446	27,582,113	28,656,494
Abstaining	4,006,614	6,280,297	5,565,475
	(15.06%)	(22.76%)	(19.42%)
Voting	22,596,850	21,301,816	23,091,019
	(84.93%)	(77.23%)	(80.57%)
Blank and void	303,549	559,758	632,131
	(1.14%)	(2.02%)	(2.20%)
Valid ballots	22,293,301	20,742,058	22,458,888
Yes	17,668,790	12,809,363	10,515,655
No	4,624,511	7,932,695	11,943,233
Percentage			
Yes	79.25%	61.75%	46.82%
No	20.74	38.24	53.17

*Referendum on the constitution of the Fifth Republic.

[†]Referendum on direct popular election of the president.

[‡]Referendum on regionalization and the reform of the Senate; its defeat led to de Gaulle's resignation.

pend them from office; most of their decisions and their budgets had to receive the *préfet's prior* approval. In each department the *préfet* was the major organ for the initiation and execution of policy, and the elected representatives (the general council) were more often than not relegated to the role of consultative assemblies.

From the monarchy through the Revolution, the two Napoleonic regimes, the four republics down to de Gaulle, and the present republic, France remained "one and indivisible." What is decided in Paris applies to all—in every department and hamlet of France and also in many of its overseas departments and territories.

Beginning with 1960, a movement in the direction of decentralization developed for a number of reasons. The central government became overloaded in at least two ways: too many decisions were thrust upon the central authority; very often it was unable to evaluate local circumstances and decide wisely. Particular conflicts could not be resolved on the spot. They were referred to the *préfet* who frequently had to refer them to the higher authorities at the ministry of the interior. The central government found itself, as a result, constantly embroiled in particular conflicts—pollution in harbors, pesticides affecting the grazing fields, conflicts about location of buildings and schools, and on, and on. It became overburdened. Even more important, French citizens found themselves separated from what touched them most—their immediate conditions of life, work, and leisure: their taxes vanished into the central administration, often without any tangible return in the form of local expenditures. Last, and obviously of critical importance, was the freedom or not of territorial units—departments and municipalities—to raise money on their own needs and interests. It had been virtually denied to them. Departmental and municipal units had scant resources and were unable to meet the growing needs of the urban population.

All these factors played a role in gradually shifting the Napoleonic administrative edifice into what has become something that looks like a gothic temple. The symmetry and the hierarchy are gone; the clear distinction of functions and roles have become blurred. A new edifice is being built. France is moving from centralization to decentralization by giving its local territorial units—the departments and the municipalities—greater autonomy and by creating new ones—the regions—that parallel them and may supersede them. It is a powerful and irreversible trend, but it will be some time before it gains roots to become a part of the political and administrative organization of the state. Some 25 major laws were enacted in the years between 1981 and 1987, and they were complemented by some 220 executive orders. It is a body of legislation that will take some time to gain roots and become operative.

The key features of decentralization are the following:

1. The *préfet* becomes now the *commissaire de la République*. Most of his powers are transferred to an elected representative—the president of the departmental councils. The *préfet* also loses his supervisory and disciplinary powers vis-à-vis the municipalities and the mayors. He can no longer suspend decisions made ·by them; his approval is no longer needed for the preparation of the municipal budget; expenditures authorized by the departmental council do not require his *prior* approval.

2. A greater degree of financial freedom is given to departments and municipalities to raise taxes and to spend. But, in addition, large subsidies (bloc grants) from the central government are provided. About half the income of local units comes from their own resources, but another half comes from state contributions and subsidies. Departments and municipalities spend about 350 billion francs (about $60–70 billion); they are also allowed to float their loans. The trend has been continuing as the central government continues to transfer resources in the form of "bloc grants" to the departments so that they can provide an ever-growing number of services—total transfers of about 160 billion francs are envisaged for 1989 (about $30 billion). What is more, the departments are free to spend as they choose.

3. There has been a trend to assimilate departmental and municipal civil services into the national civil service. A new "territorial civil service" has been established. Public civil servants who had been "borrowed" in the past by departments or municipalities will have a choice to stay permanently in local service. Over 1 million departmental and local employees are affected in this manner, and the change is likely to provide to local services the prestige, security, and benefits they lacked.

It is in terms of these trends that one can appreciate the importance of decentralization. The most pervasive figure of the French state for almost 200 years—the *préfet*—symbol of state authority and central direction is fading away. He still represents the state. He is in charge of public order. But his disciplinary powers are gone, and he can no longer intervene to block decisions of municipal and departmental councils before they are made. He is being superseded by the elected presidents of the departmental councils.

The Regions

For a long time, and irrespective of their internal organization, the departments had become too small a unit for purposes of economic planning and implementation. Regional units were created (22 in all) to implement overall programs of regional development and to participate in the planning (and execution) of public works and economic planning and development. (See Figure 2–2). But as with the department, the new regions were headed by a regional préfet—embodying central direction.

It was in 1982 that the region attained genuine territorial autonomy and independence while its overall functions were put in the hands of elected representatives—the regional councils, with the regional *préfet* disappearing. In 1986 the first elections for regional councils (and the subsequent election of their presidents) took place and the regions gained full political autonomy.

Each region includes a number of departments, but remains distinct from them.

Their functions related, as at the time of their inception, to economic matters: primarily economic development and professional training and formation. The region's elected representatives participate in the deliberation and preparation of the economic plan that sets the guidelines of investment, construction, and economic development. The region receives directly subsidies from the state for this purpose and reallocates them in turn to the departments. In addition, the regional authorities have been authorized to plan and finance the building of the advanced schools and to develop special centers of technical training and retraining. Their overall budget amounts to about 18 billion francs (about $3 billion), far below that of the departments and the municipalities put together, but their resources have been growing and are mainly devoted to public investments. The time may come when they may begin to assume more and more functions, other than economic and professional ones, and gradually become the major territorial units that will replace the 96 departments that stud metropolitan France.

THE CIVIL SERVICE

In Paris a permanent civil service is at the disposal of the cabinet. The basic unit, as in Britain, is the ministry, which is responsible for the execution, enforcement, and at times policy formulation of matters under its immediate jurisdiction. The ministries, again as in Britain, are divided into bureaus. French civil servants, like their British counterparts, form a permanent body of administrators, the top members of which are in close contact with the ministers and therefore with policy making. As with the British Treasury, the Ministry of Finance plays a predominant role, preparing the budget, formulating the estimates, collecting taxes, and to a lesser degree controlling expenditures.

Who are the French civil servants? If we include manual workers and teachers of

FRANCE
Regions—Departments—Overseas Departments

FIGURE 2-2   FRANCE Regions—Departments—Overseas Departments*

*Twenty-two regions, 96 metropolitan departments, and 4 "overseas" depart-
ments (Departments d'Outre-Mer): Guadeloupe, Martinique, Guyana, Reunion.
In addition, there are 3 overseas territories"— New Caledonia, French Polynesia,
and Wallis-and-Fortuna—and 2 units with special status: Mayotte and St. Pierre-
et-Miquelon.

grade schools and high schools, they number over 1 million persons. But if we add career military personnel and those working in the nationalized industries—railroads, gas, electricity, and other economic activities controlled by the state—the total is 3 million, or 15 percent of the work force.

Most French civil servants are engaged in subordinate tasks. Only a fraction participate in the formulation and execution of policy. This top echelon is selected on the basis of competitive examinations, as in Great Britain. the majority of its members come from certain schools known as the *grandes écoles:* the law schools, the École National d'Administration, the École Polytechnique, and a few others. Most come from the upper-middle and middle classes. Many come from families in which the father is a high-level civil servant—which indicates a high degree of cooptation. These privileged individuals are the only civil servants who have the educational background to pass the stiff written exams. As for the oral examination administered by the civil service, manners, speech, and social background continue to play important roles. It is these people who occupy the central positions in the central ministries (Interior, Foreign Affairs, and Finance) and perform the crucial functions in the other agencies. They are about 7,500 strong, and they make policy side by side with elected officials.

Since the beginning of the Fifth Republic the role of the civil service has grown, for the general trend has been to put the civil servant in the policymaking group. As we have noted, the staffs of Fifth Republic presidents have been composed of civil servants detached from their ministerial or other duties. Likewise, cabinet members have come from the ranks of experts and civil servants. In the national services and at the top of the Economic Planning Commission civil servants initiate, implement, deliberate, and often decide. It is frequently claimed that the present system is a technocracy—a government by the expert and the technician (in other words, the civil servant). But as these technocrats gain influence, the character

and role of the civil service is changing. The civil servants are no longer the "mandarins" of the past—guardians of tradition, neutral, impersonal, remote, and legal-minded. They have undertaken a "dialogue" with interest groups, regional groups, and the professions, not only about the performance of their general functions but also about economic planning and regional development. Business, production, industrial development, banking,and investment have become their preoccupations.

This development has at least three causes. First, the weakening of the Parliament, and to a great extent the parliamentary committees and subcommittees, has shifted the thrust of the interest groups. Now their attention is directed almost primarily to the civil servant, who on behalf of his minister and a cohesive cabinet has the ultimate word. The confrontation between a representative of an interest group and a civil servant often results in an agreement, a compromise, or a bargain. Second, as the state services begin to resemble those of a private firm or private industry, civil servants find themselves increasingly at home with the company director, business executive, and banker. Their concerns are common, and very very often their training is not different and their social status not dissimilar. Third, the dialogue has become increasingly institutionalized: thousands of advisory committees now bring together interest and professional groups and civil servants in a deliberative process.

Under the Fifth Republic the civil service—the bureaucracy—has gained power, prestige, and weight. The number of civil servants has doubled, and their role in the economy, as we have seen, has grown so much that in their dialogue with the private sector and its professional and interest organizations the top civil servants have the first and often the last word. Few among the businessmen and the industrialists can challenge them or alter their decisions.

But the civil service has also become, despite its alleged neutrality, increasingly politicized in at least two ways. First, some civil servants become assistants to a minister (in a so-called minister's cabinet) and help him formulate policy. While in ministerial service they retain their civil service status and position, to which they may eventually return. Some never do so, for the attraction of elective office becomes powerful. Even while in civil service they are allowed by law to run for elective office—as mayors, senators, or members of the National Assembly. Many succeed. In the legislatures of 1973–78 and 1978–81 over 25 percent of *all* deputies were civil servants. In the National Assembly elected in 1981, 23 percent of the elected deputies were civil servants. Another 33 percent consisted of teachers and professors—technically civil servants too. In the legislation of 1988, some 200 members out of 577 are "teachers" and another 75 came from the ranks of the civil service. the bureaucrats, in other words, have penetrated the National Assembly.

3

The Political Parties

INTRODUCTION

We give in this chapter an overview of the political parties. We shall situate them on the left-right continuum. The student should refer to Table 3-1. Note that virtually all the political parties we list are relatively "young"—having emerged or having replaced older formations in the last 15 years. Only the Communist party dates back to 1920—it is the oldest party of France today, except, some would say, for the Radical Socialist party that was founded in 1901. But today's "Radicals" are a far cry in spirit and strength from the old Radical Socialist party. As for the Socialists, they also date back to even before the Communists—to 1905, but the Socialist party founded in 1971-72 is a phoenix that was born from the ashes of the old Socialist party—the S.F.I.O., as the Socialists were called then (French Section of the Workers International).

THE LEFT AND THE RIGHT

Few terms in the political vocabulary of our times are as ambiguous as *left* and *right*—to which, of course, the term *center* is always added to denote those belonging to neither or sharing attitudes and beliefs common to both.

To simplify a great deal, since the beginning of the Third Republic in 1871 the left in France has been associated with three major ideologies and parties—radicalism (the Radical Socialist party), socialism (the SFIO-French Section of the Second International until 1970 and the "new" Socialist party after 1971), and communism (the Communist party after 1920). Small "left-wing" groupings have appeared and disappeared over the years.

What are the major ideological aspirations of the left? They are to place severe limitations on private property, and—with

TABLE 3-1   Party Configuration in 1988*

Extreme Left	Left	Center	Right	Extreme Right
LO: Lutte Ouvrière (1968)	PCF: Parti Communiste Français (1920)	UDF: Union pour la Democratie Française (1978):	RPR: Rassemblement Pour la Republique (1976: continuation of the Gaullists)	FN: Front National (1972)
Ligue Communiste Revolutionnaire (1969)	PC: "Renovateurs" (Communist party dissidents) (1988)	Umbrella party consisting of:	NI: Conseil National des Independents (1958)	PFN: Parti des Forces Nouvelles (1974)
Parti Socialiste Unifié (PSU) (1960)	Pour une nouvelle Politique de Gauche (Communist Dissidents) (1988)	PR: Parti Republicain (1974)	POE: Parti Ouvrier Européen (1979)	RN: Restauration Nationale— Royalists (1947)
MPPT: Mouvement pour un Parti pour les Travailleurs (1986)	PS: Parti Socialist (1971)	PSD: Parti Social Democratie		NAR: Nouvelle Action Royalists (1971)
	MRG: Movement Republicain de Gauche (1972, affiliated with PS)	URC: Union du Rassemblement et du Centre (1988)		
		Radicals (1901, 1954, 1969)		
		Ecologists "Les Verts" (1974)		

*Dates in parentheses indicate year of formation.

many qualifications and differences—to nationalize extensively industrial activity. They propose to limit income differentials to a ratio of about 1 to 5 or 1 to 7. They propose—again, with serious differences between socialists and communists—to decentralize the state apparatus and provide local and regional autonomy. They advocate industrial democracy *(autogestion)*—giving decision-making power in the running of industries (nationalized or not) to those who work in them and those who consume their products. They are imbued with a sense of social justice and equality: society through its political organs is responsible for providing genuine equality of opportunity and also as much equality as possible in the conditions of life for all. The socialists believe in individual and political freedom (the communists pay lip service). Both are nationalist, and today both claim to follow an independent foreign policy and defense destined to preserve a strong France. But the communists continue to look to the Soviet Union while the socialists (like the Gaullists) search for a middle road that will detach France

from U.S. control without allowing Soviet domination in one form or another.

The right has traditionally consisted of a number of political groupings, which in the Fifth Republic coalesced into two major political parties and some satellite fractions. The two major groups are the Gaullists and the center-right formations (including some of the radicals)—the UDF.

What do they believe in? In contrast with the overall political stance shared by the left, the political position of the right is not at all clear. Often it overlaps with positions espoused by the left. The right believe in private property, yet curiously major structural reforms of the economy, including some key nationalizations, were undertaken by General de Gaulle. The right is supposed to be conservative in economic and social matters, yet the economic expansion and modernization in France between 1960 and 1975 occurred under the Gaullist constitution and "right-wing" leadership. The right is closely associated with the Catholic church, but the number of practicing Catholics is not more than 15 percent—not a sufficient electoral base. The right favors equality of opportunity but not of material conditions, yet in the last twenty years the standard of living of the workers and the material benefits offered them in the form of direct social measures and assistance have improved as never before. The right is supposed to have a philosophy that promotes state power and centralization of authority, but many significant measures of decentralization, no matter how tentative, were suggested by the right-wing leaders who have governed France between 1958 and 1981. In fact, regionalism and decentralization have been traditionally associated with the right, yet they were implemented by the left. Finally, the right remains nationalistic. National independence was the favorite slogan of de Gaulle and his followers with regard not only to foreign policy but also to any economic or defense alliance—be it the Common Market or the Atlantic Alliance. Yet right-wing leaders have been responsible for opening the French economy to worldwide competition. Where, then, is the right? What separates it from the left?

Asking the question is in a sense answering it. The differences between the left and the right are not as profound as people believe. With regard to political institutions, the economy, social legislation, and foreign policy, the areas of agreement between the two "political families" to the right and the left are more marked than the areas of disagreement. This is supported by a number of opinion polls in which more than 30 percent of the respondents could not identify with either the left-wing or the right-wing parties; their answers amounted to a left-right "mix."

Commenting on the legislative and presidential election of 1988 one of the best students of opinion trends in France reached the same conclusion—left-right divisions were a matter of degree, not of substance. Within the left there was a strong minority that supported the views of the right and vice versa. The "distance" among political parties has been growing smaller, and on many salient issues (the European Common Market, for instance) agreement overshadows disagreement.[1]

THE PARTIES OF THE LEFT

The left is represented by two major parties—the Communists and the Socialists—and a number of leftist splinters—the extreme left.

The Extreme Left

Ever since the Bolshevik Revolution (1917) there have been all over Europe and in France small revolutionary organizations to the left of the communist parties: anarchists and anarchosyndicalists, Trotskyites in the 1930s (the Fourth International), advocates of outright violence like the Maoists, the partisans of the so-called New Left in the 1960s, and many others. The parties we list as belonging to the extreme left in France are the ones that have appeared a number of times at elections. Together these political parties and groupings have not received in any election more than 4 percent. Only in the election of 1968 that followed the student uprising of May 1968 did they manage 4.8 percent of the electoral vote, and their candidate in the presidential election of 1969 (the now Prime Minister Michel Rocard) received 3.7 percent. They are viewed as vehicles for the expression of protest against the system. No matter what the electoral system, they have never won a seat in the National Assembly, and they have been incapable of grouping together into one party. Even the efforts on the part of some Communist party dissenters in 1988 have not succeeded in forming a viable political organization to the left of the communists.

---

[1]Alain Lancelot, "L'Electorat Français s'est il recentré?" *Elections Legislatives 1988,* Le Figaro-Études Politiques, 1988, Paris, pp. 41–44.

Communists and Socialists

The left comprises the Communist and Socialist parties and some formations allied with the Socialists—notably the left-wing Radicals.

The Communist Party: One of the most remarkable phenomena in the political history of France until recently was the strength of the Communist party. In every legislative election, except one, between 1945 and 1978 the party received over 20 percent of the votes. But in the presidential election of April–May 1981 the party registered a dramatic decline, receiving 15 percent of the national vote, and in the legislative election in June of that year, it received about 16 percent of the vote. Again its strength in 1986 continued to decline with less than 10 percent of the vote—returning to about 11 percent in the 1988 legislative elections. In all subsequent elections—national, local or European, its voting strength showed no gain with regard to the number of registered voters (See Table 3–2).

The membership of the party has fluctuated considerably. From 75,000 members in the early 1930s the membership rose in the years of the Popular Front (1936–38) to over 300,000. In 1946–47 its membership reached 1 million, the highest point it ever attained. In 1981 the figure given by the party was 705,000, but there is good reason to believe

TABLE 3–2 Communist Party in Legislative Elections 1958–1988*

Year	Percentage of Voters
1958	18.89%
1962	21.87
1967	22.51
1968	20.02
1973	21.41
1978	20.81
1981	16.13
1986	9.7
1988	11.32
1989 (European Election)	7.71%

*Between 1958 and 1988 the number of registered voters increased from about 27 million to 37 million.

it was well below 400,000. It has continued to decline, and today it has not more than 175,000 members.

Organization: The structure of the French Communist party continues to resemble that of the Communist party of the Soviet Union, or of all communist parties, for that matter. It is like a pyramid, the base representing the rank and file members and the apex the leaders. The image of a pyramid also conveys the principle on which the party is founded: *democratic centralism.* In other words, the superior organs of the party make the decisions after discussion among all the members. There can be no dissension, no divergent "tendencies," no "factions" within the Communist party.

The lowest echelon of the Communist party is the *cell,* which consists of from 15 to 20 members, including a secretary. Above the cells are the *sections,* consisting of the elected delegates of the cells. They too have a secretariat or else a governing committee called a *bureau.* Like the cells, they are primarily agencies of information, propaganda, and action. The *federation* is composed of delegates chosen by the sections. There is one federation for each of the 96 French departments.

The federations are ultimately responsible for the party's activities and electioneering tactics at the departmental level. The cells, sections, and federations are under the control of the national organs: the National Congress, the Central Committee, the Politbureau, and the Secretariat. The last is headed by the secretary-general, who is the leader of the party.

The *National Congress* is composed of delegates from the membership at large. It is supposed to meet once every three years, and pass on all resolutions and policy reports submitted by the party leaders. Although in theory debates are free and open, the members rarely question the proposals that come from above—that is, from the *Central Committee.* The Central Committee in turn elects 18 members to the Politbureau, which selects the *Secretariat.* This consists of 7 persons and is headed by the secretary-general. The Politbureau and the secretary-general are the true powers of the party. They decide what the party will do in Parliament and during elections—what approach it will take among the workers in the General Confederation of Labor, which is affiliated with the party.

A number of front organizations among students, intellectuals, farmers, technicians, and of course workers provide the party leadership with opportunities to influence and mobilize the public. In the General Confederation of Labor, for example, the Communists occupy the positions of control and provide direction and organization at all levels. Communists also play a role in city and local government. There are now about 700 Communist mayors. As of 1988, only three medium-sized cities—Calais, Le Mans, and Amiens—remained in communist hands. Table 3–2 outlines this declining trend.

In the last few years the revolutionary stance of the party has been blurred. The party has abandoned its doctrinaire commitment to revolution; it has conceded that in a democracy the prospects of a dictatorship of the proletariat, which it advocated earlier, is not to be entertained; it has agreed to accept the verdict of election and to withdraw from political power in case of an adverse vote in the hypothetical case it held power; it has declared itself openly from freedom of the press and individual freedoms. It is increasingly becoming a reformist party, committed to socialism within the framework of a democratic polity and democratic institutions.

The Socialists

The French Socialist party was founded before the turn of the century but did not succeed in unifying its internal factions until 1905, just in time to ride the mounting wave of socialism that swept Europe in the early twentieth century. The party adopted a reformist social and economic policy and remained fully committed to parliamentary democracy. In the elections of 1936 the Socialists received 19 percent of the electoral vote, captured 149 seats in the legislature, and headed a coalition cabinet with the Radical Socialist party. But the victory was short-lived. Criticized from the left by the Communists and abandoned on the right by the Radicals, the Socialist prime minister, Léon Blum, resigned.

The onset of World War II and the defeat of France found the Socialists demoralized. A majority of the Socialists in the legislature voted to give full powers to the authoritarian, pro-German government of Marshall Pétain. During the German occupation the Socialists were unable to match the leadership provided by the Communists. Immediately after the Liberation they cooperated with the Communists and the center. The Communists, however, soon moved into the opposition, and the Socialists became the pivot of centrist coalitions.

Organization. Like the Communists, the Socialists purport to be a "mass party." They also emphasize internal discipline, both for members of the party and for its parliamentarians. However, a tolerance for "tendencies" and "factions" often makes it impossible for the leaders to enforce party discipline. As a result, the Socialist party has been prey to divisions.

The basic unit of the party is the *section,* a group of party members from a city, town, or village. In each department there is a *federation* composed of sections; a secretary is its spokesperson and executive. The federations control the departmental finances and make decisions about political action, not only in local matters but often in national elections as well. They enjoy considerable autonomy, especially in their electoral tactics. The supreme organ of the party is the *National Congress,* composed of delegates chosen by the party federations.

The National Congress elects the *Directing Committee* of 157 members (the number varies), which in turn nominates the 27 member *Executive Bureau.* A *Secretariat* consisting of 15 members is charged with day-to-day policy formulation and the running of the party. The secretary-general is the head of the party.

Strength. As with the Communists, the strength of the Socialists must be studied with reference to voters and members. Between World War II and 1962 the Socialists had lost over half their voters: their strength dropped from about 22 percent of the electorate to less than 10 percent. But a marked upswing began in the 1970s and today the Socialists outdistance the Communists (Table 3–3).

There are many reasons for this upswing. In 1971 François Mitterrand assumed the leadership of the Socialist party. He favored—not always unequivocally—cooperation with the Communists. In June 1972 a "Common Program of Government" was signed by the Socialists, the Communists, and the left-wing Radicals. After 1974, when Mitterrand, as the candidate of the United Left, ran again for the presidency and lost by less than 1 percent, the fortunes of the Socialist party rapidly improved. Its membership rose from 40,000–50,000 to over 200,000; its departmental organizations were strengthened, and its electoral appeal virtually doubled, surpassing that of the Communists. These trends continued through the legislative election of 1978 and were reinforced in the presidential and legislative elections of 1981 and again in 1986 and 1988.

The Socialist party replaced the Communists as the "first party of the left." In so doing it has strengthened some of its working-class support and has gained among white-collar workers, managerial personnel, and civil servants. To their traditional strongholds in the north, the Calais area, and Marseilles, the Socialists added new ones in both the east and the west. Farmers began to vote for them, and the Socialists began to gain in many traditionally conservative and Catholic departments. The middle classes, which gave their vote to centrist formations and the Gaullists, shifted—at least in part—to the Socialists.

Between 1978 and 1981 the Socialists, while cooperating with the Communists, swung to the left, moving into the ideological and electoral territories of the Communist party, which began to feel threatened. In 1981 the Socialists and their candidate for the presidency—François Mitterrand—produced a platform of sweeping economic and social reforms that appealed at the time to the French left. They won the presidency and an absolute majority in the National Assembly. Further, in a shrewd move, they asked the Communists to participate in the cabinet, thus preempting any opposition from their left. The strategy worked well—and in the 1986 and 1988 legislative elec-

TABLE 3-3 The Delcine and Upswing in the Socialist Vote in Legislative Elections, 1958–1988

	Election Year	Number of Voters	Number of Parliamentary Seats
490 seats	1958	3,176,000	40
	1962	2,319,000	65
	1967	4,224,110	117
		(including Radicals)	
	1968	3,660,200	57
	1973	4,523,400	102
	1978	6,412,819	113
	1981	9,432,362	270
577 seats	1986	8,739,995	215
	1988	8,493,702	277

Source: Adapted from François Goguel and Alfred Grosser, *La Politique en France* (Paris: Armand Colin, 1981).

tions, the Communist strength waned, while the Socialists stabilized their electoral position.

The Radical Socialists and Allied Center Formations

The Parti Républicain Radical et Radical Socialiste—in brief, the Radical Socialist party—has been a party without a program, organization, leadership, and membership. Yet this "party," under different labels and thanks to many shifting alliances, played a controlling role in the formation and life of virtually all the governments of the Third and Fourth Republics. It participated in right-wing electoral alliances only to abandon them and move to the left, but more frequently it managed to do exactly the reverse. Its internal instability both reflected and caused the instability of the cabinet and the divisions of the republic. It has had its own left (closely anchored to the Socialists and even to the Communists), its own center, and its own right (which was affiliated even with extreme right-wing groups). With the waning of the significance of anticlericalism and the general acceptance of economic planning and state social and economic controls, the Radicals found themselves not only without leaders but also without ideas. The Radical party, as it is called today, hardly exists. Some of its members are with the left (they are known as left-wing Radicals). Others are associated with the followers of Giscard d'Estaing and are one of the centrist formations that make up the Union of French Democracy.

THE CENTER-RIGHT

At least 40 percent of the French, when asked where they belong politically, say the center. Yet, though many political parties have claimed a centrist vocation, there has been no strong centrist party. Instead, the center has consisted of splinter formations: moderates, unaffiliated independents, peasants, republicans. Only in the years immediately after the Liberation did one large political party—the liberal Catholic MRP (Movement Republicain Populaire)—manage to form a coherent political formation, develop a program, and attract more than 25 percent of the voters. Thereafter the fortunes of the various centrist formations varied considerably, ranging from as little as 12 percent to almost 30 percent. Constantly pulled between the Socialists and the Gaullists, they were unable to group themselves into one political party.

It was in 1978 that the various centrist splinters united under the Union of French Democracy. The reasons for the formation of the UDF were electoral. The president of the republic decided to move his own Republican party—about 55 deputies—out of the Gaullist party and create a new "presidential" party that would attract the various centrist formations. This was in substance the UDF. But to his presidential party he gave a neo-liberal and progressive orientation. The party favored strengthening the European Common Market, supported the direct election of a European Parliament, and backed economic and social reforms, regional reforms, and social welfare measures. It claimed to be a renewed center having progressive aspirations that reflected the social and economic changes in France. Its membership rose to about 200,000.

But there are organizational, leadership, and ideological issues that plague the UDF. First and foremost, it is but an umbrella organization, consisting of a number of political parties. There are in fact at least three centrist groups.

1. *The Republican party*—heir to independents and moderates of earlier years—constantly flirting with the Gaullists and yet trying to maintain its identity.
2. *The Center for Social Democrats*—heir to the progressive Catholics—the MRP and the Democratic center. Pro-European, favoring welfare legislation, attached to the humanistic values of progressive Catholicism, this group has been unwilling to associate itself either with

the Left or with the Gaullists. In 1988 it was the most vocal group among the centrists to reject any cooperation with the extreme right-wing formation—the National Front—and to consider the prospects of cooperation with the Socialists.

3. *The Radical Socialist party*—heir to the glories, long gone by, of the "Radical-Socialists" of the Third Republic, when it was the largest political formation. It is now but a splinter of moderates. As it is the case with the PR and the CDS, membership is low—not more than 10,000.

There are, finally, a number of assorted centrist groupings and clubs.

In addition to the organizational problem, there is also the lack of ideological coherence. Some of the groups advocate social legislation and state controls, while others favor economic liberalism. Some favor the formation of a broad conservative party together with the Gaullists, while others would prefer a collaboration under preagreed conditions with the Socialists. Like all centrists, they are torn between left and right, unable to organize and impose their strength upon either or both.

Over and above the organizational and ideological predicaments, there is, as it has been always the case with French centrists, the question of leadership. Two major and two minor figures vie for it: the former president of the Republic, Giscard d'Estaign, who after all, was the founder of the UDF, and the former prime minister, Raymond Barre, who ran as a candidate in the Presidential election of 1988, along with François Leotard, the young and dynamic leader of the Republican party, arguing for the formation of a broad conservative party in association with the Gaullists, and Pierre Mehaignerie of the Social Democratic center, who is unwilling to go along and would rather flirt with the Socialists.

It is difficult to calculate the overall strength of the UDF, because it has often run in close cooperation with the Gaullists. In the presidential election of 1988, their candidate Raymond Barre received about 17 percent of the vote. In legislative elections their score has been consistently higher—about 19 percent in 1978, 21.66 percent in 1981, and almost 20 percent in the election of 1988.

THE RIGHT

The Gaullist Parties

De Gaulle and the Gaullist political formations dominated the French political scene after 1940, when the then unknown general launched a resistance movement that eventually brought him to political power in 1944. He formed a provisional government and headed it between 1944 and 1946. He then resigned to launch the first Gaullist party, the Rassemblement du Peuple Français (Rally of the French People), RPF, but it failed to capture a majority in the legislature. In 1958 de Gaulle was returned to power. He withdrew from the presidency in 1969 and died the following year. His name and legacy, however, continued to be the banner of "Gaullist" political movements under different labels. (See Table 3–4.)

With de Gaulle as president, and even for a few years after his death, the major characteristic of the Gaullist party was its catch-all

TABLE 3–4 The Gaullist Party Vote (with Allies) in Legislative Elections, 1958–1988

Election Year	Number of Votes	Percentage of All Voters
1958	4,010,787	20.3%
1962	6,580,606	35.5
1967	8,448,982	38.3
1968	9,663,605	43.65
1973	8,242,661	35.54
1978	6,329,918	22.5
1981	5,231,269	20.8
(with UDF) 1986	11,506,816	42.1
(without UDF) 1988	4,687,047	19.18
(with UDF) 1988	9,903,778	40.52

Source: Adapted from Goguel and Grosser, *La Politique en France*, 1981.

character and interclass appeal. It managed to make inroads into the regional strongholds of the left and attract many votes from workers. For instance, in 1965 more than 40 percent of the blue-collar, white-collar, and technical workers voted for de Gaulle. By 1978, however, only 14 percent of the Gaullist voters were blue-collar workers and no more than 15 percent were white-collar or technical.

The RPR

In 1976 a reorganization of the Gaullist movement took place. The major force behind it was a newcomer, Jacques Chirac, prime minister between 1974 and 1976. He removed a number of old-time Gaullists and placed many of his own followers in key party positions. In 1976 Chirac became party president. The name of the party was changed to Rassemblement pour la République (the Rally for the Republic), RPR. The party, he claimed, was to be a mass party, appealing to the middle and working classes. It was to be national and popular, reaching as de Gaulle did across class and ideological lines in the name of national independence and unity. By 1978 the new Gaullist party began to rival the Communist party in membership. It claimed over half a million members.

The party, under the leadership of Jacques Chiracm remains well organized and well financed. It is always poised to the right as the most powerful political force—a constant magnet that attracts the centrists— even the most reluctant among them. If ever the idea of a broad conservative party were to materialize, it will have to be with the RPR and cannot be except under the leadership of the RPR.

How "Gaullist" is the RPR? It claims to incarnate the national will for rank and greatness that de Gaulle embodied. It takes it for granted that France plays and will play a dominant role not only in Europe, but in the world. It is attached to the defense strategy of General de Gaulle with reliance upon the nuclear weapons, and, like de Gaulle, it has pro-

moted the German-French cooperation for defense. But otherwise the appeal and the ideology of the party has changed—it has abandoned the statist philosophy of the Gaullists. It favors increasingly economic liberalism. It has also abandoned the welfarist doctrine of the Gaullists, espousing increasingly individual effort and initiative. As a result, it appears increasingly as a middle-class and upper-middle-class party, and the working-class support that the Gaullists had enjoyed has dissipated. Unable to move to the left or to retain the leftist support de Gaulle had enjoyed, it has also found itself deprived of the support of right-wing voters because of the rise of the National Front, to which we shall turn now.

THE EXTREME RIGHT AND THE NATIONAL FRONT

The extreme right like the extreme left was also fragmented into many groups with small membership and few voters. Some share a nostalgia for the monarchy, others for fascism. Most are nationalistic and at times racist. All are antisocialist and anticommunist. Some have advocated direct actions and terrorism. The total vote for the extreme right in the legislative elections of 1978 and 1981 was about 1 percent.

The National Front

The National Front, founded in 1972, brought together various extremist right-wing splinters in an effort to represent a "social and a people's right." Its major goals were (1) to "assure the security (law and order) of the French," (2) to "reverse the wave of immigration" (in substance, immigration from North Africa and some of the former French colonies), (3) to "turn its back to socialism," and (4) to "construct a people's capitalism." Blatantly nationalistic, favoring the predominance of the French and their cultural heritage, its leader Jean-Marie Le Pen, played shrewdly also on the fears and anxieties of the French caused by terrorist acts, violence in the streets, unemployment and inflation, and, above all, the antagonisms many felt against the "colored immigrants." As with all extremist movements, there was a "scape goat" that had to be dealt with—in this case it was the colored immigrants and their families, estimated at a maximum of 2.5 million.

In the legislative election of 1973, National Front candidates received less than one-half of the vote. In the election of 1978, their vote was even smaller. In the presidential election of 1981, Le Pen failed to receive the required number of endorsers for nomination and could not run. Yet in the election for the European Parliament in 1984, it received 11 percent. The political landscape seemed radically changed and Le Pen appeared, as he was called later, its "great Perturbator." It is a change that continued as Table 3-5 shows, with Le Pen gaining almost 10 percent of the vote in the legislative election of 1986 and again in

TABLE 3-5   The Vote for the National Front, 1973–1988

Year	Result
1973 and 1978	Negligible
1981 (presidential election)	Le Pen fails to gain the required endorsement to be a candidate
1983 (municipal elections)	8–10% and in some cases 15% and over
1984 (elections for European Parliament)	11.0%
1986 (legislative elections with proportional representation)	9.7%
1988 (presidential election)	14.4% (Le Pen)
1988 (legislative elections—majority system with run-offs)	9.6%

1988, while attaining his highest score in the first ballot of the presidential election of 1988—14.4 percent. A new force appeared on the French political stage. How stable is it? Does it relate to transient factors—the economic crisis, the influx of many immigrants, and unemployment of the last ten years? Or does it represent a revival of the French right—nationalist, xenophobic, anti-Semitic, and anti-democratic? It is a question that can not be answered easily.

The strength of the National Front is, above all, in urban areas. In most of the large cities Le Pen came out strong, often vying with the Communists; relatedly, the vote for the National Front is the strongest in places (also mostly urban centers) where the number of immigrants is higher and where "safety" in the streets in uncertain; the vote is also strong in less urbanized areas, notably the south and southwest, because of the large presence of French who were forced to leave their homes in Algeria in the 1960s and continue to harbor strong hostilities against the Moslems. Its membership, estimated today at over 100,000, comes from among the young, fairly well-to-do (but with a good sprinkling also of unemployed), and relatively better educated than the average French. Le Pen has also appealed to lower middle classes among small merchants, farmers, shopkeepers, and artisans. The expression—one of Le Pen's slogans—"France, first" appeals to all French—men and women, poor and rich, cultured or not, employed or unemployed. Some 25 percent of the French (it is an astonishingly high percentage, however) agree completely or more or less with Le Pen's position on immigration and the need to take strict measures to deal with the immigrant problem in France.

4

Elections: Patterns and Trends

Under the Fifth Republic, electoral contests have been deeply influenced by a number of constraints, all of which account for some profound changes in the party system. There are constitutional constraints, constraints deriving from the electoral law used both for the election of the president and the National Assembly, and, finally, significant ideological and class changes affecting the behavior and tactics of the political parties. These factors reinforced each other, and the political parties gradually developed a majoritarian vocation forming governmental and oppositional coalitions or "blocs" that became increasingly coherent and disciplined. Multipartism was followed by a significant reduction in the number of parties, which gave place to bipolarization, which in turn accounted for an unprecedented governmental stability. (See Table 4–1.)

CONSTITUTIONAL CONSTRAINTS

French parties have been directly influenced by the constitutional reforms of the Fifth Republic. One of them was the need of a popular majority to elect the president and of a presidential majority in the National Assembly to support the president's prime minister. The political parties began to coalesce into "blocs" in favor or against the president and his policies—there was a majoritarian impulse. Relatedly, the political parties began to change their vocation—from "parties of representation"—reflecting various segments of the electorate—ideological, regional, or class—without any hope of getting a majority to form a government, to "parties of government" seeking, above all, a majority on the basis of which governments designated by the president could govern. Finally,

TABLE 4-1 Simplification of Party Configuration from Fourth Republic to Fifth Republic

1956		1988	
Party	*Seats in National Assembly*	*Party*	*Seats in National Assembly*
Communist	144	Communist	27 ⎫ 304
Progressist	6	Socialist (and affiliates)	277 ⎭
Socialist	100		
Radical	40	Union of French Democracy	130 ⎫
Dissident Radicals	20	(Centrists, Independent Republicans, etc.)	
Democratic African Rally and Democratic Socialist Union of Resistance	18	Gaullist	129 ⎬ 273
MRP	74	Nonregistered (right),	
Independents from Overseas	10	(including one deputy of FN)	14 ⎭
Rally of Republical Left	14		
Gaullist	22		
Independents	84		
Peasant	13		
Union of French Fraternity	42		
Other			
TOTAL	593	TOTAL	577

presidential elections, as in many other democracies, accentuated the personal element of leadership—the presidential candidates appealed to the electorate in terms of their personal qualities and symbolisms. In legislative elections coalitions were formed "to support the leadership" or "support the policies" of the president, provoking the organization of rival coalitions.

Constitutional arrangements—notably the right of dissolution of the National Assembly by the president (on the "advice" of his prime minister)—as well as the powers given to the prime minister to control parliamentary debate and impose his policies that we discussed in Chapter 2, disciplined the political groups—both the majority and the opposition—that gradually began to vie with each other just as it is the case with the two major parties in the British Parliament.

It is worth noting that ever since 1962 neither the presidential majority coalition nor the opposition have broken ranks in the National Assembly. No majority committed to the president has deserted him at any time (though the possibilities were raised in 1967–68); oppositions also have stood firm

and disciplined. In this manner, the political parties not only learned to cooperate within two major blocs, but voters and parties appeared at election time organized into two camps. There was, therefore, a simplification of the multiparty system into two major camps, both competing for the highest stakes—presidential power and legislative majorities to form a cabinet. It was this powerful governmental vocation that replaced the purely representative and often sectarian party concerns of the past.

ELECTORAL CONSTRAINTS

Presidential Elections

One of the most powerful reasons for the change in party attitudes and in the relationship between political parties was the method prescribed for the election of the president. The election consists of a national primary, in which as many candidates can run as they wish (subject to only minor requirements). If, in the primary, one candidate wins an absolute majority of the votes (it has never happened), then he or she is elected. A second ballot takes place two weeks after the first, limited to only the two first-placed candidates. The one with a majority is elected. (For illustration, see Table 4–2.) The primary is "expressive" and "representative"—the parties and their leaders, but often candidates without party support, develop programs that appeal to specific segments of the electorate in terms of issues, ideologies, regions of the country, classes, occupations, and groups. But it is the second ballot that counts, since it at the second ballot that the parties and their voters will have to take a position for or against one of the two candidates. Inevitably, there is nationwide mobilization, organization, and concentration for or against. The parties and the voters are forced into making a choice for the highest political office of the land. Alliances become necessary, and in the process, the original distinctions among individual political parties become blurred. Such alliances invariably crystallize into the major camps of the left and the right—but in the process, the "purity" of both camps is sullied

TABLE 4–2 The Mechanics of the French Presidential Elections (1974)

First Ballot (May 5)		
Mitterrand (leftist coalition)	11,044,373	(43.24%)
Giscard d'Estaing (Ind. Rep.)	8,326,774	(32.60%)
Chaban-Delmas (UDR-Gaullist)	3,857,728	(15.10%)
Royer (minister in Gaullist cabinet)	810,540	(3.17%)
Laguiller (Worker's Struggle—Trotskyite)	595,247	(2.33%)
Dumont (Environmentalist)	337,800	(1.32%)
Le Pen (National Front)	190,921	(0.74%)
Muller (Socialist Democratic Movement of France)	176,279	(0.69%)
Krivine (Revolutionary Communist Front—Trotskyite)	93,900	(0.36%)
Renouvin (New French Action; Action Française—Monarchist)	43,722	(0.17%)
Sebag (European Federalist Movement)	42,007	(0.16%)
Herraud (European Federalist)	19,255	(0.07%)
Second Ballot (May 19)		
Giscard d'Estaing	13,398,412	(50.80%)
Mitterrand	12,975,625	(49.20%)

Source: L'Election Presidentielle de Mai 1974, *Le Monde* (Dossiers et Documents), May 1974.

by the compromises and mutual concessions that take place. To get the vote for a leftist candidate—communists, socialists, sometimes radical-socialists, and even the extreme left and some of the moderates may have to compromise. To get the vote of the center-right alliances centrist groups will have to cooperate with the Gaullists and over and beyond; it may even become necessary to invite the extreme right. The electoral system simply simplifies choices and issues.

The Electoral System in Legislative Elections

The electoral system for legislative elections accounts also, as it is in presidential elections, for a powerful majoritarian impulse. In a legislative election many candidates run in each of the electoral districts. The election is comprised of two ballots. A candidate who wins an absolute majority of the votes on the first ballot is elected. If no candidate wins an absolute majority—the usual outcome—there is a second ballot in two weeks. But those who fail to get 12.5 percent of the registered voters on the first ballot are automatically eliminated from the second ballot. Others who receive more than 12.5 percent but whose chances appear remote may decide to withdraw in favor of one of

the more promising candidates, asking their voters to throw their support behind him or her on the second ballot. They "desist" in favor of X or Y.

These withdrawals (*désistements*) take place within each of the two coalitions. At the left, Communists withdraw for Socialists in the districts where a Socialist is ahead on the first ballot, and Socialists do exactly the same in the districts where a Communist candidate is first. The same arrangements are made for the center-right coalition, the Gaullists and the UDF (or other allied formations) throwing their support behind each other's candidates. In both coalitions, then, candidates who are automatically eliminated or who withdraw voluntarily from the second ballot ask their supporters to vote in the second ballot for one or the other of the two top candidates. (See Table 4–3.)

The support of the Communist voters (after the withdrawal of their own candidate) for the Socialist candidate in the second ballot accounted for the Socialist victory in Belle France I. However, in Belle France II the Socialist support for the Communist candidate was not sufficient. The Gaullists threw their support behind Flaubert (UDF), who also received a number of voters from Delacroix, and he won.

Mutual withdrawal accounted for the simplification that resulted in the second ballot.

TABLE 4–3   Election Results in Belle France I and Belle France II (an illustration)

	First Ballot	*Second Ballot*
Belle France I (125,000 registered voters)		
Costeau (Socialist)	31,000	60,000 + (elected)
Flambeau (Communist)	27,000	
Simenon (UDF)	29,000	48,000 −
Maigret (RPR-Gaullist)	17,000	
Bataille (extreme left)	1,000 automatic	
Fanfaille (extreme right)	2,000 elimination	
Belle France II (105,000 registered voters)		
Babillon (Socialist)	14,000	
Tiralleur (Communist)	27,000	50,000 −
Flaubert (UDF)	36,000	51,500 + (elected)
Contrare (Gaullist-RPR)	13,700	
Delacroix (independent)	6,000 automatic	
Extreme left	3,000 elimination	

Usually not more than 125 seats are decided by absolute majority on the first ballot. Over 450 or so had to be decided on the second, with only the two candidates of the opposing coalitions—left versus right—facing each other. Triangular elections have been rare.

In this manner, the majoritarian impulse provided by the mechanics of presidential elections is reinforced in the legislative election. The presidential majority becomes, in effect, a coalitional bloc of candidates running in the legislative election to support the president's program and leadership; on the other side, the other bloc makes every effort to regroup its forces and win the legislative election against the presidential coalition. The president invariably asks the electorate to give him a majority in the National Assembly; all presidents have done it. Thus the electoral system both for the election of the president and the election of the members of the National Assembly accounts for the formation of two blocs. No party can escape the logic and the weight of bipolarization with impunity.

CLASS AND IDEOLOGY

The constitutional and electoral constraints, two major socioeconomic and ideological factors, played a critical role in the simplification of the party system and the development of "governing" and an "opposition" bloc. Economic changes—new occupations, the growth of technicians, the differentiation of wages among workers, and the rapid growth of the tertiary sector—all accounted for undermining the working class and its vaunted solidarity, based on similar living conditions and similar outlooks. Different life-styles and different living conditions began to reflect differentiated incomes. An increasing number of workers began to identify themselves with the middle class. Both the militancy and the partisanship of the working class declined as it became increasingly heterogeneous; the workers' voting began to stray away from the parties of the left.

Also their numerical weight began to decline. The number of industrial workers has remained stable over the last 20 years as more and more people joined the labor force in supervisory and clerical and technical positions, to say nothing of the fast-growing service section in the economy.

With the waning of class, the distance between major political parties—the Communists and the Gaullists, for instance—grew shorter. Political ideologies were refashioned to allow for greater compromise; attitudes became more pragmatic and eclectic. Voting the issues became more important than voting the party, and often voting for a person motivated voting more than voting for political ideas. The "decline of ideology" in this way led to a broad acceptance of reformist rather than militant and ideological politics, and it goes a long way in understanding both the rapid decline of the Communist party and the growing reformism among the Socialists.

The constitutional and electoral restraints we discussed can be best understood when put in the context of a changing socioeconomic and ideological context. They reinforced each other. Consensus politics seemed to replace and shape political cleavages and intransigence gave place to compromise. The multiparty system gradually moved in the direction of bipolarity. In the period between 1958 and 1974 the Gaullists with the support of centrist groups dominated the political scene, winning the presidential and legislative elections; the trend continued until 1981, but with a centrist president—Gisccard d'Estaign—who had been closely associated with the Gaullists. In 1981 and until 1986, it was the left-wing forces with the Socialists clearly in command that won both the presidency and a clear majority in the National Assembly. It was only with the election of 1986 that the clear alternation between the leftist bloc and the center-right bloc was broken: the Gaullists and their allies won a legislative majority that confronted a Socialist president in office. We shall survey briefly these three periods and discuss in a second part the electoral contest—both presidential and legislative—of April, May, and June 1988. Table 4-4 provides a bird's-eye view of electoral returns in the Fifth Republic.

PRESIDENTIAL ELECTIONS

The first presidential election by direct popular vote was held in 1965 and was won by General Charles de Gaulle. On the first ballot the general won only 44.6 percent of the vote; the candidate of the left—François Mitterrand, who also ran in 1974 and 1981—received (with Communist support) 34.7 percent. All the other candidates were centrist or right-wing. On the second ballot, therefore, they could decide the election by switching to de Gaulle or Mitterrand. Half the centrist vote went to Mitterrand, but the shift of the other half to de Gaulle was all that the general needed to win.

The pattern has continued ever since—forcing the electorate into two camps for one or the other of the two candidates. Smaller parties are swallowed up, if not quite digested, by major parties, which in turn have to set aside their quarrels and cooperate within one or the other of the two blocs.

Gaullism Without de Gaulle

On April 28, 1969, Charles de Gaulle ceased to perform the functions of the presidency. The president of the Senate assumed the office of the presidency as prescribed by the constitution, set the date of the elections, and waited for the nomination of candidates, of whom he was to become one. Prominent individuals and parties moved rapidly onto the electoral stage, and seven candidates proceeded to run for the presidency.

First was the former Gaullist prime minister, Georges Pompidou, who declared himself a candidate as soon as de Gaulle resigned. The Gaullists, including the leaders of the Independent Republicans, rallied behind him. Alain Poher, the president of the Senate, "consented" to run as a centrist. The left was split and the Socialist-Communist alliance had no program and no leadership. The Socialists, by rejecting all cooperative arrangements with the Communists, were definitely moving to the center, and some of their leaders favored the outright endorsement of Poher. Finally, a rather confused party congress nominated the mayor of Marseilles, Gaston Defferre, as the Socialist candidate while the communists nominated their veteran leader—Jacques Duclos.

The Results. The first ballot was remarkable for the spectacular showing of the Communist candidate. With 21.5 percent of the vote, Jacques Duclos had done as well as the Communists had ever done under the Fifth Republic. Equally spectacular was the political comeback of the centrists. Poher managed to come in second with 23.4 percent and thus entered the run-off. The Socialists

TABLE 4-4 Legislative Elections in the Fifth Republic (1958–1988), Overall Trends

Major Parties	*1958*	*1962*	*1967*	*1968*	*1973*	*1978*	*1981*	*1986*	*1988*
Communists	20.58	21.87	22.51	20.02	21.41	20.61	16.13	9.7	11.3
Socialists & Allies	21.74	21.87	21.11	20.50	20.82	24.95	37.14	31.6	37.6
Centrists (Radicals, MRP, Independent, etc.)	27.39	19.39	17.35	12.41	16.67	23.89	21.66	42.1	40.5
Gaullists & Alllies	29.95	36.03	38.45	46.44	36.98	22.84	21.24		
Extreme Right (*National Front* since 1985)	—	—	—	—	—	—	—	9.7	9.8

Compiled from a survey by Alain Lancelot, *Les Elections Sous La Ve République*, Presse Universitaire de France, 1988.

suffered an ignominious defeat, barely squeezing over 5 percent. Pompidou, with slightly over 44 percent of the vote, did better, in terms of the percentage, than de Gaulle had done in 1965, but with about 700,000 fewer votes. His opponents together outdistanced him on the first ballot by 6 percent. Could they unite against him?

To the surprise of all the political forecasters, the Communists decided to abstain. Instead of using their strength and their remarkable organization to dislodge the Gaullists, they now proclaimed both Poher and Pompidou "candidates of reaction," "Tweedledee and Tweedledum," and instructed the Communist voters to abstain, which they did in great part. The issue was closed. Pompidou won.

A Non-Gaullist President

The death of President Pompidou on April 2, 1974, ushered in a new period of feverish electioneering for the highest office of the land.

The parties were unable to organize their nomination of candidates. There were too many of them—12 in all (Table 4–2)—and most were self-designated. The left—that is, the Communists, Socialists, and left-wing radicals—decided formally to support a candidate (it was again François Mitterrand). But there was disarray within every other formation, most of all the "majority." The Gaullists and their allies split, and at least two important candidates emerged: Jacques Chaban-Delmas, the choice of the orthodox Gaullists, and Valéry Giscard d'Estaing, Minister of Finance from 1962 to 1966 and 1969 to 1974.

The First Ballot. The election appeared to be an unprecedented triumph of the union of the left. The vote for Mitterrand alone—representing Communists, Socialists, Radicals of the left, and other leftists—amounted to 43.2 percent. The most dramatic aspect of the election was the collapse of the Gaullist candidate, Chaban-Delmas. With less than

15 percent of the vote, he was far behind the totals given de Gaulle and Pompidou in the previous presidential elections. Giscard d'Estaing received 33 percent, coming in far ahead of his Gaullist opponent. It was a non-Gaullist, then, who faced Mitterrand in the runoff.

The Second Ballot. The candidate of the left was defeated because of the concentration of right-center voters against him on the second ballot. But the outcome was close. Without about 900,000 more voters on the second ballot (which witnessed a record turnout), Giscard d'Estaing won with 50.8 percent. Fewer than 400,000 votes separated the two candidates (Table 4–2).

A Socialist President: In the Election of 1981

In the 1981 presidential election both the left and the center-right "majority" appeared deeply divided. There were ten candidates in all (Table 4–5), but the interest was focused on *les quatre grands*—the candidates representing the four major parties. The other six—*les petits*—were not expected to receive more than 10 percent of the votes on the first ballot. Before the first ballot there was no sign that the four major parties would cooperate on the second. The Socialist and Communist candidates were fighting each other for the dominant position within the left, and the candidates of the center-right were doing precisely the same with regard to the centrist-conservative electorate.

Mitterrand nevertheless won with 51.76 percent of the second ballot. His victory was due to two mutually reinforcing factors. Even though there was no mobilization of the Communist electorate, as there had been in the past, the Communist voters turned to Mitterrand at the rate of about 8.5 out of 10. Second, no more than 7 out of 10 voters for Chirac turned to Giscard d'Estaing. Most of the leftists and the environmentalists voted for Mitterrand. Not enough Gaullists, centrists, and supporters of the lesser conserv-

TABLE 4–5 Presidential Election of 1981

First Ballot (April 26)		
Registered voters	36,418,664	
Voting	29,529,345	
Abstaining	6,889,319	(18.91%)
Valid ballots	29,038,202	
Les Quatre Grands — Giscard d'Estaing (incumbent; UDF)	8,222,969	(28.31%)
Mitterrand (Socialist)	7,505,295	(25.84%)
Chirac (Gaullist-RPR)	5,225,720	(17.99%)
Marchais (Communist)	4,456,979	(15.34%)
Les Petits — Lalond (Environmentalist)	1,126,282	(3.87%)
Laguiller (Workers' Struggle—extreme left)	668,195	(2.30%)
Crepeau (MRG—Radical Left Movement)	642,815	(2.21%)
Debré (Gaullist candidate) (independent)	482,067	(1.66%)
Garaud (pro-Gaullist Conservative)	386,489	(1.33%)
Bouchardeau (Socialist Workers' Party—PSU)	321,391	(1.10%)
Second Ballot (May 10)		
Registered voters	36,392,678	
Voting	31,249,753	
Abstaining	5,142,925	(14.13%)
Valid ballots	30,362,385	
Mitterrand	15,714,598	(51.76%)
Giscard d'Estaing	14,647,787	(48.24%)

ative candidates voted for Giscard. Mitterrand and Giscard each held to his electoral base, but Mitterrand's was complemented by an appreciable number of Gaullists, some of whom abstained on the first ballot but voted on the second, and many of the envorinmentalists—a total of between 2 and 2.5 million voters—whereas Giscard's was narrowed by the defection of at least as many centrist and Gaullist voters. The Socialists, in short, simply did not have the votes to win, even with the support of the Communists—it was the centrists and some of the Gaullists who provided the margin of victory.

LEGISLATIVE ELECTIONS

The highest tide of Gaullism occurred in the legislative election of June 1968; the ebb came in the election of March 1978. The left

coalition was soundly defeated in 1968; it lost in both 1973 and 1978. It finally won in 1981.

A Presidential Majority: The Legislative Elections of 1981

On May 21, 1981, the leader of the Socialist party took the oath of office as president of the French republic. He immediately appointed an interim government under Premier Pierre Mauroy. It consisted mostly of Socialists with a sprinkling of left-wing radicals and even some Gaullists who had sided with Mitterrand before the election.

The moment the cabinet was formed, the president dissolved the National Assembly and announced elections for June 14 and June 21. The election was bound to be overshadowed by the presidential one. And the political parties, despite the internal rivalries—personal and political—returned to the coalitional bipolarization we have described.

The Left. To the left, the Socialists and the left-wing radicals quickly agreed to reciprocal withdrawals in the second ballot in favor of each other's better placed candidate. The old "majority," consisting of the RPR and the UDF, agreed to join forces and to cooperate fully in the election. Their respective candidates could run separately on the first ballot but agreed to support each other on the second. Better, they agreed to present a single candidate in about 340 electoral districts.

The Role of the President. During the first meeting of the Council of Ministers the new president emphasized the importance of the legislative elections. It was difficult to imagine that the French would elect him and his program and now turn around and vote for the majority that had supported Giscard d'Estaing. Without a new majority in the National Assembly pledged to him it would be difficult, indeed impossible, to implement the program on which he had been elected.

The First Ballot. The first ballot confirmed and in many respects reinforced the trend initiated in the presidential election. The total vote for the left was 55.73 percent. The center-right barely managed 43 percent. The

"environmentalists" held the remaining 1 percent. Compared with the election results from 1978, these figures represented an overall swing from the center-right to the left of almost 7 percent. The shift of voters within the left was even more remarkable. The Communists dropped from their 20.8 percent vote in 1978 to 16.17 percent and hardly managed to improve their dismal showing at the presidential election. The Socialists, on the other hand, gained about 16 percent, half of which came from the Communists and other leftists and half from centrists and others that had voted for the "majority" in 1978. The small formations were annihilated, the Big Four parties receiving almost 94 percent of the ballots. Within the Union for the New Majority the balance between the RPR and the UDF remained almost what it had been in 1978.

The Second Ballot. The second ballot reinforced the results of the first. The left won a solid victory, electing 333 deputies out of 491. Remarkably, within the left the Socialist party's 270 deputies constituted an absolute majority, independently of Communists and the left-wing Radicals (see Figure 4–1). This new majority overpowered the UFD, the RPR, and assorted independents.

The election returns of 1981 amounted to a reaffirmation of presidential government.

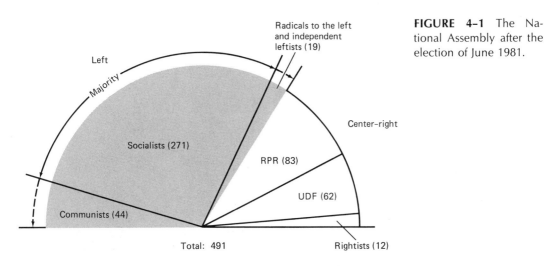

Radicals to the left and independent leftists (19)

Left

Majority

Center-right

Socialists (271)

RPR (83)

UDF (62)

Communists (44)

Total: 491

Rightists (12)

FIGURE 4–1 The National Assembly after the election of June 1981.

The presidential factor made all the difference, and it confirmed and legitimized the Gaullist constitution. The voters changed their president and then changed the parliamentary majority without which he could not implement his program. Mitterrand's coattails, in this sense, proved to be much longer than those of any American president. The logic of presidentialism was fully accepted: for a Socialist president there must be a leftist and preferably Socialist majority. The system at long last had been able to provide for "rotation," contrary to the doubts of many. The Gaullist constitution had survived as the framework within which some of the very forces that had opposed it—including the new president himself— would now operate to realize their policies. The immediate dissolution of the National Assembly gave the Socialist president a majority for five years—until the next legislative election—in 1986.

The Election for the National Assembly, March 16, 1986

The legislative election for the National Assembly held on March 16, 1986, was to be a verdict on the record of the Socialist government, led by the first Socialist president of the Fifth Republic, François Mitterrand. It was also therefore a verdict on the president. Like his predecessors, he had come out strongly for his supporters, that is to say, his party; he had claimed "responsibility" for the policies that had been pursued since 1981.

The Political Parties. The party configuration remained familiar. To the extreme left were the Lutte Ouvrière (Workers' Struggle), the Communist Revolutionary League, the MPPT (Movement for a Party of the Workers), assorted leftists, and some dissident Socialist candidates. The two left-wing parties expected to get wide support were the Communists and the Socialists. The Socialists joined forces in some departments with the "Radicals of the Left." To the center-right, the RPR (Rally for the Republic) and the

UDF (Union of French Democracy), ran candidates jointly in two-thirds of the departments (by presenting a single party list), separately in the remaining one-third of the departments—notably some of the larger ones in the Paris, Lyon, and Marseilles areas. The RPR (the neo-Gaullists) under the leadership of Jacques Chirac, was well organized, amply financed, and had mass support. The UDF consisted of a number of parties—the Republican party, the "orthodox" Radical Socialists, the National Center of the Independents and the Center of Social Democrats. It included a number of powerful, nationally known leaders, among them the former president of the Republic, Valery Giscard d'Estaing, and the former prime minister, Raymond Barre. The UDF and the RPR had joined in the preparation of a common platform and despite personal rivalries promised to support a government that would implement their programs. Finally, the National Front represented a powerful resurgence of the extreme right.

The "big" parties, then, were the Socialists, the Communists, the RPR-UDF (jointly or separately) and possibly, the National Front. These were the parties that ran candidates (party lists) in virtually all the departments of France and in the overseas departments and territories.

The Mechanics of the Elections

Under the new electoral law that introduced for the first time since 1958 proportional representation, each of the 96 departments became an electoral district in which deputies were elected at the rate of 1 for every 108,000 inhabitants. Small departments were entitled to a minimum of two seats each, and, as a result, inequalities were introduced.

In each department a party presented a "party list" of candidates whose number was equal to the number of seats alloted to the department plus 2. Voters had to vote the list; they were not allowed to make any changes or indicate any preferences in the order in which the candidates were presented. If a party won three seats, the candidates elected were those who appeared first, second, and third on the list. Party preferences determined the choice of the voters; the voters voted only for the party.

The proportional system chosen had a majoritarian bias. It discriminated against small parties. A party with a strong lead over the other parties in a department was likely to have a clear advantage over the others on the second, third, and subsequent distributions, of seats. It was estimated that a party with about 41.5 percent of the national vote would win a majority of seats in the National Assembly.[1]

The Results

The figures for the legislative election speak for themselves (Table 4–6). The center-right, the right and the extreme right—the Union of French Democracy (UDF), the Rally of the French Republic (RPR), the National Front, and assorted independent conservatives and rightists—received almost 55 percent of the ballots cast. The extreme left, the Communists, and the Socialists, together with the Radicals of the Left and assorted left-wingers, received less than 44 percent. About 10 percent of the voters had shifted from the left to the right since the election of 1981—a good 3 million voters.

Had the election of March 16, 1986, been held under the previous majority electoral system, the RPR-UDF coalition would have won easily three quarters of the seats of the National Assembly.[2] The new electoral law, however, accomplished exactly what President Mitterrand and the Socialists expected. The RPR-UDF coalition and some independent conservatives won only a slim majority of 291 (the absolute majority is 289) of the 577 seats. Only together with the extreme right—the National Front, with 35 seats—did they have some breathing room. But

---

[1] Proporttional representation was abandoned in 1988 and the previous majoritarian system was reintroduced.

[2] Under the old electoral system, most of the voters of the National Front would have voted for the RPR-UDF coalition on the second ballot, giving it a clear and strong parliamentary majority.

TABLE 4–6 Distribution of Votes: From the Left to the Right

Registered	37,162,020			
Voting	20,094,929			
Abstentions and nul	8,067,091			
Valid ballots	27,852,239*			

		Votes	*%*	*Total (%)*
	Extreme left formations	422,109	1.53	
L	Communist party	2,124,381	9.78	
E	Socialist party			43.96%
F	Union of the Left			
T	Independent leftists	9,071,294	32.65	
	Left-wing Radicals			
R	PRP-UDF (joint lists)	5,995,410	21.46	
I	RPR (separate lists)	3,063,612	11.21	
G	UDF (separate lists)	2,319,347	8.31	54.68%
H	Independent rightists	1,055,253	3.90	
T	National Front	2,705,497	9.80	
	Ecologists and minuscule parties	339,939	1.36	

*Votes cast in two small territories that elected one deputy each not included.

both UDF and RPR had expressed (at least officially) their repugnance for the policies advocated by the extreme right, and had promised not to ally themselves with it. The RPR-UDF coalition was referred to as the parliamentary right—that is, the democratic right. (See Figure 4–2.)

The Decline of the Communists. The decline of the Communist party continued. With less than 10 percent of the vote (compared to 16.5 percent in the first ballot of the legislative election of 1981) and only 35 deputies, the Communists faced political extinction. Their close attachment to the policies of the Soviet Union, the authoritarian control of the aging party leaders on the party rank and file, loss of appeal to the younger voters, and, above all, their new political tactics in considering the Socialists as a party of the right and refusing to cooperate with them, all accounted for their decline. Many Communists shifted and voted for the Socialists; some, but apparently only few, voted for the National Front.

The "Defeat" of the Socialists. The 32.5 percent of the vote that the Socialist party and its allies received, and the 216 deputies it won, amounted to a loss of not more than 5 percent from the election of 1981. Their slogan "Majority of Progress with the Presi-

dent" obviously attracted the voters. "Let us harvest what we planted" and "Give us time" were other slogans used.

The Socialist party, after five years in power, presented a strong and unified image. No factional disputes emerged during the campaign. It appeared as the only party capable of speaking for the left—but a moderate left. Yet less than one out of three voters voted for it. And by the same token, the policies of President Mitterrand were overwhelmingly disavowed. Commentators spoke of the "glorious defeat" of the Socialists.

The "Victory" of the RPR-UDF. The two-parties—running together or separately—won a majority, coming ahead of all others, with about 41 percent of the vote and 277 deputies. With the independent conservative candidates allied with them, the total was close to 44 percent of the vote and 291 deputies, out of 577. It was a slim and fragile majority. It was also the "old majority," the same one that had governed France in the years before 1981. It included 1 former president of the republic, 5 former prime ministers, and at least 60 former ministers! The heterogeneity of its composition and the age of its prominent leaders accounted for its fragility and for its lack of strong appeal. The new majority was a coalition of coali-

FIGURE 4–2   The National Assembly, 1986.

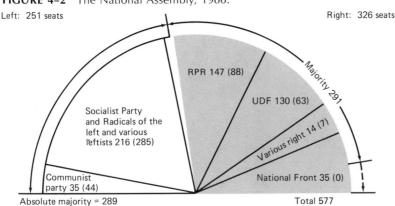

Left: 251 seats

Right: 326 seats

RPR 147 (88)

UDF 130 (63)

Majority 291

Socialist Party and Radicals of the left and various leftists 216 (285)

Various right 14 (7)

Communist party 35 (44)

National Front 35 (0)

Absolute majority = 289

Total 577

In parentheses the number of seats held by the political parties in the previous assembly as of 1 March 1986. The size of the National Assembly was increased from 491 to 577. The absolute majority needed is 289.

tions, in which the UDF comprised three different parties. There were many chiefs, few Indians!

The Surprising Showing of the National Front. The National Front represents a relatively new formation that managed to assemble and organize various extremist formations—nationalist, xenophobic, and racist—that have been active for a long time. Its leader, Jean-Marie Le Pen, was a fiery advocate of "French Algeria"—the maintenance of French rule in Algeria—in the late 1950s and early 1060s. In the election of 1981 his party received less than 1 percent of the vote. In the European election of 1984, the score rose to over 10 percent, but many discounted it because abstentions in this election were high and the stakes low. It was thought to be a protest vote that would not be repeated in the legislative election. However, on March 16 the National Front won just about 10 percent of the votes and 35 deputies—a score identical to that of the Communists. The major issue for Le Pen was the problem of the immigrant workers in France, more particularly, of the "non-European" immigrant workers—estimated, as we have seen, at at least 2 million. This issue was downright racist, but appealed to the insecurities and anxieties of the lower middle classes and the unemployed. It also promised lower taxes for the first and work for the latter, at the expense of the immigrants who would be returned to their countries of origin.

THE CRITICAL ELECTIONS OF 1988

The year 1988 was to be a critical one with the presidential election scheduled for April–May. Looming before the electorate were pressing issues that had not been resolved during the two years of cohabitation: unemployment, the status of immigrants, the overhaul of the educational system to provide for professional and technical training; the maintenance of the welfare system in a society that appeared to move increasingly in the direction of economic liberalization, relatedly, the role of the state in the economy and the impact the projected (for 1992) full economic integration of the Common Market countries into one single market was to have on France, and, finally, the defense and foreign policy options for France.

The Presidential Election: April 24–May 8, 1988

President Mitterrand's seven-year term was to end in April 1988. There were many heir apparents both within the Socialist party and, even more so, among the centrist and conservatives. The first to declare his candidacy was the leader of the National Front—Jean-Marie Le Pen who criss-crossed the country and the summer resorts in 1987 to proclaim his message of keeping France French. Two communist candidates emerged—an orthodox one, André LaJoinie—endorsed by the Communist party—and a dissenter Pierre Juquin—appealing to dissatisfied Communist voters and some leftist groups. There were, in addition, two extreme left-wingers and the inevitable environmentalist—Antoine Waechter (see Table 4–7 for candidates and results). The three "serious" candidates were Jacques Chirac (the prime minister and leader of the RPR), Raymond Barre (running for the centrists and moderates—the UDF), and the incumbent president who waited until the very last day to proclaim his candidacy, on March 24, 1988. He seemed to do so reluctantly, to save the "state" from "factions and clans" that threatened it. Thus nine candidates contested the primary on April 24, but only the two that came first would contest the final and decisive round two weeks later—on May 8, 1988.

Mitterrand did not identify himself as a Socialist. In fact, the term was hardly mentioned in the early stages of the presidential campaign. He appeared as the spokesman of a unified France, self-appointed to maintain social peace, appealing to all above and beyond parties and factions—exactly in the manner in which General de Gaulle had be-

TABLE 4–7 The Presidential Election, March 24 and May 8, 1988

Registered	38,128.507
Abstentions	7,100.535 (18.62%)
Invalid	621.934 (2.0%)
Voting	31,027.972

First Ballot (Primary)

François Mitterrand (Socialist)	10,367,220 (34.09%)
Jacques Chirac (RPR)	6,663,514 (19.94%)
Raymond Barre (UDF)	5,031,849 (16.54%)
Jean-Marie Le Pen (National Front)	4,375,894 (14.39%)
Andre Lajoinie (Communist Party)	2,055,995 (6.76%)
Antoin Waechter (Ecologist)	1,149,642 (3.78%)
Pierre Juquin (Communist-Renovation)	639,084 (2.10%)
Arlette Leguillier (Socialist left)	606,017 (1.99%)
Pierre Boussel (Extreme left)	116,823 (0.38%)
Total left and extreme left	45.32%
Center-right and extreme right	50.87%
Ecologists	3.78%

The Second Ballot

Registered	38,168,869
Voting	32,085,071
Abstentions	6,083,798 (15.9%)
Mitterrand	16,704,279 (54.01%)
Chirac	14,218,970 (45.98%)

haved. It was a personal appeal, and the campaign, in this sense, was highly personalized.

Mitterrand's program was also a personal one, issued in the form of a "letter" addressed to all French on April 6. He indicated his commitment to "social solidarity," but also his intention not to renationalize the industrial firms that were privatized and his hope that controversial issues between managerial groups and the workers could be settled by direct talks and compromises. He promised to maintain social security and even expand it by providing a minimum salary for "the new poor"—the funds to come from a tax on the "great fortunes" (i.e., the wealthy), to maintain naturalization procedures for the immigrant workers and give full rights to education, work, welfare for them and their children, and to make new efforts to improve educational and training facilities. Above all, he pledged to work for European economic integration.

There was no question that Mitterrand would come first on the primary. The most important question, therefore, was as to who would be his opponent in the decisive balloting. There were two: Jacques Chirac, the leader of the RPR, the incumbent prime minister, and Raymond Barre, a centrist, appealing to the UDF and other centrist groups but without a party base. The RPR was the largest party in terms of membership and one of the better organized ones: with a strong national appeal, but also (unlike the Gaullists) a strong commitment to the liberalization of the economy. Chirac and his associates criticized the socialist ideology and policies and asked for liberal economic reforms—privatization of nationalized industries, lower taxes, lower public spending and subsidies, in a word, a return to private initiative and competition in order to bring about economic growth and to reduce unemployment. Chirac appeared as the leader of the new, young creative forces that he claimed had been stifled by the heavy hand of socialism. His motto was "renovation." He also used, however, many slogans associated with the conservative right and even the extreme right. He promised to find ways to return immigrants to their country of origin, to introduce tough repressive legislation to combat terrorism, and, in general, to preserve "law and order." He took credit for some economic improvements in the two years he had been prime minister, including the much lower inflation and a fractional lowering of the unemployment. Chirac also outlined his personal program in a pamphlet—"A Decade of Renovation"—emphasizing some of these themes:

strict laws for naturalization, the maintenance of social security but also of flexible arrangements allowing for private schemes for retirement and health, greater aid to families with three children or more, subsidies and tax benefits to small and medium enterprises, the participation of workers in the benefits of the firms in which they worked, and special provisions for expanding education and professional training.

Raymond Barre had been, until the end 1987, highly regarded by the public, as opinion polls indicated. He was a man of experience, having been prime minister for five years. A former professor of economics, he claimed to be the real "unifier" of the forces opposed to Mitterrand. He too advanced a liberal message—to help the individual firms by reducing taxes on capital gains and on individual income, to decrease sales taxes, to reduce inheritance taxes, and to continue with privatizations. The state, however, should support industrial activity— "Between interventionist socialism and a free-for-all liberalism," he said, "there is a well-thought pragmatism and this is where I stand."

The candidate of the National Front continued to proclaim the need of safeguarding the French national "identity." He argued in favor of a preferential treatment of the French in employment, social services, social welfare, education—the exclusion of the immigrants and their return to their home countries. He promised to reimpose the death penalty, provide subsidies for the family and salaries for mothers with more than two children, rewrite the school textbooks, reform the social security, cut down spending and drastically reduce taxes, and provide mechanisms to detect AIDS victims and isolate them. A passionate man—many thought a downright demagogue—Le Pen attracted big crowds. Some were attracted by his extreme economic liberalism, others by his moral exhortations for the revival of traditional family values, while still others by his evocation of French nationalism and his promise to rid France of immigrants—the workers from North Africa.

Little need be said about the Environmentalist—representing a movement that had not gained much strength in France. The Communist candidate reiterated the orthodox communist position favoring state intervention and controls in the economy, taxing the rich, raising the minimum wage to $1000 a month and to $500 a month for those without any resources, and reducing military spending and diverting the funds to secure social justice. The message of the dissenting Communist candidate was not different, and as for the two from the extreme left-wing, they argued for the destruction of the "capitalist order"—liberal or socialist!

The Issues. In a highly personalized campaign, the issues were more often perceived and weighed with reference to the personality of the candidates than on their own merits. This was even more so when the major candidates—in this case, Mitterrand, Chirac, and Barre—agreed on some fundamental policy questions: all three were intensely European, favoring the full economic integration of Europe by the end of 1992; all three shared the same outlook about foreign policy and defense, accepting the Gaullist legacy of the French nuclear posture, but also the need of close links with the Federal Republic of Germany and cooperation with NATO forces; and all three favored the maintenance of a strong defense and the same level of defense expenditures. What divided them on many policy issues was a matter of degree—and this became even clearer when the second ballot pitted Mitterrand against Chirac.

For the French public in general the major issues of concern were:

1. Unemployment.
2. The institutional arrangements regarding relations between the president and the prime minister.
3. Education and professional training that was closely linked to employment and economic growth.
4. Economic growth and technological development.

5. *Securité,* namely, "law and order."
6. Immigration and the position of the immigrants (especially from North Africa) in the French society.

The public remained divided on the issue of privatizations versus socialism, but remained strongly united in favor of maintaining the existing social legislation (health, unemployment, and retirement benefits). None of the candidates questioned what is known as *les acquis sociaux*—"entitlements". But none of the candidates had any new proposals on how to deal with unemployment. To the very end, the issue was bypassed and only indirectly debated. The solution was sought in the full European economic integration of 1992 that all the major candidates favored and in educational and technical training to produce the workers of the future.

The Results. As Table 4–7 has indicated, the great surprise of the first ballot was the strong vote for Le Pen. Despite a late surge, Barre came in third. Chirac, however, was unable to reach 20 percent of the vote—the lowest figure ever scored by "Gaullist" candidates. The combined score of all leftist candidates was 46 percent; that of all the centrist-rightist candidates was a little over 50 percent. The Ecologists held the other 4 percent. In terms of strict arithmetic, Chirac would win on the second ballot if all the voters that had voted for him, Barre, and Le Pen voted for him on the second ballot, even if a greater percentage of the ecologists went for Mitterrand.

The Second Ballot. Between the first and the second ballot, the issues became increasingly personalized, and in a special TV debate between Chirac and Mitterrand it became apparent that the president and the prime minister were engaged in a personal duel. Overriding the personal contest was the candidates' concern over the transfer of votes from the first to the second ballot. It became apparent, however, on the basis of exit polls that the bulk of the leftist voters,

including the Communists and the extreme left and the majority of the ecologists, would hold fast behind Mitterrand. This was not to be the case with the right. Not more than 52 percent of the Le Pen voters and not more than 72 percent of the Barre voters were planning to vote for Chirac on the second ballot—*the rest going to Mitterrand or to abstention.* The issue was settled on May 8, with Mitterrand winning by 54 percent against 46 percent for Chirac.

Ironically enough, Mitterrand owed his victory to Le Pen—for two mutually reinforcing, even if contradictory, reasons! First, by accusing Chirac of sharing with Le Pen some of the same extremist ideas with regard to immigrants, Mitterrand was able to attract moderate voters from among those who had voted for Barre or to neutralize them into abstention. Second, though he sharply attacked Le Pen and his policies, he benefited from the Le Pen voters, many of them concerned with social security and benefits to unemployed, on the second ballot. According to rough estimates, Mitterrand received about 1 million votes from among the Le Pen voters and almost 1 million from Barre's. Chirac received not more than 3.5 million from Le Pen voters and about 4 million from Barre's. It was an election so personal in character that not only the ideological and policy differences became blurred, but voters from the center-right crossed in substantial numbers to vote for Mitterrand—as president. It was one of the few instances when the French right went over to the left! It was something, however, that it refused to do in the legislative elections that followed, to which we now turn.

Legislative Elections: June 1988

Elected with what appeared to be a strong personal mandate, François Mitterrand ordered the dissolution of the National Assembly on May 14 and elections for the National Assembly for June 5 and June 12. The brief period of time allowed until the first ballot—between May 14 and June 5—threw the political parties in disarray. There was no time for party conventions and the preparation of party platforms. The Socialists rallied behind the president; the Communists maintained their independent positions without committing themselves at first to cooperate with the Socialists; the UDF and the RPR, put on the defensive, agreed to unite behind a single candidate—they hurriedly formed an electoral coalition—the URC: *Union du Rassemblement et du Centre* (Union of the Rally and the Center). They excluded any cooperation and any electoral alliances with the National Front to their right. The National Front was thus isolated. Even the threat to maintain their candidate on the second ballot rather than support a URC candidate and thus splitting the right-wing vote was not taken seriously, especially since it was not expected that many of the National Front candidates would get the requisite 12.5 percent of the registered voters and be allowed to run. As a result, even though the National Front maintained its voting national strength (about 10 percent), it finished with only one seat in the National Assembly!

The haste with which the election was called gave little time to the party organizations to designate carefully their candidates. Thus, a great deal of weight was given to regional and local party leaders. There was a high degree of what the French called the "notabilization" of the elections, that is, naming local notables (an elegant term for political bosses) as candidates. They were mostly mayors and presidents of regional and departmental councils. This helped the Communists, who had retained local strongholds, and even more the Socialists, the UDF and RPR (URC); it gave them all an advantage over the National Front. To a degree, also, it "denationalized" the election, with voters voting for candidates they knew rather than for national policies and parties. Campaigning was intense at the constituency level, even though the stakes appeared to be national, namely, supporting or not supporting the president.

The electoral system was the same as it

TABLE 4–8 Legislative Election, June 1988 (1st Ballot Returns)

		Deputies in National Assembly (seats)
First Ballot		
Registered	37,945,582	27
Voting	24,944,792 (65.7%)	
Valid ballots	24,431,615 (64.4%)	
Communist Party	2,765,761 (11.3%)	
Leftists	89,065 (0.4%)	
Socialist Party	8,897,392 (37.5%)	276
Allied with Socialists	279,316	
UDF & RPR (UCR)	9,207,000 (37.7%)	273
Rightists	697,272 (1.8%)	
National Front	2,359,228 (9.7%)	1
Ecologists and splinters	102.000 (0.24%)	577*

*Absolute majority = 289.

had been since 1958, except for the election of 1986.[3] It was clear that this system would again reproduce the bipolarization between the left (Communists and Socialists) on the one side and the UDR-RPR (in the few cases where the URC had failed to designate a single candidate) on the other. But it was not at all clear whether the URC (and its voters) would support an FN candidate and whether the FN candidate (and voters) would support a URC candidate on the second ballot.

First Ballot. When the results of the balloting on June 5 became known (see Table 4–8), they caused a surprise to political experts and consternation among the Socialists.

---

[3]A majority system with two ballots (a primary and a second ballot to elect the winner). On the first ballot a candidate that receives an absolute majority of the voters is elected; in the second ballot, only candidates with 12.5 percent of the registered voters and more are allowed to run. Candidates may withdraw, however, in favor of a better placed one.

Abstention was the highest ever—34.26 percent of the registered voters, some because they were certain of the Socialist victory, others because they were simply tired of voting (it was the third national balloting is six weeks), and still others because they had become increasingly indifferent to political solutions. For instance, in a poll taken at that time, only 32 percent thought that government action would improve the unemployment situation—40 percent relied on industrial managers to do so! Finally, there were those who were simply dissatisfied with the presidential campaign, the haste with which the election was decided, and the options the political parties offered—their abstention was a protest.

The real surprise was in the returns. Despite the victory of Mitterrand in the presidential election, the Socialist party failed to gain. The Socialists won 37.8 percent (as compared to 54 percent Mitterrand had won and to almost 40 percent they had won with their allies in the legislative election of 1981). The "dynamics" of the president's victory did not benefit them as it was widely expected; there was no spill-over. To their left the Communist party remained a shadow of what it was—even if its shadow seemed a little longer. They won 11.32 percent of the vote as opposed to 9.7 percent in 1986; they still were way behind the 16.3 percent they had won in the legislative election if 1981. It was, however, the only party to improve its strength when compared to the presidential election of April–May when their two Communist candidates together had scarcely won 9 percent. The RPR, the UDF, and other centrists under the label of URC did remarkably well. Their combined vote was 40.5 percent of the total—very little below their strength in 1986, but above their combined strength of Chirac and Barre in the presidential election of 1988. As for the National Front, they fell considerably behind Le Pen's presidential score (14.4 percent) with 9.78 percent, but maintained their strength to almost what it was in the legislative election of 1986. It was a strength that seemed ominous to many.

All in all, the left, including the Communists, various other leftists and the Socialists and their allies, received 49.2 percent while the center right and extreme right, 50.3 percent. Across the political landscape of France, left and right continued to confront each other on even terms!

The Second Ballot. On the second ballot—a week later, on June 12, 1988—the constraints of the electoral system we discussed became apparent. Only in 120 districts representatives were elected by absolute majority—almost evenly distributed between the Socialists and URC, with a sprinkling of Communists. In addition, some six seats were "won" by a single candidate because all other candidates failed to get the 12.5 percent of the registered voters. There was no contest. This left about 450 seats to be decided on the second ballot. In the vast majority of cases the contest pitted a Socialist against a URC. In some 30 districts the Communist candidate had come ahead of the Socialist, and in about 10, the National Front candidate had come ahead of URC. In almost 90 percent of the districts, both the Communist and the FN candidates had failed to gain the 12.5 percent of the registered voters on the first ballot and were automatically out of the running. Thus, a total of about 450 seats were to be divided between the left (in most cases a Socialist) and the URC.

The outcome would be decided by the way in which (1) voters who had abstained returned on the second ballot to vote and (2) by the way in which voters would transfer their vote for the respective candidates of left and right.

To the left, the answer was quite clear—the old *discipline republicaine* between Communists and Socialists resurfaced. An electoral agreement was quickly made with the Communists throwing their support behind the better placed Socialist candidate and the Socialists doing likewise. To the right, the same electoral imperatives were also at work, but the situation was somewhat more complex. URC candidates came ahead of the

National Front, except in some 10 electoral districts—where the National Front came first. URC refused, however, any overt alliance with the National Front, for fear that it would antagonize moderate voters. Only in some 14 electoral districts such an alliance was explicitly made, noticeably in the Marseille area where the National Front candidate was supported by URC against Communists or Socialists and in return pledged his support to a URC candidate. In almost all other districts, the National Front had failed to receive the requisite 12.5 percent of the registered voters. No alliances were, therefore, needed.

The results of the second ballot were determined by the transfer of votes *within* the right and the left, respectively, and by the percentage of the abstentionists that returned to the voting booth. The president, realizing that the outcome was uncertain, appealed to the voters to give him a majority in the National Assembly. "I need," he stated in a speech on June 9, "in order to carry out my mission, a stable majority, ready to vote without delay the laws of social justice, equality, national solidarity and economic modernization that I proposed. . . . Ready to support a government that will implement such a policy. . . . I'm asking the French voters to confirm the vote of the second round of the Presidential election."

Only few heeded him, and the abstentionists who returned to the voting booth split their votes between the left and the right. As for the transfer of votes, with the exception of some special cases, they worked as predicted. Over 80 percent of the Communist and left-wing voters voted for the Socialist candidate on the second ballot, and at least 75 percent of the Socialist voters voted for the Communist candidate. On the other side, almost 80 percent of the National Front voters voted for a candidate of URC. It was only in the handful of districts where a National Front candidate remained on the second ballot that a fair percentage of the URC voters failed to transfer their voters to him or her—giving the victory to the Socialists. (see Table 4–9.)

TABLE 4–9 Voting Patterns from First to Second Ballot

Marseille (5th Electoral District)	
First Ballot	
Riaggini (Communist) 14.68	5,092
Echochard (Socialist) 26.01	9,019
Toga (Cent. RPR) 26.38	9,148
Sandon (Diss. RPR) 3.42	1,188
Domenech (National Front) 27.01	9,367
Second Ballot	
Ecochard (Socialist) 51.38	19,360
Domenech (National Front) 48.61	18,315

Overall Trends. The election of 1988 confirmed some trends and raised many uncertainties about the future:

1. The Socialist party (even if it did not receive the expected majority) consolidated its position. As a single party (in contrast to the URC that remains divided into a number of groups), it appears to have become a dominant party. It has received, in the last decade, over 25 percent of the vote in all presidential and legislative elections. With a Socialist as president until 1995 and with a strong departmental organization, the Socialists are likely to withstand internal factional disputes and remain united. But is it a truly socialist party, some will ask? Is it becoming increasingly a social-democratic party, moving in the direction of the center, advocating only incremental reforms and ready to form coalitions with centrist groups?

2. The National Front (FN) maintained its position with about 10 percent of the vote. Can one say that it has become a permanent part of the political landscape—one, in fact, that may attract many right-wingers from the RPR while appealing to the discontented in a society that continues to face serious economic and social problems? Or is it likely to disintegrate if it fails to cooperate with the Gaullists or the Centrists?

3. With 11 percent of the vote, the decline of the Communist strength appeared to have been arrested. The party did well in its traditional strongholds and was able to attract again voters that were disappointed with the Socialist-centrists vocation. However, the 11 percent vote is misleading. In terms of the registered voters, the percentage of Communist votes was almost the same as it had been in 1986.

Furthermore, internal dissensions about the leadership and the practices of the Communist party may continue to undermine the proverbial Communist discipline—among members and voters. The *Renovateurs*—the small group that seceded from the party, calling for its "renovation"—are ever present, even though they failed to show any strength in the legislative election.

4. The hastily formed URC was but an electoral label, thanks to which the center-right parties designated single candidates and thus prevent the dispersion of the centrist and Gaullist voters. It faces serious problems. The most serious of all is that it comprises many political groups. It is torn between the appeal of the Socialists for some and the logic of electoral politics for most. The first calls for cooperation with the "dominant" party, and experience suggests that such a cooperation will involve their subordination. Electoral politics, on the other hand, suggest that the URC is capable of winning a majority if they remain united and if they find some way to attract the FN voters, but without openly cooperating with the FN or making any concessions to its extreme positions. The URC *and* the FN together have a numerical majority. But the moment explicit alliances are formed between the URC and FN at the constituency level, many of the URC moderate voters veer to the Socialists. Thus the URC is faced exactly with the problem the Socialists faced until 1981—cooperation with the Communists made moderates and even some socialist voters move to the center-right. Now it is cooperation with the extreme right—as long as it is a threat with 10 percent and more of the vote—that will push the moderates to the left.

5. The vagaries of the electoral system should be noted. On the second ballot, some 28 contests were so close that a shift of about 2,500 voters in 15 electoral districts where the Socialists won would have given the victory to URC, and a shift of not more than 1,400 in 13 districts where the URC won would have given the victory to the Socialists. In other words, a shift of not more than about 4,000 votes—about 0.02 percent of the total could have provided an absolute majority in the National Assembly for one or the other!

6. For those who sought a clear signal and a clear direction in the electoral verdict, it was difficult to find one. The electorate simply failed to follow up the Mitterrand victory in the presidential election—it was a personal vote. The Socialist party failed to get a majority in the National Assembly. But it was also the first time when a president dissolved and, after appealing to the electorate to vote for his supporters, failed. The convergence between presidential majorities and parliamentary majorities was broken, thus undermining for the future the position of the president. Dissolution of the National Assembly is a powerful way to impose discipline or to try to get a majority in the National Assembly. But dissolution may also boomerang when the electorate fails to return the majority that the president demands.

7. Finally, the greatest irony confounding all political analysts was that in the name of unity and moderation, and while schemes of a centrist coalition were drawn by both political analysts and political leaders to bring together the Socialists and the moderate center, the election amounted to a return to the traditional political landscape of France. On the one side, Communists and Socialists joined hands on the second ballot; on the other, all the conservative groups—from moderates to the extreme right—also joined forces on the second ballot.

The profiles of left and right remain familiar: to the left the voters remain younger, have no ties to the Catholic church, are mostly working class or unemployed (but about one-fourth of the workers and the unemployed voted to the right), and belong to lower income groups of the population—among white-collar workers and second-generation immigrants (when they registered and voted). To the right, the voters are relatively older, often practicing Catholics, and come from among the farmers, the liberal professions, the self-employed, the small merchants, and artisans. Thus, a good part of the lower middle classes vote to the right; so do also managerial groups and those who are employed in the private sector as opposed to the public sector.

The traditional sociological profile is enhanced by the geographic profile of voters—despite the even spread of socialist vote across the country. The Communists maintain their waning strength in the Paris suburbs, the north and northeast and in parts of the center of the country. The center-right continues strong and, in fact, thanks to the National Front, has gained in the Mediterranean south, the southwest, in Normandie and Brittany, as well as in Alsace and Lorraine and in Paris. Behind the volatility of the French elections in the last decade there is an electoral "entropy"—with the political geography of left and right returning to its historical blueprint.

GOVERNING WITHOUT A MAJORITY

The election failed to provide the Socialists with a majority. (see Figure 4–3). It was the purpose of the framers of the 1958 constitution, as we have seen in Chapter 2, to give government (both the president of the republic and the prime minister and his cabinet) the means to govern even when (as it had been the case throughout the Third and Fourth Republics) there was no stable parliamentary majority for a government in the legislature. The essence of a "rationalized parliament" lay in the barriers erected against parliament to prevent it from unseating the prime minister and the cabinet at will and to make it impossible for it to legis-

late without regard to the prime minster's wishes. It is something of an irony that the constitutional provisions enacted in 1958 can be used to protect now a Socialist president and a Socialist prime minster and his cabinet when the Socialists do not have a majority in the National Assembly. In fact the constitutional provisions are perfectly adequate to ensure the prime minister with stability in office. They are the following:

1. The government does not need to enact legislation except in matters (to be sure of major importance) limitatively enumerated in Article 34 of the Constitution. All others can be dealt with by executive orders. What is more, executive orders can set aside legislation if such legislation is found by the Constitutional Council not to fall within the matters for which the National Assembly is empowered to legislate. More than 150 "laws" have been modified or set aside in the past in this manner.

2. The prime minister can put the question of confidence on his legislative texts. They can be refused only if a motion of censure is introduced and is passed by an absolute majority of 289 votes. (Article 49–3). The text becomes law unless there is an absolute majority against it. As noted, this procedure has been used a number of times to enact important legislative measures—that is, nationalizations and privatizations, electoral reform, and others. Mauroy, the Socialist prime minister, used it

FIGURE 4–3 The National Assembly after the election of June 1988.

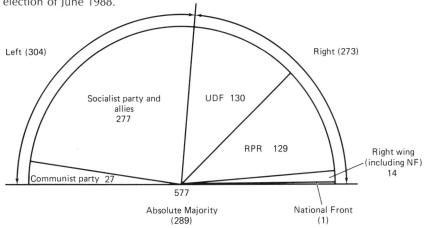

five times; Chirac, the center-right prime minister, seven times in two years. In effect, unless *all* parties in the present National Assembly, other than the Socialist, vote a motion of censure, the government can legislate! And if they were tempted to do so, the prospect of dissolution of the National Assembly and new elections may well force them to reconsider.

3. But there is yet an additional weapon in the hands of the government—a very powerful one. It can ask the National Assembly for authorization (Article 38) to legislate by executive order *(ordonnance)* on certain matters. The prime minister can ask for the enactment of a "framework law" to be implemented by ordonnances. If the National Assembly is unwilling to oblige, then the prime minister will combine his request with Article 49–3 putting the question of confidence. The only way for the National Assembly to reject the law of authorization, therefore, would be to introduce and pass a motion of censure, as described earlier. Otherwise, the framework law will be passed, and the *ordonnance* issued and signed by the president of the republic will have the force of law.

Thus the present Socialist government and the Socialist president (or for that matter any government and any president) do not need, strictly speaking, a parliamentary majority to support them, The constitutional provisions enacted in 1958 to avert the government paralysis that lack of majorities entailed in the past, suffice. As long as there is no absolute majority in the National Assembly to overthrow the prime minister, he and the president can legislate and govern.

5

Current Problems and Prospects

As the twenty-first century approaches, France faces many unresolved problems. Some date from the past, others are relatively new, while still others loom in the horizon. Many reforms have been tried and are being tried. But there has been little agreement—indeed quite frequently reforms were made only to be quickly set aside. Few of the reforms undertaken were allowed to settle in to become legitimized and operative, and, as a result, there has been considerable instability in the society and the economy. In this chapter we shall deal with a series of problem areas that confront the French polity and society.

REFORMING THE INSTITUTIONS

The constitution of the Fifth Republic and its institutions are, as we noted, solidly legitimized—perhaps more so than any other political regime was in the political history of France since the French Revolution of 1789. Constitutional reform, however, is always in the air.

The Presidential Term: One reform advocated is the shortening of the presidential term to five years. In fact, it was proposed in 1973 but never came to a conclusive vote. Both President Giscard d'Estaing and François Mitterand paid lip service to it. During the presidential election campaigns of 1988 in one of his televised addresses, Mitterrand indicated that he would support it. The argument is that a 14-year period for two consecutive presidential terms is too long for an incumbent; even the 7-year term is too long a period to sustain a mandate.

Related to the proposal for a five-year presidential term suggestions have been made to have the presidential and legislative election (the election for the National As-

127

sembly) coincide. In this manner, and contrary to the American experience, the election may lead to a clear mandate for a presidential majority. It is a suggestion that has been debated, but there is no indication that it will be formally introduced.

Referendums: Only six referendums have been held in France since the inception of the Fifth Republic, of which only two took place after de Gaulle left power in 1969. It is now suggested that the referendum be used frequently and that its scope be enlarged to include major policy questions—for instance, abortion or the death penalty or educational policy or the status of immigrants in France. The use of referendums, it is argued, will revive the public sense of participation and will take some of the most conflictual issues away from the National Assembly and the political parties directly to the people. Both Mitterrand and Chirac in their pronouncements during the presidential campaign of 1988 favored a more extensive use of referendums.

Executive-Legislative Relations: There appears to be continuing concern over the relationship between the executive and the legislature and about the subordination of parliament. Every prime minister and every president have acknowledged that the relationship is flawed and gave assurances that more autonomy will be given to the National Assembly. Virtually all of them promised (but broke their word) not to use the straightjacket procedures forcing the parliament to vote on the bills introduced by the cabinet by rejecting all amendments (the "blocked" vote) and not to use Article 49-3—whereby a bill becomes law unless the National Assembly musters an absolute majority to censure the prime minister. Yet all prime ministers have used these procedures. The National Assembly has been unable to set up investigating committees (committees of inquiry) to examine flagrant cases of executive misconduct or to use the question period when urgent and important matters are involved to force a full-dress debate and a vote—as it is the practice of the British Par-

liament. Suggestions have been made to enhance the role of investigating committees.

Limiting the Number of Elective Posts: One significant reform made in 1986 reduced the number of elective posts that one and the same person can hold—member of the European Parliament, member of the National Assembly or the Senate, member of the regional or departmental councils, mayor, sometimes in combination with a ministerial post. Now one and the same person can hold only *two* elective posts and is required to resign from all others. In this manner, personal political networks will be dismantled while a greater number of posts will be open to attract young political aspirants.

None of these issues has been divisive or even controversial. The most important "reform" of all—the gradual assumption of broader powers by the Constitutional Council to prevent legislation deemed unconstitutional from being enacted—appears to have been also accepted. Many consider it as a desirable counterweight to presidential and executive dominance.

THE ELECTORAL SYSTEM

The most controversial issue may well be the electoral law. Between 1958 and 1986 the majoritarian system with two ballots was consistently used and its majoritarian traits were progressively strengthened. The "exclusion percentage" was raised to 12.5 percent of the registered voters so that candidates who failed to get 12.5 percent of the registered voters (equivalent to at least 20 percent of those voting) were automatically eliminated from running on the second ballot. Small parties had little chance. In 1986 tactical considerations by the ruling Socialist party accounted for the abandonment of the majoritarian system in favor of proportional representation. But the moment the UDF-RPR coalition won a majority in the National Assembly in the election of 1986, it reenacted by a very narrow margin the previous majoritarian system. At present the Communists and the National Front, as well

as all smaller parties, favor a return to proportional representation, and the Socialists
remain committed "in principle" to it. As a
result, there is uncertainty as to what the future holds. A combination of the Socialist
and the Communist vote in the National Assembly (together they have a majority) may
bring forth a new electoral law. Much will depend on tactical considerations so that the
electoral system is becoming again a political issue rather than the framework within
which elections will take place and the political issues and differences decided. It is a situation that undermines the stability of political parties and constantly changes their
strategy; it affects the internal coherence of
party coalitions and affects electoral outcomes. Many argue in favor of a constitutional amendment to settle definitively the
electoral system to be used.

THE ECONOMY

Significant—at times drastic—reforms have
been made only to be unmade, in the course
of the last decade, with the economy moving
back and forth from phases of tight state
controls and nationalizations to phases of
economic liberalism, deregulation, and privatizations. During the early stages of the
first socialist government (1981–83), major
industrial sectors were nationalized, only to
be "privatized" after the UDF-RPR won the
election of 1986. Similarly, the welfare state
was expanded in the first years of the socialist government, with increases in pensions,
health care, family allocations, and unemployment benefits; wages were also raised
and job retraining programs gave the unemployed a year's respite. This social package,
however, began to be undermined after
1983. Runaway inflation and high trade deficits accounted for a policy of austerity that
reduced real wages to provide incentives to
industry and business. "Modernization", previously viewed in terms of state direction
and socialism, was now cast in terms of economic liberalism with great emphasis on the

individual entrepreneur. The French *patro-
nat* (big business and financial groups) put
also the emphasis on the individual firm.
Whereas in the past management and productivity were viewed in terms of large industrial or financial concerns, now the stress
was put on medium-sized and small ones—
"Small" became "beautiful"—allowing for
inventiveness, flexibility, and competitiveness!

The unemployment situation has remained in the last decade virtually chronic—
about 2.5 million unemployed—virtually
10 percent of the working force. No solution
was offered by either of the two major parties. Over and beyond loomed some intractable problems—the aging of the population
put added strains on those that worked and
had to pay for the welfare programs; the productivity of the French workers remained
low compared to that of many of their European partners; social legislation and wage
agreements, sponsored and defended by the
trade unions, often perpetuated high wages
in nonproductive sectors. In fact, trade
unions were concerned far more with maintaining an inflated and rigid pay scale than
coping with unemployment. Finally, there is
also the decision made to integrate the Common Market fully by 1992—to eliminate all
internal barriers so that goods, capital, and
labor can move freely across the borders of
the member states. It is a danger unless the
French manage to improve their industrial
plant and the productivity of their labor and
become competitive with the others; but it is
also a promise in that in a larger and growing European Market, the French would find
the incentives to compete and also share in
the overall economic growth that is anticipated.

NATIONALIZATIONS
AND PRIVATIZATIONS

Nationalization of banks and some key industries was aimed primarily at the control
and management of the economy, directly or

indirectly, by the state.[1] François Mitterrand gave the best reason for nationalizing; to protect French industry, the French economy, and French national security and integrity. We must, he pointed out, "give to France its industrial atomic force *(force de frappe)* to forge the sword of its industrial policy." Socialist ideology (anticapitalism and the quest for social justice) and nationalist imperatives reinforced each other to bring about the sweeping nationalizations that were introduced between September 1981 and February 1982 and have since been implemented.

By 1982–83 the Socialists themselves began to reconsider nationalizations—especially when it appeared that the goals they had set forth had failed to materialize. Not only nationalized industries were showing significant deficits, not only inflation and unemployment continued to mount, but their competitiveness within the European market and beyond began to be adversely affected. Gradually nationalizations came to a halt, and the private sector was asked to invest. Nationalized industries began to spin off some of their subsidiaries by selling them to the private sector and floating shares in the private market. "Privatizations," another word for denationalizations, and the freedom of the firm *(l'entreprise)*, became key words in the vocabulary of the political parties of the center and the right while the Socialists began to retreat from their early positions.

In March 1986, with the slim victory of the center-right parties and the defeat of the Socialists and the Communists in the legislative election, privatizations—returning what the state had taken to private hands—began in earnest and at a scale and pace greater than that undertaken by Margaret Thatcher and the Conservatives in England.

The government envisaged privatizing 65 major units—in industry, banking, communications, transportation, and insurance,

that had been nationalized. President Mitterrand did not allow the government to denationalize by executive order *(ordonnance)*, refusing to sign them. The government was forced to prepare special bills for each and every denationalization. Major nationalized units were privatized in toto or in part by floating stock in the market. Major banks such as Paribas, Sogenel (an Alsacian Bank Consortium), the Agricultural Bank of France, BTP (Construction and Public Works), Societè Génèral—a large bank that had been nationalized before 1981, and the CCF (Credit Commercial de France) were privatized, as were industrial units like Saint-Goban, Elf-Aquitane, and CGE (Companie General d'Electricité—nationalized in 1946), and the CGCT (telephone construction). In addition, radio and TV stations and many insurance companies were returned to the private sector. Half of the projected privatizations—about 30 of the projected 65 units—were enacted into law. In a period of about a year the socialist economic reforms were torn apart. The number of those that favored state ownership also declined. Only about 35 percent continued to favor it. In the presidential election of 1988 President Mitterrand took a pragmatic approach; he did not anticipate any further privatizations, but would not return to a policy of "renationalizing" either.

THE IMMIGRANTS AND THE FRENCH SOCIETY

France has had a long history of immigration—from Italy, Corsica, Poland, Spain, and Portugal and more recently from North Africa. European immigrants became easily assimilated. The cornerstone, in fact, of French policy was "assimilation"—assimilation into the French culture and tongue and nationality. But in the last 20 years, the wave of immigration from North Africa and some of the African colonies of France raised problems that defied assimilation. These immigrants—about 2.5 million—have a skin of a different color; they are Moslems—bringing with them their own religious practices; they have a

---

[1]For this brief sketch I am indebted to Jacques Blanc and Claude Brule, *Les Nationalisations Français en 1982.* La Documentation Français, 2 June 1983.

birth rate much higher than that of the French; and they often identify with the countries of their origin and not with France. Intermarriage and "assimilation" for them, or for that matter, for their children, appeared difficult.

While full employment lasted, the immigrants were not viewed as a problem. But when economic prosperity came to an end—as it did in the late 1970s—the French political leaders failed to develop a coherent policy about immigrants regarding their entry, their right to work, their claims on social services and education, the granting (if at all) of citizenship, or the terms under which they would be required or encouraged to return to their country of origin. Steps were taken to arrest the influx of new immigrants and to expel those who had entered the country illegally. Decisions were made also for granting citizenship to some. A major question, however, was the citizenship status of their children born in France: Could they become French citizens when they became 18 *automatically* or would they have to apply for citizenship and go through prescribed procedures? And what if they would fail to apply or if they would deny the citizenship when it was automatically granted?

Overriding such questions was the apparent hostile reaction of the public to foreign, that is to say, North African, immigrants. Culturally, ethnically, linguistically, and in terms of religious practices, they did not live up to the prevailing norms of French culture. The added burdens they put on the French educational and welfare expenditures provoked also the hostility of many. The situation was exploited by the extreme right-wing organization—the National Front—asking in the most unqualified terms for tight control over immigration policy and over immigrants; the granting of a preferential status in education, employment, and welfare to French citizens; and asking for the return of immigrants to their countries of origin. French "identity" was stressed, and only those that were assimilable (i.e., the European immigrants) might aspire to citizenship.

The extreme position the National Front however, has remained a minority position even though other political groups and forces echoed it. The Communists had been among the first to raise the issue of the status of immigrants after Communist mayors denied them, in some municipalities, public housing; the center parties equivocated, while many of the Gaullists began to move closer to the National Front. As a result, the immigrants and their status became a part of the political agenda and will remain on it for some time to come.

The question of French citizenship and of how to grant it to immigrants remains a complex one. Can it be granted automatically after some years of residence without satisfying any requirements of literacy and civic loyalty? Should those who refuse either to apply for it or who reject it when it is granted automatically be allowed to remain in France? Are religious differences incompatible with citizenship. (The same question can be raised about ethnicity (a gentle term for race) and language.) Above all, is "citizenship" to be distinguished from nationality? Negative answers would obviously suggest that such immigrants will have to return to the country of their origin simply because they fail to pass the test of assimilation. Positive responses, however, would suggest that France would move in the direction of a multiethnic, multiracial, multinational, and multireligious society—as in the United States and the Soviet Union. Diversity would give place to the vaunted uniformity of the French cultural tradition. The society would move into unchartered waters—at least for the French.

FRANCE IN THE WORLD

The Gaullist legacy of French independence, aloofness, and constant search for world power status and rank continues. It withdrew its forces from NATO and has relied upon its own nuclear weapons—the *force de frappe*—for its defense. It has modernized its forces with tactical nuclear weapons and has improved its delivery capabilities with seven nuclear submarines armed with multiple-targeted nuclear missiles. In addition, it has streamlined its conventional forces with a specialized and well-equipped contingent that can intervene in virtually any part of Europe and Africa—the Rapid Intervention Force. France is the only European country to maintain its military presence in many of its colonial outposts—French Equatorial and French West Africa—considered as within its "sphere of influence." The Gaullist goal of avoiding entangling alliances by playing an astute game of balance—sometimes in cooperation with its European allies—between the two superpowers continues to be pursued. But are the French means adequate?

The time has come for the question to be answered. French aspirations by far exceed its means. Not its past cultural influence, nor its economy and resources, nor its military power can compare with that of the superpowers, or for that matter, Japan or China, or the Federal Republic of Germany, of perhaps even England. Ambitious goals such as building an areospace industry, computer and communications, technology, military and nuclear weaponry, cannot be undertaken without the cooperation of European and U.S. firms. The development of a credible French defense strategy can no longer be exclusively French. It is imperative, in other words, to reconsider the Gaullist notion of "independence" in terms of genuine interdependence. Interdependence, first, with the European partners of the Common Market; interdependence, second, within the international community of industrialized nations and beyond, with the so-called Third World.

For a long time France has wavered in its commitment to European economic, let alone political, integration. Today, however, virtually the whole political class and the major political parties favor full Common Market economic integration by 1992. It calls for harmonization of taxation, welfare programs, labor and wage policies, and banking. It calls for the development of a European Reserve Bank to regulate currencies and ultimately to develop a European currency. It will allow for the full penetration of the French market by foreign (i.e., European and British) capital, foreign labor, foreign technology, and foreign investments. European "multinationals" will become the rule, and the share of the European market France gets will depend upon its resources, the productivity of its industry, and its competitiveness. France will have to get a share of the economy of Europe corresponding to the rate of growth envisaged—otherwise its economy will decline.

Growing interdependence, however, raises serious problems of common deliberation and common decision making, that is, of political integration. Political integration is in fact the second critical problem facing the French leadership. It calls for the pooling of the sovereign powers of the member states into a supranational political community. Many member states, like England, are opposed, while others favor it. France will have to play a critically important role, but as yet no clear-cut proposals for a genuine European political community have been made. Many claim that political leaders from both the left and the center-right are using Europe and European economic integration only as a way to defer hard choices needed to cope with unemployment at home without facing up to the political requirements of an integrated Europe.

French defense strategy is also entering a critical stage. With the dismantling of the INFs in Europe, U.S. deterrence has been weakened. The French deterrence, however, is not adequate, except in the context of a common European defense strategy and in conjunction with NATO. France, therefore, will have to define exactly its defense plans in cooperation with West Germany but also in cooperation with England, Italy, and the Benelux countries. It will have to decide on what kind of "sharing" it envisages with West Germany. Will it deploy its tactical missiles in the German territory? Will it accept and agree unequivocally to the notion that aggression against West German territory is also an aggression against France, thus covering Germany under its nuclear deterrent? A great deal of rhetoric has been used recently by the French leaders to indicate that they would indeed consider an aggression against West Germany to be tantamount to an aggression against France. Efforts have also been made, more on paper than in practice, to bring German and French conventional forces into binational units and to standardize European equipment and supplies. A common—even if a bilateral—defense, however, assumes procedures and institutions for the development and implementation of common strategy and a common foreign policy, in other words, of joint political decision-making arrangements. They are still to be devised or, in some cases, notably foreign policymaking for the Common Market countries, are only in the early stages of implementation. Europe continues to beckon. For some, it is a promise, for others a mirage, yet for others a prospect that will have to be realized very gradually and very carefully in the many decades to come. French political leadership will play an important role in defining the terms and the timing.[1]

Last, there is the nagging question about the adequacy even of an integrated European defense system. The dismantling of the Soviet INFs and the new opening in Soviet diplomacy under Gorbachev are viewed by some as a continuation of the same Soviet effort to "detach" Western Europe from the United States. What was not accomplished by the display of force in the later 1970s and the early 1980s may be realized now in the name of peace and coexistence. The European leadership, especially the German political leaders, may come to the conclusion that the Soviet Union is no threat and that U.S. presence in Europe is an obstacle to a rapprochement with the Soviet Union. The American protection may appear as an obstacle to the prospects of the reunification of Germany.

The manner in which France will define its relations with the Common Market countries and the relationship of the Common Market countries with the United States will, undoubtedly, be the most important defense and foreign policy issue that will be debated in the next decade. Without NATO, will Europe be able to defend itself against Soviet threats or intimidation? If not, what kind of European defense system? And what kind of links between it and the United States are needed?

BIBLIOGRAPHY

Selected Basic Sources

The following publications are indispensible for the student who knows French:

ANNÉE POLITIQUE. Published annually since 1944 by the Presses Universitaires de France. These volumes cover domestic politics, foreign relations, and economic trends.

SOFRES. Opinion surveys published annually— *L'Etat de L'Opinion,* ed. Seuil, Paris (particularly the issues for 1986 and 1987).

Since 1963, the *Revue Française de Science Politique* has regularly published articles that give excellent accounts of the development of, and trends within, political parties and elections.

Tableaux de l'Economie Française, published annually by the Institute National de Statistique et des Etudes Economiques, is an excellent compilation of social, demographic, and economic data.

The publication of *Le Monde, Cahiers et Documents,* for the presidential and legislative elections of 1981 and 1988 are of great value. Similarly, the publication of *Le Figaro, Etudes Politiques,* for the presidential and legislative elections of 1988 contain excellent analytical essays written by some of the best French political scientists.

The OECD *Annual Economic Surveys of France.* Published in English by the Organization of Economic Cooperation and Development, Washington, D.C.

The student will find an excellent overview of the first four years of socialism in

---

[1] For a fuller discussion see Part VII, The European Common Market.

France, in *The Economist,* February 9, 1985, under the title "A New Sense of Reality."

Suggested Readings

Except in a few cases, only books in English are mentioned. Detailed bibliographical material and references are found in most of the books listed.

AMBLER, JOHN S., ed. *The French Socialist Experiment.* Philadelphia: Institute for the Study of Human Issues, 1985.

ANDREWS, WILLIAM and STANLEY HOFFMANN, eds. *The Impact of the Fifth Republic on France.* Albany: State University of New York Press, 1981.

ARDAGH, J. *The New France: A Society in Transition.* Baltimore: Penguin, 1973.

ARON, ROBERT. *De Gaulle Truimphant: The Liberation of France, August 1944–May 1945.* New York: Putnams, 1964.

AVRIL, PIERRE. *Politics in France.* London: Pelican, 1969.

BIRNBAUM, PIERRE, ed. *Les élites socialistes au pouvoir. Les dirigeants socialistes face à l'Etat, 1981–1985.* Paris: Presses Universitaires de France, 1985.

CAPDEVIELLE, JACQUES, et al. *France de gauche, vote à droite.* Paris: Presses de la Fondation Nationale des Sciences Politiques, 1981.

CERNY, PHILIP G., and MARTIN A. SCHAIN, eds. *Socialism, the State and Public Policy in France.* New York: Methuen, 1985.

CHAPSAL, JACQUES. *La Vie Politiques sous la Cinquième République,* Vol. 1 (1944–73), Vol. 2 (1974–87). Paris, Presses Universitaires de France, 1988.

CHARLOT, JEAN. *The Gaullist Phenomenon.* London: Allen and Unwin, 1971.

COHEN, STEPHEN. *French Economic Planning.* London: Widenfeld & Nicolson, 1965.

CROZIER, MICHAEL. *The Stalled Society.* New York: Viking, 1973.

DeGAULLE, CHARLES. *The War Memoirs of Charles de Gaulle,* 3 vols. New York: Simon & Schuster, 1960.

———. *Memoirs of Hope and Endeavor.* New York: Simon & Schuster, 1970.

DUCHEN, CLAIRE, ed. *French Connections: Voices from the Women's Movement in France.* Amherst: The University of Massachusetts Press, 1987.

———. *Feminism in France: From May '68 to Mitterrand.* London: Routledge & Kegan Paul, 1986.

DUHAMEL, O., and JEAN-LUC PARODI. *La Constitution de la Cinquième Republique.* Paris, Presses de la Fondation Nationale des Sciences Politiques, 1988.

DUPOIRIER, ELISABETH, and GERARD GRUNBERG, eds. *Mars 1986: la drôle de defaite de la gauche.* Paris: Presses Universitaires de France, 1986.

EHRMANN, HENRY. *Politics in France,* 4th ed. Boston: Little, Brown, 1982.

GODFREY, JOHN F. *Capitalism at War: Industrial Policy and Bureaucracy in France, 1914–1918.* Leamington Spa, Hamburg, New York: Berg Publishers Limited, 1987.

GOUREVITCH, PETER. *Politics in Hard Times: Comparative Responses to International Economic Crises.* Ithaca, NY: Cornell University Press, 1986.

GRUBER, HELMUT. *Léon Blum, French Socialism, and Popular Front: A Case of Internal Contradictions.* Ithaca, NY: Center for International Studies, Cornell University (Western Societies Program Occasional Paper No. 17), 1986.

HALL, PETER. *Governing the Economy: The Politics of State Intervention in Britain and France.* New York: Oxford University Press, 1986.

HOFFMANN, STANLEY, *Decline or Renewal: France Since the 30s.* New York: Viking, 1973.

———et al. *In Search of France.* Cambridge, MA: Harvard University Press, 1963.

KEELER, JOHN T. S. *The Politics of Neocorporatism in France: Farmers, the State, and Agricultural Policymaking in the Fifth Republic.* New York: Oxford University Press, 1987.

KESSELMAN, MARK. *The Ambiguous Consensus: A Study of Local Gevernment in France.* New York: Alfred A. Knopf, 1967.

KOLODZIEJ, EDWARD A. *French International Policy Under De Gaulle and Pompidou.* Ithaca, NY: Cornell University Press, 1974.

MACRIDIS, ROY C. *French Politics in Transition: The Years After de Gaulle,* Cambridge, MA: Winthrop, 1975.

———and BERNARD BROWN. *The de Gaulle Republic: Quest for Unity.* Westport, CT: Greenwood Press, 1976.

MCMILLAN, JAMES F. *Dreyfus to De Gaulle: Politics and Society in France, 1898–1969.* London: Edward Arnold, 1985.

PARODI, MAURICE. *L'Économie et la Societé Française de 1945 à 1970.* Paris: Armand Colin, 1971.

PAXTON, ROBERT O. *Parades and Politics at Vichy: The French Officer Corps Under Marshal Pétain.* Princeton, NJ: Princeton University Press, 1966.

PENNIMAN, HOWARD. *France at the Polls: The Legisla-

tive Election of 1978. Washington, D.C.: American Enterprise Institute for Public Policy Research, 1979.

———ed. *France at the Polls: The Presidential Election of 1974.* Washington, D.C.: American Enterprise Institute for Public Policy Research, 1975.

REMOND, RENÉ. *The Right Wing in France from 1815 to de Gaulle.* Philadelphia: University of Pennsylvania Press, 1968.

RIDLEY, F., and J. BLONDELL. *Public Administration in France.* London: Routledge & Kegan Paul, 1964.

ROSE, RICHARD, and EZRA SULEIMAN, eds. *Presidents and Prime Ministers.* Washington D C: American Enterprise Institute for Public Policy Research, 1980.

ROSS, GEORGE, STANLEY HOFFMAN, and SYLVIA MALZACHER, eds. *The Mitterrand Experiment: Continuity and Change in Modern France.* Oxford: Polity Press, 1987.

SCHAIN, MARTIN A. *French Communism and Local Power: Urban Politics and Political Change.* New York: St. Martin's, 1985.

SINDER, DAVID. *Is Socialsim Doomed?* Oxford & New York: Oxford University Press, 1988.

SULEIMAN, EZRA. *Power and Bureaucracy in France: The Administrative Elite.* Princeton, NJ: Princeton University Press, 1974.

TIERSKY, RONALD. *French Communism 1920–1972.* New York: Columbia University Press, 1974.

WILLIAMS, PHILIP. *Politics and Society in De Gaulle's Republic.* Garden City, NY: Doubleday/Anchor, 1973.

———.*Crisis and Compromise: Politics in the Fourth Republic.* Garden City, NY: Doubleday/Anchor, 1973.

———. and MARTIN HARRISON. *French Politicians and Elections, 1957–1969.* Chicago: University of Chicago Press, 1970.

WILSON, FRANK L. *The French Democratic Left, 1963–69.* Stanford, CA: Stanford University Press, 1971.

WRIGHT, GORDON. *Rural Revolution in France.* Stanford, CA: Stanford University Press, 1964.

YSMAL, COLLETTE.*Le comportment electorale en France.* Paris: La Decouverte, 1986.

ZELDIN, THEODORE. *France, 1848–1945* Vol. I. Oxford: The Clarendon Press, 1973.

PART IV
THE FEDERAL REPUBLIC OF GERMANY— WEST GERMANY

*D. BRENT SMITH**

1

Introduction

Among the great industrial powers of the world, West Germany—the Federal Republic of Germany (FRG)—was clearly prosperous and stable in the late 1980s, though strained by a unique set of economic problems and internal tensions. It ranked thirteenth in population in the world (with over 61 million people), was fourth in gross national product (behind the United States, Soviet Union, and Japan), and had in 1986 become the leading export nation in the world, overtaking the United States.

While rebuilding itself from the ruins of Nazi Germany and providing jobs and housing for West Germans, the Federal Republic has found shelter and work for almost 15 million German expellees and refugees from

Eastern Europe and from Communist-ruled East Germany, called since 1949 the German Democratic Republic (GDR). Between 1960 and 1970 the Federal Republic's national income grew at almost 5 percent a year in real terms—that is, corrected for the effects of rising prices and money wages. West German national income had already outstripped the income of France by 1960 and overtook that of Britain in 1964. In the late 1960s, the average hourly wage in the Federal Republic was still less than half that of the United States, but by the mid-1970s, German industrial workers had achieved general parity with their American counterparts. The German economy withstood the world economic crises of the 1970s better than did most other industrialized nations, but in the early 1980s growth slowed markedly (with negative growth in 1981 and 1982).

Unemployment has hovered around 9 percent of the work force since 1983 while

*The author gratefully acknowledges the contribution of Karl W. Deutsch to this section in earlier editions of this volume (in particular, portions of Chapters 1–6); Deutsch and Smith coauthored the FRG section for the three previous editions.

Figure 1–1 The Changing Map of Germany.

inflation was held to less than 1 percent per year during the period between 1985 and 1987. Despite the economic downturn in the early 1980s, the FRG must be judged prosperous with a strong currency, a burgeoning trade surplus, and 1988 growth approaching 3.5 percent. In gross domestic product per capita, converted into dollars at market exchange rates, the FRG in 1988 ranked second—behind Japan and ahead of the United States.

A PICTURE OF STABILITY

Relative economic strength has been accompanied by remarkable stability in politics. Parties catering to political extremes have elicited little response from the voters. Early in the 1950s less than 3 percent of the total vote was cast for the Communists and less than 5 percent for the Sozialistische Reichspartei (SRP) and other splinter parties of the extreme right. The Federal Constitutional Court's outlawing of the SRP in 1952 and the Communist party (KPD) in 1956 was accepted with scarcely a ripple of protest by the bulk of the public. In 1967 a Communist successor party, the Deutsche Kommunistische Partei (DKP), was permitted to operate legally. Its share in subsequent federal elections has remained far less than 1 percent. On the far right, the ultranationalist National Democratic Party of Germany (NPD) received at most 8 percent of the votes in some provincial elections in 1966 and 1967. Its share in the 1969 federal election was down to 4.3 percent, and in subsequent federal elections it has remained well below 1 percent. The NPD did achieve 6.6 percent in 1989 Frankfurt municipal elections, winning representation in the Frankfurt city parliament. Another ultra right party, the Republicans, won 7.5 percent of the vote and representation in the 1989 West Berlin elections, and in the June 1989 European Parliament elections, they polled 7.1 percent nationwide.

A party of moderately conservative lean-ings, the Christian Democratic Union (CDU), and its Bavarian affiliate, the Christian Social Union (CSU), have together retained between one-third and one-half of the popular vote and, except for the period 1969–1982, political leadership of the FRG government, most often in coalition with the small Free Democratic party (FDP). Their main rival, the Social Democratic party (SPD), has concentrated on promoting the interests of labor and policies of social welfare within the framework of constitutional democracy and has relegated to second place its traditional ideological calls for socialism and the nationalization of industry. These moderate policies secured for the SPD a share increasing from one-fourth to over two-fifths of the vote until its support declined in the 1983 and 1987 elections. The SPD was a junior partner in a national coalition government with the CDU/CSU from 1966 through the 1969 election when it assumed leadership of a new coalition government with the FDP, displacing the CDU/CSU. This SPD/FDP coalition continued in power until 1982 when the FDP defected and joined forces with a new CDU/CSU government.

Despite what seemed for a time to be a trend in that direction, a two-party system has not emerged. The voting strength of the SPD never has been sufficient to carry it into federal office on its own, and the CDU/CSU has only once won a popular majority (in 1957), though it came close in both 1976 and 1983. In effect there has been a "two-and-a-half-party" or two-group" system at the national level, with both major parties—except for the 1957–1961 period of CDU/CSU rule—having been dependent on a coalition partner, in most cases the FDP. The Free Democrats provided the essential balance in both the 1969 and 1982 changes of power. In 1983, and again in 1987, delegates of the ecological, antinuclear Green party were elected to the federal parliament. Split by internal disagreement as to whether they should engage in coalition politics in the traditional sense, the Greens have joined in state government coalitions and at times have loomed as a potential partner to the SPD at the national level.

Accompanying all these developments has been a remarkable degree of social peace and political tranquility, this despite often vocal dissent and periodic terrorist activity. Changes in government have been orderly; strikes have been few and relatively easily settled. Politically steady and economically prosperous, the Federal Republic has been a picture of stability.

SOME STANDARDS FOR A MORE CRITICAL APPRAISAL

From the mid-1960s, the Federal Republic has been subjected to a rising amount of criticism, both from within (in the main, from intellectuals and university students) and from outside the society. By what yardsticks do these critics measure the success story of West Germany? Certainly they do not all speak with one voice. Their complaints vary widely, and so do their demands.

One set of critics cannot and will not forget the country's tragic past. In three great critical periods of our century, they insistently remind us, Germany chose a course of oppression and destruction. Germany had a full share in bringing on World War I. In the midst of the Great Depression, in 1933, Germany accepted and supported the dictatorship of Adolf Hitler and the National Socialist party. In 1939 Hitler's Germany incurred the major responsibility for bringing about World War II. And the Nazis were responsible for acts of genocide committed in its course.

What was it—the critics ask—what was it in the structure and institutions of German society, in the psychology and culture of the German people, that made these things possible? And if there have been some fatal flaws beneath the orderly surface of German life in the past, may not these hidden flaws still be there, ready at some future point to drive the German people into dictatorship, war, and catastrophe?

Another set of critics point to a second, related, theme, that of social structure, During the first half of this century, the governments and constitutions of Germany changed quickly and often. West Germany, either independently or as part of greater Germany, has been governed by five regimes in succession: by a monarchy (1871–1918), a unitary republic (1918–1933), the National Socialist dictatorship (1933–1945), Allied military governments (1945–1949), and a federal republic (since 1949). As noted in Figure 1–1, the territory comprising Germany has undergone change with each of the five regimes. Big business firms and rich families, such as those of Krupp and Thyssen, have remained prosperous and influential throughout all these changes. Do they not form a part, some critics ask, of an underlying social and economic structure, unequal and undemocratic but more fundamental, durable, and powerful than any change in the forms of law and government? And if so, is not the Federal Republic condemned to submit to this underlying structure at future moments of crisis and decision, and so presumably to reenact much of its past? What hope is there for democracy to become truly strong and stable as long as this basic undemocratic social structure remains undisturbed?

A third set of critics do not measure the Federal Republic by comparing it with the past; rather, they insist on measuring it against their own idealistic conception of democracy—a democracy that does not yet exist anywhere except in their thoughts and aspirations. "Differences in the conditions of life of particular social groups" were seen as "very large" by 60 percent of students and 51 percent of nonacademic youth in a survey whose results were published in 1968. At the same time, according to the survey, 60 percent of the voters and about 50 percent of the young saw "practically no chance to influence the political process in the Federal

Republic in any other way than through the formal act of voting, to be repeated every four years."[1] These results presaged the increasing disaffection of young Germans from their political system which manifested itself in the development and growth of the Greens in the late 1970s and 1980s.

Outside critics found grounds for concern in their analyses of the fortunes of the neo-Nazi NPD and follow-on ultraright movements and in what they have deemed to be repressive measures employed by the Federal Republic to combat terrorism.

The critics' portrayal of an infertile democratic climate must be weighed against manifestations since the mid-1970s of such phenomena as grass-roots voter initiatives and the infusion of members of a "successor generation" into the leadership ranks of postwar political organizations.

THE PROVISIONAL STATE

In most states both the government and the people know clearly what the territory of the state is and who its citizens are, as well as what is foreign territory and who are foreigners. Under constitutional regimes, they usually also know what the constitution of the country is. None of these matters was clear when the Federal Republic of Germany came into being in 1949. All definitions were to be provisional, pending the eventual reunification of West Germany and the Communist-ruled "Eastern Zone," which became the GDR. Only by the early 1970s did the provisional seem to become more permanent. The FRG includes two-thirds of the area of present-day "Germany" and more than three-fourths of its population. One-third of the area and 16.6 million Germans are included in the GDR.

[1]Rudolf Wildenmann and Max Kaase, *Die unruhige Generation: Eine Untersuchung zur Politik und Demokratie in der Bundesrepublik* (Mannheim: Lehrstuhl für politische Wissenschaft an der Universiät Mannheim, 1968).

It used to be widely believed in the West, and particularly in West Germany, that the Soviet-dominated government of the GDR lacked popular support, that it would fall as soon as Soviet military backing was withdrawn, and that the territory and population of the GDR would then quickly become reunited with those of the Federal Republic under a single national German government. Accordingly, the government of the Federal Republic—like that of the United States and other Western allies—long denied any type of recognition to the GDR. By the same token it officially considered only the FRG to be the forerunner and trustee of a future reunited German national state.

This reunited national state would comprise almost 80 million people and would form by far the strongest power in Europe. According to West German political and legal doctrine, the constitution of that future, reunited Germany would have to be drawn up by the representatives of its entire population. Until that time, the Federal Republic with all its laws and institutions would in theory be provisional, since nothing must take away the right of a future all-German constitutional convention to change the structure of the government.

Not only the frontiers of the Federal Republic but even those of a reunited Germany were provisional. The government of the Federal Republic, backed by the United States and other Western allies, at the outset refused to recognize the eastern frontiers of the GDR—the so-called Oder-Neisse line—and prior to 1969 it insisted on the full or partial restoration of former German territories east of that frontier.

Beginning in 1969, the SPD/FDP coalition government of Chancellor Willy Brandt worked energetically toward a settlement of these problems. In his governmental declaration in taking office, Brandt recognized the existence of "two states in one German nation." In 1970 treaties were initialed between the FRG and the Soviet Union, and the FRG and Poland, in which the inviolability of the Oder-Neisse frontier was recognized. Ratification of these treaties followed an agreement on the status of West Berlin, and of Western rights of unhampered access to that city. (The interplay of domestic and international developments in relation to Chancellor Brandt's *Ostpolitik,* Eastern policy, will be discussed more fully in Chapter 3.)

In theory, the Federal Republic is still considered provisional with respect not only to its boundaries but also to its constitution—a legalism that is contradicted in fact by the undisputed sovereignty of two German states. Since its adoption in 1949, the constitution has been referred to as a Basic Law, a name that underscores the document's temporary character. References to the provisional character of the Federal Republic's institutions have become rare with the passage of time.

The FRG continues, however, to claim to represent the entire German people, with that people's history and traditions. It backs this claim with a national policy of resettlement and indemnification of East German refugees and expellees from Eastern Europe. The policy has committed the West German taxpayer to aiding millions of persons who were citizens of the Germany of 1937, or even the Germany of 1914, solely on the grounds that they could be considered German in terms of language, culture, and political traditions.

This implied appeal to German tradition and the past has had a strange ring for some ears. For interwoven with the long and proud history of a great nation is a troubled German tradition and a turbulent past that stretches for centuries behind the four decades of peace and relative prosperity enjoyed by the Federal Republic.

Major Events of the Federal Republic of Germany Since 1945

May 8, 1945	Capitulation of German army marks end of World War II in Europe; Germany split into zones of occupation.
September 1946	British and Americans complete unification of their zones of occupation into a bizone.
June 5, 1947	U.S. Secretary of State George Marshall announces a plan for comprehensive American aid in rebuilding Europe.
June 1948	Western powers implement a currency reform in their zones of occupation and West Berlin. The Soviets retaliate by cutting off all access routes to Berlin. The Western allies organize an airlift to supply West Berliners until the blockade is lifted, May 1949.
September 1, 1948	A West German Parliamentary Council meets for the first time in Bonn.
May 23, 1949	The Basic Law (West German constitution) is officially promulgated by the Parliamentary Council, marking the birth of the Federal Republic.
August 1949	Elections for the first Bundestag take place; Konrad Adenauer is elected as the FRG's first chancellor by the Bundestag, September 15.
October 7, 1949	Establishment of the German Democratic Republic from the Soviet zone of occupation.
May 1952	The Federal Republic signs a general treaty with the three Western powers and also signs the Treaty for a European Defense Community; the GDR begins to seal off the zonal border with barbed wire.
June 17, 1953	A workers's protest demonstration in East Berlin leads to general insurrection in the GDR which is quickly put down by Soviet forces.
October 1954	The FRG joins NATO and the West European Union.

May 5, 1955	The FRG attains full sovereignty as the high commissioners of the Western occupying powers declare the Occupation Statute ended.
September 1955	Adenauer travels to Moscow to establish diplomatic relations and negotiate the release of remaining German prisoners of war.
January 1956	The West Germany Bundeswehr receives its first volunteers; universal military conscription is voted by the Bundestag in July.
March 25, 1957	The FRG signs the Treaties of Rome and joins the EEC and EURATOM.
November 1958	Khrushchev precipitates a crisis by demanding withdrawal of Allied Powers from Berlin and creation of a demilitarized free city.
November 1959	The Social Democrats adopt a new party program that marks a departure from Marxist ideology and acceptance of the FRG's social market economy.
June 1960	The SPD announces its willingness to support the concept of national defense and the FRG's Atlantic and European treaty framework.
August 13, 1961	The GDR seals off the border between East and West Berlin and begins construction of a wall.
October 1963	Adenauer steps down as chancellor and is succeeded by Ludwig Erhard.
December 1, 1966	A "Grand Coalition" of Christian Democrats/Christian Socialists with Social Democrats replaces Erhard's governing coalition.
October 21, 1969	Willy Brandt is elected chancellor by the Bundestag as a socialist/liberal coalition comes to power. The Christian Democrats/Christian Socialists go into opposition.
March 1970	Chancellor Brandt travels to Erfurt, GDR, to meet with the GDR premier. They meet again in May in Kassel, FRG.
August 12, 1970	A treaty between the FRG and the Soviet Union is signed in Moscow in which both sides agree to a renunciation of force and the recognition of the inviolability of existing borders.
December 7, 1970	Treaty similar to Moscow Treaty is signed in Warsaw between FRG and Poland.
September 1971	Four-Power Agreement on Berlin is signed.
April 1972	Brandt's governing coalition loses its effective majority through defection of deputies; an attempted constructive vote of no confidence to replace Brandt with Christian Democrat Rainer Barzel fails.
May 17, 1972	The Moscow and Warsaw Treaties are ratified in the Bundestag, with the abstention of the opposition Christian Democrats/Christian Socialists.
November 1972	A *Grundvertrag* (Basic Treaty) between the FRG and the GDR is finalized in the final days prior to new elections. Brandt is returned to power with the Social Democrats receiving their first plurality.
May 11, 1973	The *Grundvertrag* between the two German states is ratified by the Bundestag.
September 1973	Both German states are admitted to the United Nations.
May 1974	Brandt resigns as chancellor in the wake of a spy scandal and is replaced by Helmut Schmidt.
September 1977	A wave of terrorism reaches its climax with the abduction of industrialist Hanns-Martin Schleyer. In October, a Lufthansa aircraft and its passengers are taken hostage and forced to fly to Somalia where they are freed by troops from a German special unit. Imprisoned terrorist leaders commit suicide and Schleyer's body is found.
December 12, 1979	NATO decides, with FRG support, on a two-track decision with modernized American missiles to be placed in Western Europe if arms reduction negotiations are unsuccessful.

Major Events of the Federal Republic of Germany Since 1945 (cont.)

December 1981	Schmidt meets with GDR leader Honecker in the wake of strained East-West relations over Afghanistan and Poland. Soviet leader Brezhnev had visited Bonn in November.
October 1, 1982	In a constructive vote of no confidence, Helmut Kohl replaces Schmidt as chancellor as the Christian Democrats/Christian Socialists return to power in coalition with the Free Democrats (who bolted from Schmidt's coalition.)
March 6, 1983	The Kohl coalition government emerges from new elections still in power with a comfortable margin. The ecological and antinuclear Green party enters the Bundestag for the first time.
November 22, 1983	The Bundestag votes in favor of placement of U.S. Pershing II and cruise missiles (in connection with the NATO two-track decision) following stormy debate and the opposition of Social Democrats and Greens.
May 1985	Bonn hosts the Economic Summit meeting of Western leaders. Later the same week President Reagan joins in ceremonies commemorating the fortieth anniversary of the defeat of Nazi Germany, including a controversial visit to a Bitburg war cemetry with Chancellor Kohl.
January 25, 1987	Kohl's government coalition retained in federal elections with significant CDU/CSU and SPD losses and major gains by the FDP and Greens.
August 1987	Kohl pronouncement agreeing to the inclusion of FRG-maintained Pershing 1A missiles cleared the way for finalization of the U.S.-Soviet INF Treaty.
September 1987	Landmark visit of GDR leader Erich Honecker to the Federal Republic.
October 1987	Suicide of Schleswig-Holstein Minister President Uwe Barschel in wake of political scandal following revelations of "dirty tricks" employed in his September state election victory; his rival, Björn Engholm (SPD) wins landslide victory in follow-on May 1988 election.
July 1988	Major tax reform legislation enacted.
October 1988	Visit of Chancellor Kohl and five cabinet ministers to the Soviet Union for initial meetings with Mikhail Gorbachev; signing of cooperative economics and research agreements including a DM 3 billion West German bank credit for modernization of Soviet consumer goods industries.
January 1989	CDU/CSU coalition unseated in West Berlin electoral defeat with national reverberations as ultraright Republican party wins 7.5 percent of vote. SPD and Greens form governing coalition.
May 1989	President Bush visits FRG in aftermath of NATO summit during which US and FRG achieve compromise on short-range missile modernization pace and on timing for short-range missile negotiations with Soviets.
June 1989	Gorbachev visit to FRG with signing of eleven treaties and issuance of a West German-Soviet Joint Declaration.
June 1989	Republicans (extreme right) win 7.1 percent of the national vote and representation in the European Parliament; Republican votes come largely at the expense of the CDU and CSU.

The German Political Heritage

Every national political system is heavily influenced by history. The physical layout of a country, with its cities and transportation routes; its major social, economic, legal, and political structures; the language and culture of its people; and even many of their character traits and political memories—all bear the mark of the past in which they developed.

Each generation of Germans has made its own history, even though not under conditions of its choosing. Each generation made its history in an interplay between the pressures of the past and the decisions of the present, and these decisions in turn became a part of a new past in the face of which the next generation had to make its own decisions.

This chapter will focus on the major choices made in German politics over a hundred-year period that saw several different regimes: a loose confederation of particularist states, an empire under Prussian hegemony, the Weimar Republic, and a Nazi dictatorship. The vacuum created with the demise of Hitler and the foundations of the current Federal Republic of Germany are addressed in the next chapter.

IN SEARCH OF STATEHOOD: A LEGACY OF PARTICULARISM

More than 1,100 years ago, the tribes of people in what now comprises Germany were united under Karl der Grosse (Charlemagne) in a first German empire. Divided into three realms and eventually into innumberable principalities, Charlemagne's empire survived only in the guise of a Holy Roman Empire, a loose federation that ultimately came under the control of the Haps-

145

burgs, an Austrian dynasty. The German states were split further by the civil strife accompanying the religious wars during the Middle Ages. Germany became the center of the Thirty Years' War (1618–48), which engulfed Europe. Germany was ravaged by this war and its population reduced by one-third.

At a time when strong, centralized nation-states were being formed in England and France, Germany remained disunited, dominated in part by Austria and subject to the forays of the French kings. The eighteenth century witnessed the rise of Brandenburg-Prussia from a small kingdom to a European power with a preeminent position in northern Germany. Prussian administrative efficiency and military prowess won the admiration of other Germans.

In 1815, Prussia acquired the Rhineland, which included the industrial Ruhr area. Under Prussian leadership, a customs union, the *Zollverein,* from 1834 on united the territories of all the German states except Austria. In the half-hearted and short-lived revolution of 1848, German liberal leaders tried to unite Germany in a single empire on a constitutional and middle-class basis. But they failed to win either the cooperation of the Prussian court and aristocracy or the sustained support of the mass of the population, which was still predominantly rural and largely conservative.

In the following two decades, however, the growth of industry and banking, the establishment of a railroad network and postal system, and the acceptance of a unified code of commercial law all served to knit the German states more closely together than ever. Through a skillful combination of political and military moves in three wars in 1864, 1866, and 1870–1871, the Prussian statesman Otto von Bismarck greatly enlarged the territory of Prussia and then established a new unified German empire. It preserved and enhanced the power of the Prussian monarchy and aristocracy while winning almost solid middle-class consent and widespread popular support.

THE SECOND GERMAN EMPIRE, 1871–1918

This new German empire was ruled by the Prussian monarch, who now also became the German emperor, and the possessor of sweeping emergency powers under a new constitution. The emperor appointed a chancellor, who was responsible to him rather than to the legislature. The chancellor, in turn, was in control of the ministers of his cabinet; he, rather than the legislature, could appoint or dismiss them.

The imperial legislature had comparatively little power. It was divided into two chambers. One, the *Bundesrat,* consisted of delegates of the 25 states, with Prussia filling 17 out of the total of 58 seats, and usually commanding additional votes from several smaller states. Moreover, since 14 votes sufficed to block any constitutional amendment, Prussia had an effective right of veto on such matters. The Prussian delegates to the Bundesrat were appointed by the Prussian government, which was subservient to the emperor in his role as king of Prussia. The legislature in the state of Prussia was elected by an extremely unequal three-class franchise that ensured its effective control by the landowning nobility, and to a lesser extent by the upper-middle class.

In contrast with this extreme form of class franchise underlying the Prussian legislature, Bismarck's constitution for the empire provided for a second legislative chamber, the *Reichstag* (chosen by popular election), which was designed to attract a greater share of popular interest, and in time, loyalties to the empire. However, while the Reichstag made a good sounding board for speeches and debates, it had no real power to decide; even the taxes for the imperial budget could be collected and spent by the imperial government without the Reichstag's consent.

The German emperor thus had vast powers and was subject to no effective constitutional control. The first emperor, Wilhelm I, deferred to Bismarck's personal prestige and influence as chancellor, so that the system worked not too differently from the way a British prime minister and cabinet might have functioned. From 1888 on, however, the weaknesses of Bismarck's constitution became visible. A new and erratic emperor, Wilhelm II, succeeded to the throne; Bismarck himself was soon replaced by a succession of less able and more subservient chancellors; and German policy began its fateful drift toward diplomatic isolation, an arms race with Britain, France, and Russia, and the precipice of World War I.

It would be wrong, however, to see the main causes of the German drift into World War I in the personal shortcomings of Wilhelm II or in the constitutional defects of the Second Empire. Behind the constitutional forms stood the reality of a social and economic structure dominated by an alliance of the two most powerful interest groups of the country: the landowning nobility with its strong links to the army and bureaucracy and the rapidly rising big-business class in industry, commerce, and banking—the "big *bourgeoisie*," as its critics sometimes called it. The policies of high protective tariffs for industry and agriculture; of active efforts at colonial expansion; of a frantic search for international prestige; and of ever-increasing expenditures for armaments—all were backed by the most powerful interest groups and elites of the empire. In domestic politics, these policies tended to preserve or even enhance the privileges of the industrial and agrarian elites.

These policies were overwhelmingly supported by the German middle class, and had substantial support throughout the population. Between 1890 and 1914 the Germans found themselves in a world of rising tariffs and expanding colonial empires. Coming late upon the scene of colonial expansion, many of them accepted blindly the proposition then enunciated by French and British as well as by German statesmen: that any great industrial country had to win colonies, *Lebensraum* ("living space"), and "a place in

the sun" if it was not to lag behind and eventually perish in the struggle for national survival.

World War I proved devastating beyond anyone's expectations. About 2 million German soldiers lost their lives, and almost another million civilians died through the hardships of the food blockade imposed by the Allies during the war and prolonged for some time after the armistice of November 11, 1918. As a result of the war and the ensuing period of economic hardship, Germany was thoroughly spent and defeated. A popular legend persisted, however, that a German military on the brink of victory had been "stabbed in the back" by the social democratic successors to the abdicated emperor.

The Treaty of Versailles with its harsh terms and its attribution of war guilt solely to Germany was humiliating to many Germans. Germany lost all its overseas colonies, and in Europe had to give up Alsace-Lorraine to France and important territories in the east to a reconstituted Poland. There was left an impoverished and exhausted country, which now became a republic but remained burdened with a large debt of reparations imposed by the victorious Allies.

THE WEIMAR REPUBLIC, 1918–1933

The political and military collapse of the empire in 1918 found most German parties and leaders unprepared for the possibility of a Germany without an emperor, without the interlocking complex of noble landowners, high-ranking military officers, and bureaucrats, and without the concentrated elite of big industry and finance. The republic became a new façade on an old building. And since democracy had come to Germany because no alternative presented itself, rather than democracy being the end product of a popular struggle, the new republic found itself without a respected democratic leadership.

The Political Culture

About one quarter of the electorate continued to hold nationalist and militarist views. They would have preferred to see the old empire go on unchanged, with its black, white, and red flag, its arms, and its authoritarian institutions. Most of the nationalist voters came from the middle class and the peasantry. They were represented by the conservative German National People's party and by the (at first much smaller) National Socialists, the Nazis. They received significant support from segments of big business, of the landed classes, and of the high-ranking bureaucracy, particularly the judiciary and the military. These Nationalist voters never forgave the new republic for allegedly betraying all the traditions and aspirations of the army and the empire in World War I.

The Nationalists and the Nazis rejected the republic's liberal constitution, as did the Communists, who split from the German Social Democratic party (SPD) in 1918. The republic was continuously opposed by more than one-third of its population.

The majority of the socialists retained the old party name, remained oriented toward more moderate welfare and state reforms, and soon rallied to the active support of the republic. In early 1918, however, most SPD leaders had not thought seriously about anything more radical than a constitutional monarchy, and neither had the leaders and members of the moderate middle-class parties—the nationalist-liberal German People's party, the liberal German Democratic party, and the Center party, which represented the interests of Roman Catholic voters. Before 1918 none of these groups had advocated a republic for Germany. Thus, when in that year the monarchy suddenly lost so much of its former popular support that only a republic appeared practical, nobody seemed prepared to draft its constitution or make it work should difficulties arise.

The republic thus started out as a makeshift type of government—and it did so under near anarchy. To suppress the challenge from the radical left in the tense winter of 1918–1919, the SPD and the moderate middle-class parties allied themselves with the German generals and officers who still controlled army units after the armistice in November 1918. The military officers supplied the main force that suppressed radical leftist uprisings. In return, they received a great deal of formal and informal influence over the reduced armed force of the republic—the *Reichswehr,* whose strength the peace treaties eventually were to fix at 100,000 men.

The early agreement of the SPD with the generals was supplemented within a few days by an agreement between the leaders of the major trade unions and the representatives of big-business management to form the *Zentrale Arbeitsgemeinschaft* (Central Cooperative Group) for the purpose of reducing industrial conflicts and restoring production that would meet peacetime needs. These arrangements kept the number of strikes to a minimum, reduced the influence of radical groups in the factories and the unions, and tended to preserve or restore the authority of management. This was considered necessary for maintaining production, but it left big business inordinately powerful.

The agreements with the generals and with the big industrialists symbolized a larger fact. The bulk of the social and economic structure of imperial Germany was preserved in the Weimar Republic. The large landed interests, the personnel and organization of the civil service hierarchy, the class-ridden judiciary, no less than the monopolies, cartels, and near-monopolies of big business and finance and the core of the military, were taken over more or less intact. They continued to function and exercise their influence in politics and everyday life.

The Weimar Constitution

A constitution for the new republic was drafted in the small town of Weimar, symbolic as the residence of Goethe in the classic period of German literature and safely removed from the labor unrest and political turmoil of Berlin and the other industrial regions of the country. The main provisions of the constitution were remarkably democratic. In fact, it was the drafters' primary aim to bring into existence a democratic system representative enough of the people to be worthy of the adjective *democratic*. But at the same time many of the drafters recognized that it would be difficult to transform the political habits of a people overnight. Thus the framers tried to balance the democratic features of the constitution with strong executive powers as safeguards. For example, they concluded that the country needed a strong president as a focus for the people's desire for a respected authority figure standing above parties.

The constitution of Weimar gave first place to the elected legislature, the Reichstag, and it gave to that body the power to approve and dismiss the chancellor and his ministers. At the same time, however, it raised a second power to the same level: a popularly elected president was given the power to nominate the chancellor, to dissolve the Reichstag, and, in case of a national emergency, to rule by decree. Much of the power of the republic could thus become concentrated in the hands of two men, or even subservient to the will of one. A strong president with a compliant chancellor, or a strong chancellor with a compliant president, could use the vast emergency powers of government to destroy the constitutional regime.

The Record of Weimar

Since the early 1920s, many writers have argued that the weaknesses and ultimate fall of the Weimar Republic were due to the fact that the revolution of 1918, which created it, was far less thoroughgoing than the English Revolution of 1640–1649, the French Revolution of 1789–1795, or the American Revolution of 1776–1783, not to mention the vast upheaval of the Russian Revolution of 1917–1921. Each of these more far-reaching revolutions, so the argument goes, produced a fairly strong government and a stable political regime. The less far-reaching German Revolution of 1918, according to this view, went far enough to enrage its conservative enemies, but not far enough to acquire many strong beneficiaries and friends. Hence, it produced only a feeble and unstable political system.

There is some truth in this argument, but it remains one-sided. It overlooks one central fact of the 1918–1920 period: the bulk of the German people in 1918 did not want a drastic social revolution, and the majority of German workers and returning soldiers did not want it either. What they did want was peace, food, clothing, work, and a chance to start life again with their families. All these things were obtainable without a social revolution, and none of them seemed obtainable through any such deep and prolonged upheaval. After the armistice of November 11, 1918, the republic was at peace abroad. Few workers desired civil war in which they could expect to confront bitter middle-class resistance, an intact officer corps, and probable Allied intervention.

These material facts and probabilities were reinforced by cultural ones. The outbreak of the war in 1914 had shown how deeply integrated the Social Democratic party, and indeed most of German labor, had become with their national government and social system. Now, in 1918, they wanted equal political, social, and economic rights, more social welfare legislation, and a better share of the good things of the society in which they lived. Looking at the capitalist economy and middle-class culture of their country, most German workers did not want out. They wanted in.

For a time, many of them got some of the things they wanted: an eight-hour working day, greatly improved social security coverage and payments, improved union recognition and collective bargaining, somewhat better treatment at the hands of public authorities, political control of many city and town governments, improved municipal services and facilities, an intermittent share in coalition governments at the state and national levels, and by 1928 the highest real wages on the European continent.

Labor's gains under the Weimar Republic were won without dictatorship. Freedoms of speech and organization were a visible reality, with only minor exceptions, and the contrast between Weimar civil life and the increasingly repressive dictatorship in Soviet Russia was not lost on many socialist and labor voters.

The basic rights of individuals were listed in the Weimar constitution and protected by it, but far-reaching emergency provisions could be invoked by the federal government with relative ease to suspend these constitutional protections. This happened in the last years of the Weimar Republic, and these sweeping emergency powers, together with the extreme concentration of power in the hands of the president and the chancellor, did much to smooth the way to dictatorship in 1933.

The disastrous outcome, however, cannot be attributed only, or primarily, to technical mistakes in constitution drafting. The Weimar Republic suffered from political and social weaknesses even more dangerous than its legal ones. In the record, seven such weaknesses stand out.

A first weakness was a structural one. The Weimar Republic and the parties identified with it left far too much power concentrated in the hands of potential enemies. This was a fateful decision, for they might have acted otherwise. Far short of total social upheaval, they could have used the political mood and opportunities of 1918–1920 to attempt some major changes, such as a land reform in eastern Germany that would have weakened the power of the nobles—the *Junker,* as they were popularly called.

A determined republican leadership with a strong following could have organized Germany's rump army of 100,000 men more as a citizens' militia, on the model of Switzerland and of the United States in the nineteenth century, instead of letting it become a self-contained and uncontrolled power. It could have reduced the concentrated power of economic monopolies by introducing antitrust legislation similar to that in the United States, and it might have attempted to nationalize the key industries and monopolistic strongholds of coal and steel, as Britain did after World War II. It could have retired many of the antidemocratic judges and civil service bureaucrats, and reformed the judicial and civil service systems, as many countries did before and since. It could have reformed the inequitable educational system with its built-in class discrimination, at least by providing in principle a common secondary education for all children, similar to the American high school. In short, the Weimar leaders could have chosen to do a great many things that would have made democracy stronger and the gap between it and an underlying undemocratic social and economic structure less dangerous.

They did not make such choices. But in this outcome the radical left had its full share of blame. The Communist party at that time rejected reforms, insisted on total revolution, and believed in the tactic of small uprisings. Even if each such *Putsch* were defeated, the Communists thought, it would have an educational effect on the workers, making them more radical. All such uprisings were defeated, but they did have an effect—in the opposite direction.

A second weakness was at the governmental level. The republic lasted for a mere 14 years, and within that time a game of musical cabinet chairs was played in the French style, the cabinets having an average life span of nine months. In its last years the continual presidential use of emergency powers allowed conservative chancellors to govern without a majority in the legislature. Throughout the republic's existence, the civil service and the army were able to dilute or bypass their constitutional responsibility to the people's elected leaders.

A third weakness was at the level of the political parties. In the Reichstag, the legislative center of gravity continually moved to the right. From 1923 to 1930, the democratic coalition was forced to join with the moderately rightist German People's party. In 1930 the middle-class parties insisted on meeting the deepening depression with a policy of deflation, wage reductions, and cuts in welfare services. When the Social Democrats and the labor unions opposed these measures, the middle-class parties broke up the coalition, forcing new elections. In the elections of September 1930, 107 National Socialist deputies won seats in the legislature, thereby making it impossible for *any* coalition of parties to find a majority. President von Hindenburg used his emergency powers to appoint chancellors responsible to him rather than to the Reichstag. And with each successive chancellor between 1930 and 1932, the government moved more to the right, culminating in the appointment of Hitler as chancellor in January 1933.

At any one time there were usually a dozen parties represented in the legislature. They were largely parties of expression rather than of action—each tended to specialize in expressing the special demands and resentments of some group in the population, rather than in getting different groups to cooperate to get things done. Even some of the larger parties limited their appeal mainly to a single element of the population, such as the Social Democrats, who spoke for the urban workers, and the German National People's party who spoke for the landowning Junker and their rural followers.

A fourth weakness was the lack of positive popular support. The republic remained illegitimate in the eyes of roughly one-third of its population. Throughout the 1920s about 20 percent of the voters backed the German National People's party and similar rightist groups, which longed for the restoration of the monarchy and for a war to revenge the defeat suffered in World War I. About 10 percent voted for the Communists, who urged the replacement of the "bourgeois" Weimar Republic by a Soviet-style "dictator-

ship of the proletariat." This sizable minority of enemies of the republic was augmented by the growth during the late 1920s of the National Socialists.

Such extremist views, and the intense emotions of hatred and contempt that went with them, were not unusual in European politics between 1918 and 1933. What was unusual was that a large share of the electorate persisted in these attitudes in Germany throughout this period. This hostility of 30 to 40 percent of the voters in turn produced an unusually great risk of "negative majorities" in the federal legislature, unable to agree on any positive action.

A fifth weakness was in the instruments of law enforcement. Against any violent attempts to overthrow it, the Weimar Republic depended for its defense on groups that were implacably hostile to it. Against the "rightist" Kapp *Putsch* of 1920, the republic had to invoke a general strike of the workers, including the Communists; and against repeated Communist uprisings between 1919 and 1923, the republic depended on the extremely nationalistic officers and judges who remained its bitter enemies. This dependence on profoundly antidemocratic elements, in fact, undermined the entire security of the republic and left it almost paralyzed in the face of the mounting terrorism of the Nazis after 1930.

By 1928 the Weimar Republic seemed to be doing well despite these five weaknesses. The sixth and seventh ones, however, proved fatal. The sixth source of the republic's failure was the relative instability of the nation's economic institutions and the succession of disastrous economic experiences that became associated in the mind of many Germans with the Weimar Republic. The first of these experiences was the period of widespread hunger and poverty that followed the defeat of Germany in World War I and that was aggravated by the prolongation of the Allied food blockade of Germany in 1919. A second economic disaster was the runaway inflation of 1923, in which the government permitted the value of the Deutsche Mark to drop precipitously. The savings and pensions of many members of the German middle class were wiped out. Many of this group—and their children—blamed the republic, and especially the SPD, for their ruin.

After a brief period of spectacular recovery, fueled by a stream of private loans from the United States that encouraged the technological reequipment and modernization of German industry, a third disaster struck. After the Black Friday of October 1929 on the New York Stock Exchange, the flow of American credits dwindled, and the German economy suffered particularly heavily from the worldwide depression. By early 1933 about 6 million workers were unemployed—roughly one-third of the industrial work force of the country. The unemployed, their families, and particularly the young people who graduated from the schools and universities straight into unemployment blamed the republic for their misery.

From 1930 on, an increasing portion of German voters, and soon a majority, cast their votes for extremist and antidemocratic parties: the Nationalists, the Communists, and the hitherto unimportant National Socialist party of Adolf Hitler. In the face of this growing danger, a seventh weakness of the Weimar Republic was to prove decisive: the lack of imagination, competence, and courage in the economic and political policies of its leaders during its last years. The statesmen of the Weimar Republic, whatever their party, remained fearful of inflation; they clung to a policy of "sound money" and deflation, which resulted in mounting unemployment. Virtually nothing was done for the unemployed or for those shopkeepers and businessmen who lost their businesses in the depression.

THE HITLER ERA, 1933–1945

According to some of his biographers, Hitler was a man who needed to hate, to feel important, to believe in his own superiority, to be a member of a superior race, to be a great leader, and indeed to be a genius-inspired artist, molding the German people and, if possible, all of Europe and the world into the shape dictated by his visions. A poor, half-educated man, he had been on the fringe even in the provincial, middle-class society in the small town of Braunau, Austria, where he had been born. He had failed to win a scholarship to art school, and as a young man had been torn between his longing to rise to the level of the social elite and his fear of sinking down into the class of unskilled workers.

Hitler's hopes and dreams, as well as his barely suppressed fears and rages, were those of millions of his fellow Germans. He represented many of their own feelings and desires, in heightened form. Many of them vibrated to his message because it was their own tune that was being played. At the same time, his message borrowed some of the appeals of Communism; the vision of revolution, the promise of national solidarity and social justice, the emotional security and discipline of a tightly organized party, and a heady sense of historical mission.

In a nutshell, National Socialism was German nationalism plus a demogogic social promise. Adolf Hitler promised to accomplish what many Germans wanted—from high-ranking officers and industrialists all the way to many lower-middle-class clerks and small farmers. He promised to make Germany a very great power, formidably armed and universally admired and respected. And, for the German people within this greater empire, he promised the high level of economic security and standard of living that befitted a "master race."

In the electoral campaign of 1930 and thereafter, the Nazis had far more money to spend than their competitors—on posters, leaflets, advertisements, political uniforms, a private army of brown-shirted storm troopers and black-shirted "elite guards," trucks to drive their men to mass meetings, meeting halls, loudspeakers, spotlights, and all the other machinery of political propaganda. Much of this money came from the rank and file of Hitler's followers, for the Nazis were experts at collecting contributions. Much came from bank credits extended to the Nazis by big banks whose managers decided to treat this new extremist as a confidence-inspiring borrower. A good deal of money came from prominent leaders of German industry and finance, such as the steel magnate Fritz Thyssen, who saw in the Nazis not only a counterpoise to Communism but also a tool to force down the high trade union wages and to prevent implementation of the welfare state advocated by the Social Democrats.

The popular appeal of Hitler and the Nazi ideology is seen in the spectacular growth of electoral support given to the Nazis between 1928 and 1932—from 3 to 33 percent. This support was derived mainly from members of the lower-middle class who had previously voted for the liberal parties. By 1932 the middle-class liberal parties enjoyed only about one-fifth of the support they had had in 1928. At the same time, a number of small moderately rightist, nationalist, and conservative parties and groups crumbled, and their members and voters went over to the Nazis.

Hitler was finally appointed chancellor by President von Hindenburg on January 30, 1933. Not strong enough to topple the state from without, Hitler entered it by invitation and transformed it from within. Hitler thus came to sit at the head of a cabinet in which a few Nazi ministers were greatly outnumbered by conservatives. Elections were called for March 5. Two weeks before that date the empty building of the Reichstag, the German parliament, was set on fire and a Nazi rule of terror started.

Most of the evidence indicates the fire was set by the Nazis. There is no doubt that they exploited it to perfection. The Communist party was blamed for the fire and was suppressed at once. In Prussia the Nazi storm troopers were deputized as auxiliary police. Everywhere in Germany the press and the meetings of all parties still opposing the Nazis were drastically curbed: mass arrests, beatings, and torture served to intimidate opponents. Even under these conditions,

however, the Nazis got only 43 percent of the popular vote. Only together with the Nationalists, who had pooled another 8 percent, could they claim to represent a bare majority of the German electorate.

On March 23, 1933, however, a cowed parliament, including the Center party, voted Hitler an enabling bill with sweeping powers. Only the 94 votes of the Social Democrats were cast against it. The suppression of the Social Democrats and the major trade unions came in May; the Nationalists dissolved themselves in June; the Center party—disoriented by a concordat Hitler had signed with the Vatican—was obliged to follow suit in July. On July 14, 1933, the National Socialists were declared the only legal political party in Germany. A bloody purge in 1934 eliminated dissident Nazis and some conservatives, and Hitler's power became virtually absolute.

The Nazis in Power

Hitler proclaimed that the empire he was creating would last a thousand years. It lasted twelve. The main events are familiar. During the first six years Hitler achieved full employment and temporary prosperity, through controlled currency inflation and rearmament. The latter brought profits to industry and took hundreds of thousands of young men off the unemployment rolls by putting them into uniform. Added to this was an expanded program of public works—superhighways, new public buildings, and some low-cost housing—and improvements in some social benefits, such as government loans for home repairs and a popular "strength-through-joy" recreation program. As in most dictatorships, bread was supplemented by circuses. There were political and military parades, songs and martial music, and party congresses that were spectacles for millions. A network of press, film, and radio propaganda media under the virtuoso direction of Joseph Goebbels disseminated these spectacles throughout the country and completed the intoxication of the German nation.

During the same six years, the persecution of the Jews and the terror against all political opposition were systematized. The Jews played a central role in Nazi ideology. They were the scapegoats, "responsible" for inflation, depression, labor agitation, Communism, and war. They were driven from all academic and free professions, from journalism, literature, the arts, from finance and industry—where they had been much less prominent than the Nazis had pretended—and finally from practically all kinds of business and employment. They had to wear yellow stars on their clothing, and their children were barred from ordinary schools and universities. Those who did not succeed in emigrating sold their possessions piece by piece in order to live, waiting for a tomorrow that seemed ever more bleak. Thousands of Jews were imprisoned and brutally mistreated in concentration camps, and so were an even larger number of German critics of Hitler; the number of concentration-camp inmates for any given year in the 1930s has been estimated at between 20,000 and 30,000.

While "enemies" were being persecuted, the German nation was put into a totalitarian straight jacket through the process of *Gleichschaltung* (coordination) of all aspects of German life according to the Nazi pattern. All the institutions of society—political, cultural, economic, and educational—were subjected to Nazi control and a "cleansing" operation. All individuals in important positions who were thought to be unreliable were replaced by Nazi party members, and many of the remainder were fearful enough of losing their jobs to fall into the recruiting arms of the party and its auxiliary organizations. The Nazis then went one step further by creating new youth and labor organizations. They even organized at the level of the party "block"—a group of adjacent apartment houses. These organizations went further than controlling nonpolitical activities. They were also used to spy upon the population. Hitler Youth members were ordered to report their parents if they made critical remarks about the Nazis or listened to foreign radio broadcasts. Some of them complied; others merely kept their parents cowed.

The favorable surface image of Hitler's rule from 1933–1939 was reinforced by the conspicuous tolerance, if not connivance, of foreign statesmen before World War II. Between 1934 and 1936 Britain accepted the establishment of a German air force, a limited German program of battleship and submarine construction, the introduction of conscription for a new German mass army, and the remilitarization of the Rhineland—all measures explicitly forbidden under the Treaty of Versailles. Only somewhat more reluctantly, France likewise accepted each of these steps in Hitler's rearmament. In those early years of Nazism either Britain or France—or, of course, both of them together—could likely have halted the creation of the German military might that a few years later was to be turned upon them. Yet their governments chose to accept passively the creation of these German forces, hoping either that they would not be used or that they would be used only against some other country. The most obvious "other country" among the great powers was the Soviet Union, and Hitler's pose as the protector of Western civilization against Communism won him important sympathies outside Germany.

In 1938, Hitler annexed Austria, and with the sanction of appeasement-minded British and French leaders at the Munich Conference, he took over the Sudetenland—the German-speaking portion of Czechoslovakia. In March 1939, all of Czechoslovakia was occupied. In August of that year Hitler and Stalin concluded a Nazi-Soviet nonaggression pact that left Hitler free to attack Poland and make war on Germany's western front and assured him of the benevolent neutrality of the Soviet government, which during the preceding four years had loudly called for an international common front against the Nazi menace. Finally, in September 1939, Hitler took the German people into war against Poland, Britain, and France.

Poland fell, Denmark and Norway were occupied, France and the Low Countries succumbed to the German *Blitzkrieg*, Britain was saved by a heroic defense. In the summer of 1941 Hitler launched an invasion of the Soviet Union. Overextended on two massive fronts and forced to bolster a collapsing Italian ally, German forces were checked and turned back at El Alamein, at Stalingrad, and in Western Europe after the June 1944 Allied invasion. In the end, the German people were led into the depths of degradation and suffering.

Hitler's air force started the practice of large-scale bombing of civilian populations, at Warsaw in 1939 and at Rotterdam in 1940. During the first two years of war, 1939–1941, Hitler ordered five programs of mass extermination: the "euthanasia" (good death) program that killed thousands of residents of hospitals and mental asylums; the extermination of the Polish intelligentsia; the extermination of all political commissars serving with the Soviet forces; the extermination of the gypsies; and in the summer of 1941, at the peak of his military triumphs, the extermination of the Jews—men, women, and children—which he called "the final solution" of "the Jewish question." Special camps were built with gas chambers and crematoriums for the bodies. From then on, manpower, building materials, fuel, and transport were diverted from the German ar-

mies to this infamous project of the Nazis. By the end of the war in 1945, an estimated 6 million Jews had perished.

The war became a nightmare, and German defeat ever more certain. Yet the Nazi control of the German people held until the end. No German town or village rose in rebellion; no German factory crew went on strike; no German troops mutinied or surrendered without authorization. Individual Germans did resist and a conspiracy of high-ranking officers made an unsuccessful attempt on Hitler's life. But the combination of Nazi propaganda and terror remained effective, since it was backed almost everywhere by the Nazis and Nazi sympathizers among the population, who supplied the secret police with support and information.

Even under the impact of daily Allied bombings and Allied armies pushing farther and farther into German territory, the population at large remained passive and obedient. In the end, Hitler committed suicide and Germany was occupied by American, British, and, later, by French troops from the west and by Soviet forces from the east. What remained of the German armed forces surrendered on May 7 and 8, 1945, and the Allied military authorities found themselves in charge of Germany's shattered cities and people.

3

Divided Germany

PARTITION AND ALLIED MILITARY GOVERNMENT, 1945–1949

After the collapse of Hitler's German empire, Germany was reduced to a territory smaller than what had been left by the Treaty of Versailles in 1919. Land annexed by the Nazis was restored to its original owners. Thus, Austria again became independent, and the Sudetenland was returned to Czechoslovakia. Of the German territories of 1937, those to the east of the rivers Oder and Neisse (the Oder-Neisse line)—notably East Prussia and industry-rich Silesia—were detached from the rest of Germany. The northern half of East Prussia was put under the "administration" of the USSR; the southern half, together with Silesia and the rest of the Oder-Neisse territories, came under the "administration" of Poland.

In theory, the fate of all these territories was to be finally decided only by a future peace treaty among the Allies, Western and Eastern, with Germany. In fact, no such peace treaty has yet been drafted. A German-Soviet treaty, recognizing explicitly the Oder-Neisse line as the western boundary of Poland and the existence of the two German states, the FRG and GDR, was signed in 1970 with the consent of the Western allies.

The reduced Germany of 1945 was occupied by the victors and divided into four zones of occupation—Soviet, American, British, and French—in accordance with wartime agreements. The city of Berlin, which had been the capital of Germany since 1871, was similarly divided into four sectors of occupation. In theory, Germany was to be governed as an economic unit under an Allied Control Council and Berlin was to be under an Allied *Kommandatura.* In practice, the differences between the Soviet Union and the Western allies proved unbridgeable: each zone was run separately by its controlling power.

Within their zones the Western powers,

particularly the United States and Britain (the French were decidedly reluctant at the outset), tried to restore some fabric of German administrative effort and political life. After establishing German municipal administration, the Western allies proceeded to set up *Länder,* regional governments somewhat analogous to the states of the United States. During the same period the German press and radio were revived, under personnel screened by the Western allies. Political meetings and parties were permitted, and so eventually were elections to representative bodies at the municipal level (January 1946) and the *Land* level (June 1946).

From Ex-Enemy to Ally

During 1946, as it became apparent that the Soviet Union was attempting to pull Eastern Europe into the Soviet orbit, Western policies toward Germany went through a major change. In September, U.S. Secretary of State James F. Byrnes, in a speech at Stuttgart, called for a unified German economy and the early creation of a provisional German government. By implication he treated Germany as a potential ally of the West. In the same month Winston Churchill, speaking at Zurich, called for a united Europe, including Germany, that would defend Western values and traditions.

Earlier, in July 1946, the United States had proposed economic merger of its zone with any other zone, and Britain accepted the invitation. Also in July, in the first of several amnesties, the American occupation authorities had begun to allow the return of former Nazi party members into high levels of public and private employment, from which they had been ousted in large numbers by procedures of "denazification." These amnesties were intended to ease the recruitment of experienced civil servants and other personnel for the task of reconstructing West Germany, and perhaps also to help reorient the more moderate sectors of German nationalist opinion toward an eventual posture of alliance with the West.

During 1947 a German Economic Council

was created for the "bizone," a revised plan for West German industry set the 1936 level of German production as its aim, and the preparations for the Marshall Plan and the European Recovery Program opened new and increasingly attractive opportunities for German cooperation with the Western family of nations. In 1948, after the Communist takeover of Czechoslovakia, the fusion of the three occupation zones of the United States, Britain, and France into a unified West German state was accelerated. In March 1948, a Soviet walkout ended the Allied Control Council for Germany, and on June 16 a similar Soviet move put the four-power Allied Kommandatura in Berlin out of operation. Two days later, a carefully prepared currency reform was put into effect in the three Western zones and Western sectors of Berlin, greatly spurring their economic revival but severing the major previously agreed upon link between the Western- and the Soviet-occupied parts of Germany.

On June 24, the Soviet military government, taking advantage of the fact that Berlin was a landlocked enclave within the Soviet zone, announced its decision to blockade West Berlin. A dramatic airlift of food and other vital supplies by the Western allies enabled West Berlin to hold out for almost 11 months (the Soviet blockade was lifted in May 1949). By that time, three important policies had been established. The Soviet government had not attempted to dislodge the Western allies from West Berlin by force; the Western allies did not attempt to use force to break the blockade; and no Soviet pressure on West Berlin, short of force, had been able to compel the Western allies to leave the city or to abandon their plans to establish a united and democratic West German state.

The Formation of the Federal Republic

Steps toward the creation of such a state continued. On September 1, 1948, a West German "Parliamentary Council," which was in fact a constituent assembly, met in Bonn to draft a constitution for Germany. Since

Soviet-occupied eastern and central Germany were not represented, the council limited itself to drafting a Basic Law for a Federal Republic of Germany that would remain in effect until an all-German constituent assembly could replace it with a constitution agreed on by the entire German people. By the end of May 1949, this Basic Law was formally promulgated, having been adopted by the parliaments of most of the 11 Länder.

After a general election in September 1949, followed by the choice by the *Bundestag*—the popularly elected chamber—of Dr. Theodor Heuss as federal president and Dr. Konrad Adenauer as chancellor (by a majority of one vote), the Western allies were willing to see the Federal Republic actually launched. Its formal establishment was followed quickly by the creation, on October 7, 1949, of a Communist-dominated German Democratic Republic in the Soviet-occupied zone.

A CONVALESCENT REPUBLIC, 1949–1955

During its first years, the FRG's sovereignty was considerably limited. The Paris agreements of 1955, however, made the FRG in most respects sovereign. It was authorized to form its own national army, subject only to the major remaining restriction that the Federal Republic renounce certain types of heavy military and naval weapons, and particularly so-called ABC weapons—atomic/bacteriological/chemical. The Federal Republic was prohibited from equipping its own armed forces with such weapons or from producing them for any other country.

Between 1945 and 1955 about 13 million German expellees and refugees from Eastern Europe and East Germany were successfully absorbed by the Federal Republic. West German industry was rapidly reconstructed, and the country began to experience prosperity. The 1936 level of aggregate gross domestic product (GDP) was surpassed in 1950 and that of the 1936 per capita GDP in 1951. By the mid-1950s the population of the Federal Republic was better off economically than it had been before the war.

Although the United States primed the economic pump, other factors contributed markedly to the country's economic recovery. German management and labor had lost none of their traditional efficiency. The trade unions generally avoided strikes because of their belief that it was more important to increase production than to win a better distribution of the national income for workers. The millions of refugees from the East provided a cheap and plentiful labor force, willing to work especially hard to refashion their lives. Moreover, the worldwide economic boom of 1950 associated with the war in Korea came at just the right time for a Germany eager to recapture its foreign markets. Much credit also has been given to Economics Minister Ludwig Erhard for efficiently combining laissez-faire market economics with governmental incentives for industry and welfare services for labor.

Domestic Conditions and Foreign Policy

Side by side with this rapid economic reconstruction went the gradual recovery of Germany's position in international life. At home and abroad, the government of the Federal Republic strove to establish a reputation for reliability, moderation, and conservatism. It was a reputation suited to the inclinations of its leading statesmen and to the mood of a majority of the electorate. From December 1949 on, with the eventual endorsement of all major parties (after some early objections by the SPD), both the chancellor and the Bundestag put themselves on record as favoring a German military contribution to Western defense. In other words, they favored some form of German rearmament, albeit on a modest scale. After the outbreak of the war in Korea in 1950, a contribution to European defense was voted by the Bundestag in 1952, and a force of 490,000 men was promised by 1957.

In contrast with post-1945 developments in Britain, France, and Italy, no significant industries or services were nationalized, and the main emphasis of federal economic policy favored private enterprise. The social and economic structure of West Germany restored many features of the past. Property, authority, hierarchy, stability, inequality, and a good deal of monopolistic concentration were still characteristic of the structure, but fear of Communism, the felt need for the aid of the Western powers, and the hope for a speedy economic recovery made the structure increasingly popular.

At the same time, social services by federal, Land, and local authorities were maintained at a relatively high level; an "equalization-of-burdens" law (*Lastenausgleich*) further helped to improve the lot of expellees, refugees, and bombed-out families. By 1955, unemployment was down to about 4 percent of the work force, and it dwindled still more in the years that followed. In the early 1960s the West German economy not only reached the level of full employment but even had to reach into the surplus labor force of the less rapidly developing Mediterranean countries, initially Italy and Spain, to satisfy its demand for workers. The pattern was thus set for a moderately conservative welfare state in politics, combined with a notable willingness on the part of business owners and executives, politicians, and government officials to promote investment and innovation in the reequipment of industry and commerce.

In its foreign policy in the 1949–1955 period Bonn concentrated on maintaining close relations with the United States, and also with France. There were no diplomatic relations with the Soviet Union, or with any other member of the Soviet bloc. As early as March 1949, Adenauer proposed a Franco-German economic union. In 1951 the Federal Republic signed an agreement establishing the European Coal and Steel Community with France, Italy, and the Benelux countries. In the same year, after repeated intervention by Chancellor Adenauer in its favor, a reparations agreement was signed in which Germany pledged to Israel $822 million in goods over a 12-year period.

In 1954, pursuing the same policy of accommodation with France and close collaboration with the United States, West Germany ratified an agreement that would have created a Western European army (rejected, however, by the French parliament) and signed the Paris Treaties to become a member of the North Atlantic Treaty Organization. It also concluded an agreement with France to acquire the Saar territory.

BONN'S RETURN AMONG THE POWERS

The years after 1955 brought the rapid return of the Federal Republic to the ranks of such powers as Britain and France. It became not only juridically equal but increasingly able to diverge from the policies of these European powers and to apply pressure in the pursuit of its own goals. At the same time, the Bonn government showed itself increasingly independent of the day-to-day policies of its principal ally, the United States, even though the long-term alliance between Bonn and Washington remained strong.

In September 1955, Chancellor Adenauer's government initiated formal diplomatic relations with the Soviet Union. In 1956 West Germany public opinion favored Egypt against France and Britain in the Suez crisis, and the Bonn government remained friendly to Egypt. In 1958 Bonn was the first Western power to recognize the new government of Iraq, which had been installed by an anti-British revolution.

In December 1956, the Bonn government yielded readily to pressure from mass opinion and the Bundestag and cut back the term of military service for German youth from 18 months—as demanded by the NATO authorities and the German military—to a mere 12 months; the 18-month term of service was not restored until early in 1962. The target of 490,000 German troops to be placed at the disposal of NATO, which had first been promised for 1957, was not attained until the 1970s, when the term of conscriptive service was again reduced, this time to 15 months. With a markedly declining birth rate expected to take its toll on manpower by the 1990s, the government has debated returning the term of military service to 18 months.

By putting off its scheduled contribution to NATO in the 1950s and 1960s, the Federal Republic was able to devote a higher proportion of its work force and financial resources to its own industrial development than it otherwise could have done. This decision was in all likelihood in the best interests of both West Germany and her allies. Significantly, it was a decision taken by the executive and legislature of the Federal Republic against the advice of the Western powers, particularly the United States, which for so long had had a major voice in Bonn's decisions.

The Federal Republic's Growing Economic Power

From the early 1960s on, the main seat of West German power has been in the field of economics. The phenomenal growth of the 1950s was sustained until the late 1970s, apart from short-term periods of recession in 1966–1967 and 1974–1975, the latter largely the result of adverse world economic conditions. Table 3–1 reflects the growth in gross domestic product and demonstrates as well the growth of West German trade and

the relative importance of trade to the West German economy, as indicated in the ratio of trade to GDP. Note the marked increase in this ratio between 1965 and 1985. The Federal Republic has become eminently successful in redirecting a traditional German interest for a "place in the sun" into trade, paving the way for its acceptance back into the world community of nations.

A party to the European Common Market treaty of 1957, the Federal Republic was, along with France, in a dominant position in the EEC by the end of the 1960s. Its financial strength enabled the Federal Republic to make a major contribution to an agricultural fund under the Common Market. A champion of British entry and expansion of the community, the West German state found itself called upon to bear greater burdens in supporting the faltering economies of its partners, particularly Italy and Britain, in the period of galloping inflation that followed the 1973 oil crisis.

The Federal Republic's economic growth rate resumed its upward climb after the 1974–1975 recession, albeit at a lower percentage of real increase. With a remarkably low rate of inflation, a decrease in unemployment, and a surge in the value of the Deutsche Mark, the FRG continued in relative prosperity until the end of the 1970s, in contrast with the depressed economies of most major developed nations. The early

TABLE 3–1   West German GDP and Foreign Trade Ratios, 1950–1988

Year	Growth Index GDP	Growth Index (1960 = 100)	Imports	Exports	Export Surplus	Trade	Growth Index Trade Ratio (1960 = 100)	(Trade/ GDP)
1950	98	32%	11	8	−3	19	21%	19%
1960	303	100	43	48	5	91	100	30
1965	458	151	70	72	2	142	156	31
1970	679	224	110	125	15	235	258	35
1975	1,029	340	184	226	42	410	451	40
1980	1,479	488	341	350	9	691	759	47
1985	1,832	605	464	537	73	1,001	1,100	55
1988	2,129	703	440	568	128	1,008	1,108	47

(In billions of Deutsche Mark (DM), rounded off, at current prices)

Source: *Statistisches Jahrbuch fur die Bundesrepublik*, Stuttgart, 1989.

1980s brought a turn in the Federal Republic's economic fortunes, however, with stagnating growth and a major jump in unemployment. (A detailed analysis of FRG economic conditions in the 1980s is offered in Chapter 7.)

Bonn and East-West Relations

American and Soviet policies, too, came to feel the newly strengthened influence of Bonn. From 1958 to 1962 the Soviet government created an intermittent "Berlin crisis" by threatening to conclude a formal peace treaty with East Germany and to hand over to that state the control of the access routes to West Berlin. This would have forced the Western allies to choose between dealing with a new blockade or with the authorities of the GDR, which they had thus far steadily declined to recognize. President Kennedy refused to be forced to make such a choice. With the consent of American congressional and public opinion, American troops in Germany were demonstrably strengthened.

Even after the August 1961, building of the wall around West Berlin, the access rights of American and other Western allies were respected. In late 1961 and early 1962, American-Soviet negotiators searched for some agreement that might permit both great powers to retain their essential positions, as well as their prestige, but to trade sufficient concessions in nonessentials to bring about a substantial lessening of the tension between them. These American-Soviet negotiations, however, were subjected more than once to thinly disguised criticism from Bonn. Chancellor Adenauer announced that he expected little if any good to come from them, and his government made clear its objections to most of the Western steps toward a possible accommodation with the Soviet Union that had been mentioned as considerations for discussion. Bonn, of course, feared any American concessions to the Soviets at West Germany's political expense, somewhat as the Ulbricht regime in the GDR feared Soviet concessions to the West that might weaken its control.

West German policies became slightly more flexible under Adenauer's successor, Ludwig Erhard, and noticeably more so under the coalition government of Chancellor Kurt Georg Kiesinger (CDU) and Foreign Minister Willy Brandt (SPD), which undertook diplomatic overtures to several Soviet bloc countries and opened diplomatic relations with Romania in 1967.

The relative lessening of international tensions in Europe also tended to reduce somewhat the conflict between the two German states. A climate favoring negotiations developed under the Kiesinger-Brandt coalition government in 1966–1969, and talks and negotiations between the FRG and GDR, as well as among the Four Powers still legally responsible for Berlin, got under way in 1970, a few short months after the new SPD/FDP coalition government under Chancellor Willy Brandt had taken office.

West German foreign policy toward the East underwent major modification under the Brandt coalition government. The new course, commonly referred to as *Ostpolitik,* abandoned former intransigence in forging new links to the Soviet Union and the nations of Eastern Europe. Displaying a willingness to "recognize and respect" the post–World War II territorial status quo, the Brandt government was able to conduct negotiations that led in 1970 to renunciation of force agreements with the Soviet Union and Poland (Moscow and Warsaw Treaties) and ultimately to establishment of diplomatic relations with all East European states. At the same time, Four Power negotiations on Berlin culminated in a new Berlin Agreement in 1971.

The Bonn government also adopted a new strategy in its approach to the GDR, aiming to establish a dialogue between the two German states with the goal of easing the burden of division through a set of agreements. A supplemental FRG/GDR understanding in connection with the 1971 Four Power Berlin Agreement and a 1972 Basic Treaty between the two German states were results that seemed to underscore the success of this approach.

The Brandt foreign policy reestablished West German "compatibility" with the international environment as Ostpolitik became inextricably linked to movement in East-West relations. Reunification was no longer to be a prerequisite to détente; if it were to be achieved at all, it would be upon a basis of détente.

At the same time, West German foreign policy was now demonstrating greater autonomy. The Brandt government undertook its Ostpolitik in lightninglike moves without broad consultations with its Western allies. While the resulting agreements did secure the blessing of the Federal Republic's allies, it was clear that the FRG could no longer be considered a satellite power, even if it continued to remain largely dependent for its defense on the presence of U.S., British and French troops on its soil.

Powerful in diplomacy and with an economy envied by other developed nations—such was the international image of the Federal Republic by the late 1970s. Yet how much solid political strength—how much dependable civic consensus—stood behind this impressive international position? How was the political system of the Federal Republic likely to function in the face of major decisions, and how well was it likely to deal with crises, political or economic? How the Federal Republic has fared in the 1980s is addressed in Chapter 7.

THE OTHER GERMAN STATE: THE GDR

Following the creation in West Germany of the Federal Republic in 1949, the German Democratic Republic was set up in October of that same year in the Soviet zone. And after the FRG had attained substantial sovereignty through the Paris Treaties of 1954, GDR sovereignty was recognized by the USSR in September of the same year. The GDR has in effect been ruled by a Communist dictatorship, exercised through the Sozialistische Einheitspartei Deutschlands (SED) and dominated until 1971 by the veteran German Communist and SED Politburo General Secretary Walter Ulbricht. In 1971 Ulbricht retired (under some pressure from the Soviet Union) and was succeeded in leadership by an associate with similar views, Erich Honecker, a survivor of ten years in Nazi prisons. Honecker was faced with the difficult task of following Soviet prodding in achieving some measure of accommodation with the FRG under Willy Brandt.

Throughout the 1950s thousands of GDR citizens expressed their dissatisfaction with their feet. They walked out of the GDR into the Western-occupied parts of Berlin and claimed asylum. Then, after having been screened in West Berlin, they were flown to West Germany for further screening and eventual resettlement. The Soviet military authorities, as well as those of the GDR, were powerless to stop this flow, short of cutting off most of the movements of persons between East and West Berlin—a move the Western powers would have considered illegal and the Soviets inexpedient. The flow thus continued, and the government of the Federal Republic, as well as the Western allied authorities in Berlin, encouraged it. As a result of this migration through West Berlin and into the Federal Republic, the GDR from 1950 through 1961 suffered an average net loss of more than 190,000 persons each year, or a total of nearly 2.3 million. Following the loss of 565,000 in 1945–1949, this migration more than offset the GDR's natural population growth.

These figures tell a story of a serious—though not fatal—drain on the work force of the GDR. They also show that the peak period of that drain occurred during 1953–1955 and that the peak year was 1953, when the net loss rose to 320,000. On June 17, 1953, strikes and riots in East Germany approached the dimensions of revolt, challenging the dictatorial power of the East German government and the tanks of the Soviet forces backing it. The riots, however, were quickly suppressed. Earlier broadcasts from West Berlin, the Federal Republic, and the American stations in Europe had done much, wittingly or unwittingly, to encourage the spirit of revolt in East Berlin and the GDR, and the American station RIAS had been particularly emphatic. At the time of the riots, however, the West German broadcasts urged calmness and caution. The verbal attacks on the Soviet regime and the GDR, moreover, were not followed by any effective Western action supporting the rebels by force, because of the risk of local defeat by Soviet troops or the start of a new world war.

If the unrest of 1953 in the GDR was thus quickly suppressed, it nevertheless was not without results. It reminded the Communist rulers of the extent to which they had alienated popular feeling, it hastened the ending of reparations payments to the Soviet Union, and it started the transition to a policy of at least beginning concessions to consumer needs and better living standards. In the Federal Republic, the East German uprising of June 17 was taken as a promise of the early collapse of the GDR, and as a confirmation of the wisdom of Bonn's policy of consistent nonrecognition of its eastern rival.

The tide of emigration ebbed in 1959 to 150,000, down from 204,000 the previous year. But in 1960 it increased to 199,000 and rose markedly in the first seven months of 1961 to almost 200,000 for the seven-month period. In August 1961, the East German regime and its Soviet backers finally acted to halt the exodus, building a wall that completed the existing Communist system of enclosures around West Berlin. Crossings were permitted only at a very few heavily controlled checkpoints, and practically no East Berliners or inhabitants of the GDR were permitted to cross to the West. A few desperate individuals, however, still succeeded in making dramatic escapes. Until July 1987, East German border guards were under orders to shoot would-be "escapees." Electronic alarm and improved optical systems were installed in the border zone in 1985 to replace mine fields and automatic shrapnel-spraying devices. Since 1961, well over 30,000 have succeeded despite such obstacles in fleeing over the border to the FRG; around 200 have been shot in attempting to

escape. More than 600,000 have emigrated through other means—with GDR exit visas, through expulsion, or by defection via other countries.

In the early postwar period, the people of the Federal Republic remained closely connected with the population of the GDR by ties of family and old friendships, as well as of national sentiment. Today a new generation of Germans deprived of such ties of association has grown up in both states, while a significant portion of the older generation has passed on. Despite this, ties of national sentiment lingered, as dramatically evident in the reception given Willy Brandt by crowds along the way in his March 1970 journey to Erfurt to meet with the GDR premier. The granting of GDR travel permits to West Berliners and West Germans (following the 1972 Basic Treaty), as well as the relaxation of constraints by the mid-1980s on the travel of East Germans to the FRG, have undoubtedly served to renew old associations and create new ones.

Contrast with West Germany

A discussion of the institutions and politics of the GDR would go far beyond the framework of this section. They would be better discussed in a treatment of the institutions of other Soviet bloc countries, which the GDR resembles far more than it does the FRG or other Western countries.

The GDR has experienced an "economic miracle" in its own right. It eclipsed Czechoslovakia by the end of the 1960s as the leading Soviet bloc producer. Among the Soviet bloc countries it has by far the highest per capita private consumption as well as the highest per capita GDP.

According to GDR calculations, the East German economy has grown at rates not far behind those of West Germany. Economic planning has improved somewhat with experience and partial economic reforms have begun to give a freer hand to management and greater attention to sales and prices in the market. On the other hand, the GDR has antiquated factories and low productivity in comparison to the FRG and West European states. It is difficult to make general comparisons between the standards of living in the two German states given the often great disparity in the quality and availability of consumer goods and because of heavy GDR subsidization for such basic needs as housing. Although they are by no means affluent, East German citizens have improved their lot. The vast majority of GDR households have TV sets (often tuned in to West German channels), refrigerators, and washing machines; nearly half of all families now have an automobile (though the wait for one often takes months and even years). In comparison with the FRG, the GDR has double the percentage of university graduates in its work force, and it spends double the percentage of GDP on defense.

While the Federal Republic was quickly integrated into the trading and credit community of the Western countries, the GDR was integrated—much less smoothly—into the Soviet bloc, whose members were on the whole much poorer, and where international economic interchanges were less well coordinated. The Federal Republic also managed to perpetrate an effective economic boycott of the GDR that endured through the late 1960s. While carrying on a substantial "interzonal" trade itself, the FRG threatened the severing of diplomatic relations and the imposition of economic sanctions against all nations that initiated diplomatic relations with the GDR. This practice was discontinued by the Brandt government.

At the same time that West Germans have come to accept as increasingly permanent the provisional status of their state, an increasing number of East Germans (though not a strong majority) appear to have come closer to accepting a new national identity. GDR leaders, in signing agreements with the Bonn government, have been emphatic in maintaining a policy of demarcation and denying the continued existence of a single German nation.

The international environment of the two German states no longer seems biased in favor of the FRG as strongly as it has in the past. Both German states were admitted to the United Nations in 1973. Diplomatic recognition was extended to the GDR by a virtual flood of nations, including the United States, after the signing of the FRG-GDR Basic Treaty. East German teams have dominated international competition in many sports. GDR foreign trade quadrupled from a volume of 40 billion GDR marks in 1970 to 160 billion in 1983 and totaled 182 billion in 1986. Exports finally overtook imports in 1982. The GDR has sought to cultivate ties with Western trading partners, in particular France. Trade between the two German states reached a volume of 15.5 billion DM in 1984 but fell back to 14 billion DM by 1987 with an export advantage to the FRG.

Manifestations of dissent and the efforts of tens of thousands of East Germans to seek emigration permits in the aftermath of the 1975 Helsinki Agreements, which had guaranteed, among other things, freedom to emigrate, showed that the legitimacy of the GDR was still open to question. The regime began in 1977 to take action against an increasing number of its most vocal critics—including many of the country's leading artists and literary figures—expelling several to the West and placing others under house arrest. By the mid-1980s, in an effort to consolidate its domestic authority, the GDR greatly increased the number of exit permits; some 41,000 were authorized in 1984 with the number diminishing to 11,500 in 1987. An estimated 250,000 to 300,000 East Germans have applied for such permits. Beginning in February 1986, the GDR—which with few exceptions had heretofore only permitted pensioners to leave the country for visits to the FRG—began to allow citizens below retirement age to travel to the Federal Republic to visit relatives for up to two weeks. Some 573,000 nonpensioners took advantage of this relaxed policy in 1986, and in 1987, 1.2 million nonpensioners joined 2.2 million pensioners for a total of 3.4 million GDR citizens who visited the FRG, a figure equal to one-sixth of the total GDR population. Despite mandatory currency exchange at unfavorable official GDR rates, West Germans since the mid-1970s have traveled to the GDR in ever-increasing numbers. The adoption by the GDR of more liberal emigration policies and a more humane means of deterring border escapes has coincided with the issuance of major interest-free West German credits and an increase in official contacts between the two German states.

Compelled to follow the Soviet détente approach in establishing closer relations with the FRG in the early 1970s, the GDR has since then had some difficulty adapting to fluctuations in the East-West political climate. Neither German state has been willing, however, to return to an ice age in a relationship that has gained momentum and produced tangible benefits for each side. Thus intra-German relations were not seriously impaired by the placement of American intermediate-range missiles on West German soil and comparable Soviet missiles in the GDR. East German espionage infiltration of key FRG government offices has at times strained the relationship as has the housing of GDR emigres seeking asylum in FRG embassies in Prague, Budapest, and other East European capitals; such incidents have not, however, curbed the desire of both German states to pursue their own unique goals in maintaining a relationship. The September 1987 Honecker visit to the FRG and current issues with respect to intra-German relations are discussed in Chapter 7.

In relaxing restrictions on travel and emigration and in promoting closer ties with the FRG, the East German state has attempted to create a safety valve to ease internal tensions. While 99.5 percent of all GDR visitors to the FRG have returned home, dissatisfaction and protest activity have increased, sparked no doubt by a whetting of the desire for more liberalization and by the perception that the GDR regime lags far behind in letting itself be influenced by the new winds of *glasnost* and *perestroika* emanating from the Soviet Union. It remains to be seen how the GDR will deal with such internal and external challenges and whether the Honecker regime can achieve further liberalization without risking major erosion of its control over society. With Honecker in his late seventies, the question of succession looms in the near future with Moscow likely to continue to strongly influence the nature of the future GDR regime.

4

The Governmental System
of the Federal Republic

The Federal Republic has a Basic Law rather than a constitution. Its language suggests that it is provisional, and its concluding article says: "This Basic Law loses its validity on the day on which a Constitution comes into effect which has been freely decided upon by the German people." Yet its principles were intended to be permanent, and with the passage of time its provisions have increasingly come to be accepted as such.

THE MAKING OF THE BASIC LAW

The Basic Law is a constitutional document embodying an uncommon wealth of dearly bought historical experience and expert skill. The Parliamentary Council and its committees had at their disposal the advice of a number of constitutional and political experts, including distinguished specialists from the United States. Nevertheless, and despite the expressed wishes of the occupying powers—particularly France—in favor of a more strongly decentralized and federative solution, there emerged a document that was essentially German in conception and content.

One of the primary motivations of those who drafted the Basic Law was to correct what were considered the constitutional faults of the Weimar constitution, in the hope of preventing a repeat performance. Accordingly, the Basic Law decentralized the means of state power and persuasion. It left the Länder with a substantial part of the bureaucratic machinery of administration, and it left the federal government dependent on the Länder for the execution of most of its own legislation. The Länder were to be in control of the police, except for small federal units that were to be used for special purposes. One such unit is the federal border guard *Bundesgrenzschutz,* a paramilitary force based on volunteers and stationed along the borders of the FRG—especially its eastern borders.

As far as the realm of competence of the Länder is concerned, they have charge of all schools and education and of the bulk of radio and television, for the Basic Law restricted the federal power to matters delegated expressly to the federal government. It thereby left—by implication, according to some jurists—all residual powers to the Länder.

Substantial spheres of "exclusive" legislation are reserved for the federal government; the Länder may legislate only if empowered by specific federal law. In other areas of "concurrent" legislation, the Länder may legislate only to the extent that the federal government (called the *Bund,* or Federation) does not make use of its own legislative powers. In these matters, federal law overrides Land law.

The Federation is thus clearly predominant in the area of legislation, while the Länder retain the greater part of the administrative tasks and personnel. As long as government and politics remain within the confines of legality and legitimacy, federal authorities have a clear preponderance of power. In situations of crisis, however, any illegal or illegitimate attempts to establish a dictatorship or to stampede public opinion will encounter a major obstacle in the federal dependence on the administrative cooperation of the Land bureaucracies and governments, and the Land governments' control of the police forces. The arrangement increases the capabilities of the federal government for legitimate decision making, while providing for strong obstacles in the way of any *coup d'état.*

At the same time, the Federal Republic is better equipped than the Weimar Republic to maintain a stable political system, to formulate and carry out consistent policies, and to make specific decisions in accordance with them. The great powers given the federal chancellor, including his effective control over the membership of his cabinet; the provision that the chancellor can be ousted from office by the Bundestag only if the latter can agree on a successor to him (the so-called constructive vote of no confidence), which prevents purely negative majorities from dismissing a chancellor, as in Weimar days; and the narrow limits set on judicial review of federal laws and acts of the government—all tend to concentrate and stabilize the power of legitimate decision making at the federal level. The explicit recognition of political parties in the Basic Law, together with the exclusion by the electoral law of splinter parties (those that fail to receive in any one election either 5 percent of the national popular vote or a majority in at least three single-member constituencies) from the distribution of seats in the legislature (the so-called exclusion clause), tends to encourage large, powerful parties.

Guiding Values: Human and Civil Rights

The first paragraph of Article 1 of the Basic Law proclaims that the dignity of the individual must not be touched; to respect and protect it is the obligation of every state organ and authority. Article 1 has been interpreted broadly in West German legal thought as implying in itself many of the more specific basic rights. It thus outlaws torture, corporal punishment, or any physical or mental mistreatment of prisoners.

Article 1 is also particularly important because it directs that the basic rights listed thereafter are binding upon all executive and judicial authorities "as immediately valid law." The basic rights are many. They begin with the "free development of one's personality," "life and physical integrity," and "freedom of the person" (Article 2).

Further basic rights include equality before the law, equal rights for men and women, and nondiscrimination in regard to sex, descent, race, language, home and origin, or religious and political views (Article 3). Article 4 guarantees freedoms of religion, conscience, and the profession of religious or philosophic views, and the right to refuse armed military service on grounds of conscience.

Article 5 protects the freedom of opinion, research, and teaching, but adds that "the freedom to teach does not absolve from loyalty to the Basic Law." A major issue of the 1970s was the question of whether graduating radical students would qualify for teaching positions or other civil service posts.

Article 6 protects marriage and the family. It declares that "the care and education of children is the natural right of their parents." In addition, it gives "every mother" a claim to protection and care by the community and provides legitimate and illegitimate children with an equal claim to legislative protection of their social position and opportunities for personal development.

Article 7 puts all schools under the supervision of the state (i.e., the Länder). Religious instruction, according to Article 7, is to be a regular subject in the public schools, except for the "nondenominational" schools. The parents decide about the participation of their child in such instruction. Today in most Länder pupils of all denominations are educated in mixed classes. The denominational separation of the classroom prevails only during the periods of religious instruction.

The Basic Law goes on to guarantee the right of unarmed assembly without prior permission or announcement (Article 8). The right to form economic or occupational interest organizations (such as employers' organizations or labor unions) is guaranteed "for everybody and all occupations" (Article 9). Organizations whose goals or activities are criminal or "directed against the constitutional order or the idea of international understanding" are prohibited (Article 9.2).

German citizenship may not be withdrawn in any case. Even involuntary loss of citizenship may occur only on the basis of law and only if the person concerned does not become stateless (Article 16.1). No German may be extradited abroad. Article 16 thus ensures that even Nazi war criminals, if they are Germans, cannot be extradited to the countries demanding their punishment.

The politically persecuted have the right of asylum (Article 16.2). The FRG opened its doors to refugees and expellees fleeing from the GDR and East European nations, but found itself subjected by the late 1970s to a less welcome tide of political and even economic refugees, many from developing nations.

Many constitutional rights may be denied to those who misuse them in order to destroy the democratic system. Those who misuse the freedom of speech or the press, the freedom to teach, the freedom of assembly or association, the privacy of letters, mails, and telecommunications, the right of property or asylum may forfeit these basic rights. This forfeiture and its extent are subject to determination by the Federal Constitutional Court (Article 18). The same court may outlaw political parties that, "according to their aims, or according to the behavior of their adherents, tend to harm or abolish the basic libertarian democratic order, or to endanger the existence of the Federal Republic."

This broad language makes parties liable not only for their programs but for the probable behavior of their followers. This clause is influenced by the memory of the disastrous tolerance of Nazi subversion by the Weimar Republic, and by the ever-present shadow of the Communist dictatorship in the neighboring GDR. The provision for the banning of political parties acquired practical significance in the outlawing of the neo-Nazi Sozialistische Reichspartei (SRP) in 1952 and the Communist party in 1956.

The basic rights listed in Articles 1 through 18 are particularly protected by Article 19 against any later amendments that might destroy them. No part of the Basic Law may be amended except by a law passed by two-thirds majorities of the Federal Parliament. Article 20 fixes the character of the Federal Republic as a "democratic and social federal state"—a phrase that affirms in the connotations of the German word *sozial* the values of social compassion and social justice, and that gives special constitutional legitimacy to welfare legislation. The Basic Law further establishes popular sovereignty, representative government, and the separation of powers: "All power of government issues from the people. It is exercised by the people in elections and votes, and through separate organs of legislation, of the executive power, and of the judiciary" (Article 20.1–3).

Other rights or values are stated more specifically. Peace is specially protected. Actions that are both "apt and intended to disturb the peaceful coexistence of people, particularly to prepare an aggressive war, are contrary to the Basic Law. There are to be made subject to punishment." There must be no special courts. No one must be denied trial before a legally appointed judge. The death penalty is abolished. There may be neither retroactive punishment nor double jeopardy: an action may be punished only if it was legally punishable before it was committed, and no one may be punished on the basis of the general criminal laws more than once for the same action. There is an equivalent to the American right of habeas corpus: personal liberty may be limited only on the basis of law; arrested persons may not be mistreated "physically or mentally." The police may not hold anyone beyond the day after his arrest without his appearing before a judge, who must tell him the charge against him, question him, and give him an opportunity to make objections. The judge then must either order him released or issue a retroactive arrest warrant, including reasons.

Acts of terrorism by the Baader-Meinhof group, and by other leftist as well as rightist organizations, increased pressure on the government to be vigilant and to legislate antiterrorist measures. In 1978 the government passed laws seeking to curb the freedom of action of terrorist suspects, and in particular to prevent defense lawyers from passing on weapons and messages and conspiring with their clients. This legislation was attacked on the one hand by civil libertarians as abusing basic civil rights and on the other hand by the CDU/CSU parties as not going far enough. The laws—enacted in the Bundestag by a margin of only one vote—provided for installation of glass screens to separate lawyers from their clients in prison visiting rooms, the legalization of police control points and of building searches by police who are pursuing alleged terrorists, and authorization for police to detain suspects for up to 12 hours until identity has been established. In defense of this legislation, the Bonn government asserted that similar measures were already part of the legal framework in certain other parliamentary democracies.

The limited goals embodied in the Basic Law are politically realistic, and they accommodate the aspirations of the major parties. Specifically, they meet the interest of the CDU in religious instruction and in greater power for the Länder; the interest of the FDP and CDU in safeguards for private property and enterprise; and the interest of the SPD in labor unions, welfare legislation, the legitimate possibility of nationalization, and equal rights for unwed mothers and for nonreligious pupils and teachers. Even the many members of a silent political group—the former members of the Nazi party, the SS elite guard, the Gestapo secret police, and similar organizations of the Hitler period—find substantial protection in the Basic Law and in the civil and human rights it guarantees. The Basic Law forbids blanket discrimination against former members of political parties or organizations.

The Basic Law was not only a response to the ideological cleavages within the German people, but also an instrument for their modification. It aimed at establishing standards of legality and human rights, and these standards gradually won the respect and acceptance of a majority of the electorate. The progressive support of the Federal Republic and its institutions by the majority of its citizens has been due also to such extraconstitutional factors as general economic prosperity and a tolerably low level of international tension. Another factor in this success has been the efficiency of the constitutional system that the Basic Law created. The operation of the FRG's parliamentary government is in very close conformity to the Basic Law, and this has helped to legitimize parliamentary democracy.

THE BUNDESTAG

The Bundestag, the popularly elected federal chamber of parliament, was established under Articles 38–49 of the Basic Law. Half of its members are elected from 248 single-member constituencies by simple majorities or pluralities of the "first votes" cast by the voters in each district for the individual candidate of their choice. The other half are elected from party lists of candidates in each Land, by proportional representation in accordance with the share of their parties in the "second votes" cast by all voters at the same elections for the party of their preference (see Figure 4–1). The outcome is a distribution of all seats in fairly close accordance with proportional representation. Thus, it is really the second vote that counts. At the same time, however, the electorate's choice of individual candidates serves to personalize proportional representation, which otherwise usually involves voting for party lists rather than individuals.

The Electoral System

In attempting to "democratize" the parties' internal organization in imitation of the American primary and convention system, the electoral law provides that list candidates be nominated by assemblies of party members elected for that purpose in each Land and that individual candidates be nominated by similar assemblies in each of the 248 constituencies.

Parties may obtain seats from this distribution according to party lists only if they win at least 5 percent of the valid votes cast in the entire Federal Republic, or if their candidates win majorities or pluralities in at least three single-member districts. This "ex-clusion clause" eliminates most splinter and regional parties. Each of the remaining parties is entitled to its proportionate quota of seats. The difference between this proportionate quota and the number of seats a party won directly in the single-member constituencies is filled with candidates from the party list. Should a party obtain more seats from single-member constituencies than otherwise entitled by its share of the proportionate quota from "second votes," it retains these additional seats. The normal Bundestag total of 496 deputies can thus be increased to account for such additional deputies. The size and political composition of the 11 Bundestags elected between 1949 and 1987 are presented in Figure 4–2.

Bundestag deputies are elected by general, direct, free, equal, and secret vote, according to Article 38 of the Basic Law. But the electoral procedure can be, and has been, changed by ordinary federal law. According to the same article, the deputies are not subject to directions from anyone. In fact, however, the tradition of party discipline, the power of the parties over the placing of candidates in electoral districts and on Land lists, together with the need for funds to meet the costs of campaigning, have made the votes and actions of Bundestag members highly predictable.

Parliamentary Parties

Cases of defiance of important party orders by a deputy are rare, though there have been numerous cases of defection to other parties. The exclusion clause makes a deputy's reelection as an independent practically impossible. His chances of founding a new party strong enough to surmount the clauses's requirements are remote. Moreover, the great majority of voters have opted for trustworthy party labels more than for strong personalities.

All the Bundestag members of each individual party (its parliamentary party, or *Fraktion*—with the CDU/CSU combining to form one Fraktion) meet frequently, for it is in these meetings that the important decisions

FIGURE 4-1 A sample ballot from a voting district, 1983 federal election. Voters have two votes: in the left-hand column they vote directly for a candidate, and in the right-hand column they vote for a party.

regarding voting strategies are taken. The *Fraktionen* determine the general positions party deputies will take on pending legislation. They go over the Bundestag agenda point by point and take positions on each one, even going so far as to determine the public arguments and the speakers to be used to express their positions. The decisions taken in these party meetings effectively bind both the positions and the votes

of the deputies in the Bundestag. Party discipline is nearly perfect, the overwhelming majority of the deputies voting together as a block on all but a minuscule number of roll-call votes.

Examples of disintegration of party discipline abound. A growing number of FDP delegates defected from the SPD/FDP government coalition over the 1969–1972 period, unwilling to support their party's shifts

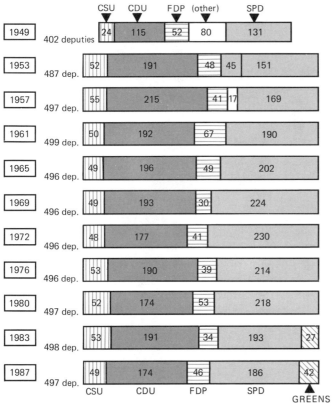

FIGURE 4-2 Distribution of Bundestag Seats Since 1949.

in policy. This defection seriously jeopardized the coalition's parliamentary majority. In another instance, the CDU/CSU, in May 1972, found itself split into factions on the Bundestag vote on the ratification of the Brandt government's treaties with the Soviet Union and Poland. A Fraktion meeting convened to attempt to forestall a split vote decided on the course of abstention. A year later, the Fraktion was split on the vote of ratification of the Basic Treaty with the GDR: a few CDU delegates voted yes, but the majority of CDU/CSU delegates were opposed. The SPD, which had in the past provided the model for party discipline, was itself rent by the refusal of a small group of maverick left-wing delegates to support the governing coalition's 1978 terrorist legislation. FDP party discipline was severely strained (more among the party rank and file than among its parliamentary Fraktion) by the September, 1982, decision of FDP

party leader Genscher to abandon his SPD coalition partner and ally the FDP with the CDU/CSU.

Committees

Most of the work of the Bundestag is done in committee, to an even greater extent than is the case in the United States Congress. There are several regular committees, corresponding to the various government departments, as well as the important budget committee. Members of committees are selected by their parliamentary parties, often with an eye to their expert knowledge in the area under the committee's jurisdiction. However, fixed party positions and tight party discipline rarely allow much flexibility for individual committee members.

Each committee may require the presence of any cabinet member at its meetings, and cabinet members and civil servants also have their own right of access to committee meetings at any time.

Special investigating committees, on any matter other than defense, must be set up whenever one quarter of the members of the Bundestag demand it. These committees may gather evidence and proof by procedures analogous to those of general criminal procedure, including the power to compel testimony. Their proceedings are public, unless a majority of the committee members votes to make a session confidential. Since their composition is proportionate to the strength of the parties in the Bundestag, any strong opposition—for example, the CDU in the Sixth Bundestag—can compel the setting up of an investigating committee, even on a subject embarrassing to the government.

Leadership and Power

The chief officer of the Bundestag is its president, who is elected by secret ballot but is taken, in fact, from the strongest party. Three vice presidents are elected by the chamber in the same manner; they are taken from the remaining parties, more or less in order of their strength. A Council of Elders, composed of these officers and other representatives of the parliamentary-party delegations, is in theory only an advisory committee for the president. But in practice it is a very important body, somewhat comparable in its power to the Rules Committee of the House of Representatives in the United States. The Council of Elders schedules the debates on particular items of legislation and allocates the times and order of speaking to the various parties and speakers.

The major sources of power and action in the Bundestag are the Fraktionen. Only parties strong enough to form a Fraktion may be represented on committees, may count on being assigned speaking time in plenary debates, may effectively initiate bills, may direct parliamentary inquiries to the government—in short, take an effective part in the work of the Bundestag. Together with the decisions of the cabinet—and primarily of the

chancellor—it is the decisions of the Fraktionen that have the greatest influence on what happens in the Bundestag, even though many details of legislation are still modified by the suggestions of civil servants and the political give-and-take of the legislative process in the Bundestag committees.

THE BUNDESRAT

The Bundesrat, or Federal Council, is a coordinate branch of the federal legislature and has a significant share in the legislative process, as well as considerable powers in emergencies. It is the specific organ through which the Länder governments cooperate in federal legislation and administration. It is composed of members of the Länder governments—that is, ordinarily the minister presidents. The minister presidents do not serve as individual deputies, but as members of the delegation of their Land, which must vote as a unit. Each Land has at least three votes; Länder with more than 2 million inhabitants have four votes, and Länder with over 6 million inhabitants have five votes. If a Land is governed by a coalition of several parties, the entire vote of its delegation is cast as a unit in accord with an agreement of the member parties, usually following the views of the strongest party, which usually is also that of the Land's minister president.

Bundesrat decisions require at least a majority of its constituent votes. Thus, abstention from voting on a proposal is equivalent to voting to reject it. Most of the Bundesrat's work is done by committees, on which other members of Länder governments, or their deputies, such as civil servants from Länder administrations, may serve. Members of the federal government have the right and, if requested, the duty to attend any meeting of the Bundesrat or its committees.

The Bundesrat has a share in all federal legislation. For constitutional amendments, a two-thirds majority of Bundesrat votes is required, just as it is of Bundestag members. About half of the legislation is composed of "federative" or "consent" laws for' which

Bundesrat consent is explicitly required by the Basic Law. Specifically, the Bundesrat must approve all federal legislation that is to be carried out by the Länder and thus may affect their administrative institutions and procedures. For all other bills, the Bundesrat has a suspensive veto, which the Bundestag may override by simple majority. If the Bundesrat rejects a bill by a two-thirds majority, however, the same majority in the Bundestag is required to override the veto.

The Bundesrat may require any bill, within two weeks of its receipt from the Bundestag, to be submitted to a Joint Conference Committee of the two chambers, composed of 11 members of the Bundesrat, 1 for each Land, and an equal number of Bundestag members. The power of the Bundesrat is reflected not only in the vetoes it casts (these are, in fact, few), but in the many compromises it forces on the Bundestag in the Joint Conference Committee, and in the extent of substantive changes it thus imposes on original draft legislation.

The role of the Bundesrat is even more significant in emergencies, or in cases of conflict between the federal government and a Land, or between different branches of the government. Bundesrat consent is required for the initiation of federal coercion against any Land that fails to fulfill its legal obligations, and the Bundesrat alone is competent to determine in the first place that such a failure has occurred.

The consent of the Bundesrat is also essential for the proclamation of a "legislative emergency" by the federal president, in the case of a deadlock between the chancellor and a negative majority in the Bundestag, and for the enactment of legislation during its duration. The federal government, without the consent of the Bundesrat, may put Länder police forces under its orders to combat a danger threatening the existence of the constitutional order of the Federal Republic or of any of the Länder. But any such emergency measure must be rescinded whenever the Bundesrat demands it.

Over the years, the Bundesrat has become increasingly inclined to play down its political and straight legislative roles, and to stress the technical and administrative aspects of its activities. In practice, this tactic has been quite effective. Technical arguments seem to lend more strength to a proposed course of action than do political ones. This fact testifies in its own way to a significant trend throughout West German politics: the increasing weight of administrative and bureaucratic considerations and the growing power of the federal executive.

THE CHANCELLOR

The federal chancellor holds the most important office in the Federal Republic (see Figure 4–3). In effect, he appoints and dismisses all members of the federal cabinet, since his proposals are binding on the president of the republic, who has the formal power of appointing and dismissing these persons. Informally, the political parties whose deputies are to elect him to his office may stipulate in their agreement of coalition that certain ministerial portfolios should be given to certain individuals or to members of certain parties. But once the chancellor is appointed, the parties have no effective control over his appointment policies, short of threatening to bring down the government by electing a new chancellor.

Position and Power

The chancellor has the power and the responsibility to determine the guidelines of public policy. His virtual subordinate, the federal minister of defense, is commander in chief of the armed forces in peacetime, but as soon as the "case of defense"—that is, war or warlike emergency—is declared, the supreme command of all forces is vested in the chancellor himself. This declaration is made by the Bundestag or, in the case of emergency, by the president of the republic, with the countersignature of the chancellor.

There are three ways in which a chancellor may be elected by the Bundestag. First, he may be nominated by the president of the

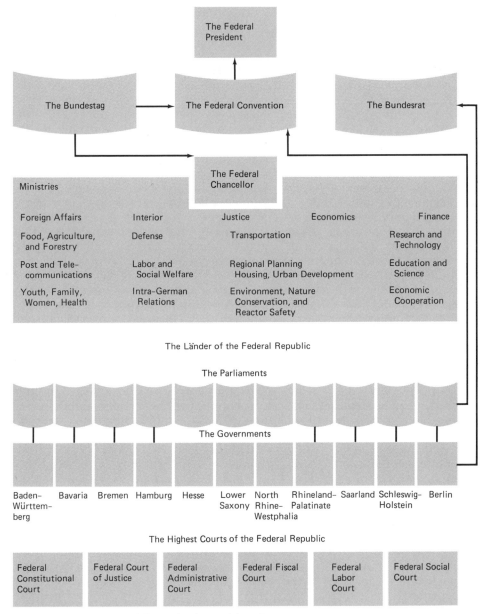

FIGURE 4–3   Organs of the Federal Republic of Germany. Source: *Globus-Kartendienst.*

republic and by the votes of the majority of the members of the Bundestag. Second, in case of the failure of the president's nominee to win such a majority, someone else may be elected chancellor within two weeks by a majority of the Bundestag members. Third, if no candidate has been elected within those two weeks, another Bundestag vote must be taken at once, in which case that candidate who gets the largest number of votes, even short of a majority, is elected. If the chancellor has been elected by such a plurality, the president of the republic must appoint him within seven days or else dissolve the Bundestag and thus bring about national elections for a new parliament.

Once elected and appointed, the chancellor is very likely to remain in office for the entire four-year period of the Bundestag. A hostile majority of Bundestag members can oust him only by a "constructive vote of no confidence"—that is, by electing another chancellor, whom the president of the republic is then obligated to appoint. In April, 1972, Chancellor Brandt narrowly missed losing his office to opposition leader Rainer Barzel in the first attempt at a constructive vote of no confidence at the federal level. Brandt's slim majority had eroded to the point that Barzel believed he had a chance. In the secret ballot that followed, however, Barzel failed, apparently not commanding all the votes of his own Fraktion. Ten years later, in October 1982, SPD Chancellor Helmut Schmidt was replaced by Helmut Kohl of the CDU in a successful application of the constructive vote of no confidence. The FDP had broken ranks with Schmidt's governing coalition and, apart from a few dissenters, threw its support behind Kohl, giving him seven votes more than the necessary absolute majority.

If the Bundestag returns a vote of no confidence against the chancellor but is unable to elect a successor, the chancellor may remain in office or else the president of the republic, if the chancellor so requests, may dissolve the Bundestag within 21 days and thus bring about new elections.

As long as a recalcitrant majority of the Bundestag cannot agree on a successor to the chancellor, the latter under certain conditions can govern quite effectively. The chancellor may even bring about the enactment of federal legislation against the will of a hostile but divided Bundestag. If he has been defeated on an important bill but is not removed from office by the election of a successor, and if the Bundestag has not been dissolved by the president, the latter, on the motion of the federal government and with the consent of the Bundesrat, may declare a "state of legislative emergency" and have the bill pass into law in the form proposed by the federal government, provided it has been approved by the Bundesrat. For a six-month period from the first declaration of such a state of legislative emergency, the chancellor may also cause any other legislative proposal of his government to be enacted in this manner, even if it has been turned down by the Bundestag. The Basic Law may not, however, be changed or suspended, wholly or partly, by such emergency procedures.

Together, and under favorable political and economic conditions, all these provisions tend to make even a weak chancellor strong and a fairly strong chancellor a great deal stronger. His initial strength depends on his position in his own party and on the strength of that party, or on the strength and stability of the coalition of parties that back him. In time, however, if his administration is successful, and particularly if it is further aided by economic prosperity and a favorable international climate, the continuing concentration of power and publicity will tend to make him a commanding figure in the nation.

The chancellor's position depends ultimately upon the support of the electorate and the confidence of his party's deputies. But given this support, the position is further enhanced by several agencies that are directly subordinate to him. Foremost among these is the federal chancellery (*Bundeskanzleramt*). This is in effect a superministry, a coordinating office for the entire federal government. It often has decisive influence on the fate of legislative drafts. Such drafts are proposed by one of the ministries, but they need the approval of the chancellor and cabinet. Thus the informal approval and guidance of the chancellery is often sought even in the early stages of drafting. The chancellery also mediates conflicts between different ministries, so that only the most important issues have to be decided by the chancellor himself.

THE PRESIDENT OF THE REPUBLIC

In spite of the concentration of powers in the chancellor and the continuing efforts to enlarge them, a chancellor may lack adequate support in his party and in the Bundestag and be much in need of cooperation from other factions, parties, and branches of the government. In such a situation, the attitudes and powers of the president of the republic may well prove crucial.

The president is the ceremonial head of the Federal Republic in domestic and international affairs. As such, he has constant opportunities to shape public opinion and the tone and style of politics and culture in the country.

The president is elected for a five-year term and may be reelected for a consecutive term only once. He is elected by a special federal convention, composed of the members of the Bundestag and of an equal number of members of Land legislatures elected on the basis of proportional representation, which brings the total to about one thousand persons. Election is by majority vote of the members of this body. If in two votes no majority has been obtained by any candidate, a plurality in the third vote suffices for election. The rationale for the president's indirect election stems from the Weimar experience, in which a popularly elected president was able to compete with the parliament in claiming to represent the electorate—a situation fraught with potential conflict and the possibility of a stalemated government. In case of the president's incapacity or of his vacating the office before the end of his term, his duties devolve upon the president of the Bundesrat.

Powers

All presidential orders and decrees are valid only if countersigned by the chancellor or by the competent federal minister. The Basic Law permits only three exceptions to this requirement: the appointment and dismissal of the chancellor, the dissolution of the Bundestag in the event of its failure to elect a chancellor by majority vote, and the order to a chancellor or federal minister to carry on the affairs of his office until the appointment of a successor.

The president, nevertheless, has important reserve powers. If the Bundestag cannot be assembled in time, it is he, together with the chancellor, who must decide whether to declare that a "case of defense" has occurred, and thus, in effect, to declare war. He must decide whom to propose first as a candidate for the post of chancellor to the Bundestag and whether to dissolve the Bundestag if no chancellor is elected by a majority vote of the members. He must decide whether to dissolve the Bundestag if it has refused the chancellor a vote of confidence but has failed to replace him by another, or whether to back a minority chancellor in such a case by declaring, at the request of the federal government, a state of legislative emergency. The president thus can lend considerable strength to a weak chancellor, or he can compel him quickly to resign.

The president can be impeached before the Federal Constitutional Court, on the grounds of willful violation of the Basic Law or any other federal law. Impeachment is voted by the Bundestag or the Bundesrat, by two-thirds of the members of the former or a majority of the votes of the latter. The motion to impeach, before it can be considered in either of these bodies, requires the backing of one quarter of the Bundestag members or of the Bundesrat votes, respectively. After impeachment the court may enjoin the president from exercising his office: if the court finds him guilty, it may deprive him of his office altogether.

These provisions underscore the separate legal responsibility of the president, which is distinct from the political responsibility of the chancellor. They tend to strengthen the president's hand in his dealings with the federal government by stressing the autonomous character of his decisions, signatures, and actions, even in cases where the government has requested them. During the controversy over the ratification of the European Defense Community treaty in

December 1952, President Heuss came close to setting a precedent when he requested an advisory opinion from the Federal Constitutional Court on the constitutionality of the treaty. After a single interview with Chancellor Adenauer, however, he withdrew the request, a few hours before the court's opinion was to be made public.

On the whole, however, no major conflicts between the chief institutions and officers of the Federal Republic have arisen thus far, and the president's reserve powers have remained largely untested. Indeed, some constitutional experts feel that the legal and political potentialities of the presidency under the Basic Law have by no means been fully utilized. Until now, most of his activities have been taken up by more formal duties of representation and government routine.

LAWMAKING

It may be convenient at this stage to summarize the roles of the different legislative and executive agencies in the normal process of legislation. The simplified flow diagram in Figure 4-4 should be largely self-explanatory.

Bills can be initiated by the federal government, the Bundestag, or the Bundesrat. Those initiated by the federal government—thus far substantially more than half the total—must first be submitted to the scrutiny

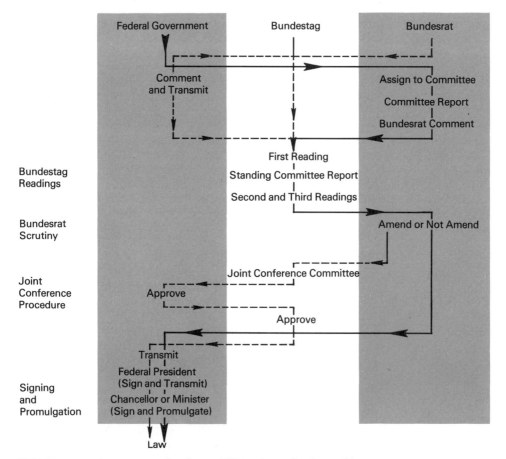

FIGURE 4-4 The passage of ordinary bills in the Federal Republic. The heavy line indicates the route of most bills.

of the Bundesrat. Those few bills originating in the Bundesrat must first be commented on by the federal government. Then, however, all bills—including those that originated in the Bundestag itself—go through the main legislative process in the Bundestag. This starts with a first reading in the full Bundestag—the plenum—of the general principles of the bill, followed by intensive work on its details in one of the standing committees of the Bundestag, which in its report produces a draft version of the bill. This is followed by a second reading in the plenum on the specific details of the bill, and a third reading and a vote. (Before a bill goes through each successive stage, there are Fraktion meetings in which decisions are made as to which position to take on the bill.)

After adoption by the Bundestag the bill goes to the Bundesrat, and if not amended there it passes on directly—as do more than nine tenths of all bills—to the president of the republic and to the chancellor or the competent federal minister for their signatures, and on to promulgation into law. For the one-tenth or fewer bills that are amended in the Bundesrat, another round of procedures is required. A compromise version is worked out in the Joint Conference Committee and approved by each of the two chambers. The approved text is then returned to the main track for executive signatures and promulgation.

The system looks somewhat cumbersome on paper, but it has worked well in practice, ensuring thorough consideration of most measures within a reasonable time. Even in a smoothly working system, however, some deadlocks and conflicts are likely to occur. To deal with these, the Basic Law provides for a Federal Constitutional Court.

THE FEDERAL CONSTITUTIONAL COURT

The chief agency for resolving constitutional conflicts is the Federal Constitutional Court. Broadly speaking, this court is competent to deal with six kinds of cases:

1. *The control of the constitutionality of laws.* There is a hierarchy of laws, in which the Basic Law ranks highest, other federal laws next, then Länder constitutions, and finally other Land legislation. Any law thus may have to be scrutinized for its compatibility with a higher one, up to the Basic Law. The Federal Constitutional Court may be invoked for this purpose by any other court of law (where in a pending case a conflict of this kind may have arisen) or by the federal government, or by any Land government, or by one third of the members of the Bundestag.

2. *Interpretations of the Basic Law, occasioned by disagreements about the limits of the rights and duties of any one of the highest organs of the Federal Republic.* Here the court may be invoked by the president of the republic, the Bundestag, the Bundesrat, the Permanent Committee of the Bundestag provided for by article 45 of the rules of the Bundestag, the federal government, or certain of the major parts of any of these, such as the one tenth or one fourth of the members of the Bundestag who have the right to initiate certain procedures there. In any case, however, the plaintiffs must show their specific legal interest in the case at issue.

3. *Disagreements about the rights and duties of the federal government or of the Länder governments.* Proceedings may be initiated only by the federal government for the federal authorities, and only by a Land government for any Länder authorities.

4. *Formal deprivations of certain constitutional rights, somewhat analogous to criminal proceedings:*
   a. Forfeiture of basic rights, on grounds of their anticonstitutional misuse.
   b. Banning of specific political parties as unconstitutional.
   c. Impeachment of the president of the republic on a motion by the federal government, by the Bundestag, or by the Bundesrat.
   d. Impeachment of federal judges, on the motion of the Bundestag.

5. *Complaints against decisions by the Bundestag in regard to the validity of an election or the acquisition or loss of membership in the Bundestag by a deputy or candidate,* on the motion of the rejected candidate, or of 101 voters, or of a Bundestag Fraktion, or of one tenth of the Bundestag members.

6. *All constitutional complaints by individuals against any alleged violation of any of their basic rights.* Such complaints may be initiated by an indi-

vidual, but ordinarily he may appeal to the Federal Constitutional Court only after exhausting his normal remedies in the regular courts. The Federal Constitutional Court, however, may accept and decide such a complaint at once if it deals with a matter of general importance or if the delays of normal legal proceedings through the courts would work serious and unavoidable harm for the plaintiff.

The Constitutional Court, located at Karlsruhe, consists of two chambers or "senates," each composed of 8 judges, or 16 for the entire court. Originally, the First Senate was to deal with conflicts between federal or Länder laws and the Basic Law or between federal and Länder laws; the Second Senate was to deal with conflicts between the highest organs of government. Experience soon showed that legal and constitutional disputes of the first kind were frequent, particularly the individual complaints (category 6), whereas top level political conflicts of the second type were rare. The court began to operate in 1951. Within the first five years the First Senate heard nearly 3,000 complaints while the Second Senate was dealing with about 30. After redistribution of the work load in 1956 and 1960, the First Senate now deals mainly with complaints against violations of civil and constitutional rights, leaving most other kinds of cases to the Second Senate, which consequently has gained somewhat in influence.

At times there has been a tendency in the Federal Republic to pass difficult political problems to the courts, particularly to the Constitutional Court, and thereby avoid the strains and stresses of seeking their resolution by legislative and executive institutions. As in other countries, this tempting practice has threatened to engage the prestige of the courts in political controversy, but respect for the courts has remained high. In a country that lacked deep-rooted habits and traditions of constitutionalism and democracy, it has been perhaps more necessary to call on the courts and the respect for law to limit political conflicts, to curb the excessive pragmatism and potential ruthlessness with which interest groups might come to press their claims, and to guard the essential rules and procedures of constitutional politics.

5

Social Structure,
Interest Groups,
and Elites

Germany has become somewhat more urban and industrial during the last four decades. By 1987, cities and towns contained some 94 percent of the population of the Federal Republic, including West Berlin. Large cities above 500,000 population accounted for 17 percent; large cities with populations between 100,000 and 500,000 accounted for another 16 percent; middle-sized cities with 20,000 to 100,000 inhabitants added 26 percent. As many as 35 percent of West Germans, however, still lived in small towns of between 2,000 and 20,000 people, and the remaining 6 percent lived in still smaller and for the most part rural communities.[1] No political party stressing mainly rural interests can hope for a majority, but since 41 percent of the voters live in communities of fewer than 20,000 people, the parties can

hardly omit making an appeal to rural and small-town voters and their values. The right-of-center parties have been significantly more successful in attracting the vote in communities of less than 20,000 people.

World War II has left its mark on the population. Of those 65 years old and older, 66 percent are women. In contrast, women make up 52 percent of the population as a whole.

In 1985 the Federal Republic had the lowest birth rate in the world, 9.6 per 1,000 inhabitants. In the late 1980s there has been a modest increase in this rate, but since 1972, the number of deaths per year has exceeded the number of live births. There are as many inhabitants aged 65 years and over as youngsters under age 15. Nearly two-thirds of all German households consist of either one or two persons. Should this trend continue, it is estimated that the West German population could shrink to half its current size by the year 2030 with a dispropor-

---

[1]These and the following data are derived from the *Statistisches Jahrbuch für die Bundesrepublik*, Stuttgart (1988), hereafter cited as *S.J.B.*

tionately high number of pensioners on the social welfare rolls.

THE STRENGTH OF OCCUPATIONAL GROUPINGS

In 1988 about 46 percent of the people of the Federal Republic were members of its work force of 28 million. The rest were their dependent children, other family members, and pensioners, the last-named group comprising some 20 percent of the total population.

Only 5 percent of the work force are engaged in agriculture, some 41 percent are engaged in mining or construction or in crafts, and the remaining 54 percent are occupied in commerce, transportation, or services, both private and public. White-collar employees now make up 48.4 percent of the work force; blue-collar workers constitute 39.8 percent. The remaining 11.8 percent of the work force consists of self-employed urban middle-class individuals and the members of their families assisting them in their enterprises. The main groups within this category are small businessmen in commerce and the service industries, artisans, and a small group of professionals. With some exceptions, there has been a strong tendency for blue-collar workers to vote for the SPD, and for employers, professional people, and farmers to vote for the CDU, CSU, or the FDP. White-collar employees are a swing group that may well decide an election.

By the early 1970s some 2.5 million foreign workers (9 percent of the work force) were employed by West German firms. The largest numbers of such *Gastarbeiter* (guest workers) came from Turkey, Yugoslavia, Italy, and Greece. The Bonn government, spurred by rising unemployment, sought to curtail the influx of foreign workers in the mid 1970s. Though most originally came with the intention of returning to their homelands, it became evident that a sizable number of Gastarbeiter and their families were seeking to establish residence. In the early 1980s the government began to offer financial inducements to encourage Gastarbeiter to leave the Federal Republic.

By the late 1970s an increasing number of political and "economic" refugees from developing countries began to take advantage of the Federal Republic's liberal policies governing the granting of asylum. The efforts of the government to deal with this influx of asylum-seekers and with the social integration of the Gastarbeiter are discussed in Chapter 7. All told, Gastarbeiter and their families, refugees, and FRG-based foreign soldiers, businessmen, and diplomats constituted nearly 4.7 million foreign residents in the Federal Republic by mid-1988.

INCOME GROUPS, STATUS GROUPS, AND SOCIAL GROUPS

The Distribution of Income

By comparison with previous German regimes and with the vast majority of nations today, the average German is very well off. There remains, however, a broad range of income distribution in the Federal Republic. On the bottom of the scale are pensioners and the unemployed, who despite inflationary trends still manage to attain a modest standard of living on government stipends, thanks to long-standing efforts to maintain an enlightened social policy. At the top are the relatively few who command a disproportionate share of the country's wealth. The holdings of the industrial entrepreneurs of the empire and the Weimar era have remained largely intact despite changes in regimes. Industrial magnates do not, however, wield the same degree of influence they did in pre-1945 Germany.

Under the Bonn government most Germans have been less interested in the just distribution of income than in seeing this total income increase, and in having their own incomes rise with it. The jump in per capita income was particularly dramatic in the 1970s. Average worker per capita income in current prices increased from DM 6,148 in 1960 to DM 13,841 in 1970, DM 29,995 in

1980, and to DM 40,778 in 1988. By the early 1980s, however, decreased purchasing power served to temper the real increase in income. West Germans are nonetheless among the most affluent people in Europe. Rising incomes and the increase in the number of those in the middle-income bracket, during a period in which German inflation was comparatively low, have contributed to this affluence.

Status Groups and Social Classes

Germans have long been a highly status-conscious people, and the distribution of status differs in some respects from the distribution of income. Occupations requiring more education and either private or public trust rank higher in status than the pay they bring indicates.

The actual distribution of social classes and status groups differed very little in the early years of the Federal Republic from the social structure of the previous several decades, but a number of factors have since contributed to greater social mobility and a lessening of divisions among classes. A primary factor has been the rising income level and the enjoyment of material benefits on a previously unmatched scale, even among those formerly counted in the lower class. Also contributing to the lessening of class differences among Germans has been the introduction of large outside groups into the country's work force—first the refugees and expellees from the GDR and the former German territories and now the Gastarbeiter. Members of both groups were willing to take on the more menial tasks in society, in effect improving the lot of lower-class West German "natives." Although the former group has become both thoroughly integrated and upwardly mobile in German society, strong cultural differences are precluding the similar assimilation of the Gastarbeiter.

Education has long been a major indicator of social class in Germany. Formerly accessible only to the privileged and rich, a university education served to demonstrate not only social cleavages but fundamental cultural cleavages as well. Higher education was maintained as the avenue for general elite membership. The educated few read different newspapers, engaged in different cultural activities, and even spoke a different language from that of the mass of Germans.

LEVELS OF EDUCATION

West German children must be enrolled full time in school for either nine or ten years depending on the policy of the individual Land. Thereafter, slightly more than one quarter of German school children go on to advanced schooling; one quarter enter the job market; the rest go on to vocational training, becoming apprentices or trainees.

Graduation from a full-fledged German academic high school—which is comparable to two years of American college—had been achieved by only 4 percent of the general population in the mid-1950s. In 1987 some 28 percent of German 13-year-olds were enrolled in academic high schools. The number of students in academic and technical programs of higher education has also increased markedly from 112,000 in 1957 to nearly 1,500,000 enrolled during the 1988 winter semester.

In 1984, of the total population of all ages, 23 of every 1,000 were attending a university or technical college versus 2 per 1,000 in 1950 and in 1932 at the end of the Weimar Republic and only 1 per 1,000 under Hitler's regime in 1938.

Quietly and without much rhetoric, the Federal Republic had by the early 1970s opened the gates of the German universities much wider than ever before. Although the West German levels are still below the United States proportion, and although marked cleavages still exist in German education, the percentage of university-educated men and women has grown significantly.

The Federal Republic has been hard-pressed to accommodate the major increase in participants in postsecondary education. The founding of several new universities did not fully alleviate crowded conditions, and limitations have been placed on student enrollment in selected fields of study. The number of university students is expected, however, to peak in the early 1990s and then to drop significantly as a result of the decline in the West German birth rate.

Those who completed higher education in the early 1980s encountered an increasingly tight job market exacerbated by the economic downturn of the period. The economy had a similar effect on vocational opportunities for those not going on to university with fewer apprenticeship slots available. By the late 1980s, however, placements had improved for both apprentices and university graduates.

REGIONAL FACTORS

It is said that Chancellor Adenauer once described Germany as being divided naturally into three parts—the Germany of wine, the Germany of beer, and the Germany of schnapps, or hard liquor—and that he expressed his love for the first, his sympathy for the second, and his willingness to do his duty for the third. Much has been written by others about the cultural and psychological differences between the wine-drinking Rhineland, beer-drinking Bavaria, and liquor-drinking northern and eastern Germany. In less picturesque language, the west, the south, the north, and the east-central regions are widely accepted as the main geographic subdivisions of Germany. The first three of these now constitute three informal regions of the Federal Republic. The fourth has now become the GDR and the Oder- Neisse territories, but it lives on in West German politics through the memories of the substantial portion of the population who are refugees or expellees.

The political and administrative structure of the Federal Republic is built upon its 11 states, or Länder. Some Länder—Bavaria, Hamburg, and Bremen, among others—continue the traditions of earlier German political units. Others, such as North Rhine–Westphalia, Baden-Württemberg, and Lower

Saxony, represent postwar mergers of earlier territorial units.

The most populous Land is North Rhine–Westphalia. It contains more than one-fourth of the population of the Federal Republic and accounts for more than one-fourth of the nation's economic activity. The second most populous state, and the largest in area, is Bavaria, followed by Baden–Württemberg and Lower Saxony. The remaining Länder have less than 6 million inhabitants each. Indeed, among them only Hesse and Rhineland–Palatinate are even middle-sized; the rest each have less than 2.6 million people.

The West German Länder

The figures in Table 5–1 illustrate the considerable differences in population, area and wealth among the Länder. The "gross domestic product" figures, technically called economic turnover, show something of the level of economic development in each state. The city states of Hamburg, Bremen, and West Berlin are noteworthy for their high per capita income. They are followed by Hesse and Baden–Württemberg. All the remaining areas are below the national average, Bavaria only slightly so. In the late 1980s, economic disparities in unemployment and the rate of economic growth among the Länder were particularly striking, with the southern states of Baden-Württemberg and Bavaria and the western states of Hesse and Rhineland-Palatinate having a higher economic growth rate and unemployment well below the national average. The converse was the case for all other states, with stagnating growth and over 10 percent unemployment in Bremen, Hamburg, West Berlin, North Rhine–Westphalia, and Lower Saxony.

As Tables 5–1 and 5–2 suggest, the postwar arrangement of Länder and regions has been unfavorable to northern Germany. That region is the smallest of the three, yet it is divided into four states. The economic "raisins" of Hamburg and Bremen are separated from the "cake" of their hinterland in

TABLE 5–1   Economic Aspects of West German Länder and Regions

| Land | 1987 Population (millions) | Area (thousands sq km) | Gross Domestic Product, 1987 | | |
			Amount (billions of DM)	% of Total	Per capita (thousands of DM)
North Rhine–Westphalia	16.7	34.1	528	26.2%	31.6
Hesse	5.5	21.1	202	10.0	36.7
Rhineland-Palatinate	3.6	19.8	108	5.4	30.0
Saarland	1.0	2.6	30	1.5	30.0
Subtotal, western region	26.8	77.6	868	43.1	32.4
Bavaria	11.0	70.6	361	17.9	32.8
Baden-Württemberg	9.4	35.8	324	16.1	34.5
Subtotal, southern region	20.4	106.4	685	34.0	33.6
Lower Saxony	7.2	47.4	195	9.7	27.1
Schleswig-Holstein	2.6	15.7	70	3.5	26.9
Hamburg	1.6	0.8	91	4.5	56.9
Bremen	0.7	0.4	28	1.4	40.0
Subtotal, northern region	12.1	64.3	384	19.1	31.7
West Berlin	1.9	0.5	76	3.8	40.0
FRG, including West Berlin	61.2	248.7	2013	100.0	32.9

Source: Derived from *S.J.B.*

TABLE 5–2   Social and Political Aspects of West German Länder and Regions

	Expellees and Refugees 1969 (% of population)	Roman Catholics 1970 (% of population)	% of 1987 Votes for CDU/CSU	Seats in Bundesrat	Governing Party or Coalition 1988
North Rhine–Westphalia	14%	52%	40.1%	5	SPD
Hesse	16	33	41.3	4	CDU/FDP
Rhineland-Palatinate	7	56	45.1	4	CDU/FDP
Saarland	1	74	41.2	3	SPD
Subtotal, western region	12	50		16	
Bavaria	16	70	55.1	5	CSU
Baden-Württemberg	14	47	46.7	5	CDU
Subtotal, southern region	15	60		10	
Lower Saxony	24	20	41.5	5	CDU/FDP
Schleswig-Holstein	26	6	41.9	4	SPD
Hamburg	10	8	37.4	3	SPD/FDP
Bremen	14	10	28.9	3	SPD
Subtotal, northern region	22	15		15	
West Berlin	6	12	*	*	SPD/Greens
FRG, including West Berlin	16	46	44.3	41	CDU/CSU/ FDP

*West Berlin, which is not legally a constituent part of the Federal Republic, does provide 22 indirectly selected, nonvoting members to the Bundestag as well as nonvoting observers to the Bundesrat. West Berlin voters do not participate in federal elections.

Source: Derived from *S.J.B.*

Lower Saxony and Schleswig-Holstein. Northern Germany is largely Protestant, small, divided, partly poor, underrepresented in most national elites, and generally less influential in national affairs than it was under the Hohenzollern empire and the Weimar Republic. The SPD has generally dominated politics in the two city-states. Lower Saxony and Schleswig-Holstein have traditionally been bastions for center-right politics, though the SPD received an absolute majority in the 1988 Schleswig-Holstein state election.

Southern Germany suffered least from the war. Its voters have stronger local attachments and markedly less interest in the rest of the country. Although southern German voters have favored German reunification, they have been much less concerned about it. Conservative and nationalist views are somewhat stronger in southern Germany, and particularly in rural and small-town Bavaria outside the metropolitan region of Munich.

The western region emerges as the one most nearly representative of the political attitudes of the entire country. It is less nationalistic and intense than the North, but less locally preoccupied than the South. In addition to its sizable population and its economic resources, this region has traditionally contributed a higher share of important national elites.

Regional diversities have been reinforced by the partial decentralization of politics through the institutions of the Länder. This has in turn enhanced the political importance of local and regional politics. The Länder system has helped government to address the inequalities of economic development among the different areas. It has permitted economically favored regions to retain some of their advantages, while using redistributive measures to assist less favored regions and thereby reduce interregional cleavages. The opportunities for governing in regional and municipal politics have been substantial enough to keep opposition parties alive with the prospect of eventually consolidating their strength and grooming their candidates for political bids at the national level. In these and other ways, regionalism and Land government have contributed substantially to the stability and adaptability of democracy in the Federal Republic.

INTEREST GROUPS AND ELITES

Political parties, especially when they are broadly based, as are the CDU and SPD, have "policy umbrellas"—platforms that cover and protect as many diverse interests as possible to maximize electoral support.

Business Interests

With the demise of large landowners, a second traditional great body of interests—big business and industry—has come into its own. Farmers and labor organizations can and often do exert effective pressure in pursuit of their specific interests, but the very much greater influence and prestige of business in the Federal Republic is conspicuous. When different business groups oppose each other their influence is weakened, but when business speaks with a united voice its views, with rare exceptions, weigh heavily in Bonn.

The business groups in the Federal Republic are organized into three *Spitzenverbände* (major organizations): the Federation of German Industries (BDI), the Diet of German Industry and Commerce (DIHT), and the Federal Union of German Employers Associations (BDA). Of these, the BDI is the wealthiest, most active and most influential. In addition, there are separate associations for banking, insurance, foreign trade, retail trade, shipping, transportation, handicrafts, and others. Serving as a coordinating committee for all these central associations is the Joint Committee of German Trades and Industries (*Gemeinschaftsausschuss der deutschen gewerblichen Wirtschaft*). This joint committee attempts to iron out difficulties among its member organizations and provide public representation for the business community as a whole.

The BDI, the BDA, and DIHT have maintained close personal contact with administrative policymakers, seeking to influence decision making and personnel choices. Influence patterns have been enhanced by the high degree of overlapping membership between business and industrial elites and administrative and parliamentary policymakers. A significant percentage of Bundestag delegates traditionally have been in effect representatives of business interest groups. These friends of business in the German parliament are not only the recognized experts on economic matters in Bundestag committees and the party caucuses; they also perform a lobbying role in their official contacts with administrative personnel in the federal ministries.

The efforts of big business firms to influence political parties and individual politicians through contributions and even financial retainers came under closer scrutiny in the mid-1980s through parliamentary investigation into the lobbying and financial dealings of the Flick industrial holding company.

The attempts of the victorious Allies to disincorporate traditional large German enterprises have largely come to naught. Industrial magnates were rehabilitated so that they could join in the thrust toward economic recovery, and were given a role within the restructured social market economy. Spurred by the "economic miracle," large conglomerates such as the chemical firms Hoechst, Bayer, and BASF; the electrical firms Siemens, Telefunken, and Bosch; the auto firms Volkswagen, Daimler-Benz, and Adam Opel; and the iron and steel firms Krupp, Thyssen, and Mannesmann continue to dominate their respective sectors.

Farmers' Organizations

The chief agricultural organization in the FRG is the League of German Farmers (*Deutscher Bauernverband*). German farm organizations have considerable political influence, which has been directed effectively toward specific demands such as agricultural subsidies and prices. As a result, German farmers have been generally well protected and effectively compensated for their high costs. Prior to the advent of a common agricultural policy in the European Economic Community, wheat prices in the Federal Republic were some 30 percent higher than in the Netherlands and almost 50 percent higher than in France. However, France's powerful bargaining position in the Common Market has since led to a significant decrease in the common price for wheat, and French, Italian, Dutch, and Danish agricultural products have been admitted more freely to the German market. At the same time, however, German agriculture has continued to be effectively compensated for high costs by governmental actions, at no small cost to the FRG federal budget.

Labor Unions and Employees Associations

There are three large labor unions in the Federal Republic. The most important is the German Confederation of Trade Unions (*Deutscher Gewerkschaftsbund,* or DGB), with 7.76 million members in 1988. The DGB includes all wage earners' unions and is also the largest organization of white-collar clerical employees. The German Employees Union (*Deutsche Angestelltengewerkschaft,* or DAG), represents nearly a half-million white-collar clerical employees. This union has tended to stress the quasi-professional characteristics of white-collar employees, contrasting their separate status and distinct interests with those of the wage earners. Nevertheless, in practice the DAG has often found itself pressing economic demands similar to those advocated by the DGB. The most professional and nonpolitical of the three great worker associations is the German Federation of Civil Servants (*Deutscher Beamtenbund*) with a membership of 786,000 civil servants in 1988.

The German labor movement—despite periods of militancy and radical expression in imperial Germany and the early years of the Weimar Republic—has ultimately proved to be in the mainstream in adjusting to and endorsing the course set by the federal administration. The necessity of collective action in the recovery effort after World War II caused union leaders to exercise restraint and tone down wage demands. This approach fostered a low-wage, high-profit trend that spurred remarkable growth and spread benefits in the economy. A marked increase in average monthly pay, especially pronounced from 1962 until the onset of an inflationary period in the early 1970s, did much to dispel any latent dissatisfaction and gave workers a stake in the system.

Labor won an important victory in gaining the support of Chancellor Adenauer for a codetermination law enacted in 1951. Under its provisions, representatives of labor join with management representatives on standing committees to consult on matters important to workers. New codetermination legislation enacted by the SPD/FDP government in July 1976 provided for equal representation of labor and management in companies employing more than 2,000 workers.

In comparison to other social market democracies, there have been relatively few strikes in the Federal Republic. However, in one major instance in the spring of 1984, against a backdrop of high unemployment and sluggish economic growth, labor organized strikes of 444,000 metal workers and 17,000 printing industry employees. The striking workers and their unions demanded wage hikes and institution of a 35-hour workweek. A settlement to the costly strike several weeks later resulted in the inauguration of a 38.5-hour workweek and a 5.3 percent wage increase.

The Churches

The influence of the churches in German political life has lessened markedly over time. In 1988, in the FRG including West Berlin, there were 26.2 million Roman Catholics and 25.4 million members of the German Evangelical (Protestant) Church. Membership in other Christian denominations is small but growing. About 27,600 Jews live in the Federal Republic. About 1.6 million Gastarbeiter are Moslems. Some 8 percent of the population either profess no religion or have withdrawn from one of the two large state churches, in many cases to avoid having church tax assessments withheld from their paychecks. These figures show a shift from 1950 when 52 percent of the FRG population were Protestant and 44 percent Catholic. Reunification with the largely Protestant GDR would increase the percentage of Protestants substantially. Since the early 1950s, average Protestant attendance has dropped to around 5 percent and Catholic attendance to 24 percent. Despite religious instruction in the schools and the continuing participation of most Germans in Church-performed baptismal, marriage, and burial ceremonies, the faithful in both denominations are a largely aging minority. Both major churches have had to contend with the rapid secularization of West German society.

The SPD in 1969, for the first time, made major inroads among Catholic workers and white-collar employees. But during electoral campaigns, Catholic audiences continue to be vigorously exhorted by bishops, the lower clergy, the church press, and lay organizations to vote according to their conscience, and not vote for irreligious parties, with specific allusions often made to the SPD. While the majority of committed Catholics continue to support the CDU and CSU, these parties—in particular the CDU—reflect a much broader focus due in no small part to the church's waning influence and the decline in the number of active Catholics.

A relatively large number of top Protestant leaders come from the eastern part of Germany, and many have strong anti-Nazi records. They have remained concerned with the political issues of peace and reunification, having a strong sense of kinship with the GDR's population and its predominantly Protestant background. Thus in 1965, in the face of the Erhard government's inaction on the question of the FRG's eastern frontiers and its present and future relationship with its eastern neighbors, the German Evangelical Church publicly took a stand in a widely discussed memorandum favoring more active and accommodating negotiations with the East, thereby helping bring that issue into the political arena.

In the early 1980s, both Catholic and Protestant lay and ecclesiastical organizations were variously involved in adding a religious dimension to the peace movement's efforts to combat the perceived threat of a nuclear buildup and the placement of American and Soviet missiles in the FRG and GDR.

Refugee and Expellee Associations

Perhaps the most vocal of all FRG interest groups with respect to foreign policy and national political issues have been the organizations representing the expellees from former eastern territories and refugees from East Germany. Remarkable success in the monumental task of integrating millions of displaced Germans into the economic and social structure of the FRG has, however, largely defused the political potency of this potentially strong revanchist element of the population.

Expellees are organized into some 24 *Landsmannschaften* (regional groups) associated in the *Bund der Vertriebenen* (League of Expelled Germans, or BDV). The *Landsmannschaften* and the BDV endeavor to preserve memories of the German heritage of the eastern territories through cultural institutes, research conferences, publications, and direct political action.

6

Political Culture, Parties, and Elections

Just as any single individual can be said to have a certain set of political attitudes, so attitudes toward different aspects of politics comprise a country's *political culture,* which is, of course, a part of its general or national culture.

POLITICAL CULTURE AND NATIONAL CHARACTERISTICS

Any study of West German political culture and political attitudes must take into account the unique political and cultural heritage of Germany's past. At the same time it should not overlook other influences that have led to some marked differences in cultural and political attitudes in the generations of West Germans who have grown up since 1945. West German attitudes have been affected by the conflicting influences of events and memories from German his-

tory, of recent or current institutions and practices in society and family life, of old and new images and ideas about human relations and politics, and of social and political developments since 1945. The long and often violent history of the German people has left them with deep-seated memories that have colored their political decisions in the past and may continue to affect future generations. These memories are embedded in German schoolbooks and in learned histories, in literature, and in the minds of individuals. These historic memories recall that for centuries the international environment has not been kind to Germany. From the horrors of the Thirty Years' War to the desperate struggles of Frederick II's Prussia and the Napoleonic wars, foreign economic and military developments are remembered as having threatened or injured Germany. To this are added memories of the overwhelmingly strong foreign coalitions that united to defeat Germany in two world wars.

Characteristic Attitudes

In the face of an environment that thus seemed often less than fair to their aspirations, many Germans, particularly those of the older generations, felt that they had to hold on to their particular virtues as a people. Outstanding among these virtues was a capacity and liking for hard work (recent surveys, however, indicate less of a preoccupation with the work ethic among members of younger generations). Most people seem to consider the members of their own nation as hard-working, but the Germans have done so to a far greater extent than others. There is no doubt that this image is based on a very real German virtue. Foreign observers, as well as Germans, have attested time and again to the energy, diligence, and thoroughness of Germans in their work, both physical and intellectual.

Yet the German "national character"—or those elements and patterns in German culture, traditions, and personality that have relevance for political behavior—is more complex. Like similar patterns in other countries, it moves often in polarities—that is, in pairs of opposites. Both German and foreign observers have spoken of a German fascination with abstract doctrines and ideas, and sometimes of the preoccupation of Germans with wealth and material success—as with the success-oriented Germans of the Federal Republic.

German attitudes toward politics have in the past swung between an insistence on the virtues of being "nonpolitical" or "above the parties" and a willingness to accept the most extreme partisan commitments of totalitarian fanaticism. By no means have all Germans at any one time been stranded on the poles of this dilemma, but a sufficient number of them have been often enough in the past to give to German political attitudes a characteristic cast and potential.

Some of these polarities can perhaps be traced back to the influences of German history, and so too can some of the potential political weaknesses they imply. German history is rich in memories of authoritarian princes and magistrates, and of the dependence of their subjects on them for protection. In this way, a strong element of authoritarianism—a willingness to submit to those in authority combined with a tendency to demand obedience from subordinates—has become part of the German national character and political culture.

POSTWAR CHANGES IN POLITICAL ATTITUDES

In the face of this complex heritage of psychological and political assets, liabilities, and contrasts, the Federal Republic has done remarkably well. It has gone far toward making the politics of compromise appear both successful and legitimate. It has increased the degree of equality in German society and politics through broader educational opportunities and a mitigation of class consciousness. More generally, it seems to have lowered the level of bitterness and tension that could be found in earlier decades in the life and outlook of the German people; this seems the more remarkable since such might have been expected to rise after a defeat in war. While not without tensions, the Federal Republic has provided stability, security, and opportunity for new generations of young Germans to grow up and reach the threshold of political life.

Are there then any changes in the political culture than can help to explain Bonn's success? That the Germans lived under a totalitarian regime for 12 years from 1933 to 1945 would seem to have played an important part in the alteration of basic political attitudes. Perhaps the single most important effect of the totalitarian experience has been the breakdown of the simple traditional German identification of "freedom" with order and with the capacity to act, and hence in practice with the powerful and authoritarian state. The tradition that merged the German quest for liberty with the acceptance of authoritarian government has been largely shattered by the experience of brutal totalitarianism combined with devastating military defeat.

The reaction to the unsuccessful totalitarian experience has also produced a more pragmatic basis for evaluating the state: what it does as the utilitarian servant of the people, and not what the people do for it. Emerging from economic and industrial ruin, the Federal Republic faced the job of reconstructing the economy. Even in the late 1950s and early 1960s, after the job of reconstruction had been more than completed and the FRG had entered a period of previously unrivaled prosperity, West Germans continued to conceive of the state's functions primarily in terms of its success in maintaining a high level of economic affluence. The Germans' support of the Bonn regime, and more generally their attachment to democratic government, grew initially out of the regime's success in overseeing the "economic miracle." This attachment seemed to have achieved some maturity by the 1980s, having weathered periods of recession and sluggish economic growth.

A Politically Cautious Pragmatism

The political culture of the early years of the FRG could be characterized primarily by pragmatic attitudes toward the democratic regime. During this period "pragmatists" far outnumbered both dedicated democrats and right- and left-wing opponents of the regime. The pragmatists seemed to have few commitments and little ideology, but in their place a lively sense of concrete benefits such as jobs, homes, and security, which they preferred to abstract slogans. A manifestation of the pragmatists' desire for security was their willingness to follow leaders and elites who seemed to promote this value. The main Christian Democratic poster in the 1957 election showed only the impressive sun-bronzed face of Chancellor Adenauer and the slogan "No Experiments!" It was developed with the advice of experts in public opinion and persuasion, and it was a resounding success.

Since 1945, the great majority of West Germans have had no interest in policies en-

tailing elements of risk. They very much want peace, and they have shown no inclination to underrate the strength of either the United States or the Soviet Union. When asked in 1965 if they thought that Germany would ever become a major world power again, only 17 percent said yes.[1] This sentiment was repeatedly stressed by Chancellor Helmut Schmidt in the late 1970s at a time when the Federal Republic's economic prowess suggested the capability of becoming a great power.

The Federal Republic's leaders have succeeded in maintaining democracy, moderation, and a limited consensus. Though the economic boom slackened and terrorist activity and a growing counterculture threatened domestic tranquility, successive governments have managed to maintain economic solvency and civic peace.

West German democracy has been based largely on the collaboration of a small yet increasing number of committed democrats with a large number of "fair-weather" democrats whose allegiance is based primarily upon what they expect to get. This chiefly pragmatic orientation is by no means the best cultural foundation for democracy—nor is it the worst. In the case of the FRG, the foundation has been sufficient for democracy to take hold.

The Popular Rejection of Communism

The Communists, who attracted an average of 13 percent of the votes cast in each of the seven national elections between 1924 and 1933, have dwindled into insignificance in the Federal Republic. This change was complete even before the outlawing of their party in 1956. In the first Bundestag election in 1949, the Communist party won only 5.7 percent of the vote and 15 seats. In 1953 its strength fell to little more than 2 percent and no Bundestag representation. In the elections since 1969, when Communist parties were again permitted, their share of the

---

[1] Unpublished report of the Institut für Demoskopie, Allensbach (June 1965).

vote has been minuscule—this despite the modest growth of a dissident, leftist segment of the population. This segment has increasingly identified with the Green party and Land-based "alternative" groupings, rather than with the reconstituted Communist party.

Popular revulsion against Communism in West Germany may have been promoted by the continuing stream of expellees and refugees from Communist-ruled areas; by the inflow of these intensely anticommunist millions into the least skilled and worst paid occupations, where the Communists otherwise might have hoped for converts; and most important of all, by the unprecedented rise and spread of economic prosperity after 1948, combined with effective social welfare legislation.

Nazi Ideology and the Extreme Right

A sizable but waning minority of West Germans could be identified through the late 1960s as supporters of Nazi or neo-Nazi causes. In a 1953 poll, 13 percent said they would welcome the attempt of a new Nazi party to seize power; 5 percent promised their active support. In repeated polls during the years 1949–1963, proportions of 7 to 15 percent (1) admired Hitler and his propaganda minister, Joseph Goebbels, (2) professed Nazi race doctrines about the Jews, and (3) blamed foreign powers, and not Germany, for the outbreak of World War II.[2] The reality of the attitudes indicated by these poll results was demonstrated in December 1959 and January 1960 when a Jewish tombstone and a synagogue in Cologne were disfigured with anti-Jewish slogans and Nazi swastikas. These acts of vandalism received wide and unfavorable publicity in the West German press, radio, and television, but were followed within about four weeks

by 170 similar incidents in all the states of the Federal Republic. The West German authorities, both state and federal, were quick and unequivocal in condemning these outrages, and so were most articulate Germans.

The phenomenon of measurable electoral support for the right-wing National Democratic party (NPD) from 1965 through the 1969 federal election indicated that neo-Nazi supporters still existed. The National Democrats received only 2 percent of the vote in the 1965 Bundestag election. However, in four Landtag elections in 1966 and 1967—in Schleswig–Holstein, Hesse, Bavaria, and Bremen—they polled between 7 and 12 percent of the vote. The NPD subsequently succeeded in entering three more Land legislatures, but the Bundestag election of 1969 proved the turning point for this party. With only 4.3 percent of the popular vote, the NPD was blocked from entry into the Bundestag by the exclusion clause of the electoral law. The disintegration of the party became apparent in early 1970, when the two vice chairmen of the party and many high-ranking functionaries renounced their membership. In the next round of Landtag elections the NPD lost its representation, in most cases not even fielding candidates. Its share of the electorate in national elections shrank to 0.6 percent in 1972 and in subsequent federal elections through 1987 has remained at this level or below. Other small right-wing parties have emerged at the local level such as the Republican party, which won over 3 percent in the October 1986 Bavarian state elections. The Republicans achieved national prominence by winning representation (with 7.5 percent of the vote) in the West Berlin city parliament in January 1989 and by becoming the first ultraright party to break the 5 percent hurdle in a nationwide vote with a 7.1 percent showing in the June 1989 European Parliament election.

The Nazi past and the issue of right-wing extremism have continued to command attention in the domestic political arena and have led to increasing international concerns about the Federal Republic. A fascination

[2]See Elisabeth Noelle-Neumann and Erich Peter Neumann, *Jahrbuch I; Jahrbuch II* (Allensbach: Verlag für Demoskopie), and Karl W. Deutsch and L. J. Edinger, *Germany Rejoins the Powers* (Berkeley, Calif.: Stanford University Press, 1959), pp. 40–42.

with the Third Reich and Adolf Hitler manifested itself in a "Hitler wave" of publications and motion pictures in the late 1970s, not all of them critical. Efforts in early 1979 to show the American television series "Holocaust" in the Federal Republic were at first frustrated by the refusal of the two national networks to carry the series, reportedly because of its "soap-opera-like artistic quality." But both Chancellor Schmidt and opposition leader Kohl urged that the series be shown, and the Federal Republic's five regional networks carried the series to an audience estimated at 41 percent of all viewers by the final program. "Holocaust" was instrumental in exposing a broad cross section of the population, and particularly the younger generation, to the record of Nazi atrocities that had heretofore received scant mention and little reflection in German postwar society. German television has itself recently produced documentaries on the Nazi period. In July 1979, the Bundestag, in a relatively close vote, abolished the statute of limitations that would have allowed Nazi-era war-crime suspects to escape prosecution for murder following a 30-year period scheduled to end January 1, 1980. As of early 1987, federal authorities were still investigating 1,112 cases involving Nazi war crimes. Of a total of 91,160 cases pursued since 1945, sentencing has occurred in only 6,482 instances.

Despite the apparent decline in the hardcore Nazi following and the waning of NPD membership and electoral support, there remained cause for concern in the formation and growth of right-wing extremist paramilitary groups in the late 1970s and early 1980s. Some of these organizations, such as the *Wehrsportgruppe Hoffmann* (Hoffmann Defense Sport Group), engaged in paramilitary exercises and acts of political violence. It was a member of this particular group who was implicated in a September 1980 bombing that killed 13 and injured scores more at the crowded entrance to Munich's *Oktoberfest.* This incident provoked a much greater public awareness of the threat to society of terror by the right wing. The federal government took steps in 1983 to ban neo-Nazi paramilitary organizations and to prosecute their leaders.

With controversies in Austria and France relating to the wartime activities of Kurt Waldheim and Klaus Barbie, West Germans have noted that they are not alone in having to shoulder the burden of the Nazi past. In fact a major controversy raging since 1986 among West German historians (the so-called *Historikerstreit*) has addressed the issue of whether the Holocaust was a singular historical event, unique in its manifestation of Nazi barbarity, or whether it can be relativized and examined comparatively in connection with other organized atrocities, in particular Stalin–era liquidations. Amid outpourings of international concern, the FRG's chancellor and president have affirmed their convictions that the Holocaust remains unique and can not be diminished by historical comparisons with other campaigns of extermination.

The commemoration in the 1980s of anniversaries—50 years since Hitler's accession to power, 40 years since the capitulation of Nazi Germany, and 50 years since the November 9, 1938, *Kristallnacht* pogrom—provided an impetus for Germans to seek a new understanding of their country's Nazi past. Also demonstrated, however, was the difficulty in healing wounds dating from this period—as witnessed in the furor over President Reagan's visit to the Bitburg war cemetery and the resignation in November 1988 of Bundestag President Philipp Jenninger after an address commemorating *Kristallnacht,* which, due to textual deficiencies and poor delivery, sounded like an uncritical appraisal of the Nazi era.

Attitudes of the "Successor Generation"

West Germans born since 1945 have now become a majority of the total population. A great deal of attention is being focused on the FRG's university-educated elites who have grown to maturity in a Federal Republic preoccupied with economic well-being and firmly anchored in the Western alliance. Members of these postwar elites are now taking over prime positions of leadership from those who participated in the founding and development of the FRG's political and social institutions. While a great many members of this "successor generation" share the attitudes and values of their parents' generation, a significant portion have adopted more critical attitudes and what have been termed "postmaterialist" values.

In the late 1960s there was a strong trend to the political left among university students and some nontenured junior faculty members, in contrast with the strong conservatism of students in previous periods. The percentage of students and junior academic personnel in the German university population had increased nearly three-fold, but their political influence, social status, and economic status had not risen in proportion. At the same time that students became more numerous and more frustrated, many of them became enraged by what they perceived to be contradictory information given them by their studies and by the mass media, and by the normative and cognitive dissonance between their ideas and aspirations and their perceptions of the realities of the world in which they lived.

Such feelings had been growing during the 1960s, particularly from 1966 on. In 1967 and 1968 they erupted in large student demonstrations, occupations of buildings, disruptions of academic work, and demands for university reform, more permissiveness in matters of sex and life-style, and more far-reaching political changes. The United States and its alleged materialist influences and imperialist policies became a frequent target of demonstrations and invective.

By the early 1970s a turbulent and variegated movement had developed—a significant counterculture. It displayed marked differences from the political views and cultural values of postwar West German society. Alienated from that society and finding little support among working-class supporters of the governing SPD/FDP national coalition, student leftists played a major role in the founding and development of alternative political groups, most notably the Green

party. Ultimately their influence was evident in the SPD, particularly in galvanizing opposition to placement of Pershing II and cruise missiles on West German soil. A particular rallying point for dissidents came in opposition to the Extremists Decree issued in early 1972 by the minister presidents of the Länder with the support of the Brandt coalition government. Designed to exclude radicals from the civil service and, in particular, the teaching profession, the decree was variously administered by individual Länder—usually through administration of a questionnaire, but sometimes through the initiation of cumbersome background investigations.

While student leftists and their counterculture have undoubtedly contributed to the polarization of West German society, their concerns have had an impact on the culture as a whole, and in particular on the attitudes of other members of their generation. People of virtually all political persuasions have become concerned about protecting their environment; the West German peace movement has enjoyed broad support; citizens of the Federal Republic are more likely than ever before to be critical of the policies of the United States. Certainly previous generations of Germans have had their share of critics and dissidents. While there are indications that the next generation in the FRG will be more conservative and pragmatic, a significant proportion of the generation now about to assume leadership positions appear to be imbued with alternative political and cultural attitudes.

THE CHANGING PARTY SYSTEM

Since the founding of the Reich in 1871, Germany has undergone spectacular but uneven changes. Its constitutional arrangements have changed most often and most dramatically. Its political parties have changed somewhat less, and its most influential interest groups have changed relatively least.

Throughout the empire and the Weimar

Republic, the voting strength of the center and the right had been scattered over many parties, the only exception being in 1933 when the Nazis united a large part of it for their adventure in extremism. Before the days of the Federal Republic, no moderate party had ever succeeded in uniting under its leadership the bulk of this potential right and center vote, let alone keeping it together election after election. All this the CDU accomplished, and in doing so it became Germany's first example of a moderate and successful party of political integration.

Founded as a militant working-class party in 1863, the SPD received the largest share of any party with 29 percent of the vote in the 1912 election. It became more moderate in the Weimar Republic, when it was outflanked on the left by Communists and independent socialists, and moved toward the center in the Federal Republic. In doing so it steadily gained in its share of the vote, capturing more than 40 percent in 1969 and becoming the largest Fraktion from 1972 through 1976 (Table 6-1).

As we have seen, parties at the ends of the political spectrum have not fared well in the Federal Republic. Nationalists and conservatives have largely found a home in the CDU/CSU, though they have emerged as the standard-bearers in movements such as the NPD and the Republicans. The specter of Communism in the other German state effectively undermined the chances of the left in the early period of the Federal Republic and dictated the SPD move to the center. The Free Democrats have demonstrated remarkable staying power as an alternative force. In the 1950s minor parties disappeared or were successfully integrated, particularly into the CDU/CSU. No other party overcame the 5 percent hurdle for representation in the Bundestag until the Greens did so in 1983.

Apart from the mandate given the CDU/CSU in 1957, no one party has been able to govern alone. The resulting coalitions—the FDP with the CDU/CSU through 1956, from 1961–1966, and again after 1982; the FDP with the SPD from 1969 to 1982; and the in-

TABLE 6-1 Party Strength and Coalition Formation in the Federal Republic of Germany, 1949–1987, in Terms of Percentages of the Voting Electorate

Year	CDU/CSU	FDP	SPD	Other Parties
1949	31.0%	11.9%	29.2%	27.9%
1953	45.2	9.5	28.8	16.5
1957	50.2	7.7	31.8	10.3
1961	45.3	12.8	36.2	5.6
1965	47.6	9.5	39.3	3.6
December 1966–September 1969: CDU/CSU/SPD Grand Coalition				
1969	46.1	5.8	42.7	5.4
1972	44.9	8.4	45.8	0.9
1976	48.6	7.9	42.6	0.9
1980	44.5	10.6	42.9	2.0
1983	48.8	7.0	38.2	5.6*/0.5
1987	44.3	9.1	37.0	8.3*/1.3

*The Green party successfully entered the Bundestag with 5.6 percent of the vote in 1983 and 8.3 percent in 1987. Other parties had 0.5 percent in 1983 and 1.3 percent in 1987.

The shaded figures represent the parties forming the government coalition in each Bundestag. The 1966–1969 Grand Coalition was formed upon dissolution of a CDU/CSU/FDP coalition government.

Voter turnout was 78.5 percent in 1949, an average of 87 percent for the five elections from 1953 through 1969, 91 percent for both 1972 and 1976, 89 percent for both 1980 and 1983, and 84 percent in 1987. The 1949 governing coalition contained other minor parties; the 1969 SPD/FDP coalition has been the only case in which the governing parties have been elected by less than 50 percent of the voting electorate.

terim 1966–1969 CDU/CSU/SPD Grand Coalition—all have served to moderate German politics and have predetermined a centrist approach. Clearly not a two-party system, the Federal Republic has often been termed a two-group system, a coalition government facing parliamentary opposition with the Free Democrats providing the balance between the two. With the staying power of the Greens and the potential for Republican entry into the Bundestag in the 1990 election, and given the often uncertain coalition allegiance of the FDP, there is some merit in characterizing the FRG's current political structure as an emerging multiparty system.

A Broad and Growing Consensus

Whereas the left-wing and right-wing parties under Weimar were separated by a wide chasm of ideologies, the major parties in the Federal Republic—leaving aside the Greens—have shown a great deal of affinity in their programs. Competing for the more numerous votes near the center of the political spectrum, the major parties have, for the most part, come to emphasize moderate, middle-of-the-road policies. Although the right wing of the CDU and the left wing of the SPD still exercise a good deal of constraint upon their respective party leaders, the center of gravity in both parties has generally resided with the more moderate elements. The relatively smooth formation of the CDU/CSU/SPD coalition government in 1966 and the easy shift of power to the SPD/FDP in 1969 shows how far this consensus had developed by the end of the Federal Republic's second decade.

The conflict between the supporters of democratic and dictatorial forms of government has been largely settled, for the CDU/CSU, the SPD, the FDP, and the Greens have all made it clear that they accept the democratic rules of the game. Unlike the situation in the French Fourth and Fifth Republics, Bonn's parties have not had major disagreements with each other about procedural (i.e., constitutional) issues. Church-state issues have receded into the background at the federal level and have lost most of their bitterness at the Land level.

The conflict between nationalization of industry and the free enterprise system has also been effectively muted. On the one hand, the Socialists have accepted the idea of a largely free market economy; on the other hand, the CDU has accepted some government intervention and antimonopolistic measures that have, in the interests of the consumer, placed limitations upon business competition.

Thus the differences among political parties have often become blurred, though campaign slogans and platforms in election years attempt to play them up, even among former coalition partners. A 1964 cabaret joke had it that the SPD was "the best CDU we ever had." The Grand Coalition government of the CDU/CSU with the SPD, controlling over 90 percent of the Bundestag, occasioned much concern. Its critics argued that such absence of competition boded ill for democracy. The spirited competition since 1969, with first the CDU/CSU, then the SPD in opposition, has pointed up differences and drawn political lines more clearly.

With the FDP providing the balance in governing coalitions since 1969, centrist politics have prevailed. The possibility of a future government coalition involving the Greens and a more left-oriented SPD could challenge the centrist course of the Federal Republic and lead to increased polarization. Should the Republicans gain Bundestag representation, a CDU/CSU thus outflanked on the right might be induced to seek a "Grand Coalition" with the SPD.

THE CHRISTIAN DEMOCRATIC UNION

The Christian Democratic Union (CDU), together with its Bavarian sister party, the Christian Social Union (CSU), is the successor of the old Catholic Center party, some small Protestant nonsocialist parties, and parts of several middle-class and moderately conservative parties, such as the German People's party (*Deutsche Volkspartei*). For the first time in the history of German political parties, one party—the CDU/CSU—succeeded in 1949 in uniting strongly committed Catholics and Protestants, together with voters of less intense religious feelings. At the same time, it united rural and urban voters, farmers and businesspersons, artisans and white-collar workers, professionals and housewives, employers and labor union members. This broad party has largely succeeded in maintaining its significant appeal to these diverse interests and groups, though some degree of defection—particularly among white-collar workers—was apparent by the 1969 federal election.

Prior to 1969 the CDU/CSU was getting twice as much support from Roman Catholics as from Protestants, and more of the votes of farmers, professional people, and businessmen, both big and small, than any other party. It was getting more of the votes of the wealthy and the well-off, but was doing well in every income group. It has consistently had a strong appeal for voters over 60 years of age. The CDU/CSU has traditionally done least well, but still not too badly, among Protestants, skilled workers, nonskilled workers, and rural laborers. By 1986 the CDU counted 719,000 members. The CSU has some 183,000 members.

The sources of the party's electoral support are reflected in the composition of its leading bodies. The formal decision-making body of the party, its national executive (*Bundesvorstand*), mirrors the diversity of the party's supporters and its strong local roots, particularly in southern and western Germany. Formal power in this executive is divided between leaders of regional organizations (*Landesverbände*) and the party's chief representatives in the federal government and in the Bundestag, between Protestants and Catholics, and between trade union leaders and representatives of business and industry. This multiplicity of interests and the breadth of the party's electoral support, however, have given the party and its leaders a measure of independence against any single pressure group.

Breadth of support also increases the importance of the highly visible national leaders, who after years of successful performance in government have become unifying symbols for their party and its electorate. Chancellor Adenauer's power over his party was well known. Chancellors Erhard and Kiesinger and the CDU/CSU leaders in opposition, Rainer Barzel and Helmut Kohl, all built significant reputations, with Kohl able in 1982 to oust Chancellor Schmidt as a result of a successful constructive vote of no confidence. Regional CDU leaders Gerhard Stoltenberg (Schleswig–Holstein), Ernst Albrecht (Lower Saxony), and Lothar Spaeth (Baden–Württemberg) have achieved increasing nationwide visibility. Franz Josef Strauss, former leader of the CSU, from the 1950s played a prominent role in CDU politics and wielded a formidable influence in CDU/CSU–led government coalition politics until his death in October 1988.

In opposition from 1969 through 1982, after two decades of governing, the CDU/CSU found itself playing an unaccustomed role. While in opposition, it attempted to revamp its image as a party of moderate reform at the same time seeking to capitalize on the fears of socialism among its sizable conservative constituency. The CDU/CSU returned to power in 1982 when Schmidt's government coalition broke apart. With Helmut Kohl as chancellor, the coalition won the 1983 and 1987 federal elections. Kohl has had to deal with internal divisions within his coalition, in particular polarity on several issues between the CSU and the FDP. The current status of the CDU/CSU and the performance of the Kohl government are addressed in Chapter 7.

THE SOCIAL DEMOCRATIC PARTY

The leaders and many of the members of the Social Democratic party (SPD) think of it as a grand old party with a great tradition going back 125 years to the days of Ferdinand Lasalle, August Bebel, and even—although this is stressed less often—Karl Marx. They are particularly proud of the party's long history of firm commitment to democracy, which was maintained in the years of Nazi persecution, as well as its success against the appeals and threats of Communism.

Although the party has long since shed much of the vocabulary of Marx, much of its concern for ideology, and much of its old, sharply focused class appeal to industrial labor, many of its old symbols—the red flag, the labor union songs, and the salutation "comrade"—still kindle in members the hope for a bright and fraternal future. The revised party platform of 1959 largely deemphasized the party's former demands for nationalization of industries and stressed instead indirect economic controls reminiscent of Keynesian economics and the American New Deal and New Frontier.

In the 1950s the SPD had a more intense interest than the CDU in German reunification and the recovery of former German territories, from which much of the SPD's strength was drawn before 1933. The party was cool toward the NATO military alliance and might have been amenable to buying reunification at the price of neutrality and disarmament, provided that reunification could bring genuinely free elections in the GDR. The Soviet Union, in an attempt to forestall FRG integration in the Western defense alliance, hinted in March 1952 at the possibility of some such arrangement, but this overture was not deemed credible either by the Western allies or the Adenauer government. Gradually the SPD came to accept the essentials of Adenauer's foreign policy, including German membership in NATO and the Common Market and the policy of firm alliance and increasing integration with the West. Willy Brandt, the former mayor of West Berlin who as leader of the SPD became foreign minister in the CDU/CSU/SPD coalition government of 1966–1969, became the symbol of this new SPD stress on bipartisan unity.

These major shifts in the SPD's economic and foreign policies paid off in the rising fortunes of the party at the polls. In entering into the 1966–1969 Grand Coalition with the CDU/CSU, the SPD proved that it could govern. The success of SPD-sponsored measures in combating the economic recession of the late 1960s, and the growing popularity of new approaches in foreign policy advocated by its leaders, brought the SPD national renown and helped it win electoral victory in the 1969 election. The SPD attracted 42.7 percent of the votes, breaking through the "40 percent barrier" beneath which its share of votes in the Federal Republic and most of the Länder had so long been confined. The party's impressive victory in the 1972 federal election made it the largest single Fraktion in the Bundestag. Although it sustained losses in the 1976 and 1980 elections under popular Chancellor Helmut Schmidt, the SPD, continuing in coalition with the FDP, held on to the reins of government until the FDP defected to the opposition CDU/CSU in 1982.

The SPD continues, though to a lesser degree than during the 1950s, to derive its most reliable voting support from trade union members, skilled workers, unskilled workers, nonchurchgoers, men, large-city residents, pensionees and trainees, and the lower-middle and low-income groups—in roughly that order. In the late 1960s the SPD attracted white-collar workers from the CDU but has since had varying success holding on to voters outside of its core support groups.

The SPD has traditionally had a strong and disciplined membership. In 1932, before the Nazi dictatorship, the SPD had about 980,000 members; in 1946 the re-emerging party in the much smaller Federal Republic already had 710,000 members. Membership rose to 840,000 in 1948, declined to 600,000 in 1957, swelled to a peak of 1,022,000 in 1980, and then declined to 919,000 in 1986. Membership dues collected amounted annually to about DM 70 million by 1980, a clear indication of the consolidation and loyalty of the membership and a guarantee of the substantial financial independence of the party.

The highest authority of the SPD is its biennial congress, but the real power lies in the party's national executive committee—the *Parteivorstand*—and in the leadership group of the SPD delegation in the Bundestag. The executive committee is effectively in control of the party. The most prominent SPD parliamentarians are members of the party executive as well, and many deputies are also employees of the party, or of some organization under its control.

From the early 1950s until his retirement in 1983, the party was tightly governed by its deputy chairman Herbert Wehner, who served from 1969 on as SPD Bundestag Fraktion leader. Next to Chancellor Helmut Schmidt and party chairman Willy Brandt, he played the role of an energetic whip and organizer, ensuring discipline and unity. Party discipline became increasingly difficult given the resurgence of the party's left wing during the 1970s. The *Jusos* (Young Socialists), with 270,000 members by 1983, were particularly vocal in their advocacy of leftist alternatives to a party that was attempting to steer a centrist course while in government. Chancellor Schmidt thus faced opposition and strife within his own party to policies he was trying to implement. Intraparty opposition was strongest with regard to government defense policy, in particular Schmidt's advocacy in the late 1970s of the two-track approach which foresaw placement of U.S. Pershing II and cruise missiles in Western Europe in the event of failure of negotiations with the Soviets to limit "European-theater" nuclear forces.

When the SPD went into opposition with Schmidt's ouster in October 1982, leftist forces in the party gained strength. Schmidt declined to run for chancellor in the 1983 election and retired from party politics in November 1983, in the wake of the SPD's strong "no" vote on implementation of the two-track missile decision. Former justice minister Hans-Jochen Vogel and Minister President Johannes Rau of North Rhine–Westphalia were unsuccessful as SPD chancellor candidates in the 1983 and 1987 elections, respectively. Brandt retained the party chairmanship until he was forced to resign in March 1987 due to strong opposition to his appointment of a nonparty member as the party's first female spokesperson. Vogel succeeded Brandt as party chairman. Aspirants to future SPD leadership roles include two "successor-generation" politicians—Oskar Lafontaine of the Saar and Björn Engholm of Schleswig-Holstein—who like Rau have gained political stature through resounding victories in their respective Länder.

THE FREE DEMOCRATIC PARTY

A small party that has managed to serve in government longer than any other West German party, the Free Democratic party (FDP) has a somewhat divided character and heritage. It continues from Weimar days the tradition both of the liberal-progressive Democratic party and of the moderate-conservative German Nationalist People's party (DVP), which in turn was a successor to the National Liberals of the pre-1914 era. The progressive tradition of the party links the FDP to the liberal, middle-class Protestants of southern Germany, and the conservative tradition ties it to the Protestant and anticlerical business and professional elements in the northern and western regions of the country. Until the Grand Coalition period, the adherents of conservative parties regarded the FDP as a party somewhat to the left of center, but most supporters saw it as a party of the right. The latter view was the more realistic.

For a time, power within the FDP shifted from the liberal wing represented by the first president of the republic, Theodor Heuss, to the somewhat more nationalistic and business-oriented views of Erich Mende, who was party leader until late 1967. During its time in opposition, from 1966 to 1969, the FDP underwent a remarkable transformation. With support from its younger members, the new leadership under chairman Walter Scheel made headlines with its demand for a new Ostpolitik.

In 1969, after this change in leadership and the lessening of the party's financial dependence upon the business class thanks to the advent of government subsidies for political parties, the FDP was able to join a national coalition with the SPD.

This change of course caused the defection of enough FDP conservative delegates (including Mende) to imperil the Brandt government and erode its already slim majority. The FDP also lost a great many voters in Länder elections in 1970 and 1971; it had barely attained the 5 percent level in the 1969 federal election. The future of the party was uncertain. The 1972 federal election proved, however, that the FDP had a staying power of its own: it garnered over 8 percent of the vote and again helped provide the majority necessary to maintain the social-liberal coalition in power. Doubtless it had attracted a new constituency of liberal voters, who, though they supported the coalition, were wary of the SPD. When FDP chairman Walter Scheel became federal president in 1974, he was succeeded in his party post by Hans-Dietrich Genscher, who also assumed Scheel's positions of foreign minister and vice chancellor. By 1976, the FDP was represented in all Länder parliaments.

The FDP in coalition with the SPD served at times to brake the actions of the larger party, resulting in a more moderate government coalition approach to social policy and domestic measures such as codetermination and tax reform. Courted by moderates in the CDU, the FDP nevertheless elected to continue its alliance with the SPD in the 1976 and 1980 national elections, though on two occasions in the mid-1970s the FDP did join in coalition governments with the CDU at the Land level.

In the early 1980s, the pendulum in the FDP swung back again to a more conservative orientation with FDP Economics Minister Count Lambsdorff openly supporting business interests in opposition to the government's economic policies. A major rift ensued in the SPD/FDP governing coalition. The defection of FDP cabinet members led by Genscher in September 1982 brought down the Schmidt government. The alliance of these FDP party leaders with the new coalition under CDU leader Kohl split the FDP and led to widespread disaffection among adherents of the party's liberal tradition. The party, with 80,000 members at the time of the 1980 election, entered the 1983 election campaign with the loss of one-sixth of its prior membership. It survived the election with 7 percent of the vote. Genscher held on as foreign minister and vice chancellor but relinquished party leadership in early 1985 to Martin Bangemann who had replaced Lambsdorff as economics minister when the latter resigned in the wake of the Flick political donations scandal.

Although its membership has shrunk to 67,000, the FDP has indeed survived and has regained its pivotal role in German electoral politics. It garnered a healthy 9.1 percent of the vote in the 1987 federal election. Genscher's ratings have soared in public opinion polls; he is seen as an effective counterbalance to the CSU in the government coalition. In 1985 the FDP was represented in only 6 of the 11 state parliaments with a role in state government only in West Berlin. By 1989 it was represented in all but three state parliaments and participated in four governing coalitions at the state level.

THE GREEN PARTY

In the 1983 election, for the first time in over 20 years, a new party—the Greens—overcame the 5 percent hurdle and was elected to the Bundestag. The party is a loose amalgamation of factions, founded at the national level in the late 1970s· as an "antiparty." The party's name symbolizes the unifying original goals of the founders: protecting the environment from the ravages of industry, urbanization, and nuclear power.

The Greens reflect the influences of multiple legacies going back to the pacifist movement of the 1950s and an extraparliamentary opposition to the Grand Coalition in the late 1960s. The new party includes members of environmental voters' initiatives, Marxists, disaffected SPD members and liberal deserters from the FDP. Above all, it has appealed to the young and well educated. In some university towns, the Greens have garnered the second largest number of votes. In alliance with Land-based "alternative list" slates of delegates, the Greens entered the Bremen Land parliament in 1979 and by 1982 were seated in 6 of the 11 state parliaments. Winning only 1.5 percent of the vote in the 1980 federal election, the Greens improved their share in the 1983 election, gaining 5.6 percent of the vote and 28 seats. In the June, 1984, European Parliament elections the Greens replaced the FDP as the third West German party to be represented. In the 1987 federal election the party won 8.3 percent of the vote, increasing its Bundestag representation by more than 50 percent to 42 seats and thereby proving that it was not a short-lived phenomenon. The Greens have some 39,000 members but obviously a much greater reservoir of supporters.

The party has been governed on the basis of radically democratic principles that have led to dissension and disarray. Elected members of parliaments and the Bundestag are to contribute major portions of their salaries to a party fund. Seats are to be rotated among other party members. A number of prominent Greens elected to the Bundestag have balked at relinquishing their seats, contending that doing so would dilute the party's ability to pursue its program in a sustained manner. The major divisive issue dividing the party has been a feud between pragmatic *Realos,* who contend that the party should consider coalitions with other parties to accomplish its aims, and the *Fundi* purists who fear the dilution of ideological principles through any coalition. Realo-leaning Greens in the Hesse state parliament agreed in October 1985 to join in coalition with a minority SPD government, the Greens securing the post of environment minister and two deputy minister posts. The Hesse Greens took this step in defiance of the Fundi-dominated Green national executive committee. The Hesse coalition lasted a little over a year when its breakup over the SPD partner's unwillingness to immediately halt commissioning of a nuclear power plant led to an election that was won by the CDU/FDP. By 1989, the Greens participated in the governing coalition in West Berlin and were represented in all but 3 of the 11 state parliaments—significantly, these three were Länder in which the SPD commanded outright majorities.

Unkempt and uncombed, Green delegates have added color to the Bundestag. In the main pursuing a role of vocal opposition to the policies of the Kohl coalition government, the Greens have achieved a measure of credibility in their championing of environmental issues. They had long been judged to be free from complicity in the types of party financial scandals that have plagued all other Bundestag parties, but in 1988 the Greens became embroiled in their own scandal, this in connection with financial discrepancies relating to the renovation of a new party headquarters building. While the Greens will likely continue to maintain a following in upcoming state and federal elections, the internal stability and viability of their party structure remain in question.

ELECTIONS
IN THE FEDERAL REPUBLIC

Federal elections take place every four years, except in the case of an early dissolution of the Bundestag on a vote of no confidence in the chancellor and his government. Voters elect delegates to the Bundestag who subsequently elect a chancellor. The chancellor then forms the government.

Federal election laws provide for the election of 496 deputies to the Bundestag by a dual procedure. Half are elected in direct balloting in their respective constituencies. The remaining half are selected by a predetermined proportional method from party lists of candidates in each of the Länder. As outlined in Chapter 4, each voter in a federal election casts two votes—one for a candidate in his voting district and one for a specific party list.

Länder elections are also held once every four years though premature elections follow the dissolution of state parliaments. They are held at staggered intervals, and as a result, their outcomes have been variously interpreted as barometers of support by both the government in power and its parliamentary opposition. The political composition of the Bundesrat is directly affected by the outcome of these Länder elections. Although the CDU/CSU was out of government from 1969 through 1982, it enjoyed a Bundesrat majority, consolidating its strength in the Länder while being in opposition in the Bundestag.

Election campaigns in the FRG have been run in a manner increasingly similar to those in the United States. Intense saturation of the voting public with media advertising, billboards and handouts, the fixing of party platforms and campaign slogans, an increasing willingness of members of the electorate to engage in "voters' initiatives" for the political party of their choice, the televising of debates among the major candidates, and increased press and media coverage and electoral predictions have all demonstrated the greater level of public involvement among citizens of the Federal Republic.

Figure 6-1 shows the share of major party votes in the 11 federal elections from 1949 through 1987. Some trends are evident: the steady rise of the SPD and its moderate decline in 1976 and more precipitous decline since 1980, the staying power of the FDP in maintaining its strength above the 5 percent level, the advent of the Greens, and the formidable and fairly consistent strength of the CDU/CSU.

Elections: 1949–1965

The first two decades of federal parliamentary history saw the domination of one parliamentary group, the CDU/CSU. For much of this period one man, Konrad Ade-

nauer, dominated the party and the government as well. The central figure in German politics as the Federal Republic's first chancellor, Adenauer effectively waged a personality campaign. A figure who stood for order and restoration, but also for change and prosperity, Adenauer left his imprint on German politics. His style of governing became known as *Kanzlerdemokratie* (chancellor democracy). Subsequent chancellors and indeed all West German political figures have been measured against the standards he set.

The CDU/CSU was quite successful in increasing its Fraktion membership at the expense of the small parties of the center and right. Leaders of these parties were typically given cabinet posts in Adenauer coalition governments, then persuaded to change their party loyalty. This absorption of minor parties was a major contributing factor in the smashing successes enjoyed by the CDU/CSU in the 1953 and 1957 elections, particularly in the latter case, when it received an absolute majority (50.2 percent) of the vote—something never before achieved in German history by a single party in a free election.

A factor of equal importance was the marked failure of the SPD to mount a suc-

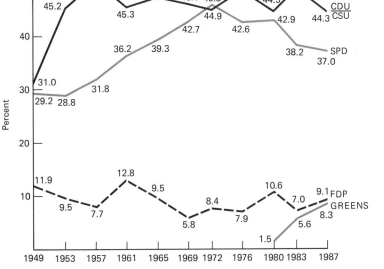

FIGURE 6-1 Results of Second Votes Cast in Bundestag Elections, 1949–1987 (in percentages) Source: *Globus-Kartendienst.*

cessful opposition. The SPD opposition to West German rearmament (which had effectively been coupled by Adenauer to the regaining of West German sovereignty) and to the initial phases of West European integration impressed the electorate as being more negative than constructive in its tone.

The chief slogans of the CDU/CSU in the 1953 and 1957 campaigns emphasized prosperity, security, and no experiments. The Adenauer government could point to a doubling of industrial and agricultural output, to a strong currency, and to rapidly rising living standards. The ravages of war and displacement were no longer evident. Adenauer effectively isolated the SPD on the security issue. He was in turn charged by the opposition as having sold out German interests as a "chancellor of the Allies." But the popularity of West German integration into the Western alliance and of participation with other West European nations in a coal and steel community and the Treaty of Rome caused these charges to backfire on the SPD. After the 1957 CDU/CSU electoral victory the SPD seemed doomed to perpetual opposition.

But by 1961 much had changed. The SPD had undergone a fundamental transformation in both its platform and its leadership. Committed to both the social-market economy and West German foreign policy, it sought to dispel the image of negativism that had plagued it. The CDU/CSU, on the other hand, was in the throes of an internal crisis. Adenauer would not step down to make way for the popular social market economist, Ludwig Erhard, as candidate for chancellor. His SPD opponent, West Berlin's mayor Willy Brandt, was in turn encumbered by his illegitimate birth and his record of having fought against Germany in the war. The erection of the Berlin wall, and the government's inability to prevent it, became an issue in the campaign. The returns demonstrated that the shift in course had paid off for the SPD. The CDU/CSU lost its absolute majority and was forced to make concessions to the Free Democrats in forming a coalition.

Distinctions between the two major parties became increasingly blurred in the early 1960s, with both the SPD and FDP supporting the Western alliance policy of the federal government. Adenauer's hold on government became increasingly tenuous and he finally stepped down in 1963. Ludwig Erhard became chancellor and defeated Brandt in the 1965 election. The CDU gained votes at the expense of the FDP, while the SPD nearly attained the long-elusive 40 percent. An economic crisis in 1966 precipitated the fall of the Erhard government and the entry of the SPD into a Grand Coalition with the CDU/CSU, with Kurt Georg Kiesinger of the CDU as chancellor. The SPD welcomed the chance to become a partner in government and found its position vastly improved for the September 1969 federal election.

The 1969 Election

The members of the Grand Coalition parted ways to conduct their own campaigns in the summer of 1969. An alliance between the SPD and the FDP seemed increasingly likely, given the convergence of the two parties on Ostpolitik and the fact that the FDP had collaborated with the SPD to elect Social Democrat Gustav Heinemann as federal president earlier that year.

The CDU/CSU remained the largest parliamentary party in the September election. The NPD did not achieve Bundestag representation; the FDP remained in, but by the smallest of margins. The substantial showing of the SPD enabled it to form a governing coalition with the FDP. The new government, with Willy Brandt as chancellor, had a parliamentary majority of only 12 seats. It remained to be seen if this majority could hold, particularly with the threat of FDP disintegration. The CDU/CSU entered the opposition for the first time, ill prepared for the loss of the benefits accruing to the governing party.

The *Machtwechsel,* or transfer of power, to the social-liberal coalition was the first such peaceful instance in German history. A number of CDU/CSU politicians continued to question the legitimacy of the new government. The first Brandt administration faced a strong opposition and stormy parliamentary sessions reminiscent of the 1950s. The upcoming Länder elections were of critical importance in testing whether the social-liberal coalition could survive. The FDP's loss of its Landtag representation in Lower Saxony and the Saar in June 1970 and in Schleswig-Holstein in April 1971 increased the chance that the coalition at the federal level would break up.

The 1972 Election

The erosion of the thin SPD/FDP governing majority in the spring of 1972—chiefly over the issue of Ostpolitik and ratification of the treaties with Moscow and Warsaw—led to a stalemate in parliament. The CDU/CSU failed in an attempt, using the constructive vote of no confidence, to elect its leader Rainer Barzel as chancellor. The treaties were ratified in May, the opposition abstaining. It soon became clear that neither the coalition nor the opposition could muster a majority. All parties opted for early elections, although the FDP was apprehensive about its ability to survive.

Brandt himself staged a vote of no confidence in September that paved the way for November elections. The government's foreign policy stood to be a major issue in the campaign, as the pursuit of a new and more flexible Ostpolitik had been stressed to a far greater extent than any domestic measures during the legislative period. Despite its divisive nature, Ostpolitik had proved to be a popular policy with the German public. Brandt's own popularity increased after he was awarded the 1971 Nobel Peace Prize and it became clear that he enjoyed the support of the Western allies.

All efforts by the CDU leadership and its candidate for chancellor, Rainer Barzel, to play down the issue of foreign policy were eclipsed by the precipitous conclusion of negotiations for a Basic Treaty between the Federal Republic and the GDR. The initialing of this treaty on November 8 in Bonn was the turning point in the campaign. Brandt called upon the opposition to speak out on the treaty so that voters could be apprised of its position in casting their ballots. Strong conservative sentiment in the CDU/CSU caused the opposition to hedge on the issue. Barzel even suggested that a CDU/CSU government might seek to renegotiate the treaty.

The November 19 election produced a clear victory for the Brandt government. The nature of the election was reflected in the 91 percent voter turnout, high even by West German standards. The SPD, for the first time in the Federal Republic's history, captured the most votes (45.8 percent to 44.9 percent for the CDU/CSU), and it won 152 direct seats, many for the first time in traditional CDU strongholds. The social-liberal coalition garnered a comfortable 48-seat majority.

The 1976 Election

All three major parties underwent changes in leadership midway through the legislative period. Brandt resigned as chancellor in May 1974, the victim of an espionage affair (a GDR agent was found among his close advisors). He was succeeded as chancellor by Helmut Schmidt, minister of economics and formerly defense minister in the social-liberal coalition. Hans-Dietrich Genscher succeeded Scheel as FDP leader and the coalition's foreign minister when the latter was elected federal president in 1974; CDU leader Rainer Barzel resigned his party leadership posts in 1973, and Helmut Kohl, minister president of the Rhineland-Palatinate, consolidated his support for the post of party leader and emerged as the CDU/CSU chancellor candidate for 1976. Kohl was often dependent, however, on the support of CSU strongman Strauss.

The October 3 election, which featured a 91 percent voter turnout, was the closest in the history of the Federal Republic. The social-liberal coalition held on, but with a bare 10-seat majority. The SPD, down to 42.6 percent of the vote, won only 113 direct seats, sustaining the loss of 39 of its previous constituencies to CDU/CSU candidates. The

CDU/CSU, with 48.6 percent of the vote, failed to obtain an absolute majority. The FDP, making it clear before the election that it remained loyal to the coalition, sustained moderate losses.

As a result of the election Schmidt continued to govern, but his slim majority threatened to become precarious. A one-month walkout in late 1976 by CSU delegates from the CDU/CSU Fraktion suggested, however, that this opposition would not be as potent as the opposition that forced the dissolution of the Bundestag in 1972.

The 1980 Election

During the eighth legislative period the Federal Republic gained increasing international stature and seemed, at least from the outside, the model of a successful economy, an island surrounded by neighboring systems beset with rising unemployment and galloping inflation. Chancellor Schmidt won increased recognition abroad as a premier among statesmen, and at home a degree of support matched previously only by Adenauer. This success was punctuated, however, by a number of crises: heightened terrorist activity, political scandal, internal political disarray, and increasing dissonance in the government's relationship with its major ally, the United States. The government coalition with its bare majority withstood all such crises, but not without the widespread dissipation of SPD party unity, the failure of the FDP to remain above the 5 percent hurdle in important state elections, and the successful inroads of the environmentalist Green party (which won representation in the Bremen and Baden-Württemberg Landtag elections) in the ranks of the social-liberal constituency.

The CDU/CSU in a surprising move nominated Franz Josef Strauss over CDU Chairman Kohl's favorite, Lower Saxony Minister President Ernst Albrecht, as its chancellor candidate to run against Schmidt. The controversial Bavarian CSU leader refrained from his customary combative political stance early in the campaign, stressing bipartisan interest, particularly in the conduct of foreign policy. But after the FDP lost its representation in the North Rhine–Westphalia parliament through election defeat in May 1980 and in criticism of Schmidt's decision to be the first Western leader to travel to Moscow following its invasion of Afghanistan, Strauss declared an end to the truce and increased the tempo of his campaign.

With the North Rhine–Westphalia election, SPD leaders came to realize that an absolute majority in the coming election was not likely and that the party's continuation in power might well be contingent on the FDP remaining in the Bundestag. Party leader Brandt consequently proclaimed the goal of a relative SPD majority. Despite dissent in the ranks of party leftists and among party regulars such as Wehner, the chancellor's election strategists carefully avoided open antagonism of the FDP while waging a personality campaign against Strauss, charging him with instability and an inability to preserve peace.

The 88.7 percent of the West German voters who turned out on October 5 retained the governing SPD/FDP coalition, increasing its majority to a comfortable 45 seats. The results could be variously read: an endorsement of Schmidt, a repudiation of Strauss, a vote for the coalition but against left-wing influences in the SPD. A major surprise was the showing of the FDP, which received 10.6 percent of the vote, well beyond the share predicted by pollsters—making it the only real winner in the election. Gaining the support of an additional 1 million voters, the FDP was definitely the beneficiary of vote splitting, not only by SPD voters but by CDU voters as well. The SPD failed to capitalize on the Schmidt record and the Strauss candidacy, gaining but a 0.3 percent increase (to 42.9 percent). The CDU/CSU remained the largest Fraktion, but lost 1.5 million votes. CDU losses were particularly heavy in the Protestant North and in Baden-Württemberg. The Green party achieved only 1.5 percent of the vote, demonstrating its difficulty in building more than a regional appeal at this point.

The 1983 Election

After almost 13 years in office, the SPD/FDP coalition broke up with the desertion of FDP Vice Chancellor Genscher and other FDP ministers, and with the support of the majority of FDP delegates for Helmut Kohl's election as chancellor through a constructive vote of no confidence on October 1, 1982. The dismal state of the economy—negligible growth and steadily increasing unemployment—had exacerbated tensions in the governing coalition. SPD support in public opinion polls had sunk to 30 percent in mid-1982.

Although the next federal election was not scheduled until fall 1984, both major parties favored earlier elections, albeit for differing reasons. Kohl and the CDU sought to legitimize the change in power. The SPD hoped for a backlash of voter disfavor over the ouster of the still highly popular Schmidt. Strauss and the CSU pushed for immediate elections in the hope of a CDU/CSU absolute majority and thereby added stature for the CSU. The FDP, suffering major internal defection, was less enthusiastic about new elections but committed to them as Kohl's junior coalition partner.

The way to new elections on March 6, 1983 was paved through Kohl's deliberate loss in December 1982 of a vote of no confidence (his supporters abstained) and President Carstens's dissolving the Bundestag in early January 1983 on the strength of "the overwhelming will of both Government and Opposition to have new elections." Four Bundestag delegates challenged the constitutionality of this sequence of events, but in a 6 to 2 decision the Federal Constitutional Court ruled the March election to be consistent with the Basic Law.

The SPD entered the election campaign at a decided disadvantage. With unemployment continuing to increase to now over 10 percent, it could not escape being charged

with the underlying responsibility for the current economic situation. Its efforts to brand the five-month-old CDU/CSU/FDP government with complicity never achieved credibility. With Schmidt bowing out, Hans-Jochen Vogel, opposition leader in the West Berlin Senate and former justice minister, was selected as the party's candidate for chancellor. Lacking Schmidt's charisma and far behind in the polls, Vogel faced an uphill battle. Early in the campaign the SPD flirted with the idea of a left-of-center coalition with the Greens, only to abandon it in the campaign's closing days, realizing that it was thereby losing former supporters both to the CDU and the Greens. After trips to Washington and Moscow, Vogel seized on the issue of the placement of Pershing II and cruise missiles in Western Europe. He called on both of the superpowers to negotiate more seriously. He declared that as chancellor he would agree to missile deployment only under extreme circumstances, at the same time charging that Kohl was a "missile chancellor."

With slogans of "vote for the upturn" and "upwards in Germany," the CDU/CSU focused on economics. Kohl vowed to revitalize the economy and reduce unemployment. In attempting to counter issues raised by both the SPD and the Greens, Kohl staked out a CDU position on protection of the environment and called for "peace with fewer and fewer weapons." The FDP was fighting for its life, having been turned out of three state parliaments in 1982. It was hovering perilously below 5 percent in all opinion polls at the beginning of the campaign. In its platform, the FDP advocated continuation of its coalition under Kohl, tax breaks for business, environmental protection, and support for a "zero solution" with no intermediate-range missiles in Europe. The FDP openly sought the second votes of CDU supporters to keep it alive in the Bundestag, pointing out that with its departure Strauss was certain to succeed Genscher as foreign minister and vice chancellor. The Greens, with a great deal of momentum from gaining representation in Länder parliament elections, charged that all the major parties had failed in their attempts to govern. The Greens focused on opposition to missiles and nuclear power and pointed to the growing involvement of the other parties in party financial scandals.

The results signaled a major loss for the SPD (38.2 percent) and a major victory for the CDU/CSU—but, with 48.8 percent, not enough for an absolute majority. The FDP received 7.0 percent of the vote, the Greens 5.6 percent. The 1983 election marked the first time in over two decades that a fourth Fraktion was constituted in the Bundestag. The CDU scored massive gains in North Rhine–Westphalia and the northern states, winning 59 direct seats outright from the SPD. The Greens did best in university towns and won the votes of nearly one in four first-time voters. The FDP survived on the strength of "loaned" second votes.

The Kohl governing coalition was confirmed in office with a comfortable majority of 58 seats. The CSU garnered five ministerial positions to three for the FDP. Genscher stayed on as foreign minister.

The 1987 Election

Beset by scandals and internal coalition squabbles, the CDU/CSU trailed in opinion polls when the SPD announced Johannes Rau as its chancellor candidate for the January 1987 election. The SPD had momentum following landslide state election victories in spring 1985 in the Saar and Rau's own North Rhine–Westphalia. As a moderate, Rau demonstrated some difficulty in representing an SPD platform that called for a halt to commissioning of nuclear energy plants and for the FRG to negotiate directly the removal of U.S. missiles. Rau made it clear that he would not favor a coalition government with the Greens, instead declaring a goal of seeking an SPD absolute majority.

The SPD momentum was stopped in the early summer of 1986 in the aftermath of the

Chernobyl nuclear plant incident when the CDU, despite major losses, was barely able to form a coalition with the FDP after a Lower Saxony state election the SPD and Greens had been predicted to win. By this time charges against Kohl in relation to the Flick scandal had been dropped and the economy was benefiting from a -0.2 inflation rate, significant wage increases and a slight dip in still high unemployment. The SPD was unable to capitalize on other major issues as the Kohl government itself jumped on the ecological bandwagon and Soviet/American missile reduction negotiations entered an earnest phase. The SPD was itself touched by a scandal involving the near bankruptcy of a trade union–operated low-cost housing corporation. Disastrous SPD showings in the October 1986 Bavarian and November 1986 Hamburg state elections forced Rau to abandon the goal of an absolute majority and caused him to even consider withdrawing his candidacy. The SPD reformulated its election goal, declaring its intent to prevent an absolute CDU/CSU majority. The Greens, focusing on the twin issues of ecology and peace, indicated their willingness to cooperate in a SPD coalition government contingent on the closing of all nuclear plants and the removal of all U.S. missiles.

The CDU/CSU campaigned against the specter of a "Red-Green" government with Strauss and the CSU also mounting a campaign against the FDP and Genscher's foreign policy. The FDP, for its part, pointed to its liberal braking function in the coalition, effectively capitalizing on concerns that Strauss would be directing foreign policy in a CDU/CSU government.

In the January 25, 1987, election, Kohl's coalition was retained but at the expense of major CDU/CSU losses that transferred into FDP gains—in losing 4.5 percent from its 1983 showing, the CDU/CSU at 44.3 percent had its worst result since 1949. The SPD at 37.0 percent was down 1.2 percent, significantly below the 40 percent threshold. The beneficiaries were the two small parties. The

FDP polled 9.1 percent, attracting some 900,000 CDU voters and ensuring its continued existence at the national level. Genscher emerged the real victor of the election with the FDP able to subsequently gain another cabinet seat at the expense of the CDU. The Greens achieved 8.3 percent, assuring themselves a more permanent status in the Bundestag and making sizable inroads in the service sector and among first-time voters.

7

The Federal Republic Today:
Performance and Issues

Today, four decades after its establishment, the Federal Republic has a record of relative stability and success. It has been accepted as a legitimate form of government by the overwhelming majority of its citizens, who no longer view past periods in German history as having been more prosperous. But does this commitment extend to the Federal Republic's institutional framework and to democracy in general? Or is it based primarily on the degree of affluence and well-being of its citizens?

A number of democratic yardsticks can be employed to measure the performance of a government and the incidence of democratic values in a nation's political and social infrastructure. Is majority rule established? Are minority rights protected? Are basic freedoms and rights embodied in a constitution? Are there opportunities for citizens to participate directly in government? Is there

relative equality, not only of opportunity but also of probable attainment? Does government get things done, and is it responsive to the needs of its citizens? Can it adjust to new realities and put aside invalid methods and disproved policies?

By such yardsticks, it is apparent that the Federal Republic has made great strides. Some vestiges of its authoritarian heritage persist, and doubtless will for some time to come. But the experiment in democratic government of 1949 has proved viable. Democratic norms have attained great validity in its political sphere.

As we have seen, Bonn's governments have been more stable than those of the Weimar Republic. Thanks to a high degree of political consensus enjoyed by the Federal Republic from its outset, transitions in government have been relatively smooth; in only one instance has a government in power been toppled, and this was through the successful application of the constructive vote of no confidence procedure. No major political party or interest group has questioned the legitimacy of the system— even the Green party has opted to work within the system. Economic crises to date have not had severe repercussions on the political system, as in Weimar. Heated national debates over the course of the Federal Republic's foreign policy in the 1950s and again in the early 1970s did not disturb the consensual climate. Despite the concerns engendered by resurgent neo-Nazi movements and left-wing terrorists, extremism has not flourished in the Federal Republic. The democratic loyalties of a large number of repatriated Nazi supporters and sympathizers may deserve to be questioned, but the participation of ex-Nazis in all levels of public administration has not undermined democratic development.

Disparities of wealth, social status, and educational opportunity persist. But as we have seen, there has been some closing of the gap that has long existed in German society between the wealthy and the average German worker and between the relatively few university-educated and the mass of the rest. The disparity between the promises of democracy and what is actually achieved often leads, however, to the type of malaise and disaffection manifested in both the student protest movement of the late 1960s and early 1970s and the protest activities of peace and environmentalist groups starting in the late 1970s. While such malaise has affected the political and cultural outlooks of a growing number of the Federal Republic's "successor generation," the majority of the West German population, recognizing that it is better off, displays few signs of disaffection with a system that it credits with its much improved lot.

But again the question must be raised: What type of commitment does this represent? Germany has had a legacy of passive submission to authoritarian regimes, so that a high voter turnout cannot be accepted as a fully valid indicator of democratic commitment. But other indicators have demonstrated growing attachment to active participation in the processes of government. Both a marked rise in political-party membership figures in the mid-1970s and the phenomenon, recurrent in federal elections since 1969, of active participation of citizens groups and individuals in "voter initiatives" revealed a newly found faith in the effectiveness of participation. Such positive developments must be weighed, however, against incidents such as the fall 1987 Schleswig-Holstein election scandal (to be discussed in this chapter), an event that has dampened public enthusiasm in the efficacy of political activity.

An assessment of governmental performance—either of the CDU/CSU/FDP coalition in power since 1982 or the SPD/FDP coalition that preceded it—can be made by focusing in greater detail on the range of issues confronting any West German government during this period: the lengthening world economic recession, the twin specters of inflation and unemployment, the continuing problem of dealing with a large number of nonindigenous residents, the growing awareness of major environmental problems, outbreaks of terrorism and dissent, divisiveness within parties and within the governing coalition itself, the steering of a foreign policy course that does not foreclose the improvement of relations with the other German state, and the need to serve German defense and economic interests while pursuing collaboration with the Federal Republic's allies.

THE ECONOMY

Memories of runaway inflation in the early 1920s, of the economic depression and high unemployment of the early 1930s, and of the economic disarray of the period immediately following World War II have made Germans more prone than most peoples to panic when the economy falters. Accustomed to a sustained high rate of growth and an ever-rising standard of living during the first two decades of the Federal Republic, West Germans were thereafter psychologically ill-equipped to deal with a decline or even a stoppage in the growth rate.

The effects of the world economic crises following the precipitous increases in the price of OPEC oil were of far greater magnitude for the West German economy than a previous economic recession in 1966–67. Economic growth slowed from nearly 5 percent in 1973 to 0.4 percent in 1974 and to a decline of −1.8 percent in 1975. Inflation and unemployment increased and in 1975 exports dipped for the first time in postwar history. The economy rebounded in 1976, however, with a 5.3 percent growth rate and a surge in exports. The Schmidt government took action in the late 1970s to keep inflation down by maintaining a tight-money policy. It thereby incurred the disapproval of some of its allies, notably the U.S. administration, who felt that the Federal Republic should pursue expansionist policies as a "locomotive" to the world economy. Indeed, the Federal Republic withstood the world recession of the mid-1970s better than other Western industrialized nations. While unemployment continued to hover around 4 percent, the West German economy remained intact and steady. The German mark was revalued, and next to the Swiss franc, it became the world's strongest currency.

A second marked increase in OPEC prices in 1979 sent further tremors through the world economy. This time the FRG could not withstand the effects. From a 4.5 percent growth rate in 1979 and a 3.6 percent in the first half of 1980, the decline was precipitous. Growth was only 0.2 percent in the last half of 1980; negative growth of 0.3 percent in 1981 was followed by an even greater dip to −1.2 percent in 1982. Unemployment jumped from under 800,000 in the summer of 1980 to 1.7 million at the end of 1981 with 500,000 additional workers on shortened shifts. The number of unemployed climbed

to 2.48 million (some 10.2 percent of the work force) by January 1983, a statistic that none of the major parties could disclaim responsibility for in the then ongoing election campaign. With seasonal fluctuations, the unemployment rate has fluctuated between 8 and 10 percent through 1988 with over 2 million out of work. Inflation of 5 to 6 percent in the early 1980s moderated to 2.4 percent in 1984 and fell to a negative 0.2 percent in 1986. Growing from 0.5 percent in 1987 to around 1.5 percent in 1988, it is projected to reach 2.5 percent in 1989.

Meager wage increases during the early 1980s did not keep pace with inflation, resulting in tangible reductions in the buying power of most West Germans. Still, the FRC was relatively well off; its low rate of inflation was matched only by Japan's, and its unemployment rate was equaled or surpassed by that of most major developed countries. Wage increases in real terms of more than 3 percent in both 1986 and 1987 coupled with a resurgence of the mark in relation to the dollar left German workers in a much better economic situation than their counterparts elsewhere.

The Kohl government succeeded in achieving modest economic growth—1.4 percent in 1983, 3.3 percent in 1984, falling gradually to 1.8 percent in 1987 (all figures adjusted for inflation)—with an economic upturn in 1988 to 3.4 percent, and 3.5 percent growth expected for 1989.

It was clear by the mid-1980s that the German economy was facing acute structural problems. Unemployment was highest in mining, steel, shipbuilding, and textiles—traditional sectors of the West German economy. In these and other sectors the FRG found its share of the world market increasingly threatened by the burgeoning economies of Japan and Southeast Asian nations. The German federal railroad, coal mines, and other no-growth, state-owned businesses have required massive subsidization. Although the Federal Republic spends proportionately more on research and development than the United States—though not quite as much as Japan—it has not kept pace technologically with either nation and has shown sizable trade deficits in the importation of high-technology products from both countries. In the 1980s the FRG has been challenged to diversify its economy, to promote the growth of venture capital, and to develop new jobs for the unemployed and young Germans entering the work force.

Despite the economic slowdown, German exports have remained strong overall. With a 12 percent share of world trade, the FRG in 1986 overtook the United States as the leading exporter. It has maintained this position largely due to the decline of the dollar (from DM 3.47 per dollar in February 1985 to DM 1.58 in December 1987, with more modest fluctuation in the dollar's value thereafter). The FRG share of exports to GDP was 26.2 percent in 1987, roughly twice the comparable share for Japan and five times that of the United States. In the late 1980s the FRG has enjoyed a trade surplus running in excess of DM 100 billion per year, helped in no small measure by a reduction in its dollar-denominated oil import figures. Its only sizable trade deficit is with Japan.

The FRG has come under renewed U.S. pressure to stimulate its economy and increase its economic growth rate and domestic demand to thereby presumably contribute to a "locomotive" effect on the world economy. As in the mid-1970s, the FRG has largely resisted such pressure, willing to endure persisting high unemployment rather than risk intolerable inflation. But following the October 1987 stock market crash, the government undertook some rather timid measures to stimulate the economy, reducing key interest rates and initiating a government loan program. These limited measures did not fully satisfy the United States and were labeled by critics at home as "a German ornament for the conference table of international economic diplomacy." German economic policy will likely continue in the main

to be dictated by purely German concerns and perceptions.

DOMESTIC ISSUES

The Federal Republic faced a major challenge in the 1980s in the assimilation of several different groups of nonindigenous residents into West German society. The number of ethnic German resettlers from the GDR and Eastern Europe increased in the late 1980s at a rate unequaled since the mid-1950s. Of 78,500 such resettlers from Eastern Europe in 1987, almost two-thirds came from Poland. The Soviet Union has eased emigration of ethnic Germans with a 50-fold increase in the number of exit permits granted over a two-year period beginning in 1986. In the wake of a major increase in the number of ethnic German resettlers from Eastern Europe to 202,600 in 1988, the Kohl government established an interministerial task force to focus on the problem of assimilating these German resettlers, most of whom have had very limited post-1945 contact with West Germany and its citizenry. It remains to be seen whether the FRG will be able to assimilate this influx as successfully as it did millions of German expellees and refugees in the 1940s and 1950s.

A second group, the Gastarbeiter, or foreign workers, have posed more of a challenge. By the mid-1980s, more than half had been living in the FRG for over ten years with little incentive to return to their homelands. Some 1.5 million Turks, 600,000 Yugoslavs, 555,000 Italians, and significant numbers of Greeks, Poles, Spanish, and Portuguese live in overcrowded and expensive dwellings and fraternize very little with the German population. They make up the majority of a foreign population of 4.7 million. Foreign residents amount to 7.7 percent of the total West German population but have disproportionately greater birth and unemployment rates. The Gastarbeiter are concentrated in large cities; Frankfurt leads with a 25 percent share of foreign residents in its population.

The rapidly increasing Gastarbeiter population was by the late 1970s perceived to be a "social time bomb," in particular with respect to the integration of foreign children into the country's school systems and the potential major drain on the German welfare and social security system. A federal commission for the integration of foreign workers was organized, and in 1980 the Bundestag enacted legislation designed to relax naturalization requirements and encourage the institution of special education classes for foreign children. These classes were subject to implementation by the individual Länder. Gastarbeiter were given the right to participate in elections of representatives to company work councils but—with the exception of plans underway for enfranchisement for local elections in the city states of Hamburg and Bremen—have not been granted the right to vote. The SPD and Greens have called for legislation that would give Gastarbeiter this right. With the downturn in the economy, there has been a renewed effort to curtail the influx of new Gastarbeiter through the institution of visa requirements for citizens from certain non-European Community countries, and the payment of sums up to DM 10,500 to induce foreign workers to return home. Other propositions, such as lowering the age limit of Gastarbeiter dependents who may be brought to the FRG, have been hotly debated among political parties. The Kohl government is in the process of drafting legislation that may result in greater assimilation of Gastarbeiter who came to the FRG prior to the initial 1973 effort to curb emigration while at the same time seeking to impose an eight-year residency limit on all others. FRG treatment of Gastarbeiter from European Community countries could likely become an issue in the broader context of the EC's plans for internal integration.

A third nonindigenous group has consisted of a growing number of non-German refugees, seekers either of political asylum or relief from economic want, who have seen in the economic prosperity of the FRG and its liberal provision of refuge a promised land. Sizable numbers have come from Iran, Poland, Lebanon, Turkey, Ghana, and Sri Lanka. Increasing from about 5,000 per year in the early 1970s, the tide of those seeking asylum reached an alarming 108,000 in 1980, dropped off to around 20,000 in 1983, but increased again to the 100,000 level by 1986. Without abridging the obligation—derived from the Basic Law—to provide a haven for the politically persecuted, efforts have been made to contain the flow by allowing for local determination at the point of entry of the validity of the asylum-seeker's claims. Stricter guidelines and the willingness of the GDR to stem the flow of asylum seekers entering West Berlin via East Berlin—heretofore a major entry route—led to a drop in the number seeking asylum to 57,400 in 1987. Applicants increased again, though, to 103,000 in 1988. Even though less than 10 percent are eventually granted asylum, each case must be examined in a process that typically takes up to five years. Legislation tightening the regulations relating to the granting of asylum is to be expected.

Although in the past the Federal Republic has opened its doors wide, it has not become a melting pot for non-German nationals. Despite increased awareness of the need to accommodate foreign residents within the country's social and educational spheres, it remains doubtful that non-German immigrants can be fully integrated into West German society. The large concentration of Turks poses a particular challenge; marked by major cultural and religious differences, Turks have created their own ghettos in major German cities. A volatile situation exists given the latent hostility toward foreigners of a sizable minority of Germans together with the incomplete integration of a generation of those who have grown up without a distinct national identity.

The tranquility of West German society was shattered in the early 1970s by a wave of terrorism whose culmination in the fall of

1977 brought the country to a standstill. Born in the wake of student protests in Berlin and the conflagration of department stores in Frankfurt, and fueled by the ideology of radical members of an "extraparliamentary opposition" formed in the late 1960s, small groups of terrorists undertook a nationwide offensive of bombings in the spring of 1972. The capture and imprisonment of the movement's leadership delayed but did not deter further development of the phenomenon, for a generation of converts to the cause developed a revolutionary cell infrastructure throughout the Federal Republic. This reconsolidation was ingeniously directed from behind prison walls, posing a direct threat to the underpinnings of the German legal system and provoking the government response noted in Chapter 4. Terror was escalated within prison by hunger strikes and outside by assassinations, the taking of hostages, and indiscriminate violence. The campaign climaxed in the fall of 1977 with the abduction and ultimate slaying of industrialist Hanns-Martin Schleyer; the freeing by German commandos of the passengers of a Lufthansa jet highjacked by terrorists to Mogadishu, Somalia; and the subsequent suicides of movement leaders Andreas Baader and Gudrun Ensslin. Since then, there have been quiet periods punctuated by new outbreaks of violence. Calling itself the Red Army Faction, the movement continues to regenerate itself despite the capture of key leaders, the seizure of weapon caches, and increased government vigilance. By the mid-1980s, terrorist activities were increasingly aimed at installations of NATO and U.S. forces; they spread beyond German borders through collaboration with counterpart groups in other West European countries. The linked assassinations in early 1985 of a West German arms industrialist and a French defense ministry official prompted the FRG and France to establish an antiterror working group. Assassinations in 1986 of a Siemens Company nuclear physicist reputedly involved in Strategic Defense Initiative research and of the head of the Foreign Ministry's political office prompted the enactment of new antiterrorist legislation by the government coalition. The FDP balked, however, in agreeing at that time to tougher antidemonstration measures and to immunity for terrorists who testified on behalf of the state. Following a public outcry upon the murder of two policemen at a November 1987 demonstration at Frankfurt airport, the FDP leadership at a special party congress voted to support the additional measures which in July, 1988, were enacted into law over SPD and Green objections. Right-wing terrorism has also continued, though on a much reduced scale due to increased surveillance and the prosecution of the key perpetrators of neo-Nazi paramilitary activities.

The environment became a major concern in the Federal Republic in the 1980s. Initially an issue exploited with limited success by the Green party and local activists who sought to block construction of nuclear facilities and airport runways, the state of the environment—in particular, the plight of Germany's forests—captured the attention of the public and all political parties. The *Waldsterben,* or dying of forests, has become an issue of acute concern. In the Black Forest, two-thirds of all trees are visibly damaged, one-half of these severely so. Damage is judged to be at a comparable level in other German forests. Industrial and chemical plant pollution, auto emissions, and acid rain contributed to this calamity. The April 1986 Chernobyl nuclear power plant incident, with the resulting threat of radiation contamination of the West German food supply, the November 1986 major spillage of hazardous chemicals from a Swiss chemical plant into the Rhine River, and the death of thousands of North and Baltic sea seals and fish due to exposure to toxic waste in fall of 1988 have catapulted the environment into a major issue of concern to all.

The Kohl government reacted to Chernobyl by establishing a new Ministry of Environment, Nature Conservation, and Reactor Safety, naming the CDU mayor of Frankfurt as minister. The future of West German nuclear energy operations and construction became the political issue of the day. The government pledged to focus attention on reactor safety and to investigate alternative energy sources. The Greens demanded the immediate closing of all nuclear facilities and stepped up demonstrations at new construction sites. SPD politicians took a middle course, advocating the quickest possible development of alternative energy sources with divestiture by legal means of existing nuclear facilities. The divergence in approaches between the SPD and Greens led, in February 1987, to the collapse of the fragile SPD/Green coalition government in Hesse.

The breaking up of the SPD/FDP governing coalition and ouster of Chancellor Schmidt through a constructive vote of no confidence in October 1982 signaled for many a *Wende*, or turning point, in West German politics as 13 years of social-liberal leadership came to an end. (It can be argued, however, that the Wende occurred as early as the mid- 1970s with the more conservative leadership of Schmidt and Genscher as well as economic austerity combining to stifle the reform euphoria that had marked the earlier years of the coalition under Brandt and Scheel.) The CDU/CSU/FDP coalition that came to power in 1982 and had its mandate to rule legitimized through its March 1983 electoral victory brought with it the momentum of a power-starved opposition eager to implement its own programs.

The Kohl government's achievements—upturn in the economy with reduction of the national debt and improved relations with its closest ally, the United States—were initially obscured by a series of political misfortunes and scandals that called into question Kohl's leadership abilities and at times challenged the staying power of his coalition. Kohl has been particularly hard-pressed to reconcile the differing factions within his coalition. The CSU in particular has challenged the coalition rights of the FDP and the foreign policy leadership of Genscher. The FDP has tenaciously held on to both the Foreign and Economic Ministries in the Schmidt and Kohl cabinets; neither of these important ministries has had a CDU/CSU minister since 1966. The CSU, in control of the Interior Ministry until spring 1989, advocated the curbing of demonstration rights of protestors, favored introduction of a mandatory personal identification card, and proposed strong restrictions on the granting of asylum and on extension of rights to foreign residents (all of which pitted it against the FDP's championing of civil liberties—the FDP has controlled the Justice Ministry). The CSU has clashed with its coalition partners in balking at establishment of restrictive FRG policies against South Africa and Chile.

The political landscape in the Federal Republic was overshadowed in the mid-1980s by the Flick affair. Public confidence was severely shaken by revelations that politicians from all major parties save the Greens were implicated in the acceptance of large sums of money from the Flick industrial holding company. A special investigative committee of the Bundestag collected evidence and heard testimony of payments made purportedly as contributions to political parties. Investigation focused on cases in which the donations had "strings attached" or in which politicians pocketed the money. The scandal unraveled in Watergate fashion with allegations of involvement leading to the resignations of FDP Economics Minister Otto Graf Lambsdorff and Bundestag President Rainer Barzel, former party chairman of the CDU.

Lambsdorff and his predecessor as economics minister, Hans Friderichs, were both indicted and brought to trial in late 1985. Helmut Kohl testified to the investigative committee that he accepted cash donations from the Flick company on behalf of the CDU in the late 1970s and had turned all money over to the party treasurer. Two investigations of Kohl's conduct in this matter were subsequently dropped because of insufficient evidence. Lambsdorff and Friderichs were fined for tax evasion but acquitted of more serious bribery charges in February 1987, following an 18-month trial. The Flick scandal not only raised the specter of political corruption; it also called into question the means of political party financing in the Federal Republic. The FDP, CDU, and CSU, in particular, have relied on donations. New rules legislated in the wake of the Flick scandal set limits on tax deductions for contributors and require that donors' names be revealed on all donations in excess of DM 20,000.

The Kohl government was shaken in the summer of 1985 by the defection to the GDR of Hans Joachim Tiedge, the director of operations against East German agents in the FRG. His defection set off a spate of similar defections that included, among others, the chief secretary of FDP Economics Minister Bangemann, and secretaries from both the chancellery and the federal president's office. The unveiling of East bloc spies in responsible positions in the FRG bureaucracy, while not unique in the history of the Federal Republic, nevertheless underscored the concern Bonn's allies have in sharing sensitive information with the FRG.

Kohl came under public fire at home and abroad in connection with the controversy involving President Reagan's visit to the Bitburg war cemetery during public observances associated with the fortieth anniversary of the capitulation of Nazi Germany. Here, he suffered from comparison with the federal president, Richard von Weizsäcker. In a memorable speech on May 8, 1985, Weizsäcker noted that this day, 40 years ago, was a day of liberation, but also a day that could not be separated from January 30, 1933, the day Hitler came to power. In publicly stating German responsibility for the war, the Holocaust, and for the division of Europe ensuing from the war, von Weizsäcker eased the furor caused by Bitburg and eloquently stated the German desire for atonement, a declaration that was not, however, popular with all Germans.

Von Weizsäcker, a liberal CDU politician, former West Berlin mayor and lay Evangelical church official, was elected to the presidency in 1984 and again in 1989, both times with the solid support of the SPD. With a measure of independence from his own

party, he has in the fulfillment of the duties of his office made important state visits and received visiting heads of state, but has also acted informally in speaking out on timely and important subjects. Von Weizsäcker has thereby unwittingly transcended party politics and, in the view of many observers, has challenged Kohl's position of authority and leadership. Thus far, the two have not been brought into conflict in the exercise of their prescribed roles. While von Weizsäcker has proven to be a strong president, he has not sought to overstep the bounds placed on his office.

Elected in January 1987 to his second full term as chancellor, Kohl succeeded in uniting his coalition partners in forming a new government. Having previously weathered the domestic tumult associated with the decision to go ahead with the placement of Pershing II and cruise missiles on West German soil, the Kohl government now positioned itself as a strong supporter of superpower efforts to dismantle and remove the missiles (though not without some concerns relating to ultimate West German security as will be noted later).

The government and indeed the country were rocked in the fall of 1987 by a political scandal associated with the state election in Schleswig-Holstein, a scandal that was judged by many observers to have grave implications for the health of participatory democracy in the Federal Republic. Schleswig-Holstein Minister President Uwe Barschel faced a strong challenge from SPD candidate Björn Engholm in his bid for reelection. Barschel was the protégé of Schleswig-Holstein's CDU party chairman, Gerhard Stoltenberg, finance minister in Bonn and a Kohl rival for national party leadership. On September 12, 1987, the day prior to the election, the German news magazine, *Der Spiegel*, published allegations of a Barschel press aide that he had helped carry out a "dirty tricks" campaign masterminded by Barschel against Engholm. The campaign included surveillance of Engholm's private life, an anonymous letter to tax authorities charging Engholm with tax fraud and a plan to accuse Engholm in connection with installation of a wiretap in Barschel's office. The CDU lost 6.4 percent and its outright majority in the September 13 election; Barschel's ability to form a government became contingent on the FDP and the small Danish minority party (which permanently elects one seat in the Schleswig-Holstein parliament). In mounting furor, Barschel resigned on September 25, strongly denying any wrongdoing. On October 11, he was found dead in a Geneva, Switzerland, hotel room, one day before he was to testify before an investigating committee. Variously speculated to be either suicide or murder, an autopsy revealed his death attributable to an overdose of sedatives. A final February 1988 investigative report found that Barschel had abused his authority and had been abetted in his wrongdoing by state officials and CDU politicians. In a follow-up election in May 1988, Engholm won a commanding victory with a 54.8 percent majority, ousting the CDU from 38 years in power. The CDU lost an additional 9.3 percent for a total 15.7 percentage loss over the eight-month period of the two elections. The Barschel election scandal undoubtedly damaged respect for politicians and bred public disillusion. The shock was strongly felt in Bonn. While the impact of this one particular instance should not be exaggerated, it remains to be seen what long-term effect the scandal might have on the fortunes of the CDU and the West German party state as a whole.

Finance Minister Stoltenberg was a key and often embattled figure in the struggle to enact landmark tax reform legislation which finally passed the Bundestag in June 1988, winning Bundesrat approval the following month. To get the necessary votes for passage, the Kohl government had to agree ultimately to abandon a disputed aviation fuel tax exemption for private pilots (that had been energetically pushed by CSU leader Strauss) and had to guarantee major federal subsidies for economically weak Länder, the latter being the price for Lower Saxony's vote for the tax reform measure in the Bundesrat.

With the tax reform package enacted, Kohl pledged in the time remaining before the fall 1990 election to pursue health care and pension reform as well as to focus on reducing unemployment.

Even with the unexpected death of Strauss in October 1988, Kohl has his hands full in maintaining unity in his coalition, given increasing signs that at least some FDP politicians are beginning to consider the merits of a new coalition with the SPD. Although Kohl has survived a number of domestic crises and has established strong personal relationships with both Bush and Gorbachev, his personal approval rating and that of his party have been subject to dips in public opinion polls, raising the question as to how long he will remain the standard bearer of the CDU/CSU. While Stoltenberg is now less likely a credible rival, Baden-Württemberg Minister President Lothar Spaeth is one possible alternative to whom the CDU and CSU might turn. Kohl's political future beyond the fall 1990 election will also of course depend on how strong a chancellor candidate the SPD fields.

The fortunes of the governing coalition sank even further with the results of the January 1989 Berlin election, of 1989 local elections in Hesse, the Saar, and the Rhineland-Palatinate, and of the June 1989 election for the European Parliament. In West Berlin, the popular CDU mayor lost his majority as the ultraright Republicans—with no previous voter base in Berlin—won 7.5 percent of the vote, essentially a protest vote on the asylum issue. Also, the CDU's FDP coalition partner fell below the 5 percent hurdle. West Berlin government leadership passed to a coalition of the SPD with the Alternative List, an affiliate of the Greens. In Hesse local elections the CDU suffered major losses in all municipalities; in Frankfurt the CDU mayor was replaced by the SPD candidate, and the NPD, with 6.6 percent of the vote, won representation in the municipal council.

CDU losses on the right further escalated intra-party and intra-coalition strife, with the new CSU leadership in particular critical of the Kohl government's inability to effectively handle the emigration and asylum issues. In April 1989, Kohl dealt with the political crisis by reorganizing his cabinet. He succeeded in persuading CSU Party Chairman Theo Waigel to share responsibility for coalition fortunes by joining the cabinet as finance minister. Stoltenberg moved to occupy the defense minister portfolio. The government undertook to deal anew with the emigration and asylum issue by signalling its intentions to encourage ethnic Germans to remain in their Eastern European homelands and to introduce visa requirements for travel to the FRG by additional nationalities, including Poles. At the same time Kohl sought to shore up his coalition on the right, he aligned himself with Foreign Minister Genscher and overwhelming public sentiment in favor of the dismantling of short-range nuclear forces. He called both for postponement of any NATO decision on short-range missile modernization and for early superpower negotiations on significant reductions in short-range missiles in Central Europe. This shift in course by Kohl served to rob the opposition SPD of a likely major issue and to curb prospects for an FDP-SPD rapprochment on defense and foreign policy issues. But in moving thus to consolidate his domestic political position, Kohl risked a major rift with the new Bush administration.

The elections in mid-June for the European Parliament and for local assemblies in the Saar and Rhineland-Palatinate resulted in further electoral losses for the CDU and CSU, this despite the energetic image Kohl had displayed in achieving a compromise with the U.S. on missile policy and in hosting both Bush and Gorbachev in the weeks preceding the elections. The CDU/CSU lost 8.1 percent of the vote compared to the previous European Parliament election, and in Saar and Rhineland-Palatinate local elections the CDU lost 6.9 percent and 7.8 percent respectively. The FDP, with 5.6 percent of the vote, returned to the European Parliament after five years' absence. The Republicans became the fifth German party in the European Parliament with 7.1 percent; their

share of the vote in Bavaria reached 14.6 percent. Despite this poor showing of the CDU/CSU, Kohl's party leadership and role as chancellor was not challenged by other aspirants within his party.

Should the Republicans achieve Bundestag representation in the 1990 election along with the Greens and the FDP, it is conceivable that neither large party, the CDU/CSU nor the SPD, would be able to put together a majority coalition—the CDU/CSU with the FDP, or the SPD with the Greens. Assuming that neither party would in such circumstances accept the Republicans as a coalition partner, then there would appear to be only two possible options for a governing majority: an SPD/Greens/FDP coalition if it constitutes a majority (and if the Greens and FDP can work together), or the remaking of a Grand Coalition of the CDU/CSU with the SPD. The fate of the Kohl governing coalition appears thus to rest with the fortunes of the Republicans.

The death of Strauss marked the end of an era. His successors— Waigel and Bavarian Minister President Max Streibl—cannot expect to wield as much influence on a national scale.

The FDP also underwent a leadership change in the fall of 1988 in connection with Martin Bangemann's announced departure to become a member of the European Commission in Brussels. In a close party convention vote, Otto Count Lambsdorff was selected new party chairman over Irmgard Adam-Schwaetzer, this despite his earlier party finance tax evasion conviction. Although he has made no move to return to a role of leadership within the party, Foreign Minister Genscher remains the most prominent FDP politician and indeed the most popular political figure in the FRG. FDP politicians including Lambsdorff have favored a more independent role for the party vis-à-vis the Kohl coalition and have welcomed the more centrist course being pursued by the SPD. While not beyond the realm of possibility, it would seem that Genscher and Lambsdorff—who themselves precipitated the fall of the Schmidt government—would face rather formidable obstacles in steering their party back into a coalition with the SPD. While there is a greater appreciation of the FDP's role in providing the political balance, it remains to be seen whether a newly consolidated party rank and file would go along with yet another shift in political direction. The precedent has already been set in the FDP forming a coalition with the Social Democrats in the city-state of Hamburg.

SPD Party Chairmen Vogel consolidated his claim to leadership at the party's September 1988 convention, being reelected with 99 percent of the vote. Rau and Lafontaine were reelected deputy chairmen, Lafontaine with a much reduced margin due in part to labor union criticism of his call for civil servants to forgo pay raises in order to help create new jobs for the unemployed. Although not as popular among the population as a whole, Vogel would appear to be the most likely SPD candidate to challenge Kohl with perhaps better prospects than he had in 1983.

There will be several political events on the path to the December 1990 federal election: with prior state elections planned for the Saar, North Rhine–Westphalia, Lower Saxony, Bavaria, and Hamburg. Each should prove a test of political party strength and contribute to the running barometer that will, as in the past, influence the issues and the outcome of the Bundestag election. The role of the two small parties and of the Republicans should be of greater importance than heretofore. The more sophisticated West German electorate is by now experienced in vote splitting and more prone to switch their party support on the basis of judgment of issues and performance.

FOREIGN POLICY ISSUES

Over the last four decades, the interaction of the West German political system with the international system has revealed a complex dichotomy of penetration and autonomy, complicated by the nature of the international system. And in the Federal Republic itself, foreign policy has had such an effect on the formulation of domestic and social policy, and domestic policy has at times so affected the formulation of foreign policy, that it is difficult to define what is internal and what is external. Such blurring of foreign and domestic politics in the Federal Republic is nowhere more evident than in the way the Bonn government approaches its relationship with the other German state, the GDR. The evolution of the relationship between the two Germanies is recounted in Chapter 3. The myth of a single German nation has been officially kept alive by the Bonn government for whom the GDR is not foreign territory.

The primacy of this special relationship brings with it certain constraints on West German policymaking. While firmly entrenched in the Western alliance, the FRG has since the advent of the Brandt/Scheel coalition not been willing to let intra-German relations be subjected to the vicissitudes of the East-West political climate. West German efforts to improve ties to the GDR—and thereby to improve the lot of GDR citizens—continued unabated despite the passing of détente and the placement of Pershing II missiles in the Federal Republic and Soviet missiles in the GDR. The Kohl government has continued the efforts initiated by its predecessors. Franz-Josef Strauss was particularly active in helping to secure West German financial credits for the GDR and in engaging GDR leader Erich Honecker in dialogue. Movement in intra-German relations proceeded at a slow pace in the early 1980s, with Moscow blocking a planned September 1984 Honecker visit to the FRG. With new leadership in the Kremlin and the advent of U.S.-Soviet summit diplomacy, conditions were by early 1987 ripe for further development of relations between the two German states. A series of overtures and understandings involving both sides culminated in Honecker's landmark visit to the FRG in September 1987. The spectacle of Honecker being received as a visiting head of state reinforced the reality of two distinctly separate states, but the visit also served effectively to illustrate common elements that bind the two states together. Honecker noted on more than one occasion that the borders between the two German states "are not as they should be." A joint communiqué announced that both sides would undertake efforts to increase travel, expand trade and technical cooperation, and participate in more sport and cultural exchanges. It remains to be seen on what terms the two Germanies can move even more closely together and whether allusions made by Honecker to an eventual normalization of borders are within the realm of possibility. While concrete results have already been achieved, the pace has been slow and further movement in intra-German relations will likely continue to take place in incremental steps.

Concerned with maintaining its special relationship with the GDR, and at the same time acutely aware of its vulnerable position on the East-West front, the Federal Republic has been a firm proponent of the continuation of East-West arms reduction negotiations. The Schmidt government supported a December 1979 two-track NATO ministers' agreement to accept deployment beginning in 1983 of 572 U.S.-built Pershing II missiles and cruise missiles in west-central Europe and the United Kingdom to counter Soviet intermediate-range missiles already in place in east-central Europe. The ministers also agreed that the West should seek to negotiate with Moscow on limiting the use of these "European theater" nuclear forces. The Soviets countered with an announcement of planned reductions of Soviet forces in the GDR and an offer to reduce the number of its Eastern Europe–based missiles if NATO would refrain from any new deployment of U.S. missiles in Western Europe. This offer was greeted as an indication of Soviet good intentions by the SPD's left wing and also by Egon Bahr, the party's Eastern policy strategist. This forced the Schmidt government not only to deal with dissent in its own ranks but also to push for the initiation by the West of missile reduction talks at a time

when events in Afghanistan and Poland were freezing the East-West climate. Schmidt thus welcomed the Reagan administration's announcement in May 1981 of its decision to initiate such talks with Moscow.

When negotiations in Geneva failed to achieve any resolution, the Soviet Union under Yuri Andropov launched a public relations campaign to appeal to West European public opinion. The question of the placement of Pershing II and cruise missiles became a dominant issue in the West German election campaign in early 1983 with the victor, Helmut Kohl, committed to carry out the NATO two-track agreement but increasingly concerned about the divisiveness of the issue amid seeming American intransigence. As the year progressed without agreement in Geneva, a West German peace movement— some 5 million strong, embracing a spectrum from bishops and lay religious officials to the West German Communist party— staged massive rallies in solidarity with their counterparts in other West European countries. The climax came in a Bundestag debate and vote November 22, 1983, as thousands of demonstrators converged on Bonn. The Bundestag approved the deployment by a vote of 286 to 226 with one abstention. The SPD had decided in a Fraktion meeting to vote "no" on deployment, in opposition to the recommendation of Helmut Schmidt.

The Federal Republic under Helmut Kohl exercised less of a role in strategic matters than did the Schmidt government as the dynamics of the East-West relationship were dominated by the superpowers themselves, once they agreed to bilateral negotiations. The Federal Republic was relegated to a consultative role, and in this situation it was often unable to influence decisions made in Washington. West German public opinion was concerned initially at U.S. intransigence in the East-West negotiations, then by concern that Western Europe's umbrella of protection might be removed. Kohl was placed in the difficult position of being expected to be a Western alliance team player, and at the same time having to deal at home with lack of understanding and support for the U.S.

position. President Reagan's Strategic Defense Initiative (SDI) has been a case in point: the majority of the West German public have opposed it, the SPD and Greens decidedly oppose it, and key members of the governing coalition have expressed strong reservations. The Kohl government elected to have the German Economics Ministry conclude a cooperative SDI agreement with the U.S. Department of Defense thereby ensuring a role for German industrial participation while avoiding the delicate issue of a Defense Ministry relationship.

By mid-1987 the superpowers were on the verge of finalizing a treaty on intermediate-range missile (300 to 3400 miles) nuclear force (INF) reduction. The issue of German maintenance of aging U.S. Pershing-IA missiles (with U.S.- controlled nuclear warheads) became the last stumbling block in U.S.-Soviet INF negotiations. Against vocal opposition from within the CDU/CSU and with the opposition seeking to capitalize on government intransigence in upcoming state elections, Kohl announced in late August 1987 that the FRG agreed to the inclusion of the Pershing-IAs in the treaty. The general euphoria that greeted the signing of the INF treaty by Reagan and Gorbachev was tempered by the realization of the increased vulnerability of the two Germanies as the potential battleground in a conventional war in which tactical nuclear warheads could be employed. The FRG succeeded through an appeal to the United States to at least temporarily forestall modernization of NATO's short-range Lance missile in favor of a full-scale review and development of a revised, comprehensive NATO defense strategy. Kohl would clearly like to have the 1990 election behind him before the FRG has to face the issue of short-range missile modernization. Foreign Minister Genscher and CDU/CSU Fraktion leader Dregger have been—along with SPD politicians—vocal proponents for new approaches that would lessen the threat of regionalized nuclear conflict. It remains to be seen how vulnerable the FRG might be to renewed attempts by the Soviets

to woo West Germans, along with other West Europeans, away from NATO security positions traditionally advocated by the United States. It is clear that West Germans desire an atmosphere in East-West relations that is conducive to good relations with the East and to continued improvement in relations with the GDR.

In contrast to the dramatic events that fashioned the Brandt/Scheel government's Ostpolitik with the Soviet Union and other East bloc states in the early 1970s, further movement in the area of Ostpolitik has been much more incremental. The period of initial euphoria led to some disillusionment as many expectations remained unmet. Since then, the governments of Schmidt and Kohl, and with them the West German citizenry, have adjusted their expectations to reflect a greater understanding of reality. The FRG's Ostpolitik was dealt a blow with the passing of détente following the Soviet invasion of Afghanistan. While agreeing not to field a team at the 1980 Moscow Olympics, the Federal Republic balked at imposing strong sanctions in connection with the imposition of martial law in Poland. A succession of changes in Kremlin leadership and the lessening of FRG foreign policy autonomy under Kohl had decidedly cooled West German–Soviet relations by the mid-1980s. Soviet charges of West German revanchism were revived and the Kremlin exercised its influence on the GDR to prevent Honecker from following up on his plans to visit the Federal Republic in September, 1984. Bonn's position was not helped by German expellees from Poland reasserting their claim to Silesia and other former German eastern territories. While Kohl insisted that the FRG accepted current Eastern European borders, the fact that he and other CDU/CSU leaders accepted invitations to address expellees' rallies contributed to East bloc mistrust. With the dawn of the Gorbachev era, an initially brief thaw in Soviet-FRG relations was thwarted by Kohl's unfortunate October 1986 comparison of Gorbachev's public relations campaign to that of Nazi propagandist Joseph Goebbels and by German intransigence in including its Pershing-IA missiles in the INF treaty.

Following in the wake of the INF treaty negotiations, a new West German Ostpolitik is beginning to unfold. President von Weizsäcker made a state visit to the USSR in July, 1987. Honecker's trip to the FRG took place two months later. Cold warrior Strauss, traveling to Moscow in December 1987, praised Gorbachev and declared that the postwar period was over and a new era had begun. In January 1988, Kohl visited Prague and Genscher traveled to Warsaw. A Gorbachev letter to Kohl in April 1988 expressed a desire for intensification of Soviet-FRG relations. In May, German banks announced a DM 3.5 billion credit for the Soviet Union to assist in the modernization of Soviet food processing industries. Kohl and five cabinet ministers visited the Soviet Union for four days in October 1988, signing agreements and undertaking discussions with Gorbachev and his colleagues on an intensification of economic, cultural, scientific research and environmental protection ties. Kohl also undertook discussions on the issues of disarmament and human rights. His effort to secure Gorbachev's recognition of the FRG's position in inclusion of West Berlin in all agreements was less successful with the issue being relegated to future discussions between Soviet and FRG foreign ministers.

Gorbachev's follow-up visit to the FRG took place in June 1989, two weeks after the visit of Bush. Not since John F. Kennedy had a foreign leader so won the acclaim and captured the adulation of West Germans. To repeated choruses of "Gorbi," Gorbachev and his party engaged in highly public activities in a number of cities. Kohl and Gorbachev issued a Joint Declaration, announcing a common goal of working toward peace and cooperation in what they repeatedly termed "a common European house." Both sides took care to recognize the role of respective allies, in particular the United States, and Gorbachev chose the occasion of his FRG visit to comment favorably on President

Bush's recent NATO summit proposals for conventional arms reductions. The two sides signed 11 treaties promoting various aspects of economic and technological cooperation, with incorporation of West Berlin in each agreement.

Spurred by Ostpolitik, West German trade with the East bloc increased through the 1970s. In terms of proportionate share of all FRG trade, however, East bloc trade has not exceeded 5 or 6 percent per annum and in 1987 fell to 4.3 percent due to the sharp decline in hard currency reserves in Eastern Europe. (Such figures do not include the GDR, with whom, it should be noted, a special "interzonal" trading arrangement has been maintained.) Trade with the Soviet Union has increased in particular as a result of joint efforts in connection with development of a pipeline supplying the FRG and other West European states with gas in exchange for steel pipe, compressors, turbines, and other construction-related materials.

Despite any autonomy it has gained in pursuit of its Ostpolitik, the Federal Republic has remained firmly anchored in the Western alliance and closely tied to its chief ally, the United States. Fears that the Federal Republic could become a Trojan horse for Soviet designs toward a neutralized Western Europe appear unfounded at this time, though it should be noted that Gorbachev's stock in West German opinion polls has risen sharply at the same time that concerns about a Soviet threat to peace have greatly diminished.

The close relationship between Kohl and Reagan was evidenced by Reagan's stubborn insistence on joining Kohl in memorial services at the Bitburg cemetery. This relationship stood in contrast to the often acrimonious one between their predecessors, Schmidt and Carter. In being the first foreign leader to travel to Washington to meet with President-elect Bush, Kohl underscored the value he attaches to the U.S. relationship. While he is less inclined than his predecessor to steer an independent course, Kohl has not hesitated to back German interests—as reflected in the implementation of the pipeline deal with the Soviet Union, in German insistence on trying an accused Lebanese terrorist wanted for murder in connection with the 1985 hijacking of a TWA flight rather than extraditing him to the United States, in Bonn's refusal on the grounds of constitutional limitations to send warships to the Persian Gulf in support of U.S. naval operations, and in expression of German concerns over high U.S. interest rates and the large budget and trade deficits of the Reagan and Bush administrations. Additional irritants in U.S.-German relations came as a result of German efforts to restrict flights of low-flying aircraft and to ban airshows after an August 1988 disaster that killed 70 participants and onlookers at Ramstein Air Base, and in connection with FRG denials and then admissions of West German chemical firm involvement in development of a chemical weapons plant in Rabta, Libya.

Kohl's independence from Washington in pressing in early 1989 for postponement until 1992 (well after the next FRG federal election) of a Western alliance decision on short-range missile modernization and his subsequent call for negotiations with the Soviets on short-range missile reductions underscored the potential for differences with the U.S., but this time the stakes were higher as NATO unanimity appeared threatened and Washington was put on the defensive in having to develop initiatives to defuse the impact of the Gorbachev peace offensive on the FRG. The keen sense of post-INF vulnerability felt by Germans was seen alternatively by some U.S. policymakers as a desire to seek new opportunities in relations with the East and a willingness to abandon Western ties. American willingness to go along with a delay in the decision on short-range missile modernization, President Bush's May 1989 NATO summit initiative for cuts in conventional forces, and the compromise NATO decision to agree to pursue negotiations with the Soviet Union toward partial reduc-

tions in short-range missiles—but only after implementation is underway for negotiated conventional arms reductions—all served for the time being to smooth over differences between the two allies, easing Bush's trip to the FRG in the aftermath of the NATO summit and two weeks before Gorbachev's planned arrival in Bonn. In the near-term future the FRG will likely continue to be a critical focal point for initiatives and counter-initiatives proposed by both sides in the efforts of East and West to move beyond the Cold War era. While it is clear that Washington can best deal with a CDU-led government in Bonn, it is unlikely that an SPD-led government could easily abrogate longstanding West German alliance commitments. Any FRG government must represent the clear desire of its population to remove the threat of nuclear vulnerability. For the time being, even with Gorbachev's immense popularity and the favorable impression of changes taking place in the Soviet Union and Eastern Europe, a large majority of West Germans continue to support NATO membership and the presence of U.S. troops as a "tripwire" to ensure full U.S. engagement in the event of military conflict. Should the perception of a Soviet threat diminish further, the rationale for continued presence of sizable numbers of U.S. troops may be open to question in both Bonn and Washington. Maintenance of the Bundeswehr at current levels may also be subject to modification. The Federal Republic remains the linchpin of the Western alliance; the future of NATO will depend in large part on the willingness of West Germans to fully participate in the alliance under U.S. leadership.

Both the FRG and U.S. governments have embarked on a concerted effort to increase transatlantic exchanges among their citizens, particularly members of the "successor generation." The tricentennial of German settlement in North America was celebrated with much fanfare in 1983. A West German scientist was the first non-American to fly on a space shuttle mission. Both the Bundestag and the U.S. Congress are sponsoring intern programs to provide exchange opportunities for young citizens of both countries.

The FRG also maintains a special relationship with France, its chief partner in Europe. Kohl and President Mitterrand meet biannually, maintaining intact the senior-level relationship inaugurated by Adenauer and De Gaulle in 1963. Both sides have long recognized that any form of West European integration will require Franco-German support. In the wake of the INF treaty, both leaders met in January 1988 and endorsed a plan to create a French/German brigade as a first step toward closer defense collaboration.

Political and economic power beget responsibility, as the FRG has realized in viewing the recent state of affairs in the European Community. The task has on several occasions fallen to the Federal Republic to "bail out" the Community. FRG credits were extended to bolster a sagging Italian economy, and the Federal Republic pledged a $1.4 billion contribution in June 1980 at an emergency EEC session in Brussels that largely offset a cut of $1.6 billion in Great Britain's dues announced by the Thatcher government. The FRG has since then been less willing to agree to disproportionate contributions to the maintenance of the Community but was influential in pushing in March 1988 for a reform of the Community's financial structure—with assessments to be based on each country's GDP and value added tax—with the result that the German contribution to the Community will cost DM 30 billion more each year through 1992.

Public opinion in the FRG has traditionally supported the concept of a politically united Europe, though this level of support has not been evident in the relatively low turnout of West German voters in elections for the European Parliament. Chancellor Kohl joined with French President Mitterrand in jointly submitting at a June 1985 European Council summit meeting a draft proposal for a European Union as a further development of the European Community

with closer integration in the areas of foreign and security policy. Fully committed to the 1992 attainment of a common internal market within the Community, the Federal Republic will, along with other Community member states, have to wrestle with a necessary surrender of national sovereignty to be able to address the social dimensions of an internal market and attain eventual economic and monetary union.

Export expansion and developmental aid have been the twin hallmarks of West German policy toward the non-Western world. German industry has enjoyed the strong support of the federal and state governments in opening up markets in the world abroad. China, South Asia, and Latin America were areas of particular focus for German trade in the 1980s. The FRG has sought to avoid choosing sides in the conflicts between the Arab states and Israel. While recognizing the special responsibility it bears toward Israel, it has supported the European Community's position that Palestinian claims must be considered in any Middle East settlement. German industry has entertained particular ambitions with regard to a lucrative market for German armaments in the Arab states. Revelations relating to the involvement of German firms in the development of a Libyan chemical weapons factory have led to a toughening of West German export laws. The Bonn government's dealings with South Africa and with the Latin American states of Chile, Nicaragua, and El Salvador have been subject to ideological dispute within the FRG in the 1980s. Astute development aid policies have helped the FRG to remain the friend of a number of developing nations. In 1987 the Federal Republic provided DM 7.9 billion in developmental assistance. In 1988 the FRG waived DM 3.3 billion in debt payments coming due from poorer developing nations, adding to a sum of DM 4.2 billion previously waived. One troublesome problem for FRG foreign policy has been the Bonn government's requirement that the FRG's special administrative responsibility for West Berlin (subject to Four Power rights to Berlin as a whole) be recognized in all bilateral and multilateral agreements entered into.

THE FUTURE

The Federal Republic will be faced with significant challenges in the early 1990s. Will it be able to reduce unemployment and achieve sustained and significant economic growth? Will it be able to accommodate what has become a large and more permanent population of foreign inhabitants? Can extremism of the right and the left continue to be contained? Can the disenchantment and the political activism of critical members of the "successor generation" be channeled into societal development rather than disaffection and disruption? Will upcoming elections continue to produce viable coalitions that can govern effectively at the federal and state levels? Will the FRG's citizens continue to participate actively in the political process and can politicians inspire sustained public confidence? Will the CDU and CSU be able to prevent an erosion of their voter base toward the Republicans and other ultraright groups? Will the SPD complete its return to the center and emerge as a viable contender to provide government leadership in both domestic and foreign policy? Will the FDP continue to be represented in the Bundestag and to maintain its now traditional role as coalition partner to the government in power? Will the Greens consolidate their forces and remain a permanent fixture in the federal and state parliaments?

Will there be further movement and "normalization" in the relationship with the GDR? And what will be the future of the GDR after Honecker and with Gorbachev in power in Moscow? What will be the future basis for West German security in the aftermath of the INF treaty? Can Bonn enjoy a measure of autonomy in pursuing its own interests consistent with its Western alliance and European Community ties? Finally, do the indicators of democratic development that have been observed now for four decades conclusively demonstrate a real shift in attitudes and a commitment to democratic principles in the FRG?

While legally remaining a provisional state, it should by now be amply apparent that the Federal Republic has a mature political system and is fully integrated into the international political community. While it yet faces many challenges, it stands as a successful model for the development and survival of democracy in a modern industrial society.

Editor's Note: With the fall of Honecker and the virtual dissolution of the top Communist Party leadership and the promise to convene a Party Congress, open demonstration against the Communist Party rule, the exodus of East Germans to the Federal Republic, the opening of the Berlin Wall and the promise of free election but above all the prospects of German reunification in one form or another, sooner or later, the challenge to the leadership of the FRG has become more pressing than ever. By the end of 1989 few could predict with assurance the course of events in the 90s and, beyond, of the kind of political order that will emerge in Europe in the 21st century.

BIBLIOGRAPHY

Basic Reference Sources

Federal Republic of Germany. *Statistisches Jahrbuch für die Bundesrepublik Deutschland.* Stuttgart: W. Kohlhammer, 1952–current.

German Democratic Republic. *Statistisches Jahrbuch der Deutschen Demokratischen Republik.* Berlin (East): Staatsverlag der DDR, 1955–current.

MERRITT, RICHARD L., and ANNA J. MERRITT. *Politics, Economics and Society in the Two Germanies, 1945–1975: A Bibliography of English-Language Works.* Urbana: University of Illinois Press, 1978.

Press and Information Office of the Federal Government. *The Basic Law.* Bonn, 1973.

Books and Articles

BAKER, KENDALL L., RUSSELL DALTON, and KAI HILDEBRANDT. *Germany Transformed.* Cambridge, MA: Harvard University Press, 1981.

BRACHER, KARL D. *The German Dictatorship: The Origins, Structure, and Effects of National Socialism.* New York: Praeger, 1970.

BRANDT, WILLY. *A Peace Policy for Europe.* New York: Holt, Rinehart and Winston, 1969.

BRAUNTHAL, GERARD. *The West German Social Democrats, 1969–1982: Profile of a Party in Power.* Boulder, Co: Westview, 1983.

———. *The West German Legislative Process.* Ithaca, NY: Cornell University Press, 1972.

BURDICK, CHARLES, HANS-ADOLF JACOBSEN, and WINFRIED KUDSZUS, eds. *Contemporary Germany: Politics and Culture.* Boulder, CO: Westview, 1984.

CHALMERS, DOUGLAS A. *The Social Democratic Party of Germany.* New Haven, CT: Yale University Press. 1964.

CHILDS, DAVID, ed. *Honecker's Germany.* Boston: Allen & Unwin, 1985.

CONRADT, DAVID P. *The German Polity,* 4th ed. New York: Longman, 1989.

COONEY, JAMES A., GORDON A. CRAIG, HANS-PETER SCHWARZ, and FRITZ STERN, eds. *The Federal Republic of Germany and the United States: Changing Political, Social and Economic Relations.* Boulder, CO: Westview, 1984.

CRAIG, GORDON, *The Germans.* New York: Putnam, 1982.

———. *From Bismarck to Adenauer: Aspects of German Statecraft,* rev. ed. New York: Harper & Row, 1965.

DAHRENDORF, RALF. *Society and Democracy in Germany.* Garden City, NY: Doubleday, 1967.

DEUTSCH, KARL W. and LEWIS J. EDINGER. *Germany Rejoins the Powers: Mass Opinion, Interest Groups and Elites in German Foreign Policy.* Stanford, CA: Stanford University Press, 1959.

EDINGER, LEWIS J. *West German Politics.* New York: Columbia University Press, 1986.

FEST, JOACHIM. *Hitler.* New York: Random House, 1975.

FISCHER, FRITZ. *From Kaiserreich to Third Reich: Elements of Continuity in German History, 1871–1945.* Boston: Allen & Unwin, 1986.

FRAENKEL, ERNEST. "Historical Obstacles to Parliamentary Government in Germany." In Theodor Eschenburg, ed. *The Path to Dictatorship.* Garden City, NY: Doubleday/Anchor, 1966.

FRIEDRICH, CARL J. "Rebuilding the German Constitution." *American Political Science Review,* June 1949.

GROSSER, ALFRED. *Germany in Our Time.* New York: Praeger, 1971.

———. *The Federal Republic of Germany: A Concise History.* New York: Praeger, 1964.

GUNLICKS, ARTHUR B. *Local Government in the Ger-*

HANHARDT, ARTHUR M. *The German Democratic Reman Federal System.* Raleigh, NC: Duke University Press, 1986.

public. Baltimore, MD: Johns Hopkins University Press, 1968.

HANRIEDER, WOLFRAM, ed. *Arms Control, the FRG, and the Future of East-West Relations.* Boulder, CO: Westview, 1987.

———,*Germany, America, Europe: Forty Years of German Foreign Policy.* New Haven: Yale University Press, 1989.

HEIDENHEIMER, ARNOLD J. *Adenauer and the CDU.* The Hague: Nijhoff, 1960.

HOLBORN, HAJO. *A History of Modern Germany, 1840–1945.* New York: Alfred A. Knopf, 1970.

KAISER, KARL. *German Foreign Policy in Transition.* London: Oxford University Press, 1968.

KATZENSTEIN, PETER J. *Policy and Politics in West Germany; the Growth of a Semisovereign State.* Philadelphia: Temple University Press, 1987.

LAQUEUR, WALTER. *Germany Today: A Personal Report.* Boston: Little, Brown, 1985.

LOEWENBERG, GERHARD. *Parliament in the German Political System.* Ithaca, NY: Cornell University Press, 1966.

MARKOVITS, ANDREI S. *The Political Economy of West Germany: Modell Deutschland.* New York, Praeger, 1982.

MERKL, PETER H. *The Origin of the West German Republic.* New York: Oxford University Press, 1963.

NOELLE-NEUMANN, ELISABETH. *The Germans: Public Opinion Polls, 1967–1980.* Westport, CT: Greenwood Press, 1981.

NOELLE-NEUMANN, ELISABETH, and ERICH P. NEUMANN. *The Germans: Public Opinion Polls, 1947–1966.* Allensbach: Verlag für Demoskopie, 1967.

REINHARDT, KURT F. *Germany: 2000 Years.* 2 vols., rev. ed. New York: Ungar, 1962.

SCHMIDT, HELMUT. *Perspectives on Politics.* (ed. Wolfram Hanrieder.) Boulder, CO: Westview, 1982.

SCHWEIGLER, GEBHARD. *West German Foreign Policy: The Domestic Setting.* New York: Praeger, 1984.

SMITH, D. BRENT. "The Opposition to Ostpolitik: Foreign Policy as an Issue in West German Politics, 1969–1972." Ph.D. thesis, Harvard University, Cambridge, MA, 1976.

SONTHEIMER, KURT. *The Government and Politics of West Germany.* London: Hutchinson, 1972.

STRAUSS, FRANZ JOSEF. *Challenge and Response: A Program for Europe.* New York: Atheneum, 1970.

SZABO, STEPHEN F. *The Successor Generation: Interna-*

tional Perspectives of Postwar Europeans. London: Butterworths, 1983.

TROSSMANN, HANS. *The German Bundestag: Organization and Operation.* Darmstadt: Neue Darmstädter Verlagsanstalt, 1965.

VERBA, SIDNEY. "Germany: The Remaking of Political Culture." In Lucian W. Pye and Sidney Verba, eds. *Political Culture and Political Develop-*

ment. Princeton, NJ: Princeton University Press, 1965.

VON WEIZSÄCKER, RICHARD. *A Voice from Germany.* London: Weidenfeld and Nicolson, 1986.

WALLACH, PETER and GEORGE K. ROMOSER. *West German Politics in the Mid-Eighties: Crisis and Continuity.* New York: Praeger, 1985.

PART V
MEDITERRANEAN EUROPE: STABILIZED DEMOCRACIES?

*THOMAS D. LANCASTER**

1

Introduction

This part provides an overview of the politics of the Mediterranean countries—Italy, Portugal, Spain, and Greece. These nations have different historical backgrounds, cultures, and political institutions. There are also significant differences between Italy and the other three countries in the timing of modernization and the process of democratization. Despite the differences, these countries share a common experience: a relatively recent transition to democracy from an authoritarian regime. The recentness of this change reflects a tendency in all four countries toward political instability. These four countries' political institutions and regimes are struggling to gain legitimacy. Today, expectations and demands press on

their relatively new and often weak governmental structures. These structures attempt either to channel demands into public decisions or to contain them.

When viewed over a period of time—at least since the turn of the nineteenth century—the politics of the Mediterranean countries contrast sharply with those of the Scandinavian region discussed in Part VI. Scandinavia can be characterized, as we have seen, by well-established democratic procedures and long periods of governmental stability. The Mediterranean systems, in contrast, struggle with gaining acceptance for relatively young democratic institutions, with government and regime instability, and, except in Italy, with the frequent intervention of the military into politics. Some have been relatively more successful than others in their transitions to democracy. These four southern European countries dif-

*The author gratefully acknowledges the research assistance provided by Michael Duclos.

fer from one another in many aspects of economic growth, social structures, and policy outputs. And each country is undergoing a process of uneven and rapid economic development and experiencing a clash between traditional and more modern social norms.

CONTINUITY AND CHANGE

What is political instability? Most political and social scientists would agree that political instability involves change. But the crucial questions are how much change, what kind of change and, perhaps even more important, how does change take place. As late as the middle of the nineteenth century, the Scandinavian countries had not even begun industrialization. They were near-subsistence economies in which the peasantry constituted the mass of the population. Since then, they have industrialized rapidly to reach levels comparable to and even surpassing those of Great Britain, France, and West Germany. In contrast, until World War II the Mediterranean world remained in a virtually preindustrial stage. Italy had made rapid industrial progress in the north, but southern Italy remained backward.

Scandinavia shows us that dramatic socioeconomic changes can occur without major disruption of political structures and institutions, without revolution and violence. The Mediterranean world gives us an historic, panoramic view of constant regime changes, violence, revolution, and the intrusion of the military even when there are no appreciable socioeconomic changes. But we should not conclude that under certain circumstances rapid socioeconomic change will produce stability. The two major variables—political stability and socioeconomic change—cannot be linked without reference to many other factors, the most important of which may be the political culture and the institutional arrangements characteristic of a country's political history.

POLITICAL AND GOVERNMENTAL STABILITY

One important misunderstanding often arises in discussions of political stability. Such discussions often blur the distinction between a regime and a government. A regime is a particular pattern of political institutions that operates under a determined set of rules and procedures. The French Fourth Republic and Weimar Republic, for example, were distinctive regimes, as are the Fifth Republic and the current Federal Republic of Germany. A government, on the other hand, is a particular team of individuals, generally under the leadership of one person, that holds the positions of power within a regime at a given period. In this sense, one refers to the Thatcher government in Great Britain, the Mitterrand government in France, or the Bush administration in the United States.

The very nature of a democratic regime should permit the change of governing personnel without any necessary change in the political ground rules. It has been common practice, however, to refer to countries in which governments are rapidly overturned as "politically unstable." The classic instances are France of the Third and Fourth Republics and contemporary Italy. The pattern in these cases is of multiparty systems producing an ever-shifting set of coalition governments. Such governmental instability, however, is not necessarily associated with a serious challenge to the existing regime. The French Third Republic was a democratic regime that lasted for 70 years, despite government instability and frequent challenges to the regime by antisystem groups and parties during a period when many other Western nations succumbed to dictatorship. Similarly, the present Italian republic has lasted for more than 43 years even with rapid cabinet turnovers and governmental instability. For these reasons, the distinction between the stability of the political regime and the stability of the government is an important one. The stability and legitimacy of the political regime rather than the stability of government is the most important consideration in assessing the prospects of a democratic political system.

MEDITERRANEAN PROFILE

Socioeconomic Characteristics

The Mediterranean countries show many similarities in their socioeconomic configuration. In all of them, there continues to exist a large gap between the countries' elite and their masses. Elite members are literate and wealthy and able to pass on their status and wealth to their children. Wealth was traditionally measured in terms of landed property, but in recent decades commercial, business, industrial, and banking interests have gained ascendency.

A small percentage of people has owned the greater part of the land, with the mass of the peasantry working as agricultural laborers or tenant farmers cultivating small private holdings. As in Latin America, the need for land reform and redistribution has been one of the most potent sources of violence and revolution. Sometimes land reforms took place early enough to avert violence, as in Greece. Sometimes they were delayed for a long time, as in Italy and Spain. Portugal undertook the expropriation of large estates and the establishment of cooperatives and collectives only after its 1974 revolution.

The distance between the poor and the rich—in effect the existence of two separate societies—has been buttressed by educational opportunities. If we take into account the loose standards used to define literacy, at least 20 percent of all Portuguese are illiterate. The corresponding figures for Spain, Greece, and Italy vary between 5 and 10 percent, but many, many more have only a rudimentary knowledge of reading and writing.

Economically, the four countries we discuss here are the poorest in Western Europe, despite Italy's and Spain's record of economic industrialization and modernization

and a similar, even if not as impressive, growth in the other two. As of 1986, Italy's per capita income was $8,550 (the highest of the four), Spain's $4,860, Greece's $3,680, and $2,250 in Portugal. The average per capita income of the four is about half of what it is in the other countries of the Common Market. However, averages are misleading. The distribution of income is so slanted in the four Mediterranean countries that well over half the people in each of them may be earning below $3,000 a year. Another 30 to 35 percent hover around the national average, and a small minority earn well above it. Italy has developed comprehensive welfare measures, but elsewhere comprehensive legislation for health, old age, and retirement—which would lessen this disparity in income—has much room for improvement.

Except in Italy, where there has been a sharp drop in the number of farmers (they represent today about 10 percent of those gainfully employed), agriculture continues to be an important occupation, despite the rapid urbanization and modernization of the last two decades. Over 22 percent of the population in Portugal, 15 percent in Spain, and a little less than 30 percent in Greece still till the soil, often on small, unproductive holdings. Conditions for farmers and much of the rural population in general remain underdeveloped. Many still live in the world bequeathed them by their grandfathers and great-grandfathers, without electricity, running water, and decent housing. Only a move to the city or emigration can offer relief. As a consequence, Portugal, Spain, Greece, and southern Italy have had the greatest rate of emigration within Europe, generally to the more advanced economies of France, West Germany, and Switzerland. This emigration may well have contained social and political pressures and allowed a transition to democracy.

The rapid economic modernization that began after 1950 accounted for some dramatic changes in the composition of the working force and in the social structure. The number of farmers declined steadily while the number of manual, semiskilled, and skilled workers and employees in industry, commerce, and service occupations (notably tourism) steadily rose. There was rapid urbanization. Many cities in Mediterranean Europe face many of the same insurmountable problems of urban areas in other parts of the world. The rate of urbanization and of the exodus from the land to the industries and service occupations has been far more rapid in the Mediterranean countries than anywhere else in the world. The change has had far-reaching and destabilizing impacts on habits, expectations, and values. It has created internal tensions and social conflicts as well as great disparities in development and growth from one region to another.

In short, a socioeconomic profile of all the countries we survey shows marked similarities. First, modernization came late, with Italy leading the way after the turn of the century, and particularly after 1945. In Greece it became especially noticeable after 1950, whereas Spain and Portugal were literally forced to begin to modernize only in the mid-1950s. These three countries, therefore, have attempted to become "European" only in the last 35 years or so. Second, the phenomena associated with industrialization were common to all: rapid urbanization, considerable though uneven exodus of farmers to the towns, massive emigration abroad, growth and expansion of education services, lessening of the distance between town and country, expansion of national communications media, and improvement in the gross national product and per capita income.

Cultural Factors

The socioeconomic distance between the elite and the masses was reinforced by a system of beliefs that fostered deference to elite groups in Italy and Greece to a lesser extent than in Spain and Portugal. The political cultures of the four countries included, to use the terms of Almond and Verba's classic comparative study *The Civic Culture,* a greater number of "parochials" and "subjects" than "participants." Subjection was taught through the elementary educational system. Secular values were downplayed and other worldly considerations emphasized and often reinforced by outright repression. In all four countries, the church was and remains a socializing force inculcating deference and obedience. Only in the last two decades or so has the church in each country begun to play a truly active role in fostering social and political awareness and promoting political participation. In Italy, the hold of the Catholic Church has weakened considerably, as shown by the adoption of legislation permitting divorce and abortion. Similar steps have also been taken in Spain and Portugal since their recent transitions to democracy.

In all four countries, authoritarian regimes discouraged popular participation and encouraged distance between the privileged few and the many. Most citizens therefore failed to identify with their country's regime. The authoritarian regimes were suspected and feared. They showed no sensitivity to the demands of the people. They resorted to repressive measures. Voting, when allowed, was carefully limited to a small percentage of the people or was rigidly controlled by the administration and the army. Political parties were either abolished or reduced to only one.

In Portugal, there were no political parties during Salazar's long stay in power (1932–1968) and only limited reforms between 1968 and 1974 during the rule of Caetano, Salazar's successor. Following the Spanish Civil War of 1936–1939, Franco permitted only the Falange (later transformed into the *Movimiento*), an authoritarian, intensely nationalistic organization that cooperated with the military, the landed aristocracy, and part of the middle class. Some workers were attracted to it because of its syndicalist aspirations, but not many. The Fascist party was the only party in Italy from 1924 to 1944, although it never assumed the cohesive organization or attained the power of the Nazis in Germany. Greece has had a more varied history: political parties grew rapidly, only to be dealt a death blow every time the military took over. The parties were abolished in 1936, only to surface in 1945. They led a precarious life until 1967, when they were declared illegal again. They remained outlawed until 1974 when the military dictatorship collapsed.

In each of these Mediterranean countries, the only real link between the people and the state had been the personality of the leader—Salazar and Caetano in Portugal, Franco in Spain, Mussolini in Italy, and various leaders in Greece. When voting was introduced, notables and political bosses in various regions, provinces, and localities provided a link between the people and the central authorities by trading favors in return for support at the polls. This phenomenon—the "patron-client" relationship—developed into a network of personal ties, the patron providing services for and, in turn, commanding the loyalty of minor local officials and notables. It was only after World War II in Italy and only in the last decade in the other Mediterranean countries that mature democratic political parties developed to provide a linkage between the public and the state, thus beginning to undermine patron-client relations.

Cleavages

Sharp cleavages characterize all the Mediterranean systems. At least four general types can be noted: (1) class cleavages, (2) regional cleavages, (3) church-lay cleavages, and (4) cleavages about the regime. These divisions are only very slowly being overcome. They continue to exist, to varying degrees, in these four countries as antagonistic and often mutually exclusive forces. Only in Italy and Spain has a trend developed toward compromise. Portugal may begin to follow this trend now that it has finally found a parliamentary majority. In these countries, rational patterns of policy making are evolving, in which participation for all may become acceptable to all.

Class Cleavages. These exist at three levels: landowners versus small farmers, tenant farmers, and agricultural workers; workers versus industrialists and managers; poor versus rich. The conflict between poor and rich is naturally a diffuse one, pitting the majority of the people against the elites. It provides a general context within which class cleavages take place, but the poor have no organization or leadership and usually are passive. Few are directly involved in politics and party activity. The same is generally the case for most of the non-unionized workers. They vote, but a good number, especially in the smaller cities, do not vote for the left. It is among the unionized workers, hardly more than 25 percent of the labor force, that one finds a genuine feeling of class, an organization, and a direct connection with left-wing political parties—communist or socialist. Of course there are significant variations among the four Mediterranean countries. Italy again shows the way with a strong trade union movement representing almost half the workers. Trade unions began to play a direct role in policymaking through consultations and negotiations.

Some trade unions are attracted to compromise and peaceful means of political action, as advocated today by many of the Mediterranean communist parties. Others, however, share some severe reservations about the current democratic regime and a deep hostility toward the "capitalist class." They have not forgotten that some of these elites supported the authoritarian regimes and might be disposed to do so again if conditions were to take a turn for the worse.

In the 1970s, Eurocommunism gained ascendancy in Italy and Spain, but not in Greece or Portugal. Eurocommunism is the term used in Western and Southern Europe to describe the communist parties' new ideological position: they have abandoned revolutionary Marxism in favor of participating in their respective democratic systems, they accept reformist policies and tactics rather than openly revolutionary ones, and they seek cooperation with other political parties—even conservative ones. Eurocommunism has introduced an element of moderation and independence from the Soviet Union, even though the acceptance of democratic regime by Eurocommunist parties is still doubtful to many. The Mediterranean countries' socialist parties also present a broad reformist appeal, making them similar in many ways to the British Labour party and the German Social Democratic party.

Regional Cleavages. There are at least two types of regional cleavage: conflict between the center (the capital) and the periphery (the provinces) and conflict among specific regions having distinct ethnic or national characteristics and different levels of economic development. Ethnic cleavages are much more significant and potentially far more dangerous to regime stability. They take the form of outright separatist movements directed not only against the capital and its government and administration, but nationalist parties that advocate independence and secession from the regime and the nation-state. The most visible example here is in northern Spain where Basque separatist groups have continued the deadly violence against Spain's democratic regime that it began during the Franco period. Addressing the separatist movements' call for independence, and other regionalists' desire for autonomy in a multilingual nation-state, is the most threatening problem Spain's democratic leaders face today.

Regional cleavages do not produce such regime-threatening political consequences in Italy, Portugal, and Greece. Despite sharp disparities in political culture, economy, and standard of living between the populations of northern and southern Italy, there is no separatist movement, properly speaking, in the south or in Sicily. Nor are there any such movements in Portugal or Greece. More peaceful demands for regionalization and local authority are prevalent.

Church versus State. Politically, the old conflicts between a "religious" and "lay" culture are today mostly matters of voting, partisanship, and policy advocacy—for instance, the issues of divorce and abortion in Italy and Spain. Memories still linger, however, because the church supported authoritarian solutions in the past and continues to encourage conservative political formations. Sizable percentages of workers and especially farmers support the church, and the majority of women remain deeply attached to it. They vote for political parties that are conservative, and in Italy, Spain, and Portugal, are influenced by the Catholic hierarchy. The Greek Orthodox Church has a lesser degree of influence in that country.

Regime Cleavages. Three overall political orientations can be identified: right-wing traditionalism and authoritarianism, liberal democracy, and left-wing authoritarianism. Each reflects different visions of how society should be organized politically and different means of political action. They reflect, in other words, basic and strongly felt attitudes about the overall organization and structure of political life.

The conflict between authoritarian movements from the left and the right is the most debilitating to regime stability. In Italy and to some extent in Spain, socialists and communists agree on the overall goals of economic and social transformation and see parliamentary democracy as the means of bringing it about. In Greece and Portugal, however, the communists and the authoritarian right are prone to call for violence. The recent development of democratic regimes and the changing attitude of the communists in favor of parliamentary government have nevertheless blunted the sharpness of the conflict. Italy's maintenance of a republic since the end of World War II is a good illustration of how conflict about the regime can be lessened. Portugal, Spain, and Greece appear to have learned from this lesson as they traverse the difficult path to democracy.

2

Italian Politics

Italy, which in many respects projects a political and socioeconomic profile somewhat different from the other three Mediterranean countries we discuss, went through a long period of authoritarianism before emerging as a democracy after World War II. Whereas questions about the stability of democracy are still raised in the other three countries, Italy has accommodated itself to democratic norms quite well. Its democratic constitution is now more than 41 years old. As a parliamentary system, the current Italian regime provides for a prime minister and a cabinet, both of whom are directly responsible to the popularly elected bicameral parliament, and a relatively powerless president of the republic. As a liberal democracy, the present Italian system also seeks to guarantee the individual freedoms of its citizens.

With the spread of education and the economic growth and modernization that the country has experienced since World War II (despite some downturns and, more noticeably, the stagnation that afflicted all industrialized societies during the 1970s and into the 1980s), a body of citizens has developed that is alert, interested in, and aware of political problems. Italian citizens also tend to be inclined to participate in political affairs. Much of the credit for this goes, strangely enough, to the Communist party of Italy, which, as we shall see, developed a political style and political tactics different from any other Communist party and managed to mobilize various segments of the population from apathy to participation in a broad democratic political system. Although few Italians seem to be proud of their political system—indeed, many consider it ineffective—and although there have been periods of terrorism and violent demonstrations, Italians seem to have come to terms with democracy.

Democracy seems to be the system that today best accommodates Italy's social and political cleavages. The Communist party itself has fully accepted democracy, has operated within it, and has repeatedly promised to uphold its norms and values. Democracy provides opportunities to build the widest possible consensus and to reconcile old and new conflicts. Liberal democracy excludes the imposition of political values or policies by a minority upon others; it even goes so far as to deny a majority the right to impose its views upon a minority. Agreement is to be sought but disagreements are respected in a liberal democratic system. As a result, the sharp cleavages of Italy's past have been mitigated. This is particularly true of the conflicts between the church, on the one hand, and the state and many political parties, on the other. The church's influence is eroding. This is also the case with the sharp conflict between left (Communists) and right (Christian Democrats).

The Communist party has been fully legitimized within the system—indeed as Italy's second largest party in the parliament it has become one of the pillars of the regime. The distance between communism and Catholicism has narrowed. The conflict between the industrialized wealthy north and the agrarian and underdeveloped south has also diminished. Some of the sharp differences of the past have been bridged. Finally, Italy's position in the world seems to divide the Italian people and their leaders very little. Italy, as a member of the Common Market and NATO, follows a policy of noninvolvement. Most political parties accept this position.

While we can speak of a growing "regime stability" in Italy, we must more negatively assess the stability and effectiveness of the government. Since 1945, Italy has had 48 different cabinets headed by as many as 31 different prime ministers—even though one party, the Christian Democrats, has always been in a dominant position. Central direction and leadership have suffered, internal order seems often to amount to disorder, terrorism has spread, factionalism within the governmental services has grown, and crucial public services fail to perform their functions. "Protest movements"—*constestazione*—have spread through all social and economic institutions, allowing small groups a veto power over decisions.

Yet while many groups seem to be acting directly, and some violently, within the democratic system, there is no movement directed against the democracy—except by some very weak fascist groups and extreme left groups. Few Italians reflect upon the fascist period of Benito Mussolini (1923–1943) with pride.

THE AUTHORITARIAN LEGACY

Italy became a nation-state when various independent states, many under papal jurisdiction, were united around 1865. Proclaiming itself a republic, it went through a "liberal era" that lasted until the establishment of an authoritarian and fascist system in 1922. In truth, liberal and democratic institutions and values were not fully developed and legitimized during this early democratic period. Illiteracy and a restricted franchise limited voting to less than 15 percent of the population. The church remained opposed to the republic and counseled the faithful not to participate and vote. The political parities were weak, controlled by notables and bosses through a personal network of contacts and patron-client relationships. With the exception of the Socialists, parties remained personal and membership small. Prime ministers were chosen and cabinets formed on the basis of tenuous coalitions, and cabinet instability was high.

In addition there were three basic cleavages that often affected politics and voting. The first was that between the church and the state. The Catholic Church demanded recognition of its right to maintain controls over education, to speak authoritatively in all matters regarding the family and the upbringing of children, and to address itself to issues of civic conscience. It claimed to be a state within a state and to have a jurisdiction of its own. The state could not accept these claims without undermining its own legitimacy and control.

A second cleavage was that between the

north and the south of Italy. If, in the early years of this century, we were to have drawn a line across Italy somewhere north of Naples, we would have found that the regions south of the line were poor and culturally and educationally underdeveloped (this remains the case today). An agreement between the industrialists of the north and the southern landowners to provide support for the farmers and subsidies for the landowners did not promote the modernization of the south. Instead, there was a flow of emigration from the south to the north, or to the United States. Southern Italy's high birth rate nevertheless meant continued population growth.

Last, there was the conflict between workers and industrialists. The workers attempted to form trade unions and develop bargaining procedures to improve their dismal conditions of living and raise their wages. The industrialists tried to thwart them. Some of the workers resented organized movements, such as trade unions and parties; they preferred direct action. Some were anarchists. The conflict between militant workers and the industrialists often assumed the form of a private war, with the state unable or unwilling to intervene. In 1921, a Communist party was formed, along the lines of the Bolshevik party of the Soviet Union. It split from the Socialist party and became a member of the Third International. The Socialists and the Communist party took a revolutionary stance, urging the overthrow of the capitalist order.

Immediately following World War I, as these various cleavages became more pronounced amid widespread inflation and an economic crisis, the Socialists and the small Communist party intensified their appeal for revolution and the transformation of the existing socioeconomic order. Demonstrations, riots, occupation of factories, and strikes spread throughout Italy, to be countered by private armies that came increasingly under the control of the newly founded Fascist party. The democratic state was unable to impose order and put an end to this strife.

The Rise of Italian Fascism

Fascism capitalized on the nationalistic fervor that followed World War I. The Fascist party emerged in Italy at about the same time as did the Nazis in Germany. The Fascists, however, took power in Italy on October 28, 1922—a decade before Hitler. Italy's parliamentary institutions could not cope with the postwar problems facing the country. There were many political parties, sharply divided on ideological and policy matters. Democratic institutions were not valued by major sections of the population, and Italy's experience with democracy and representative government had been limited.

The workers joined powerful leftist movements, some led by the Socialist party, some by anarchists and syndicalists, and some by the Communist party, who after 1921 began to infiltrate several trade unions. This "red menace" threatened not only the conservative forces—the church, the industrial elites, and the monarchy—but also the middle classes, the lower-middle classes, and the peasants in regions where the church was particularly influential.

Against this background, vigilante nationalist groups led by former army officers and veterans began to spread rapidly, many in the countryside and among the peasants. They took the law into their own hands in fighting the leftists, with the complicity of national and local governmental authorities. The newly formed Fascist party began to play the leading role in combating "the reds." Late in 1922, Benito Mussolini, the leader of the Fascist party, organized his "March on Rome." His squads occupied various localities, and tens of thousands moved into Rome and its outskirts. King Victor Emmanuel III received Mussolini and asked him to take office. The fascist state was thus born.

Fascism was Italy's answer to liberal democracy: it sought to eliminate competition and individualism. The new regime hoped to create unity and cooperation, discipline and joint effort, for the realization of collective purpose under the state. "Believe, Obey, Work, Fight" was one of the fascist mottoes. "Everything within the State; nothing outside the State" was another.

Under Mussolini, the Fascist party monopolized representation, office holding, and mobilization and recruitment. It controlled opinion, the education of the young, and all the media. It outlawed all opposition and through its various agencies intimidated those who were of a different mind. All agencies of the state were in the hands of party members.

ITALY SINCE WORLD WAR II: THE REPUBLICAN SYNTHESIS

The problems facing Italy after the collapse of the fascist regime in 1943 were compounded by the fragility of the new political regime and the uncertain prospects of a genuine republican synthesis. The basic cleavages remained, but the new constitution, adopted in 1947, resolved at least one issue—that of the monarchy. King Emmanuel III had severely damaged the traditional apolitical role of the crown through his collaboration and support of Mussolini. The Italians agreed by a narrow margin in a referendum held on June 2, 1946, to abolish the monarchy and adopt a republican form of government. Almost 11 million Italians voted to preserve the monarchy with about 13 million against it.

Italy's republican constitution was modeled after those of other Western parliamentary democracies. The parliament is bicameral, consisting of a Chamber of Deputies and a Senate, with equal powers. The premier is the head of government. The president of the republic is the titular head of state, yet possesses few real powers.

Government Instability

Italy's central policymaking organ is the cabinet, which is headed by the premier and is accountable to both chambers of parliament. The premier forms the cabinet. Consistent with the procedures of other parliamentary systems such as those of Great Britain, West Germany, and Sweden, the cabinet—or "government"—must control a majority of the members of parliament or run the risk of falling from power through (or under the threat of) a vote of no confidence. The combination of proportional representation and a multiparty system has produced in Italy a situation in which, as in France under the Fourth Republic, only coalition cabinets can be formed. Italian cabinets consist of the leaders of many parties, even when one party has a dominant position. These coalition governments are inherently unstable; stalemate is a frequent occurrence. When coalitional politics fails, the device of a "minority" government may be used. A minority cabinet is one that has no majority support in the parliament. Given this precarious position, such a government is always at the mercy of an adverse parliamentary majority. As long as the cabinet is tolerated by parliament, it can govern. However, such an arrangement constitutes a powerful restraint on the government's freedom of action.

Cabinet instability has been particularly high in Italy. As seen in Table 2–1, between 1945 and 1988 there have been 48 different cabinets—with an average life span of a little less than 11 months. Italy's multiparty system is not the only reason for this. Instability at the government level has been primarily due to the inability of the parties and their leaders to form binding coalitions, as is the case in other multiparty systems. In turn—and this is perhaps the root of government instability—this is due to the failure of the Italians to learn the politics of accommodation and compromise. Consensus has been weak from the start, and the attitudes of the parties undermine it even more. Lack of consensus is often evident within the same party. On crucial questions such as divorce, regionalization, abortion, and social and economic policies, many of the parties are internally divided. In some instances, strong factions have formed within a party—notably the Christian Democrats—to challenge the leadership from a local or ideological

TABLE 2-1 Cabinet Instability in Italy, 1945–1988

Premier	Period	Coalition
Perri	June 1945–December 1945	
DeGasperi	December 1945–July 1946	
DeGasperi	July 1946–January 1947	
DeGasperi	February 1947–May 1947	
DeGasperi	May 1947–May 1948	Centrist
DeGasperi	May 1948–January 1950	Centrist
DeGasperi	January 1950–July 1951	Centrist
DeGasperi	July 1951–July 1953	Centrist
DeGasperi	July 1953–August 1953	Centrist
Piela	August 1953–January 1954	Center-right
Fanfani	January 1954–February 1954	Centrist
Seelba	February 1954–July 1955	Centrist
Segni	July 1955–May 1957	Centrist
Zoli	May 1957–July 1958	Center-right
Fanfani	July 1958–February 1959	Centrist
Segni	February 1959–March 1960	Center-right
Tambroni	March 1960–July 1960	Center-right
Fanfani	July 1960–February 1962	Center-left
Fanfani	February 1962–February 1963	Center-left
Leone	May 1963–November 1963	Center-left
Moro	December 1963–August 1964	Center-left
Moro	August 1964–February 1966	Center-left
Moro	February 1966–June 1968	Center-left
Leone	June 1968–November 1968	Center-left
Rumor	December 1968–July 1969	Center-left
Rumor	August 1969–February 1970	Center-left
Rumor	February 1970–August 1970	Center-left
Colombo	August 1970–February 1972	Center-left
Andreotti	February 1972–June 1972	Centrist
Andreotti	June 1972–June 1973	Centrist
Rumor	June 1973–March 1974	Center-left
Rumor	March 1974–December 1974	Center-left
Moro	December 1974–January 1976	Center-left
Moro	January 1976–June 1976	Center-left
Andreotti	July 1976–July 1977	Center
Andreotti	March 1977–March 1978	Christian Democrat with Communist support
Andreotti	March 1978–August 1979	Center-left
Cossigli	August 1979–April 1980	Center-right
Cossigli	April 1980–October 1980	Right
Forlani	October 1980–May 1981	Right-center
Spadolini	June 1981–August 1982	Center-left
Spadolini	August 1982–November 1982	Center-left
Fanfani	November 1982–June 1983	Center-left
Craxi	June 1983–July 1986	Left-center
Craxi	August 1986–April 1987	Left-center
Fanfani	April 1987–July 1987	Center-left
Goria	July 1987–April 1988	Center-left
DeMita	April 1988–May 1989	Center-left
Andreotti	July 1989	Center-left

Adapted and updated from J. Sani, "Mass Constraints and Political Realignments: Perception of Anti-Party Systems in Italy," *British Journal of Political Science*, January 1976.

base. There is hope that the April 1988 abolishment of the use of secret ballot in parliament will hinder rebellions within party ranks. Nevertheless, the breakdown of Italy's coalitions has frequently been the result of internal quarrels about the distribution of favors and "spoils" by the government.

THE GOVERNMENT AND THE POLITICAL PARTIES

A government in a multiparty parliamentary system, if it is to govern, needs most of all a few well-organized parties that can compromise their differences, in case none has a majority, and form stable coalitions. In contrast with France and West Germany, in Italy there has been no such simplification of the party configuration. There does seem, however, to be a trend in the direction of bipolarization—the growth of two powerful political parties.

There are at least 13 political parties in Italy today. From the extreme left to the extreme right, they range as follows:

DP: Proletarian Democrats

PDUP (also listed as PSIUP): Party of Proletarian Unity

Lotta Continua (Continuing Struggle)

Workers Vanguard

PCI: Italian Communist party

Radical party

PSI: Italian Socialist party

DC: Christian Democrats

PSDI: Italian Social Democratic party

PRI: Italian Republican party

PLI: Italian Liberal party

MSI: Italian Social Movement (neo-fascist)

SVP: Popular South Tyrolean party

We cannot deal individually with all these parties. Many are too small to merit attention. Others are going through a period of transition and are likely to merge with the stronger parties. Still others depend almost exclusively on the personality of their present leader and are likely to disappear with him. We shall concentrate on the major parties: the Italian Communist party (PCI), the Christian Democrats (DC), and briefly, the Socialists.

The Communist Party

Founded in 1921 after splitting from the Socialist party and joining the Third International, the Italian Communist party has been Italy's best organized party. Its electoral strength increased dramatically from 27.2 percent in 1972 and reached its peak at 34.4 percent in 1976. After that, the PCI's electoral support fell to 30.4 percent in 1979, to 29.9 percent in 1983, and still farther to 26.6 percent in the 1987 Chamber of Deputies election. Its 1986 membership was 1.55 million, about three times that of the French Communist party.

After World War II, the Italian Communist party took a far more open, European, and reformist stance than the French Communist party. The PCI's "Eurocommunist" direction meant favoring broad cooperation with various organizations, associations, interest groups, and social classes as a means of permeating them and modifying their behavior, and in the process gaining influence over them. The Italian communists were convinced that only a gradual change of the institutions of society could modify fixed ideological positions and make reform possible. In short, they abandoned the Leninist idea of capturing the state through armed conflict and strove rather to modify the social institutions surrounding the state and the ideas people held about them. They gave up all ideas of centralized authoritarian control and accepted parliamentary institutions and electoral politics. This enabled them to make deep inroads during the early and mid-1970s into the electoral strength of the other parties, with whom they continue to favor cooperation.

The PCI took a cautious stance on the church-state cleavage and the clerical-anticlerical confrontation. It allowed its members to be practicing Catholics. The party did not impose the strict and rigid scrutiny that non-Eurocommunist Marxist parties apply to new members, nor did it demand the strict discipline that those parties require. The PCI abandoned a strict class appeal in favor of "alliance politics." It sought to penetrate, influence, and establish good contacts with as many socioeconomic groups and voluntary organizations as possible. Alliance politics in this sense can be viewed as the building of multiple, reinforcing networks of influence and support. Finally, the Italian Communists were the first of the Western Communist parties to disagree openly with the Soviet Communist party. They professed that theirs was an open and independent party, adapted to Italian conditions and to the realities of the Italian geographic and international position.

In many respects, the Italian Communists' strategy was successful. They increased their strength and influence at the local and regional level. More than 1,200 mayors are Communists, and the party has a majority or heads a left-wing coalition in many of Italy's 15 regions. Its administration has been generally efficient, and the way in which it manages municipal and regional affairs has alleviated the fears of many anti-Communists.

The PCI's ongoing quest for legitimacy forced the late secretary-general of the party, Enrico Belinguer, to announce in 1973 the need for a compromise—the "historic compromise"—with the Christian Democrats. Even a PCI victory with 51 percent of the vote, Belinguer admitted at the time, was insufficient; the PCI could not govern Italy with such a slim majority. The PCI would have to cooperate with the Christian Democrats, establish agreement on a given number of policies, and provide Communist party support and cooperation in their implementation. The alternative would be economic and social chaos, possible civil strife, if not civil war.

Table 2-2 presents some recent results of general elections in Italy. In the 1976 election, the PCI obtained its highest proportion of votes—34.4 percent with over 16.6 million votes, which made it the largest electoral force among all the Communist parties in the West. Given Italy's electoral system of proportional representation, this strong showing translated into 211 of a total of 630 seats in the Chamber of Deputies. The PCI also won 109 of the Senate's 315 seats. Since reaching this electoral high point in 1976, the party has slipped slightly in the three most recent elections. It lost 4 percent of the electorate in the balloting of 1979. In the 1983 elections, its electoral strength dropped, but by only 0.5 percent. Nevertheless, it lost another 3.3 percent in 1987. Since the Christian Democrats experienced a similar decline in 1979 and 1983, some Italian political analysts suggested that this loss of support reflects an emerging trend away from Italy's two major parties and toward the smaller ones. This insight seemed to be substantiated in 1987 when the PCI's losses

TABLE 2-2 The Electoral Strength of Italy's Parties, 1972–1987

	1972	1976	1979	1983	1987
DC	38.8%	38.7%	38.3%	32.9%	34.3%
PCI	27.2	34.4	30.4	29.9	26.6
PSI	9.6	9.6	9.8	11.4	14.3
MSI	8.7	6.1	5.3	6.8	5.9
PRI	2.9	3.1	3.0	5.1	3.7
PSDI	5.1	3.4	3.8	4.1	3.0
PLI	3.9	1.3	1.9	2.9	2.1
PR	—	1.1	3.4	2.2	2.6
Greens	—	—	—	—	2.5
Others	3.8	2.3	4.1	4.7	3.3

translated into gains for the Socialists. If this decline of support for the major parties is correctly interpreted as an indication of increased political frustration, Italy may be facing increased political instability.

The PCI's present position differs from that of the recent past in that it is spearheading Eurocommunism: it now calls for continued electoral participation *and* respect for Italy's party system, a willingness to surrender power if it were to win an election and form the government and then be defeated at the polls, and a renunciation of the term "dictatorship of the proletariat." It now asserts that the "parliamentary road" is the only way for it to assume power. Having abandoned the "historic compromise," the PCI continues compromise politics. It will have to confront in a constructive manner, nevertheless, its prolonged electoral slump and the absence of effective leadership caused by the death of its longtime leader, Enrico Belinguer.

The Christian Democrats

The Christian Democratic party (DC) seemed to be the best means the Catholic Church could find after Mussolini's fall to ensure the participation and the support of the mass of Catholic believers. The DC is a loose regional association of factions whose total membership is estimated at 1.3 million. Factions within it range from extreme clerical conservatives to progressive and reformist Catholic and lay groups. Like the Christian Democrats in Germany, the DC receives support from many nonbelievers and nonpracticing Catholics, especially those in the middle- and upper-income groups. The "glue" that holds the party together has been anticommunism, deference to the Pope and the Church, and the grip on governmental power that it held until 1981 and regained in July 1987. It has relied heavily on the Catholic Church to secure the support of the voters—notably women, farmers, and the populations of the regions in the northeast where the church's influence has historically been strong. The DC also receives support from workers through the Italian Association of Christian Workers. Upper-income groups see the DC as the best protector of their privileges, interests, and status. The DC has nevertheless developed an appeal to all groups and classes, a catch-all approach that also helps to ensure the coexistence of several factions within the party.

The Christian Democrats' balancing act between its left and right factions has not been an easy one. The DC contains factions that include left-of-center members who are motivated by a Christian social orientation and right-of-center followers who are more concerned with matters of liberal economics. As a party looking to the left, the DC has sought to form alliances and coalition cabinets in cooperation with the Social Democrats and the Socialists, even if not with the Communists. As a centrist party, it has often tilted toward the conservative groups, forming coalitions with them and seeking their support. An "opening to the left" (i.e., cooperation with left-wing forces) was opposed by the Vatican, while a rightist orientation eroded the party's strength among many of its progressive members. When cooperation with the Socialists finally seemed acceptable, the welfare and reform implications of such collaboration frightened the more conservative forces, including, of course, big business. The party was thus torn between left and right. Its ambivalence caused a loss of support and, even more important, made the Communists by default the spearhead of social and economic reform policies.

The Christian Democratic party has been Italy's dominant party since 1945. Until June 1981, it formed all the governments in Italy. (When the Republican leader Spadolini formed a non-DC–led government, he claimed that it was the first "lay" cabinet in Italy's modern political history!) The Christian Democratic dominance weakened after the 1976 election when, as seen in Table 2–2, its electoral strength peaked. In the 1976 legislative elections and again in 1979, the Christian Democrats received about 38 percent of the vote. In the 1983 elections, however, the Christian Democratic party fell to an all-time low of 32.9 percent of the vote. Yet, in 1987 the DC gained support while the Communists continued their decline. This increased strength helped the Christian Democrats to regain the premiership in 1987.

The Christian Democrats' loss of support in the late 1970s and early 1980s could be attributed, in part, to internal factionalism, personal rivalries, and corruption. The resulting cabinet instability raised questions about the regime itself. The DC, reluctant for so long to establish communications and dialogue with the left, was forced to consider some types of cooperation in line with the logic of the "historic compromise" suggested by the Communist party's leadership. Given the shrinking strength of the Christian Democratic party, to form stable coalition governments, the office of premier was passed on to leadership of several of Italy's smaller parties. Italy's Republican party first held the premier's office under Spadolini. More recently, the country was governed by the Socialist Bettino Craxi. The Christian Democrats, however, have now returned to the center stage of the Italian political scene, once again controlling the office of the premier.

The Socialists

Socialists in Italy are split into distinct parties: the Italian Socialist party (PSI) and the Italian Social Democratic party (PSDI). Founded in 1892, the PSI is Italy's oldest political party. It presently has approximately 350,000 members. In the 1979 legislative elections, it gained almost 10.0 percent of the share of the vote and about 60 seats in the Chamber of Deputies. In the 1983 elections, the Socialists' percentage of the vote rose to 11.4 percent with about 73 seats in the Chamber of Deputies. This constant rise in electoral strength permitted the Socialists under the leadership of Craxi to form a government in June 1983. This Craxi government set the record for the longest-lasting government in Italy since World War II in 1985 despite a near-collapse over the hijack-

ing of the *Achille Lauro*. This government held together until July 1986. The party continued its electoral rise in 1987, gaining 14.3 percent of the vote. Despite this rise, Craxi had to hand over the office of the premier to the Christian Democrats who also increased their support. The Socialists have thus emerged as one of Italy's pivotal small parties, and their role is likely to remain very important both in the Chamber of Deputies and in future cabinets. Many analysts suggest they may eventually replace the PCI as the major party of the political left in Italy. This seems unlikely, but they are increasingly a political force in Italy.

Other Parties

As indicated before, there are at least seven more political parties, all of which have very small memberships and electoral strength. They cannot survive except in coalition with the two larger parties, and most of them are likely to give their support to the DC. The only genuinely authoritarian party, indeed the only neo-fascist party, is the Italian Social Movement (MSI). It has a membership of not more than 40,000. It received 6.6 percent in 1976, 5.3 percent in 1979, 6.8 percent in 1983, and 5.9 percent in 1987. (See Table 2–3.) The MSI consists of activists

TABLE 2–3 Parliamentary Composition After June 1987 Election

	Chamber	*Senate*
DC (Christian Democrat)	234	125
PCI (Italian Communist Party)	177	100
PSI (Socialist Party)	94	36
MSI (neo-fascist)	35	17
PSDI (Social Democrat)	17	5
(PR) Radicals	13	3
PRI (Republican)	21	8
PLI (Liberal)	11	3
Prol. Democrats (DP)	8	1
Greens	13	1
Others	13	16
Total	630	315

ready for violent political confrontation rather than electioneering.

A Multiparty System

A multiparty system remains one of the characteristics of Italian politics and a basis for cabinet instability. If the two major parties cooperated as they did tacitly between 1976 and 1979, when the Communists pledged to support (at least not to turn out) a center-left cabinet led by the Christian Democrats, stability might result. But since 1980, when the Communists withdrew their support for such an accord, the Christian Democrats have had to seek allies among the socialists, centrists, and even the MSI on the far right. The DC's giving up of the premiership between 1981 and 1987 made this a central aspect of this process of coalition building. Even in 1987, Craxi and the Socialists were able to veto which DC leader became prime minister. The difficulty of creating stable coalitions from such disparate political forces remains problematic.

One of the reasons for Italy's multiparty system is the electoral system of proportional representation. In such a system, the strength of the parties in the parliament is proportionate to the number of votes they receive in the country. For instance, if a party receives 10 percent of the national vote, it is given about 10 percent of the seats in the legislature. Small parties can therefore survive. Local parties are always assured of a small percentage of votes and a small representation in the Chamber of Deputies. And ideological parties are assured of a few seats as long as they hold on to a small number of their faithful. In contrast with the British and U.S. single-member district plurality systems, the Italian electoral system perpetuates a multiparty system.

Yet, as noted, a proportional representation system performs a vital political function in societies that are highly divided. Proportional representation incorporates a great deal of diversity into the political process by permitting many groups, ideas, programs, and interests to gain representation.

Negotiation to reach decisions becomes the norm. Significant groups or interests cannot be ignored or politically stepped upon. A process of give-and-take, no matter how laborious and ineffective, promotes protection for all. Proportional representation thus attenuates conflicts at the expense of efficiency and governmental stability. It is a calculated risk that many political systems have to take to avoid conflict.

PROSPECTS

Until World War II, there was minimal legitimacy, stability, or popular participation in Italian politics. What of the present postwar republican period? Has there been a change in terms of regime acceptance and conflict resolution? On the surface, we still observe a great deal of negative sentiment toward the regime and its decision-making processes. There are, however, some positive indications. The social, economic, and political cleavages discussed earlier have by no means disappeared, but they seem to have less of a polarizing effect than in the past. Indeed, they even seem amenable to reconciliation. The controversy over issues such as divorce and abortion continues. Southern Italy is still woefully underdeveloped and continues to lose inhabitants to the prosperous north. The continued strength of the Communist party has maintained the old socialist-capitalist dichotomy. But none of these conflicts fundamentally affects the regime itself. Even the socialist-capitalist split has to a great degree been lessened in intensity with communist acceptance of the capitalist economy.

Serious difficulties persist, but they revolve around policy issues, not regime survival. These problems include (1) the continuing economic crisis and the government's inability to cope with it; (2) the loss of support for the Christian Democrats due to factionalism and corruption; (3) the changing nature of the balance of power within the coalition-building process given the new found strength of the Socialist party; and (4) the country's immobile, inefficient, and often corrupt bureaucracy, the result of the Christian Democrats' hold on political power for over 30 consecutive years. The central problems of Italian politics at present concern representation and governmental efficiency rather than legitimacy. We thus have a crisis of policymaking and government rather than a crisis of legitimacy and the regime.

In fact, regime acceptance and popular participation seem to have increased. Voter turnout is high, the parties have large memberships, and the political dialogue continues unimpeded. In Italy, democracy appears to be preferred to the extremist and authoritarian alternatives of the past.

Major Events in Italy Since 1945

April 28, 1945	Mussolini killed and publicly hanged in northern Italy.
April 29, 1945	World War II ends in Italy.
June 2, 1946	National referendum abolishes monarchy and establishes a democratic republic.
May 1947	Communists and Socialists removed from cabinet.
September 15, 1947	World War II peace treaty takes effect.
January 1, 1948	New republican constitution goes into effect.
April 18, 1948	Christian Democrats gain absolute majority of parliamentary seats in first national elections.
1949	Italy becomes founding member of NATO.
1952	Marshall Plan ends after providing Italy with more than $1.5 billion in economic aid. Italy joins the European Coal and Steel Community.
1955	Italy joins the United Nations.
March 25, 1957	Italy becomes charter member of the European Economic Community when it signs the Treaties of Rome.
1956–1959	Socialists and Communists in strong ideological disagreements. Communists begin their "Italian Way to Socialism."
1959–1963	The "opening to the left" by the Christian Democrats.
December 1963	First center-left coalition government.
October 1966	Socialists and Christian Democrats unite temporarily only to split again in July 1969.
1968	Italian Communist party becomes the first Communist party to condemn the Soviet invasion of Czechoslovakia, advocating ideological positions and an independent foreign policy stance later to become known as Eurocommunism.
October–December 1969	The Italian labor movement's "Hot Autumn": strikes and confrontations.
December 1969	Emergence of terrorist violence.
June 1970	Regional elections mark the beginning of regional autonomy and administration in Italy.
1972	Divorce legalized. Enrico Berlinguer becomes PCI's party secretary.
September 1973	Berlinguer proposes the "historic compromise."
October 1973	Oil embargo begins serious economic problems for Italy and other western nations.
May 1974	National referendum upholds divorce law.
January 1975	Socialists leave center-left coalition.
June 1975	Communists make large gains in regional and local elections.
June 1976	Communist party makes gains in national election.
August 1976	For first time, PCI does not vote against a Christian Democratic government. Andreotti forms government and PCI receives several important posts in parliament.
March 1978	Communists and Socialists become part of majority supporting the government led by Christian Democrats.
March 1978	Former prime minister Aldo Moro kidnapped and murdered (in May) by leftist terrorists. Socialist Sandro Pertini elected Italy's president after 16 parliamentary votes in 12 days.
January 1979	PCI withdraws support to Christian Democratic government.
June 1979	National election produces PCI's first decline in votes.

Major Events in Italy Since 1945

March 1980	Socialists join government, producing new center-left coalition.
May 1980	Law passed permitting abortion under certain circumstances.
October 1980	New four-party center-left coalition government.
May 1981	National referendum upholds abortion law.
June 21, 1981	Giovanni Spadolini, a Republican, becomes the first non-Christian Democrat prime minister in Italy since World War II.
December 1981	U.S. Brigadier General James Dozier kidnapped by the Red Brigades—an extreme left group.
January 1982	Italian antiterrorist unit frees General Dozier. Information obtained in raid leads to massive roundup of suspected terrorists.
June 1983	Socialists make large gains in national elections; Christian Democrats and PCI decline. The Socialist's Bettino Craxi becomes prime minister.
June 22, 1984	European Parliament elections, in which the Communist party comes first, for the first time in Italian history.
June 24, 1985	Christian Democrat Francesco Cossiga elected Italy's president by the parliament with PCI's assistance.
October 1985	Italian cruise ship *Achille Lauro* hijacked. Affair produces government crisis.
November 1985	President Cossiga refuses to accept Craxi's resignation. Same five-party government continues, becoming Italy's longest-lasting postwar government.
February 10, 1986	Largest trial of Mafia suspects opens in Palermo (474 defendants).
May 18, 1986	PLI selects Renato Altissimo as new party secretary.
June 26, 1986	Finance bill defeated; Craxi resigns after heading government for a record 1,050 days.
July 10, 1986	Giulio Androetti (DC) is asked to form new government.
August 1, 1986	Craxi forms new government after Androetti fails in his attempt.
March 3, 1987	Craxi resigns.
April 18, 1987	Fanfani (DC) sworn in as head of Italy's forty-sixth government since World War II. Minority government.
April 28, 1987	Fanfani government falls; Cossiga dissolves the parliament and elections are called, with Fanfani continuing as caretaker.
June 15, 1987	Christian Democrats and Socialists gain, and PCI slips in general election.
July 29, 1987	Goria (DC) becomes head of new government (same five parties in coalition).
November 8, 1987	Voters support referendum proposals on nuclear power, parliamentary oversight, and judicial accountability.
November 18, 1987	Goria avoids crisis as Liberals, who bolted from the government, rejoined the coalition (dispute over budget).
December 14, 1987	Gianfranco Fini becomes leader of the neo-fascist MSI.
December 16, 1987	Mafia trial ends in Sicily with 338 convicted.
January 6, 1988	Sergio Stanzani becomes new leader of PR.
February 10, 1988	Goria resigns after losing several key votes on budget (president asks him to stay in power until a budget is passed).
February 29, 1988	Antonia Cariglia becomes new PSDI leader.
March 11, 1988	Goria resigns over issue of constructing nuclear power plants.
April 13, 1988	De Mita (DC) becomes premier of forty-eighth government (same five parties); planned reforms include increased taxes (to reduce deficit), increased government efficiency (including reform of use of secret ballot in parliament), and a speeded-up implementation of EC directives.
May 30, 1988	PSI and DC gain ground in local elections (at Communist party expense).
June 13, 1988	Natta formally resigns as head of PCI after suffering heart attack.
June 21, 1988	PCE installs Achille Occhetto as leader.
June 30, 1988	Italy agrees to take 72 U.S. F-16 fighter planes from Spain (to be placed in base in Southern Italy).
February 22, 1989	Arnaldo Forlain elected new general secretary of the Christian Democrats in their 18th National Congress.
March 18, 1989	At 28th Congress, the Communist Party takes a more moderate stance under the leadership of Achille Occhetto. Party does better than expected in June European elections.
May 1989	Labor unrest and other problems force new governmental crisis. Ciriaco De Mita resigns as prime minister.
July 1989	New government formed by the same five parties with Guilio Andreotti returning as prime minister.

Iberian Politics: Portugal and Spain

On April 25, 1974, a leftist military revolt in Portugal brought down the authoritarian regime that had ruled since 1932. On November 20, 1975, General Francisco Franco died in Spain. Franco had imposed an authoritarian regime following the victory of his Nationalists in the Spanish Civil War of 1936–1939 and ruled Spain thereafter. His death ushered in a feverish period of political activity that led to the establishment of constitutional government and parliamentary democracy.

Today, both Portugal and Spain are constitutional democracies. Constitutions were drafted and ratified by the people in both countries. Freedom of the press and civil rights have been introduced. Political parties, including viable Communist parties, have been allowed to compete for votes and offices, and elections with a high rate of voter participation have taken place regularly. These two countries appear to have successfully made the difficult transition from authoritarianism to democracy. Many reforms and many political difficulties, however, are still being faced. Long-term regime stability in both cases and appears likely, but not a certainty.

THE CASE OF PORTUGAL

When Portugal became a constitutional monarchy in 1882, the country was in the midst of a century-long period of power struggles, political infighting, and instability. Competition for power was intense. On the one hand were conservatives, different monarchical groups, and the nobility, all of whom supported the Catholic Church; on the other hand were liberals who sought to limit their power. Regime instability led to the assassination of King Carlos I and the crown prince in 1908, produced the fall of the monarchy as an institution, and resulted in the establishment of a parliamentary republic in 1910. For the next 16 years, the Portuguese parliamentary system was plagued by political factionalism, economic strife, many forms of public violence, and government instability. There were three governments a year, on average.

In the name of political peace, the military stepped in during 1926. When the military leaders appointed Dr. Antonio de Oliveira Salazar as finance minister in 1928, it paved the way for his becoming Portugal's dictator in 1932. Salazar established a fascist-like state, which he called *Estado Novo,* the New State. His constitution provided for some "appropriate" institutions such as a unicameral National Assembly and a directly elected president, but these did not diminish the dictatorial nature of the political system, a regime that lasted until the Revolution of 1974.

Beginning in the 1960s, external pressures stemming from revolts in Portugal's African colonies—among them Angola and Mozambique—began to affect the authoritarian regime. Portugal's leaders found it necessary to step up military expenditures and recruit a number of junior officers and noncommissioned officers from the lower-middle classes. These recruitment patterns produced the social basis for a leftist political orientation among many younger men in the Portuguese army. These younger soldiers' political ideology became manifest as the colonial wars threatened the army with the loss of status, for it faced certain defeat. There was resentment among many officers and a desire to change the political system that had brought about their predicament. There were also popular manifestations: strikes for higher wages and protests against inflationary pressures became pronounced after 1972. In addition, the Catholic Church began to disassociate itself from the regime.

The fall of authoritarianism was imminent. Salazar had a stroke in 1968. Marcello Caetano replaced him. Caetano retained the support of the traditional forces, including the church, but he did not have the personal stature of his predecessor. Caetano contin-

ued the African wars. The army, aware of its inability to win or even to maintain the African colonies in some kind of confederation with "internal" autonomy, began to balk. On April 25, 1974, leftist army officers overthrew Portugal's long-standing authoritarian. They immediately announced a program of sweeping reforms, including representative institutions and socialist-orientated economic and social changes. Political parties and trade unions were legalized. There were to be elections for a constituent assembly that would draft a new constitution. The Armed Forces movement, representing all ranks in the army, promised freedom under a military surveillance that was to be only temporary. The army, however, needed popular support. This it found in the Communist party, which, with its usual skill and organization, began to attract members and to staff the various organs of the state. The Communist party's membership grew from not more than 10,000 to over 60,000. It gradually assumed control of the press and the radio; it gained directive positions in many of the newly nationalized banks and insurance companies. The Armed Forces movement became increasingly radicalized. In 1975, while paying lip service to democracy, its leadership claimed to be the "vanguard" of the people in cooperation with the Communist party. The Socialists and the other parties were unable to compete with the organization and determination of the Communists. However, the Communists and the Armed Forces movement miscalculated in calling elections for April 1975. In this first election for a constituent assembly, the Communists received only 12.5 percent of the vote, thus fully exposing their lack of popular support. In this election, the Socialists received 37.9 percent and the People's Democratic party (a center-right coalition) 26.4 percent.

By mid-1975, internal conflicts and disagreements had arrested the radicalization within the Armed Forces movement. Many senior officers became concerned about the infiltration of the Communists, about the inevitable withdrawal of Portugal from NATO if the country's leftward political direction continued, and about their own future status. Pressures from abroad, especially from the Socialist parties of Western Europe, the inability of the Communist-inspired leadership to obtain economic loans and credits, and the reaction of many of the conservative forces, supported by popular demonstrations, encouraged these conservatives and the Socialists to resist. On November 25, 1975, when the Communists openly attempted to take power through a coup, a new alignment of senior army officers and some military units, the Socialists, the conservative forces, and the church was able to stop them.

The long-term consequence of Portugal's flirtation with far leftist control was twofold. First, and most important, since 1976 Portugal has consolidated its transition to democracy in a rather nonradical, moderate manner. The uncertainty of the first two years of the transition gave a standard by which to view the future quest for regime stability. Second, several of the institutional arrangements, particularly economic ones, still bear the mark of the leftist-oriented times. Many of Portugal's more moderate governments have found their hands tied by nationalizations and political procedures that were institutionalized during the early years.

In 1976, a new democratic constitution came into force, and new elections were held, this time for an Assembly of the Republic. The Socialists gained 35 percent of the vote, compared with 14 percent for the Communists, 24 percent for the Popular Democrats, and 16 percent for the Social Democratic Center party (CDS). A new president was elected—General Ramalho Eanes, a high-ranking centrist officer who had been instrumental in putting down the 1975 coup attempt. Within about two years, the transition from authoritarian regime to democracy was thus made. The big monopolies—the banks, the insurance companies, and some industries—were taken over by the state. Freedom of the press and of association were consolidated. The military was pushed to the background, and the Communist party appeared unable to make a new bid for power.

Institutionally, Portugal's 1976 constitution created a "mixed" form of democracy in that it contains elements of both a presidential and a parliamentary system. The Portuguese political system operates much like Italy's parliamentary system with a prime minister who is elected by the parliament itself. The prime minister forms a government—a cabinet—that is accountable to the parliament and may be turned out of power through a vote of no confidence. Unlike Italy, however, Portugal also has a directly elected president who holds considerable power. The president has the power to dissolve the parliament, call new elections, and take a direct role in forming governments in the event that a parliamentary majority cannot be readily found. President Eanes exercised this last power several times during the late 1970s. Portugal's "mixed" presidential-parliamentary system is thus more similar in many respects to the French Fifth Republic with its strong presidential position than to the Italian and Spanish parliamentary systems. As in France, the exact nature of the president–prime minister–government relationship has developed over time and has often been influenced strongly by the personalities involved. This institutional development will, in the near future, probably continue to produce some highly visible conflicts within Portugal's new democratic regime.

THE POLITICAL FORCES IN PORTUGAL

The character of Portugal's political forces, especially the political parties, is linked critically to ongoing economic modernization. The question is whether modernization will be associated with democratic forms and institutions or will lead to renewed political strife and instability. What follows is a survey of the developing party configuration in Portugal since the revolution. There are four major Portuguese political formations: the Portuguese Communist party (PCP), the Portuguese Socialist party (PS), the Social Democratic party (PSD), and the Social Democratic Center party. The Democratic Renewal party (PRD) competed for the first time in 1985. There are also, of course, splinter groups on the left and the right, most of them electorally insignificant.

The Left

The Portuguese left consists of the Communists and the Socialists. Their respective parties initially engaged in a fierce competition over which would dominate. The Communist party held a political advantage during the turbulent years of 1974–1976. During the more recent years of stable electoral competition, the Socialist party has been at the forefront on the political left. The PCP, nevertheless, remains strong.

The PCP. The Portuguese Communist party, unlike its Italian, Spanish, and French counterparts, has not taken the Eurocommunist direction. Instead, it remains more revolutionary in its rhetoric and goals. Founded in 1921, the PCP was declared illegal following the military coup of May 29, 1926, which overthrew the republic and eventually led to the dictatorship of Antonio de Oliveira Salazar and Marcello Caetano. It was legalized in 1974. Its membership is estimated at no more than 75,000.

Since 1961, the PCP's secretary-general has been Alvaro Cunhal, who spent some 14 years in Salazar's prisons and another 14 years in exile. Five days after the April 25, 1975, coup, Cunhal proposed a 5-point program for the revolution: (1) to consolidate and make irreversible the gains achieved by the Armed Forces movement; (2) to secure democratic freedoms, including freedom for political parties; (3) to put an end to the wars in Africa; (4) to "fulfill" the workers' most urgent needs; and (5) to guarantee free elections to a constitutional assembly.

In April 1976, the PCP announced its economic platform for the parliamentary elections. It called for the consolidation of the revolution's gains (notably nationalization and the right of labor to organize), the expansion of the public sector of the economy, speedy and comprehensive agrarian reforms, and sweeping wage increases and social benefits for the workers. Regarding the important indication of support for Portugal's transition to democracy, however, the Communist leader struck an ominous note in an interview by stating, "We Communists do not accept the game of elections ... I promise you there will be no parliament in Portugal. For me democracy means getting rid of capitalism. Portugal will not be a country with democratic freedoms and monopolies, it will not be a fellow traveler of your bourgeois democracies, because we will not allow it ... we will certainly not have a social democratic Portugal." Since then, however, the PCP, without abandoning its pro-Soviet position, has accommodated itself to electoral politics. The PCP's association with the Armed Forces movement and its role during the turbulent years of 1974–1976, however, leave it suspect in the eyes of many more moderate Portuguese political leaders and voters.

The PSP. The Socialist party of Portugal was founded in Geneva in 1963 and became a member of the Second International in April 1973. In general, the PSP follows the line of the other European Socialist parities; it has particularly close links with the German Social Democrats. It is a reformist party that favors pluralistic democracy, selective state control and nationalization of the economy, and comprehensive agrarian reform. It does not, however, agree with the Communist advocacy of outright seizure of landed estates.

An earlier party leader, Mario Soares, was the first prime minister of the new republic. More recently, the PSP again took a leading role in governing Portugal. Soares returned to the office of prime minister in 1983 and held that position at the head of a coalitional government until the October 1985 elections. Soares is now president of the republic. The nonrevolutionary and moderate stance of the party is best exemplified by the fact that during its period of governmental control in 1983–1985, the Soares government—like the González-led Spanish Socialists and Mitterrand in France—took very stern and difficult economic measures which cost it heavily politically. Soares's attempts to manage a bad economic situation did not permit the Portuguese Socialists the opportunity to promote more socialist-oriented policy reforms in other areas. The 1985 and 1987 elections proved extremely costly to the party and its position in the government. Only the hard campaigning and personal figure of Soares saved it in the 1986 presidential election. The party is now seeking to regain its past strength under the leadership of Vitor Constancio.

The Democratic Alliance

Portugal's Social Democratic party and the Social Democratic Center party operated as an electoral alliance during the 1979 and 1980 elections. They have since returned to their prealliance political identity, although the CDS is now calling itself a Christian Democratic party. Both parties claim to offer the people the only genuine alternative to the left. Both call for a free market economy, denationalization of industry and banks, and the suspension of agrarian reform.

The Social Democratic party, founded in 1974, is a left-of-center party that has moved toward the right since the revolution along with the entire Portuguese party system. The party is comprised primarily of professional people, the self-employed, businesspersons, and intellectuals. The party leadership has tended, however, to be more to the left than its supporters. Under the pragmatic direction of Cavaco Silva, however, the party has grown and prospered. In July 1987, he led the party to the first majority victory by any party in Portugal since the 1974 Revolution.

The Social Democratic Center party is concentrated in the conservative north of Portugal. It has represented the traditional farmers' associations in their fights against state takeovers of land. The CDS's conservative philosophy is also reflected in its vote against Portugal's socialist constitution; its stressing of personal initiative and protection for small traders, entrepreneurs, and farmers; and its international links with Germany's Christian Democratic party and Britain's Conservative party.

Although clearly favoring capitalism, the PSD and the CDS have among their leaders a number of competent administrators and technocrats who would not shrink, if necessary, from social reforms and state controls, following the example of the Gaullists in France. Both the Social Democratic party and the Social Democratic Center party, it should be emphasized, are firmly opposed to Marxism.

Earlier Elections

The turbulent period of Portugal's transition to democracy ended in 1976 when two important elections were held in the country, those for parliament in April and for the presidency in June. These elections marked the beginning of a more moderate transition. The Socialists showed remarkable strength, the Communists declined, and, at the same time, the entire party system showed an unmistakable trend to the right, a trend that has continued to the present. The Socialists received almost 35 percent of the vote and gained 107 seats in the National Assembly; the Communists managed only 14.5 percent and 40 seats. The centrist Social Democratic party received over 24 percent of the vote and 73 representatives; the rightist Social Democratic Center party received over 24 percent of the vote and 73 representatives; the rightist Social Democratic Center party received almost 16 percent and 42 representatives. In the presidential election, the Communist-backed candidate received only 7.5 percent of the vote. The successful candidate, General Ramalho Eanes, who was supported by the Socialists, the Social Democrats, and the Social Democratic Center, received 61.5 percent of the popular vote. Thus, the pendulum after the revolution seemed to be swinging to the center and even to the right. The prospects for a Socialist minority government without either Communist support or centrist and rightist support seemed uncertain.

This moderate trend in Portuguese general elections has continued. (See Table 3–1.) In subsequent elections, the five largest parties (including Eanes's Democratic Renewal party in 1985 and 1987) have received about 94 percent of the votes and virtually all the seats in the legislature.

The Democratic Alliance between the Social Democratic party and the Social Democratic Center party in the 1979 and 1980 elections produced right-of-center governments. While the Portuguese system clearly remained divided between right and left, these elections permitted the country the time and the opportunity to continue backing away from the leftist direction it had taken between 1974 and 1976. The 1983 election produced a new moderate alignment with a center-left government led by the Socialists in coalition with the Social Democrats. Between 1983 and 1985, Socialist Prime Minister Soares, like his Socialist counterparts in Italy (Craxi), Spain (González), France (Mitterrand), and Greece (Pa-

pandreou) has had to govern a country facing severe economic problems. Austerity policies ultimately helped produce a potentially unstable governmental coalition following the 1985 election. This election saw the Social Democratic party return to control the prime minister's position, but, the success of President Eanes's new Democratic Renewal party—which received 18 percent of the votes—introduces a question mark in the balance of the Portuguese party system. However, the partisan political battles no longer appear to be between left and right but, rather, within the political center. This bodes well for Portugal's long-term regime stability.

The 1986 Presidential and 1987 Parliamentary Elections

In early 1986, Portugal held its scheduled presidential elections as President Eanes completed his five-year term. This election was anxiously awaited given the rather inconclusive nature of the October 1985 parliamentary elections. The first round of the presidential election was held on January 26. Diogo Freitas do Amaral, the Center Democratic candidate, won 46 percent of the vote, and Mario Soares, the Socialist candidate and former Portuguese prime minister, won

TABLE 3–1 Portugal's Legislative Elections, 1976–1987 (seats in parentheses)

	1976	1979	1980	1983	1985	1987
Communist Party (PCP)	14.6%	18.8%	16.8%	18.2%	15.5%	12.1%
United People's Alliance (APU)	(40)	(47)	(41)	(44)	(37)	(31)
Socialist Party (PS)	35.0	27.3	27.8	36.3	20.8	22.2
Republican & Socialist Front (FRS)	(107)	(74)	(74)	(101)	(55)	(60)
Democratic Renewal Party (PSD)	—	—	—	—	18.0	4.9
					(43)	(7)
Social Democratic Party (PSD)	24.4			27.0	29.9	50.2
	(73)			(76)	(85)	(148)
Democratic Alliance (AD)		45.3	46.7			
		(128)	(134)			
Social Democratic Center Party (CDS)	16.0			12.4	9.8	4.4
	(42)			(29)	(20)	(4)
Total	100.0%	100.0%	100.0%	100.0%	100.0%	100.0%
	(262)	(250)	(250)	(250)	(250)	(250)

24 percent. These results were sufficient to advance these two men to the election's second round. Soares's strong showing came as a surprise given the defeat suffered by the Socialists in the parliamentary elections when they mustered only 20 percent of the vote. Furthermore, Salgado Zenha, another left-of-center candidate who won 21 percent of the vote, had the backing of the current prime minister, Anibal Cavaco Silva, whose minority Social Democratic government is supported in parliament by President Eanes's new Democratic Renewal party.

The election's second round saw Mario Soares narrowly defeat Freitas do Amaral by a 51.3 percent to 48.7 percent margin, a difference of 151,000 votes. This election demonstrated Soares's ability to rebound from the Socialists' earlier defeat. But it also showed in the conservative Freitas do Amaral's narrow defeat that Portugal's democratic right now has a strong base of support. Portugal's leftist revolution of a decade earlier has been moderated to the point that the right is now considered a viable alternative by at least half the population.

In Portugal's parliament, the years of coalitional uncertainty since the revolution had continued following the general elections of 1985. The coalition government led by the Social Democratic leader Anibal Cavaco Silva experienced difficulties in pushing its program through parliament. It was continually challenged from without and even from within by the other political parties in the coalitional government. As another of Portugal's shaky coalitional governments, it had to face several votes of confidence. When it lost in such a parliamentary vote in April 1987, President Soares called for new elections.

The general elections of July 1987 produced a result Portuguese democracy had not enjoyed since the 1974 revolution—a parliamentary majority. Cavaco Silva adroitly campaigned on the issue of parliamentary instability and asked the people to give his Social Democratic party the majority it needed to run the country effectively. This plea and his personality hit a responsive

chord in the electorate. The consolidation of democracy thus took a new turn in Portugal, something that has not occurred in Italy. The PSD received 50.2 percent of the vote and 148 of the 250 seats in parliament. The party received support rather evenly across the entire nation. It severely hurt the Democratic Renewal party which had done so well in the election. But it also drew from voters who had previously cast ballots for other established parties. This mandate gave a Portugese government, for the first time, an opportunity to carry out its programs.

Given the results of these elections, the Portuguese political system is in some ways in a position similar to France following the French parliamentary elections of March 1986 that we discussed in Part III. In both mixed presidential-parliamentary systems (or semipresidential systems) the Socialist president—Soares in Portugal and Mitterrand in France—must work or "cohabit" with a parliament where an opposition has a majority. Portugal is different from France, however, in that Portugal's five-party parliament has become accustomed—with the exception of the Communists—to the compromise inherent in coalition politics. Also, President Soares does not have the same constitutional prerogatives that the French President enjoys. This, together with the narrowness of Soares's victory and the uniqueness of a majority government, suggests that Portugal's president may not play a politically important role.

PROSPECTS

The unfinished nature of the Portuguese revolution of 1974 left uncertain the long-term success of the establishment of democracy itself. Only recently have the political parties been able to overcome the need to form a coalitional government. Personal politics still dominate, and the parties have still not proven they can form viable long-term coalitions. Most significantly, the revolution initially divided the people and their leaders into several hostile camps: those who accepted the leftist direction and wanted to work within democracy and the new social and economic structural reforms, including nationalizations; those who preferred a more centrist democratic direction; and those who opposed democracy altogether. The first group had the upper hand between 1974 and 1976. The more moderate forces have dominated since. The former president of the republic—General Eanes, reelected in November 1980—was centrist, but appreciated some of the accomplishments of the revolution and the continuing role of the army. Some analysts thought that his entry into more active political affairs through the Democratic Renewal party, following his stepping down from the presidency in early 1986, would prove to be an important development for the Portuguese political system. The election of 1987 suggested it did not. Now it appears the new majoritarian government of Cavaco Silva has given Portugal a chance to experience governmental stability. If this stability is short-lived, the forces against the revolution may gain strength, and the possibility of a bipolarization that will bring the left and the right back into open conflict cannot be excluded.

Until the election of October 1980, when the Democratic Alliance secured a tentative working majority, governmental instability had been the rule in Portugal. Between 1974 and 1981, there were 11 cabinets and 4 legislative elections. The Communist party had maintained its strength. The Socialists, while they made many gains, continued to experience many political ups and downs. The nationalization of Portugal's banks and some industries continued to be contested as the political system became more moderate. The establishment of rural cooperatives was delayed, and many of the dispossessed owners reclaimed their lands. The armed forces were removed from the center of the political arena but continue to maintain their presence in politics. The army was also becoming an increasingly conservative force, putting hierarchy and order above reform and change. Now, given its parliamentary majority which has produced a workable government, Portugal appears to be resolving favorably many conflicts arising out of its institutional arrangements, even if not as rapidly as is Spain. Such a process, nevertheless, is characteristic of most successful transitions to democracy.

Major Events in Portugal Since the End of Dictatorship, 1974–1989

April 25, 1974	Military uprising. Fall of authoritarian dictatorship of Caetano.
May 15, 1974	General Spinola becomes president of the republic; center-right government formed under Da Palma Carlos.
July 9, 1974	Resignation of Da Palma Carlos.
July 17, 1974	Colonel (later General) Vasco Concalves becomes head of the government.
September 30, 1974	General Spinola resigns as president of republic and is replaced by General Costa Gomes.
March 11, 1975	Coup attempted by Spinola fails.
April 25, 1975	Elections for a constituent assembly.
July 10, 1975	Resignation of all Socialist ministers from cabinet; conflict between Socialists and Communists.
August 7, 1975	Moderates in the Armed Forces movement manifest against left-wing orientation of the government supported by Communists and the radical elements of the army.
November 25, 1974	The extreme left in the military, with Communist support, organizes an abortive coup.
April 25, 1976	Legislative elections.
June 27, 1976	General Ramalho Eanes is elected president of the republic with an absolute majority of votes on the first ballot.
July 22, 1976	Formation of all-Socialist cabinet under Prime Minister Mario Soares.
January 1978	New government under Soares.
July 27, 1978	Fall of the second Soares government and appointment of Nobre de Costa—"the president's man."
September 22, 1978	Fall of de Costa's cabinet.
November 22, 1978	New government composed of "technicians" under Premier Mota Pinto.

Major Events in Portugal Since the End of Dictatorship, 1974–1989

December 2, 1979	Legislative elections: Democratic Alliance wins a razor-thin majority (128 out of 250 seats).
December 10, 1979	Francisco Sa Carneiro, leader of the Democratic Alliance, becomes prime minister.
October 5, 1980	Legislative elections: Democratic Alliance and Sa Carneiro win majority (134 out of 250 seats).
December 5, 1980	Death of Sa Carneiro in plane crash.
December 7, 1980	Reelection of Eanes as president.
January 1981	Diogo F. do Amaral replaces Sa Carneiro as prime minister and leader of Democratic Alliance.
September 2, 1981	Balsano forms new government (Democratic Alliance).
August 13, 1982	Revolutionary Council of the Armed Forces is disbanded.
December 19, 1982	Balsano resigns.
December 29, 1982	do Amaral, leader of Christian Democrats, quits the government.
February 4, 1983	Eanes dissolves parliament.
April 5, 1983	General elections. Socialist party, led by Soares, obtains the largest percentage of votes.
June 9, 1983	Soares as premier in coalition with Social Democratic party under Carlos Mota Pinto.
February 5, 1985	Pinto, leader of Social Democrats, resigns.
June 1985	Portugal and Spain sign the Treaty of Adhesion to the European Community following years of negotiation.
June 13, 1985	Social Democratic party withdraws from the coalition.
October 6, 1985	General election; Social Democrats receive largest percentage of votes.
October 29, 1985	President Eanes asks the Social Democratic leader Anibal Cavaco Silva to become prime minister and form a coalition government.
January 1, 1986	Portugal and Spain become members of the European Economic Community (EEC).
February 16, 1986	The Socialist leader Mario Soares is elected president on the second ballot by a very narrow margin, becoming the first civilian president in over 60 years.
February 26, 1986	Minority government of Cavaco Silva wins a vote of confidence.
June 29, 1986	Vitor Constancio elected head of PSP; replaced Soares who resigned after being elected president.
April 13, 1987	Portugal signs pact with China to return Macao by 1999.
April 28, 1987	Soares calls for elections after censure vote brings down the government of Cavaco Silva.
July 19, 1987	Cavaco Silva's Social Democratic party wins majority in the parliamentary elections; gives Portugal its first majority government since the 1974 revolution.
August 13, 1987	Cavaco Silva presents his new government.
January 4, 1988	Portugal reports its unemployment rate at 8 percent (lowest in four years).
May 30, 1988	Constitutional court rules against the Social Democratic government's plan to reprivatize state companies and liberalize labor laws.
Mid-Summer 1988	Parliament approves an agricultural reform law ending the agricultural reforms initiated with the 1974–1975 Revolution. The government sells 49% of several state companies: first break with the "irreversibility" of the nationalizations decreed after the Revolution.
January 5, 1989	Socialist President Mario Soares harshly criticizes the Social Democratic government of Anibal Cavaco Silva.
June 5, 1989	Parliament concludes revisions of 1976 Constitution to permit structural changes necessary for economic reform.

THE CASE OF SPAIN

On November 20, 1975, Generalissimo Francisco Franco, who had ruled Spain for 37 years, died. The country he had ruled had experienced developments that in general paralleled those in Portugal: modernization and industrialization, foreign investment, increased demands for reform among some of the elites, including elements of the Catholic Church. Immediately after Franco's death, King Juan Carlos I, appointed successor by Franco himself in 1967, assumed the throne. The restoration of the Bourbon monarchy—Juan Carlos's grandfather Alfonso XIII was king until 1931—technically place Juan Carlos in the position to be the last absolute monarch in Europe. Franco's supporters hoped he would govern as one. Juan Carlos, however, proved to be a very modern and liberal monarch, clearly supportive of democratic reforms. He initiated measures to liberalize the regime, legalized political parties (including the Communists), granted freedom to the press, reestablished freedom of association, and endorsed a new constitution allowing for representative government One year after assuming power and on the anniversary of Franco's death, Juan Carlos had maneuvered around the old Franquist elite successfully enough—particularly through his collaboration with the young lower-level politican Adolfo Suárez—to promise to hold elections within the year and to establish parliamentary government. Juan Carlos kept these promises.

AN EMERGING DEMOCRATIC POLITY?

The Spanish government revealed its proposal for constitutional reform on September 12, 1976. The Law of Fundamental Reform, as the proposal was called, recognized popular sovereignty and universal suffrage. It scrapped the corporatist arrangement based on functional representation that was in force under Franco. The proposal was submitted to the people in a referendum held on December 15, 1976 and was overwhelmingly approved.

The Reform Law, and later the Constitution of 1978, established Spain as a parliamentary democracy, institutionally similar to those in other European countries such as Italy, West Germany, and Great Britain. The executive—the government—is comprised of the cabinet members led by the prime minister. It must command majority support in the lower house of parliament. The prime minister decides who is to be a member of the cabinet. Once formed, the executive has several strengths, including the ability to dissolve either or both houses of parliament under certain circumstances. As in Germany, it can only be replaced with a constructive vote of no confidence.

The bicameral legislature (the Cortes) consists of a lower house, the Congress of Deputies (350 delegates, elected through a proportional representation system), and an upper house, the Senate (204 senators, 4 from each province and 2 each from Melilla and Ceuta, elected by a majority system). Each house elects a president, draws up its own rules, and faces reelection at least once every four years. The constitution clearly outlines the superiority of the Congress over the Senate. The deputies deliberate on bills submitted by the government, with a majority needed for approval. If approved, the bill goes to the Senate, which must vote on the exact text agreed upon by the lower house. If the Senate does not approve the deputies' bill within two months, the Congress can override the bill with a simple majority vote. Furthermore, the Senate has only 20 days to act on a bill the Congress or government considers urgent.

A bill revising the constitution goes to the king, who has the option of either signing it into law or submitting it to popular referendum. Similar to France, referenda may be called not only on constitutional revisions but also on "questions of national interest," such as the one on NATO discussed shortly.

The Spanish Constitution of 1978 also established a Constitutional Court with the power to declare laws unconstitutional. This "check" on the parliament and the country's executive is a totally new institutional feature in Spain. The Constitutional Court has already demonstrated in several important cases its ability to stand firm against other institutional and political powers. Such developments in the powers of the judiciary will probably assist in the long-term preservation of democracy in Spain.

THE POLITICAL FORCES IN SPAIN

Spain's apparently successful transition to democracy, and the difficulties the country has had to overcome, can readily be seen in its party system. The country's national party system has basically contained four major groups throughout the transition: the Popular Alliance, the Union of the Democratic Center (UCD), the Socialists, and the Communists. (See Table 3–3.) The disintegration of the UCD following its 1982 electoral defeat, however, left open some intriguing developments in future Spanish politics, given the void in the political center. Furthermore, the continued strength of the many regional and ethnically oriented nationalist parties throughout this multilingual country adds an additional question to the long term development of Spain's party system and the type of politics it both reflects and promotes.

The Right

The Extreme Right. The Spanish right has had many different small and extremist parties, some of which have competed at different times in both the general and regional elections. Table 3–3 lists a few examples of these. As with the many extreme leftist parties, most of these rightist parties are small and not competitive electorally. Most, in fact, are small groups that view the Franco years nostalgically and seek to carry on the traditions of Spanish nationalism, fascism,

TABLE 3–3 Political Parties in Spain

Right	
	Spanish Falange
	New Force (Fuerza Nueva)
	Spanish Solidarity
AP	Popular Alliance

Center	
UCD	Union of the Democratic Center
CDS	Social and Democratic Center
PRD	Democratic Reform party
PNV	Basque National party
CiU	Catalan Convergence & Union

Left	
PS	Socialist party
PSOE	Spanish Socialist Workers' party
PCE	Spanish Communist party
HB	Herri Batasuna
EE	Euzkadi Left
	Spanish Communist party (Marxist Leninist)

and other forms of extremism on the political right. These parties are, for the most part, only a persistent reminder of the past and what Spain's transition to democracy has sought to overcome. Many of these parties have died given a lack of interest.

The Popular Alliance. Spain's major conservative party was organized and led until late 1986 by Manuel Fraga, formerly Franco's minister of information. Many of its original members also served under Franco. This rightist party initially consisted of a number of groups, many of which sought to limit parliamentary government throughout the country's transition. Its original platform stressed opposition to any "rupture" of the "legacy of the past," speaking of the necessity to establish a Spanish democracy, yet in such a manner as not to break totally with the past. Following the early stages of the transition, however, Popular Alliance appeared to become a more moderate party, comparable in many respects to the British Conservative party and the German Christian Democrats. Today its platform emphasizes economic development based on a free economy, a "strong social program," and fiscal reform. The Alliance receives support from the big banks and major financial interests and, of course, the Catholic Church. It is the second largest party in Spain today. It favors fiscal reforms that would increase the ability of Spanish business to finance and expand its operations. It has received help from the Bavarian stronghold of the German Christian Democratic party.

Popular Alliance's political fortunes did not appear particularly promising during the transition's early stages. Its right-wing philosophy, often pro-Franco, prevented the party from becoming a mass party in the European sense. This has changed in recent years as Popular Alliance worked to modify its image. The party's showing in the 1982 election helped legitimize it. In that year, the party filled the center-right political vacuum. Under Fraga's leadership, despite the hostile memories he stirred among many voters to the left of center, the Popular Alliance has become the leader of the parliamentary opposition. Given these memories and the question of whether the party could win under his leadership, Fraga resigned as party leader in December 1986. Two years later, however, he returned as party leader. The party has also changed its name to the Popular party.

The Center

Adolfo Suárez created the Union of the Democratic Center shortly before the 1977 election as a federation of many small parties and groups. With governmental power as its focal point—given Suárez's position at the time as a royally appointed prime minister—UCD brought together many different political forces ranging ideologically from left-of-center to center-right, including social democrats, liberals, and Christian democrats. Under Suárez's leadership, UCD governments were committed to free elections open to all, guarantees of the right to form political parties and labor associations, suppression of the special tribunals set up under Franco to deal with terrorism, the immediate granting of amnesty to all political prisoners, and the recognition of Spain's ethnic diversity. Most important, Suárez led the party throughout Spain's transition to democracy by implementing many of these critical political reforms. Once the major elements for a successful transition to democracy were in place, however, the party fell on hard times. Many ideological conflicts within the party ultimately led to its demise.

Adolfo Suárez left the UCD in 1982 and formed a new left-of-center party, the Social and Democratic Center party. This formation is an attempt to reestablish a viable centrist political party in Spain mostly along the lines of a moderate social democratic party. The party did not meet with a great deal of success in its initial electoral contest in 1982, neither nationally nor regionally. Several factors help explain this poor performance: organizational difficulties; policy moderation by the Socialists to its left and Popular Alliance to its political right, leading to in-

creased competition; and challenges from other new and small centrist parties such as Miguel Roca's Democratic Reform Party (PRD). Roca, a spokesman for the Catalan group in Spain's national parliament, is one of the country's most popular political personalities. The PRD competed directly against the CDS in the 1986 national election, with Suárez's CDS achieving impressive gains and the PRD being completely shut out of the parliament. The CDS thus seems to have established a foothold in the electoral center in Spain.

The Left

The Spanish left is split into two major political parties, the Socialists and the Communists, and many smaller and often more extremist parties. Small and extreme parties on the political left in Spain include many that do not support the country's new democratic values and several regional parties that promote their causes—often independence from Madrid—through the use of armed violence. Some of these smaller parties are listed in Table 3–3. In terms of peaceful electoral competition, the Spanish Socialists have been much more successful in adapting to democratic competition than the Communists. The Spanish Communist party is currently openly split by several factions and questions of political leadership.

The Socialists. The Spanish Socialist Workers' Party (PSOE) has grown to become Spain's largest party in terms of electoral appeal. The PSOE has a long and tradition-filled history. It is the only Spanish Socialist party recognized by the Socialist International and has ties to the other European Socialist parties, particularly the German SPD. The PSOE's victories in 1982 and 1986 stemmed in large part from an organizational foundation laid during the last years of the Franco regime. Unlike the Communists who generally lived in exile and worked from outside Spain, the PSOE was firmly positioned within the country. It thus got a competitive edge over the other leftist parties. This permitted the party's leadership—Felipe González and Alfonso Guerra—and its membership to play an immediate role in the early stages of political transition. For example, the PSOE developed its ideological and organizational ties with the trade union movement, particularly the General Workers' Union (UGT). With its organizational base essentially in place, the party was ready to change its role as the political climate changed. Throughout the transition, the PSOE supported moderate liberal democratic reforms while insisting on a complete break with the Franco regime—*ruptura democrática.* The PSOE has consistently supported efforts toward pluralist democracy, autonomy for Spain's ethnic and regional groups, and the freedom to organize labor unions, business groups, and other political, economic, and social organizations. Today the Spanish Socialists continue to be a very moderate left-of-center party, advocating reforms that are generally more "modern" than "socialist." They have pushed for the liberalization of divorce, greater state participation in the schools, conditions more conducive to operating efficient businesses, and a more outward-looking foreign policy, including membership in the European Economic Community and, after much debate, NATO. The PSOE draws much of its support from Spain's middle and working classes, white-collar employees, and civil servants.

The Communists. The Spanish Communist party (PCE) is an open "Eurocommunist" party. It has more in common with the Italian and French Communist parties than with those in Portugal and Greece. It broke with the Communist party of the Soviet Union over the Czechoslovakian invasion of 1968, the treatment of dissidents within the USSR, and the repressive policies of the Soviet system. It claims that one-party rule is justifiable only in poor countries, not Western Europe. It has consistently supported a pluralist democracy; a "peaceful road to socialism"; recognition of Spain's diverse ethnic composition; membership in the EEC; and the modernization of social, political,

and economic institutions. The PCE has not, however, been afraid to demonstrate openly yet peacefully against the government on such issues as NATO membership and economic issues it believes are harmful to working-class people.

During the transition to democracy, the PCE came under the leadership of Santiago Carrillo, one of the few active political leaders in Spain who also participated in the pre-Franco democracy. The PCE's Eurocommunism, however, has led to severe internal conflicts within the party, with a strong, militant revolutionary and pro-Soviet wing challenging the present leadership. Further exacerbating the PCE's factional problems is the fact that the party's leadership, now under Julio Anguita, still struggles with the followers of Carrillo, even though he has now left the party. Such internal problems have not helped the party to confront its steady decline in electoral support, its increased loss in membership, and the continued difficulties that the Workers' Commissions (the PCE's trade union and the party's source of strength) has had in competing in the workplace against the Socialists' UGT.

Elections and Referendums

Since the death of Franco, Spain has had five national legislative elections and three referenda in addition to its many regional and local elections. Participation, perhaps even enthusiasm, was high in the beginning. On December 15, 1976, there was a referendum on the political reforms undertaken by King Juan Carlos and his prime minister Adolfo Suárez in the direction of democracy, reforms that signaled a departure from the legacy and the institutions of Franco. They were approved by 94 percent of the voters. On June 15, 1977, the Spanish elected representatives for the first time in 40 years. Again participation was high—almost 80 percent. The results of these elections overwhelmingly rejected the past pattern of authoritarian rule and reflected a desire for democratic forms of government. As seen in Table 3-4, the 1977 general election saw

TABLE 3-4 Spanish National Elections (seats won in parentheses)

	1977	1979	1982	1986
Popular Alliance (AP)	8.3%	6.0%	26.5%	26.2%
	(16)	(9)	(107)	(105)
Democratic Center Union	34.4	35.0	6.7	—
(UCD)	(166)	(168)	(11)	
Social & Democratic Center	—	—	2.8	9.3
			(2)	(19)
Socialist (PSOE)	29.3	30.5	48.4	44.1
	(118)	(121)	(202)	(184)
Communist (PCE)	9.4	10.8	4.1	4.6
	(20)	(23)	(4)	(7)
Others	18.6	17.7	11.5	15.8
	(30)	(29)	(26)	(35)
Total	100.0%	100.0%	100.0%	100.0%
	(350)	(350)	(350)	(350)

Suárez's centrist UCD receive 34.4 percent of the vote. The Socialists placed second with 29.3 percent. The Communists were third with 9.4 percent—a percentage viewed at the time as significantly large for a new Communist party pledged to support the constitution and the monarchy and committed to reform rather than revolution. The rightist Popular Alliance received a mere 8.3 percent. The rest of the vote went to splinter organizations such as the nationalist groups of Catalonia and the Basque region. In the Congress of Deputies, the Union of Christian Democracy held 166 seats, the Socialists 118, the Communists 20. The remaining 21 seats went to independents or regional autonomist candidates. Thus no party was able to gain an absolute majority of seats (176), but it appeared relatively easy for Suárez to gain enough support from smaller centrist parties to obtain a majority.

On December 6, 1978, the new democratic constitution formulated by the parliament elected some 18 months before was presented to the people in a referendum. The Spanish voters overwhelmingly approved it. Though the percentage of abstentions was significant (32 percent), 87.7 percent of those voting endorsed the new constitution. It provided for a parliamentary monarchy, recognized religious freedom, guaranteed the right of nationalities to seek autonomy, established the familiar democratic freedoms of association and the press, and protected the right to vote and other individual rights.

With the ratification of the new constitution behind him, Prime Minister Suárez called an election for March 3, 1979. These second legislative elections virtually duplicated the first. Most political parties maintained their strength: each retained almost the same number of representatives in the lower house. The UCD could now get on with the task of governing the country.

A general feeling of disenchantment had, however, set in. Many Spaniards had lost the sense of excitement over this new experience known as democracy. People realized that many problems of Spanish society remained intractable and that new difficulties had appeared. For one thing, after more than a decade of economic growth and relative well-being, Spain experienced the same symptoms of economic depression that began to afflict all industrial societies in the late 1970s: unemployment, inflation, and stagnation. But beyond that, Spain continued to face a crisis of legitimacy, a challenge by regional groups to its territorial integrity, and a constant danger of army intervention and the imposition of an authoritarian solution.

THE CRISIS OF LEGITIMACY

The crisis of legitimacy was manifested in terrorism from both the left and the right. Army officers and policemen were murdered daily, many by the militants of the autonomist movements in Catalonia and the Basque region. These assassinations provoked a reaction in kind from the nationalist and right-wing forces. The search for ethnic autonomy in the Basque region and Catalonia continued despite legislation providing the two areas with self-government. They demanded full separation. Autonomist movements appeared in other provinces, and many commentators referred to a widespread "autonomania" that threatened to dismember the state.

The army, which had never fully accepted the dismantling of the Franco regime and its institutions, remained ready to step in. This was clearly demonstrated when an officer of the paramilitary civil guard and some soldiers entered the Cortes on February 23, 1981, interrupted the proceedings, and held the parliamentarians prisoner. Other army units seized the national radio and television complex and began to broadcast martial music. Military movements were observed in provinces, and it was expected that General Milans de Bosch—a pro-Franco figure highly regarded in the army—would momentarily take command on behalf of the king. The general, in fact, communicated his plans to a number of regional commanders. There was no prime minister at the time. Suárez had resigned, and the parliament had met to nominate his successor, Leopoldo Calvo Sotelo. The fate of the republic rested in the hands of King Juan Carlos. If he had consented, a military dictatorship would have been imposed. He refused. Spanish democracy was saved by the only remaining Bourbon monarch!

The subsequent investigations and trial showed that the attempted coup had deep roots. The demand for stability and order escalated and most major political forces responded. The UCD and the PSOE backed off many controversial policies. Democratic leaders proceeded only tentatively for a time. All of Spain had been reminded of how uncertain the transition to democracy remained.

THE SOCIALIST VICTORIES

This uncertain stage in Spain's democratization essentially came to an end in late 1982 when the Socialist party peacefully assumed power without incident, following its October electoral victory. In this election, the PSOE won a large majority of the seats in the parliament—202 of 350. With 48.4 percent of the vote, the Socialists far outpassed the UCD's returns in the previous two elections. (As previously mentioned, the Communists lost a great deal of support to the Socialists.) The Spanish electorate selected a government with a clear mandate. The Popular Alliance emerged as the major opposition party, following the total defeat of the UCD. This victory established the AP in its new role as the leading political group on Spain's political right-of-center; it generated some comments concerning the settling of the Spanish party system into a multiparty system with two major parties.

The Socialists' rise to power proved to most political observers that the old antidemocratic forces of the far right had finally lost their influence. Spain's full transition to a stable democratic regime now appears assured. Memories of the start of the Spanish Civil War in 1936 under somewhat similar circumstances suggest that the army, the civil guard, and other rightist forces, while still strong, do not have enough power or supporters to alter Spain's democratic direction.

Spain and the PSOE resolved a major foreign policy question when, on March 12,

1986, it voted in a nationwide consultative referendum in favor of continued membership in NATO. The referendum's outcome was 52.5 percent voting "yes" for continued membership, 39.8 percent "no," and 7.6 percent casting null or blank ballots. This result reinforced the direction Spain began with its transition to democracy and its membership in the EEC in terms of developing closer ties to the other Western European nations. This "yes" vote, however, surprised most Spaniards as well as the many outside observers who watched closely this first referendum on membership by any NATO member country. Most public opinion polls had predicted a large "no" vote and thus a defeat for the Socialist party and the Socialist government on the issue.

Spain originally joined NATO in 1982 when the UCD government won parliamentary approval for membership. Since then, however, many of Spain's foreign policy issues were placed on hold until this bitterly contested issue was resolved. The Spanish Communists strongly opposed membership. For its part, the Socialist party had originally agreed with the Spanish Communists in their opposition to NATO membership. As a matter of fact, Felipe González suggested the holding of the NATO referendum itself as a campaign promise during the 1982 general election because of this opposition to NATO. Once in office, however, González changed this anti-NATO position and began a campaign in favor of continued membership. This Socialist campaign for Spain's continued membership in NATO culminated in the referendum in March 1986 that produced a slim majority in favor of continuing participation. Spanish membership in the EEC and NATO indicates that Spain will continue its new path of being an active member in the main international organizations to which most Western European countries belong.

PSOE's decisions regarding NATO and other policy matters seem to have been accepted by a majority of the population. For a second time, the party was given an absolute majority, thus establishing their position with the 1982 and 1986 elections in much the same way that the 1977 and 1979 elections did for the UCD. However, unlike the UCD, the Socialists appear to have the ability to remain in Spain's political arena for a long time to come. Having firmly established themselves and given the lack of a viable alternative, some people suggest the PSOE may have a semipermanent role in government, much like the Christian Democrats in Italy.

In sum, the PSOE government, under Felipe González's leadership, has undertaken many moderate reforms helping to assure democratic stability. Initial reforms of the armed forces have been implemented. Spain has become a member of the European Economic Community. Judicial and other legal reforms have occurred; social and educational reforms have been undertaken. In sum, since the death of Franco, Spain seems to have successfully faced the challenges of democratic legitimacy, institutional reorganization, and international cooperation— which bodes well for its future as a member of Europe's democratic political systems.

Major Events in Spain Since the End of Dictatorship, 1975–1989

November 20, 1975	Death of General Franco.
November 22, 1975	Prince Juan Carlos is proclaimed Juan Carlos I, king of Spain.
December 1975	Carlos Arias Navarro, prime minister under Franco, forms a government.
July 1, 1976	Navarro resigns.
July 3, 1976	King Juan Carlos I asks centrist Adolfo Suárez to form a government.
August 1976	General amnesty is ordered for political crimes.
December 15, 1976	Referendum on democratic political reforms approved overwhelmingly.
June 15, 1977	Legislative elections.
July 6, 1977	New government under Suárez.
September 29, 1977	Autonomous administration for Catalonia reestablished.

Major Events in Spain Since the End of Dictatorship, 1975–1989

February 17, 1978	Reestablishment of regional representative council in the Basque region.
December 6, 1978	Approval of the constitution.
March 1, 1979	Legislative elections.
May 14, 1979	Neo-fascist demonstrations.
August 8, 1979	Granting of autonomy for Catalonia.
February 23, 1981	Military right-wing coup fails.
February 25, 1981	Leopoldo Calvo Sotelo becomes prime minister following Suárez's resignation.
June 1981	Enactment of divorce law.
December 1981	Parliament passes bill approving Spain's membership in NATO.
July 1982	Calvo Sotelo resigns as UCD party leader.
August 1982	Suárez leaves the UCD.
October 1982	General election results in overwhelming Socialist victory. Felipe González becomes prime minister.
June 1985	Spain and Portugal sign the Treaty of Adhesion to the European Economic Community following years of negotiation.
July 1985	Major cabinet shakeup under Felipe González.
November 20, 1985	Tenth anniversary of Franco's death. Major demonstrations by rightists in Madrid as well as anti-NATO demonstrations.
January 1, 1986	Spain and Portugal become EEC members.
January 30, 1986	Prince Felipe of Asturias sworn in as the heir apparent to the Spanish throne; reaffirms the continuation of a constitutional monarchy.
March 12, 1986	Referendum on NATO membership; the "yes" vote wins by a very small margin.
June 22, 1986	PSOE loses some seats in the general elections but maintains its clear majority.
July 19, 1986	France begins handing over suspected ETA terrorists directly to Spanish authorities as the two countries work closer to combat violence.
December 2, 1986	Manuel Fraga resigns as leader of AP after leading it for ten years.
January 14, 1987	Talks with Britain over the status of Gibraltar still produce no change.
January–February 1987	Sectarian strife in Melilla as Moslems protest poor living conditions and citizenship status.
February 7, 1987	Hernández Mancha elected as leader of Popular Alliance.
February 27, 1987	ETA-military leader Abasolo Domingo Iturbe killed in auto accident in Algeria.
June 10, 1987	PSOE and AP lose ground in regional elections while the CDS gains.
November 10, 1987	Spain serves notice that current agreement over U.S. bases on its soil will not be extended.
January 15, 1988	U.S. promises to remove F-16 fighter planes from Spain to preserve the remaining military presence in the country.
February 19, 1988	Government accepts ETA proposal to begin talks.
February 22, 1988	Julio Anguita elected as new leader of PCE to succeed Gerardo Iglesia.
December 14, 1988	General strike led by the major labor unions against the Socialist government's policy paralyzes Spain.
January 1989	Popular Alliance reorganized as the Popular party. Manuel Fraga returned as party president.
June 29, 1989	First victory in campaign begun in April by Popular party and the Social and Democratic Center party calling for motions of censure against Socialist mayors in many cities. Juan Barranco (Socialist) is replaced by Agustín Rodríquez Sahangín (CDS) as mayor of Madrid.
October 29, 1989	New general parliamentary elections.

4

The Politics of Greece

Greece returned to parliamentary government in 1974 after seven years of the most repressive military government it had ever experienced. As in Portugal, a particular event precipitated the collapse of Greece's dictatorship: Turkey successfully invaded the island of Cyprus, an independent nation yet predominately Greek in its ethnic population. Greece's military junta was unable to respond. As in Portugal and Spain, widespread opposition had already existed to the military regime. The rule of "the Colonels," as the junta was known, was opposed by many of Greece's elites, party leaders, and students. Investments from abroad, rapid economic growth, and modernization increased the mobilization of many groups against the military's repressive tactics.

The rise and fall of the Colonels followed a pattern of instability that has characterized Greece since its independence in 1821. This instability has taken Greece through various forms of dictatorship and democracy. It has also cost many lives, especially during the bloody Civil War of 1946–1949. As seen in Table 4–1, several factors account for this instability. First, political trust still does not run very deep either among the elites or in the population as a whole. Too many memories linger about past battles over ideology, the monarchy, and the civil war. Second, the entire population, but especially the middle class, has fundamentally disagreed for a long time about the very nature of the political regime itself: democracy or dictatorship, monarchy or republic. Third, and perhaps even more fundamental, the Greek elites have traditionally had a strong "dependence" on outside powers: first Britain and then the United States since World War II. Throughout the twentieth century these powers have openly intervened in Greek politics.

The restoration of democracy in 1974 brought to the forefront many of these problems and issues in Greek politics. The ques-

TABLE 4-1 Regime Instability in Greece, 1824–1974

1821	Proclamation of Independence and Republic
1830	Absolute monarchy
	Uprising, 1843
	First parliamentary election, 1844
	Uprising, 1862; deposition of king
1863	Constitutional monarchy
	Revolt of military, 1909
	Accession of King Constantine, 1913
	Political and military uprising; king forced into exile, 1917
	Return of Constantine, 1920
	Military coup; second exile and abdication of the king, 1922
1924	Second Republic
	Military coup, 1925
	Military dictatorship, 1925–26
	Attempted military coups, 1933, 1935
1935	Constitutional monarchy
	George II becomes king
1936	Dictatorship under General Metaxas
1940–41	Greek-Italian war
1941–44	Military occupation by Germany
1944–45	Regency of Archbishop Damaskinos
1946	Constitutional monarchy
	Referendum and return of George II
	Civil war, 1946–49
	King Paul succeeds George II, 1951
	Death of King Paul and accession of King Constantine, 1964
1967	Military junta; exile of king
1974	Junta collapses; monarchy abolished by referendum
1974	Third Republic

tion of the monarchy was the first to be addressed. Shortly after the return of democratic rule, the Greek voters abolished the monarchy in a referendum. This conflict between monarchy and republic has deep roots in Greece. A different style of rule has been associated with each, since they tend to be supported by different socioeconomic and political forces. The Greek monarchy amounted to a semiauthoritarian system in which the king maintained some basic powers. Foreign policy and defense—the Armed Forces—remained in the monarch's hands, often exercised in close cooperation with foreign powers. The upper bourgeoisie, some of the middle class, and the majority of farmers, especially those from the poorer regions of the country, supported the monarchy. On the other side, the majority of the middle class, urban residents, workers, and other sections of the country such as the island of Crete traditionally supported a republican form of democracy. This conflict reached another stalemate between 1963 and 1967, when neither the proponents of parliamentary democracy nor the supporters of the monarchy were able to prevail. The army then stepped in and established its repressive military dictatorship.

GREEK DEMOCRACY

The contemporary political system of Greece is a republic form of parliamentary democracy. Institutionally, it therefore has many similarities with the other southern and western European countries discussed in this volume. For example, the abolition of the monarchy means the president acts as "head of state." As will be discussed shortly in more detail, the Greek president is now relatively powerless, in much the same way as the presidents of Italy and the Federal Republic of Germany.

As a parliamentary democracy, executive functions in Greece are carried out by a cabinet under the direction of the prime minister who acts as "head of government." In a manner similar to many other European countries including Britain, Spain, and Italy, the prime minister and his team of ministers are accountable to the parliament. This "government" remains in power as long as it holds the confidence of a majority of the parliament. The parliament—the Vouli—is the center of legislative activity in Greece. Besides electing the prime minister, it must pass all important legislative acts, is the center of debate for governmental bills, and provides the opposition with the opportunity to criticize government policy.

Again as do most European democracies, parliamentary and all other political activity in Greece is generally carried out through the political parties. However, the Greek party system was fragmented as was that in Italy. This party fragmentation not only led in the past to governmental instability during periods of democracy, but also to regime instability. The current democratic system in Greece has attempted to remedy this in several ways. For example, one way has been through the use of an electoral system that often excludes smaller parties from representation in the Vouli. While West Germany has effectively used its 5 percent clause, the Greek electoral system of proportional representation penalizes parties that receive less than 17 percent of the national vote.

THE FRAGILITY OF THE PARTY SYSTEM

Between 1944 and 1967 when the Colonels took power, Greece held 13 legislative elections. At least 35 parties competed in these elections. More than 30 governments had to be formed, similar in its cabinet instability to modern Italy. This instability in the party system can be easily seen in the elections. Except for the election of 1964, no party obtained a majority and no stable party coalitions or alliances could be found to provide one. Early dissolution of the legislature occurred five times. If we cluster the political parties of 1946 and 1964 into ideological formations of the right, center, and left, some 10 parties on the right received as little as 35 percent of the vote and as much as 82 percent. The 14 parties of the center ranged from 17 to 57 percent. And the left-wing parties obtained between 8 and 30 percent of the vote. The average shift of the popular vote from one political "family" to the others was as much as 30 percent from one election to the next.

Besides fragmented parties and wide shifts in voting patterns, Greece's parties system have been "leader parties"—formed, led, and sustained by the founder. Such personality-oriented parties tend to remain intact only as long as the leader is present.

Meetings of party congresses and executive committees are often only a formality. Powerful bosses and their followers frequently desert one party to form or join another. Continuous shuffling among the parties aggravated their inherent instability and made them increasingly susceptible to extraparliamentary pressures—from the monarch, the army, or foreign powers. Greek parties in general were characterized by weak membership; a lack of internal organization; a lack of institutionalized methods for selecting leaders and establishing relationships between leaders and the rank and file, internal party decentralization, with emphasis on local and regional party bosses; and a lack of coherent programs. Such parties have found it difficult to translate political demands into policies.

Greece's party system has become greatly stabilized since the return to democracy in 1974. There has been a noticeable reduction in the number of parties, due in part to the highly restrictive election laws. The trend toward party simplification began in the election of 1974 and has continued to the present.

Despite the current stabilization of Greece's party system, many past practices continue. The most significant of these is that the political parties remain "personal parties." This can clearly be seen in contemporary Greece's two major parties—New Democracy and PASOK. Constantine Karamanlis established New Democracy as a moderate right-wing party upon his return from exile following the fall of the military junta in 1974. Likewise, Andreas Papandreou organized and inspired PASOK—the Panhellenic Socialist movement. PASOK managed to create a strong, centralized organization and mass membership, but today it remains beholden to its founder and leader. In contrast to New Democracy and PASOK, the centrist group, formerly the Centrist Liberals and more recently the Center Union, demonstrated the inability of Greek parties to operate without a charismatic leader. It quickly lost its support in this new stage of Greek democracy. The Communists also remain divided into competing factions but the pro-Soviet wing (the KKE) has remained dominant.

In sum, Greece's political parties today still demonstrate many characteristics of past parties. They tend to be loose formations of confederate leaders and local magnates rather than centralized, disciplined entities. They remain prone to factionalism and fragmentation, regardless of whether they are on the political left or right. They tend to be intense in their ideological rhetoric while inconsistent in their programs. Above all they remain "leader parties," deriving their strength from the charisma of the leader.

PARLIAMENTARY ELECTIONS OF 1974 AND 1977

The first four parliamentary elections following Greece's return to democracy can best be viewed analytically as two pairs of two, in a manner remarkably similar to post-authoritarian Spain. New Democracy won the first two elections—in 1974 and 1977—and PASOK received a clear majority in 1981 and 1985. The moderate right thus controlled the Greek government under the leadership of Karamanlis and New Democracy until the Socialists came to power in 1981 (see Tables 4–2 and 4–3).

TABLE 4–2 Major Political Parties in Greece, Elections of 1974

Right, Right-Center	
EDE	National Democratic Union (nationalist right-wing)
ND	New Democracy
Center	
	Center Union
Left	
PASOK	Panhellenic Socialist Movement
KKE (Es.)	Communist party of Greece "interior" (Eurocommunist)
KKE (Ex.)	Communist party of Greece "exterior" (pro-Soviet)

The parliamentary elections of November 1974 were Greece's most fairly conducted elections since World War II. The Greek people voted for the center-right and the center. This support for the moderate right in the first election since the restoration of democracy was similar to what occurred in Spain but in contrast to Portugal and Italy, which voted heavily for the Socialists and the Communists. Karamanlis and his New Democracy party won overwhelming pluralities and majorities in virtually all regions of the country. The center-right received more than 74 percent of the total vote (New Democracy 54 percent and the Center Union 20 percent). In its initial electoral contest, the New Socialist party PASOK came in a poor third with 13.6 percent of the vote. The Communists (the United Left) retained their traditional hard-core support of about 10 percent. New Democracy's clear victory translated into overwhelming control of the parliament: it secured 220 of the 300 seats in the Vouli.

As promised, the referendum on the king's return was held three weeks after this general election. The Greek people chose between a parliamentary monarch, along the lines of Britain's, or a republican form of parliamentary democracy, with a president, similar to either the strong president in the French Fifth Republic or the weak president of the Federal Republic of Germany. Presidential powers were to be defined later by the new legislative assembly, which was given the power to revise the constitution. As seen in Table 4–3, the response was overwhelmingly against the monarchy.

The period between the election of November 19, 1974 and the second general elections on November 20, 1977 was one of unprecedented stability in Greek political history. There were no cabinet crises, no military coups, not even any serious threats from left-wing or right-wing groups. The usual strikes occurred as well as student demonstrations with occasional confrontations with the police, but otherwise matters of state were handled by a stable government that enjoyed solid support in the par-

TABLE 4-3   Election and Referendum Results, November–December 1974

	Election		Referendum (king's return)	
Party	*Votes*	*Percentage*	*Yes*	*No*
New Democracy	2,631,531	54.51%	1,445,857	3,244,748
Center Union	984,584	20.40	(30.8%)	(69.2%)
PASOK (Socialist)	656,466	13.60		
United Left	448,362	9.29		
EDE (extreme right)	53,418	1.10		
Independent	51,601	1.07		

liament. Under Karamanlis's leadership, New Democracy maintained its majority by remaining cohesive and disciplined. The other parties demonstrated discipline as well.

This political stability was even more remarkable given the many serious economic and international issues. Greece sought full membership in the Common Market, and negotiations for entry were being actively pursued with the European Commission. The government undertook to renegotiate its position in NATO; rework its relationship with the United States, which was tarnished during the period of the Colonels; and reach a new agreement on the future role and control of the American military bases in Greece. Large sums were appropriated for defense in the face of Turkey's claims to the Aegean islands. Defense expenditures contributed to Greece's high rate of inflation—at least 20 percent a year. Long-awaited reforms in agriculture, education, industrial development, health, social security, and regional reorganization were yet to be undertaken. Nevertheless, Greece survived as a democracy.

The election of 1977 was conducted with an electoral system almost identical to the one used in 1974. This was another indication of stability since Greece has often seen the electoral system itself become highly politicized: incumbents change the election laws to enhance their own prospects for reelection. The election was free, open, and hard fought, with all protagonists given

equal opportunity to use the media, including television. Party positions paralleled those of 1974. Prime Minister Karamanlis and his New Democracy party highlighted their record of stability, democracy, and incremental reforms while promising more drastic ones. New Democracy grew in its open commitment to democracy and social reform when a militant, proroyalist group emerged to campaign on the extreme right. This party ultimately received almost 7 percent of the vote. Karmanlis's party disassociated itself from these extremists and moved closer to the center. As seen in Table 4–4, it lost votes to this extreme right group, finishing with 42 percent of the vote, compared to 54.4 percent in 1974. The combined vote for New Democracy and the extreme right,

TABLE 4-4   Election of November 20, 1977

Party	*Votes*	*Percentage*	*Seats*
National Front (extreme right)	346,800	6.84%	5
New Democracy	2,122,894	41.88	173
Democratic Center Union	607,985	12.00	15
PASOK (Panhellenic Socialist Movement)	1,282,577	25.31	92
Coalition of the Left	136,712	2.70	2
KKE (pro-Soviet)	470,852	9.29	11
Other	100,147	1.98	2
Total			300

nevertheless, was only 6 percent below what New Democracy had received in 1974.

The greatest electoral shift in 1977 was at the center and center-left. Without strong leadership, the Center Union party virtually collapsed. It received only 12 percent of the vote, down from 20.4 percent in 1974. Most of these centrist votes went to the Panhellenic Socialist Movement, led by Andreas Papandreou. PASOK appeared to be the election's real winner. Except for the extreme right, it was the only party to show an appreciable gain, increasing its national vote from 13.5 percent in 1974 to 25.3 in 1977. The Communist party split prior to this election into the two factions it maintains today: a pro-Soviet Communist party of the Exterior and a "Eurocommunist party" of the Interior. The Communist party of the Exterior (KKE-Ex.) maintained its strength with 9.3 percent of the vote, while a leftist coalition of several left-wing splinter groups, including the Communist party of the Interior, lost strength.

THE TURN TO THE LEFT: PASOK'S FIRST VICTORY

Center-right control of the Greek government ended in 1981 in the third election fol-lowing the restoration of democracy. The same year Spain had a similar result. In both countries, the Socialists had grown in strength while in opposition and were now ready to assume power. As seen in Table 4–5, in Greece PASOK increased its strength and won 48 percent of the national vote. It returned 173 deputies to parliament out of the total 300—a clear majority. PASOK's leader, Andreas Papandreou, became prime minister. The Communist party (of the Exterior) won almost 11 percent of the vote and 13 deputies. The Left—PASOK and the Communists—thus received almost 60 percent of the ballots cast. Together they had the required 180 votes in parliament to elect the next president of the republic in March 1985.

On the right, New Democracy lost the parliamentary majority it had enjoyed since 1974. The party dropped more than 15 percent of its 1974 votes, despite forming an alliance with the National Front, some Liberal groups, and a number of powerful individual political leaders. The smaller centrist parties were simply crushed between New Democracy on the right and PASOK on the left. These centrist parties barely received 4 percent of the vote. Greece's traditional fragmented party system had given way to party bipolarization.

TABLE 4–5 Election of October 18, 1981

	Greek Parliament			*European Parliament*		
	Votes	*Percentage*	*Seats*	*Votes*	*Percentage*	*Seats*
New Democracy	2,033,584	35.86	115	1,686,976	31.53	8
PASOK	2,725,132	48.06	172	2,155,434	40.29	10
Center	23,723	0.42	—	60,843	1.14	—
Communist Party	619,292	10.92	13	678,236	12.86	3
Communist (Interior)	77,461	1.37	—	275,731	5.15	1
Liberals and Assorted Centrists	165,653	3.30	—	311,000	7.90	2
Extreme Left	12,500	0.20	—			
Independent	12,750	0.21	—			
Total			300			24

The Two Major Parties

New Democracy lost the election of 1981 for several reasons. One was that Constantine Karamanlis, its charismatic leader, had earlier been elected president of the republic. In his absence, the party was plagued with dissension among its other top leaders. In characteristic Greek fashion, New Democracy remained a party of notables and bosses. It had failed, despite many efforts, to develop a strong structure and grass-roots organization. In the election campaign, it chose to stand on its record of over seven years in office. New Democracy ran on the platform of "renewal" (*Ananeossis*).

While in power, New Democracy's leadership had scrupulously maintained all constitutional liberties, it had brought Greece into the European Economic Community, it had kept Greece with the lowest unemployment rate in Europe, and it had promoted economic growth. On the negative side, however, inflation marred the record, averaging 20 percent a year. Urban living conditions and services had deteriorated, something particularly troublesome since more than 65 percent of all Greeks live in urban centers, with more than one-third of the population in greater Athens. Pollution also continued to grow as a serious problem. Despite the establishment of provincial university centers, educational facilities continued to be inadequate. The civil service remained bloated and inefficient. And, above all, corruption remained unchecked. As a traditional party of notables, New Democracy distributed favors and subsidies on the basis of patron-client considerations. After seven years in office, it faced a backlog of unfulfilled pledges and mounting grievances.

On the other hand, PASOK chose "Change" (*Allaghi*) as its slogan for the 1981 election. It had a strong leader, Andreas Papandreou, who provided the leadership New Democracy lacked. It had also developed a powerful organization throughout the country, a phenomenon unprecedented in Greek political history. PASOK thus emerged as a party with both leadership and organization. Ideologically, Papandreou's socialism focused on the cooperation of as many social groups and classes as possible. He promised to nationalize many sectors of the economy, to decentralize the state apparatus, giving self-government to the regions and provinces, and to create cooperatives for the farmers. This program appealed to a number of groups: workers and farmers, students and intellectuals, the lower-middle class and much of the middle class, urban dwellers and those living in the countryside, older Greeks on pensions, parents of school children given its promise of radical education reforms, and army officers. But perhaps the most important aspect of PASOK's appeal was its nationalist posture. PASOK took an intransigent position with regard to Turkey, pledged to protect the interests of the Greeks in Cyprus, appealed to the army to defend the Greek territory, and proclaimed its intentions to move Greece out of NATO and to close the American military bases. Papandreou also argued for the withdrawal of Greece from the European Common Market, or at least a renegotiation of its terms of membership. PASOK's appeal thus appeared to be both socialist and nationalist. It successfully cast its net wide enough to catch many voters with grievances and protests.

Shallow Electoral Roots

The election of 1981 reminds us of a central feature of Greek politics: electoral volatility and the weak foundation of the party system and individual party identification. The "swing" from the center-right to the left in 1981 included more than 25 percent of the voters. This suggests about 12 percent of those who voted for the centrist groups in 1977 and 13 percent who voted for New Democracy and the extreme right switched to PASOK. The magnitude of such an electoral swing is uncharacteristic of more established European democracies. It leads us to make the following observations about the study of modern Greek politics.

Volatility. The Greek political parties have not well organized or structured a large portion of the electorate. Many Greek citizens do not closely identify with any particular party, moving instead from one position and party to another. For example, this volatile group of voters supported the center parties in the mid-1960s, they switched to New Democracy in 1974, and they voted for PASOK in 1981. PASOK's nationalist appeal may well account for its ability to attract these voters from the extreme right and New Democracy. Only time will tell if PASOK or some other party will be able to develop stronger roots and individual party identification as in the other European democracies.

Heterogeneous Support. PASOK voters do not have a clear social, economic, or regional identity. They come from all groups and share almost the same strength throughout the country. PASOK's vote fell below 40 percent in only a few electoral districts. However, the same applied to New Democracy, except in the greater Athens area where it lost heavily.

Unpredictability. With a catch-all program, PASOK's leadership was able to move in a number of directions in policymaking once in government. On one hand, this is characteristic of modern, mass parties in Western Europe. On the other hand, it makes it difficult to predict the course of Greek politics since so much depends on the leadership. For example, given his nationalistic and anti-Turkey rhetoric, who would have guessed that Papandreou would have made history by meeting with Turkey's president in January 1988 seeking better relations. Nevertheless, the fact that many voters chose PASOK as a protest in 1981 means that these same voters may turn against it in the future.

PASOK's Record in Government

After its 1981 victory, PASOK consolidated its position within the governmental structure. The civil service was purged and new appointments were made on the basis of political considerations similar to what New Democracy had done earlier. The armed forces, for long the spearhead of rightist coups, were brought under civilian control. Radio and television were also placed under the government's control and have been used to promote and defend the government's program and policies. PASOK and its deputies in parliament increasingly fell under Papandreou's control. He has continued the Greek tradition of strong personal rule, but within the structure of his party. As party leader, he has the power to establish electoral lists for his party's candidates in order of his preference.

The PASOK government undertook some long-awaited and much needed reforms after its 1981 victory, in a manner similar to the Socialists in Spain at the same time. The Greek socialists liberalized the divorce laws, promoted greater equality for women, abolished the institution of the dowry, and provided liberal pensions for the aged and the farmers, including women who work on the land. The rural areas benefited from the reforms and the establishment of agricultural cooperatives provided new structures for the improvement of agricultural production. With its control over most governmental agencies and many private or autonomous organizations such as the universities and the private sector of the economy, PASOK continued the Greek tradition of strong political control of the nation's institutional life. Such political dominance, however, has not come at the expense of individual and civil freedoms. In this regard, Greek democracy has stabilized in a manner similar to other European liberal democracies.

THE GREEK PRESIDENCY, 1985

The Greek constitution as it was revised in 1975 gave independent powers to the president of the republic. Constantine Karamanlis, the incumbent, had led Greece back to democracy as prime minister in 1974 and had been president since June 1980. He had, however, chosen to use few of the presidential powers legally at his disposal. Nevertheless, many considered Karamanlis's personality and popularity a genuine brake on Prime Minister Papandreou's ambitious policies, especially in foreign affairs. Karamanlis was pro-European, attached to the Common Market, unwilling to see Greece withdraw from NATO, and reconciled to the presence of the American military bases in Greece. As New Democracy's former leader, he thus provided a significant ideological counterbalance to Socialist control of the state apparatus after 1981.

The Greek president is elected by the parliament for a five-year term. A two-thirds majority (200 votes) is required on the first and second ballots. If unattained, a third and final ballot is held with a requirement of 180 votes for election. If no candidate obtains this minimum, the parliament is automatically dissolved and a new general election is held.

The question in 1985 was, given Karamanlis's personal popularity, whether PASOK would agree to help reelect him? Without PASOK support, no party could muster the requisite minimum of 180 votes to elect its own candidate without the votes of the Communists. March 1985 brought Greece through a constitutional crisis similar to many in its past. PASOK proposed a radical revision of the constitution in order to deprive the president of his personal powers (the right of dissolution under certain circumstances; the right to call for a referendum; the right to nominate a Prime Minister, etc.). Papandreou then withdrew his previously promised support for Karamanlis. After that, President Karamanlis decided to resign rather than use his constitutional powers to dissolve the parliament and call a new election. In April 1985, PASOK and the Communists together mustered the minimum requisite 180 votes to elect Christos Sartzetakis as Greece's new president. Later the parliament proceeded to revise the constitution and remove all personal powers from the president. Now, the Greek presi-

dency resembles institutionally the presidency in West Germany rather than the French or Portuguese presidencies. All personal powers have been transferred to the prime minister.

PASOK'S REELECTION, 1985

The general election of June 2, 1985 was a repetition of that of 1981. PASOK and its leader insisted on the continuation of *Allaghi* (change) and stressed the same themes of socialism and nationalism, the latter directed against Turkey. It warned voters that defeat would usher in turmoil and a rightist dictatorship. New Democracy, as the center-right and major opposition party, had Constantine Mitsotakis as its new leader. It urged modernization in the context of economic freedoms and private enterprise, the reduction of the state-controlled sectors of the economy, and a vigorous program of investments with proper guarantees to private and foreign investors. Of course, it too pointed out the dangers of democracy that the recent constitutional crisis had highlighted. Mitsotakis accused Prime Minister Papandreou of plotting to establish a one-party political system. A lack of political trust had clearly resurfaced.

As seen in Table 4–6, the election continued the recent trend toward a sharp bipolarization in Greek politics. The two major parties, PASOK and New Democracy, together received almost 87 percent of the total vote. The Center Union Party ceased to exist and its leaders, and other centrists and independents, moved to join the two major parties. The Communist party (of the Exterior) was the only third party to survive. However, it received less than 10 percent of the vote. All the other political parties together received less than 4 percent of the total popular vote. This continued and growing bipolarization threatens to put a heavy strain on democracy given the intense ideological divide that separates them.

PASOK's second consecutive electoral victory gave it the opportunity to consolidate

TABLE 4-6 The Legislative Election of June 9, 1985

	Votes	Percentage	Seats
New Democracy	2,599,949	40.84%	126
PASOK	2,916,450	45.82	161
KKE (Communist Ex.)	629,518	9.89	12
All other	314,954	3.45	1
Total			300

Eligible voters	8,119,410
Votes cast	6,422,352
Valid votes	6,365,039

Legislative majority (PASOK and KKE): 151 (majority needed for revision of the constitution and election of the president: 180)

its governmental position. The Socialists gained in the countryside but did not do as well in the cities as previously. In Greece as a whole, it received almost 46 percent of the vote—only 2.5 percent less than in 1981. This was 2.9 million votes. New Democracy, on the other hand, improved from about 36 percent in 1981 to almost 41 percent, with some 2.5 million votes. These results translated into a parliamentary majority for PASOK. PASOK held a safe even if slender majority in parliament—161 of the 300 seats. New Democracy held 126 seats, the Communist party 12, and the Eurocommunist party 1 seat. Equally important, however, PASOK did not achieve the three-fifths majority it sought, even with Communist support, to undertake a major revision of the constitution or to elect the new president.

PASOK's Foreign Policy

As in 1981, PASOK's victory resulted from the personality of Papandreou, the nationalist theme of his campaign, and the distinctive populist fervor he imparted. PASOK continued to cast itself as the party of the "little man" against the powers of privilege and status. With a strong nationalistic tone, he attacked Greece's traditional foreign enemies. Turkey was a particular focus of his verbal attack. In the past, PASOK had refused to negotiate with Turkey on various points of dispute—including Cyprus; the Ae-gean islands; air, navigational, and mineral rights in the Aegean Sea; and other important issues. The division of Cyprus into two ethnic territories and the proclamation of an independent ethnic Turkish state on the island's north side continues to be a major source of controversy. Yet Greece and Turkey are both members of NATO, a mutual defense association dominated by the United States. PASOK and its leaders have repeatedly asserted that NATO does not protect Greece from Turkey. In other words, PASOK's anti-Turkey stance has often forced it to question the nature of Greece's relationship with the United States and NATO. Under PASOK, Greece has thus asserted it was searching for more independence in its foreign relations.

PASOK's nationalism and anti-Americanism have been good for its domestic political fortunes, in both the elections of 1981 and 1985. Nevertheless, it is hard to envision any radical change in Greece's relationship with the West and the United States within NATO. One must separate the rhetoric from the reality in PASOK's rule. Papandreou criticized the Common Market in 1981 only to find Greece's membership in it very profitable. He called Turkey Greece's worst enemy and then shook hands with President Ozal in 1988. He is thus likely to continue to see Greece's interests in a manner consistent with the other Western European democracies.

PASOK's Economic Policies

The Greek economy did not perform much better during PASOK's second term than it did during the first. Growth of Greece's economy remained quite slow in comparison to that of the other southern European countries. Inflation also remained a major problem. Greece's five-year average for the annual increase in consumer prices was 19.3 percent in 1987, compared to Spain's 8.5 percent and Italy's 7.6 percent during the same period.

The Papandreou government introduced a policy of economic austerity in October 1985 to battle Greece's economic problems. The policy was continued for several years. At the beginning of the program, the government devalued the drachma by about 15 percent. Wages were frozen. And, in critical areas, the policy of indexation—allowing wage increases to match inflation—were abandoned. The government also established stricter exchange controls. The severity of this and related economic policies by the PASOK government is best revealed by the fact that the average wage increase for the five years ending in 1986 was 0.7 percent in Greece, compared to 17.4 percent in Spain, 12.6 percent in Italy, and 23.6 percent in Portugal. And this by a socialist government! Inflation, nevertheless, continued to be high. Such inflation is a political liability since welfare benefits PASOK provided have been swallowed up by the increases in prices.

Ideological and nationalist rhetoric helped PASOK win the elections of 1981 and 1985. Such rhetoric, however, cannot be reconciled with a stable economic policy that calls for strong investment and thus heavy borrowing from abroad. Papandreou had to turn his back on many political demands and insist on economic austerity while he sought credits from the international money markets. This need has come into conflict with his frequent challenges to the West and the United States. Economic planning and controls became necessary, along with post-ponement of the fulfillment of promises made to consumers.

PROSPECTS

PASOK's ideological rhetoric continues to be that of the old populist slogans of nationalism and *Allaghi* while its governmental style has generally been one of pragmatism. During its time in government, PASOK has upheld the authority of the state and met the requirements of the consolidation of the democratic regime. Its pragmatic outlook on policy and government professionalism helped qualify its nationalism, not to mention its desire to remain in power. Despite occasional bursts of rhetoric, the Papandreou government has apparently accepted Greek participation in the European Economic Community. The terms for the U.S. military bases in Greece, to be renegotiated in 1989, provide economic benefits for the country. The status quo has been maintained in Cyprus. And the Papandreou government has taken some pragmatic steps toward economic growth and modernization.

However, the Papandreou government's popularity has been low as it approaches the next general election in the summer of 1989. The prime minister's rhetoric and his governmental style has continued as in the past. However, several of his actions have drawn wide attention, often negative. These actions have occurred in the area of domestic politics, international affairs, and his personal life. Domestically, the PASOK government directly challenged the Greek church over land owned and controlled by the church. The Greek Orthodox Church is conservative, so it is not a natural political ally of the socialists. But, for some people, it is a fundamental part of traditional and populist Greek life. The PASOK government antagonized the religious segment of the Greek population with its policy that questioned the church's land holdings and the church's more general role in the country. More important politically, the PASOK government eventually lost this clash with the church in the eyes of many.

The same is true with his decision to "nationalize" all private schools. It has provoked the hostility of many middle- and upper-middle-class parents who wish to give their children the quality education that public schools no longer provide.

Internationally, Papandreou took a big, and politically risky, step in January 1988 when he met with Turkey's President Ozal to discuss their mutual problems and poor relations. This courageous diplomatic move may, in the long run, prove to be the beginning of neighborly relations with Greece's traditional enemy. However, many nationalistic Greeks—the very people PASOK has appealed to in the past—viewed this as tantamount to capitulation to Turkey. This view was held, in part, because no agenda was set, no concessions demanded for the meeting itself.

Finally, the prime minister became involved in a heavily publicized affair with an attractive, 33-year-old airline stewardess. Papandreou ultimately announced he would divorce his American wife of 37 years to marry his mistress. While not a matter of government, Papandreou's personal life has negatively affected his own and his government's popularity. This matter adds to the political questions many voters may raise about domestic, international, and economic affairs when they return to the polls in mid-1989.

THE PARLIAMENTARY ELECTION OF JUNE 18, 1989: INSTABILITY

In the last months before the parliamentary election of June 18 Papandreou attempted desperately to salvage his and PASOK's failing fortunes. Opinion polls indicated clearly that PASOK was trailing and that the election under the electoral system in force would give a majority to New Democracy. As a result the electoral law was modified by PASOK, that continued to have, despite a number of defections, a majority in the Parliament. The new law provided for greater proportionality, and made it possible for parties and candidates with more than 1 percent and less than 3 percent of the vote to receive from one to three seats. It was estimated that a party to win the majority of 151 seats (out of 300) would need about 48 percent of the national vote. The law was aimed to deny a majority to any party.

The electoral campaign during the months of March and April and the first three weeks of June was a personal campaign dealing with Papandreou's deeds and misdeeds. The opposition leader—Mitsotakis—promised a purge ("Catharsis") of those in the government that had participated in the financial scandal and the prosecution of Cabinet members and possibly the Prime Minister himself. Papandreou defended his record and appealed, as before, to Greek independence and national pride. The real issues—the state of the economy, action against terrorism, educational reform, and civil service reform were hardly touched upon. Personal politics dominated the scene—as had been the case so often in the political history of the country.

The new electoral law encouraged party fragmentation—and some 25 parties and "independent" candidates ran. The most significant change was the organization of a "leftist front," under the leadership of the Communist party, that included the splinter "Communist Party of the Interior," a number of PASOK dissidents, and a scattering of left-wing and "progressive" leaders. It became the third largest formation, after PASOK and New Democracy, and it expected to emerge as a third force arbitrating between PASOK and New Democracy, thus playing a role disproportionate to its strength.

The results of the election (Table 4–7) of June 18 reintroduced political instability—reminiscent of the years after the Greek Civil War, in the period from 1949 to 1967. New Democracy won with about 45 percent of the vote—but only 144 seats in the legisla-

TABLE 4-7 The Election of June 18, 1989

	Percentage of Vote*	Seats in Parliament (Needed majority 151)
PASOK	39%	125
Nea Democratia	44%	145
Communist-Led Coalition	13%	28
Other	4%	2
	100%	300

*Percentages rounded

ture; PASOK received 39 percent, almost ten percent less than in the election of 1985, and 125 seats compared to the 161 it held in the previous parliament. The Communist coalition was the only winner—improving its position from the previous election by about two percent of the vote but raising its strength in the legislature to 29 seats from the 13 the Communists had held. Two independents were elected and the total vote for them and all other parties did not amount to more than 3 percent. It was what the British call a "hung" parliament—one in which there was no majority to govern. Within two weeks after the election a temporary coalition was formed between the New Democracy and the Communists—much to the surprise of most commentators. The new government formed had only one objective: to deliberate and bring forth indictments against the PASOK Ministers, including Papandreou, accused of fraud. Indictments were brought forth on September 24 against four Ministers and Papandreou who are to be tried by a special court. New elections were scheduled for Nov. 5, 1989. They are to be held amidst an unprecedented—even for Greece—political turmoil. They will again pit New Democracy against PASOK, but with the position of its leader—Papandreou—in jeopardy. The Communist Party may emerge again as a broker. After almost 15 years of stability the spectre of bitter political conflicts and a political stalemate haunts again the country.

Major Events in Greece Since the Fall of the Dictatorship, 1974–1989

August 1974	Turkish forces invade Cyprus; military junta falls; Constantine Karamanlis, Andreas Papandreou, and other political leaders return from prison or abroad.
September 1974	Formation of provisional government, including many centrists, under Karamanlis; amnesty followed by imprisonment of junta leaders.
November 1974	Legislative elections for a parliament with authority to revise constitution.
December 1974	Referendum on monarchy; democracy approved by seven voters out of ten.
June 1975	Promulgation of new constitution prepared by parliament (two-thirds majority required) of Constantine Tsatsos as president of the republic; Karamanlis remains prime minister.
November 1977	New legislative elections; New Democracy maintains a narrow majority.
June 1979	Ceremonies for Greece's accession to Common Market.
June 1980	Constantine Karamanlis elected president to replace Tsatsos, whose term expires. George Rallis elected leader of New Democracy and nominated as prime minister by the president.
January 1981	Greece attains full membership in Common Market.
March–April 1981	Greece rejoins NATO.
October 18, 1981	Legislative elections. Victory of the left. PASOK—Panhellenic Socialist Movement—receives 48 percent of the vote and wins an absolute majority in Parliament: 172 out of 300 seats.
October 20, 1981	Andreas Papandreou—PASOK leader—becomes prime minister.
October 1982	Municipal elections. PASOK maintains its position, despite some losses. More than two-thirds of the townships came under PASOK/Communist control.
1983	Agreement between United States and Greece to maintain U.S. military bases for five years.
June 1984	Elections for the European Parliament. PASOK retains a slim plurality of the popular vote.

Major Events in Greece Since the Fall of the Dictatorship, 1974–1989

April 1985	With new presidential elections in sight, Karamanlis withdraws and a new president—Sartzetakis, the candidate of PASOK and the Communist party—is elected by the minimum requisite number of votes on the third and final ballot.
May 1985	The constitution is revised to deprive the president of the republic of all independent powers.
June 2, 1985	New legislative elections. PASOK maintains its majority despite some losses and continues to have an absolute majority in parliament. Papandreou remains prime minister.
September–October 1985	Austerity measures introduced.
February 1986	Constitution formally revised by the new parliament withdrawing all personal powers from the president of the republic.
June 13, 1986	Government passes law allowing abortion in first 12 weeks of pregnancy despite strong opposition from the church.
September 23, 1986	Greece and Italy sign accord to cooperate against terrorism, drug trafficking, and organized crime.
October 19, 1986	PASOK suffers significant defeats in municipal elections while New Democracy shows great strength.
April 3, 1987	Government passes law allowing takeover of most church land to give them to farm cooperatives under PASOK control.
August 18, 1987	Strong opposition from the church and its supporters force the government to revoke a decree implementing the expropriation of the church lands.
September 5, 1987	Papandreou announces that austerity measures were achieving their goals and would end.
September 17, 1987	Papandreou meets with church leader and both agree to establish a committee dealing with the problems of church/state relations.
October 1987	Reported affair of Papandreou and a 33-year-old stewardess weakens the government as his popularity fades.
October 8, 1987	Former president Constantine Tsatsos dies.
October 9, 1987	United States and Greece hold the first meeting on the future of U.S. bases in Greece.
November 3, 1987	Church and government agree on the transfer of some of the church's land to the state; seen as a victory for the church.
January 31, 1988	Papandreou and Turkish Prime Minister Ozal meet in Davos, Switzerland; promised to establish better relations and solve problems between the two nations.
July 13, 1988	Greece says it will close U.S. military bases if accords are not successfully renegotiated by the end of the year.
September 15, 1988	Ailing Papandreou announces he will divorce his American wife of 37 years and marry his mistress as PASOK's support falls well below that of New Democracy; criticism of Papandreou comes from both the right and the left.
November–December 1988	Financial scandals rock Papandreou government; a number of ministers resign as some seem implicated. Nonetheless Papandreou wins narrowly a vote of confidence in parliament (156 to 138) in which both Communists and New Democracy vote against him.
March, 1989	New electoral law introduced—enhanced proportional representation calculated to form small parties and penalize large ones
April–May 1989	Electoral campaign
June 18, 1989	Parliamentary elections. PASOK loses majority (39%) to New Democracy (44%); Communist "Front" (13%) holds balance.
September 24, 1989	Parliament brings indictments against Papandreou and four of his ministers. They are to be tried for bribery, stealing public funds, breach of faith, and (for Papandreou) wire-tapping.
November 5, 1989	New elections for Parliament.

BIBLIOGRAPHY

General

DAVIS J. *People of the Mediterranean.* London: Routledge & Kegan Paul, 1977.

DELZELL, CHARLES F., ed. *Mediterranean Fascism 1919–1945.* New York: Harper & Row, 1970.

HERZ, JOHN H., ed. *From Dictatorship to Democracy.* Westport, CT: Greenwood, 1982.

KOHLER, BEATE. *Political Forces in Spain, Greece and Portugal.* London: Butterworth Scientific, 1982.

LANGE, P., and VANNICELLI, M., eds. *The Communist Parties of Italy, France and Spain.* Cambridge, MA: Allen & Unwin, 1981.

O'DONNELL, GUILLERMO, PHILIPPE C. SCHMITTER, and LAURENCE WHITEHEAD, eds. *Transitions from Authoritarian Rule: Southern Europe.* Baltimore, MD: Johns Hopkins University Press, 1986.

PRIDHAM, GEOFFREY, ed. *The New Mediterranean Democracies: Regime Transition in Spain, Greece and Portugal.* London: Frank Cass, 1984.

TSOUKALIS, LOUKAS. *The European Community and its Mediterranean Enlargement.* London: George Allen & Unwin, 1981.

Italy

ALLUM, P. A. *Italy: Republic Without Government?* New York: W. W. Norton, 1973.

BARNES, SAMUEL H. *Representation in Italy: Institutionalized Tradition and Electoral Choice.* Chicago: University of Chicago Press, 1977.

BARZINI, LUIGI. *The Italians.* New York: Bantam Books, 1965.

DIPALMA, GUISEPPE. *Surviving Without Governing: The Italian Parties in Parliament.* Berkeley: University of California Press, 1977.

GERMINO, DANTE. *The Italian Fascist Party in Power: A Study in Totalitarian Rule.* New York: H. Fertig, 1971.

KOGAN, NORMAN. *A Political History of Italy: The Postwar Years.* New York: Praeger, 1983.

LANGE, PETER, and SIDNEY TARROW, eds. *Italy in Transition: Conflict and Consensus.* London: Frank Cass, 1980.

LAPALOMBARA, JOSEPH. *Democracy, Italian Style.* New Haven, CT: Yale University Press, 1987.

PENNIMAN, HOWARD R., ed. *Italy at the Polls: The Parliamentary Elections of 1979.* Washington, DC: American Enterprise Institute, 1981.

SASSOON, DONALD. *Contemporary Italy: Politics, Economy & Society Since 1945.* London: Longman, 1986.

SPOTTS, FREDERIC, and THEODOR WIESER. *Italy: A Difficult Democracy.* Cambridge: Cambridge University Press, 1986.

ZARISKI, RAPHAEL. *Italy: The Politics of Uneven Development.* Hinsdale, IL: Dryden, 1972.

ZUCKERMAN, ALAN S. *The Politics of Faction: Christian Democratic Rule in Italy.* New Haven, CT, and London: Yale University Press, 1979.

Portugal

BRAGA DE MACEDO, JORGE. *Portugal Since the Revolution: Economic and Political Perspectives.* Boulder, CO: Westview, 1981.

BRUNEAU, THOMAS C., and ALEX MACLEOD. *Politics in Contemporary Portugal.* Boulder, CO: Lynne Rienner, 1986.

GALLAGHER, TOM. *Portugal: A Twentieth-Century Interpretation.* Manchester: Manchester University Press, 1983.

GRAHAM, LAWRENCE S., and HARRY M. MAKLER, eds. *Contemporary Portugal: The Revolution and Its Antecedents.* Austin: University of Texas Press, 1979.

GRAHAM, LAWRENCE S., and DOUGLAS L. WHEELER, eds. *In Search of Modern Portugal: The Revolution & Its Consequences.* Madison: University of Wisconsin Press, 1983.

MAXWELL, KENNETH, ed. *Portugal in the 1980's: Dilemmas of Democratic Consolidation.* New York: Greenwood, 1986.

MORRISON, RODNEY J. *Portugal: Revolutionary Change in an Open Economy.* Boston: Auburn House, 1981.

OPELLO, WALTER C., Jr. *Portugal's Political Development.* Boulder, CO: Westview Special Studies, 1985.

PAYNE, STANLEY G. *A History of Spain and Portugal,* 2 vols. Madison: University of Wisconsin Press, 1973.

ROBINSON, R. A. H. *Contemporary Portugal.* London: Allen & Unwin, 1979.

WIARDA, HOWARD J. *Corporatism and Development: The Portuguese Experience.* Amherst: University of Massachusetts Press, 1977.

Spain

BONIME-BLANC, ANDREA. *Spain's Transition to Democracy.* Boulder, CO: Westview, 1987.

BRENAN, GERALD. *The Spanish Labyrinth: An Account of the Social and Political Background of the Spanish Civil War.* Cambridge: Cambridge University Press, 1960.

CARR, RAYMOND. *The Spanish Tragedy: The Civil War in Perspective.* London: Weidenfeld & Nicolson, 1977.

CARR, RAYMOND, and JUAN P. FUSI. *Spain: Dictatorship to Democracy.* London: Allen & Unwin, 1979.

CLARK, ROBERT P., and MICHAEL H. HALTZEL, eds. *Spain in the 1980's.* Cambridge, MA: Ballinger, 1987.

DONAGHY, PETER J., and MICHAEL T. NEWTON. *Spain: A Guide to Political and Economic Institutions.* Cambridge: Cambridge University Press, 1987.

GRAHAM, ROBERT. *Spain: Change of a Nation.* London: Michael Joseph, 1984.

GUNTHER, RICHARD, GIACOMO SANI, and GOLDIE SHADAD. *Spain After Franco: The Making of a Competitive Party System.* Berkeley: University of California Press, 1988.

LANCASTER, THOMAS D., and GARY PREVOST, eds. *Politics and Change in Spain.* New York: Praeger, 1985.

MARVALL, JOSÉ. *The Transition to Democracy in Spain.* New York: St. Martin's, 1982.

MUJAL-LEON, EUSEBIO. *Communism and Political Change in Spain.* Bloomington: Indiana University Press, 1983.

PAYNE, STANLEY G., ed. *The Politics of Democratic Spain.* Chicago: The Chicago Council on Foreign Relations, 1986.

PENNIMAN, HOWARD R., and EUSEBIO M. MUJAL-LEÓN, eds. *Spain at the Polls, 1977, 1979, and 1982.* Durham, NC: Duke University Press & AEI, 1985.

PRESTON, PAUL. *The Triumph of Democracy in Spain.* London: Methuen, 1986.

SHARE, DONALD. *The Making of Spanish Democracy.* New York: Praeger, 1986.

THOMAS, HUGH. *The Spanish Civil War,* rev. ed. New York: Harper & Row, 1977.

Greece

CAMPBELL, J. S., and P. SHERRARD. *Modern Greece.* New York: Praeger, 1968.

CLOGG, RICHARD. *A Short History of Modern Greece.* 2nd ed. Cambridge: Cambridge University Press, 1986.

CLOGG, RICHARD. *Parties and Elections in Greece.* Durham, NC: Duke University Press, 1987.

CLOGG, RICHARD, and G. YANNOPOULOS. *Greece Under Military Rule.* New York: Basic Books, 1972.

DAKIN, D. *The Unification of Greece 1870–1923.* New York: St. Martin's, 1972.

FEATHERSTONE, KEVIN, and DIMITRIOS K. KATSOUDAS, eds. *Political Change in Greece: Before and After the Colonels.* London: Croom Helm, 1987.

LEGG, KEITH R. *Politics in Modern Greece.* Stanford, CA: Stanford University Press, 1969.

MACRIDIS, ROY C. *Greek Politics at the Crossroads: What Kind of Socialism?* Stanford, CA: Hoover Institution Press, 1981.

PENNIMAN, HOWARD R., ed. *Greece at the Polls: The National Elections of 1974 and 1977.* Washington, DC: American Enterprise Institute, 1981.

TZANNATOS, ZAFIRIS, ed. *Socialism in Greece.* Hants, England: Gower, 1986.

VATIKIOTIS, P. J. *Greece: A Political Essay.* Beverly Hills, CA: Sage, 1974.

FRANCIS G. CASTLES AND DIANE SAINSBURY

1

The Nature
of Scandinavian Democracy

Culturally, and to some extent linguistically, it is possible to identify a Nordic area comprising Iceland, Finland, Denmark, Norway, and Sweden. In territorial terms, however, the last three countries constitute a more defined Scandinavian region, whose closely interrelated historical development has resulted in a distinctive modern political structure and culture. Consequently, we concentrate on politics in Denmark, Norway, and Sweden and discuss the other Nordic countries only to the extent that they illuminate our understanding of the Scandinavian phenomenon.

The contrast between Scandinavia and much of the rest of Europe is dramatic. Whereas the Mediterranean region and the majority of the larger European nation-states have experienced considerable governmental and regime instability, Scandinavia has had long periods of governmental stability, stable institutional structures, and long-established democratic procedures un-

threatened by the dangers of internal military or totalitarian takeover. There are differences, too, in Scandinavia's economic growth, types of social structures, the nature of policy outcomes, and the overall character of the democratic form which has emerged in the process of historical development.

On the one hand, much of Europe is still experiencing, or bears the political scars inflicted by, a process of uneven economic development. There has been an alternation between poles of policy management designed to favor either a tiny elite of the wealthy or the vast mass of the impoverished. The Scandinavian countries have achieved an almost completely peaceful transition to economic and social modernity and have in recent decades become the exemplars of social-welfare policies, a push toward social and economic quality and moderate reform. Moreover, that reformism is not just a matter of the policy content of democracy. It has become a part of the fabric of the democratic process itself and has led to a style of politics which emphasizes the right to and the desirability of popular participation to a degree, arguably, greater than in any other countries.

Contrasts as great as these make Scandinavian politics an area of considerable interest. In particular, they offer us the opportunity to explore the basic nature of democratic political stability and to examine a variant of democratic practice rather unfamiliar to those of us brought up to take the Anglo-American model as the norm of democratic behavior. By exploring the economic, social, and political circumstances associated with political stability in Scandinavia, we can acquire a picture of the total configuration that lends endurance to democratic political institutions. Such a picture is valuable for both scientific and practical reasons. From a scientific point of view, it enhances our knowledge of the causes and correlates of political stability. From a practical point of view, it may suggest lessons for those who would preserve political democracy. By examining a policy profile which emphasizes the need to create greater equality and a policy process which emphasizes democratic participation as something more than the formal right to vote, we can learn other lessons. In particular, it can help us to appreciate that democracy is compatible with a wide range of policy options and very different institutional practices. In the process, it can help us to be less insular about our own democracy and even possibly to think of ways of making it better.

Those who look at Scandinavian politics with these considerations in mind should remember three important points. The first is that the three countries are by no means identical. Here our concern is to stress the political similarities of the Scandinavian region, but each of its countries exhibits unique characteristics that may also be relevant to its political life. The second point is that politics change over time. Our interest is in contemporary Scandinavia and the historical and cultural forces that have shaped

its politics, but, as we shall show, the Scandinavian scene is itself changing. In particular, the once assured dominance of moderate democratic socialism is no longer as certain as it was in the immediate postwar decades. Finally, in drawing up a list of the characteristics of democratic stability and participatory democracy in Scandinavia, we should not imagine that we have uncovered the causes of those phenomena. The comparative method demands that we find a single circumstance that differentiates between different phenomena,[1] but Scandinavian politics and society differ so greatly from those of much of the rest of Europe that this is virtually impossible. Naturally, in what follows, arguments will be presented to show the importance of some factors rather than others, but the conclusions about Scandinavian political stability and democratic participation are by no means necessarily the same thing as conclusions about democratic stability and participatory democracy as such.

CONTINUITY AND CHANGE

A discussion of political stability involves substantial definitional problems. Most commentators would agree that the criterion distinguishing between stability and instability is the extent of change. But the crucial questions are what sort of change and how much change. As we saw in Part V of this book, the Mediterranean countries are generally unstable, but in many respects the Scandinavian nations have undergone far greater change during the last century than have those of southern Europe. This is clearly the case in reard to economic and social structure. In the middle of the nineteenth century, none of the Scandinavian countries had really begun industrialization. They were near-subsistence economies in which the peasantry composed the mass of the popula-

---

[1] J. S. Mill, *A System of Logic* (London: Longmans, 1967), p. 255.

TABLE 1-1   Basic Statistics, 1986

Country	Production (GDP per capita)	Agriculture	Employment Industry	Services
United States	$17,324	3.1%	27.7%	69.3%
Denmark	16,130	5.9	28.2	65.9
Finland	14,326	11.0	32.0	57.0
Iceland	15,984	10.3	36.7	53.0
Norway	16,746	7.2	26.7	66.1
Sweden	15,661	4.2	30.1	65.6
United Kingdom	9,651	2.5	30.9	66.6
West Germany	14,611	5.3	40.9	53.7
France	13,077	7.3	31.3	61.3
Greece	3,987	28.5	28.1	43.4
Spain	5,925	16.1	32.0	51.8
Portugal	2,984	21.7	34.8	43.5

Source: *OECD Historical Statistics, 1960–86*, Paris, 1988.

tion. Toward the end of that century the comparison between Scandinavia on the one side and Britain, France, and Germany on the other was one between poverty and the beginnings of affluence based on industrial might. Sweden, today among the richest countries of Western Europe, was then described as "Europe's fortress poorhouse." The data in Table 1–1 illustrate the extent of the changes that have taken place in Scandinavia and the other Nordic countries, the extent to which they have caught up with the major countries of Western Europe, and the contrast with the Mediterranean area.

The nature of the changes in Scandinavia is demonstrated not only by high average incomes (gross national product per capita) but also by a drastically altered employment structure in which agriculture has ceased to be the predominant sector. The tertiary or service economy has outstripped industrial production. Certainly, then, we cannot equate stability with an absence of economic and social change. Indeed, in the case of Scandinavia at least, one of the central problems in discussing the nature of political stability is the question of how such dramatic and rapid change can have occurred without a major disruption of political life.

Lipset has argued that affluence is related to political stability, but both he and Olson have also argued that rapid economic growth

is a destabilizing force.[2] By changing the established patterns of economic expectations and tearing individuals from their traditional social and territorial surroundings, rapid growth becomes a source of discontent and protest that can easily lead to the disruption of the political structure. Yet this did not happen in Scandinavia. Sweden, with Europe's highest sustained growth rate over the last hundred years, is possibly its most stable polity. Why that should have been so is one of the crucial issues we tackle in the coming pages.

But if stability cannot simply be seen in terms of economic and social change, it cannot simply be equated with an absence of political change. Within the space of a century, all the Scandinavian countries have been transformed from conservative oligarchies into democratic political systems in which working-class parties play a major role, and in which welfare-state policies have in many respects been developed further than in other advanced nations. In the past half-century, the strong Social Democratic parties of Sweden, Norway, and Denmark have been associated with policy innovations designed to achieve a greater level of egalitarianism in

---

[2] S. M. Lipset, *Political Man* (London: Mercury, 1963); M. Olson, Jr., "Rapid Growth as a Destabilizing Force," *Journal of Economic History*, Vol. 23 (1963).

society in levels of welfare and income distribution, and more recently in terms of power in industry. Moreover, as we shall see shortly, these changes have been allied with others in the character of political participation. From conservative oligarchy to the beginnings of industrial democracy, to what is almost certainly the most influential interest group politics in the world and to the highest level of female legislative participation in the Western world are mighty changes in the course of less than a century. Again, in terms of both policy and participation we might be tempted to argue that it was Scandinavia that had undergone a major transformation and the Mediterranean countries that had stayed the same.

But in one respect at least, Denmark, Norway, and Sweden have changed far less than the countries of southern Europe. In the same period of a century in which economic, social, and policy change was so rapid, the pattern of institutional arrangements through which political issues are decided has remained remarkably constant. Constitutions and practices of government have been gradually modified to meet new conditions, and in particular to allow broader popular participation, but there is an essential continuity. We may argue if we wish that in each of the Scandinavian countries there has been one change of regime—from oligarchic to democratic. But it may be more instructive to view even that change as a modification rather than a transformation of existing institutions. For the adoption of democratic practices, which came about in the late nineteenth and early twentieth centuries, was largely the result of a series of accommodations between the traditional ruling elite and the new classes clamoring for participation. It came about neither through coup nor through revolution, but through the gradual, though sometimes grudging, acknowledgement by these two groups that they could preserve more of the existing system by making concessions than by fighting for privileges. Thus our assertion that Scandinavia is politically stable is essentially about the form of government rather than

its content. Policies and personnel may change, but they remain stable in the sense that political institutions show "a capacity to endure without great or important changes in pattern."[3]

One final point that is vital to any discussion of political stability is the need to distinguish between regime stability and governmental stability. A democratic regime remains such despite frequent changes of government so long as governmental change is effected by due democratic process. Governmental stability means that a particular party or coalition of parties stays in office for long periods. What was said in the previous paragraph refers to the stability of democratic regimes in Scandinavia this century. In addition, it is also true that for a period from the 1930s to the 1970s Social Democratic Party governmental stability was the Scandinavian norm, and one important question we shall attempt to answer is the extent to which Scandinavia's distinctive policies and participatory democracy are a function of that governmental stability of a democratic socialist variety. Since the 1970s, Social Democratic political dominance has been less obvious, with conservative and center parties in office for various periods in all three countries. That could have implications for the future course of policy and participation in Scandinavia. What it does not mean is that Scandinavia has suddenly begun to experience instability of its *democratic regimes*.

THE MEANING OF DEMOCRATIC PARTICIPATION

It is not just political stability that requires definition. Democratic participation also covers a spectrum of meanings. At a minimum level, we usually take it to imply the existence of "a representative government elected by an electorate consisting of the entire adult population, whose votes carry

---

[3] H. Eckstein, *Divisions and Cohesions in Democracy* (Princeton, NJ: Princeton University Press, 1966), p. 227.

TABLE 1-2 Measures of Democratic Participation—Mid- to Late 1980s

Country	Voter Turnout (various dates in 1980s)	Female Legislators 1988	Trade Union Density 1985	Government Expenditure 1986
United States	55%	5.3%	15.7%	36.9%
Denmark	87.,5	29.0	78.2	55.4
Finland	75.0	31.5	n.a.	42.3
Iceland	89.3	20.6	n.a.	36.6
Norway	83.9	35.0	65.1	52.0
Sweden	86.0	38.0	87.7	63.5
United Kingdom	76.3	6.3	43.3	46.2
West Germany	87.7	16.0	36.7	46.6
France	74.7	5.4	19.3	52.4
Greece	83.1	2.7	35.5	42.8
Spain	69.3	6.4	21.0	42.2
Portugal	77.4	7.6	n.a.	43.9

Sources: Total government expenditure as a percentage of GDP from OECD, *Historical Statistics 1960–86*, Paris. Other information from various reference texts and embassies.

equal weight and who are allowed to vote for any opinion without intimidation by the state apparatus."[4] In that sense, all the countries covered in this volume, bar those of the Soviet bloc, are characterized by democratic participation, although in the case of several of the Mediterranean countries the right to such participation is newly won.

But participation can carry additional meanings. First, it may refer not merely to the existence of democratic rights, but also to their actualization. The questions then become not ones of who has the right to vote and has the right to be a representative, but of how many people actually do vote and who actually are the representatives. For instance, we can, as in Table 1–2, look at the differential voter turnout of democratic nations or the extent to which women are represented in their legislature.

In both respects, it will immediately be noted that Scandinavia scores very high compared with most democratic nations, and the contrast between the levels of female legislative representation in Scandinavia and the Anglo-Saxon countries is particularly dramatic. That participation can imply a real change in the locus of political

power may be seen from the fact that nearly 40 percent of the Norwegian social democratic cabinet is female including the prime minister, Gro Harlem Brundtland.

Second, democratic participation may refer to the range of channels through which individuals may participate in decision making. As we shall see, organized opinion can influence policy not merely through the vote, but also through pressure group activity. Pressure groups are exceptionally strong in Scandinavia, as is dramatically illustrated by the figures for trade union membership, also provided in Table 1–2.

Third, participation may be fostered or hindered by the character of the institutional arrangements through which electoral or organized opinion may be exerted. We shall note at many points the exceptional extent to which the Scandinavian polities have encouraged the development of arrangements allowing the widest possible accommodation and incorporation of diverse sectional opinion. In Chapter 3 we use the term "corporate pluralism" to describe these arrangements. Terms like "societal bargaining" or "corporatism" have been used by other writers to denote much the same phenomenon.

Finally, the degree of participation may refer to the arenas in which popular representation or control is possible. One, possi-

---

[4] G. Therborn, "The Rule of Capital and the Rise of Democracy," *New Left Review* (May–June 1977), p. 4.

bly contestable, measure of that is the extent to which the government controls the economy, measured in Table 1–2 by government expenditure as a percentage of gross domestic product. Scandinavia comes out very high on that measure, and it is also in these countries that the greatest effort has been made to democratize industry and the economy by insisting that wage earners have a right to a say in the way firms are run and a share in their profits. To many Americans or British this broadening of the areas of popular control is the very antithesis of democracy—it takes away rights deriving from private ownership. However, the very fact that many Scandinavians do not see things in that light both illustrates the variety of meanings that may be attached to the notion of participatory democracy and makes it particularly interesting to understand how the nations of Scandinavia came to adopt their particularly distinctive democratic institutions.

Sweden: Major Political Events Since 1945

June 1945	National coalition replaced by a Social Democratic government.
November 1946	Sweden joins the United Nations.
1947–48	Adoption of several major social reforms: universal flat-rate old-age pensions, general child allowance, housing subsidies and allowances. Tax reform introducing steeper taxes on inheritances, wealth, and high incomes.
September 1948	*Riksdag* elections. Despite losses, Social Democrats retain office.
1950	Introduction of nine-year comprehensive school on trial basis. Death of King Gustaf V. Gustaf VI Adolf ascends the throne.
October 1951	Formation of Social Democratic–Agrarian government headed by Erlander.
September 1952	*Riksdag* elections. Social Democratic and Agrarian losses.
1955	National health insurance. Reimbursement for medical fees, sickness benefits as a percentage of earnings, and universal flat-rate maternity allowance.
September 1956	*Riksdag* elections. Continued losses for the governing parties.
October 1957	Referendum on proposed supplementary pension reform produces government crisis. Social Democratic minority government under Erlander.
June 1958	Extra election called because of pension issue. Results in equal number of seats for socialist and centrist bourgeois blocs.
May 1959	Supplementary pension scheme adopted by centrists (115 against 114) when a Liberal MP decides to abstain.
September 1960	*Riksdag* elections with the pension reform as a major issue. Social Democratic gains and Conservative losses.
1962	Parliamentary decision to adopt the comprehensive school on a permanent basis.
September 1964	*Riksdag* elections. Negligible losses by Social Democrats and Communist gains.
May 1967	Communists change their name to the Left Party–Communists and adopt a new program. Dissident factions leave the party.
September 1968	*Riksdag* elections. Social Democrats win an absolute majority.
1969	Adoption of parliamentary reform introducing a unicameral *Riksdag*.
Autumn 1969	Olof Palme succeeds Erlander as prime minister.
1970	Tax reform introducing individual taxation irrespective of sex and marital status.
September 1970	*Riksdag* elections. Despite losses Social Democrats maintain a majority.
1973	Death of Gustaf VI Adolf. Succeed by Carl XVI Gustaf.
September 1973	*Riksdag* elections result in a "tie" parliament. The Palme Social Democrat government remains in office.
1974	Adoption of new constitution. Parental benefit for either parent replaces maternity allowance. Improvement of sickness benefits (90 percent compensation for earnings). Introduction of national dental insurance.
1975	Revision of Social Democratic party program putting greater emphasis on economic democracy and employee ownership.
1976	Passage of the Co-determination Act which enhances employee and union influence.
September 1976	*Riksdag* elections. Bourgeois majority ends Social Democrats' 44 years in power. Bourgeois coalition Thorbjörn Fälldin, center, prime minister.

1978	Work environment legislation strengthening role of unions.
Autumn 1978	Dissension over nuclear energy issue leads to the fall of the bourgeois government. Liberals form a minority government headed by Ola Ullsten.
September 1979	*Riksdag* elections. Bourgeois majority (175/176). New bourgeois coalition under Fälldin.
1980	Public spending reaches around 60 percent of the GNP.
March 1980	Referendum on nuclear energy. Majority for operation of nuclear plants until 2010.
April–May 1981	Breakup of the bourgeois coalition on taxation issue. Center and Liberals form a new government.
September 1981	Founding of the Greens.
September 1982	*Riksdag* elections. Social Democrats return to power. Olof Palme prime minister.
September 1985	*Riksdag* elections. Social Democratic losses but socialist majority.
February 1986	Assassination of Olof Palme. Ingvar Carlsson prime minister.
September 1988	*Riksdag* elections. Greens elected to parliament but socialist bloc retains a majority of seats in parliament.

Norway: Major Political Events Since 1945

May 1945	Liberation of Norway.
	All parties endorse the Joint Program for the Reconstruction of Norway entailing strict price controls, economic and regional planning, state ownership of a limited number of key industrial enterprises, and long-range commitment to social reforms.
October 1945	*Storting* elections. Social Democratic majority for the first time (76/74). Einar Gerhardsen prime minister.
1946	Introduction of general child allowance for the second child and all consecutive children.
1949	Norway joins NATO.
October 1949	*Storting* elections. Major gains for Social Democrats (85/65).
January 1951	Gerhardsen resigns. Oscar Torp prime minister.
1952	New electoral law decreasing the overrepresentation of large parties.
October 1953	*Storting* elections. Social Democratic majority.
1954	Reorientation in economic policy: relaxation of controls and more reliance on market forces.
	Comprehensive schools introduced on trial basis.
January 1955	Torp resigns, Gerhardsen returns as prime minister.
1956	Introduction of universal flat-rate old-age pensions.
1957	Adoption of national health insurance.
October 1957	*Storting* elections. Social Democratic gains.
	Death of King Haakon VII. Olav V ascends the throne.
Spring 1961	Splinter group in the Social Democratic party, opposed to NATO, forms the Socialist People's party.
September 1961	*Storting* elections. Social Democrats (74), bourgeois parties (74), and Socialist People's party (2).
August–September 1963	Kings Bay mining accident brings down Gerhardsen's government. Replaced by bourgeois coalition which lasts four weeks. Gerhardsen forms new government.
September 1965	*Storting* elections. Bourgeois majority (80/70) results in a four-party coalition government headed by Per Borten, Center.
1966	Introduction of supplementary pensions and consolidation of various public pension schemes.
1968	Discovery of North Sea oil.
1969	Legislation to make comprehensive schools permanent.
September 1969	*Storting* elections. Bourgeois parties retain a bare majority (76/74).
1970	Introduction of general child allowance for the first child.
March 1971	Bourgeois government falls because of indiscretions concerning negotiations for EEC membership. Replaced by Social Democratic minority government under Trygve Bratteli.
1971	Incorporation of health, unemployment, and occupational injury insurance into the National Insurance Scheme.
1972	Legislation to increase employee influence through the "company assembly" and representatives on company boards.

Norway: Major Political Events Since 1945

September 1972	EEC referendum with 53.3 percent against membership. Bratteli resigns and a "mini" coalition formed, consisting of the Christian People's party, Center and anti–EEC Liberals.
Spring 1973	Formation of the Socialist Electoral Alliance consisting of Communists, the Socialist People's Party and anti–EEC Social Democrats. Anders Lange's party—an antitax party—is founded.
September 1973	*Storting* elections. Major defeat for the Social Democrats but a socialist majority (78/77). A new Social Democratic government under Bratteli.
March 1975	Sections of the Socialist electoral alliance establish a new party—the Socialist Left party.
January 1976	Odvar Nordli prime minister.
September 1977	*Storting* elections. Social Democrats recoup most of their losses.
1978	Improvement of sickness benefit (100 percent compensation of earnings).
February 1981	Gro Harlem Brundtland replaces Nordli as prime minister—first woman prime minister in the Scandinavian countries.
September 1981	*Storting* elections. Gains by Conservatives who form a minority government. Kåre Willoch prime minister.
June 1983	Conservatives broaden government to include the Center and Christian People's parties.
September 1985	*Storting* elections. Socialist parties (77), governing parties (78), and Progress party (2). Governing parties retain office.
April 1986	Bourgeois coalition replaced by Social Democrats with Brundtland as prime minister.
September 1987	Local elections. Progress party jumps to more than 10 percent.
May 1988	Major reform of the electoral system, introducing a 4 percent threshold and 8 seats at large to achieve greater proportionality.
Summer 1989	Highest rate of unemployment (4%) since the end of World War II.
September 1989	***Editor's Note:*** Storting election provides unprecedented changes. The Right Wing Progress party (anti-tax, free enterprise, and favoring stringent controls on immigrant workers) increases its strength from 2 to 22 seats with 22 percent of the vote; the farther left Socialist People's party increases its strength from 6 to 17 seats with more than 12 percent of the vote; the Social Democrats (the Labor party) falls from 41 percent to 34 percent and from 71 seats to 63; the Conservatives fall to about 22 percent of the vote with 37 seats; the combined "bourgeois" parties hold 84 seats, and the socialist parties, 81 seats.

Denmark: Major Political Events Since 1945

May 1945	Liberation of Denmark.
October 1945	Major gains for Communists and heavy losses for Social Democrats. Liberals form a minority government. Knud Kristensen prime minister.
1947	Death of King Christian X. Frederick IX ascends the throne.
October 1947	Vote of no confidence against prime minister because of statements on the Schleswig question. New elections result in Social Democratic wins. Hans Hedtoft prime minister.
1949	Denmark joins NATO.
Autumn 1950	*Folketing* elections. Major changes in strength of Conservatives and Liberals. Resignation of the Social Democratic government. Liberal-Conservative coalition under Erik Eriksen, Liberal.
June 1953	New constitution that abolishes the upper chamber and broadens the use of a mandatory referendum.
September 1953	*Folketing* elections. Social Democratic–Radical majority. Social Democrats form a minority government.
February 1955	Death of prime minister Hedtoft. H. C. Hansen prime minister.
1956	Introduction of universal flat-rate old-age pensions with means-tested supplement.
1957	Denmark and Norway refuse to accept the presence of NATO nuclear weapons on their territory.
May 1957	*Folketing* elections. Formation of a coalition government of Social Democrats, Radicals, and Justice party.
February 1959	The Socialist People's party is founded.

1960	Health insurance reform to provide universal coverage.
November 1960	*Folketing* elections. A coalition of Social Democrats and Radicals formed under Viggo Kampmann.
1961	New public assistance act eliminating concept of the "undeserving poor."
August 1962	Kampmann resigns. Jens Otto Krag prime minister.
September 1964	*Folketing* elections. Resignation of Social Democrat–Radical cabinet. Krag forms a Social Democratic minority government.
1964	Pension reform increasing the amount of the pension and eliminating the means-tested supplement.
November 1966	*Folketing* elections. Socialist majority in *Folketing* for first time. Socialist People's party supports Social Democratic government, popularly known as the "Red Cabinet."
1967	Introduction of general child allowance and flat-rate maternity allowance. Unemployment benefit raised to 90 percent of previous earnings.
January 1968	Split in Socialist People's party over cooperation with Social Democrats. Formation of the Left Socialist party.
	Folketing elections. Losses for socialist bloc. Bourgeois majority coalition government. Hilmer Baunsgaard, Radical, prime minister.
September 1971	*Folketing* elections. Nearly even split between the socialist and bourgeois parties. Social Democratic minority government.
Autumn 1972	The Progress party founded by Mogens Glistrup.
1972	Improvement of sickness benefit.
	Compulsory education extended from seven to nine years.
	Legislation for employee representatives on company boards.
	Death of Frederick IX. Margaret II ascends the throne.
October 1972	EEC Referendum, 63 percent for membership. The next day prime minister Krag unexpectedly resigns. Succeeded by Anker Jørgensen.
1973	Legislation for employee representatives on company boards.
November–December 1973	Split in Social Democratic party and formation of Center Democrats leads to the fall of Jørgensen's government. "Protest election" doubling the number of parties in the *Folketing*. Liberals, under Poul Hartling, form a minority government.
January 1975	*Folketing* elections. Sizable gains for Social Democrats and Liberals. Social Democrats form a minority government. Anker Jørgensen prime minister.
1975	Comprehensive school reform adopted.
February 1977	*Folketing* elections. Main victor Social Democrats whose polling strength returns to its 1971 level.
August 1978	Social Democrats form a coalition with the Liberals.
Autumn 1979	Coalition collapses over incomes policy. New elections result in socialist bloc gains. Jørgensen forms a new Social Democratic government but relies on support from the center parties.
December 1981	*Folketing* elections. Gains by the Socialist People's party and Center Democrats. Social Democratic losses but the party stays in office.
September 1982	Jørgensen government resigns. Bourgeois government composed of Conservatives, Liberals, Christian People's party and Center Democrats. Poul Schlüter, Conservative, prime minister.
January 1984	*Folketing* elections. Conservative advances. Governing parties, together with the Radicals, command a majority.
January–February 1986	*Folketing* majority (Socialist bloc + Radicals) refuse to support the EEC reform package. The government calls for a referendum to decide the issue. A majority of 56 percent votes for the reform package.
September 1987	*Folketing* elections. Despite losses for the governing parties and the withdrawal of Radical support, the Schlüter government stays on. Jørgensen resigns as Social Democratic leader. His successor is Svend Auken.
Spring 1988	*Folketing* majority votes to require NATO vessels in Danish ports to state if nuclear weapons on board. New elections. Rightward shift in the electorate resulting in gains for Progress party and losses for the Conservatives. The Radicals join in a coalition government with the Conservatives and Liberals. Schlüter continues as prime minister.

2

Political Development and Political Culture

To understand the workings of any contemporary political system, we need to do more than describe the nature of contemporary political behavior and the operation of political institutions. Both behavior and institutions are set in an historical and attitudinal context that conditions their performance. We cannot study politics without understanding the historical forces that have determined the shape of institutions and the issues of political debate. Similarly, an understanding of why people act in one way rather than another can come only through a knowledge of individuals' beliefs and attitudes about political action. In every society there are different conceptions about the nature of politics, and the level and type of political participation that is acceptable.

Moreover, although the effects of political development may be apparent in the form institutions take, political culture is often the agency through which historical

events influence political life. This can easily be illustrated for France, where the events of 1789 are perpetuated in a revolutionary tradition that can still lead to direct intervention in politics. In Scandinavia, a long series of political conflicts settled by compromise and rational debate has resulted in the "habituation" of this mechanism of conflict resolution. Thus, our first step toward an understanding of both regime stability and the character of participatory democracy will be to examine the traditional structures of the Scandinavian polities, the manner in which they coped with two great crises of development (industrialization and democratization), and the extent to which both are reflected in contemporary political attitudes and beliefs.

Rather than describing the separate historical development of the three Scandinavian countries, we intend to locate the significant ways in which their traditional political structures varied from the European norm. What is significant is by no means always a consequence of identical development. Much that we now think of as distinctively Scandinavian is a consequence of the spread of customs, ideas, and institutions through complicated dynastic struggles that ended only in this century with Norway's independence from Sweden in 1905 and Finland's independence from Russia in 1917.

One characteristic all Scandinavian countries have in common is a predemocratic political structure based on the exercise of group authority within the peasant community. This reached its highest constitutional expression in the "republic" set up in 930 A.D. by a number of farmers who had migrated from Norway to Iceland. They created the *Althing*, the world's oldest parliament, in which supreme lawmaking and judicial control was vested. Throughout Scandinavia the local organ of peasant self-government in the tenth to twelfth centuries was the *ting*, or assembly, consisting of those heads of families who were free men; their functions included the regulation of community life and the administration of justice. From the thirteenth century onward, the *ting* went into decline as a consequence of rivalries between the aristocracy and the monarchy. But these very rivalries prevented the emergence of feudalism in Norway and Sweden, although not in Denmark.

In Sweden, the balance between monarchy and aristocracy was so close as to lead to a series of constitutional developments such that Sweden was, apart from Britain, the only European country to enter the modern era with a living predemocratic political tradition. The Swedish equivalent of Magna Charta was Magnus Ericsson's *landslag* of 1350, which restricted the king's powers and declared that the monarchy must be elective and the king must swear to carry out certain obligations. The nobility was also instrumental in the calling of the first *Riksdags*, or parliaments, to express their grievances against the crown. By the seventeenth century, what had been an occasional assembly of peers

and commoners had become an institutionalized and constitutionally regulated assembly of the realm.

On the other side, the monarchy frequently intervened to protect his own prerogatives. When in the seventeenth century the nobility managed to exert its influence to the extent that peasant freeholding was fast disappearing, Charles XI decreed the Great Reduction (1680), by which the crown resumed alienated crown land. At one stroke he diminished aristocratic power and removed the danger to peasant ownership.

The alternation between royal and aristocratic dominance was so frequent that neither was able to exert absolute control over the peasantry, which consequently preserved something of its previous influence. Indeed, the need to enlist the peasantry on one side or the other meant that the peasantry was integrated into the political structure in a way that occurred nowhere else in Europe. Only in Sweden did the peasantry play an institutionalized role in a parliament that constitutionally required the assent of all four groups in society (aristocracy, clergy, bourgeoisie, peasantry) to alter its basis of representation. Along with political influence went a degree of economic independence. After the Great Reduction, peasant freeholding gradually increased until by the early nineteenth century, it covered more than 50 percent of the land.

Thus, when Scandinavia emerged into its era of modern constitution building, it was with a heritage of predemocratic peasant political institutions, some tradition of constitutional barriers against absolute authority, and, in Sweden, a strong constitutional structure with a substantial measure of representation for the peasantry. A case can be made that the antecedents of a participatory political culture in Scandinavia—and particularly in Sweden—had a firmer historical foundation than almost anywhere else in Europe. In the brief period between the end of Danish rule and the union with Sweden, Norway adopted in 1814 what was among the most liberal constitutions of its time. It recognized, on the American model, the principles of popular sovereignty and political equality, offering the vote to a substantial part of the adult male population (mostly peasant landholders). Operating in the context of the union with Sweden, it was to be seven decades before the provisions implying parliamentary sovereignty over government could become a reality, but nonetheless it offered an institutionalized platform for pressing such demands.

In Denmark, it was only at the end of the eighteenth century that the system of feudalism was finally abolished and the number of independent farmers started to increase. Yet the June Constitution of 1849 included a lower house selected by direct election and balanced only partially by an indirectly elected upper house. A constitutional amendment of 1866 attempted to strengthen the latter in the hope that a coalition of farmers would ensure political stability. Instead it only guaranteed the radicalization of the conflict between a majority in the lower house demanding parliamentary sovereignty and an upper house dominated by the aristocracy and the bureaucracy.

It was in fact Sweden, which had the most vital constitutional tradition, that lagged farthest behind in the creation of a modern representative assembly. A new constitution was promulgated in 1809, but it was still based on the four estates. It was not until 1866 that Sweden adopted a two-chamber parliamentary assembly. The second chamber largely represented independent farmers and had effective veto power, whereas the first chamber, composed of aristocracy and new urban magnates, had the power to initiate policy. Such a lag was exactly consonant with Swedish constitutional arrangements, since the peasantry had already obtained an established role in the system of government. Changes in the system were a question not so much of opposition to the status quo as of mutual accommodation and compromise. Thus, by the seventh decade of the nineteenth century the Scandinavian states had abandoned their traditional political structures and introduced representative assemblies.

INDUSTRIALIZATION AND DEMOCRATIZATION

Although the pace of democratic evolution in the first half of the nineteenth century varied somewhat in the Scandinavian countries, in none of them was it very rapid. This was because the impact of industrialization was experienced later than in Britain and much of the rest of Continental Europe. But although industrialization came late, it came with extreme rapidity and potentially disastrous consequences for the maintenance of political stability.

Even at its most gradual, industrialization must be seen as a major instrument of social and political transformation. Not only does it destroy the traditional village way of life, it brings individuals into a new and unfamiliar urban setting and subjects them to the artificial rhythms of the factory environment. Moreover, although industry increases the overall product of society, it may well create, particularly in its early stages, a small class of wealthy entrepreneurs whose ability to accumulate capital is bought at the cost of the impoverishment of the vast majority.

Perhaps even more important than the physical changes brought by industrialization is the extent of social mobilization and the demands for enhanced participation that accompanies it. Social mobilization denotes the phenomenon by which individuals who did not previously participate in politics are enabled to seek remedy through explicit political action. Early in the industrialization process the two major sources of social mobilization are to be found in the spread of literacy and increased urbanization. Literacy creates a greater ability to express political protest. Urbanization simultaneously causes protest because of poor living conditions and facilitates its expression by creating an environment in which riots and demonstrations can become a natural channel of political activity.

In discussing the process of industrialization in Scandinavia, however, we encounter a crucial paradox of political development. Extremely rapid economic development was accompanied by a wholesale democratic transformation without any dramatic change in the structure of political institutions and without any mass violence. A comparison of the rate of industrial change as measured by the growth of per capita production in the major European countries (Table 2–1) demonstrates the speed of industrial development in Scandinavia, and particularly the extent to which the Swedish rate exceeded that of the larger and earlier industrializing nations. During the first 50 years of this economic transformation each of the Scandinavian countries experienced the growth of Liberal parties, whose major policy platform was the extension of the suffrage and the introduction of true parliamentarianism—that is, the responsibility of the government of the day to popular sovereignty expressed through a majority in the lower chamber of parliament.

Moreover, it was not to be much later that these parties' demands were reinforced by the development of working-class–based Social Democratic parties to whom parliamentary democracy was merely a first step to the radical transformation of society. Norway, with its theoretically more liberal constitution, was the first to establish parliamentarianism, in 1884. Denmark followed in 1901, when the virtual elimination of Conservative representation in the lower house made impossible the continuation of a system in which the government ruled by the assent of king and upper house alone. Sweden was the last to change, but when it did the political transformation reflected the rapidity of economic growth. Indeed, as one commentator notes, the pace of change was so rapid that the first Social Democratic government was formed in Sweden in 1920, even though neither the Liberal nor the Social Democratic party had been represented in the *Riksdag* 25 years before. Moreover, although in these decades the pace of political change was faster than elsewhere in Europe, it occurred in Sweden without bloodshed.

A clue to the Scandinavian paradox of

TABLE 2–1 Rate of Industrial Change

Country	Length of Period (years)	Rate of Increase per Decade (Percentage)		
		GNP	Population	GNP per Capita
Great Britain 1855–60 to 1957–59	101	21.1%	6.1%	14.1%
France 1841–50 to 1960–62	105.5	20.8	2.5	17.9
Germany (W. Germany) 1871–75 to 1960–62	88	31.1	11.2	17.9
The Netherlands 1900–04 to 1960–62	59	29.7	14.3	13.5
Switzerland 1890–99 to 1957–59	63.5	25.7	8.3	16.1
Denmark 1870–74 to 1960–62	89	31.8	10.4	19.4
Norway 1865–74 to 1960–62	91.5	29.0	8.4	19.0
Sweden 1861–65 to 1960–62	98	36.9	6.7	28.3

Source: S. Kuznets, *Modern Economic Growth–Rate, Structure and Spread.* (New Haven, CT: Yale University Press, 1966).

major economic and political transformation without political instability may be found in Huntington's distinction between civic and praetorian political systems.[1] A praetorian system is one in which demands for enhanced political participation are high in relation to the level of political institutionalization and consequently are subject to attempts by social forces to act directly in the political arena. In civil systems, the relationship between participation and institutionalization is reversed, and social forces tend to act through existing political mechanisms to procure their demands. Clearly, Scandinavian politics are civic in character. In these terms, what happened in Scandinavia was that in a period of rapid economic transformation the extent of political institutionalization remained greater than demands for political participation.

INSTITUTIONAL ADAPTABILITY

That a number of factors mitigated the intensity of demands for political participation is not in itself a sufficient explanation for the relative stability and absence of violence experienced by Scandinavia. To explain a civic rather than a praetorian outcome, it is also necessary to show that the demands for political participation that did exist were outweighed by a higher level of political institutionalization. What is required for such an explanation is an account of the factors making for strong political institutions readily adaptable to changing conditions.

Adaptability of this kind of easiest to demonstrate in the case of Sweden. Throughout the centuries, its living constitutional tradition had never permitted any one of the three major social forces in the community—the monarchy, the aristocracy, and the peasantry—absolute power. The final establishment of a stable and lasting balance among these forces was signaled by the con-

stitutional settlement of 1809. A constitutional monarchy was set up in which strong executive power vested in the king was balanced by an independent judiciary and the legislature, which had joint legislative powers as well as power over finances. From that time on, the system was such that it facilitated the gradual accommodation of new aspirants to greater political participation.

Although the 1866 bicameral reform enfranchised only 20 percent of the adult male population, it led to a situation where, ten years later, the lower house was composed overwhelmingly of independent farmers. Moreover, the 1866 reform was itself a consequence of the need to give representation to the newly emerging force of bourgeois urban industrialists, who had no place in the system. Finally, the strong representation of the independent farmers in the lower house prevented an aristocratic-bourgeois coalition from taking power after the Prussian pattern. The parliamentary battles of the final decades of the nineteenth century centered on the conflict between the upper and lower chambers. Although the latter never secured initiative in policymaking, it did hold the line until industrialization created a middle class and working class capable of pressing their own demands.

The growth of the Liberal and Social Democratic parties at the end of the nineteenth century, together with an increasing per capita income, which enabled many of their supporters to vote, led to the incorporation of some members of those parties pressing for equal suffrage and parliamentarianism within the existing political structure. By 1909 their strength was such that a compromise was reached. In return for equal manhood suffrage, the Liberals and Socialists conceded the principle of proportional representation and the continuance of the upper house, both guarantees against the swamping of Conservative forces by democracy. The final triumph of constitutional democracy came with the establishment of a Liberal-Social Democratic coalition responsible to a majority in the lower house in 1917. The next year the Conservatives, aware

---

[1] S. P. Huntington, *Political Order in Changing Societies* (New Haven, CT: Yale University Press, 1968), p. 78.

of the revolutionary events in Germany and Russia, abandoned their last position with the establishment of universal suffrage.

The processes outlined here reveal the considerable adaptability of Swedish political institutions. Within the constitutional provisions adopted in 1809, they could incorporate both the greater influence of the existing independent farmers and then the new middle and working classes produced by industrialization. But to describe such adaptability is not the same thing as to explain it. In the Swedish case, we can offer reasons inherent in the traditional and continuing political structure for the high degree of adaptability.

These reasons may be found in the way in which elite attitudes were shaped by constitutional developments. Constitutionalism, or the limitation of autocratic political power, is itself a view implying that policy should be the outcome of a balance of forces. Moreover, in Sweden the unique position of the independent peasantry in premodern times meant that the principle that politics was not a game for aristocracy and monarchy alone had long been accepted. Both had been forced by the situation to realize that the peasantry had some right to be consulted in political affairs and the consensus-seeking procedures of such consultation reinforced an attitude of compromise. Thus, in seeking an explanation of the adaptability of Swedish political institutions, we must stress the impact of the traditional heritage in creating an elite political culture that emphasized compromise, participation by major social groups, and the effort to create a *modus vivendi* among them.[2]

In Norway and Denmark, the development of parliamentary institutions came somewhat earlier than in Sweden. Norway's semicolonial status rendered every attempt to assert the parliamentary principle not only part of the general movement of democratic ideas, but also an assertion of the right to national independence. By opposing the bureaucratic elite that dominated the government, the farmers in the legislative assembly (the *Storting*) were in effect opposing the Swedish king. Again, the institutionalized role of the peasantry in the constitutional system established in 1814 made it impossible for the elite to ignore the peasants' demands, since they could apply constitutional remedies when the *Storting*'s will was too arrogantly flouted. Thus, after the king had vetoed a bill that tied ministers more closely to parliament by entitling them to take part in its debate, the *Storting* responded by impeaching all those ministers who had approved the use of the veto. As a result of the ensuing constitutional deadlock, the king was forced to appoint a ministry enjoying the confidence of parliament.

Denmark, given its long history of absolutism and feudal serfdom, was later than either Sweden or Norway in giving a measure of representation to the peasantry. But once this was conceded with the June Constitution of 1849, the consequences were rather similar. The parliamentary struggle, as in Sweden, was between a lower house dominated by the Liberal party, representing largely peasant interests, and a government supported by the king and the Conservatives entrenched in the upper house. As we have already stated, the struggle was resolved in favor of parliamentarianism when the 1901 elections almost eliminated all Conservative representation in the lower house and the king was forced to appoint a Liberal cabinet.

In each of the three major Scandinavian countries, the institutions of constitutional monarchy adopted in the first half of the nineteenth century proved adaptable enough to cope with increasing demands for democratic participation. In each case this adaptability may be attributed largely to a willingness for compromise and accommodation on the part of an elite faced by constitutionally entrenched peasant participation. Scandinavian history may provide a gloss on Huntington's theory by suggesting that political participation is a self-generating phe-

---

[2] For a fascinating account of how traditional class alignments can affect political forms, see Barrington Moore, *Social Origins of Dictatorship and Democracy* (Boston: Beacon Press, 1966).

nomenon, since, under appropriate circumstances, it creates the institutional arrangements that allow it to be enhanced still further.

THE EMERGENT POLITICAL CULTURE

The term *political culture* describes the political attitudes and beliefs of a given population. Political culture is itself an historical product, slowly changed and modified in the course of development. We have already seen something of the evolution of the Scandinavian political culture in the emergence of elite attitudes of compromise and accommodation and the way in which the early development of universal literacy channeled protest into popular organizations. In this section, which is concerned with the development of the Scandinavian political culture during the twentieth century, we shall examine first the joint impact of the traditional political culture and the processes of modernization in producing the lines of social and political cleavage in contemporary Scandinavian society. Next, we shall look at the further evolution of participatory attitudes and their role in the resolution of social and political conflict. Finally, we shall suggest that the sum total of these historical influences may have produced in Sweden, and to a lesser extent elsewhere in Scandinavia, an image of society significantly different from that found elsewhere in Europe.

Cleavage Structures in Scandinavia

Discussions of political culture in the 1960s tended to make use of a simple scheme: they described political cultures as homogeneous or fragmented. *Homogeneity* described a culture in which the degree of political differentiation was small, and in which the similarity of sentiment among individuals removed many of the potential causes of conflict from the political arena. *Fragmentation*, in contrast, implied a degree of division and cleavage sufficient to endan-

ger the continuity of state and nation. Such a simplification has proved wholly inadequate in describing or understanding the complexities of the European nations, and nowhere has this been more true than Scandinavia. At a minimum, we require an account of the number and nature of social cleavages, their salience (the extent to which they are reflected in everyday politics), and their intensity.

It would be mistaken to describe the Scandinavian political cultures as homogeneous, since each has several cleavages. It is more accurate to suggest that in each there has on the whole been a tendency for the salience of cultural divisions to decline. Indeed, it would be almost silly to argue for Norwegian homogeneity, since Norwegian political scientists have used their own country as a prime example in studying cleavage structures.

What happened in Norway, under the combined pressure of early peasant mobilization and the struggle for national liberation, was only a more intense version of similar divisions elsewhere in Scandinavia. As we have already noted in discussing the traditional political structure, the linkages between urban and rural elites were weak, and power rested predominantly with the urban bureaucratic aristocracy. Given the lateness and rapidity of industrialization in Scandinavia, the development of a political conflict between town and country occurred at much the same time that the lower classes were demanding access to the political system. In consequence, there was no development along British lines of an upper-class party allying the interests of the urban and rural elite against the political demands of the lower classes.

Party divisions are a reflection of cleavage structures, and the Scandinavian pattern of division came to be reflected in a system of four basic blocks. (For a more detailed discussion of contemporary parties, see Chapter 3.) The Conservatives expressed the interests of the urban elite. The left, or Liberals, were in part the party of the rural counterculture and in part the party whose historical mission was to establish parliamentarianism and universal suffrage. The Agrarians promoted the economic interests of the farming community, and the Social Democrats expressed the demands of industrial labor. Thus it can be seen that Scandinavian multipartyism owes as much to a divided political culture as to electoral mechanisms like proportional representation. In Scandinavia, proportional representation may be seen as a device deliberately adopted to allow cultural differences to be represented in accordance with their weight in the community, a device, in other words, to create a fairer kind of participatory democracy.

Organized groups, in particular popular movements, have also been closely related to cleavage structures. The strong temperance movement of the late nineteenth and early twentieth centuries was another aspect of the defense of the rural counterculture against the alien aspects of urban life. Its strength in Sweden, and not merely Norway, provides evidence for a similar, if weaker, cultural tendency there. In the case of the farmers, the networks of producer cooperatives that came to dominate agricultural production throughout Scandinavia from the latter half of the nineteenth century actually predated the establishment of exclusively agrarian parties. The two arms of the labor movement, the industrial trade unions and the Social Democratic party, developed in much the same way.

The impact of cultural cleavages, and the fact that they were not similar throughout Scandinavia, may also be seen in the political repercussions of the Russian Revolution. In Rokkan's view, the crucial variable was the extent to which national independence had been firmly established. Denmark and Sweden, both of them long-established nation-states, were barely affected by the Socialist-Communist division. Finland, in contrast, experienced a complete and intense rift in its labor movement between those whose loyalties were to the national culture and social hierarchy and those whose bonds were with their revolutionary comrades. Norway,

having recently emerged from semicolonial status, was somewhere in between. Its Labor party briefly joined the Communist Third International before returning to the democratic fold. This radicalization, which deeply divided the Norwegian labor movement through much of the 1920s, probably owed much to the discontinuities in political development that led to an early mobilization of the peasantry and the rapid victory of parliamentarianism. Whereas in Denmark and Sweden the Social Democrats had some part in the struggle for democracy, in Norway social democracy emerged after the victory of parliamentarianism.

What is true of Norway is even more so of Denmark and Sweden. There are a number of cleavages, which are reflected in the structure of parties and organized groups, but for the most part they have been relatively unintense. There are some signs that this could change in the future, with old divisions assuming new forms and a new salience. This could well apply in respect to ecological issues and it may be significant that the first new party to obtain parliamentary status in Sweden since the 1920s was the "Green" party campaigning on environmental issues in 1988. However, the most intense division until recent decades had in all instances arisen from the demands of the lower classes for greater redistributive justice, and it was fought as much by organized groups as by political parties. Rights to organize and to enter into free collective bargaining were frequently won through protracted strikes and lockouts. As late as 1931, three workers were killed by the civil authorities in Ådalen in Sweden in an armed confrontation over the right of employers to use strikebreakers. Since that time, the political and industrial wings of the labor movement have won an established role in the decision-making process, and the intensity of conflict has declined until labor relations in postwar Scandinavia have become the envy of the rest of Europe.

In general, the old urban-rural divide seems to have declined with the decrease in the agricultural population. The farmers' parties in Sweden and Norway have both changed their names to the Center party in the hope of attracting the white-collar groups in the towns. In Norway, issues involving national independence are capable of infusing new life into the politics of the rural counterculture, as was demonstrated in the national referendum on entry into the European Economic Community in 1972. Here it was the parties of economic modernity—the Social Democrats and the Conservatives—that proposed entry into the EEC and the parties of the rural counterculture that opposed. The latter's victory, despite the much greater parliamentary strength of the former two groups, illustrates not only the power such issues still have in Norway but also the fact that in normal times they are submerged in the routine of running a social-welfare society.

One of the side effects of the social-welfare society may show the first signs of a new cleavage structure in Scandinavia. It is not the desirability of social welfare itself that is questioned. That has been accepted by all parties, including the Conservatives. The Swedish Conservatives even signaled their conversion by changing their name to the Moderate Unity party. The problem that has caused real trouble in recent years is that of finding the resources to pay for social welfare. Average tax rates in all three Scandinavian kingdoms are exceedingly high, for they must finance a public expenditure in excess of 50 percent of national income, and larger and larger numbers are expressing their discontent through the ballot box. In 1973 the established Danish party system was almost devastated by the rise of new parties, among which the largest by far was the Progress party. Its platform was the drastic reduction of taxation and public expenditure. Although at the same time a similar party in Norway was much less successful, by the late 1980s opinion polls suggest that the Progress party could have a similar devastating effect in the election scheduled for autumn 1989.

In Denmark and Norway nonsocialist coalitions had held office in the late 1960s and could be regarded as just as accountable for high tax levels as the Social Democrats. The consequence is that discontent has had to be channeled outside the established party system. This has not yet occurred in Sweden. In September 1976 the long reign of the Swedish Social Democrats came to an end in an election in which one of the major issues was the level of taxation. Even though the bourgeois parties won a second election in 1979,[3] there have been few, if any, signs of a marked change in welfare-state priorities. What has happened—and a similar trend was apparent in Norway until the recent rise of the Progress party—is that the Conservatives, who take the strongest stand against high progessive rates of taxation, have recently gained strength at the expense of the other bourgeois parties.

Attitudes to Participation

The rise of democracy implies a massive extension of participation in political decision making, but, as we have already noted in Scandinavia, that participation takes a rather distinctive form. There, individual participation through the ballot box to choose who will be the decision makers is only one aspect of the democratic process. Just as important is collective participation through organized groups whose balance of strength is at any given time the most important single influence on the nature of policy outputs. Whereas in Britain a Labour or Conservative government will attempt to implement those policies it put before the electorate at the previous election, in Scandinavia the emphasis is on a compromise with other social forces, which, though outvoted in parliament, have strong channels of participation through organized groups.

The origins of Scandinavia's uniquely strong organizational life lie in the development of popular movements reflecting emergent cultural cleavages in a highly literate population. The most interesting characteristic of these organizations, which makes them extraordinarily suitable agencies of

---

[3] Throughout Scandinavia *bourgeois* is the term used for the non-Socialist parties.

compromise, is their strange combination of democratic participation and deference to leadership. Both have their origins in the period at which the popular movements developed, but each represents a wholly different side of the cultural tradition. The popular movements were organizations that represented the participatory demands of those who were on the disadvantaged side of any given cleavage. Since the way forward for all of them was the widening of the democratic sphere, all adopted democratic procedures of election, and the accountability of leaders.[4]

Policymaking in contemporary Scandinavia is, as we shall see, largely a question of compromises and trade-offs among a wide variety of organizational and political elites. That such compromises usually prove possible should not surprise us, given the declining intensity of cultural cleavage, and economic circumstances which have made the primary issue the division of shares in a growing economic pie. What is much less obvious is how compromise emerged as the primary mechanism of conflict resolution at a time when cleavages were much stronger. The one answer that clearly will not do is to see compromise as some sort of national characteristic. To argue, as does Roland Huntford, that

The Swedes have a horror of controversy as something unpleasant, inefficient and vaguely immoral. They require for peace of mind, not confrontation, but consensus. Consensus guides everything: private conversation, intellectual life and the running of the State.[5]

is to suggest that the Swedes have always been like that. But we know that political

and industrial confrontation sometimes had to reach major proportions over a period of decades before a compromise was arrived at. Some cultural factors may be involved, but their operation can only be understood in the context of the historical circumstances that made a particular ruling elite feel the time was ripe to make concessions to popular demands.

Thus the cultural norms of the Swedish bureaucratic elite in the nineteenth century contained a strong emphasis on "objectivity"—a belief that the national interest could best be served by cooperation and that one should attempt to use reason to arrive at solutions in a way best calculated to further human progress. Clearly, this administrative creed was more conducive to reforms, concessions, and compromise than an ethic of authority based on the prerogatives conferred by ownership. But it cannot be a sufficient explanation of a fundamental change like that to parliamentarianism, since that change meant the bureaucratic elite's giving up its right to rule, a right based precisely on its "objectivity" in policymaking. A similar argument is appropriate to the view that Norway's transition to parliamentarianism in 1884 needs to be looked at in the light of the Norwegian bureaucratic elite's weak ascriptive values and resulting tendency to coopt new elements. This then led to a further tendency to appease rather than fight new demands.

In both cases a balanced account of the factors promoting compromise requires that we examine the forces creating political conflict as well as traditional cultural influences mitigating its disruptive impact on the society. We have examined the evolution of the fundamental democratic compromises in the Scandinavian countries in the section on institutional adaptability. Once they were effected, further compromises came about. The most important was the mutual acceptance on the part of trade unions and employers' associations of each other's legitimate sphere of influence. Here, the very strength of Scandinavian organized groups was a strong impetus to compromise. Ex-

---

[4] For an account of the crucial impact of the popular movements in shaping the content as much as the form of modern Swedish democracy, see G. Therborn, "Pillarisation" and "Popular Movements," in *Two Variants of Welfare State Capitalism: The Netherlands and Sweden*, Francis G. Castles, ed., *The Comparative History of Public Policy* (Cambridge: Polity Press, 1989).

[5] R. Huntford, *The New Totalitarians* (London: Allen Lane, 1971), p. 109.

tremely powerful, centralized organizations were in a position to hold each other and the community as a whole to ransom. This possibility a democratic government could not tolerate, and it became increasingly unsatisfactory to the groups themselves.

Once all the new leadership elites had been accepted as part of the democratic decision-making process, there was a strong incentive to divide influence roughly in accordance with power in the community. No single political force, with the exception of the Swedish Social Democrats, has ever managed to mobilize a majority of the voters. This means not only that there must be formal and informal coalition agreements apportioning influence, but also that any government proposing policies completely in favor of one side is taking grave risks with its electoral future. The Norwegian referendum on entry into the EEC is an example of the risks of not compromising. The problem was that there were only two solutions—to enter or stay out—and winner-takes-all politics of this kind is not the Scandinavian way.

The Scandinavian Image of Society

Political participation, individually through the ballot box and collectively through organized groupings, is only one aspect of a dualism that runs through the whole Scandinavian conception of what is considered appropriate social, economic, and political action—in other words, through their whole image of society. This dualism is manifested in a series of what seems paradoxes to the outside observer. The Swedes and Norwegians are considered the most private of people. Yet these same people have developed agricultural and consumer cooperatives to the extent that one commentator could consider them the basis of a new type of society. Another contrast is a press freedom unparalleled elsewhere in Europe. In Sweden, for example, a citizen has the constitutional right to look at and publish any document possessed by state or local authorities. These are safeguards against state interference with personal liberties, but they are bought at the expense of individual privacy.

A similar paradox is the phenomenon of highly centralized states, with all the powers implied by extensive social-welfare structures, high taxation, and a large public sector, appointing parliamentary commissioners (ombudsmen) to ensure that government officials do not step beyond the law. Another seeming contradiction is to be found in a trade union movement, stronger and more centralized then elsewhere in Europe, that considers one of its major tasks to be making capitalist industry more efficient. This raises the issue that always engages the outsider's attention more forcibly: Are the Scandinavian countries socialist or not? On the one side, they display high levels of social welfare, a considerable leveling of incomes, extensive government control of the economy, and Social Democratic parties in office for extended periods. Yet in comparison with major European nations such as Britain and France, they have until recently lacked the most important distinguishing characteristic of socialism—large-scale public ownership of industry. Paradoxically, the moderate increase in public ownership in Scandinavia since the early 1970s has been as much or more under auspices of nonsocialist governments.

M. D. Hancock has described the Swedes as "cooperative individualists," and this term captures exactly the dualism inherent in Scandinavian culture and society.[6] In many nations individualism and collectivism are the basis for rival political collectivities, but in Scandinavia they seem to appear together in each individual's image of society and in the various institutions of which he or she is a member. The reasons why Scandinavia should be distinctive in this sense lie once again in the complex interrelationship of the traditional political structure and the processes of industrialization and democratization. To put the argument in its simplest form, late and rapid industrialization

---

[6] See M. D. Hancock, *Sweden: The Politics of Postindustrial Change* (Hinsdale, IL: Dryden, 1972), pp. 36–60.

prevented the growth of a sizable urban bourgeoisie, which elsewhere in Europe was the chief agency of laissez-faire ideas and liberal ideology. Moreover, nowhere in Scandinavia were Liberal parties outstandingly successful unless allied with peasant interests. That they were underdog parties pressing for a place in the system made them emphasize egalitarianism and social reform in a way not wholly dissimilar from that of the Social Democrats. Again, egalitarianism was an important peasant cultural value, preserved by the lateness of the impact of industrialization and the institutionalized position of that sector in the legislative assemblies of the nineteenth century. All these factors were compounded by the rapidity of industrial growth, which meant an equally rapid rise of working-class parties. Nowhere was there a gap of more than 50 years between the institution of parliamentarianism and the formation of the first Social Democratic cabinet.

Together, the length of this gap (briefest in Sweden and longest in Norway) and the relative strength of the urban bourgeoisie (greatest in Denmark and least in Sweden) may well explain the comparative dominance of the Social Democratic party in the three Scandinavian kingdoms. But the general point to be emphasized is that the short span between the fall of a conservative, bureaucratic oligarchy and the rise of a collectivist government dedicated to welfare and egalitarianism allowed little opportunity for the cultural dominance of liberalism. Elsewhere in Europe such dominance created a division between the individualist right and the collectivist left. Conservative paternalism and democratic socialism have in common a belief in the desirability of compromise among social groups as a means of avoiding political conflict, and a view that collective action may be necessary to overcome individual ills. They also share a belief that organized collectivities are as much or more important as social actors than the individual voter and for that reason tend to define relevant forms of political participation in a manner quite different from liberal individualism. Such notions are strongly reflected in Scandinavian political and governmental institutions and practices, and it is to these we now turn.

3

The Politics of Organized Participation: Organized Groups and Political Parties

Modern democracies are distinguished from other types of political systems by the importance of the role played by mechanisms of political participation. Individuals play a part in the selection of governing personnel and of policy alternatives by their participation in elections and a variety of political groupings. Of such groupings, the political party, which acts as the agency of electoral mobilization and governmental recruitment, is usually the most important. In what follows, we shall mention the major party groupings that have developed in Scandinavia and sketch the evolution of a party system that has been dominated primarily by the Social Democratic party. This latter is one of the important distinguishing features of Scandinavian democracy, but it is allied with a further element of distinctiveness: organized groups play a political role probably greater than anywhere else in Europe and the proportion of the adult population belonging to associations is much higher in Scandinavia than in the rest of Western Europe.

CORPORATE PLURALISM

We follow Stein Rokkan in describing the Scandinavian system of organized groups as *corporate pluralism*. In doing so, we depart from the contemporary intellectual fashion of using the term "corporatism" to denote all systems which depart from the Anglo-American model of interest group pluralism. As far as we are concerned, the corporatist notion has three main problems as applied to Scandinavia. First, corporatist arrangements are often taken to include a routinized and high-level consultation between organized groups and government.

Certainly, this does occur to some extent in Scandinavia, but there are many important arenas in which it does not. For instance, in Sweden, the government seeks to keep out of the industrial relations arena and the trade unions and employers try to ensure that they do keep out. Second, corporatism is often taken to imply strong consensus-seeking activity. Again, while that does often happen in Scandinavia, an equally common pattern is for a strong group to fight hard for its viewpoint and to use the participative mechanism to persuade other interests of the validity of its case. Third, just because the corporatist model is an intellectual fashion, it has been applied somewhat indiscriminately to many countries with very different characteristics, including Japan, Germany, and Switzerland, as well as Scandinavia. We prefer to use the narrower term *corporate pluralism* to denote characteristics that the Scandinavian countries have in common.

Predominance of Groups

Swedish and Norwegian politics may be described as *group-dominant* in the sense that organized groups constitute the primary focus for political activity; this description also applies to Denmark. The preeminant position of organized groupings is demonstrated in a variety of ways. First, their membership is high. In each country economic interest groups representing the industrial workers and their employers are fully represented, and the same goes for producer cooperatives in the agricultural sector. In addition to cooperative organizations, the farmers in each nation have strong interest groups representing their general economic demands.

Moreover, since World War II that section of the economy traditionally most difficult to organize, the salaried white-collar workers, has recorded a higher and higher group membership. Productive relationships have not been the only basis for group membership: in each country, consumer cooperatives have played a major role in retailing. In addition, idealistic associations—notably the temperance movement, professional associations, and educational associations—are all strongly supported, and groups that are often unorganized or weakly organized in other societies, such as tenants, pensioners, the handicapped, and immigrants, have relatively strong organizations. Indeed, one can point not merely to the high level of Scandinavian group membership, but also to the fact that organized groups cover virtually every aspect of human activity.

The second aspect of group dominance, and one that certainly does distinguish corporate pluralism from the Anglo-American system of interest representation, is the strong tendency toward centralized organization. This is a particular feature of economic interest groups. High degrees of industrial concentration have led to the creation of strong centralized employers' associations covering whole industries and centralization by the employers forced the trade unions to respond in kind. In Norway and Sweden highly centralized trade union confederations (*Landsorganisationen*, or *LO*) emerged, and despite greater craft divisions in Denmark, the tendency there has been in a similar direction. On both sides of industry, centralization is shown by the control the confederations have over their members. Individual unions cannot strike without prior permission by the LO, and individual firms cannot institute a lockout against the dictates of the employers' association. Collective wage agreements are arrived at by negotiation between LO and the respective employers' association. Although there is often some scope for further bargaining at the plant and industry level, agreements are generally binding for the labor market as a whole. Moreover, centralization permits the trade unions and employers to pursue objectives as a collectivity. Perhaps the most interesting example of this is the consistent attempt by the Swedish LO to procure an equalization of wage levels throughout the industry by the so-called wage policy of solidarity.

Political Functions of Groups

A third feature of group preeminence in Scandinavia is demonstrated by the multiplicity of political functions the groups perform. Where Anglo-American interest group theory suggests that the major function of organized groups is to propagandize to the parties, legislature, and executive in favor of their policy demands, in Scandinavian politics as a whole they have crucial policymaking and administrative roles as well. In Sweden and Norway, the right of groups to be involved in the policymaking process is institutionalized through the *remiss* system, whereby a ministry contemplating legislative or administrative action relevant to the concerns of a particular interest is obliged to consult that interest. Even more important in each country are the many routine committees and royal commissions that discuss policymaking proposals, and on which the relevant interests are always represented. The crucial decisions on economic and public policy issues are rarely the province of the parties and parliament alone. They are made at the bargaining table where the representatives of organized groups meet government officials.

The integration of organized groups can be seen at its clearest in what is traditionally regarded as a governmental function, the administration of policy. The boards and agencies responsible for the administration of much of the public domain are frequently composed of a mixture of government officials and parliamentarians plus representatives of the relevant organizations. Thus, to take a single example, the Danish Tariff Council draws half its members from parliament and the other half from representatives of trade and shipping, industry, handicrafts, and agriculture. Norway has carried this type of development to its ultimate extent: 48 percent of the membership of its administrative boards is composed of interest group representatives. Extensive group participation in policymaking and policy administration tends to ensure that policy outputs will be acceptable to the majority of interested parties, and at the same time that those interested parties take a partial responsibility for governmental proposals.

Authority of Groups

A fourth aspect of organized group dominance has been pointed out by a commentator on Danish groups who argues that interest groups have acquired legal authority to regulate, administer, police, or otherwise manage many of their own affairs. This can be illustrated by the labor courts of the various Scandinavian countries, which make judgments as to whether employers or employees have violated the legislation on collective contracts. They draw the majority of their judges from the trade unions and employers' associations. Perhaps even more crucial is the extent to which opposing groups have collaborated to avoid coming under the legal authority of the state in the first place. Here, again, industrial relations are the most important example. The early decades of the twentieth century were years of extensive industrial conflict throughout Scandinavia, expressed in prolonged and frequent strikes and lockouts. The creation of labor courts was one response to this situation, but clearly it was by itself inadequate.

In a series of negotiations between 1936 and 1938, the workers' and employers' organizations hammered out a basic agreement on how disputes between them would be regulated in the future. In effect, they set up an institutionalized system of collective bargaining, on the basis of which a whole series of agreements have since been arrived at. These have, of course, involved wage settlements, and also provisions for progressively greater worker influence on management, safety regulations, educational leave, work environment, and a host of other issues. Although the exact circumstances in which basic procedural agreements were entered into in Denmark and Norway are somewhat different, the result has been virtually the same. Many issues that can arise in an industrial society are resolved by compromise between trade unions and employers, without government involvement.

Organized Groups as a Mode of Participation

A final aspect of group dominance is that organizations and associations offer an attractive avenue for achieving political influence and promoting policy preferences—or what has been called the organizational/corporate channel of participation. As a result, not only can organized groups boast of high membership but the proportion of Scandinavians who belong to organizations is very high indeed. Roughly 90 percent of all Danes and Swedes and around 70 percent of the Norwegians report membership in at least one association. Although many are not more than nominal members, between one-third and two-fifths of all Scandinavians claim to be active members in an organization, and one-fifth hold office in an association. Furthermore, membership and participation in organizations and associations experienced an upswing during the 1970s and into the 1980s.

One trait of participation in the organizational/corporate channel is that it appears to be related to education and income more than participation in the party/electoral channel. Nonetheless, the strong organizations of LO serve to modify this tendency. In Sweden, for example, the proportion of workers who were members of at least one organization was above the national average, as was the proportion of skilled workers who reported active participation in an organization, held an elected position, and attempted to influence organizational decisions. Similarly, workers as organizational joiners (members of at least four organizations) were on a par with other occupational groups.

Corporate Pluralism as a System

Three important points emerge from this brief discussion of Scandinavian corporate pluralism. The first is that the institutionalization of conflict in labor relations has minimized the most destabilizing influence in modern industrial societies—the divide between labor and management. The relative lack of intensity of this cleavage in Scandinavia may be demonstrated by its strike statistics, which compare extremely favorably with those of Britain, France, and the United States.

The second point is that the compromises inherent in policymaking through corporate pluralist channels are particularly conducive to governmental stability. Because policy is invariably mediated by a strong element of group compromise, it is that much less likely that a government's policy outputs will alienate large numbers of supporters, or even seriously annoy those who oppose it.

Third, corporate pluralism with its wide consultation and inclusion of organized groups, combined with the pervasiveness of organization, provides an additional channel for citizen involvement in politics and potential influence on policies and their implementation. Furthermore, in several instances the potential for influence through participation in organizations is enhanced by ties with the political parties. Several associations are party supportive organizations which provide resources (financial contributions, members, and leaders) to the parties.

Despite the contributions that strong, institutionalized groups make to political stability and opportunities for participation, the system is not without defects and critics. On the rare occasions that compromise fails, disputes are likely to be costly precisely because of organizational strength. Moreover, critics of the system argue that the established group leadership is divorced from the membership by the very nature of centralization and by closeness to the administrative elites with which they compromise. Criticisms of this kind amount to a charge that the system is oligarchic rather than democratic, and frequently unresponsive to new demands. Certainly, it is true that, despite the demands of New Left activists that the established groups be bypassed by more direct forms of democratic participation, the established arrangements remain largely untouched. On the other hand, as we shall show in the final section of the chapter the demand for new forms of participation has had a major impact in creating further channels of access for previously disadvantaged interests.

A FUNCTIONING MULTIPARTY SYSTEM

The danger of a multiparty system based on proportional representation is that it will lead to governmental instability, but certainly until the 1970s this was not the Scandinavian experience. Instead, as shown in Figure 3–1, government stability has been the rule. An examination of the major factors

that have accounted for stability in the Scandinavian countries will offer us an opportunity to look at the major party groupings and to trace the evolution of the party system as a whole as well as to discuss the strains it has faced since the early 1970s.

Proportional Representation

The first point to note is that in Sweden, but also to a degree in Denmark and Norway, proportional representation was introduced early this century as a means of avoiding too dramatic political change. In effect, it was a part of the historic compromise whereby the Conservatives conceded democratization in return for a device that would ensure that the rapidly growing working class would acquire political dominance only gradually. A plurality voting system implies instant change in the dominant party the moment the supporters of a new aspirant to power become the largest single element in the electorate. Proportionalism reflects the incremental changes in the electorate as they take place. Proportional repre-

Figure 3–1   Scandinavian Cabinets since the 1930s

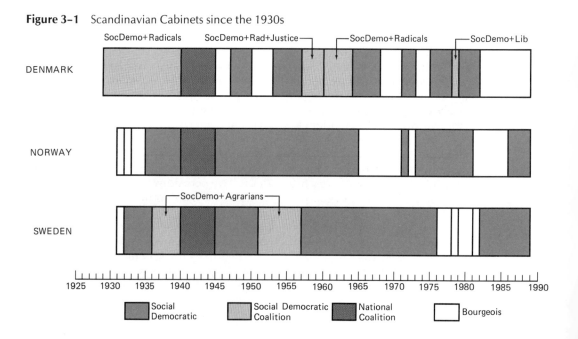

sentation according to some gave Sweden a breathing space: before the Social Democrats came to power they had abandoned their more extreme positions on pacificism, republicanism, and anticlericalism.

Moreover, proportionalism in a situation of complex cross-cutting cleavages makes possible the representation of particular interests without forcing them into the confines of a party whose primary objectives lie elsewhere. The emergence of distinct agrarian parties in Norway and Sweden in a period when agriculture was declining but still of some economic importance illustrates this effect. The most serious dangers that proportional representation can present for political stability as such as the substantial representation of antisystem parties and the rapid rise of new parties where the electorate is unstable.

The first of these dangers depends on the political alienation of a sizable proportion of the electorate. Since the acceptance of democratization and the progressive emergence of the system of corporate pluralism, it has become increasingly unlikely that alienation of such dimensions could develop in Scandinavia. The obvious exception is the radicalization of the Norwegian Labor party in the 1920s, but that in a sense merely proves the rule, since the Labor party rapidly reentered the democratic fold. By 1932 it had abandoned the threat of violence in favor of a commitment to parliamentarianism and a program of public works for combating unemployment. Otherwise, extremism has had little success in Scandinavia. The second danger—the rise of new parties in combination with increasing voter volatility—is a fairly recent phenomenon creating new pressures on the party system, which we discuss shortly.

A Bipolar System and Social Democratic Dominance

Although proportional representation cannot be said to have had disastrous political effects in Scandinavia, the governmental stability that has accompanied the multi-

party system cannot be seen as an effect of proportionalism as such. Rather, it has been the result of a configuration of stable party divisions and gradually changing party strengths, which led to what has in effect been a bipolar political system. Two rival blocs of parties have confronted each other as potential governments (see the listing in Table 3–1 and review Table 3–2). In Sweden and Norway the system came to be weighted in favor of the Social Democrats, and for long periods the socialist bloc has won a majority of the electorate. In Denmark the Social Democrats have not commanded the same position of strength, and a socialist majority has been a rare occurrence. Thus the Danish Social Democrats' dominance of the executive has often necessarily rested upon the tacit or open support of at least one of the nonsocialist parties.

The immediate effect of proportional representation in the parliamentary arena was to produce four major party groupings. The rapid advance of industrialization made for an increasingly large working-class constituency. It was the basis for the Social Democrats, the party of collectivist egalitarianism, to succeed the Liberals, the party of democratization, as the largest parliamentary grouping by the 1920s. Although the Bolshevik Revolution created competition for the loyalties of the working class through the eventual establishment of communist parties, their role has been marginal especially in Denmark and Norway. In addition to the Liberals, whose support in each of the Scandinavian countries came from a balance of peasant farmers and urban radicals, there was a Conservative party, whose organization involved a regrouping of the old right. It had opposed democratization, and now, having grudgingly accepted it, wanted to stem the tide of radical change as much as possible. Moreover, the Liberals were under internal pressures from two directions. In addition to urban middle-class intellectuals, these parties contained a clear agricultural economic interest, which in Norway and Sweden gave rise to separate agrarian parties. In Denmark, where the economy as a

TABLE 3-1 Characteristics of Major Parties

Denmark

Social Democrat: Became largest party in 1924 with 36 percent of vote. Generally won at least that percentage until 1968. Fell below 30 pecent in 1973 as a consequence of splintering of party system, but recovered substantially to become the major source of stability in the system. During the period 1929–1982 in power, alone or in coalition, for about forty years but in opposition since 1982. Stands for a moderate social-welfare program egalitarian economic policy.

Liberal: Party of agrarian liberalism and for much of the century the major opponent of the Social Democrats. Included in all bourgeois governments during the postwar period. Obtained between 20 and 25 percent of the vote in the 1950s but down to around 12 percent in the 1970s and 1980s. Stands for a free economy, but does not see this as incompatible with social welfare. The party of farm interests. Member of government since 1982.

Conservative: Originally the party of antiparliamentarianism. Now, the urban defender of free enterprise—again, not opposed to social-welfare programs. Like the other established parties of the era 1920–1960, drastically lost support in the early 1970s, but since 1984 has won around 20 percent of the vote. Party of the prime minister since 1982.

Radical: Social-liberal party somewhat to left of other bourgeois parties, receiving support from smaller farmers and urban intellectuals. Usually fourth or fifth in electoral support. In the 1980s has tended to vote with the other bourgeois parties on economic issues but with socialist parties on foreign affairs and defense. Used to have a major role in coalition with Social Democrats, but moved closer to the other bourgeois parties from the late 1960s. Entered the bourgeois government following the 1988 election.

Socialist People's: Founded in 1959. Has replaced the Communists as the major party to the left of the Social Democrats through its democratic left-wing policies and neutralist stance. In the 1980s has polled more than 10 percent of the vote.

Progress: Main agent for disruption of traditional parties attracting more than 10 percent of the vote in the 1970s. Declined in the 1980s, but did well in the 1988 election, receiving just under 10 percent. Opposed to high taxation, bureaucracy, and the welfare-state consensus.

Norway

Labor (Social Democrat): Between 1933 and 1969 never polled less than 40 percent. Suffered a sharp electoral decline in 1973, but formed minority administrations from 1973 to 1981. A moderate social-welfare party on the lines of the other Scandinavian Social Democrats. The greater importance of nationalization in Norway reflects the early more radical traditions of the party. Recovered appreciably in 1977, fell below 40 percent again in 1981. Made gains in 1985 (41 percent) and back in office since 1986.

Liberal: Founded in 1884 and the dominant party until the early 1920s. Much of its support has been agrarian, and its policy one of social reform in the context of liberal democracy. Since the 1920s it has suffered splits and a declining vote. It could obtain only two seats in the Storting in 1977 and 1981—and none in 1985.

Conservative: Having declined between the wars, it has become the second largest party since World War II (30 percent of the vote in 1985). No serious divergences with the other parties on social legislation, but an advocate of lower taxes and greater economic freedom. A wholehearted supporter of EEC entry. Main party of government between 1981 and 1986.

Center (previously Agrarian): A splinter from Liberals in 1920s. Represents farmers' interests in close association with farmers' pressure group. Since 1950s has attempted to broaden its appeal to the towns, but recently seems to be losing support to the Conservatives. Polled nearly 7 percent of the vote in 1985. Center prime minister in nonsocialist coalition, 1965–1971. Opposed to socialism, but favors extensive social and economic planning. Opposed to EEC entry.

Christian People's: Founded 1933 to support a Christian and moral stance in politics. Strongest support in Protestant southwest. Polled around 12 percent in 1970s but declined below 10 percent in 1980s. A major interest in cultural, religious, and educational matters. Strongly opposed to "liberal" legislation on abortion.

Socialist Left (previously Socialist People's): Founded in 1961, takes an anti–NATO, anti–EEC line as well as advocating more "genuine" socialism. A Socialist alliance of which it was part gained 11 percent of vote in aftermath of EEC referendum. In 1975 part of the alliance formed the Socialist Left party which has obtained around 5 percent of the vote in recent elections.

Progress: Antitax party established in the early 1970s, generally polling around 4–5 percent through the mid-1980s. With only two seats after the 1985 election it became the power broker between the bourgeois and socialist parties. Experienced major gains in 1987 local elections, winning 12 percent of the vote. Poll ratings of over 20 percent in 1988, challenging the Conservatives as second largest party. See page 288 for update.

TABLE 3-1 Characteristics of Major Parties

Sweden

Social Democrat: Largest party since 1914, polling over 40 percent at every election since 1932. In office continuously from 1932 to 1976, either in coalition or alone. Lost office in 1976 but back in power since 1982. Pragmatic party advocating extensive social welfare, economic equality, and industrial democracy.

Liberal: Major party of democratization. Suffered splits in 1920s but reunited in the mid-1930s. The largest bourgeois party during the first two decades of the postwar period but declined after 1968, polling only 6 percent in 1982. Staged a comeback in 1985, winning 14 percent. Favors marginally less taxation than Social Democrats, but few differences on welfare.

Conservative: After losing struggles against franchise extension and parliamentarianism, has fluctuated considerably. Since 1979 has been the largest bourgeois party, with around 20 percent of the vote. Changed name to the Moderate Unity party at the end of the 1960s. Opposes high taxation, demands greater economic freedom, and favors privatization of social services.

Center (previously Agrarian): Gained considerable support in urban areas after change in name and widening of policies. Largest bourgeois party from 1968 to 1979, and its leader was prime minister during five of the six years of bourgeois administrations (1976–1982). In social and economic policy not that different from Social Democrats, but advocates substantial decentralization of power. Opposition to expansion of nuclear industry a major contribution to bourgeois victory in 1976, but its stance on this issue led to the fall of the coalition in the autumn of 1978. Substantial decline in support since the mid-1970s.

Left-Party Communist: Successor to Communist party when it decided to embrace a democratic, parliamentary road to socialism. Influential in New Left upsurge of late 1960s and expected to do well in 1968 elections until invasion of Czechoslovakia. Just manages to obtain the 4 percent of the vote necessary for parliamentary representation in Sweden.

Greens: Founded in 1981, espousing a program to shape society and the economy in accordance with ecological principles. Received over 5 percent of the vote in the 1988 election to become the first new party elected to the Riksdag in nearly seven decades.

whole was more oriented to agriculture, these pressures led to the early emergence of a Radical party, supported by small landholders and urban intellectuals, that pursued a more radical line than the agrarian-based Liberals. The other pressure came from the dissenting Protestant church allied to the temperance movement, which created a temporary split in the Swedish Liberals in the 1920s. In Norway in the 1930s these groups formed the basis for a small party, the Christian Democrats, who drew their strength from the southwest, where religious dissent was strongest.

For the most part, the party groupings that crystallized during the 1920s have until very recently remained the major participants in the parliamentary system. There are two reasons for this stability. The first seems common to the majority of Western democracies: the parties that managed to create mass organizations and gain an established place in local government structures before the final extension of the suffrage have proved strongest. These parties were able to establish loyalties among the electorate, and so deny openings for support to new claimants to participation.

The second reason is that the party system as established coincided closely with natural divisions in the electorate. That party divisions have been along natural cleavage lines separating labor from management, primary from secondary industry, and town from country has provided a continuous rationale for their existence. Interests within the electorate have changed somewhat over the years, and with them the policies of the parties, but the fact that there are such distinct interests, and that the parties cater to the more important views within the electorate, has become questionable only since the 1960s.

The overall stability of the party system is only the beginning of an explanation of the Scandinavian tendency to bipolarism and the resulting governmental stability. Here again two factors seem important. The first is the progressive growth of the Social Democratic party. This came about with industri-

TABLE 3-2 The Bipolar Pattern in Danish, Norwegian, and Swedish Politics,[a] 1929–1988

Denmark (% of votes in *Folketing* elections)

Year	Bourgeois	Socialist	(SD)
1929	57.3%	42.0%	41.8%
1932	55.5	43.8	42.7
1935	47.3	47.7	46.1
1939	47.5	45.3	42.9
1943	50.0	44.5	44.5
1945	54.8	45.3	32.8
1947	52.6	46.8	40.0
1950	55.5	44.2	39.6
1953 (Apr.)	53.6	45.2	40.4
1953 (Sept.)	53.2	45.6	41.3
1957	57.1	42.5	39.4
1960	50.3	49.3	42.1
1964	50.6	48.9	41.9
1966	50.1	49.9	38.2
1968	56.0	43.3	34.2
1971	50.4	49.4	37.3
1973	47.4	36.7	25.6
1975	45.3	41.2	29.9
1977	37.2	47.3	37.0
1979	38.8	50.2	38.3
1981	42.9	48.2	32.9
1984	49.8	46.5	31.6
1987	45.2	48.4	29.3
1988	43.4	46.1	29.8

Norway (% of votes in *Storting* elections)

Year	Bourgeois	Socialist	(SD)
1927	56.1%	40.8%	36.8%
1930	63.5	33.1	31.4
1933	52.1	41.9	40.1
1936	51.3	42.8	42.5
1945	46.8	52.9	41.0
1949	47.8	51.5	45.7
1953	48.2	51.8	46.7
1957	48.1	51.7	48.3
1961	47.8	52.1	46.7
1965	49.5	50.5	43.1
1969	48.9	51.0	46.5
1973	44.2	46.9	35.3
1977	49.0	47.5	42.3
1981	51.6	43.1	37.2
1985	48.6	47.1	40.8

Sweden (% of votes in *Riksdag* elections)

Year	Bourgeois	Socialist	(SD)
1928	56.5%	43.4%	37.0%
1932	49.3	50.0	41.7
1936	44.8	53.6	45.9
1940	42.0	57.3	53.8
1944	42.4	57.0	46.7
1948	47.5	52.4	46.1
1952	49.5	50.4	46.1
1956	50.3	49.6	44.6
1958	50.4	49.6	46.2
1960	47.6	52.3	47.8
1964	43.9	52.5	47.3
1968	42.9	53.1	50.1
1970	47.6	50.5	45.3
1973	48.8	48.9	43.6
1976	50.8	47.8	42.7
1979	49.0	48.8	43.2
1982	45.0	51.2	45.6
1985	47.9	50.1	44.7
1988	42.1	49.4	43.5

[a]The socialist bloc is comprised of the Social Democrats (SD) and the parties to their left. In Denmark the bourgeois bloc includes all non-socialist parties except the Progressives whose support has been shunned as well as the Schleswig party. In Norway, bourgeois parties include the Left (Liberals), Conservatives, Agrarians, and Christian Democrats. In Sweden they include the Liberals, Conservatives, and Agrarians (Center).

alization and the development of an industrial working class. A large industrial working class is not, of course, a guarantee of the parliamentary supremacy of socialism. In many European countries, religious fragmentation, deference to the traditional ruling elite, and divisions fostered by the victory of the Bolsheviks in Russia have acted to fragment the political left or to direct working class votes to other political groupings. In Scandinavia, as our previous discussion as shown, none of these factors was operative. Moreover, the left has also been better able to overcome cultural cleavage than its competitors. Recently, this has been demonstrated by the ability of the Social Democrats to obtain a large percentage of the white-collar vote. The strength of the Scandinavian Social Democratic parties has been a major agency of bipolarism, simply because they were the one party that could hope to obtain a parliamentary majority by themselves. They have been the most viable source of minority government particularly when the difficulty of the smaller left parties in doing anything other than giving them tacit support is taken into account.

The only real possibility of an alternative to the Social Democrats has been a coalition of the so-called "bourgeois" parties. The second major reason for governmental stability based on Social Democratic dominance has been these parties' relative failure to overcome their differences. Indeed, the end of the era of minority parliamentarianism in the 1920s was in every case marked by the willingness of one of these parties to enter into a formal or informal agreement with the Social Democrats. In Sweden and Norway the agreement was with the Agrarians. They were able to accept an extensive program of public works to maintain employment in return for measures to alleviate the indebtedness of the farming community, which was as much affected by the economic depression as the workers. This alliance was facilitated by the long-standing cultural cleavage between peasant landholders and urban Conservatives, which made it natural for the Agrarians to unite with the Social

Democrats against the official establishment. This coalition of workers and farmers has ceased to be practical politics today, but that has not always made it easier for the bourgeois parties to reach agreement.

In Norway a bourgeois coalition was formed between 1965 and 1971, but it foundered on differences between the Conservatives and the Center party on the EEC issue. The most recent bourgeois coalition (1983–1986) fell when it failed to win the necessary support of the Progressives for a taxation proposal. In Sweden the bourgeois coalition formed in 1976 was bedeviled by serious differences on the issue of the extent of the domestic nuclear energy program, and the coalition split in the autumn of 1978. A new three-party bourgeois coalition formed after the 1979 election was dissolved in 1981 after dissension concerning taxation. Because of the somewhat weaker position of the Social Democrats in Denmark, when they have been in office it has been in coalition with, or with the tacit support of, at least one other party. From the 1920s to the early 1960s that support usually came from the Radical party, which shows once again the disunity of the bourgeois forces.

The Party System Under Pressure

Until recent decades few new parties obtained parliamentary representation and fewer still retained it. The Socialist People's parties' successes in Denmark and Norway may well have marked the end of an era in which new parties found it difficult to enter the political arena. Certainly the most phenomenal instance of the emergence of new parties occurred in the 1973 Danish election when the number of parties in the *Folketing* doubled, increasing from five to ten, and resulting in a fragmentation of the left, center, and right of the political spectrum. In Norway divisions over the EEC referendum in 1972 also seemed to auger political fragmentation, but the major effect of this event was virtually to wipe out the Liberal party, which split into warring factions in its aftermath. In the 1980s, however, the Progress party, somewhat similar to the Danish party and founded at the same time, has come to be an increasingly important factor in Norwegian politics. Following the 1985 elections the Progress party held the balance between the traditional rival blocs. Finally, in Sweden for the first time since the introduction of universal and equal suffrage a new party—the Greens—succeeded in getting elected to parliament in the 1988 election.

These developments raise fundamental questions about the future of the party system in Scandinavia. As we have seen, the dominant position of the Social Democrats has been an underlying factor contributing to the continuity of government and the stability of the party system. The basis of this dominance has stemmed from the party's own polling strength, the socialist bloc's share of the vote, the pivotal position of the Social Democrats which has allowed them to form left-center alliances when expedient, and the disunity of the bourgeois parties. A major question concerns the extent to which the preconditions for Social Democratic preeminence have been eroded in the three countries.

Clearly events in Denmark have put the most severe strains on the previously functioning multiparty system. And in Denmark the strength of the Social Democrats has deteriorated on several counts during the past two decades. In the elections during the 1980s the party has mustered on an average only slightly over 30 percent of the vote, substantially down from its election results in the late 1970s (see Table 3–2). Because of the frequent lack of a socialist majority, the pivotal position of the Social Democrats has always been crucial in its ability to remain in government. In the 1970s with the emergence of the antitax Progress party and serious party fragmentation, there was a tendency for the Social Democrats to take a balancing role in the political system and for the established bourgeois parties to lend them more or less formalized degrees of support in order to protect the established political system. Since the early 1980s the Conservatives have assumed the key role as

the party of the prime minister, forming a minority four-party coalition government which demonstrated the existence of a viable alternative to Social Democratic party administrations. The Social Democrats' pivotal position has also been undermined by their inability to resurrect a working alliance with the Radicals for one reason because an alliance commanding a majority must now also include or rely on the support of the Socialist People's party.

Divisions continue to plague the bourgeois bloc. The fact that during most of the 1980s the Radicals have sided with the socialist bloc on foreign policy and defense issues as well as other matters, such as the environment, civil liberties, and certain social policies, has meant the lack of a parliamentary majority for the bourgeois government on these issues. Equally significant, the existence of the Progress party detracts from the strength of the bourgeois bloc as long as the party is considered to be outside the bounds of respectability. The importance of the Progressives declined with its electoral fortunes in the 1980s and the substantial gains of the Conservatives in the 1984 election. However, the party's recent minor resurgence in the 1987 and 1988 elections and gains in subsequent polls, largely at the expense of the Conservatives, suggests that the Progressives as a disruptive force in Danish politics may not have yet run full course. If the party were to experience further gains in strength and remain outside the bourgeois fold, this could result in the Social Democrats once again assuming a balancing role.

In Norway the Social Democrats until 1989 had not experienced electoral erosion on the same scale as the Danish party. However, there has been a downward trend in support combined with alternating victories and losses in every other election since the early 1960s. Nor has there been a socialist majority in the electorate since the 1969 election. Furthermore, from the late 1970s into the mid-1980s the Conservative party seemed to present a major challenge to the Social Democratic dominance. The Conservatives attracted Labor voters and began to rival the party in size. In the late 1980s, however, the Conservative threat has eased. Bourgeois disunity led to the formation of a Social Democratic minority government in 1986 and thwarted efforts to bring down the new government. The growing popularity of the Progress party, is likely to undercut the Conservatives, something that happened in the election of September 1989.

In Sweden the 1980s witnessed the return of a socialist majority in the electorate and the Social Democrats as the party of government and hence the reassertion of the features typifying the party system since the early 1930s. At the same time the Greens' entry into the *Riksdag* has altered the party landscape. The emergence of the Greens possibly signals a new dimension in Swedish politics and has created an element of uncertainty with respect to eventual repercussions on bloc politics. The immediate effects, however, have been to leave the strength of the socialist bloc relatively intact and to weaken the three bourgeois parties whose combined share of the vote fell to its lowest point in history.

THE IMPACT OF SOCIAL DEMOCRATIC DOMINANCE

Two of the most distinctive features of Scandinavian politics have been the system of corporate pluralism and the functioning multiparty system. A third has been the dominance of the Social Democratic party[1] and, what is not necessarily quite the same thing, the hegemony of the Social Democratic image of society. In outlining the major reasons for social democracy's success in Scandinavia and the ideas that have motivated policymaking, we will point to further mechanisms promoting the political stability and democratic participation that is typical of the Scandinavia nations.

[1] For an extended discussion of this topic, see F. G. Castles, *The Social Democratic Image of Society* (London: Routledge & Kegan Paul, 1978).

Peaceful Transformation versus Radical Reform

We have shown that Social Democratic success was largely a function of the capacity to mobilize working-class electoral support. But how was it that Social Democratic policies evolved over the years so as to evoke such massive electoral support and to act as the agency for the peaceful transformation of society? At the end of the nineteenth century, peaceful transformation was the last thing that might have been expected of Socialist parties, whose ideological stance was a direct translation of the Marxist view that the workers could procure freedom and justice only through the abolition of the bourgeois state and its institutions. An understanding of social democracy's success as a parliamentary party can be gained only through an explanation of the forces that made it replace the doctrine of class warfare with an emphasis on parliamentary gradualism and its role as an instrument of radical reform on behalf of the community as a whole.

Part of this explanation lies in the timing of the two revolutions of industrialization and democratization. In Denmark and Sweden the immediate problem faced by the young Socialist parties was securing a forum for the expression of their views. This forced them into collaboration with Liberal parties pressing for an extension of the suffrage. In the course of such cooperation they came to consider democracy itself not only a means but a fundamental principle. The same phenomenon was apparent in Denmark. It was only in Norway that the early advent of parliamentarianism isolated the workers' movement from other democratic forces and that a radical antidemocratic stance perished for any length of time. But even in Norway a number of other factors conducive to gradualist reformist throughout Scandinavia were operative by the early 1930s. One was the nature of the political culture and political development, which made the Social Democrats realize that support was dependent on compromising their views. An early sign of this was the abandonment of the exclusively urban focus of Marxism.

By the 1930s the Danish and Swedish parties were wedded to a reformist strategy that portrayed the Social Democratic party as the representative of the interests of the community as a whole. This was made clear in 1935 when Per Albin Hansson, the Swedish Social Democratic prime minister, used the old conservative slogan "The People's Home" to characterize his party's attachment to the national community. By 1949 a similar principle was enshrined in the Norwegian Social Democrats' program: "[The Labor party] no longer stands as the representative of a single class or group of the nation; it now represents all those willing to find their place in a society built upon the principles of cooperation and community of interest."

The Social Democratic Society

Gradualism and compromise are crucial elements in the continuing success of any moderate socialist party insofar as they help to reassure other groups and parties, as well as its own potential supporters, that demands for reform are not attempts to undermine the existing framework of political institutions. But to look at Social Democratic dominance in these terms alone is to present an entirely negative picture of how the Social Democrats have come to accept goals similar to those of the community as a whole. The positive side of the picture lies in the impact of Social Democratic ideology on the goals of society, on the Scandinavian image of society.

Compromise is a two-sided process in which both parties adopt what is to them a second best solution for the sake of preserving social harmony. Such agreements are sometimes seen as a consequence of consensus, but it is perhaps more accurate to see them as partial accommodations of differing views. Their effect is, however, to produce a constantly changing consensus. For as the parties to a compromise move on to new areas of disagreement, they learn to live with, then to accept, and finally to embrace

what was originally a situation about which they had grave reservations. This, as we have seen, was the process by which Social Democrats came to accept parliamentary reformism. It is also the process by which the other groups and parties have come to accept the Social Democratic ideology of an egalitarian welfare state.

Even though nationalization of the means of production has been one of the traditional socialist policies to become a victim of reformist gradualism, this does not mean that ideological concerns have not motivated their actions. For the Social Democrats, the three enduring ideological themes have been security, equality, and control of the economy. A concern for the security of the individual was the prime incentive for the public works programs adopted in the 1930s to combat unemployment. A commitment to full employment was the first socialist goal to be embraced by all opposition parties. The late 1930s also saw the elaboration of a variety of welfare measures that in succeeding decades were to become the basis for comprehensive schemes covering old-age pensions, the provisions of free or subsidized health facilities, unemployment insurance, and child endowments.

Security and welfare have been seen as aspects of a wider egalitarian objective, which has in part been served by the social transfer payments made through the welfare system and also by the steeply progressive income taxes that finance them. Egalitarianism, like social welfare, is a goal that can be pursued in an even wider context. Measures for the extension of educational opportunity and the contemporary emphasis on schemes for industrial democracy and co-ownership by workers' organizations testify to the Social Democrats' continuing urge to equality. Control of the economy, through the impact of public sector spending, the percentages of investment funds held for welfare purposes, and government intervention in the labor market, is seen as a means to both welfare and equality. A sound and growing economy is regarded as an essential condition of greater welfare and a leveling of incomes. It is for these reasons that the Social Democrats attempt to enhance the productivity of capitalist enterprise. At the same time, regulation is considered necessary to avoid periodic unemployment, to prevent massive disparities in income, and to ensure that the ownership of wealth is not used to social disadvantage.

The control of the governments of the Scandinavian countries over their economies is in effect the Social Democrats' answer to their traditional socialist detractors, for what they are saying is that they can increase social justice while harnessing all the advantages and suffering none of the disadvantages of a capitalist economic system. It is this Social Democratic ideology combining welfare, egalitarianism, and economic control with the continued dominance of individual ownership that gives rise to the paradox we have already mentioned: in any outsiders' discussion of Scandinavia, the nature of politics is as likely to be described as capitalist by a socialist as it is to be described as socialist by a capitalist.

Those who live under systems in which compromise is not commonplace may not recognize the accommodations between Social Democrats and bourgeois forces for what they are. Over the decades of Social Democratic electoral dominance, the bourgeois parties have come to accept the Social Democratic image of the humane welfare society, as earlier the Social Democrats came to accept parliamentary reformism. It would, of course, be quite wrong to see this process of compromise and accommodation as somehow unchanging and involving no policy conflict. The lines of consensus are ever-changing, and the lines of policy conflict change with them. Today, the welfare society is accepted by all parties to the political contest, but the traditional Social Democratic means of financing it by higher and more progressive taxation are not. Clearly, the Social Democrats' electoral reverses in recent years owe much to this factor, and their hopes of further reform within the structure of capitalist society must depend on their capacity to overcome this impasse.

Toward a More Participatory Society

An additional feature of the Social Democratic image of society is an emphasis on citizen participation in political life but also in social and economic organization or what Timothy Tilton has termed *integrative democracy*.[2] Originally this notion focused on the fuller participation of workers and the working classes in society as championed by the Social Democrats, but it has also come to encompass weak and underrepresented groups in society. This ideal shaped the demands for participation and new forms of representation put forward in the 1970s; it also tempered the response to these demands.

In Scandinavia the demands came from both the established parties and alternative groups. The socialists (the Social Democrats and parties to their left) championed the issues of greater equality, democracy in the workplace and employee influence, democratization of schools, and increased influence for residents in community planning and services. In addition, the center parties called for decentralization and more local autonomy, and in Sweden the party revised its program to include ecological demands. At the same time, alternative groups—feminist organizations, university students, and community and environmentalist action groups—pressed for similar demands.

The response to these demands can be illustrated by three areas where the perimeters of representation and participation have been clearly altered. First, labor reforms enacted in the 1970s expanded employee influence. The reforms included schemes for workers' representatives on company boards, the establishment of new codetermination bodies in the workplace, and strengthening the unions' negotiation powers by extending the number of areas subject to collective bargaining. Most significantly, the design of the reforms has generally enhanced the potential for participation

---

[2] T. Tilton, *The Political Theory of Swedish Social Democracy* (Oxford: Oxford University Press, 1989).

of individual workers and simultaneously strengthened the union organizations.

Second, the ideal of integrative democracy is also manifested in the rapid increase in women's political representation during the 1970s and 1980s. Representation has expanded at all levels of government, even within the cabinet where gains have been most striking in Sweden and especially Norway. Although feminist organizations have been important in changing attitudes and bringing women's issues to the top of the political agenda, increased representation is primarily a result of the endeavors of women in party organizations.

Third, the ideal of integrative democracy has influenced immigration policy. The influx of foreigners during the postwar period has eroded the homogeneous character of Scandinavian society. This development has proceeded furthest in Sweden where roughly 8 percent of the population are foreign born. However, in contrast to the German *gastarbeiter* policy and the creation of incentives for immigrants to return to the country of their origin, the Scandinavian approach has been inclusive with efforts to integrate immigrants into political and organizational life. In Sweden foreign nationals after three years of residence have had the right to vote and run for office in local and regional elections since 1976. A few years later Norway and Denmark adopted similar policies.

The end result has been an overall increase in participation—both with respect to who participates and how people participate. Demonstrations, protest meetings, petition campaigns, and boycotts have a long tradition in Scandinavia. From the late 1960s onward, however, there has been an upsurge in these activities. The figures for signing petitions are over 60 percent, and participation in demonstrations is much more widespread in Scandinavia than in many countries. As elsewhere in the advanced industrial countries, participation in ad hoc politics has increased rather dramatically in the past two decades. What is perhaps more unusual is that in Scandinavia this increase has been accompanied by a growth in participation in the organizational/corporate channel and by high rates in participation in the party/electoral channel. New forms of participation have not replaced other modes of participation but instead coexist. The traditional modes of participation probably owe much of their vitality to the high level of institutionalization of parties and organizations that existed prior to the 1970s and made them appear as viable avenues of influence.

In the context of cross-national comparisons, Scandinavians rank extremely high on a wide variety of gauges of participation, for example, voting, party membership, organizational activities, signing petitions, participating in demonstrations, and contacting officials. As distinct from the United States where political participation is related to high socioeconomic status,[3] differences in rates of participation in Scandinavia as in many European countries have been equalized through the existence of the LO unions and the Social Democratic parties. As distinct from the other West European countries discussed in this volume, membership in associations and participation in the organizational/corporate channel of politics are far more prevalent in Scandinavia. Furthermore, in Norway and Sweden the organizational strength of the political parties (members as a percentage of the electorate), with a few exceptions, has shown an increase in the 1970s and 1980s—a trend that contrasts with party development in several West European countries.

Governmental Structure and Performance

In our discussion of political stability and democratic participation in Scandinavia, the main focus has been on political culture and political actors. To complete our account, it is necessary to pay some attention both to governmental structure and performance. We need to ask how far the stability and participatory emphasis of Scandinavian politics has been conditioned by the institutional context from which it has emerged and we also wish to show how the distinctive arrangements of Scandinavian politics have in turn conditioned public policy outcomes.

PARLIAMENTARY GOVERNMENT

The political institutions of the Scandinavian kingdoms are not unlike those of Europe's other major parliamentary democracies. Constitutional monarchy has developed into parliamentary monarchy. The monarch is formally head of state but has in fact relinquished all governmental functions in favor of ministerial rule dependent on the confidence of parliament. Gradual accretion of political authority in the hands of parliament and later, during the era of greater government intervention in the economy, in the hands of the ministerial bureaucracy, has been only very slowly formalized by constitutional amendment. Sweden operated until 1974 on the basis of Europe's oldest written constitution. It was only in that year, and after considerable discussion and debate, that a number of changes were made. These were for the most part a codification of the immense political changes that had transformed the country from an unrepresentative constitutional monarchy into a parliamentary democracy in which political authority emanated from popularly elected representatives. In Denmark, constitutional change occurred somewhat earlier (in 1953), but even today Norway's political system operates under the rules set up in its constitution of 1814. Throughout Scandinavia it has been a question of new wine in old bottles, the existing political institutions proving almost infinitely adaptable in changed social and political conditions.

Indeed, constitutional change in Denmark and Sweden has really been a consequence of the relatively undemocratic structure of the legislatures in an era of full popular sovereignty. In Denmark the upper chamber, with its system of indirect election, higher voting age, and formally coequal powers, stood as an important conservative guarantee against full parliamentary supremacy. Since early in the twentieth century Social Democrats and Radicals had been pledged to the abolition of a chamber that stood in the way of radical reform, but this constitutional amendment was not practical until 1953. It could be argued that it was this failure of full democratization that prevented the Radical party from allying itself with the other bourgeois parties. In Sweden the problem was not so acute, since the first chamber eventually lost its conservative bias. Unicameral reform had to wait until 1970, when it was a result of a more general process of deliberation and compromise begun by a royal commission appointed 16 years earlier.

Because the Eidsvold Convention, which in 1814 wrote the Norwegian constitution, provided for a unicameral legislature in the first instance, it has not proved necessary to undo its handiwork. The monarch (in Sweden the speaker of the House) appoints a prime minister and cabinet from the party that has a parliamentary majority. When no single party has a majority, he selects as prime minister that party leader who enjoys the temporary confidence of parliament. Such confidence may be explicit in the form of a coalition agreement by a number of parties, who decide on a stipulated program. Or it may be implicit, one or more parties forming a minority cabinet and relying on the tacit support of other parliamentary groups

not to defeat them. When no cabinet appears viable in Denmark and Sweden, the prime minister may advise the dissolution of parliament in the hope that a majority may emerge. In Denmark elections must be held every four years, but an election that results from a premature dissolution constitutes the starting point for a new electoral period. In Sweden premature dissolution does not affect the predetermined three-year electoral cycle for the *Riksdag*.

Norway is unique among parliamentary democracies in having no provisions for dissolution during its four-year electoral cycle. This might be regarded as a recipe for political instability in a situation in which no parliamentary grouping could form a viable majority, but as the brief minority government headed by a Christian Democrat and supported by less than one-third of the *Storting* illustrated in 1973, the extent of political consensus is more than sufficient to tide the system over such temporary difficulties. A similar point emerges from the dead heat in the Swedish election of 1973, in which the Social Democrats' and Left-Party Communists' total of 175 seats was exactly matched by the bourgeois parties. This did not prevent Olof Palme, the Social Democratic prime minister remaining in office, from making an agreement with the Liberals on economic policy, relying on the nonpartisan manner in which most issues are debated to secure the passage of legislation, and being willing to accept a final decision by lottery where votes were tied. Again, as we have already noted, Danish governments have proved singularly effective in translating policy intentions into legislation despite the necessity for coalitions and minority governments. In all three countries, therefore, the emergence of policy initiatives through compromise among organized groups and political parties, and the development of a degree of consensus on the legitimate goals of policy, facilitate governmental stability and effective performance under precisely those circumstances in which they would be endangered elsewhere.

GOVERNMENT AND ADMINISTRATION

Apart from the formulation of legislation, the government's major responsibility is for its administration. The cabinet consists of a prime minister and a number of other ministers, most of whom are responsible for the affairs of one of the departments of state. In the Scandinavian countries, as in all Western democracies, the range of governmental functions has expanded widely in this century: there are ministries covering such areas as social welfare, economic affairs, education, commerce, housing, and culture. Much of the legislative and administrative activities in each of these areas falls within the province of individual ministers. The cabinet acts largely as an agency of coordination and a forum for final decisions on issues. Within the cabinet, the prime minister has considerable authority in his role as party and national leader. His position is limited to some extent by the deference accorded departmental expertise, and his major roles are as chairman and coordinator. The cabinet as a whole is responsible to the legislature, which may inquire into the government's actions through parliamentary questions and debate and may in the last instance register its disapproval by a vote of no confidence.

In formal terms there is a major distinction between the administrative systems of Denmark and Norway, which are organized on a strict departmental pattern with a minister responsible for the actions of all those civil servants in his jurisdiction, and that of Sweden, which is far more decentralized. Swedish ministers are in charge of relatively small policymaking units, and most civil servants work for independent administrative agencies and boards whose major function is routine administration. In reality, however, the practical differences between the two systems should not be unduly stressed. The proliferation of the administrative functions of government in this century has led to the emergence of a number of extraministerial agencies in both Norway and Denmark. The need for greater economic coordination has made the independent agencies of Swedish administration take more notice of ministerial directives. In all the Scandinavian polities, public servants enjoy considerable security of tenure and protection from arbitrary dismissal. They have considerable influence on policymaking in conjunction with the representatives of organized groupings and political parties.

This brings us to one of the distinctive aspects of the Scandinavian governmental structure—the extent to which it facilitates access to policymaking by organized group interests. The *remiss* procedure in Sweden and Norway has already been mentioned as a means by which organized groups are formally incorporated in the structure of decision making. Moreover, because of the decentralized administrative structure in Sweden, a similar procedure exists by which boards and agencies are required to submit their opinion on proposed measures that affect them. More important in Scandinavia as a whole is the role of royal commissions in the legislative process. The functions of such commissions are basically investigatory, and they may be set up on the initiative of the government itself or as a consequence of concern expressed by legislators. Their membership is generally not large, although it usually contains some balance among the various shades of parliamentary opinion, the representatives of organized groups, members of the appropriate administrative agency, and expert, usually university, personnel.

Royal commissions have a long tradition as a part of the Scandinavian administrative structure and owe much to the spirit of "objectivity" that was a feature of the nineteenth-century official culture. They have played a major role in the elaboration of social-welfare policy. As early as 1884, the Swedish *Riksdag* appointed a commission to investigate all aspects of social insurance. It consisted of a Liberal member of parliament, a provincial governor, the farmers' leader, several representatives of the employers, and even a worker. It is possible that, as governmental stability has become rather more precarious since the early 1970s, such commissions have been used more than they once were to shelve issues, but their more normal role has been as a forum in which new policy initiatives can be explored in a nonpartisan spirit. They are an attempt to arrive at solutions that can provide the basis for noncontroversial legislation. Royal commissions can therefore be said to be an institutionalized mechanism of corporate pluralism. All those involved in the making and implementation of a policy, as well as the official representatives of those likely to be affected by it, can thus have some influence on its form and content.

In addition, standing and special legislative committees have offered the opposition parties the opportunity to collaborate with— and, in effect, participate in—government. Frequently condemned to long periods out of office, the opposition parties use parliamentary committees as a means for gaining compromise solutions. Such a situation sometimes makes it difficult to know which are the opposition parties, since opposition to the government may change from issue to issue and over the duration of a parliament. Indeed, as commentators on all three Scandinavian countries have argued, the very term *opposition* may be misleading in a governmental system that allows such extensive access to organized groups, bureaucratic agencies, and nongovernmental parties.

The impact of widespread access on government performance has a number of consequences. It generally ensures that policy initiatives are acceptable to the major organized interests in society and do not become a source of bitterness and political divisiveness. Because this is so, there is a greater tendency for continuity of policy than in nations whose governments are marked by greater partisanship. Furthermore, the extensive consideration policy proposals receive from so many bodies guarantees a degree of rational appraisal unrivaled in other systems. The provision of factual and analytic information may enable the government to avoid party strife and prepare the ground for the general acceptance of necessary reforms. On the other side, the operation of these access mechanisms can be excessively slow. Another possible defect is the extent to which incorporation of all the relevant policymaking elites in a close-knit group in which discussion is led by experts can exclude the public from comprehending the real issues at stake. This was certainly one complaint of those advocating an extension of direct democracy in the 1970s.

STATE AND CITIZEN

One safeguard against the political dangers of hegemony by political elites would be a resort to some form of popular initiative. Referendums have occurred in all the Scandinavian countries in recent decades. In Denmark there is a constitutional provision for using such means as a check on arbitrary government action. Even here, the rules do not allow popular initiatives, but are designed to prevent governments with a small majority from adopting extreme policies. In effect the referendum is a means for ensuring the viability of compromise politics, as was illustrated by its use in 1963 to defeat a number of measures passed by the Social Democratic–Radical government on land use in Denmark. In Sweden the option of a mandatory referendum was introduced in 1980, but its use is limited to constitutional amendments. Otherwise referendums are consultative, as demonstrated by the Swedish government's decision to change the traffic system from left-hand to right-hand drive a decade after this proposal had been decisively rejected in a referendum.

If there are no real constitutional safeguards for the citizen against the corporate policymaking elite, the situation is markedly different in regard to his position vis-à-vis the administrative agencies of government. Here again the Swedish administrative structure is distinctive. One of its features, the ombudsman, has been copied throughout

Scandinavia and is being adopted in other countries as well. The 1809 Swedish Constitution provided for the appointment of an ombudsman for civil affairs responsible to parliament for ensuring the compliance of government and civil service with its will. Over the years the increasing range of governmental activity has meant a proliferation of duties. The ombudsmen's jurisdiction covers the conduct of courts and judges, and the activities of military personnel and public servants at both national and local levels. The vast majority of the cases with which the ombudsmen deal—and they may be initiated by complaints from the public or *Riksdag* members as well as by their own investigations—are handled without recourse to legal action. But the ombudsmen may also use the courts to proceed against officials who have broken the law or not performed their duties properly.

The institution of the ombudsman, devised in the early nineteenth century, has become particularly appropriate in the era of the social-welfare state, when ordinary citizens are dependent on officials' correct performance of their duties in order to obtain their rights. Denmark in 1953 and Norway in 1962 adopted similar institutions, although in both the competence of the ombudsman is somewhat more limited than in Sweden. In 1972 Norway appointed an ombudsman to protect consumers from powerful business interests and to ensure that marketing practices are not being misused within the meaning of the law. In both Norway and Sweden ombudsmen have been appointed to ensure the observation of legislation intended to guarantee equality between the sexes. Once again this is an illustration of the way in which political institutions in Scandinavia tend to be adapted and extended to cope with contemporary problems that could not have been foreseen when they were first established.

The rights of the citizen in Scandinavia are protected by other devices as well. In Sweden all official documents issued or filed by state or municipal public authorities are available for inspection on demand. This is a major instrument for public control, particularly because such access is used by the press in investigations of bureaucratic actions. It is also, of course, a mechanism that transforms formal participative rights into the actuality of participation on the basis of informed knowledge. Furthermore, in Norway and Denmark, the courts play a major part in the control of the administration. They may decide whether laws and legislation delegated to the administrative agencies are in accord with valid law. None of these means of administrative control seems to have any serious impact on the effective performance of government, although in many other democratic systems, it has been claimed that such intense public scrutiny might well make the job of administration impossible.

THE WELFARE STATE

We have already seen how welfare-state objectives have constituted a major aspect of the ideological perspective of social democracy, and the extent to which welfare goals are now commonly accepted by all established groups and parties in Scandinavian society. This ideological commitment is reflected in economic and administrative structures dominated by the welfare system. In each of the Scandinavian nations more than 50 percent of the gross national product goes to make up public sector revenue in the form of direct and indirect taxation and contributory payments to various social insurance and pension schemes. This should not, of course, be taken as an indication of the extent to which private consumption as a whole is reduced, since between 30 and 50 percent of that revenue is returned in the form of social transfer payments. The real effect of these transfer payments should be considered less in terms of the reduction of private spending power and more in terms of redistribution.

Redistribution can be of two types, one involving the vertical leveling of disparate income groups, and the other the horizontal equalization of an individual's lifetime earnings. Both effects are notable in Scandinavia. The poor in all nations are more subject to fluctuations in fortune than are the middle classes, since the latter possess capital or savings to tide them over economic dislocations caused by illness, unemployment, increased family size, and old age. Thus, the major impact of social transfer payments financed by taxation is that individuals are compelled to save an appreciable part of their income in good times to cover the possibility of economic misfortune. That the general level of income equality is rather high in Scandinavia is less a consequence of the welfare system than it is of the high productivity of an advanced industrial society and extremely strong trade unions that can exploit their position in the labor market.

In terms of administrative structure, the major effect of welfare legislation is to increase the size and number of administrative agencies as well as the number of personnel they employ. Only a small part of the increase in personnel can be attributed to high levels of transfer payments. Far more are occupied in the collective services provided by the state, which is the other main aspect of the Scandinavian welfare system. Such services include medical care, free education up to and including the college level, and social work agencies for the rehabilitation of the sick, the elderly, and the handicapped.

As Rudolf Meidner, formerly the chief economist of the Swedish LO, has pointed out, there is absolutely no reason to suppose that the demand for such collective services has been filled by the level of service already offered. On the contrary, the tendency in Sweden has been for need to rise faster than the level of services. This has been particularly true in preventive medicine, where advances in technology have markedly increased the average life span, and have simultaneously created an urgent need for nursing and other forms of care for the elderly. Sweden, with 37 percent of the working population in government employment, has probably the highest level of collective

service in the world, although the other Scandinavian countries do not come far behind. Meidner's prediction for the end of the century is a public sector employing more than 50 percent of the working population.[1]

Even at the current level, the welfare state is not without its economic and administrative problems. On an economic level the problem is one of finance, and questions of economic growth and taxation loom large as political issues as in other countries. In recent years, even the Social Democrats have seen the necessity to make marginal cuts in public expenditures under adverse economic conditions. Moreover, they have been persuaded that extremely high marginal tax rates are hardly the way to make collective consumption and welfare acceptable to the electorate. Thus, while total tax burdens have not declined appreciably, the incidence of taxation has, with an appreciable shift from direct income taxes to indirect taxes on consumption.

In administrative terms, the dangers presented by an ever-growing public sector lie in the increasing power that this must necessarily confer on the bureaucracy. To date, the administrative safeguards already noted seem to have been adequate to protect the citizen from the power of officialdom, but if the public sector grows further, new forms of protection may have to be devised. Problems of taxation and bureaucratic control constitute the major challenge to the established Scandinavian welfare-state societies, and it is on these issues that many of the political battles of the next few decades are likely to center.

Two other problems sometimes raised by critics of the welfare state have hitherto been of somewhat lesser importance. Conservative parties throughout Scandinavia, and most recently the Swedish Employers' Con-

---

[1] R. Meidner, "The Trade Union Movement and the Public Sector," speech delivered at the Twentieth Convention of Public Services International, New York, October 10, 1973.

federation (SAF), have suggested that the high level of certain welfare payments are a disincentive to work. They have attributed high levels of absenteeism in certain industrial companies to this cause. However, in evaluating this argument one should remember that the general level of industrial productivity in Scandinavia is extremely high. Although the fear of unemployment and poverty have become rare, other motivations, such as the desire to get ahead, are strong.

The other supposed problem is the disinclination to invest capital in economic systems as tightly controlled as those of Scandinavia. Until the early 1970s, this problem seemed to be of more ideological than practical significance, as illustrated by the continuingly high rates of economic growth in all three Scandinavian kingdoms. Although wealth is taxed, it has been at rates that have not prevented the accumulation of capital, and, in general, the philosophy has been one of cooperation between government and business in the belief that that conflict between the classes is itself a major impediment to economic performance.[2] The big question is whether such cooperation, and the economic growth it has hitherto encouraged, is likely to persist in a changed economic climate. The evidence of the 1970s and the early 1980s is that most Scandinavian governments have been willing to endure temporary international indebtedness and reduced economic growth to preserve the main features of their welfare programs. However, the word temporary is the operative one. Having failed to sacrifice the welfare state on the altar of economic rationality in the period of the second oil crisis, the Scandinavian countries under both bourgeois and social democratic administrations have set about the task of restoring a good economic climate for investment. Indeed, the Swedish Social Democrats almost certainly owe a large part of their electoral victories in 1985 and 1988 to their reputation as sound economic managers.

POLICY PERFORMANCE, POLITICAL STABILITY, AND DEMOCRATIC PARTICIPATION

Throughout this section we have tried to demonstrate the operation of political institutions and practices in Scandinavia and to show the major reasons why they have developed as they have. But all political analysis involves the exercise of judgment. In talking about politics it is part of our task to evaluate the effectiveness, the performance, and therefore the desirability of the institutions and processes we examine. In concluding, we will suggest some ways in which policy performance may be linked to both political stability and democratic participation.

Economic Performance

In terms of economic performance, several points about the Scandinavian countries are notable. First, there can be no question whatsoever as to economic success. Each of the nations has an advanced industrial structure, each has until recently enjoyed high rates of economic growth, and each has high average levels of per capita income. As we have seen in Table 1–1, all three Scandinavian countries are among the richer countries and lag only slightly behind the United States.

Second, we can question the extent to which economic success is attributable to governmental action. In some respects, all three countries have been extremely fortunate. Both Sweden and Norway have had a raw materials base for their developing export economies (timber and iron ore in Sweden and timber and hydroelectricity in Norway, now augmented in the latter by North Sea oil). Denmark, a small country specializing in the export of animal products, found a natural market in the burgeoning demand

---

[2] G. Adler-Karlsson, *Functional Socialism: A Swedish Theory for Socialization* (Stockholm: Bokforlaget Prisma, 1969), p. 18.

of other industrializing European nations. By pursuing a policy of neutrality, all three countries avoided much of the economic dislocation of World War I, and Sweden has succeeded in avoiding international conflict for over a century and a half. But government policy has also played a part.

In the depression of the mid-1970s caused by the impact of increased oil prices, Norway and Sweden experienced lower unemployment, lower inflation, and higher rates of economic growth than did the majority of European nations. During the crisis that has affected most European countries in the last decade, both countries have kept unemployment levels well below the average for advanced Western states.

Finally, it is clear that economic success, whether measured by recent performance or by the rapid economic growth of the last century, has had a major influence on continuing political and governmental stability. The fact that the national cake has grown bigger and bigger has meant that individuals have seen a continuous improvement in their position. This could not fail to be reflected in adherence to the political and governmental system that made it possible. Indeed, it is notable that high rates of inflation in Denmark in the 1970s have coincided with the fragmentation of the established party system.

Social Welfare

There can be no debate about the extent to which welfare policies designed to alleviate the misfortunes facing the individual are a consequence of governmental performance. In Scandinavia in general it is fair to argue that the level of security and protection offered the individual is greater than in any other nations in the world. Moreover, although this has meant a heavy and increasing tax burden, the high level of average income has made it possible to combine welfare with levels of disposable income in no way inferior to those in the other advanced countries of Western Europe. As we have been at pains to stress throughout, enhanced security through social welfare has

been a vital tenet of the Social Democratic image of society. However, although the emergent consensus on ever-greater degrees of welfare has been a product of Social Democratic success, humane collectivist solutions have had a part in the Scandinavian political culture since the nineteenth century.

The development of welfare policy in Scandinavia has not involved discontinuity and conflict, but rather the gradual development of a set of attitudes and beliefs consonant with the preexisting political tradition. For this reason, the emergence of the welfare society has not been the source of destabilizing conflict between the adherents of individualism and collectivism. Rather, it has been a factor binding the community more closely together by ensuring that the major potential areas of protest and dissatisfaction in an industrial society have been minimized. Only today have the issues of massive taxation and the extent of bureaucratic influence inherent in an economy providing so great a level of public service raised any real question of the further extension of the welfare state. Nor is the question one of the desirability of public welfare. Rather, it is one of the economic and institutional means to achieve it.

Social and Political Harmony

The performance of political institutions and governmental structures in facilitating social and political harmony has been the underlying theme of this section. In nonparticipatory political systems, stability is maintained by the repression of dissenting opinion. In participatory or democratic political systems, stability may result from one of two mechanisms. Where sections of the community and political opinion are deeply divided, stability may be a consequence of a willingness to live and let live, to allow the expression of opposing views, and to permit that group having a temporary majority in the community to make its policies effective. Alternatively, stability may rest on an attempt to seek political accommodation through encouraging enhanced and varied forms of democratic participation. No democratic political system is purely one or the other, and in each can be found some balance between divisions and consensus.

What we would argue, however, is that Scandinavian polities have hitherto sought to use the mechanisms of a constantly extended participatory democracy to achieve the accommodation-seeking alternative as nearly as possible. This is reflected not merely in the fact that policy is designed to achieve compromise. The institutional mechanisms of corporate pluralism are of a kind that put a premium on the achievement of harmony, although, as the label "corporate *pluralism*" suggests, the conflict of interests and individuals channeled through effective participative arrangements is considered the primary means to that end. In essence, corporate pluralism involves widening the sphere of politics and government so that the major groups in society are brought together in the policymaking and administrative process. In Scandinavia, the institutional dividing lines between state and society are drawn less clearly than in other societies. As we have seen, the organized groups in society do not merely press the government to take actions in accord with their interests; they are involved as participants in the policymaking and administrative processes.

In the emergence of such a system, groups have ceased to be merely the agents of particular interests and have acquired a political responsibility that has made them prefer mutual accommodation to outright conflict. The extent to which the political performance of such a system fosters continuing stability depends fundamentally on the extent to which the political elites represent their members' views. Although radical critics of Scandinavian society have argued that recent years have witnessed the emergence of an organizational oligarchy among the established groups in the system, the twin traditions of democratic participation and regime deference have at least until now guaranteed the ability to respond to new views with both effective policymaking and

an extension of the participatory sphere itself.

BIBLIOGRAPHY

Scandinavia

ALLARDT, ERIK, et al., eds. *Nordic Democracy.* Copenhagen: Det danske selskab, 1981.

BERGLUND, STEN, and ULF LINDSTRÖM. *The Scandinavian Party System(s).* Lund: Studentlitteratur, 1978.

BORRE, OLE. "Critical Electoral Change in Scandinavia." In Russell J. Dalton, Scott C. Flannigan, and Paul Allen Beck, *Electoral Change in Advanced Industrial Democracies: Realignment or Dealignment?* Princeton, NJ: Princeton University Press, 1984.

CASTLES, FRANCIS G. *The Social Democratic Image of Society.* London: Routledge & Kegan Paul, 1978.

CERNY, KARL H., ed. *Scandinavia at the Polls.* Washington, DC: American Enterprise Institute, 1977.

DERRY, T. K. *A History of Scandinavia.* Minneapolis: University of Minnesota Press, 1979.

EINHORN, ERIC S., and JOHN LOGUE, *Modern Welfare States: Politics and Policy in Social Democratic Scandinavia.* New York: Praeger, 1989.

ELDER, NEIL, et al. *The Consensual Democracies? The Government and Politics of the Scandinavian States,* 2nd ed. Oxford: Basil Blackwell, 1988.

ESPING-ANDERSON, GØSTA. *Politics Against Markets: The Social Democratic Road to Power.* Princeton, NJ: Princeton University Press, 1985.

FLORA, PETER, ed. *Growth to Limits.* Vol. 1, *Sweden, Norway, Denmark, Finland.* Berlin: de Gruyter, 1986.

GRAUBARD, STEPHEN R., ed. *Norden—The Passion for Equality.* Oslo: Norwegian University Press, 1986.

HAAVIO-MANNILA, ELINA, et al. *Unfinished Democracy: Women in Nordic Politics.* Oxford: Pergamon, 1985.

HECKSCHER, GUNNAR. *The Welfare State and Beyond.* Minneapolis: University of Minnesota Press, 1984.

INGHAM, GEOFFREY K. *Strikes and Industrial Conflict: Britain and Scandinavia.* London: Macmillan, 1974.

LOGUE, JOHN, ed. "Rethinking the Welfare State." *Scandinavian Studies,* special issue (Spring 1987).

SAINSBURY, DIANE. "Scandinavian Party Politics

Re-examined: Social Democracy in Decline?" *West European Politics*, Vol. 7 (1984).

SARLVIK, BO. "Coalition Politics and Policy Output in Scandinavia." In Vernon Bogdanor, ed., *Coalition Government in Western Europe*. London: Heinemann, 1983.

SJOBLOM, GUNNAR. "The Role of Political Parties in Denmark and Sweden 1970–1984." In Richard S. Katz, ed., *Party Governments: European and American Experiences*. Berlin: de Gruyter, 1987.

Denmark

BORRE, OLE. "The Social Basis of Danish Electoral Behaviour." In Richard Rose, ed., *Electoral Participation. A Comparative Analysis*. Beverly Hills: Sage, 1980.

FITZMAURICE, JOHN. *Politics in Denmark*. London: Hurst, 1981.

LOGUE, JOHN. *Socialism and Abundance*. Minneapolis: University of Minnesota Press, 1982.

PEDERSON, MOGENS N. "The Defeat of all Parties: The Danish Folketing Election 1973." In Kay Lawson and Peter H. Merkl, eds., *When Parties Fail*. Princeton, NJ: Princeton University Press, 1988.

———. "The Danish 'Working Multiparty System': Breakdown or Adaptation?" In Hans Daalder, ed., *Party Systems in Denmark, Austria, Switzerland, the Netherlands and Belgium*. London: Frances Pinter, 1987.

Norway

ECKSTEIN, HARRY. *Division and Cohesion in Democracy*. Princeton, NJ: Princeton University Press, 1966.

KVAVIK, ROBERT. *Interest Groups in Norwegian Politics*. Oslo: Universitetsforlaget, 1976.

LAFFERTY, WILLIAM M. "Decision-Making Involvement in Norway: The Nature and Scope of Citizen Access in a Social Democratic Polity." *European Journal of Political Research*. (March 1984).

———. *Participation and Democracy in Norway: The "Distant Democracy" Revisited*. Oslo: Universitetsforlaget, 1981.

MARTINUSSEN, WILLY. *The Distant Democracy. Social Inequality, Political Resources and Political Influence in Norway*. London: John Wiley, 1977.

OLSEN, JOHAN P. *Organized Democracy. Political Institutions in a Welfare State—The Case of Norway*. Oslo: Universitetsforlaget, 1983.

ROKKAN, STEIN. "Geography, Religion and Social Class: Crosscutting Cleavages in Norwegian Politics." In S. M. Lipset and S. Rokkan, eds., *Party Systems and Voter Alignments*. New York: Free Press, 1967.

———. "Norway: Numerical Democracy and Corporate Pluralism." In Robert A. Dahl, ed., *Political Oppositions in Western Democracies*. New Haven, CT: Yale University Press, 1966.

VALEN, HENRY, and DANIEL KATZ. *Political Parties in Norway*. London: Tavistock, 1964.

Sweden

ANTON, THOMAS J. *Administered Politics*. Boston: Nijhoff, 1980.

CASTLES, FRANCIS G. "The Political Functions of Organized Groups: The Swedish Case." *Political Studies*, Vol. 21 (1973).

GRANBERG, DONALD, and SOREN HOLMBERG. *The Political System Matters: Social Psychology and Voting Behavior in Sweden and the United States*. Cambridge: Cambridge University Press, 1988.

HAMILTON, MALCOLM B. *Democratic Socialism in Britain and Sweden*. London: Macmillan, 1988.

HANCOCK, M. DONALD. *Sweden: The Politics of Postindustrial Change*. Hinsdale, IL: Dryden, 1975.

HECLO, HUGH. *Modern Social Politics in Britain and Sweden*. New Haven, CT: Yale University Press, 1974.

HECLO, HUGH, and HENRIK JESS MADSEN. *Policy and Politics in Sweden*. Philadelphia: Temple University Press, 1987.

KORPI, WALTER. *The Democratic Class Struggle*. London: Routledge & Kegan Paul, 1983.

LEWIN, LEIF. *Governing Trade Unions in Sweden*. Cambridge, MA: Harvard University Press, 1980.

RUSTOW, DANKWART A. "Sweden's Transition to Democracy: Some Notes Towards a Genetic Theory." *Scandinavian Political Studies*, 1971.

———. "Scandinavia: Working Multiparty Systems." In S. Neumann, ed., *Modern Political Parties*. Chicago: University of Chicago Press, 1956.

SAINSBURY, DIANE. "The 1988 Swedish Election: The Breakthrough of the Greens." *West European Politics*, April, 1989.

TILTON, TIMOTHY A. *The Political Theory of Swedish Social Democracy*. Oxford: Oxford University Press, 1989.

TINGSTEN, HERBERT. *The Swedish Social Democrats*. Totowa, NJ: Bedminster, 1973.

VEDUNG, EVERT. "The Swedish Five-Party Syndrome and the Environmentalists." In Kay

Lawson and Peter H. Merkl, eds., *When Parties Fail*. Princeton, NJ: Princeton University Press, 1988.

WHEELER, CHRISTOPHER. *White-Collar Power: Changing Patterns of Interest Group Behavior in Sweden*. Urbana: University of Illinois Press, 1975.

Finland

ALAPURO, RISTO, et al., eds. *Small States in Comparative Perspective*. Oslo: Norwegian University Press, 1985.

ARTER, DAVID. *Politics and Policy-Making in Finland*. New York: St. Martin's, 1987.

NOUSIAINEN, JAAKKO. *The Finnish Political System*. Cambridge, MA: Harvard University Press, 1971.

PESONEN, PERTTI. *An Election in Finland*. New Haven, CT: Yale University Press, 1968.

TÖRNUDD, KLAUS. *The Electoral System of Finland*. London: Evelyn, 1968.

Annual Publications

OECD *Economic Surveys*. Separate publications for Denmark, Finland, Norway, and Sweden.

Scandinavian Political Studies. Oslo: Universitetsforlaget.

PART VII
THE EUROPEAN ECONOMIC COMMUNITY: ECONOMIC AND POLITICAL UNION

FRANÇOISE DE LA SERRE

1

Introduction

EDITOR'S NOTE - *Few developments in the post-World War II period (since 1945) have attracted so much attention as the on-going efforts of the Europeans—first the Federal Republic of Germany, France, Italy and the Benelux countries in 1958, later England, Ireland and Denmark (1973), and more recently Greece, Spain and Portugal (1981 and 1986)—to form first an economic and ultimately a political union. After decades of deliberations and negotiations, finally the Single European Act—providing for a complete economic union—will come into force on January 1, 1993. All trade barriers among the twelve member states of the European Community will be eliminated, and rules and regulations are being drafted to harmonize social and welfare policies, taxation, to restructure the common agricultural policy, establish free exchange of currencies and labor, and ultimately to set up a common European currency and a central European bank similar to the Federal Reserve Board. Looming even larger than economic union is the prospect of a political union in which ulti-mately the individual member states will relinquish their sovereign powers to a European political entity that will, in the course of time, assume the power to make laws for all members and conduct a common defense and foreign policy. Such a political union will involve the growth of a strong European Assembly, a European executive representing a European electorate and acting on its behalf, and a European Court ruling on all disputes among member states and between individuals and member states. It will also involve the emergence of a truly European public opinion. But how soon institutional structure will be fully in place is uncertain.*

As the representatives of the twelve states constantly meet and deliberate and as we read about their efforts in the press, anyone with a sense of history cannot but be exhilarated. European nations—Spain, France, England and, for a short and frightening period, Nazi Germany—one after the other had assumed ascendancy over all other nations and made their power felt throughout the world. National rivalries among the European states led to constant wars and brought both the United States and Russia into these conflicts.

In 1945, too weak and exhausted, all European nations had to accept in one form or another Soviet or American control or domination. Gradually, like a phoenix rising from the ashes of World War II, the European nations began again to reassert themselves, but no longer in rivalry with each other. Gradually, the realization of common interests that transcended national ones began to emerge; gradually a European reality began to assert itself. The European Community to which this section is devoted is an effort to give to this reality new institutions and new goals: first, to create an economic union; second, to avoid the recurrence of force in the resolution of conflicts; third, to provide mechanism for cooperation and common decisions in all matters that concern the member states individ-

ually and in all matters that concern them collectively with the rest of the world. Only in this manner will a European reality gain precedence over the nation states that still comprise Europe. It has been and it remains a daring and exciting prospect.

Unlike the American states that sent their representatives to Philadelphia to make a Federal constitution that united them on all crucial matters of governance, the European Union is being fashioned step by step, regulation by regulation, meeting after meeting, sector by sector. It is to this grinding, at times halting, process that this section is mostly addressed. "The interstices of law are in procedures," wrote a famous British jurist. The ultimate goals of a European community and its formation lie in specific institutional arrangements of binding community agreements that grind down the individual sovereignty of the states in favor of a community organization that transcends them.

One of the most significant political developments since the end of World War II has been the proliferation of nation-states, independent and sovereign, with representatives in the United Nations. The number will swell to 185 by the end of 1990. Yet World War II showed conclusively that only very large nation-states—the United States, the Soviet Union, possibly China and India—could command the resources needed for the maintenance of their independence and security. And they too are subject to forces over which they have no absolute control, and to economic, political, and military considerations that often underscore the kind of interdependence that calls for cooperation and reciprocity.

In Europe after World War II, the need to "unify" was keenly felt. Western Europe had emerged from the war economically weakened, politically in disarray, and militarily completely overshadowed by the power of the Soviet Union. Massive American support was needed to deter the Soviet forces and to permit European revival.

The idea of European unity was not new. It had been sustained and nourished over the years after the breakup of the Holy Ro-

man Empire, which had maintained the symbolism of the unity of the European Christian world until the beginning of the nineteenth century. It was shattered by World War I and the devastation it brought. But the moment peace came, the movement for unity sprang up again with renewed force precisely because of the general revulsion to the war and the fear of another one. A pan-European Union was drafted for the purpose of organizing a United Europe, with a European Council consisting of delegates of the various states, a parliament consisting of delegates chosen by the national parliaments, and a high court.

Perhaps the most significant move in the direction of European unity was made by the French statesman Aristide Briand in a memorandum dated May 17, 1930. Brushing aside all arguments favoring a limited economic or customs union, Briand went straight to the heart of the problem. Economic union is unavoidably related to security, he argued; security is a matter related to collective political decisions and a collective political will. It is therefore necessary to consider an economic union in political terms. It is only when political structures and insti-

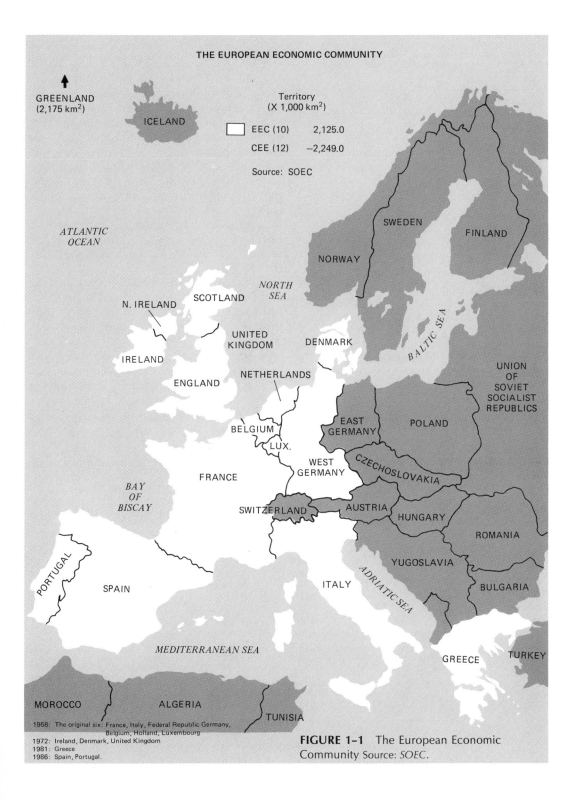

FIGURE 1-1 The European Economic Community Source: *SOEC*.

331

TABLE 1-1   The Growth of the Economic Community Since 1958

Founding Members

- Fed. Republic Germany
- France
- Italy
- Belgium
- Netherlands
- Luxembourg

New Entrants

- United Kingdom (1973)
- Ireland (1973)
- Denmark (1973)
- Greece (1981)
- Spain (1986)
- Portugal (1986)

Applicants for membership

- Turkey

tutions are established, Briand pointed out, that customs, trade, and even the development of a "common market" (he used the term) can be decided upon and implemented.

Briand's dream lived on during World War II. From Italy, Holland, and France came bold plans for a federation with real supranational powers. Even in Britain and in the United States, where some of the pan-Europeanists had taken refuge, plans for federation were made—some on a European scale, others on a world scale. Leaders such as Jean Monnet (who later founded the Action Committee for the United States of Europe and became known as the "father of Europe"), Paul-Henri Spaak, the Belgian political leader who was to become the author of the report for the establishment of the European Economic Community, and even orthodox nationalists like Winston Churchill and Charles de Gaulle outlined thoughts in favor of European "federation." Sometimes this body was to be limited to economic matters, sometimes to cultural and social matters. Sometimes it was to be endowed with genuine, supranational powers even in security and defense. The word *federation* was in the air, and people began to search desperately for ways to bring it to life.

TABLE 1-2   The Economic Weight of the Community

EUROPEAN COMMUNITY: THE SUM OF ITS PARTS			
	Area (000 km²)	Population (000)	(GDP)[a] per head $
Belgium	30.5	9,855.3	10,603
Denmark	43.1	5,111.6	14,946
Germany	248.7	61,175.1	13,509
Greece	132.0	9,895.8	4,325
Spain	504.8	38,386.8	5,632
France	544.0	54,947.1	12,280
Ireland	68.9	3,535.0	6,817
Italy	301.3	57,004.9	8,297
Luxembourg	2.6	365.9	12,876
Netherlands	41.2	14,424.2	11,460
Portugal	92.1	10,089.3	2,705
United Kingdom	244.1	56,487.8	10,533
Community Total	2,253.3	321,278.8	10.055
United States	9,372.7	236,681.0	21,851
Japan	372.3	120,018.0	14,617

[a]Gross domestic product.
Source: *Eurostat*, 1988 (In basic statistics of the community), 4th ed., Brussels.

THE FORMS OF UNITY

Before we examine the steps taken toward European unity, it is worth looking at the three basic types of unity—intergovernmental, functional, and political—that at one time or another influenced the construction of a unified Europe. The *intergovernmental* type envisaged "union" as an ongoing consultation and cooperation among national governmental organs. Heads of state, ministers, ambassadors would meet several times a year to reach common conclusions and arrive at common policy positions. There would be no permanent structure for deliberation and implementation of the decisions. There would be no federation. No supranationality would be granted to the intergovernmental organs, and there would be no way to reach decisions except by unanimous vote. De Gaulle was by far the perfect representative of this school of thought.

The *functional* type of unity stressed the primacy of economic and social cooperation and integration in the form of common tariffs, common social policies, common banking and investment policies, even the creation of a common currency. It was the hope of the functionalists and also that of men like Jean Monnet that upon integration of the economic sectors common political institutions would become a necessity. The functional plan saw political union as a result of economic and social unification. It tended therefore to be gradualistic and incremental and to defer the establishment of common political institutions and a common decision-making machinery until a time when the economies had in fact become more European than national.

The third type of union was the affirmation of political unity through political organization and structures, with a power and an authority that transcended the governments of individual states. This political union could be a confederation in which the powers of a European political body were very limited, and exercised only under stringent conditions requiring weighted majorities. Or it could be a federation like the United States, where the delegation of power to the national government comes broadly and directly from the people. Advocates of the political type of union subordinated all economic and social matters to the establishment of a political authority. Without it, without some degree of genuine federalism and supranationalism, they argued, Europe would remain a grouping of independent states whose viability would depend upon the uncertain convergence of national interests.

The three types we have outlined are not of the "either-or" variety; not one of them excludes the others. In fact, the three co-existed in the various stages of the formation of the EEC. They still coexist.

In its present form (see Figure 1–1 and Tables 1–1 and 1–2), the Community's development is the result of two frequently conflicting trends that have marked the evolution of European unification since the early 1950s: the logic of integration and that of state sovereignty.[1] And only by studying the realization of European Union since the 1950s can we gauge the direction in which it is, or, as the case may be, is not moving.

---

[1] Francoise de la Serre, ed., "Foreign Policy of the European Community," in Roy Macridis, *Foreign Policy in World Politics*, 7th ed. (Englewood Cliffs, NJ: Prentice Hall, 1989).

Landmarks in European Economic and Political Union

September 9, 1946	Address by Winston Churchill in Zurich suggesting the establishment of a United States of Europe.
June 5, 1947	Announcement of the Marshall Plan by the United States to help in the reconstruction of Europe.

Landmarks in European Economic and Political Union

April 16, 1948	Creation of Organization of European Economic Cooperation (OEEC) for the implementation of the Marshall Plan.
April 4, 1949	Signing of the North Atlantic Treaty.
May 5, 1949	Creation of the Council of Europe.
May 9, 1950	Statement of Robert Schuman, French minister of foreign affairs, proposing a "Franco-German pool of coal and steel."
April 18, 1951	Treaty of Paris establishes the Coal and Steel Community; France, the Federal Republic of Germany, Italy, Belgium, Holland, and Luxembourg are members.
June 1–3, 1955	Meeting at Messina of the foreign ministers of West Germany, Belgium, France, Italy, Luxembourg, and Holland. They envisage a Common Market for the whole economy as well as for nuclear energy. A committee of experts, presided over by Paul-Henri Spaak, is charged with the preparation of a report. Great Britain is invited to take part but refuses.
March 25, 1957	Signing in Rome of the treaties constituting the European Economic Community and the European Atomic Energy Community (EURATOM) by the six counries. The goal of the Common Market is to establish a customs union by eliminating all tariffs and obstacles to free trade and also to put into effect a common political economy for the six countries in the Community. To realize these objectives, Community institutions are created: the European Commission, the Council of Ministers, the European Parliament, and the Court of Justice.
January 1, 1958	The treaties of Rome come into effect.
January 1, 1961	First steps to bring national customs tariffs of the six together.
August 9, 1961	Great Britain applies for entry to the Common Market and is followed by Denmark, Ireland, and Norway.
October 10, 1961	Opening of negotiations for the admission of Great Britain to the Common Market.
January 14, 1963	General de Gaulle announces at a press conference that Britain is not ready to enter the Common Market.
May 11, 1967	Great Britain reapplies for entry to the Common Market.
July 1, 1968	The customs union comes into effect: total elimination of customs among the six; establishment of common customs tariff.
December 1–2, 1969	Meeting at The Hague of the chiefs of state and of the governments of the six: agreement in principle on the agricultural policy and financing; decision to start negotiations with Great Britain
April 22, 1970	Treaty relating to the strengthening of the budgetary powers of the European Parliament is signed; establishment of independent resources for the Community.
October 27, 1970	Adoption of a project for political cooperation to coordinate the foreign policy of the member states.
February 9, 1971	Agreement among the six on the European economic and monetary union (Plan Werner).
January 22, 1972	The treaties for the expansion of the Community and the entry of four countries (Britain, Ireland, Denmark, and Norway) are signed.
April 23, 1972	Referendum in France on the expansion of the Common Market (67.7 percent in favor).
May 10, 1972	Referendum in Ireland on entry in Community (83 percent in favor).
September 26, 1972	Referendum in Norway (53 percent against).
October 2, 1972	Referendum in Denmark (63.5 percent in favor).
October 19–20, 1972	First summit conference of the nine heads of state of the enlarged Community, in Paris.
July 23, 1973	The Copenhagen Report favoring the strengthening of political cooperation.
December 9–10, 1974	Paris summit decision to elect the European Parliament by direct vote and to create the European Council. (Periodic meetings of Heads of State.)
March, 1975	Report on strengthening European union (Tindemans report).
June 5, 1975	Britain holds a referendum on membership in the European community (67.2 percent in favor).
July 27, 1976	Opening of negotiations for the entry of Greece.
October, 1978	Opening of negotiations for the entry of Portugal.
December 4–5, 1978	The European Council decides to establish a European Monetary System to stabilize the rates of exchange of the various currencies.
February 5, 1979	Opening of negotiations for the entry of Spain.

May 28, 1979	Treaty of Accession of Greece to Community signed in Athens.
June 7–10, 1979	First direct popular election of the European Parliament (410 members).
January 1, 1981	Greece becomes the tenth member.
June 17–19, 1983	Adoption by the European Council of a solemn declaration in favor of European union.
June 14–17, 1984	Second election of the European Parliament by universal suffrage (434 members).
June 25–26, 1984	The European Council decides to augment the independent resources of the Community, to reform the CAP and to adopt a budgetary discipline.
June 29–30, 1985	The European Council adopts a resolution calling for an intergovernmental conference to elaborate a new treaty on European union. This meets in Luxembourg, September 1985.
1 January, 1986	Spain and Portugal become the eleventh and twelfth members.
February 17–18, 1986	Signing of the Single European Act.
July 1, 1987	The Single European Act comes into effect; its provisions to come into full force on January 1, 1993.
June 1988	Free movement of capital decided; to become effective in 1990.
June 18, 1989	Elections for the European Parliament. Right-wing and left-wing parties evenly divided. Socialists show gains; Environmentalists show remarkable strength; Extreme Right makes gains, while Communists decline (518 members). See pages 342–343.
June 26, 1989	Meeting of European Council at Madrid.
July 1, 1989	France assumes the presidency of the Council.

2

Economic Integration: The Common Market and Its Institutions and Policies

THE EUROPEAN COAL AND STEEL COMMUNITY

The first genuine step toward integration in Western Europe was the European Coal and Steel Community (ECSC) established by the Treaty of Paris in 1951. The plan for it had all the earmarks of the functional approach, while equally emphasizing the political approach through the creation of institutions. On May 3, 1950, Robert Schuman, French minister of foreign affairs, announced at a French cabinet meeting the prospects of establishing "a Franco-German pool of coal and steel" open to all European countries. "We have not managed to make 'Europe,'" he said, "but Europe cannot be made all at once, nor can it be constructed as a whole. It will be made step by step through measures that will create a 'de facto solidarity.'"[1]

[1] Political and Economic Planning, *European Unity: Cooperation and Integration* (London: Allen & Unwin, 1969), p. 76.

The new organization was a functional arrangement for the accomplishment of broad political goals: to establish a community of peace in Western Europe and then to federate it. Its immediate task, however, was the integration of one important sector of the Western European economy, namely, steel and coal. But within this narrow area, the institutions established to bring about integration were supranational. The ECSC agreement was signed in 1951 and came into effect in 1952. It established a set of institutions having power over production, pricing, research and development, investment, discriminatory practices, cartels and mergers, labor conditions, and so on, as these affected the production and selling of coal, iron, and steel among the six member states: France, West Germany, Italy, Holland, Belgium, and Luxembourg. The institutions established were the High Authority, the Council of Ministers, the European Parliament, and the Court of Justice.

Among the institutions established, the

most original by far was the High Authority. For the first time in their history, governments of Europe accepted to delegate a portion of their sovereignty to a "High Authority" consisting of nine officials chosen by the governments but independent and able to make decisions binding the member-states.

The High Authority could, among other things, make loans, and undertake investment policies, without the consent of the Council of Ministers. Such decisions could be made by straight majority vote. Whenever the opinion of the Council of Ministers was required, it could be given by qualified majority vote or unanimous consent, depending on the particular issues set forth by the treaty.

What made the supranational status of the High Authority secure was its right to levy a tax on business turnover of steel and coal, after consultation with the Council, and with the consent of the latter by two-thirds majority. The levy could not exceed 1 percent of the business turnover of an enterprise. The proceeds went directly to the Authority and could be disbursed by it. The Court of Justice decided on disputes between the High Authority and the member states and between it and private organizations. The assembly did not have the power to legislate; it only deliberated and made recommendations.

FORMATION AND EXPANSION OF THE EUROPEAN ECONOMIC COMMUNITY

Following the establishment of the ECSC, the movement in favor of European unification rapidly gave rise to the creation of two new communities: the EDC (European Defense Community) that was the object of the treaty signed by member-states on May 27, 1952, and the European Political Community that complemented the EDC. Although of French initiative, the EDC providing for the integration of European armies, was nevertheless rejected two years later by a coalition of political forces in the French National Assembly that were highly critical of German rearmament. In August 1954, the National Assembly refused to ratify the treaty and thus terminated any hopes for a project of a European army, and for the political community that was to accompany it.

Following this setback, the Benelux countries suggested pursuing and expanding economic integration objectives. The basic idea was to integrate progressively the economies of member-states through common policies and institutions, leaving defense aside.

This approach gave birth to the Treaty of Rome, signed in 1957 by France, West Germany, Italy, and the Benelux countries, creating the European Economic Community (EEC), and the European Atomic Energy Community (EAEC). This was the third step in the process toward the unification of Western Europe.

Usually called the Common Market, the Community is based on the sectorial (i.e., functional) approach even if the goal remains political union: the treaty stipulated that its purpose is "to establish the foundations of an ever-closer union among the peoples of Europe."

Over the years, the EEC has increasingly attracted its European neighbors (including those who initially expressed hostility at the creation of a unified Europe). Genuine economic success and its increasing international weight rapidly attracted new membership applications.

On January 1, 1973, after long and difficult negotiations, the Common Market was enlarged to include Great Britain, Ireland, and Denmark (Norway refused to join). On January 1, 1981, Greece became the tenth member, and five years later, on January 1, 1986, Portugal and Spain joined. Thus the original 6 have become 12. Politically, the inclusion of countries like Spain, Portugal, and Greece strengthens the democratic regimes in these countries. Economically, the expansion of the Community amounts to the formation of a regional bloc that compares favorably in terms of population and resources with Japan and the United States, even though Ireland and the newer Mediterranean member countries are less developed than the original six. In terms of population, the Common Market has progressed with the inclusion of Spain and Portugal in 1986 from about 265 to 320 million.

The Treaty of Rome remains the fundamental Charter of European construction. However, successive enlargements, serious economic disparities among the partners, as well as acute difficulties in managing a Community that over 30 years grew from 6 to 12 members, have compelled member-states to review the Treaty of Rome. With the intention of reaffirming the final objective of European unity (see Chapter 3), a text, the Single European Act, was negotiated, signed, and ratified by all EEC member-states. It came into effect July 1, 1987, represents an updating of the Treaty of Rome, and takes into account developments and events of the past 30 years. It includes a revision of certain articles, allowing for an accelerated integration (i.e., a genuine single market, as of January 1, 1993), and widens the scope of EEC competence to new areas (technology, environment, and monetary matters). Although not fundamentally modifying the initial institutional system it nevertheless grants additional powers to the European Parliament.

EEC INSTITUTIONS

The EEC institutions do not fit easily into any of the legal categories with which we are familiar. They contain elements of federalism that could develop into a genuine supranational federation. But there are also elements of intergovernmental cooperation that safeguard the national interests of the states involved. The balance between the two remains very delicate.[2]

The European Economic Community comprises the following institutions: a Commission, a Council of Ministers, a European Parliament, and a European Court of Justice. These date from the founding of the EEC.[3] As we shall see, a new institution—the European Council—has been added and has gained importance. (See Figure 2–1).

The Commission

The Commission consists of 17 officials (the commissioners) designated with the consent of all member-states by the individual governments—2 each for France, Italy, Great Britain, the Federal Republic of Germany, and Spain and 1 each for the other 7 members. They hold office for four years. According to the Treaty of Rome, the Commission acts in the general interest of the European Community and the commissioners cannot receive instructions from the governments that designated them.

The Commission therefore represents the federal component. It has a supranational character. The guardian of treaties, it overlooks the proper implementation of the Community's bylaws. It is also the policy-initiating body: virtually all policy decisions originate with the Commission and is entrusted with the execution of all decisions. It is supposed to make sure that all decisions are enforced in such a way that national laws do not infringe on Community regulations. The Commission is assisted by a large staff of civil servants (commonly referred to as "Eurocrats"). It is internally divided into directorates general, that is, administrative departments responsible for specific areas— agriculture, internal markets, social affairs, transportation, and so on. One might think

---

[2] See W. Wallace, "Less than a Federation, More than a Regime: The Community as a political system," in H. Wallace, W. Wallace, and C. Webb, eds., *Policy-making in the European Community*, 2nd ed. London: John Wiley, 1983, pp. 403–435.

[3] In 1967, the merger of the previously separate institutions of the communities (CSCE, EEC, and Euratom) took place. As of now, there exists only *one* council and *one* commission for the three communities. The parliamentary assembly, presently called the European Parliament, and the European Court of Justice have always been common to all three communities.

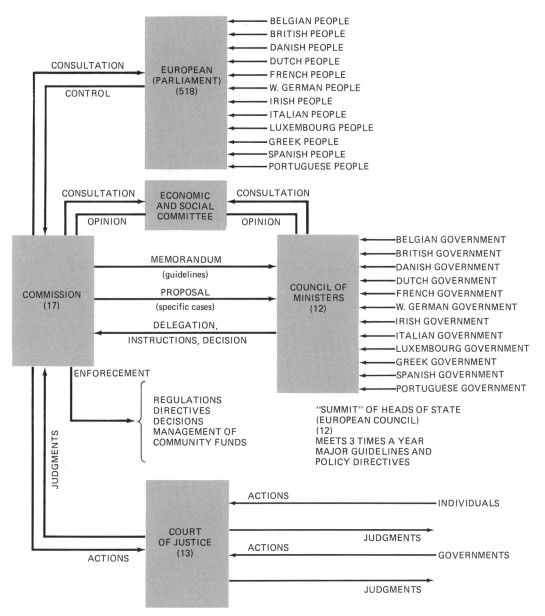

FIGURE 2-1   Institutions of the European Community

of the Commission as the "energizing" element of the Community: it initiates policy and passes on to the Council of Ministers the measures recommended that will lead to policy. But the Commission is not the policy-making body.

The Council of Ministers

The policymaking body of the Community is the Council of Ministers. It consists of the foreign ministers of the member states. These, however, may be represented by other ministers depending on the problem discussed: agriculture, finances, transport, energy, and so on. The presidency of the council rotates every six months among the member-states.

The originality of the decision-making process in the Community can be found in the dialogue between the Commission and Council. In effect, the Council can only make decisions based on Commission proposals. While the Council can adopt or reject the Commission's proposals, it only can amend them by a unanimous vote. The Treaty of Rome provided a powerful federal ingredient by stipulating that after January 1, 1966, decisions in the Council could be made by a qualified majority—in which the role of the large states is weighed more heavily and where two-thirds or three-fourths majority is required—except for some special cases in which unanimity was required. However, in June 1965, this was contested by the French, who insisted on unanimity whenever one country considered that its vital interests were at stake.

These positions provoked, within the Community, a serious crisis that was only partially resolved with the "Luxembourg arrangement" in January 1966. More of an "agreement to differ" than a reconciliation of positions, the text only recorded the French refusal to a majority vote whenever "vital" interests were at stake. From a legal standpoint, the Treaty was in no way modified. However, in practice (and since 1973 with the active support of Great Britain, opposed to any drift toward supranationality), the search for consensus has replaced majority vote and has often paralyzed the Council. In the recent past, however, dangers of hindering the very functioning of the Community have progressively led to more "majority voting." This trend was confirmed by the Single European Act to bring about integration by 1993 that enlarged the field of majority voting. This has influenced the 12 member-states to invoke the "Luxembourg compromise" as an exception; in 1986, for example, approximately 100 decisions were made by qualified majority votes. Neverthe-

less, this qualified majority is not easy to obtain, and a minority of 23 votes to block a decision can easily be found. For example, a coalition of three large nation-states, or since the enlargement of the Community, a coalition of the southern member-states, can block any decision.

With the enlargement of the community after January 1, 1986, the voting strength of the member states in the Council are weighed as follows: Great Britain, France, the Federal Republic of Germany, and Italy—10 votes each; Spain—8; Belgium, Greece, Portugal, Holland—5; Ireland and Denmark—3; Luxembourg—2. A qualified majority requires 54 "votes."

The European Parliament

The popular and representative component of the Community is the European Parliament. As of January 1, 1986, the European Parliament consists of 518 members (see Figure 2–2). Elected members are grouped together politically, not by the nation-states they represent, but in European political groups—groups that transcend individual states. They are supposed to speak, act, and vote on the basis of European—that is, transnational—considerations and imperatives.

Originally, the representatives were designated by the parliaments of the member states. It was only in December 1974 that an agreement was reached for the direct election of the European Parliament. The first direct popular election was held in June 1979.

The June 1979 election was a milestone. It was the first time that the peoples of nine European countries were asked to elect representatives directly to the common European assembly. There was no question of increasing the powers of the assembly. The purpose of the election was mostly symbolic. No matter what the legal and formal powers of the European Parliament were, a popular election, it was expected, would give it additional weight.

The prospect that the European assembly might gain in power agitated political lead-

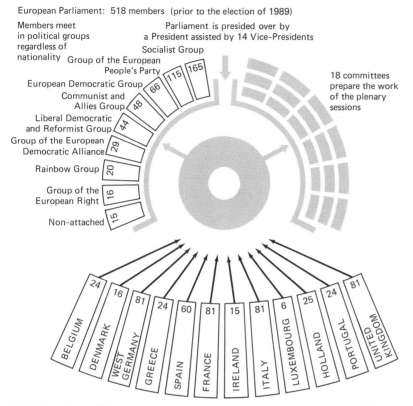

European Parliament: 518 members (prior to the election of 1989)

Members meet in political groups regardless of nationality

Parliament is presided over by a President assisted by 14 Vice-Presidents

Socialist Group

Group of the European People's Party — 115 | 165

European Democratic Group — 66

Communist and Allies Group — 48

Liberal Democratic and Reformist Group — 44

Group of the European Democratic Alliance — 29

Rainbow Group — 20

Group of the European Right — 16

Non-attached — 15

18 committees prepare the work of the plenary sessions

BELGIUM 24 | DENMARK 16 | WEST GERMANY 81 | GREECE 24 | SPAIN 60 | FRANCE 81 | IRELAND 15 | ITALY 81 | LUXEMBOURG 6 | HOLLAND 25 | PORTUGAL 24 | UNITED KINGDOM 81

FIGURE 2–2 Political Composition of the European Parliament (518 members), as of June 13, 1988. Adapted from *Working Together: The Institution of the European Community,* official publication of the European Community, Luxembourg, 1988.

ers in a number of countries. Anti-Community sentiment was strong in Denmark, among the Labour party's followers in Great Britain, and also among the Communists and Gaullists in France. A popularly elected European Parliament, many felt, would naturally use its representative and popular character to snatch power from the sovereign states of the Community and offset the major executive organs—notably the Council of Ministers. In fact, nationalist sentiment remained very strong, and was voiced in the slogans of major national political parties.

Voter participation was considerably lower than it is generally for the respective national parliamentary elections. The best showing—86 percent—was in Italy (where voting is mandatory); the lowest—a mere 31 percent—was in Britain. The other states averaged about 65 percent.

A major outcome of the returns was that "anti-European" or "reluctant-European" parties lost—this was clearly the case with the Labour party representatives in England and the Gaullists in France. Parties that were pro-European fared well. They held a majority in the European assembly.

About 120 million voters elected their 434 representatives in the second direct election, held in June of 1984.[4] Voter participation was on the average a little lower than in

---

[4] Spain and Portugal elected their representatives to the European Parliament in 1987.

1979—60 percent instead of 62 percent. Denmark showed a higher rate of participation, but only half the eligible voters came out to vote in Ireland and only one-third in Britain. With the exception of Britain, which maintained its traditional majoritarian system, all member-states used the proportional representation system (but with variations).

The election did not bring about serious changes in the configuration of the European Parliament, or in the distribution of the political forces and groups. The center-right groups, despite some losses, retained a slim majority. The Socialists continued to show strength despite losses by the French Socialists and the German Social Democrats. They were offset by the gains of the Belgian Socialists and the British Labour party. In fact, the Socialist group became the most powerful one in the assembly. The Communists maintained their position although the French Communist party went down to 10 members from 19. The two most significant characteristics of the election were the growth of the Greens and of the extreme right. The Greens gained strength not only in Germany but also in Holland and Belgium. Together with "ecologists" in other countries, some members of the extreme left and some anti–EEC Danish members, they constitute the "Rainbow group." As for the extreme right, it consists of a group of ten French representatives (members of the French National Front), five Italian right-wingers, and one from Greece.

EDITOR'S NOTE: The Elections for the European Parliament (June 18, 1989)

As we shall see the European parliament has gradually increased its powers. It is expected to represent increasingly the needs and aspirations of a European electorate. Hence the importance of the elections of June 18, 1989—the third one to take place by direct popular vote.

The election produced mixed results so much so that it is difficult to gauge any important trends. First and above all the rate of abstention indicated that there was a great deal of apathy. About 56% of the electorate voted—compared to the average

voting rate in national elections of nearly 80%. National issues overshadowed European ones and the voters used the occasion to express their dissatisfaction with their national governments—as was notably the case in England and to a lesser degree the Federal Republic of Germany, Greece, Ireland and Luxembourg. In Britain the Labor Party candidates won a majority for the first time since 1979. In France the Socialists failed to gain the votes they had received in the last presidential and legislative election of 1988. In overall terms, the socialists gained however, in the European parliament while the Communist strength declined. [See attached Table 2–1]

There was one major "winner" in the election: the Environmentalists or Ecologists (generally referred to as "The Greens"). They received 15% of the vote in England (but due to the electoral system no seats in the European Assembly), 14% in Belgium, 11% in France and 8.4% in the Federal Republic of Germany. The other "winner" was the Extreme Right. In France the National Front maintained its strength with 12% of the vote while in the Federal Republic of Germany the newly-founded extreme right wing (some say neo-Nazi) party—the "Republicans"—under the leadership of an ex-Nazi sergeant, Franz Schönhuber, received 7% of the vote. Intensely nationalistic, xenophobic

TABLE 2-1 Left and Right in the European Parliament (518 Seats)—1989

		Election of June 1989
LEFT		
Communists & Allies	48	41
Rainbow Group [Greens]	20	39
Socialists	165	180
Total	233	260
CENTER-RIGHT		
Independents	15	16
Christian Democrats	115	123
European Democratic Alliance	29	44
Liberal Democratic Reformists	44	20
European Democrats	63	34
European Extreme Right	16	21
Total	282	258

if not downright racist, the extreme right will have 21 seats in the European parliament.

Left and Center-Right divided almost evenly— (See Table 2–1) with the left coming slightly ahead and holding at least arithmetically a majority— 260 out of the 518 seats. But the left-right division cannot be easily translated into policy commitments and policy outcomes. The Left is divided, especially since many of the Greens belong rather to the center on economic issues. There is no clear cut commitment either from the Right or the Left on the speed of economic integration, to say nothing of political union. With a divided European parliament, it is likely that until the new election the major European policies regarding social and welfare measures, a comprehensive European wage policy, agricultural policy, the harmonization of taxes, the establishment of a Common European Currency, a Central European Bank, and the development of a common European defense and foreign policy will continue to come from the Summit, the Council of Ministers, and the European Commission. But within these three bodies, powerful national imperatives continue to play a dominant role, and important disagreements continue to raise questions about the future of the Community. England continues to remain unwilling to allow for a common European currency and a Central Bank and, under Margaret Thatcher, to consider common wage and welfare policies. The Federal Republic of Germany on the other hand—which has the greatest economic weight and favors speedy economic integration—may begin to pay more attention to its relations with Eastern Europe and the Soviet Union and even to the prospects of reunification with East Germany. The role of France will be of critical importance.

Organization and Powers

The European assembly meets once a month—about ten weekly sessions a year. There are also provisions for special meetings. The business of the assembly and its various bodies is conducted by the president, assisted by 12 vice presidents. These elected officers form a bureau responsible for the day-to-day running of the assembly.

The chairmen of the political groups usually attend the general meetings of the bureau.

Within the assembly are 18 specialized committees, each dealing with a particular area of Community activity, the committees keep in touch with the Commission, and in some cases with the Council, between sessions.

Power entrusted to the European Parliament cannot be compared to those of national parliaments.

The European Parliament does not legislate, nor can it hold the executive organs of the Community—notably the Commission—directly responsible to it and replace them. It can force the Commission to resign only by introducing and passing a motion of censure. But this motion must be carried by two-thirds of the votes cast. In the past 20 years, a number of motions of censure have been proposed. They have all failed.

The assembly can submit written or oral questions to the Commission and thus exercises a certain control over the Community's activity. For the year 1987, for instance, 2,591 questions were submitted to the Commission and 201 to the Council.

According to the Treaty of Rome, the assembly only participates in the drafting of Community laws in expressing an opinion on the Commission's proposals before they are adopted by the Council. However this consultative role has become less and less satisfying to Euro-deputies, especially since their direct election, and they have not ceased to demand an equal say with the Council in the legislative domain.

The Single European Act has not fully satisfied this demand and has only slightly increased the powers granted to the European Parliament. Henceforth, any future enlargement of the EEC (for example, the eventual membership of Turkey or Austria), and any new "association agreement" (for example, the renewal of the Lomé Convention) must receive the "assent" of the absolute majority of the European Parliament.

In addition, the Single Act has implemented, essentially with regard to the internal market, a "cooperation procedure" that increases the influence of the European Parliament within the legislative process, requiring the Council and Commission to consider, more than in the past, the European Parliament's amendments. But it is within the budgetary field that the European Parliament is beginning to possess some real power. This was granted to the Parliament when the Community was endowed with its own resources designed to finance common policies. The Parliament amends and adopts the budget at the end of a procedure which establishes a dialogue between it and the Council of Ministers. Often, the budget has been rejected, and differences involving budgetary provisions between the Council and Parliament have required the intervention of the Court of Justice.

With regard to the budgetary powers of the European Parliament, a distinction should be made between the "mandatory" and the "optional" expenditures. The first amount to over 71 percent of the total expenditures (66 percent of total expenditure is earmarked for financing the CAP—the Community Agricultural Policy).

The European Parliament, despite all recent efforts, has virtually no say about these expenditures. It can make recommendations, but the Council of Ministers can reject them by a qualified majority vote. On the "optional" expenditures that comprise less than one-third of the total budget, however, the Parliament has considerable powers. It can vote the appropriations and increase or lower, within limits, the expenditures envisaged. Even if relatively small, these expenditures involve significant policy matters—in social policy, research, regional development programs, and the like.

It is clear that over the past years, the role of the European Parliament in budgetary procedures has grown, the deputies have often succeeded, despite numerous difficulties, in imposing their viewpoint. A substantial increase in their legislative as well as budgetary powers obviously represents the declared goal of Parliament. But there is no indication that the majority of the governments of the Twelve are willing.

The European Court of Justice

The overall purpose of the Court is to see that the Treaty of Rome is observed and that all decisions and regulations made are in accord with it and are respected by the parties concerned. It can hear cases directly from member states, from the Commission, from firms, and from individuals. It is the court of last resort. It can impose fines to force compliance; it can sanction non-compliance. The Court's decisions are made by majority, but dissenting views are not made public.

The Court of Justice consists of 13 justices designated with the consent of all member states. They serve for a period of six years. Once designated, they act on behalf of the Community and cannot receive instructions from their member-states.

Over the years, the Court has been instrumental in developing a "Community law"—that is, in establishing the validity and supremacy of the treaty and the decisions based upon it. Concerned with economic problems such as tariffs, restrictions of trade, antitrust legislation, discriminatory practices, and the like, it has gradually and cautiously established itself as the body that can authoritatively interpret the treaties and Community legislation. It has also established that community law takes precedence over national legislation. Community law, so far developed, covers primarily economic, trade, and social matters. Thus, when France imposed preferential rates on loans to exporters to promote exports and avoid a capital outflow, the Commission declared this to be contrary to the provisions of the Treaty of Rome prohibiting subsidies. The Court upheld the Commission against France.

The Court has left no doubt that Community law supersedes national law. It has welcomed appeals from national courts who seek its advice in conflicts between national law and Community law. "The effect of Community law," the Court has argued, "is to divest national courts of the right to apply a contrary national law." Community law applies everywhere within the Community: "In giving up to the Community the rights and powers corresponding to the Treaty provisions, the member states have brought about a definitive limitation of their sovereign rights that no national statute may restore."[5] Students who know American constitutional history will recognize in these words the reasoning of the U.S. Supreme Court in its decisions upholding the supremacy of the U.S. Constitution against individual states.

The European Council

The European Council is a new institution that was not provided for in the Treaty of Rome, but whose existence was formally recognized by the Single European Act (Article II). It consists of periodic meetings, held at least twice a year, of the heads and foreign ministers of the member-states and the president of the Commission. It is often referred to as the "European Summit." It was instituted in 1974 at the same time that it was decided to hold direct popular elections for the European Parliament. Since then, the Council has gained strength as the major energizing force in the development of Community policies. It decided on the direct European elections, on the European monetary system, and on the entry of new members (Greece, Spain, and Portugal) and took the initiative for major reforms in agricultural policy and the allocation of new resources to the Community. However, the very existence of the European Council has also hindered the normal development of Community work. The Council of Ministers, in effect, has tended to consider it as a Court of Appeals or an organ of arbitration, thus letting the heads of state handle the thorny problems. While Parliament represents the popular component, the European Council (or "Summit") remains an intergovernmen-

tal body in which decisions are usually made by unanimous vote. The convening of the intergovernmental Conference that was meant to establish the Single European Act, was nonetheless decided through a majority vote (against Great Britain, Greece, and Denmark) at the European Council in July 1985.

Resources

In assessing the degree of supranationality of the Community, we must take into consideration the manner in which the Community derives its resources. Until 1970, most of the resources of the Community were derived from contribution of the member-states. Since the Treaty of April 1970, however, the Community has its own independent resources. They come from the tariffs collected on imports of industrial goods and from the levies on agricultural goods imported from outside the Community. A third source, and by far the most important (64.5 percent), introduced in 1979, is the automatic allocation of 1 percent (since 1986, 1.4 percent) of the value added tax (a sales tax) collected by the member-states.

Faced with the increase in Community expenditures, these resources still remained insufficient as of 1987. In 1988, a new system was adopted, including, at the same time, a fourth resource emanating from the GNP of member state was introduced. The 1987 budget amounted to 36 billion ECUs (the European Currency Unit corresponding to roughly $1.20). This represents only one percent of the Gross National Product of the Community and three percent of the combined budgets of the Twelve.

ECONOMIC INTEGRATION: HOW FAR HAS IT GONE?

As we noted, the framers of the Treaty of Rome aimed to achieve economic integration and thus pave the way for political union. The planners stated that their pur-

---

[5] Cited in H. Smith and P. Herzog, *The Law of the European Communities* (New York: Mathew Bender, 1976).

pose was "to ensure the economic and social progress of their countries," to improve "the living and working conditions of the people," and to provide "a harmonious development of economic activities." These objectives they resolved to attain by "establishing a common market and progressively approximating the economic policies of the member states" (Article 2).

Thus, the Treaty of Rome aimed to regulate the entire economies of the member states, including their trade with the outside world. There was no question of establishing only a custom union with a common tariff for all. The Common Market was to be a comprehensive economic union aimed at the genuine integration of economic policies and practices across the borders of the member states. It would ultimately allow the free exchange of goods, free movement of persons and capital, and free access to employment on the basis of the same general conditions, common forms of taxation, common social security provisions, the same currency, and the same banking practices and rules for the control of credit. Its goal was to create a big market, like that of the United States.

The specific economic arrangements have involved difficult and careful compromises. All members have seemed determined to meet, cooperate, and deliberate until a decision is reached. There have been notable successes and occasional setbacks.

While it is true that the European Community has not managed to realize all its major objectives, its accomplishments are impressive. First, a custom union has been established with a common tariff for all member states for all goods coming from outside. Second, within the Community tariffs have virtually disappeared. There is free trade and free circulation of goods. They have accounted for a spectacular increase in inter-Community trade. This has grown between 1958 and 1980 almost 23-fold and accounts today for over 50 percent of the total trade of the Community members. Trade relations with the outside world are no longer negotiated and made by individual states—they are negotiated by the Community for all members. It is the Community representatives that meet and negotiate with other states with regard to tariffs and trade arrangements with all other countries, including the Third World.

It should be noted that freedom in the movement of persons has also been realized at least in part. Since 1970, no person can be discriminated against because of his or her nationality in securing employment, in remuneration, or in working conditions. The free circulation of travelers within the Community has been fully guaranteed, and since January 1985, all citizens of the member states can use a common European passport.

Together with common customs and the gradual development of a common internal market for all the member states, the development of a common agricultural policy is considered by many to be one of the major accomplishments of the Community. The Common Agricultural Policy aimed to provide an equitable income for the farmers, and at the same time keep agricultural prices at reasonable levels. To do so four major principles were adopted: free circulation of agricultural commodities, common prices, preference for all Community agricultural products, and a common financial arrangement. Producers of agricultural products are guaranteed fixed prices fixed by the Council of Ministers each year. A Community preference is realized by taxing importers of products an amount equal to the price differentials they represent. Thus, for example, if U.S. chickens can be sold at 90 percent of the Community price, importers will be taxed by 10 percent. By the same token, when European prices are lower than world prices, then the European producers are given export subsidies that correspond to the difference between the European prices and the higher world prices.

Finally, with regard to the fourth principle of the CAP (financial solidarity), financing the agricultural policy is taken care of by the Community budget and no longer by the national treasuries.

If the global evaluation of the CAP is

rather positive, given the fact that it contributed less to the modernization of agriculture, it has provoked a series of criticisms. On the one hand, overproduction in numerous fields (milk products, cereals, wine) brought on a rapid increase in agricultural costs, preventing the Community budget from financing other projects. On the other hand, the Community was criticized for demonstrating a protectionist attitude due to policies of "Community preferences" and engaging in a disloyal competition on the international market. This is precisely where the United States and the EEC have often been at odds.

Since 1984, the EEC has become involved in a CAP reform whose main objective is to manage surpluses and to diminish costs. European farmers have seen guaranteed prices diminish in real value. Production ceilings were imposed on them, and the EEC adopted a program of land freeze.

With the exception of fishing, no other Community policy has achieved the same degree of integration than the customs union and the CAP. Nevertheless, Community institutions have established a certain number of landmarks edging toward some common social and regional policies. Of particular interest has been the establishment of a Community Social Fund to provide direct help to workers who must move from one job to another for resettlement and vocational retraining. Significant efforts have been also made by the Community to modernize backward areas. The European Investment Bank and the European Fund for Regional Development have provided economic aid to underdeveloped areas in southern Italy, Greece, Ireland, and Corsica and also to declining industrial centers—particularly coal and textile centers in Britain, France, and Belgium.

One of the most obvious signs of the incomplete economic integration of the 12 member-states remains, to this day, the absence of a genuine monetary Union. This objective has, ever since the early 1970s appeared on the Community agenda and has inspired multiple projects and ambitious constructions. But the collapse of the Bretton Woods System and generalized currency fluctuations have noticeably disturbed the European project. Of course, a decisive step was taken in 1979 with the creation of the European Monetary System (EMS) whose main objective is to preserve stable yet adjustable exchange rates between the currencies of member-states. The EMS is based on three main elements: a European monetary unit, the ECU (the "currency basket" constituted from participating currencies and reflecting the economic weight of each), an exchange-rate mechanism (currencies may fluctuate among each other, within a margin of 2.25 percent above or below the central rate established for each currency), and mechanisms for mutual credit to correct the margins of fluctuation. Although the British sterling and the Greek drachma participate in the ECU currency basket,[6] they do not participate in the exchange-rate mechanism. In addition, and by special derogation, the Italian lira is authorized to fluctuate at a ± 6 percent rate of its central rate.[7] Ten years following its creation, the EMS appears to have been successful. Still, 11 parity adjustments have intervened between European currencies, leading essentially to German mark and Dutch florin reevaluations, while most of the other currencies were devalued. But those adjustments were agreed upon, thus proving the reality of monetary cooperation and proper collaboration of central banks. In addition, variations among European currencies have remained lower than the fluctuations with outside currencies—the dollar, yen, and so on. However, a genuine agreement over exchange-rate policies, especially with regard to the dollar, has not yet been established, and the European Monetary Fund, provided for at the outset to receive transfers of national gold reserves

---

[6] In principle, the Spanish peseta and the Portuguese escudo will join the currency basket by 1989.

[7] L. Tsoukalis, "Money and the Process of Integration," in Wallace, Wallace, and Webb, eds., *Policy-making in the European Community*, pp. 115–141.

and foreign currencies, has yet to come into existence.

A Single Market in 1993?

Even though this brief account gives a positive evaluation of European realizations one should not underestimate the many drawbacks that remain. Thirty years following its advent, European construction does not fully deserve the name of "Common Market" since many of the original barriers to the internal market have remained, and new ones have sprung up.

The free circulation of goods continues to be beset by many obstacles. Some of these derive from administrative and technical regulations, from special advantages given to national firms, or from special research and subsidy practices. Custom officials continue to inspect merchandise at the borders of individual members-states and apply complicated rules and procedures.

Concerning unrestricted circulation of individuals and capital that should have accompanied Customs Union, it has been only partially realized. And there were many sectors (technology for instance) that were left beyond community control.

In the mid-1980s the Commission decided to sensitize governments and public opinion in the imperfections of the situation. In its June 1985 White Paper,[8] it established the cost of "Non-Europe" (see Table 2–2) and reviewed the main obstacles which prevent the creation of a genuine internal market. More specifically, to boost the construction of Europe, it proposed to the 12 member-states the priority objective of creating by 1992 an economic area where all barriers would be removed. Through the adoption of the Single European Act, the 12 subscribed to this priority. In fact this text favors an approach that reminds us of the initial methods of integration: the creation of economic solidarities designed to foster political union.

---

[8] Commission of the European Communities, *Completing the Internal Market* (The White Paper), COM 85/310, Brussels, June 1985.

TABLE 2–2   The Cost of non-Europe: Potential Gains from Removing Barriers

Although it is difficult to obtain exact figures for the costs to governments, consumers, and industry of all these barriers, the best available and most recent findings indicate that the lack of a single market in Europe has been costing industry billions. These findings confirm that the removal, finally, of the barriers which still fragment the Community's economy will provide major opportunities for economic growth, for job creation and for economies of scale.

Total savings from the abolition of administrative formalities and border controls	13–24 billion ECU*
Potential savings from opening up public procurement markets	±17.5 billion ECU*
Labor market	2–5 million new jobs (depending on the macroeconomic policies accompanying the 1992 program)
Benefits from increasing the scale of production of manufactured goods	2% of GDP

Source: *Europe Without Frontiers: Completing the International Market,* 2nd edition, EEC (Luxembourg, 1988).
*An ECU is equivalent to about $1.20.

The realization of an internal market, however, by January 1, 1993 will not be easily accomplished. To unify this huge market of 320 million consumers requires that member-states agree upon the removal of all types of barriers (physical, technical, and fiscal). According to the Commission's paper approximately 300 Community "laws" will be required to organize and complete free circulation of goods, capital, services, and people.

Is it realistic to imagine that the Community will be able to achieve by 1990 what it has been unable to accomplish in 30 years? Although it is legitimate to doubt that all goals of the Single Act can be realized, one may be reasonably optimistic given the progress already achieved.

In the first place, economic and social factors, as well as public opinion in general (see Chapter 3), demonstrate interest and just may well exert an important influence on governments for the implementation of this market. One may look to the multiple takeover bids and industrial concentrations that, at the eve of 1993, may contribute to a reshaping of the European financial and industrial landscape. Faced with U.S., Japanese, and newly industrialized nations' competition, Europeans have become aware of the strength that a closer integration might offer them.

Second, the prospects for genuine integration are reinforced, as we noted, by the modest, yet significant, reform of voting procedures within the Council. To accelerate the completion of the internal market, the Single Act provides for the extension of the qualifier-majority vote to sectors in which, according to the Treaty of Rome, and up to now, unanimity was required. (However, decisions concerning fiscal harmonization, free movement of peoples and rights of workers still require unanimous consent.)

More important, and here we find an essential point, the listing of measures adopted in the past two years and aiming at the completion of the internal market, leads one to believe that a great deal has already been accomplished that is irreversible. At the end of 1988 the Council had in fact adopted a third of the contemplated measures. In the field of free circulation of goods much progress has been made— through mutual recognition—to remove technical barriers due to national standards and regulations. In the field of services, until now the orphan of economic integration, important steps have been taken concerning insurance, air and marine transport, and financial services. Equally, the efforts toward mutual recognition of national professional qualifications and higher education diplomas have progressed, the final aim being to allow European citizens to practice their profession in any Community country. Yet without a doubt, the adoption of measures relative to the liberalization of capital movements has been in the eyes of world opinion the most decisive sign of European determination. In June 1988, finance ministers de-

cided that the free movement of capital, which is the first requirement for an internal market in financial services, will come into effect in 1990.

Of course, a large number of important problems remain to be resolved especially in the fields of fiscal policy and of the free movement of people. Although the value added tax system exists throughout the Community, the rates differ widely from one country to another. It will also be necessary if one wants to avoid capital evasion to fiscal paradises such as Luxembourg, to harmonize tax rates on savings from one country to the other. Another sticky problem is raised by the free circulation of individuals: How can one reconcile the alleviation of customs formalities for travelers and the controls designed to prevent arms and drug traffic, illegal immigration, and terrorism? Measures in these domains will be even more difficult to adopt since they require a unanimous vote, and not a qualified majority vote, within the Council.

Despite these difficulties, Community partners within the international system still consider the 1993 deadline in earnest. A great interest is shown by virtually all countries in the world along with certain apprehensions. Without being able to base their fears on concrete facts, certain trading partners of the Twelve, in particular Japan and, to a lesser degree, the United States, fear the possibility of the Community becoming a "Fortress Europe."[9] This perception is, however, misleading since the realization of the internal market will not modify international, bilateral, or multilateral obligations already subscribed to by the Community in the field of commerce. It might even offer to trading partners of the EEC opportunities of expanded trade due to the expected growth of the single market and to free circulation among the Twelve. The Community will favor a maximum liberalization of trade, provided that its partners offer reciprocity.

[9] See "The Growing American Fear of a "Fortress Europe," *The New York Times*, October 23, 1988.

3

Toward European Union?

In this context of a reinforced economic integration, what are the prospects for political union? As we have seen, a degree of genuine integration in the form of confederate and federal structures to make decisions may have been reached for some of the economic matters explicitly covered by the Treaty of Rome. But the Community, even as an economic entity, has remained half finished, and the problem of political, as opposed to economic integration is still a critical one. Ever since the beginning of European construction, there have been constant arguments and debate as to how to honor the preamble of the Treaty of Rome—to establish "an even closer union among the peoples of Europe."

Following the failure in 1954 of the European Defense Community and of the Political Community, which was to complement it, hopes for political unification have not materialized: neither those of "the federalists," who had anticipated that the creation of eco-nomic solidarities and supranational institutions would automatically lead to some form of political integration, nor those of General de Gaulle, who stated in the early 1960s that the union would be an organized coopera-tion of states. For the French president, the states were in fact "the only entities possess-ing the right to command and the power to be obeyed." Accordingly, the European po-litical union and its evolution toward a con-federation had to pass through an intergov-ernmental cooperation in the fields of foreign policy and defense. But France's partners believed that the "European Eu-rope" envisaged by Paris lacked the much needed ingredient of supranationality. They refused the Gaullist scheme of "organized cooperation," and had to wait until the end of the 1960s to timidly resume talks around political union. In 1969, The Hague summit allowed foreign ministers to "study the most optimal means of implementing progress in the realm of political unification." The following year foreign policy coordination through "political cooperation" became the instrument of these new hopes.[1] With the summit convened in Paris in October 1972, on the eve of the first enlargement of the EEC, the term "political union" was replaced with "European union." The nine member-states declared their intention "to transform before 1980 the totality of their relations into a European union." Nevertheless European leaders remained uncertain about the procedures to follow to achieve the goal.

The Tindemans Report

M. Tindemans, the Belgian prime minister, was requested to report on possible outlines for the future European union. Presented at the end of December 1975 the Tindemans report underscored the many difficulties ahead: "Our peoples ... realize that political union does not automatically follow from economic integration.... Too many fruitless discussions cast doubt on the credibility and topicality of our joint endeavour; to this extent the European idea is also a victim of its failures." Tindemans, on the basis of consultations with European statesmen and the many reports prepared by various organs of the Community, pointed to a series of failures even in the economic area. He hinted strongly that these failures were due to the lack of political union. Economic or "sectorial" integration can proceed up to a certain point, but can go no further without supranational institutions and the political will to use them.

To set the stage for the realization of European union, the Tindemans report proposed a series of steps: a genuinely common foreign policy, economic and monetary union, common social and regional policies, and common policies in key industrial and

technological sectors. What was also of great importance in the report was the suggestion that European unification could move in different sectors at different speeds, thus allowing member-states to accommodate themselves at different rhythms to the construction of Europe. One implicit hint was that Europe could be constructed on a "two-tier" approach, with the original six members moving faster toward integration and the other three moving more slowly in the same direction.

The proposed reforms would give the European Parliament the power to consider, discuss, initiate, and pass resolution on all matters within the competence of the Community, whether or not explicitly covered by the Rome treaty. The report also suggested to do away with the distinction between "economic" matters handled by the Community institutions and "political" matters—like political cooperation—handled exclusively by intergovernmental consultations. It also recommended that the qualified majority vote should apply to all decisions in the Council of Ministers.

Towards European Union

The suggestions of the Tindemans report were not accepted at the time by the member-states. However, ever since 1981, there has been a considerable effort to strengthen the European union, and a number of the report's proposals have resurfaced in one form or another.

In November 1981, German and Italian foreign affairs ministers, Genscher and Colombo, proposed to their partners a reassessment of the political objectives of the European endeavor. The model envisaged seemed to be inspired by a confederal approach: it proposed to strengthen cooperation of the (then) Ten, to render it more coherent, to enlarge it to other domains notably to matters of security and culture. It also suggested strengthening the role of the European Council and giving to the European Parliament a greater say in the development of European union. In addition, to avoid sys-

---

[1] For a detailed presentation of the procedures and results of political cooperation, see Francoise de la Serre, "Foreign Policy of the European Community," in Roy Macridis, ed., *Foreign Policy in World Politics*, 7th ed. (Englewood Cliffs, NJ: Prentice Hall, 1985).

tematically relying upon the unanimity vote, the text stipulated that "vital" interests could only be exceptionally invoked, and suggested to the countries that disagreed abstention so as to avoid hindering decision making.

This initiative gave rise in June 1983 to the adoption by European governments of the "Solemn Declaration on European Union" that was essentially symbolic. The "Stuttgart declaration" codified and formalized institutions and practices implemented over the past ten years; it did not offer any new or radical changes.

Faced with the indecision of the European governments, the European Parliament went into action. In July 1981, it decided to establish a permanent institutional committee, chaired by a well-known federalist, Altiero Spinelli, to consider reforms in the direction of European unity. It prepared a "draft treaty" and submitted it, in 1984, to the European Parliament, which endorsed it by a large majority.

This treaty, modest in comparison to many expectations, did not truly reflect a demanding federalist orthodoxy, even if it went beyond what the majority of governments could accept. The EEC, as it existed and functioned, with its institutions, policies, and realizations, remained the cornerstone of the proposal. The project's originality consisted in temporarily allowing for the coexistence of an essentially federalist economic integration and a confederalist inspired political cooperation. The Union's methods remained those of community action and of interstate cooperation. The extension of Union's competence required, depending on the policy area involved, a majority or a unanimity vote. However, one must underline an important point: over a period of ten years, when a member-state invoked "a vital national interest," the vote would be postponed and the question reexamined. In summary, what the Spinelli draft proposals amounted to was to provide a political and institutional structure for integration *only if* the political will to implement it were there!

The challenge of the draft treaty and its overwhelming endorsement by the European Parliament galvanized the European governments into action. They took up again the issue of how to move in the direction of European union and in the European Council of 1984, meeting at Fontainbleau, established an "ad hoc committee for institutional matters" composed of representatives of heads of states and presided over by the Irish senator, Mr. Dooge. This committee submitted, in the spring of 1985, a report suggesting the creation of a genuine political entity, in other words, a European union. In addition to the creation of an internal integrated economic space through the achievement of an internal market, the reinforcement of the monetary system and the systematic search of a common foreign policy, it was to be extended to problems of security and defense. To achieve these goals, the committee emphasized the need for more efficient and democratic institutions. This implied that the rule of majority vote could only be exceptionally waived.

The role of the European Parliament was strengthened by granting it—in the legislative domain—an equal say with the Council and—in the budgetary domain—new responsibility in raising taxes. Insofar as methods are concerned, the Committee proposed to organize an intergovernmental conference entrusted with the task of drafting a new treaty on European Union that would take into consideration the Community realizations, its own report, and the draft treaty voted by the European Parliament. Three member states—Great Britain, Denmark, and Greece—after voicing reservations concerning certain report suggestions, did not desire the convening of this conference. Nevertheless the Milan European Council (June 29–30, 1985) decided, contrary to the recommendations from these three countries, to convoke this conference. It opened in September in Luxembourg, with the mandate of reforming Community institutions and preparing a treaty on political cooperation. Faced with the prospect of a new treaty, the three recalcitrant countries finally decided to participate. The conference resulted in the elaboration of the January 27, 1986 Single European Act (SEA).[2]

THE SINGLE EUROPEAN ACT

Just what is this unusually worded text? The title itself says very little. First, it reflects a lowering of initial ambitions: instead of being established, European Union is once again considered a goal to be achieved. However, the vocabulary used indicates that modifications of the Treaty of Rome, dealing with economic integration, and a treaty of political cooperation, aiming at the progressive implementation of "a common European foreign policy" are grouped together. Thus, through the Single European Act are reconciled the two trends that, up to now, have been in conflict in the history of the European Community: intergovernmental cooperation and the supranational approach. Economic and political matters are brought together to be dealt with as a whole.

In effect, the text states that "The European Communities and European Political Cooperation shall have as their objective to contribute together to making concrete progress towards European unity."

If this Single Act is viewed in terms of the evolution of European integration, it is surprising to see to what extent it borrows elements from certain models and methods proposed during the last decade: the Tindemans Report, the Colombo-Genscher Project, and others. Title II of the Single Act does include modest institutional reforms, but they are linked to the pursuit of a priority objective: the realization of a "Europe without frontiers in 1993" (see Chapter 2). It is this desire to accelerate the advent of a genuine internal market that has allowed for a modest but real modification of the Treaty of Rome, in particular the voting procedures. Even before the opening of the intergovernmental conference, the Commission had indeed realized that a reform of the de-

cision-making process would have no chance of being accepted if it were not linked with the implementation of a single economic internal market. The qualified majority vote is thus expanded, and the European Parliament has more say on Community legislation. However, the Luxembourg "compromise" of January 1966 was not formally affected. It remains the ultimate protection of member-states' "vital interests." It may be invoked by a member-state, within the Council, in last resort, and call for unanimity.

Beyond these essential goals of establishing the internal market and the means to implement it, it should be noted that the SEA continues to insist upon the Community's vocation to become more than a free trade area. It leads the way to an integrated economic and social entity by establishing a broadening of community powers to areas not provided for by the Treaty of Rome: research, environment, technology, and above all, social and regional policies. It was obvious that drastic measures were necessary to aid less advanced economies of the Community to help them support the shock of the single market. To benefit all member-states, and not only the industrialized northern countries, an "economic and social cohesion" provision was added to the Treaty of Rome. It aims at reducing the gap of economic development between the various regions of the community, and at organizing, for the benefit of poorer countries, an important financial aid through the community budget (infrastructure, professional training, and so on). For just about three years the amount (about 52 billion ECU) of this aid will be greater, in real terms, than the Marshall Plan for Europe after the war. Thus, one may now find, in the revised Treaty of Rome, the principle of solidarity among member-states that, up to now, was implicit but not clearly defined.

However, it is important to underline the fact that the extension of Community powers to new domains remains more limited than it had been proposed and expected. In particular, the Single Act fails to organize the economic and monetary coop-

[2] Text in the *European Communities Bulletin* (February 1986).

eration between the Twelve, which, logically, should have complemented the creation of the single market. In fact the Single Act does not really change the situation that has up to now prevailed: the European monetary system will continue to function within an intergovernmental framework; its reinforcement has not been the object of explicit provisions.

One may equally wonder whether the Single Act offers something radically new in the search for a European foreign policy. The Treaty on Political Cooperation (Title III of the SEA) remains essentially a codification of what has been gradually achieved over the last 15 years. Principles and institutions[3] remain the same. At the most, the text underlines the necessity of consistency between Community policies and political cooperation. It also stresses that the Twelve are committed to an improved "coordination of their positions with regard to political and economic aspects of security." This includes, for example, problems of disarmament, but not as yet a common defense. In the present state of European construction, the Treaty on Political Cooperation clearly reveals the limits to consensus that exist between governments on what should be a genuine European foreign policy and resulting consequences on national and defense policies.[4]

PROSPECTS

This rapid examination of the state of European Union requires some additional remarks and raises questions for the future.

The first remark concerns the situation

created by the Single Act. Naturally, the Single Act preamble continues to assert that member-states "are moved by the will to transform relations as a whole among their states into a European Union." But within the Single Act, this European union is once again considered a goal to achieve. Although there is a broadening of Community competence, it does not include decisive areas such as defense. As for foreign policy, only a loose system of intergovernmental cooperation exists.

We thus find ourselves today, insofar as the future of European union is concerned, in a situation where this union is defined more in terms of "concrete progress," common actions, and procedures than in terms of institutional reforms and large-scale legal and constitutional construction. Although one may note here a certain influence of British pragmatism (and the strong opposition of Mrs. Thatcher to a vast institutional scheme trespassing on national sovereignty), one nevertheless is struck by the fact that the situation resembles that of the beginning of European integration. The approach suggested by the Single Act, that is, the acceleration of integration through the creation of a genuine internal market, renews those methods advocated by J. Monnet in the early 1950s.

The problem of political unification has simply been postponed. It is a fact that today the Twelve find themselves in a process of state disengagement and of erosion of national sovereignties under the double influence of liberalization and the growing interdependence of their economies. Economic and social factors, as well as public opinion (see Tables 3–1 and 3–2) globally favor these developments. But just how far can this go? Over the past 30 years, the experience of European construction has shown that national sovereignty could not easily be circumvented through the automatic workings of economic integration. In sensitive fields such as the fiscal system or the free circulation of people, the single market will not be easy to implement. In addition, for this

---

[3] However, one must take note of the creation of a Political Cooperation Secretariat, a minor administrative organism responsible for management and organizational tasks.

[4] See Francoise de la Serre, "The Scope of National Adaptation to EPC," in A. Pijpers et al., eds., *European Political Cooperation in the 80's* (Dordrecht/Boston: Ninhoff, 1988), pp. 124–211, and La Serre, "Foreign Policy of the European Community," in Macridis, ed., *Foreign Policy in World Politics*, op. cit.

TABLE 3-1 Advantages of the Single Common European Market in 1992, Spring (S) 1988 and Autumn (A) 1987

EC12	Advantage		Disadvantage		d.k./n.a.	
	S	A	S	A	S	A
The ability to make payments without complication within the whole European Community (MAKE PAYMENTS)	79	80	7	8	15	13
The possibility to take any amount of money with you when you travel to other countries of the European Community (CARRY MONEY)	79	79	10	12	11	10
The possibility to buy in one's own country any product lawfully sold in other countries of the European Community (BUY PRODUCTS)	77	81	12	11	11	9
The opportunity for any citizen of a country within the European Community to go and live without limitation in any country of the Community for instance to retire there or to study there (RESIDENCE)	77	79	14	13	9	7
The opportunity for any citizen of a country within the European Community to go and work in any other country of the European Community (WORK)	76	80	16	14	8	7
The possibility to open a bank account in any country of the European Community (BANK ACCOUNT)	70	70	15	16	15	14
The possibility to buy land or property throughout the Community (BUY PROPERTY)	68	69	17	17	15	14
Bringing closer together the rates of value added tax applied in the various countries of the Community so that products are sold under similar cost conditions (V.A.T. CLOSER)	66	69	16	16	18	16
Elimination of custom controls when crossing frontiers between countries inside the European Community (BORDER CONTROL)	64	67	27	26	9	8
The possibility for a contractor from another country to be in charge of public works (for instance, building a bridge or a road) in our country if his offer is cheaper at the same level of quality (PUBLIC WORKS)	52	54	34	32	14	14

Source: *Euro Barometer* (June 1988).
d.k. – Don't know.
n.a. – Not available.

single market to function, it must be accompanied by measures affecting decisively national sovereignty, especially in the monetary field—such as the adoption of a European currency or the establishment of a Central European Bank. In fact, it is indeed difficult to imagine that a genuine internal market, wherein complete freedom of capital movements exists, can function without the existence, in one form or another, of monetary union. This problem is actually at the heart of the European debate and will

TABLE 3-2 Attitudes on the SEA in Spring (S) 1988 and Autumn (A) 1978 (by country, percentages)

	B		DK		D		GR		S		F		IRL		I		L		H		P		UK		EC12	
	S	A	S	A	S	A	S	A	S	A	S	A	S	A	S	A	S	A	S	A	S	A	S	A	S	A
A good thing	59	66	33	29	49	53	45	54	58	59	53	56	58	55	74	77	45	61	52	57	48	60	39	43	53	57
Neither good nor bad	26	22	26	28	31	33	27	20	19	17	35	32	15	17	19	13	25	25	33	28	21	12	30	29	27	25
A bad thing	4	3	25	23	7	5	9	7	4	4	6	6	5	5	2	2	13	5	5	3	2	2	19	15	8	6
d.k.	11	10	16	20	14	10	19	19	19	20	6	7	21	23	6	8	17	10	10	12	29	26	11	14	12	12
Total	100	101	100	100	101	101	100	100	100	100	100	101	99	100	101	100	100	101	100	100	100	100	99	101	100	100
Mean score*	2.62	2.70	2.10	2.07	2.48	2.53	2.45	2.58	2.67	2.68	2.50	2.53	2.67	2.65	2.77	2.81	2.38	2.62	2.52	2.62	2.64	2.79	2.22	2.33	2.52	2.57

*Assigning 3 to "good thing," 2 to "neither . . . nor," 1 to "bad thing"; excluding d.k., ("don't know"). Source: *Eurobarometer* (June 1988).

prove to be an excellent test of real intentions on the part of the governments of the Twelve and of their willingness to delegate, for example, to a central European bank, some of the most tangible prerogatives of their sovereignty. The European Council meeting in Madrid on June 26–27, 1989, failed to make a decision.

More generally, the problem of transferring national powers to a supernational Community authority and the modes used to carry out this transfer will represent the major challenge that governments will have to face. Possibly, the European Single Act, in framing the internal market with imperatives for economic and social cohesion, has paved the road toward a European power possessing means, notably budgetary ones, to manage a genuine solidarity among the Twelve. But such an evolution presupposes the creation of a genuine political system organizing the democratic control of the Community executive by a parliment endowed with real powers.

Are governments and the peoples of the European states ready to envisage such an evolution? At a rhetorical level, a majority probably is. However, obstacles will be difficult to overcome. In the present situation, only Great Britain and Mrs. Thatcher have explicitly expressed their double opposition to any formal abandonment of sovereignty and to any reconstitution of a European welfare state controlling and shaping market forces. But other difficulties are predictable, be they (among others) inherent resistance of centralized states such as France, lack of German enthusiasm to be the paymaster of the Community, or the Danish lack of enthusiasm for a European union. As for the peoples of Europe, despite a positive and, at times, strong disposition in favor, it will be some time before they transfer their involvement and loyalties from their own state to a European supranational entity. Even if the Single Act represents a decisive step in this lengthy process it is difficult to predict easily today how long it will take the Europeans to attain the goal of political union.

BIBLIOGRAPHY

Books and Articles

ALLEN, D., R. RUMMEL, and W. WESSELS, eds. *European Political Cooperation*. London: Butterworth, 1982.

BALASSA, BELA. *European Economic Integration*. New York: American Elsevier, 1975.

BIBES, G., F. DE LA SERRE, et al. *Europe Elects Its Parliament*. London: Policy Studies Institute, 1980.

COMMISSION OF THE EUROPEAN COMMUNITIES. "Completing the Internal Market" (The White Paper), Brussels, June 14, 1985.

CECCHINI, PADO. *1992 The European Challenge. The Benefits of the Single Market*. Aldershot: Gower, 1988.

FELD, WERNER. *Western Europe's Global Reach: Regional Cooperation and Worldwide Aspirations*. New York: Pergamon, 1980.

HARTLEY, TREVOR. *The Foundations of the European Community Law*. Oxford: Oxford University Press, 1987.

HILL, CHRISTOPHER, ed. *National Foreign Policies and European Political Cooperation*. London: RIIA/Allen & Unwin, 1983.

HODGES, M., and W. WALLACE. *Economic Divergence in the EC*. London: Allen & Unwin, 1981.

JANSEN, MAX. *History of European Integration 1945–1975*. Amsterdam: Amsterdam University Press, 1975.

KAISER, KARL, et al. *The European Community: Progress or Decline?* London: Chatham House, RIIA, 1983.

KERR, ANTHONY. *The Common Market and How It Works*. Oxford: Pergamon, 1983.

KIRCHNER, EMILE. *The European Parliament. Performance and Prospects*. Aldershot: Gower, 1984.

LUDLOW, PETER. *The Making of the European Monetary System*. London: Butterworth, 1982.

MORGAN, ANNETTE. *From Summit to Council: Evolution in the EEC*. London: Political and Economic Planning, European Series, no. 27, 1976.

PALMER, M. *The European Parliament. What It Is. What It Does. How It Works*. Oxford: Pergamon, 1981.

PAXTON, JOHN. *The Developing Common Market: The Structure of the EEC in Theory and in Practice*. Boulder, CO: Westview, 1976.

PELKMANS, J., and A. WINTERS. *Europe's Domestic Market*. London/New York: Chatham House, Routledge RIIA, 1988.

PIJPERS, A., et al., eds. *European Political Cooperation in the 80s.* Dordrecht/Boston: Ninhoff, 1988.

PRYCE, ROY. *The Dynamics of European Union.* London, 1987.

SCHOUTHEETE, PHILIPPE DE. *La cooperation politique europeene.* Paris-Brussels: Nathan-Labor, 1980.

A survey of Europe's internal market, The Economist, July 9, 1988.

TAYLOR, PAUL. *The Limits of European Integration.* New York: Columbia University Press, 1983.

TSOUKALIS, LOUKAS. *The European Community. Past, Present and Future.* Oxford: Blackwell, 1983.

WALLACE, H., W. WALLACE, and C. WEBB. *Policymaking in the European Community,* 2nd ed. London: John Wiley, 1983.

WILLIS, ROY F. *European Integration.* New York: New Viewpoints, 1975.

ZWAAN, JAAF W. "The Single European Act: Conclusion of a Unique Document." *Common Market Law Review,* Vol. 23, no. 4 (Winter 1986), pp. 747–765.

Journals

Bulletin of the European Communities, Commission of the EC, Office for Official Publications, Luxembourg. Monthly.

Common Market Law Review, Fred B. Rothman and Co., 57 Leuning St., So. Hackensack, NJ 17606. Quarterly review on legal developments in the Community.

European Yearbook, Manhattan Publishing, 225 Lafayette St., New York, NY 10012. Annual account of the work of European organizations.

Journal of Common Market Studies, Basil Blackwell, Oxford, England. Quarterly journal on integration in Europe and Latin America.

European Affairs, Elsevier, Amsterdam. Quarterly.

PART VIII
THE SOVIET UNION: POLITICS AND SOCIETY IN FLUX

STEVEN L. BURG

1

Introduction

The Soviet social and political order is undergoing rapid and dramatic changes under the leadership of Mikhail Gorbachev, general secretary of the Communist party of the Soviet Union (CPSU) and chairman of the Presidium of the Supreme Soviet (president of the Soviet Union). The modern Soviet regime of which Gorbachev assumed leadership in March 1985 reflected the almost seven-decades–long marriage of an authoritarian, revolutionary movement to the centuries-long Russian historical legacy of bureaucratized autocracy. The Stalinist system produced by this marriage during the 1920s and 1930s provided the political, organizational, and ideological instruments for the transformation of the former Russian empire into a modern military and industrial power.

But that transformation was enormously costly. The Stalin regime's major instruments for mobilizing and controlling the population were arrests, deportations to forced labor camps in remote and inhospitable regions of the country, and executions; in short, a system of terror that affected millions of individuals. The regime mobilized, allocated, and consumed its material resources by means of a woefully inefficient, centrally planned economy and a collective system of agriculture that destroyed the peasants' incentives to produce. By the 1980s, it had become apparent even to many of the country's own leaders that the Stalinist system, despite changes adopted in the 1950s and 1960s, was exhausted.

The Stalinist system was sustainable only as long as quantity counted as much as quality in the process of economic development. The transformation of the developmental tasks confronting the Soviet regime in the contemporary period has rendered it not only obsolete, but self-defeating. Thus, Gorbachev is today faced with a daunting political challenge: he must substitute a modern economy for the Stalinist one. To do so, he must carry out revolutionary social and political changes. These, in turn, bring him and his supporters into conflict with some of the most powerful forces in the Soviet Union—the party apparatus, the state bureaucracies, the military establishment, and the scores of other groups that benefit from the arrangements that evolved under Stalin and that, in turn, reflect powerful Russian cultural, social, and historical influences.

Thus, Gorbachev today confronts the powerful legacies of Imperial Russian development, the Bolshevik revolutionary tradition, and the Stalinist dictatorship. Their strength was demonstrated during the Khrushchev period, when radical reforms of a very different character from those being attempted by Gorbachev failed, and during the Brezhnev era, when the elite generation raised up by Stalin settled into a long period of complacent resistance to change.

To overcome these legacies, Gorbachev will have to unfetter new social forces and mobilize them in opposition to the old order. But, to perform these feats, he will have to amass enormous personal power. It is not clear whether Gorbachev can do the former without creating social unrest that prompts a reactionary assault from Stalinist forces and sweeps him and his reforms away. Nor is it clear whether he can do the latter without himself undermining the very essence of his reforms. These are the central questions raised by any attempt to understand contemporary Soviet politics.

Major Events in Soviet Domestic Politics Since World War II

September 1945	State Defense Committee disbanded; powers transferred to government (Council of People's Commissars).
October 1952	Nineteenth Party Congress meets; first since 1939. Politburo enlarged and renamed Presidium; Malenkov in role of "heir apparent."
March 1953	Stalin dies; Malenkov assumes leadership; Presidium reduced in size; party and government reorganized.
	Malenkov relinquishes position in party Secretariat while retaining post as chairman of Council of Ministers (prime minister).
	Khrushchev becomes senior party secretary.
June 1953	Beria, Stalin's secret police chief, removed from leadership; later tried and executed, marking end of the use of violence within the leadership.
September 1953	Khrushchev named "first secretary" of the Central Committee, giving him predominate role in party.
February 1954	Khrushchev launches "virgin lands" program, opening vast new territories to agricultural exploitation.
February 1955	Malenkov ousted from prime ministership, but retains membership in Presidium; Khrushchev emerges as predominant leader.
February 1956	Twentieth Party Congress; Khrushchev denounces Stalin in "Secret Speech" to Congress; de-Stalinization campaign begins; sixth five-year plan adopted; over 60 percent of Central Committee appointed in 1952 is reappointed.
October 1956	De-Stalinization destabilizes Eastern Europe; anti-Communist uprising in Hungary suppressed by Soviet troops; reformist leadership seizes control of Polish party.
February 1957	Khrushchev announces reform that decentralizes the economy; central government bureaucracies reduced in number, size, and authority.
June 1957	Malenkov and leading figures of the Stalinist era—Molotov and Kaganovich—along with majority of the Presidium attempt to oust Khrushchev; Central Committee membership supports Khrushchev, ousts his opponents from the leadership instead, labeling them the "Anti-Party Group."
March 1958	Khrushchev ousts his erstwhile ally, Bulganin, and assumes the prime ministership—combining leadership of both party and state.
January 1959	Twenty-first (Extraordinary) Party Congress meets; no changes in Central Committee or leadership; five-year plan replaced by new "seven-year plan."
October 1961	Twenty-second Party Congress meets; new party "program" adopted; de-Stalinization campaign revitalized with removal of Stalin's body from Red Square mausoleum; less

than half of Central Committee is reappointed, reflecting extensive changes in party apparatus carried out by Khrushchev since last Congress.

November 1962	Khrushchev announces reorganization of party and economy; splits party organization into industrial and agricultural divisions.
March 1963	Seven-year plan abandoned as failure.
October 1964	Khrushchev removed from power by other members of the Presidium; Brezhnev becomes first secretary of the party; Kosygin becomes prime minister.
September 1965	Economy recentralized; Kosygin program for economic reform initiated; renewed suppression of writers, artists, and dissident intellectuals.
March 1966	Twenty-third Party Congress meets; Presidium renamed Politburo; Brezhnev named general secretary; over 79 percent of Central Committee reappointed, reflecting new emphasis on "stability of cadres."
June 1968	After 10 years of quiet political activity, Soviet physicist Andrei Sakharov publishes underground manifesto entitled *Progress, Coexistence, and Intellectual Freedom,* which galvanizes dissent and thrusts Sakharov into its leadership
August 1968	Soviet troops invade Czechoslovakia to suppress Communist liberal reform movement; invasion stimulates intellectual dissent in USSR, stimulates flood of *samizdat,* or underground literature.
November 1970	Sakharov and others form Committee on Human Rights.
March 1971	Twenty-fourth Party Congress; over three quarters of Central Committee is reappointed.
1973	Politburo oligarchy expanded with addition of KGB chief (Andropov), defense minister (Grechko), and foreign minister (Gromyko) as full members.
1975	Sakharov awarded Nobel Peace Prize.
July 1975	Helsinki Agreement, including human rights guarantees, signed by Western and Soviet bloc countries; stimulates rise of dissident human rights groups throughout the bloc.
February 1976	Twenty-fifth Party Congress meets; over 80 percent of Central Committee is reappointed.
April 1976	Death of Politburo member and Defense Minister Grechko marks beginning of series of deaths in the aging leadership of the Brezhnev era.
June 1977	Brezhnev assumes presidency of the USSR while retaining post as general secretary.
October 1977	New Constitution is adopted.
July 1978	Politburo member and party secretary for agriculture Kulakov dies.
November 1978	Gorbachev promoted to party secretaryship for agriculture.
November 1979	Gorbachev appointed candidate member of Politburo.
October 1980	Politburo membver Masherov dies; Kosygin resigns for health reasons; Gorbachev promoted to full member.
December 1980	Kosygin dies.
March 1981	Twenty-sixth Party Congress meets under the shadow of labor unrest and rise of *Solidarity* movement in Poland.
January 1982	Politburo member and party secretary Suslov dies.
May 1982	Andropov replaces Suslov as secretary for ideology, making him senior party secretary after Brezhnev.
November 1982	Brezhnev dies; Andropov appointed general secretary.
December 1983	Andropov appoints Ligachev party secretary in charge of cadres.
February 1984	Andropov dies; Chernenko appointed general secretary.
March 1985	Chernenko dies; Gorbachev apppointed general secretary.
February 1986	Twenty-seventh Party Congress meets; over 40 percent of the newly-appointed, smaller Central Committee are new members.
December 1986	Kazakhs demonstrate in Alma-Ata and other cities of Kazakhstan, demanding greater concessions to local autonomy.
January 1987	Gorbachev calls for sweeping political "democratization."
June 1987	Gorbachev unveils program for radical economic reform.
February/March 1988	Massive nationalist demonstrations break out in Armenia, focusing on status of Nagorno-Karabakh (an ethnically Armenian region of Azerbaidzhan). These prompt ethnic violence in Azerbaidzhani city of Sumgait, directed against Armenians. Conflict continues unabated for many months.
June 1988	Nineteenth Party Conference convenes; sharp criticism and debate over economic and political reform is heard. Nationalities issue comes to the fore.
October 1988	Gorbachev completes the removal of holdovers from the Brezhnev era; restructures the party leadership, calls for constitutional reforms and reorganization of the state and government.

Major Events in Soviet Domestic Politics Since World War II

March 1989	Elections to Congress of People's Deputies produces stunning defeat for party-nominated candidates.
April 1989	Demonstrators in Georgia are violently attacked by troops.
	Gorbachev ousts 110 aged members of Central Committee, promotes own supporters to additional leadership positions.
May 1989	Congress of People's Deputies Convenes; sharp criticism and open debate accompanies election of Gorbachev as President of the Soviet Union.
June 1989	New Supreme Soviet convenes.
	Ethnic rioting reported in Uzbekistan, Kazakhstan.
August 1989	Two million people demonstrate peacefully in Latvia, Lithuania, and Estonia to protest the annexation of these countries by the U.S.S.R. in 1940.
September 1989	Gorbachev removes additional opponents of change from Politburo leadership.

The Legacy of Imperial Russia and the Bolshevik Revolution

THE AUTOCRACY

The political system of the Russian empire was based on the autocracy. The tsar was the apex of a political hierarchy comprising the court nobility and the landed aristocracy, the state administrative bureaucracies and the bureaucrats who staffed them, the military and secret police organizations, the Russian Orthodox Church, and certain economic and cultural elites. The broad masses of the common people were completely excluded from political participation until revolutionary unrest compelled the last Russian tsar, Nicholas II, to permit the introduction of a limited constitutional order in 1905.

The autocracy has evolved over hundreds of years of Russian history and was buttressed by each of the elements in the political hierarchy. The Russian Orthodox Church, the official state church of Imperial Russia, provided the organizational founda-

tion for the propagation of both a conservative, anti-Western religion and a romanticized Russian nationalism. The state bureaucracies not only performed the administrative tasks of government, but also directly enriched the Imperial household. The military and secret police hierarchies protected the empire from enemies abroad and within. To perform the latter task, an extensive network of police spies and informers was established throughout the empire, and any form of opposition to any aspect of the existing order was subjected to brutal repression.

The Imperial order benefited certain key groups beyond the tsar and royal family. The chief beneficiaries were the court nobility, who shared in the prerogatives of the court. The status of the landed aristocracy, or gentry, was protected by the autocracy, and they produced the human capital that staffed the military and civilian bureaucracies of the state. A very small strata of economic entrepreneurs benefited from the industrialization and development effort sponsored by the autocracy in the late nineteenth and early twentieth centuries.

In comparison to Western Europe, Russia was a late-developing country. Industrialization began in earnest in the late nineteenth century and was carried out largely by foreign entrepreneurs, using foreign capital and dependent on foreign technology. It was concentrated in a relatively small number of enterprises, constructed on an enormous scale, in a few regions of the country. And it was concentrated largely on sectors of the economy significant for the development of the military capabilities of the empire. The entire effort was carried out under the control of the state.

As a result of this pattern of development, the empire was characterized by a relatively small native Russian bourgeoisie, or class of capitalist entrepreneurs, and a weak labor, or trade union, movement. The absence of such social groups represented a major obstacle to political development along Western democratic lines. The autocracy was so powerful, and other social forces were so weak, that the autocracy was able to avoid any expansion in the scope of popular participation, or limitation on the powers of the state and its rulers until the early twentieth century; changes that had characterized earlier periods of industrialization in the West. The forces that exerted such pressures in the West—the urban middle classes—were nearly absent in Russia.

PRESSURES FOR CHANGE

Pressures for change were building up in Russia, however. Early in the nineteenth century the "Decembrists," military officers who had participated in the defeat of Napoleon and had fallen under the influence of French political ideals, formed secret societies and carried out an unsuccessful revolt in

December 1825. A broad political "awakening" of the intelligentsia was also taking place, manifest in a literature featuring self-reliant, activist hero-liberators, or their antithesis. And, by the later 1800s, a populist revolutionary movement, focused on mobilizing the peasants' land hunger in support of a socialist political program, was spreading among intellectuals. This movement had little effect on the Empire because the peasantry, although freed from serfdom only in 1861 and generally impoverished, remained naturally suspicious of the urban strangers who came to their villages, and loyal to the church and its tsar. By the early 1900s, however, the poverty and land hunger of the peasantry—who constituted over 80 percent of the population—became manifest in widespread, spontaneous peasant uprisings.

The late nineteenth and early twentieth centuries were also a period of unrest among the urban industrial workers, or proletariat. Rapid industrialization stimulated the migration to the cities of impoverished peasants. As workers, their strike activity focused in the beginning on improving working conditions and wages. But, under agitation from revolutionary groups, strikes gradually became more overtly political in nature. An attempt by the tsarist secret police to bring the urban proletariat under the control of trade unions led by police agents enjoyed brief success in the early 1900s. But a widespread general strike in 1903 was followed by further strike activity in 1904 and rising popular discontent with the autocracy. That discontent became intensified by a disastrous war with Japan in 1904 and 1905 and produced the revolutionary upheaval of 1905.

Widespread strikes became general strikes. In the capital, St. Petersburg (now Leningrad), a general strike gave birth to a Soviet of Workers Deputies, comprising delegates of activist worker-revolutionaries of all inclinations and led by Trotsky. The St. Petersburg Soviet soon became the focus of worker loyalties and an authoritative institution rivaling the government. Against the background of continuing peasant unrest, the additional threat of revolutionary action by the urban proletariat was enough to persuade Tsar Nicholas II to issue a conciliatory manifesto in October 1905, ostensibly transforming Russia into a limited constitutional monarchy. At the same time, however, both urban and rural unrest were forcibly suppressed.

THE CONSTITUTIONAL FACADE

It was sections of the lesser nobility, the so-called liberal gentry, that provided the leadership and support for the short-lived constitutional movement and the Duma, or parliament, of the post-1905 period. These nobility could not bring themselves to respond with great sympathy to the deepest sources of social unrest in the late Imperial period. The more radical, revolutionary groups refused to participate.

The Duma, or parliament, was granted only a very limited set of competencies, and no actual political autonomy. Although political parties were legalized for the first time in Russia, there were strict limitations imposed on the franchise, so as to ensure overrepresentation of the classes and parties most sympathetic to the autocracy, and underrepresentation of its potential opponents. The power of elected delegates to the Duma was further constrained by the creation of a second, upper house, half of whose members were to be appointed by the tsar. The tsar reserved "supreme autocratic power" for himself even in the very act defining the new constitutional order.

The demands of the Constitutional Democrats, the largest party in the Duma, for political changes were rejected outright by the tsar's government, and the Duma itself was dissolved by the tsar after only 73 days. The second Duma lasted not much longer. By changing the electoral law and through outright pressure on the electorate, the autocracy partially disenfranchised the peasantry, the urban proletariat, and the national minorities in the elections for the third Duma. As a result, a deeply conservative Duma was elected. It was a largely irrelevant institution and served its full term. The fourth Duma became relevant only with the collapse of the autocracy in 1917.

THE COLLAPSE OF THE AUTOCRACY

Early twentieth-century Russia was thus a society still in the early stages of industrialization, social modernization, and political development. These processes were beginning to transform the traditional society on which the autocracy rested, but there were as yet few organizations or institutions to mediate between the autocracy, on the one hand, and mass society, on the other. While the emergence of such institutions proceeded slowly, the collapse of the autocracy was accelerated by the effects of war—first, with Japan and, then, the world war. World War I brought massive disorganization, destruction, and demoralization, undermining both the legitimacy and organizational bases of the autocracy.

Although literacy levels were still low, education was improving in early twentieth-century Russia. Industrialization had given rise to urbanization. The combination of these processes produced the social mobilization of the urban masses and created increasing demands for political participation from this still relatively small, but disproportionately important, sector of the populace. The slow, indeed, reluctant creation of new institutions to accommodate these demands reflected the rigidity of the autocracy. It simply could not be adapted to new circumstances, yet it was powerless to prevent their rise.

In effect, conditions in late Imperial Russia were ideal for the political mobilization of the masses for revolution. It fell to the

Bolsheviks, almost by default, to perform this task.

RUSSIAN MARXISM BEFORE 1917

Bolshevism was only one of the many tendencies in the Marxist movement that emerged in reaction to the failure of peasant-oriented revolutionary groups in the nineteenth century. All the Marxist groups were antipeasant in temperament. And most of their leaders were forced into exile by the autocracy.

Some of the Marxist groups of the pre-1917 period were composed of "orthodox" Marxists who, consistent with the precepts of Marxist theory, saw their task as helping the Russian bourgeoisie carry out its own, democratic revolution. Marx had anticipated revolution in advanced industrial and bourgeois capitalist countries. In such countries, Marx argued, increasingly exploitive patterns of economic development would lead to the emergence of working-class consciousness and, ultimately, a working-class–led revolution. From this perspective, Russia—still a relatively underdeveloped and predominately peasant country—would need to undergo substantial economic and political development before such a revolution might be expected to take place. "Orthodox" Marxists were, therefore, not inclined to become "mobilizers."

Other Marxists were more impatient with history, and more "revolutionary" or "interventionist" in orientation. Trotsky, who led the St. Peterburg Soviet in revolutionary directions, was one such Marxist. For him, the backwardness of Russia would be overcome by the revolutionary proletariat, who would first carry out the bourgeois democratic revolution on behalf of the small and insufficiently powerful Russian bourgeoisie, and then proceed immediately to carry out a socialist revolution for itself. Trotsky's theory of "permanent revolution" also had an international dimension: revolution in Russia would lead to revolutions in the more developed countries of Europe and the support of the revolutionary proletariats of those countries would ensure the survival of the Russian Revolution. Despite the brilliance he displayed as a revolutionary orator and leader, however, Trotsky offered no formula for mobilizing the popular support that would be necessary to carry out such a revolution.

LENINISM

The organizational blueprints for revolution were provided by Lenin in two key prerevolutionary tracts, *What Is to Be Done?* and *Two Tactics of Revolution,* and in the "April theses" he delivered upon his return to Russia in 1917.

In *What Is to Be Done?*, written in 1902, Lenin set out an elitist, conspiratorial formula for the organization of the revolutionary party. He argued that revolutionary class consciousness could be brought to the working class only from without, by a professional revolutionary party organization, the so-called "vanguard of the proletariat." While the masses might successfully act against police and troops on the street, and would in fact determine the outcome of the revolution, political struggle against the autocracy could be carried out only by professional political revolutionaries. He called for revolutionaries to carry out their action within broader workers' organizations, especially trade unions, that would serve as "fronts" for the revolutionary party. The conditions of autocracy, he argued, demanded that the party itself be organized secretly. Only full-time, professional revolutionaries were to be admitted to membership. And he called for a highly centralized organization, with much if not all initiatives in the hands of the leadership.

This formula ran contrary to the heretofore-dominant democratic tradition in the Russian Social-Democratic Labor party (RSDLP) or Russian Marxist movement. At the second Congress of the RSDLP, held in Brussels in 1903, Lenin's views were opposed by a majority of the delegates. Trotsky, then an opponent of Lenin, suggested that Lenin's formulas meant that "the organization of the party takes the place of the party itself; the Central Committee takes the place of the organization; and finally the dictator takes the place of the Central Committee." But, ultimately, it was Lenin's conception of the revolutionary party that proved triumphant.

His first triumph, however, was tactical. As the result of a series of splits among the delegates attending the second Congress in 1903, the faction led by Lenin eventually secured a majority. Using their majority, they won a short-lived victory on questions of revolutionary organization. The more enduring and more significant result of this victory, however, was that the Leninist faction came to be known within the revolutionary movement as the "majority-ites," or "Bolsheviks," while their more orthodox Marxist opponents acquired the misleading label of "minority-ites," or "Mensheviks." In fact, at any given moment the majority of Marxist revolutionaries shared Menshevik views, and those loyal to Lenin's views and responsive to his personal leadership were in the minority.

Lenin's prescription for revolutionary tactics also clashed with the more democratic orientation of many of the more orthodox Marxists. In his "two-tactics" tract of 1905, Lenin emphasized the "provisional character" of any alliance with non-Bolshevik forces and "the duty to carefully watch our ally as if he were an enemy." When the goal of strengthening the proletariat had been secured, such allies were to be subjected to suppression by the dictatorship of the proletariat. Of course, by "the proletariat" Lenin meant the revolutionary party, and by "the dictatorship of the proletariat" he meant the dictatorship of the party.

Thus, Leninism boils down to a formula for highly centralized, authoritarian, and elitist political organization, dedicated to the pursuit of revolution. Unlike more orthodox Marxists, Lenin was ready to sacrifice

ideological fidelity on the altar of political expediency. He was a pragmatic revolutionary first and a Marxist idealist second.

Ironically, it was not too long after Lenin had developed these views that Robert Michels, the German sociologist, published his own study of power and influence in political organizations (*Political Parties,* 1911), in which he argued that

it is organization which gives birth to the domination of the elected over the electors, of the mandatories over the mandators, of the delegates over the delegators. Who says organization says oligarchy.[1]

Michels developed this "iron law of oligarchy" by studying the operation of democratic party organizations with ostensibly democratic organizational and operational principles. It has applied with even greater force to the Leninist party: a party of self-selected individuals with no commitment to democratic procedure or to democratic political relations in society, but rather to revolution.

This is not to argue that the Stalinist dictatorship that emerged in the late 1920s and early 1930s was inevitable. Rather, it is to say that precisely those characteristics of the Bolshevik organization and of Lenin's leading role in it that enabled Lenin and the Bolsheviks to carry out a successful coup d'état in 1917 and to consolidate their power in the period 1918–1920 also contained the seeds of dictatorship.

In fact, there is no necessary contradiction between hierarchical organizational principles—even dictatorial ones—and political democracy as long as these principles are not applied uniformly across society, to the exclusion of others. American experience, for example, suggests the compatibility of authoritarian organizations such as business corporations and other private groups, on the one hand, and a democratic political

---

[1]Robert Michels, *Political Parties,* trans. by Eden and Cedar Paul (New York: Free Press, 1962), p. 365.

order, on the other. It is the autonomy of and competition among these organizations and groups that preserve the broader democracy. But, as the views Lenin was advancing might have suggested, he and the Bolsheviks proved intolerant of either autonomy or competition in the revolutionary movement and moved to suppress both with the establishment of the new Soviet state.

THE COLLAPSE OF THE OLD REGIME

In theory, revolution might eventually have occurred in Russia as the orthodox Marxists were led to anticipate, that is, as the result of the inevitable development of class consciousness on the part of an industrial proletariat which, as the result of capitalist development, had become the majority in society. Or it might have occurred as Lenin anticipated, as the result of the determined action of a professional revolutionary party engaged in what we now call mass mobilization. In fact, the revolution of March 1917 came about as the result of the collapse of the old order.

Military failures and domestic privations resulting from World War I eroded support for the autocracy among the military, the police, the state bureaucracies, the landed gentry, and the native Russian bourgeoisie. Defeatism was widespread among the troops of the rear. The strains on the railway transport net associated with moving military supplies made it difficult to supply cities and industrial centers with food. The result was growing unrest among urban industrial workers. Massive workers' strikes broke out in Petrograd (St. Petersburg, the Germanic name of the capital had been Russianized early in the war) in February 1917.

The Provisional Government that assumed power after the abdication of Nicholas II in March 1917 was a hybrid composed of moderate members of the fourth Duma and representatives of a workers' and soldiers' Soviet that had sprung up spontaneously in Petrograd. Unlike 1905, however, the revolutionary leaders of the Petrograd Soviet were determined to prevent a reversal of the revolutionary developments. As a hybrid, the Provisional Government was torn between the conservative tendencies of the Duma politicians intent on preserving much of the old social order and the more radical tendencies of those drawn from the Soviet.

The Petrograd Soviet immediately commanded the loyalty of those opposed to the old order. Its leaders moved to assume certain governmental functions, such as securing food supplies for the city and organizing a workers' militia to maintain public order. They also issued their famous "Order Number One," which destroyed discipline in the military by calling for the transfer of authority from individual officers to committees of common soldiers and sailors. In this way, the Soviet undermined the ability of the Provisional Government to enforce its authority. Yet, in comparison to Lenin, those in the Soviet, which was largely under the sway of the more populist and more idealistic Socialist Revolutionaries and the more orthodox Mensheviks, were relatively moderate in their views. They were inclined to support the war effort, and even the liberal revolution of the bourgeois Duma politicians. Not even the Bolshevik leaders in Petrograd at the time, Stalin and Kamenev, were as radical in their views as Lenin.

Lenin, however, was impatient for revolution. He arranged to return to Russia and immediately issued his "April theses." He called for an end to support for the war, and an openly revolutionary program. His views were initially rejected by the Bolshevik leadership, but Lenin gradually mobilized support for them and assumed leadership of the revolution. He advanced several dramatic themes. He called for "peace" to mobilize the support of those opposed to continuing the war. He called for "bread" to mobilize the support of the hungry urban population. He called for "land" to mobilize the support of the peasants who were already seizing the land on their own. And he called for "workers' control" to mobilize the support of the industrial proletariat who were already seizing control of the factories on their own.

THE BOLSHEVIK COUP

Under Lenin's leadership, the Bolsheviks pursued a dual strategy for waging revolution in the course of 1917. Where they held influence, they attempted to destroy existing institutions and organizations from within. At the same time, they attempted to organize and mobilize opposition forces in support of alternative institutions. They built up support throughout the network of Soviets that were springing up spontaneously across the country, but especially in the Petrograd Soviet, where agitation in the factories won them support among the workers and eventual control over the workers' section of the Soviet. By doing so, the Bolsheviks were able, eventually, to seize the mantle of revolutionary legitimacy.

This was not a smooth path to power, however, as suggested by the changing Bolshevik slogan. From March to July, the Bolsheviks advanced the slogan "All power to the Soviets," reflecting their growing influence in these institutions. After street demonstrations in July led to a government crackdown on the Bolsheviks, the Soviets were denounced as "fig leaves of the counterrevolution." But, after the Bolsheviks helped to put down an attempted countercoup by the military in September, their popular support grew dramatically, and the slogan "all power to the Soviets" was restored.

The October Bolshevik revolution was actually a coup d'état, carried out on the evening of October 24 and morning of October 25 (since a change of calendar in February 1918 that brought Russia in line with the prevailing system, the anniversary of the revolution has been celebrated on November 7). The military aspects of the coup were carried out under the command of Trotsky, who had in the course of 1917 emerged as one of Lenin's most loyal supporters, and under the cover of the "Military Revolutionary Committee" of the Petrograd Soviet. The Bolsheviks commanded the services of the "Bolshevik Military Organization" (a group of about 1,000 commissars), the "Red Guard" of workers' militia (about 20,000 strong), the sailors of the Kronstadt naval base in the Petrograd harbor, and (less reliably) the Petrograd army garrison.

Resistance proved minor, and the Bolsheviks quickly seized control of the government. On the evening of October 25 (November 7) a gathering of delegates from Soviets across the country, the Second All-Russian Congress of Soviets, convened. Bolsheviks and their supporters comprised 390 out of the 650 delegates. This reflected the sharp increase in their strength since June, when there had been only 137 Bolshevik delegates out of the 1,090 attending the first Congress. The Congress immediately appointed a new all-Bolshevik government, the "Council of Peoples' Commissars" (Sovnarkom), with Lenin as its chairman and Trotsky as commissar for Foreign Affairs. Stalin became commissar for the Nationalities, a post that would place him in the center of efforts to define political relations between Russia and the Russians, on the one hand, and the non-Russian peoples and territories of the former empire, on the other.

Thus, instead of destroying the state apparatus of the old order, instead of proceeding to construct a new order, Lenin and the Bolsheviks in large part simply seized the old order for their own. Control over the governmental bureaucracies provided them with a powerful organizational base for the consolidation of their power. But the Bolsheviks had no real plan for governing the country.

THE CHALLENGES OF POWER

Lenin's *State and Revolution* is the only serious prerevolutionary attempt to set out the features of a postrevolutionary state. The bourgeois capitalist state, Lenin argued, is an "organ of class domination" designed to legalize and perpetuate oppression. Universal suffrage and parliamentarism are merely facades to disguise the use of secret channels and government departments and staffs by the wealthy to protect their interests. It is, in effect, a dictatorship of the bourgeoisie. Lenin proposed, therefore, to replace this with a dictatorship of the proletariat, to be established through violent revolution.

The new dictatorship would, however, differ from the old. Lenin argued that industrialization and concomitant social modernization had simplified the tasks of government, reducing them to "registration," "filing," and "checking." These simple "management" tasks were well within the capabilities of any literate person. The state apparatus, therefore, could be depoliticized. Those who performed such managerial functions could be controlled through elections and recall procedures and pay scales kept to the equivalent of those of ordinary workers. Executive and legislative functions could be unified in a single representative institution, further reducing the size and complexity of the state. Supression of the minority, that is, of the remaining exploiters, would still be necessary. But it could be carried out without the establishment of a special machinery of repression. Repression would be aimed only at individuals, not whole classes. These would be the features of the so-called transitional state, through which the revolution would proceed to the construction of socialism.

In the socialist period, the means of production would belong to the whole of society, but the division of goods would be governed by the principle "to each according to what he has given to society," or "he who does not work neither shall he eat." Therefore, inequalities would continue to exist, but not exploitation. Only with movement beyond the transitional, socialist stage of development, toward "communism," would the process of the "withering away of the state" begin.

The communist period of development would be characterized by the disappearance of the distinction between mental and manual labor. More important, both social consciousness and labor productivity would increase to the point that the division of goods would be governed by the principle "from each according to his ability, to each according to his needs."

In fact, neither Lenin and the Bolsheviks of the revolutionary leadership, nor succeeding leaderships in the USSR ever implemented the utopian, democratic, and egalitarian principles of the transitional, socialist state described in *State and Revolution*. Those principles were to become the platform of the revolutionary idealists, or Leftists, of the 1920s. Instead, the Bolsheviks and their successors turned toward the principles underlying Lenin's more basic work, *What Is to Be Done?* The authoritarianism inherent in these principles was tempered only by pragmatic considerations of political survival.

Even if one accepts Lenin's formulas at face value as evidence of a commitment to achieve such a utopian change, a number of serious obstacles stood in the way of Lenin and the Bolsheviks in 1917. They had to work out patterns of authority within the ruling Bolshevik party and between the party and society. They faced the immense task of simply establishing control over the vast areas of the country as yet untouched by Bolshevism or even the revolution. They had to reorganize the shattered industrial base of the country, which included the reestablishment of labor discipline. They had to arrange for the production and distribution of food. And they had to settle the relationship between Russia and the other countries of the world; especially Germany, with which they were still at war and which still occupied vast portions of their country.

To establish their authority, the Bolsheviks had to legitimize their power. The most immediate obstacle to establishing their legitimacy was the Constituent Assembly, or constitutional convention, called by the Provisional Government to determine the post-Imperial political order. The Bolsheviks were extremely weakly represented in it. Of 707 deputies, only 175 were Bolshevik.

Three hundred and seventy deputies were Socialist Revolutionaries, a more radical, populist revolutionary party. Faced with the prospect that the Assembly might not have endorsed their coup, the Bolsheviks decided simply to dissolve it by force. Contrary to even the Bolsheviks' own expectations, the action generated little public protest.

Dissolution of the Constituent Assembly was followed by rigged elections to a Third All-Russian Congress of Soviets, convened in January 1918. The Bolsheviks manipulated this Congress to provide ex post facto authorization for the dissolution of the Constituent Assembly and legitimation for the Bolshevik coup and the use of violence against the Bolsheviks' opponents. The latter were attacked as "enemies of the people" or "counterrevolutionary conspirators."

The most immediate issue confronting the Bolsheviks was the question of peace with the Germans. The Bolshevik decision to open negotiations with the Germans at Brest-Litovsk met with opposition from the revolutionary left. Those committed to the concept of revolutionary war, of bringing revolution to the proletariats of the West, argued that to conclude peace with the Germans would be to fail to fulfill revolutionary obligations. Only Lenin's threat to resign, and the resumption by the Germans of an offensive that threatened to crush the new regime, won their support for peace, which was concluded in March 1918. The treaty of Brest-Litovsk marked the end of the alliance between the Bolsheviks and those seeking the rapid implementation of revolutionary goals.

CIVIL WAR
AND WAR COMMUNISM

By summer 1918, Russia was plunged into civil war. The Bolsheviks were opposed by several different forces: the "Whites," or forces seeking to restore the monarchy; troops of the Allied powers attempting to restore the provisional regime; nationalist forces of the non-Russian peoples; and even other revolutionary groups. To win the war, the Bolsheviks were compelled to adopt a set of policies that on the face looked like extremely radical attempts to establish communism immediately. Hence, they came to be known as "war communism." These policies won the Bolsheviks the support of some left communists. But they also alienated broad segments of Russian and Soviet society and made the legitimation of Bolshevik power more difficult. Their abandonment at the end of the war introduced new divisions into the Bolshevik leadership.

The peasants continued to seize land throughout the revolutionary period. The Bolsheviks could not stop them and so endorsed their actions. This won an enthusiastic response from the peasantry and helped to mobilize them in support of the Bolshevik cause. However, agricultural production remained insufficient to meet the needs of the urban population. Hunger and the general chaos of revolution produced a mass exodus to the villages by former peasants eager to share in the land.

The Bolsheviks attempted to secure bread for the urban populace by seizing grain from the peasantry by force. This was carried out by armed food detachments sent out from the cities. With few consumer goods being produced, there was little incentive for peasants to produce surplus crops for the market. The food detachments therefore seized even the nonsurplus grain intended for the peasants' own consumption. This led, of course, to widespread alienation of the peasantry, hoarding, and a precipitous decline in food production. It also led to the breakdown of the money economy and the rise of a system of barter. But, as long as the Bolsheviks remained the only force opposed to the return of the landlords, the peasants continued to support them.

In industry, revolution brought the seizure of factories by committees of workers and a precipitous decline in production. The Bolsheviks nationalized major enterprises and centralized the control of industry and labor under a supreme council of the national economy (*Verkhsovnarkhoz*). They concentrated their efforts on producing the materials required for the Red Army to win the civil war. Labor was subjected to military-like discipline. Workers' control was soon supplanted by collegial boards and, in 1919, by one-man management. These changes, of course, led to the increasing alienation of the industrial proletariat. But, as long as the Bolsheviks controlled the food supplies, survival required subservience.

The Bolshevik victory in the civil war can be attributed to several factors. First, military intervention in support of the "Whites" by the Allied powers during the summer of 1918 allowed the Bolsheviks to assume the mantle of Russian nationalism. Because the Bolsheviks were the only political force not under the influence of external powers, the Red Army under Trotsky's command was able to mobilize the support and the military skills of former tsarist officers motivated by simple Russian patriotism. The combination of Trotsky's organizational skills and their military expertise gave the Red Army superiority over each of its military opponents. Second, the German surrender to the Allied powers in November 1918 returned large portions of the country to the Bolsheviks, including the industrial and agricultural lands of the Ukraine and the Volga. It also led to the withdrawal of foreign support for the "Whites." Third, Bolshevik tolerance for land seizures and concessions to nationalist sentiments in the non-Russian peripheries of the empire stood in sharp contrast to the intolerant and chauvinist policies of the Whites. Thus, the Bolsheviks could command at least the grudging support of the peasantry and the non-Russian nationalities as long as the threat of restoration continued.

THE CONSOLIDATION OF BOLSHEVIK POWER

The end of the civil war in 1920 marked the establishment of Bolshevik power. Over the course of the next eight years that power would be consolidated by a series of tactical concessions to the peasantry and to "bourgeois specialists," managers, and individual entrepreneurs in the economy. These concessions were called "the New Economic Policy," or NEP, and resulted in the creation of a mixed economy—socialist control of the major enterprises and economic resources, and widespread private economic activity, in the context of a limited market economy. The contrast between the policies of "war communism" and the NEP gave rise to open conflict within the party over the organization of the economic and political order, between those with a "leftist" orientation, intent on rapid and revolutionary transformation of society, and those with a more "rightist" orientation, willing to continue the more gradual approach of the NEP. The initial victory of the rightist orientation was made possible by the personal authority of Lenin, who conceived the policies of the NEP period, and by the continuing growth of the authoritatian party organization he had created.

As the Bolsheviks secured their power, the party organization began to grow. Up to 1919, the party leadership consisted of the Central Committee. Party policies were the product of open, sometimes intensely conflictual, debate in the committee. In 1919, at the Eighth Congress, two additional central party bodies were created: the political bureau, or Politburo, to act as an authoritative policy making subcommittee of the full Central Committee and an organizational bureau, or *Orgburo*, to carry out the increasingly demanding internal administration of the party itself. The Congress also centralized control over both the assignments of party workers, or cadres, and the administration of lower-level party elections in the hands of the Central Committee. Within a year, the need for a full-time administrative staff became apparent, and a Secretariat was established in March 1920.

The Secretariat rapidly assumed enormous decisional autonomy by virtue of its organizational position, interposed between the leading organs and the party masses. One indicator of its growing importance was its very rapid growth from a staff of about 150 workers when it was created to over 600 after one year of operation. At the same time, the Secretariat's internal organization grew more complex, as departments for party organization and cadres training (*orgotdel*), personnel management (*uchraspred*), party statistics (*informotdel*), and other specialized party functions were created. Although these were formally subordinated to the Central Committee, they were in reality subordinated to the Secretariat.

One factor that accelerated this process was the death of Sverdlov in March 1919. Sverdlov had been the only party secretary, and chairman of the central executive committee of the Congress of Soviets, the state hierarchy. He dominated administration of the country through the network of Soviets. The party organization, which, as secretary, he also headed, had played only support functions. Paradoxically, Lenin, too, held formal office only in a state body. As chairman of the Council of People's Commissars, or government, he relied on state institutions rather than the party to implement policy. Up until 1922, there was no one assigned full-time to the administration of party affairs. With the growth of the party after the revolution, and the expansion of distinct central party organs, however, such administration was essential. In 1922, Stalin, already a member of the party's *Politburo* and *Orgburo*, was chosen by the leadership to become the general secretary of the party, and was placed in control of the party apparatus. This placed Stalin in control of a growing organizational base and supporting network for the exercise of power.

The increasing exercise of central control reinforced the tendencies toward internal authoritarianism and elitism that had characterized party life since Lenin first formulated the principles of party organization in *What Is to Be Done?* In 1919 and 1920 two groups within the party organized themselves in support of internal democracy and the representation of working class interests. These were the Democratic Centralists and the Workers' Opposition, respectively.

The Democratic Centralists focused their opposition on the growing centralization of power and loss of democracy within the party itself. The Workers' Opposition, led by proletarian worker-communists, mounted the last serious opposition to the reestablishment of a bureaucratic, authoritarian regime in Russia. Alexandra Kollentai, the intellectual female revolutionary who became the most articulate spokesperson for the opposition, called for the deprofessionalization of the ruling elite by requiring every party member to perform physical labor for a part of each year; for more direct participation in the government by the workers themselves, organized into democratic unions; and, for direct self-management by the workers in the factories. "In whom will our party place the trust of building up the communist economy," she asked, "in the Supreme Council of the National Economy with all its bureaucratic branches or in the industrial unions?"

A bitter debate over the organization of the economy, over the nature of relations within the party, and over the nature of the political regime being constructed by the Bolsheviks soon developed. These issues divided both the leadership and the broader membership as the party convened its Tenth Congress in March 1921. At the same time, popular challenges to party rule were arising. Peasant revolts, workers' strikes, and even an anti-Bolshevik uprising at the Kronstadt naval base, the stronghold of the Bolsheviks at the time of the revolution, were breaking out.

Some members of the leadership, Trotsky most prominent among them, urged a radically authoritarian response to these difficulties. He called for the "militarization" of labor. The whole population, he argued, should be subject to the imposition of strict central controls, and mobilized for use in accordance with the economic plans of the state. Those plans, in turn, should focus on the rapid industrialization of the economy. These positions were entirely consistent with his earlier calls for "permanent revolution" and represented a precursor of the approach taken by Stalin after 1928.

In March 1921, however, the Bolsheviks were still too weak, and resistance among workers and peasants was too strong to permit anything but a concessionary approach toward economic and social development. Hence, Lenin proposed, and won, the support of the Tenth Congress for policies designed to appease the peasants, both those in the countryside producing the food so desperately needed by the regime and those in the Army on whose continued loyalty the defense of the regime rested. The new economic policy adopted in 1921 replaced the expropriation of foodstuffs with a graduated tax-in-kind. Private enterprise was reintroduced in commerce and small-scale industry, and a limited market was established for the whole of agricultural production and consumer goods. Within two years of the adoption of NEP, the economy was revived and popular hardships reduced. This created a valuable "breathing space" during which the Bolsheviks could consolidate their victory.

Lenin offered no meaningful concessions with respect to the internal authoritarianism and elitism of the party itself, however. Instead, he won support for two historic resolutions limiting the freedom of discussion of party members and asserting party control over nonparty organizations. The resolution on "party unity" banned the formation of groups or factions within the party and subjected those who did so to expulsion by the Central Committee. The resolution on "the Syndicalist/Anarchist Deviation in Our Party" condemned the Workers' Opposition and reasserted the party's monopoly over the organization and representation of the working class. With respect to labor itself, Lenin urged a gradual transition to discipline through persuasion, but did not preclude the use of "proletarian compulsion."

Having defeated the Workers' Opposition and put in place a program for appeasing the peasantry and the workers, the Bolshevik leadership turned to the suppression of the political opposition outside the party. Immediately upon the conclusion of the Tenth Congress, the Kronstadt rebellion was brutally suppressed. The All-Russian Extraordinary Commission for Combating Counter-Revolution, Sabotage and Speculation (the *Vecheka*) and its local affiliates (the *Cheka*) were repackaged in early 1922 as the state political directorate (the *GPU*) of the People's Commissariat for Internal Affairs (the *NKVD*), or secret police. The ruthless elimination of perceived political opponents outside the party, including by summary executions, was thus transformed from a widespread, but by definition "extraordinary" activity of the revolution period, to a routine, bureaucratized function of the new Soviet state.

The decisions of the Tenth Congress in 1921 provided the basis for the creation of an organizational monolith. Authoritarian state and social organizations would be subordinated to party control. And the party itself would be forged into a centralized and authoritarian hierarchy. The ban on factional activity created the mechanisms for suppressing debate and disciplining opponents within the party that would permit the seizure of this hierarchy of control by a single individual.

As long as Lenin remained alive, these authoritarian and elitist tendencies were tempered by his own tolerance for debate. But these decisions were to be his last effective intervention in Soviet political development. Lenin was forced because of failing health to abandon full-time work in late 1921. He suffered a stroke in May 1922 and died in January 1924. The implementation of these decisions was left instead in the hands of the party's day-to-day administrator: Stalin.

3

Stalin and Stalinism

Stalin transformed the Leninist oligarchy of revolutionary leaders into a personal dictatorship. He was aided in this by the Russian tradition of autocracy. But the primary foundation was provided by Bolshevism as shaped by Lenin. Bolshevik insistence on the possibility of reshaping society from above through "revolutionary action," the Bolshevik formula for organizational penetration of society, the Bolshevik "culture" of unity that established the party as the sole repository of revolutionary "truth" and led broad segments of the party to view debate and conflict inside the party as "pathological" and opposition outside the party as the treasonous activity of "enemies of the people," and Bolshevik reliance on the bureaucratic state apparatus as instruments of rule all contributed to creating the Stalinist dictatorship.

THE STALIN MACHINE

During the brief periods in 1922 and 1923 when he was able to work, Lenin showed concern about the apparent bureaucratization of the party, and especially for the personality defects of Stalin, who was assuming ever-increasing power. In December 1922, he suggested that Stalin, "having become General Secretary, has concentrated an enormous power in his hands; and I am not sure that he always knows how to use that power with sufficient caution." In January 1923 he called on his comrades "to find a way to remove Stalin from that position and appoint to it another man who in all respects differs from Stalin only in superiority—namely, more patient, more loyal, more polite and more attentive to comrades, less capricious, etc."[1]

The suggestion was a futile one. By this time Stalin was already the master of a growing party apparatus. The Secretariat, through its assignments department, was already controlling the appointment of thou-

---

[1]V. I. Lenin, "Testament," in Samuel Hendel, ed., *The Soviet Crucible,* 5th ed. (North Scituate, MA: Duxbury Press, 1980), pp. 112, 113.

sands of responsible officials in the local and regional party organizations and expanding its activity to include appointments to the state apparatus and key social and economic posts. Representatives of the Secretariat were being dispatched to monitor local activities directly, and new administrative units were being created within the Secretariat to maintain direct supervision of them.

The power of the secretariat to control appointments was used by Stalin to break up opposition groups, such as the Workers Opposition, Trotskyists, and others. Key positions throughout the hierarchy were staffed with loyal Stalinists or with new personnel socialized into the values of the party apparatus. These values, and loyalty to the man at the top, were reinforced by a network of material privileges reserved for full-time workers in the party apparatus—the *apparatchiki*.

Lenin, already concerned by the growth and bureaucratization of the party apparatus in December 1922, suggested expanding the central party organs as a means of making them more democratic. Stalin readily supported this suggestion and implemented it in 1923. It allowed him to "pack" the Central Committee, the central Control Commission (which had been created in 1920 to hear complaints against the party apparatus, but which after 1921 became a major instrument for the enforcement of party discipline), and the Politburo itself, with his supporters. Similar expansions took place in 1924 and 1925. With each expansion, the number of Stalinists in the leading party bodies increased.

Thus, Stalin was able to use his control over the appointment process to extend his influence throughout the party apparatus. The increasing subordination of other organizations to the party, in turn, allowed him to control such vital political resources as the press and mobilize support for his positions.

Stalin's task was made easier by the vast increase in party membership following the death of Lenin in January 1924. This brought hundreds of thousands of new members into the party unfamiliar with either the history of the party and its revolution or recent political debates within it. These new members could be easily persuaded by the official "party line."

Stalin also moved to seize ideological leadership of the party. In a series of lectures in April 1924 on the theme "the foundations of Leninism," Stalin defended the importance of the party in transforming the Soviet Union. He argued that, to defend the dictatorship of the proletariat, the party would have to remain the militarized, conspiratorial organization it had become in the revolutionary period. It would also continue to serve as the vanguard of the proletariat, which as yet had not developed proletarian consciousness. The party, not broad social forces, would transform the country. And, as he argued in his polemics against Trotsky, it would be able to do so despite the absence of revolutions elsewhere. In contrast to Trotsky's theory of "permanent revolution," and its insistence on the necessity of revolutions elsewhere for the success of the revolution in Russia, Stalin held out the possibility of "socialism in one country," thereby appealing to Russian patriotism in support of Bolshevism.

Stalin's men dominated the proceedings of the Fourteenth Party Congress in December 1925, and he was acclaimed *Vozhd*, or leader.

ECONOMICS AND POLITICS

The period following the death of Lenin was dominated by a renewed debate over how best to develop the economic foundations for a socialist order. This debate was intensified by the simultaneous struggle for power among the remaining party leaders. Stalin exploited his superior organizational strength first to defeat the proponents of more rapid industrialization, or the "left," and then reversed his own position and turned his political resources against his erstwhile allies on the "right." Having gained superiority over all other political leaders by 1928, Stalin then began a revolutionary transformation of the Soviet Union "from above."

The NEP concessions to the peasantry had revived agricultural production, as shown by the figures in Table 3–1. But industrial development after 1922 suffered for lack of investment capital. The resulting shortage of consumer goods produced a steep rise in their prices, while those of agricultural goods fell. This produced a "scissors crisis," named after the image of the intersecting trend lines produced by a graph of agricultural and industrial prices. Although peasants were producing more foodstuffs, the absence of consumer goods left them with little incentive to deliver their surplus to the market. Instead, they consumed more of it themselves, or simply withheld it in the hope of improved prices. The government's commercial grain procurements—the tax-in-kind had been replaced by a tax in cash in 1924—were insufficient to fulfill demand. The cooperative movement encouraged by the Bolsheviks as an alternative to individual farming was, like the industrial sector, undercapitalized.

At first, Stalin allied himself with Bukharin and other proponents of continued reliance on the growing prosperity of the peasantry. As peasant purchasing power increased, they argued, capital would flow to industrial sectors producing goods for the peasants' consumption and the expansion of these sectors, in turn, would create demand for machinery and other products of heavy industry. Gradually, the heavy industrial sector, and the proletariat employed by it,

would assume a dominant role in the economy. This position was opposed by more leftist-oriented communists, who advocated the more accelerated development of industry, fearing that gradualism would result in the creation of a bourgeois, not a socialist state.

Trotsky was the most prominent leader among the leftists. But neither he nor his allies were any match for the organizational resources at Stalin's command. Trotsky was defeated early on in this debate, stripped of his positions in the leadership, expelled from the party in 1927, and sent into exile abroad in 1929. In 1940, he was assassinated in Mexico by an agent of Stalin.

By late 1927, however, the party was experiencing both political and economic problems. In the countryside, the spread of Bolshevik power was being frustrated by the increased influence of peasants who, taking advantage of the NEP, had become more wealthy and more active politically. In elections to local Soviets, nonparty peasants were defeating party-picked candidates. In the cities, growing food shortages led to rationing in 1920. This included, in 1929, Moscow and Leningrad. In response, the Bolsheviks turned once again to forcible expropriations, at first, as a temporary measure in late 1927, but again in 1928 when agricultural production declined. The more violent expropriations of 1928, however, yielded less grain because of increased peasant resistance.

Against this background of growing crisis, Stalin reversed himself and assumed a leftist position. He called for the abandonment of NEP concessions to private, individual agriculture and industry and their replacement

TABLE 3–1 Economic Recovery Under the NEP, 1920–1928 (1913 = 100)

	1920	1924	1925	1925	1927	1928
Industrial production	22	51	73	98	111	132
Agricultural production	67	90	112	118	121	124

Source: Gosudarstvennyi komitet SSSR po statistike (Goskomstat), *Narodnoe khoziaistvo SSSR za 70 let* (*NK SSSR za 70 let*) (Moskva: Finansy i statistika, 1987), p. 32.

by the collectivization of agriculture and the elimination of private ownership in industry. And, he called for the replacement of the market by a centrally determined economic plan emphasizing the rapid development of heavy industry. This led to a split between Stalin and his former allies on the right.

Bukharin openly defended the rightist policies of the NEP period in his article "Notes of an Economist" in *Pravda* in September 1928. In January 1929, he again defended the NEP in an article with the provocative title "Lenin's Political Testament," which revived Lenin's call for "a radical change" in strategy from "political struggle" to "peaceful organizational and cultural work" and evoked the memory of Lenin's 1923 call for the removal of Stalin. But by this time the party elite was, with the exception of a few individuals in the highest party organs, now solidly behind Stalin. References to Lenin had lost their emotional appeal for party cadres dependent on the secretariat for career advancement. Bukharin was accused of "collaboration with capitalist elements" and expelled from the leadership.

COLLECTIVIZATION AND INDUSTRIALIZATION

The defeat of Bukharin and the rightists in 1929 cleared the path for Stalin to carry out the leftist policies of forced collectivization and accelerated industrialization. Collectivization began in late 1929. It was planned at first to take place gradually, but was accelerated in 1930. The peasantry resisted the seizure of their lands furiously, engaging the OGPU (formerly the GPU) troops and the thousands of young party workers from the cities sent to the countryside in warlike battles. Widespread arrests, deportations, killings, and wholesale confiscations of personal possessions took place. The violence of these events led to a slowdown in the process during 1930, but by 1934 three quarters of all peasant holdings had been collectivized, and, as the figures in Table 3–2 reveal,

TABLE 3–2   Collectivization 1927–1939 (as a percentage)

1927	0.8
1928	1.7
1929	3.9
1930	23.6
1931	52.7
1932	61.5
1937	93.0
1939	95.6

Source: Goskomstat, *NK SSSR za 70 let*, p. 35.

veal, by 1940 collectivization was nearly complete.

The costs of collectivization were enormous. The most productive, and therefore most wealthy, peasants—the *kulaks*—were singled out by the regime for particularly brutal treatment. Half of all livestock and one quarter of productive capacity was destroyed. Despite disastrously declining production, state procurements increased dramatically. This left little food in the countryside for personal consumption, producing a man-made famine in 1932–1934. Some 5 million peasants died of hunger and disease as the result of collectivization, 3 million of them in the Ukraine alone. An additional 3 million were sent to forced labor camps.[2]

After 1933, arbitrary state procurements that amounted to little more than forced expropriations were replaced by fixed obligations based on acreage planted. Production beyond this amount reverted to the peasants of the collective farm, who were free to consume or market it themselves. This introduced a certain degree of stability in the countryside and contributed to the improvement of production. The former private peasants forced into becoming collective

---

[2]The estimate of 5 million is widely held. See, for example, Leonard Schapiro, *The Communist Party of the Soviet Union*, 2nd ed., revised and enlarged (New York: Vintage Books, 1971), p. 390. For a detailed account of the collectivization process, see Merle Fainsod, *Smolensk Under Soviet Rule* (New York: Vintage Books, n.d.), pp. 238–264.

farmers never reconciled themselves to their fate, however. The collective farmers dedicated more effort to tending the small private plots of land and the few cattle, sheep, and goats permitted to each collective farm family for their own use than they did to the collective farm itself. As a result, these private plots have continued to play an enormously important role in supplying the Soviet population with basic foodstuffs.

The collectivization of agriculture eased the task of state procurements by reducing the number of farming units in the countryside. Improved state procurements allowed the regime to establish a secure, if not generous, food supply for the urban population and to export more grain during the 1930s than at any time since the revolution. The export of grain raised the capital necessary for industrial development.

The blueprint for rapid industrialization was contained in the first "five-year plan," introduced in 1928. The plan established impossibly high goals for industrial production. To achieve them, strict central controls were imposed on the entire economy. Capital investment was focused on heavy industry, that is, on the production of materials, equipment and resources used as inputs in later stages of industrial production, and finished industrial goods used for nonconsumption purposes, such as military equipment. The production of light industrial, or consumption-oriented industries, such as food processing, textiles, and clothing, was intentionally suppressed. To maximize the amount of capital available, wages were kept artificially low, workers were compelled to purchase state bonds, taxes were increased, and foodstuffs were purchased from the peasantry at artificially low prices and resold at higher ones. Despite food shortages at home, grain exports were increased, contributing to the onset of widespread famine in the countryside in 1932–1934. Imports were limited to equipment and supplies intended to support the industrialization effort. As a result, private consumption fell off sharply between 1928 and 1932.

To enforce these policies, the industrial

proletariat was subjected to severe disciplinary measures. The free movement of labor was forbidden, and forced transfers of labor—including transfers to remote, inhospitable, and ill-supplied regions of the country—were introduced. The internal passport was reintroduced to reinforce these controls. The food supplies expropriated from the peasantry were placed under the control of factory managers and used as a weapon to maintain labor discipline, and prison sentences were established for violations. Vast inequalities in pay and access to material goods were introduced. And piecework, the system of individual pay based on the number of pieces produced that Marx had characterized as a "weapon of capitalist exploitation," was introduced—with the norms for production set at the highest levels possible.

Efficiency and quality were secondary considerations in the Stalinist industrialization effort. Large amounts of resources were mobilized for the construction of vast development projects. Production, or "output," was increased by increasing the number of production units brought into operation and the amount of capital, labor, and material resources, or "inputs" available, rather than by increasing the efficiency with which production facilities were operated and "inputs" consumed. This pattern of increasing "inputs" as a means of increasing "outputs" is called "extensive" development. It results in both dramatic increases in production and enormous waste of resources.

Stalin declared the first five-year plan "fulfilled" after only a little more than four years, in January 1933. Although many of the stated goals of the plan had not, in fact, been met, impressive gains in industrial production were achieved, as indicated in Table 3–3. Even more impressive gains were registered during the second five-year plan period, 1933–1937, and in the period up to the outbreak of World War II. To concentrate resources on development, private consumption continued to be suppressed, except where it could be used to provide incentives to key personnel. As a result, expanded industrial output was accompanied by the ini-

TABLE 3–3 Prewar Economic Development, Selected
Indicators, 1932–1940 (1928 = 100)

	1932	*1937*	*1940*
Social product	160	340	450
National income produced	180	390	510
Industrial production	200	450	650
Agricultural production	90	110	130
Capital investment	320	520	670
Labor productivity			
In industry	130	240	310
In agriculture	110	160	170

Source: Goskomstat, *NK SSSR za 70 let,* p. 41.

tial impoverishment and deprivation of broad segments of the population, from which there was only a partial recovery before the onset of war. Consumption began to increase, and then did so very rapidly, only in the late 1950s, after a period of additional sacrifice associated with economic recovery in the immediate postwar years.

STALIN, THE PARTY, AND THE STATE

By the end of the first five-year plan period, Stalin had forged the party and the state apparatuses into huge engines of command, coercion, and communication, each under his personal control. That control was exercised through both the party secretariat and a personal secretariat. By 1934, Stalin's personal secretariat had assumed control over the entire party and state apparatuses. It had become the de facto cabinet of the Soviet political order. The basis of its control lay in the personal secretariat's monopoly over cadres assignments in all areas related to security, over access to the secret internal communications network of the party and state, and over the secret party archives, including personnel records.

In addition, from the very beginning of his tenure as general secretary, members of Stalin's personal secretariat were assigned to serve as heads of key administrative bureaucracies, such as the secret police (GPU,

OGPU, NKVD, and so on) and the network of political commissars in the army (under the "main political administration" of the Red Army). These bureaucracies not only managed the economy, but directly controlled vast resources, including human labor. The number of prisoners in labor camps skyrocketed, and their uncompensated labor was mobilized for vast development projects. Thus, the party organization that exercised overall supervision and control, the state bureaucracies that executed the administrative tasks of development, and the coercive powers of the military and secret police came to be under the direct control of individuals personally loyal to Stalin and staffed by individuals selected by them or by the secretariats under Stalin's control.

Although united under a single command, the party, police, and administrative bureaucracies were not yet integrated into a single organizational hierarchy at this time. Party members, for example, could be arrested by the secret police, but their punishment remained in the hands of party organs. The continuing reluctance of even Stalin's own handpicked leaders to employ extreme measures against internal dissent was demonstrated in 1932, when the *Politburo* refused Stalin's demand that Riutin, the leader of a rightist faction bitterly critical of Stalin personally, be put to death, allegedly for having threatened Stalin's life, and voted instead for expulsion from the party.

Resistance to Stalin may also explain certain changes adopted at the Seventeenth Party Congress, in February 1934. This congress was labeled the "Congress of Victors," to denote the successful completion of the first five-year plan, including collectivization and industrialization. Yet, this congress adopted more modest goals for the second five-year plan. Several former opponents of Stalin, including Bukharin, were permitted to speak and were elected to membership in the Central Committee. And, finally, the party secretaries appointed by the Congress included Kirov, the Leningrad party secretary who was alleged to oppose the use of violence against party members and to favor a general reduction in the level of social strife. The rise of Kirov seemed to make him a potential competitor for power.

All sources of opposition to Stalin—whether real, potential, or only imagined—were soon eliminated, however. In late 1934 Stalin began a violent campaign of arrests and executions that swept away almost all the party, government, economic, and cultural elites of the revolutionary period and the 1920s and 1930s. This assault on society has come to be known as the period of "the great purges," or "the great terror." It began with the assassination of Kirov in his Leningrad office on December 1, 1934.

THE GREAT PURGES

Although a "smoking gun" is unlikely ever to be discovered, it seems clear that Stalin was responsible for the assassination of Kirov. His death led to a redistribution of positions and a strengthening of the role of Stalin proteges in the leadership. The Kirov murder also became the pretext for a purge of the party. In January 1935, Zinoviev, Kamenev, and other former opponents of Stalin were indicted for having organized an alleged secret opposition. This marked the beginning of a series of trials of Stalin's former leading opponents, first of the left, and then of the right. They were accused of participating in a variety of conspiracies against the regime, including conspiring with the exiled Trotsky. These trials culminated in March 1938 with the prosecution of Bukharin and other former leaders of the party, in what has come to be known as "the great show trial." In each case, the trials resulted in the conviction and execution of the defendants.

These trials were only the most open expression of a broader and deeper terrorization of Soviet society. Beginning in 1935 and lasting until late 1938, Stalin and his closest assistants directed a massive campaign of arrests, deportations, and executions. Unlike the violence that accompanied collectivization and, to a lesser extent, industrialization, this terror was also directed against the regime's own elites. Although accurate data are not available, careful estimates suggest that some $8\frac{1}{2}$ million people, or about 5 percent of the general population, were arrested. Some 1 million of these were party members, so that about 35 percent of the party was arrested. Former prisoners estimate that about 10 percent of all those arrested were executed, for a total of around 800,000 victims. Among party members, the execution rate may have been as high as 50 percent. Other sources suggest that executions may have amounted to as many as 2 to 3 million persons.[3]

The purges destroyed the overwhelming majority of the Soviet elite. Of the 1,966 delegates to the Seventeenth Congress in February 1934, 1,108 or 56.3 percent were killed. Of the 139 Central Committee members elected at the Congress, 98 (70.8 percent) were killed; others committed suicide.[4] Eighty-five percent of provincial party secretaries perished in the purges. In the Red Army, one-third of the officer corps was exe-

---

[3]The most careful calculation of victims is to be found in Robert Conquest, *The Great Terror* (Hamronsworth, England: Pelican Books, 1971), Appendix A: Casualty Figures, pp. 699–713.

[4]Figures revealed by Khrushchev in his denunciation of Stalin. Nikita S, Khrushchev, *The Crimes of the Stalin Era*, Special Report to the 20th Congress of the Communist Party of the Soviet Union (in closed session, February 1956) (New York: The New Leader, 1962).

cuted, including 3 of 5 marshals, all but 1 of the fleet commanders, 13 of 15 generals of the army, all commanders of military districts, all corps commanders, almost all brigade and division commanders, and one-half of all regimental commanders. The military academies, the political commissars, and even the military intelligence networks were all swept by the purges.[5]

This campaign of terror was not simply the product of Stalin's madness, although any such campaign is, of course, prima facie evidence of madness. Nor can one discount the role of possible defects in Stalin's personal psychology in explaining it. Nor can the terror be explained as an attempt to prod the population to greater effort. Productivity actually declined in the period following the purges. Moreover, the purges produced an enormous waste of human resources. Nor can the terror be explained as an attempt to root out an internal enemy in preparation for a coming war. For war was not imminent when the purges began, and they turned against the military precisely when the threat of war became very real.

Nor can the terror be explained as an attempt to bring loyal, Soviet-trained managers, political functionaries, scientists, engineers, and technicians into positions of leadership. For the industrialization effort of the first five-year plan had already created an enormous demand for personnel at all levels of the economic and administrative hierarchies. Even collectivization had created new demands for managers and technical specialists. This demand was met by a new generation of youth trained in the universities and technical schools. This was the "Brezhnev generation" of cadres, who achieved their first key positions in 1938 and advanced up the hierarchy until they took over everything in 1964.

The terror can only be explained as a conscious attempt by Stalin to consolidate his personal rule over the immense, centralized machinery of command, control, and communications that he had created. He had to

destroy the organizational autonomy of the vast bureaucratic hierarchies under his command and subject them to his personal intervention. He had to prevent the entrenchment of lower officials, the creation of informal networks of communication, influence, and loyalties that might serve as the basis for resistance to commands from above. He had to establish what Aristotle called tyranny. For this, Stalin had to acquire the power of life and death over his subjects, including even those in positions of authority. And this is precisely what he achieved through the terror he imposed on the Soviet Union.

The end of the purges in 1938 marked the consolidation of the Stalinist system whose main features remained largely intact until Gorbachev's attack on it nearly 50 years later. Stalin enjoyed the use of an unprecedented machinery of societal penetration that eliminated all barriers to the tyrant. He created what were, for his time, technologically advanced systems of communication, observation and monitoring, reporting, information processing, economic planning, resource mobilization, transportation, persuasion, and coercion. This did not mean, however, that Stalin decided everything in the USSR. That would have been impossible. But it did mean that he could intervene in any process, or make any decision, without constraint.

COERCION

The main foundation of the Stalinist system was coercion. Almost immediately upon seizing power, the Bolsheviks established a national network of "extraordinary commissions," the *Cheka,* to arrest and execute perceived opponents of the new regime. With the conclusion of the civil war and adoption of the NEP, the *Cheka* was transformed into the state political directorate (GPU), under the People's Commissariat for Internal Affairs (NKVD), and certain formal legal restraints were imposed on it. In practice, the GPU remained subject to few con-

---

[5]Conquest, *The Great Terror,* pp. 277–374.

straints, as it pursued class enemies, former Whites, and even the non-Bolshevik left. The GPU became a de facto independent ministry in 1924, when it became the OGPU, and undertook much broader tasks with the onset of collectivization and industrialization. It became the instrument for carrying out the arrests, deportation, and violence, and administered a greatly expanded network of forced-labor camps with a population in the millions.

In 1934 the OGPU took control over all instruments of coercion and control outside the military, including the civil police and fire departments, and penal system, in addition to all the functions of internal security. By this time, the OGPU had established a nationwide network of organizations at all levels. Control over this organization culminated in Stalin's personal Secretariat. With the onset of the Great Purges, the NKVD assumed unlimited power to terrorize the population. Although the fiction of "the leading role of the party" was maintained during this period, the NKVD was restrained only by personal instructions from Stalin. The terror appeared to be limitless and was so widespread as to give the impression that anyone could become its victim at any moment. The insecurities and anxieties that these conditions induced in the Soviet population destroyed the bases of potential resistance to commands from above.

The end of the terror came abruptly, and for no obvious reason. It was brought to a halt in 1938, when Stalin placed Beria in command of the NKVD, and he purged the purgers. The organizational base of the terror remained intact, however. The possibility that it could be revived as suddenly as it was concluded remained a powerful, even if only implicit, coercive threat to the population.

On the eve of World War II, the external security and internal secret police functions were separated from the simple internal civilian public safety functions and apportioned among separate agencies: the People's Commissariats, later ministries, for state security (MGB) and for internal affairs

(MVD), respectively. The MGB became the instrument through which Stalin appeared to be preparing for another round of purges and terror when his plans were cut short by his death in March 1953.

This division of functions has persisted for most of the postwar period. With the turn away from terror as an instrument of control in the period since Stalin's death, the secret police and security functions were placed under the administration of officials with political rather than police careers. The focus of repression turned toward the persecution of more specific groups, such as religious believers and various dissidents. Such repression remained unconstrained by considerations of "legality" and preserved the implicit threat to the population at large of a potential revival of the Stalinist terror. At present, the KGB—the (State) Committee for State Security—carries out the security and secret police functions. The MVD—Ministry of Internal Affairs—carries out the more routine public safety functions.

PERSUASION

To elicit the positive cooperation and support of key segments of society, the Stalinist system balanced coercion with positive incentives consisting of status, privilege, wealth, and power. The young, new scientific and technical intelligentsia—already the beneficiaries of the rapid turnover in elite positions produced by the purges—were rewarded for loyal performance with social status and privileged access to goods in short supply, from food to housing. This gave them the equivalent of wealth. Similar incentives were made available to the cultural intelligentsia willing to produce and enforce the official culture. For political functionaries, status, privilege, and wealth were reinforced by power.

A whole stratum of new elites, all of them in positions subject to control by the party's appointments process, was created. Not all individuals in such positions were rewarded equally, of course. The Stalinist system was

TABLE 3–4 Specialists in the National Economy, 1913–1941 (in thousands)

	1913	1928	1941
With higher education	136	233	909
With specialized secondary education	54	288	1,492
Total	190	521	2,401

Source: *N.K. SSSR za 70 let,* p. 39.

characterized by substantial inequalities. Collectively, however, they came to be known as "the *nomenklatura,*" after the lists of positions, or *nomenklatura,* under the control of the party.

Each party organization controlled its own *nomenklatura,* although not all elite positions were within its control. Some were reserved for control by higher bodies. The *nomenklatura* under the direct control of Stalin's personal Secretariat, working at times through the cadres department of the party Secretariat, constituted the "ruling elite" of the Stalinist system. This *nomenklatura* system has remained in operation in the Soviet Union to this day, although it appears to have become a highly bureaucratized process carried out by the party Secretariat. Control over it appears to be shared by all members of the leadership rather than under the control of any single individual. Nonetheless, the *nomenklatura* system, because it places appointments to key positions throughout the Soviet system under the control of the party, remains the most important foundation of the party's continuing power, and the most enduring element of Stalin's legacy.

The Stalinist system also produced benefits for, and thereby elicited support from, those not part of either the *nomenklatura* or the scientific, technical, and cultural elite. Expanded educational opportunities in the prewar period brought near-universal literacy to the urban population and transformed a predominately illiterate rural population into a predominately literate one. Rapid industrialization brought expanded opportunities for upward social mobility for former peasants, who migrated to the cities in large numbers during this period. The urban population increased from 17.9 percent of the total in 1926, to 32.9 percent in 1939.[6] Opportunities were particularly enhanced for those who acquired specialized secondary and higher education. As indicated in Table 3–4, the number of such "specialists" increased more than fourfold during the period of industrialization. Economic development also was accompanied by the establishment of an expanded public health system. In a survey conducted in the postwar period, these benefits were acknowledged by former Soviet citizens who fled the USSR during World War II and later settled in the West as major accomplishments worth preserving.[7]

Soviet social welfare policies, and the material benefits delivered to the population, improved rapidly in the 1960s and 1970s. The ability of the regime to deliver material well-being remained an important basis of its popular legitimacy and support. In response to a survey conducted in the early 1980s, for example, the most recent generation of Soviet emigres, who arrived in the West in the 1970s, also attached a strong positive value to these same features of the Soviet system.[8]

[6]Warren W. Eason, "Demography," in Ellen Mickiewicz, ed., *Handbook of Soviet Social Science Data* (New York: Free Press, 1973), p. 54.

[7]Alex Inkeles and Raymond Bauer, *The Soviet Citizen* (New York: Atheneum, 1968, originally published in 1959 by Harvard University Press), pp. 233–254.

[8]Brian D. Silver, "Political Beliefs of the Soviet Citizen: Sources of Support for Regime Norms," Working Paper No. 6, *Soviet Interview Project* (University of Illinois Urbana-Champaign, December 1985).

Popular compliance and support were also encouraged through a comprehensive network of agitation and propaganda. Agitation comprises party-led activities designed to elicit the participation of the populace in officially sponsored activities such as voting. Propaganda work consists of imparting information to the population in such a manner as to lend support to the regime's policies. Organized lectures in workplaces, residential communities, and other locations constitute a major element of propaganda work. Such lectures provided an important alternative channel for informing the population at large or selective elite groups within it of issues and developments that the leadership wishes to keep out of the mass media. Khrushchev's secret speech denouncing Stalin in February 1956, for example, was disseminated to the party in this way.

To eliminate information and views inconsistent with those of the leadership, an elaborate system of censorship was established. Careful censorship of the Soviet media was accompanied by efforts to insulate the country from external influences. In this way, the Soviet Union became a "closed society."

ADMINISTRATION

Day-to-day administration of the economy was in the hands of the central state bureaucracies. These increased in number gradually from 1917 to 1936. Thereafter, a rapid proliferation of specialized state bureaucracies took place to meet the demands of overseeing the rapid industrialization of the 1930s, and the mobilization and coordination of civilian and military tasks during World War II. By 1947, a hypercentralized, centrally planned economy administered by numerous highly specialized central state bureaucracies was firmly established. This pattern has lasted until the present day.

A limited attempt was made to streamline the central administration in the postwar period, and the number of ministries was cut in half as the result of a reorganization following Stalin's death. Nonetheless, the number of central bureaucracies expanded again rapidly, to the highest number since 1947.

Khrushchev attempted to reverse this tendency toward hypercentralization by introducing a major reorganization of the economic administration along regional lines in 1957. Thereafter, however, a gradual recentralization of economic administration and reestablishment of central bureaucracies took place. As long as the economy continued to be based on central planning, the tasks of coordination required large central bureaucracies. In 1965, after the ouster of Khrushchev, his successors reorganized the central state administration, creating 71 highly specialized ministries, state committees, and other bodies. These grew to 83 in 1971 and 108 in 1983. The array of central bureaucracies, as it existed in late 1987, is shown in Figure 3–1.

The Council of Ministers, or government, is composed of the heads of all the ministries, state committees, and other agencies with ministerial status. As such, it is an extremely large and unwieldy body, incapable of actually coordinating the management of the economy. The increasing functional specialization of the central ministries, committees, and other agencies has been counterbalanced instead by several high-level commissions created to carry out oversight and coordination functions for broad areas of economic activity and by a smaller executive organ, the Presidium of the Council of Ministers. The chairman of the Presidium is the head of the state administration, or government, and is sometimes referred to as the "prime minister" or "premier."

Each ministerial organization was fully penetrated by both the secret police and the party during the Stalin era. The police enforced security. The party ensured the fulfillment of tasks imposed from above. Under Stalin, the role of the party gradually declined. After 1938, the Soviet system became more bureaucratized, less revolutionary, more conservative, and more traditionally Russian, or "national" in character. Moreover, the growing emphasis on "rationaliza-

FIGURE 3–1 The Central State Bureaucracies, 1987

Presidium of the USSR
Council of Ministers

Chairman, USSR Council of Ministries
First Deputy Chairmen (5)
Deputy Chairmen (10)

Other Organs of the Council of Ministers

Bureau for Social Development
USSR Permanent Representative to COMECON
Bureau for Fuel and Energy Complex
Bureau for Machine Building

Commissions of the Presidium

For Environmental Protection and Rational Use of Natural Resources
For Improving Administration, Planning, and the Economic Mechanism
Foreign Economic Commission
Military-Industrial Commission

All-Union Ministries

Automotive Industry
Aviation Industry
Chemical Industry
Chemical and Petroleum Machine Building
Civil Aviation
Communications Equipment
Construction in Eastern Regions
Construction in Northern and Western Regions
Construction in Southern Regions
Construction in the Urals and Western Siberia
Construction of Petroleum and Gas Industry Enterprises
Construction, Road, and Municipal Machine Building
Defense
Defense Industry

Union-Republic Ministries

Coal Industry
Communications
Construction Materials Industry
Culture
Education
Ferrous Metallurgy
Finance
Fish Industry
Foreign Affairs
Geology
Grain Products
Health
Higher and Secondary Specialized Education
Installation and Special Construction Work
Internal Affairs
Justice
Land Reclamation and Water Resources
Light Industry
Nonferrous Metallurgy
Petroleum Refining and Petrochemical Industry
Power and Electrification

All-Union State Committees with the Status of Ministries

Computer Technology and Information Science
Foreign Economic Relations
Hydrometeorology and Environmental Control
Inventions and Discoveries
Science and Technology
Standards
Supervision of Safe Working Practices in the Atomic Power Industry

Union-Republic State Committees with the Status of Ministries

Planning (Gosplan)
Agroindustrial Construction
Material and Technical Supply
Cinematography
Foreign Tourism
Forestry
Labor and Social Relations
Physical Culture and Sports
Prices
Publishing Houses, Printing Plants, and the Book Trade
State Security (KGB)
Supervision of Safe Working Practices in Industry and for Mine Supervision
Supply of Petroleum Products
Television and Radio Broadcasting (*Gosteleradio*)

Other Agencies with Ministerial Status

Administration of Affairs of the Council of Ministers
Secretariat of the Chairman of the Council of Ministers
Central Statistical Administration[a]
USSR State Bank (*Gosbank*)
Committee for People's Control
Chairmen of Councils of Ministers of the Union Republics (15)

Agencies without Ministerial Status

State Board of Arbitration
Main Archives Administration
All-Union Bank for Financing Capital Investment (*Stroibank*)
Main Administration for State Customs Control
Higher Certification Commission
Main Administration of Geodesy and Cartography
Commission for the Establishment of Personal Pensions
Committee for Lenin Prizes and State Prizes in Literature, Art and Architecture

Electrical Equipment Industry
Electronics Industry
Foreign Trade
Gas Industry
General Machine Building
Heavy and Transport Machine Building
Instrument Making, Automation Equipment, and Control Systems
Machine Building
Machine Building for Animal Husbandry and Fodder Production
Machine Building for Light and Food Industry and Household Appliances
Machine Tool and Tool Building Industry
Maritime Fleet
Medium Machine Building
Nuclear Energy
Petroleum Industry
Power Machine Building
Production of Mineral Fertilizers
Radio Industry
Railways
Shipbuilding Industry
Tractor and Agricultural Machine Building
Transport Construction

Timber, Pulp and Paper Industry
Wood Processing Industry
Trade

Vocational and Technical Education

Committee for Lenin Prizes and State Prizes in Science and Technology
State Commission for Oversight of Aircraft Flight Safety
Council for Religious Affairs
Main Administration for Safeguarding State Secrets in the Press (*Glavlit*)
State Commission for Stockpiling Useful Minerals
Telegraph Agency of the Soviet Union (*TASS*)
State Committee for Utilization of Atomic Energy
Academy for the National Economy
Main Administration for Exhibition of Achievements of the National Economy of the USSR
Commission for Prizes for the Development and Implementation of Outstanding Construction Projects
Main Administration for the Creation and Utilization of Space Technology for the National Economy and Scientific Research

aReorganized in July 1987 into higher-status union-republic State Committee on Statistics (*Goskomstat*).

tion" of economic administration in this period was more compatible with the technocratic values of the state administration than with the revolutionary values of the party. The role of the state was further enhanced when Stalin became chairman of the Council of People's Commissars, or head of the government, just before the outbreak of war. He chaired the State Committee for Defense during the war, and retained the chairmanship of the Council of Ministers in the postwar period.

PARTY ORGANIZATION

Even as the state bureaucracies grew in importance, the party retained its oversight functions. Its most important power, however, remained its control over cadres assignments. The enormous expansion of demand for specialized personnel created by the collectivization and industrialization effort led to a corresponding expansion in the structure of the party Secretariat. The assignments to the party apparatus and to the administrative and economic apparatus were divided between separate departments in 1930. Administrative and economic assignments, in turn, were handled by specialized subdepartments for particular branches of the economy. As the tasks of administrative and economic oversight increased in importance, the Secretariat was reorganized again in 1939 into specialized departments, some of them responsible for party affairs, some for specific policy areas and others for sectors of the economy. Each specialized department was vested with control over personnel issues in its particular area. Since then, the internal organization of the party secretariat has become increasingly specialized. Through the departments of the Secretariat, the party leadership has exercised close supervision over the military, the political and civilian police, the mass media, key sectors of the economy, the intellectual establishment, and the party organization itself. By 1983, however, there were still only about 22 specialized departments, leaving

the party with a significantly smaller central apparatus than that of the state (see Figure 3–2.)

The central party apparatus is formally subordinated to the Central Committee, although in fact it is subordinated to the Secretariat. The Central Committee is the most authoritative party organ between party Congresses, which are held once every five years. The Central Committee is composed mostly of professional party workers from the central party apparatus, first secretaries of the provincial party organizations, and leading figures from the state bureaucracies. Although politically powerless as an institution after about 1934, the Central Committee has assumed increasing importance in the years since Stalin's death. At present, it functions as the Soviet political system's closest equivalent to a parliamentary body, although its membership is handpicked by the members of the *Politburo* and not elected.

The strength of the party, however, lies not in its central organs, but in its ability to mobilize the efforts of party members throughout Soviet society. Party members and party organizations are found in all major, and most of the minor, institutions and organizations in the country and exercise direct supervision over their operation.

The party is organized both territorially and functionally. In addition to the leading party organs of the CPSU in Moscow, which exercise control over the entire party, there are separate party organizations for 14 of the 15 union republics comprised by the federation. Only the Russian republic has no party organization of its own. Instead, the national organization operates as the de facto Russian organization, and each of the regional (*krai*) and provincial (*oblast*) party organizations of the Russian republic remains directly subordinated to the CPSU leadership.

Each of the 14 republic party organizations has its own central committee and party secretariat, which are subordinated directly to the CPSU organs in Moscow. The provincial party organizations within the non-Russian republics are subordinated to

FIGURE 3-2 The Central Party Apparatus, 1987

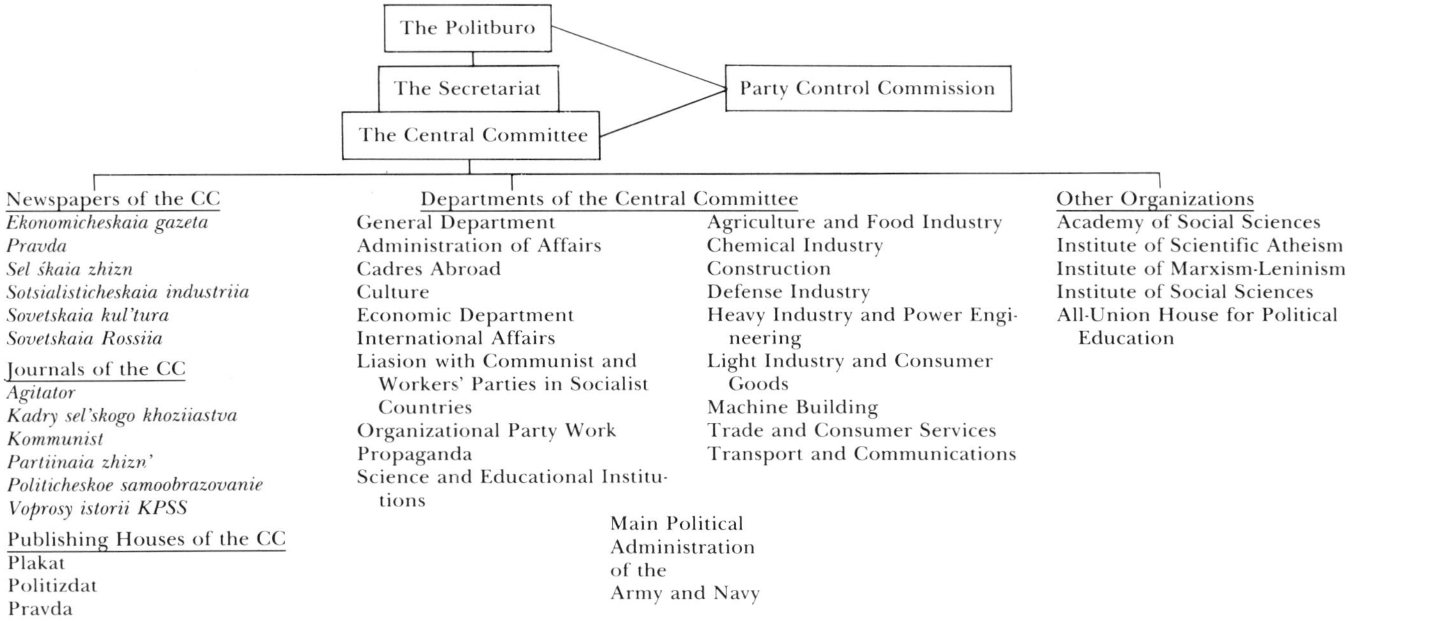

The Politburo

Party Control Commission

The Secretariat

The Central Committee

Departments of the Central Committee

General Department
Administration of Affairs
Cadres Abroad
Culture
Economic Department
International Affairs
Liasion with Communist and Workers' Parties in Socialist Countries
Organizational Party Work
Propaganda
Science and Educational Institutions

Agriculture and Food Industry
Chemical Industry
Construction
Defense Industry
Heavy Industry and Power Engineering
Light Industry and Consumer Goods
Machine Building
Trade and Consumer Services
Transport and Communications

Main Political Administration of the Army and Navy

Other Organizations
Academy of Social Sciences
Institute of Scientific Atheism
Institute of Marxism-Leninism
Institute of Social Sciences
All-Union House for Political Education

Newspapers of the CC
Ekonomicheskaia gazeta
Pravda
Sel'skaia zhizn
Sotsialisticheskaia industriia
Sovetskaia kul'tura
Sovetskaia Rossiia

Journals of the CC
Agitator
Kadry sel'skogo khoziiastva
Kommunist
Partiinaia zhizn'
Politicheskoe samoobrazovanie
Voprosy istorii KPSS

Publishing Houses of the CC
Plakat
Politizdat
Pravda

Source: Adapted from Alexandr Rahr, "The Apparatus of the Central Committee of the CPSU," *Radio Liberty Research*, RL 136, April 10, 1987.

both Moscow and their respective republic leaderships, as indicated in Figure 3–3. Similar organizations exist for urban centers. In the case of political, administrative, and economic centers, these can be larger and more complex than an average provincial organization. These structures are repeated for lower, district (*raion, okrug*) organizations.

Up to late 1988, primary party organizations in social and economic organizations and institutions, the basic units of the party, were subordinated to both their respective territorial party organization and a vertical hierarchy of local, provincial, republic and central party secretariat departments responsible for overseeing their functional area of activity. With the onset of economic reforms intended to increase the autonomy of enterprises, and the reorganization of the central party secretariat in October 1988, the future lines of subordination remain unclear. But it is highly unlikely that provincial party secretaries (the *obkom* first secretaries), who up to now have been the most powerful actors in their respective territories, will give up their power easily.

THE STALINIST "POLICE STATE"

The lines of distinction between the major organizational hierarchies of the Stalin period cannot be drawn too distinctly. The lines of division between the party and state hierarchies became blurred. Some have argued that there was an overlapping of administrative hierarchies and responsibilities that served as a "check" on the inherent powers of the bureaucracies. However, the interpenetration of party and state administrative hierarchies was so complete that they became fused into a single, all-embracing organizational hierarchy, culminating in the personal Secretariat around Stalin. This system was characterized by an inherent conflict between tendencies toward rational, rule-oriented behavior arising out of the bureaucratized nature of the hierarchy itself and rule-breaking behavior arising out of the absolute need to fulfill the tasks imposed on the system by the tyrant or his agents.

The Stalinist tyranny itself rested on the overall superiority of the secret police network which penetrated the party-state hierarchies at all levels. Control over the coercive powers of the police rested in the personal Secretariat. They could be—and were—used against party and state officials with impunity.

Even after the terror had subsided, party and state officials remained vulnerable to police persecution. To fulfill tasks imposed on them from above, they simply had to break formal rules and laws. The need to fulfill tasks "at any cost" placed a premium on certain forms of patrimonial behavior by responsible officials at all levels of the system. They were compelled to rely on interpersonal relations and loyalties to secure support and to advance their own career and the careers of their supporters. Loyalty tended to obscure less subjective, performance-based criteria. Responsible officials were also obliged to tolerate, and even participate themselves, in behaviors that were formally illegal. Black marketeering and other forms of unofficial exchange, for example, became essential to fulfilling production assignments in the centrally planned, nonmarket economy. Soviet elites therefore came to rely on personal loyalties to protect themselves from liability for such behaviors.

As the economy of the Soviet Union grew more complex, internally differentiated and functionally specific, the administrative bureaucracies of the state, and the technocrats who staffed them, grew more powerful. This transfer of power from party to state institutions was reinforced by the increasing identification of Stalin and his closest lieutenants with the institutions of the state, a process accelerated by the onset of World War II and the creation of an all-powerful State Committee for Defense to oversee the entire war effort, military and civilian.

The increasing economic and military importance of technical expertise, and the increasing prominence of technically trained

FIGURE 3-3 The Hierarchy of Territorial Party Organizations

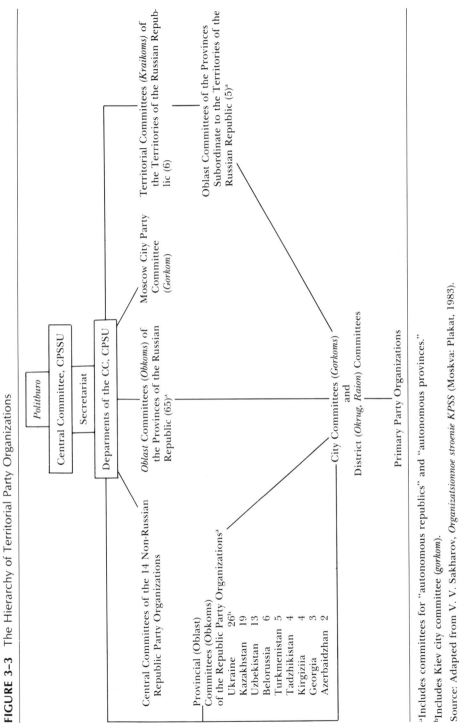

[a]Includes committees for "autonomous republics" and "autonomous provinces."

[b]Includes Kiev city committee (*gorkom*).

Source: Adapted from V. V. Sakharov, *Organizatsionnoe stroenie KPSS* (Moskva: Plakat, 1983).

administrators among the Stalinist leadership, resulted in the assertion of technocratic values such as organizational autonomy and rule observance. These values had to be suppressed, or at least overridden, when they conflicted with the Stalinist commitment to achieving goals regardless of the costs involved. The party provided a powerful network of authoritative command, control, and communication by which to oppose the natural tendency of the state administrative bureaucracies to become focused on their own narrow departmental or ministerial interests at the expense of system goals. The highly centralized, but territorially dispersed, party organization also provided an instrument by which to combat constant tendencies toward regionalism and localism. In effect, the party continued to carry out the function for which Lenin had created it. Under Stalin, however, mobilization was focused on directing human and material resources toward the creation of economic growth and military power, not revolution.

The assertion of goals, or ends, over means remained the central feature of the Stalinist system. The secret police apparatus, and the coercive force it could bring to bear on party and state officials alike, represented the ultimate guarantor of compliance. At the time of his death, in March 1953, Stalin was preparing another campaign of terror. It appeared to be a response to the emergence during the war of entrenched interests powerful enough to resist central direction. With Stalin's death, however, the terror was averted, and the dispersion and institutionalization of power underway since 1939 continued.

THE CONSTITUTIONAL FACADE

The Stalinist police state functioned behind the facade of a constitution, adopted in 1936, which established formal institutions and procedures that imitated those of liberal democratic political systems. It vested all power in the hands of the people. It formally established socialist ownership of the means of production, including state ownership of the land, resources, and social services. On the collective farms, it provided for the existence of small private plots. The constitution obligated each able-bodied citizen to work for the common good.

The constitution granted Soviet citizens the right to employment, housing, an education, and health and other social services. It also granted them the civil liberties familiar in Western democracies, including the rights to free speech and assembly. But, even in the constitution itself, these rights were rendered moot by provisions limiting their use to activity that conformed to the interests of the broader community, as defined by the Communist party. The revised constitution adopted in 1977[9] preserved the rights granted in 1936, and even marginally enhanced them. But it also preserved and even strengthened the leading role granted to the party in the political life of the nation. It elevated the authoritarian principles of decision making established by Lenin, and characteristic of the party since the Tenth Congress in 1921, to a constitutional principle valid for all organizations and institutions.

The constitutions of the Soviet Union have established a set of electoral and representative institutions, the system of "soviets," or legislatures, at each level of the governmental system. The soviets were organized hierarchically and culminated in a central or Supreme Soviet for the country as a whole. The soviets remained essentially moribund during the Stalin erea. During the Khrushchev era, however, mass participation in the political process received new emphasis, and both the electoral process and the system of Soviets was gradually allowed to assume a greater, but nonetheless ceremonial function. With the turn toward oligarchy under Brezhnev, and the concomitantly increased emphasis on consultation and consensus, the Soviets assumed the role of arenas for

---

[9]*Konstitutsiia (osnovnoi zakon) Soiuza Sovetskikh Sotsialisticheskikh Respublik* (Moskva: Izdatel'stvo Izvestiia Sovetov Deputatov Trudiashchikhsia SSSR, 1977).

consultations during the preparation of legislation among government and party officials, on the one hand, and specialists and representatives of interested parties, on the other.

The legislative chambers of the Supreme Soviet consisted of a Soviet of the Union, comprising 750 delegates elected from across the country, and a Soviet of Nationalities, comprising 750 delegates apportioned among the various federal territories: 32 from each of the 15 "union republics," 11 from each of the 20 "autonomous republics," 5 from each of the "autonomous regions," and 1 from each of the 10 "autonomous areas." Despite the adoption of a new constitution in 1977, the Supreme Soviet and lower-level legislative bodies remained rubber-stamp bodies that convened for only a few days each year to conduct the entire legislative business of the state.

The role of the Supreme Soviet was enhanced only marginally when Brezhnev assumed the presidency of the Soviet Union in 1977. This position is formally the chairmanship of the Presidium of the Supreme Soviet, the Presidium being the executive committee of the Supreme Soviet. Its assumption by the general secretary gave him the formal constitutional authority to exercise his de facto power over the institutions of the state, but did little to increase the role of the Supreme Soviet itself in the central policymaking process.

Membership in the Supreme Soviet, as well as in lower-level bodies, has been carefully controlled through manipulation of the electoral process. The delegates include a large bloc of individuals selected as representatives of the common citizenry. But they also include many of the country's political, economic, and cultural elites. There is extensive overlap, for example, between the memberships of the party's Central Committee and the Supreme Soviet—at both the national and republic levels.

Despite the officially reported 99.9 percent participation level, however, undisguised manipulation of the electoral process emptied it of any real meaning for the average Soviet citizen. With changes introduced by Gorbachev in 1987 and 1988, however, the electoral process is now taking on more than mere symbolic importance in Soviet politics. The introduction of multiple candidates, and increased opportunities for direct citizen participation in the candidate nominating process, have resulted in the election of some genuine representatives of popular interests. This may breathe new political life into the network of soviets.

The constitutions of the Soviet Union have sustained the fiction that the Union of Soviet Socialist Republics, or federation, was formed as the result of the voluntary union of the ethnic groups, or nationalities, whose homelands roughly correspond to the union republics. By the end of World War II, there were 15 so-called "Socialist republics" in the union. The largest, the Russian Soviet Federated Socialist Republic (RSFSR), or Russian republic, now includes within its boundaries 16 lesser ranking political subdivisions of the federation, called "autonomous republics." These correspond to the territories of settlement of the larger indigenous ethnic minorities, such as the Tatars. Other republics with large, territorially compact, national minorities also contain corresponding "autonomous republics." Smaller minorities within the RSFSR have been granted administrative subdivisions of lower status, called "autonomous territories" or "autonomous regions." These territorial units, and their corresponding administrative bodies are listed in Figure 3–4.

The actual administrative authority of the constituent republics has varied over time. Republic governments tend to have little influence over all-union ministries based in Moscow or the enterprises they supervise in the republics. They tend to have greater influence over union-republic ministries. But the number of such ministries has remained small, and the functions they control tend to be of less economic consequence. Even during the brief periods when decentralization of administration has occurred, the center has remained the dominant force in Soviet government and administration.

FIGURE 3-4 The Federal Structure of Government

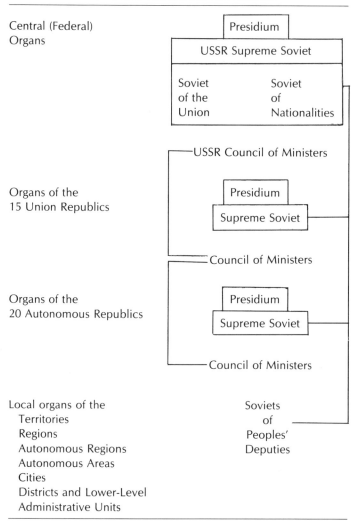

Central (Federal) Organs	Presidium
Organs of the 15 Union Republics	
Organs of the 20 Autonomous Republics	
Local organs of the Territories Regions Autonomous Regions Autonomous Areas Cities Districts and Lower-Level Administrative Units	

Although each of the 15 union republics has the constitutional right to secede, this right cannot be exercised. This fiction has been maintained largely as part of an effort to sustain the myth that membership in the union represents the free exercise of the right of self-determination of each of the country's major ethnic minorities. Some of these territories, such as the Georgian republic, were forcibly prevented by the Bolsheviks from becoming independent states in the post-revolutionary period. Others, such as the republic of Central Asia, are artificial creations of the Bolsheviks, intended to introduce political-administrative and linguistic divisions among a larger people for the purpose of rendering them easier to rule. Still others, the Baltic republics, were formerly independent countries annexed by the Soviets in 1940.

The USSR is a multinational state. Each of the republics, "autonomous" republics, and lower-level "autonomous" territories is the homeland of a particular nationality, or ethnic group. Thus, the Ukrainian Soviet Socialist Republic is the homeland of the Ukrainians, who constituted almost 74 percent of the republic population in 1979. Not every group constitutes a majority in its own home republic or territory, however. Kazakhs, for example, constituted only 36 percent, and Russians over 40 percent of the population of Kazakhstan in 1979.[10] In the USSR as a whole, Russians constitute a slim, and declining majority of the population. Together with the other major Slavic nationalities, the Ukrainians and Byelorussians, they comprise over 70 percent of the population. The major nationality groups, and their share in the total Soviet population, are shown in Table 3–5.

The union republics are distinguished by more than the ethnic differences among their populations. There are also significant economic differences among them. The union republics can be grouped into a "developed northwest" comprising the Baltic republics, Ukraine, the European RSFSR, and the Transcaucasian republics of Georgia and Armenia; an "underdeveloped but resource-rich East" comprising the Siberian and Far Eastern regions of the RSFSR and northern Kazakhstan; and an "underdeveloped South" comprising southern Kazakhstan, the Central Asian republics of Uzbekistan, Turkmenistan, Tadzhikistan and Kirgiziia, and the Transcaucasian republic of Azerbaidzhan. These republics and regions differ not only with respect to the level of development, but also with respect to the composition of their economies, or "mix" of economic activities that takes place within them. These differences are manipulated by Moscow to ensure their economic dependence on Moscow.

Each of the union republics is endowed with a governmental and administrative apparatus and, except for the Russian republic, party organization of its own. Since the 1950s, indigenous, or ethnically native, elites

TABLE 3–5 Major Nationalities of the USSR (in percent)

Nationality	1959	1979
Russians	54.6	52.4
Ukrainians	17.8	16.2
Byelorussians	3.8	3.6
Moldavians	1.1	1.1
Lativans	0.7	0.5
Lithuanians	1.1	1.1
Estonians	0.5	0.4
Georgians	1.3	1.4
Armenians	1.3	1.6
Azerbaidzhanis	1.4	2.1
Kazakhs	1.7	2.5
Uzbeks	2.9	4.8
Turkmen	0.5	0.8
Tadzhiks	0.7	1.1
Kirghiz	0.5	0.7
Tatars	2.4	2.4
Germans	0.8	0.7
Jews	1.1	0.7
Chuvash	0.7	0.7
Daghestanis	0.5	0.6
Bashkirs	0.5	0.5
Mordivinians	0.6	0.5
Poles	0.7	0.4

Source: Tsentral'noe statistilcheskoe upravlenie SSSR (TsSU SSR), *Itogi vsesoiuznoi perepisi naseleniia 1970 goda* Vol. 4 (Moskva: Statistika, 1973), p. 9
TsSU SSSR, *Chislennost' i sostav naseleniia SSSR* (Moskva: Finansy i Statistika, 1984), p. 71

have played increasingly prominent roles in the local government and party organizations. This has established the trappings of political self-rule. But actual power and control is exercised from Moscow, through the placement of Russian and other Slavic personnel in positions from which they can control the local *nomenklatura,* and the secret police organization, or KGB. These Slavs tend to be drawn from among cadres serving in the central party apparatus in Moscow. But they are also drawn from among the Slavic populations resident in these territories for decades, or even centuries. In addition, territorial military commands are firmly under the control of Slavs. This pattern of apparent self-rule but actual central control is reproduced at each level of the federal hierarchy.

---

[10]TsSU SSSR, *Chislennost' i sostav naseleniia SSSR* (Moskva: Finansy: Statistika, 1984), pp. 102–116.

4

Social and Political Change After Stalin

The basic features of the modern Soviet political system were shaped by Stalin. The organizational characteristics of the party and state administration, the relationships among institutions, and the distribution of power are all part of the Stalinist legacy. This legacy shaped the outcome of the succession struggle which followed his death and established the parameters within which successive leaders of the system have been compelled to operate.

FROM STALIN TO KHRUSHCHEV

The death of Stalin left intact the vast networks of totalitarian controls he had created. None of the surviving leaders, however, enjoyed enough personal authority or political power to assume control over the entire apparatus. A struggle to secure such a dominant position began among them almost immediately. To prevent this struggle

from becoming violent and, potentially, even fatal, the post-Stalin leadership agreed to put an end to the use of violence within the elite. To protect themselves personally, they removed Stalin's secret police chief, Beria, from power. He became the last Soviet leader executed for political reasons. They halted the preparations Stalin had begun for a renewal of the purges and reversed the expansion of the central leadership that Stalin had carried out at the Nineteenth Congress in 1952. These changes transformed the Politburo, renamed Presidium in 1952, from a powerless reservoir of leading cadres into the actual political leadership of the Soviet Union.

To disperse among the members of the Presidium the power Stalin had concentrated, the leadership broke up Stalin's personal Secretariat. They appear to have subordinated the security organs and other agencies of coercion to oversight by a department of the Secretariat (the "administrative organs" department) and to have relegated the remaining parts of the personal Secretariat to serving as the general administrative staff of the central leadership (the "general department"). They also separated leadership of the party organization from leadership of the state administration and assigned these two posts to two separate individuals: Malenkov, who was appointed chairman of the Presidium of the Council of Ministers, or head of government, and Khrushchev, who was appointed first secretary of the Central Committee.

Malenkov was a former member of Stalin's personal secretariat and secretary of the Central Committee. He had been in charge of the cadres appointment process for most of the 1940s. With the outbreak of the war, Stalin picked Malenkov to serve on the State Committee for Defense. Malenkov emerged as the leading administrator of the wartime economy and was placed in charge of the postwar reconstruction effort. These responsibilities allowed him to build up substantial support in the state bureaucracies. Stalin appeared to have selected Malenkov as his successor by casting him in the leading role at the Nineteenth Congress in 1952.

Malenkov attempted to secure his claim to leadership of the Soviet Union by exploiting the trend toward increasing state power and authority established under Stalin. He used the state bureaucracies to assert control over the domestic and foreign policymaking processes. In effect, he was attempting to assume the powers and prerogatives of a prime minister within the emerging cabinet-like body, the Presidium. Khrushchev, in contrast, had assumed the leadership of the party at a time when its role was substantially diminished. However, Khrushchev had several important resources at his command, the most important of these being the *nomenklatura* system and the party's historical claim to leadership of the Soviet system.

Khrushchev immediately turned to the *nomenklatura* system to build up his support throughout the party. Just as Stalin had done earlier, Khrushchev placed his supporters in positions that qualified them for membership in the party's nominal decision-making body, the Central Committee. Also like Stalin, however, Khrushchev was unable to effect any changes in the membership of the Presidium (formerly called the Politburo), the real locus of decision making in the post-Stalin period. Even when Khrushchev was able to force Malenkov to resign as head of the government in January 1955, he was unable to secure Malenkov's removal from the Presidium. The other members of the leadership were reluctant to permit him to accumulate too much power over them.

For the next year and a half, Khrushchev conducted a political campaign to build up his personal power and authority and thus free himself from the constraints of "collective leadership." A central component of this campaign was the open rejection of the Stalinist terror and an attempt to discredit all those associated with it, including his main opponents in the Presidium. At the Twentieth Party Congress in February 1956, Khrushchev delivered a lengthy, but selective, condemnation of the Stalinist terror, known as "the secret speech" because he delivered it to a closed session of the Congress, but which was read to all party members at local meetings and copies of which soon became available in the West. Khrushchev faulted Stalin for his violent attack on the party after 1934, not for the violence attending the previous five years of collectivization and industrialization. He also attacked the "cult of personality" that was built up around Stalin and the accompanying demise of "collective leadership." And he accused his current political opponents in the Presidium of complicity in Stalin's "crimes," while carefully dissociating himself and his supporters from them.

Khrushchev's revelations about Stalin sent shock waves throughout the communist world. By attacking Stalin, Khrushchev not only undermined the authority of his domestic opponents, he also undermined the authority of the Stalinist leaderships that had been installed by Moscow throughout the Eastern European satellites, often by means of violent purges of the local leaderships.

Within months, both Poland and Hungary experienced political upheavals. The de-Stalinization campaign that followed the Twentieth Congress also created the foundation for a growing political conflict with China, whose leaders still remained loyal to the Stalinist system. In the Soviet Union itself, de-Stalinization led to a political "thaw" and increased intellectual unrest. It also raised an implicit political threat to the chief beneficiaries of the terror: the entire generation of incumbent officials who had entered the elite as the result of the purges.

In June 1957, Khrushchev's opponents in the Presidium had secured a majority of seven of the members and attempted to force him to resign. Khrushchev refused. Instead, he made the unprecedented demand that the Central Committee, which had formally "elected" him, be convened to decide the issue. There, he enjoyed broader support and defeated his opponents. Khrushchev's victory allowed him to begin to remove his opponents from the Presidium and to add several of his supporters to it. It also reconfirmed the circular basis of power in the Soviet system first established by Stalin in the 1920s.

Stalin and Khrushchev each manipulated the circular basis of power to secure their control over the political system. They used the power of the central party Secretariat over the *nomenklatura* system to secure the appointment of known supporters as regional party secretaries and to exchange career advancement for support. Through the regional party secretaries, each gained control over the selection of delegates to the party congress. Control over the party congress, in turn, permitted each to secure the "election" of their supporters to the Central Committee. And, finally, each was able to use the support of the Central Committee to remove opponents from the leading party organs.

Khrushchev's reliance on the Central Committee in 1957 strengthened its role as a central legitimizing institution in elite politics. Khrushchev later used open policy debate in the Central Committee to overwhelm his opponents in the Presidium, inviting supportive, nonmember experts to participate in committee deliberations. This helped to transform the committee and the departments formally subordinated to it into a semiparliamentary body through which representatives of various organizational, regional, and functional interests achieved limited participation in the central policymaking process. Contrary to Khrushchev's clear intentions, this reinforced the dispersion of power in the Soviet system.

FROM KHRUSHCHEV TO BREZHNEV

Although Khrushchev took over as head of government as well as head of the party in 1958, he never was able to secure as much personal power as Stalin had had. The increasing autonomy of central institutions and organizations, the consequent dispersion of authority, and the delegitimation of terror in the post-Stalin period severely constrained his ability to eliminate his opponents. To counteract these trends, Khrushchev turned to dramatic organizational changes in the economy, the state administration, and the party itself and attempted to use the resulting organizational turmoil to increase his opportunities to remove key officials and appoint new ones. But a minority in the Presidium and the Central Committee continued to oppose him even after June 1957.

By 1964, Khrushchev had suffered a series of foreign policy defeats, including the Polish and Hungarian unrest of 1956, the destruction of an emerging "détente" with the West in the aftermath of the May 1960 downing of an American U-2 spy plane over the Soviet Union, the public airing in 1960 of the conflict with the still-Stalinist Chinese leadership and its intensification thereafter, and the embarrassing retreat from confrontation with the United States during the 1962 Cuban missile crisis. He had also alienated the very core of his political support.

Khrushchev renewed his de-Stalinization

efforts at the Twenty-First party Congress in October 1961. He secured the removal of Stalin's body from Lenin's mausoleum on Red Square, and its interment in a less prominent location directly behind the mausoleum. But he was unable to extend de-Stalinization to the political arena. And, beginning in February 1963, a process of re-Stalinization began.

The halt to revelations about the past, the gradual reimposition of tight artistic and cultural controls, and the attempt to retain a place of honor for Stalin in Soviet history was fueled by the growing resentment among Soviet elites of Khrushchev's challenges to their positions. De-Stalinization was enough of an indirect threat to those whose careers had benefited from Stalin's purges to make many of them uneasy. But, in November 1962, Khrushchev pushed through a change in the party organization that threatened them more directly. He divided local and regional party organizations into separate agricultural and industrial committees, each to be headed by its own party secretary. The incumbent secretaries appointed by Khrushchev in prior years had been selected for their special competence with respect to agricultural issues, reflecting Khrushchev's earlier concerns. Now, these secretaries, the core of Khrushchev's support in the Central Committee, were to be assigned to the smaller, less powerful, agricultural divisions of their organizations and new secretaries were to be appointed to lead the larger, and politically more powerful, industrial divisions. Furthermore, by late 1964 Khrushchev appeared ready to carry out a similar division of the central party organs.

The prospect of demotion for a large number of the incumbent members of the Presidium leadership, against the background of foreign policy fiascos and domestic discontent, galvanized them into action. In October 1964, the other members of the Presidium—many of them appointed by Khrushchev himself—carried out a swift and peaceful coup. They convened a meeting of the Presidium, demanded that Khrushchev resign, and convened a meeting of the Central Committee the next day to ratify their demand. Unlike the course of events in 1957, Khrushchev now enjoyed little support in the committee.

The dispersion of organizational and institutional powers in the post-Stalin period, and the circular basis of building personal power and authority in the Soviet system, had allowed the senior members of the Presidium around Khrushchev to build up their own authority at his expense. Khrushchev's actions had created a basis of shared opposition between his increasingly powerful lieutenants in the party Secretariat and the broader Soviet political elite. And the coup was carried out in the name of collective leadership. Khrushchev was consigned to historical anonymity and lived out his life in peaceful retirement. No other member of the leadership was removed from power, although some secondary figures closely associated with Khrushchev were removed.

The post-Khrushchev leadership reaffirmed and strengthened the dispersion of power and authority adopted after the death of Stalin. The very act of convening the Central Committee to ratify Khrushchev's removal further increased the importance of that body. The posts of party leader (renamed general secretary at the Twenty-Second party Congress in April 1966) and head of government (chairman of the Council of Ministers) were once again divided between separate individuals. Brezhnev assumed the former post, Kosygin the latter. Within a few months, the presidency of the Soviet Union (formally, the chairmanship of the Presidium of the Supreme Soviet) was assumed by a third member of the leadership, Podgorny. Positions in the party Secretariat were distributed among several of the oligarchs, who exercised joint control over the *nomenklatura*. Lesser members of the leadership were assigned to other key positions, such as heading the KGB, and subordinated directly to the Presidium (renamed Politburo in April 1966). In this way, a true oligarchy was established.

The post-Khrushchev oligarchy also moved quickly to reassure the broader Soviet elite. They restored the unified organizational structure of the party and recentralized the state administration, undoing the changes that had been adopted under Khrushchev. They also stressed a personnel policy based on "stability of cadres," resulting in a dramatic slowdown in turnover in the elite. Central Committee members, for example, were removed with decreasing frequency, and the size of the committee grew steadily over time, as more and more members of the political generation that came to power as the result of the Stalinist purges were granted elite status.

Under these conditions, the Politburo was gradually transformed into a cabinetlike body. The senior party secretaries, key regional party leaders, the heads of the most important governmental ministries, the military and security chiefs, and other key figures were gradually incorporated into its membership. Although the Politburo itself was a body that transcended both state and party, its staff support continued to be located within the central party apparatus, in the General Department that was formally subordinated to the Central Committee. The Politburo rapidly became the indisputably most important policy making body in the Soviet Union.

Oligarchic control was extended to military and defense issues through the institution of the Defense Council. Until 1977, when the new constitution formally defined it as a state organ subordinate to the Presidium of the Supreme Soviet, the council functioned as a subcommittee of the Politburo. It was chaired by the general secretary and included senior members of the Politburo, military leaders, and other relevant state and party officials. Since 1977, chairmanship of the council has been assumed by each successive general secretary as a means of taking over the direction of military and defense policies. But, in doing so, each has been constrained by the participation of other members of the leadership.

The establishment of an oligarchy centered in the Politburo and resting on shared control over the *nomenklatura* institutional-

ized the devolution of power and authority that had been taking place since the death of Stalin and reaffirmed the division of functions between the state and party. Central state bureaucracies reassumed control over the day-to-day management of the economy. The number of functionally specialized central ministries and state committees proliferated, their role as sources of expertise in the policymaking process was enhanced, and their autonomous influence over the implementation of policies adopted by the Politburo increased. The central party apparatus exercised oversight over the operations of state institutions to ensure the implementation of party policies and served as an alternative source of expertise in the policymaking process. The broader party organization retained its role in the mobilization of popular effort.

Policy debates became more open than in the past, as institutional actors came to advocate competing positions on a broad range of policies. But the oligarchy retained policymaking authority. The Politburo set careful limits on the degree of institutional autonomy, and enforced them through their control over the *nomenklatura*. Meaningful participation was strictly limited to official, institutionalized channels. Establishment of the oligarchy was accompanied by the abandonment of de-Stalinization. Some degree of honor was restored to Stalin personally. A modest monument was erected over his gravesite, and he was credited with having achieved the rapid industrialization of the Soviet Union. The moderate relaxation of control over the arts and intellectual life that had taken place under Khrushchev was reversed. Those who chose to engage in unofficial or dissident activity were subjected to brutal suppression, including imprisonment in harsh labor camps and even psychiatric torture. For the population at large, however, obedience was purchased through moderate enhancements in the social welfare policies of the regime and greater emphasis on—and investment in—the production of food and consumer goods.

The establishment of an oligarchy did not

change the basis of power in the Soviet system. However, it did make the appointment of one's supporters to key positions, and the accumulation of personal power, a slower, more long-term process. Within the Politburo, open challengers to the oligarchic principle itself or those who persistently remained outside the policy "consensus" could be eliminated. But, under conditions of more open debate, simple policy differences alone no longer were sufficient basis for removal. Outside the Politburo, throughout the party and state apparatuses, the emphasis on "stability of cadres" also reduced opportunities for exploitation of the *nomenklatura* system.

Even under these conditions, however, Brezhnev enjoyed an important advantage over the other oligarchs. His career had been a diverse one. He had served as party secretary in the central apparatus and in regional apparatuses. He had overseen the party organization in the military and the state administration. He had foreign policy experience. And he had served as de facto "second secretary," the number two position in the leadership usually associated with administration of personnel policies. As a result, Brezhnev had accumulated substantial policymaking experience and developed leadership skills that made him a capable actor in a collective setting. He had also developed a vast number of personal relationships and career associations with other Soviet elites of his own generation on which he could build personal support.

Brezhnev's generally cautious and conservative "style" of leadership, and especially his preference for "consensual" over "conflictual" decision making, reduced the threat posed to the other oligarchs by accretions to his power. Nonetheless, it took ten years for him to achieve the status of *primus inter pares*. And, even then, his rule was marked by the further incorporation of more actors into the ruling oligarchy. During his tenure, many new faces were added to the leadership, but almost all of them were drawn from the generation of officials who, like Brezhnev himself, first reached

elite status in the aftermath of the Great Purges.

After 1976, most changes in the top leadership consisted of transfers from one position to another within the broader ruling bodies: Politburo, Secretariat, Council of Ministers Presidium, and the Presidium of the Supreme Soviet. Only the removal of Podgorny from the presidency of the Soviet Union in 1977 and his replacement by Brezhnev represented a significant increase in Brezhnev's status. Most other changes in the leadership during this period were due to the deaths of incumbents.

The oligarchic nature of the leadership, and especially the emphasis on consensual decision making, constrained the policy process, making it resistant to change. This resistance was reinforced by the emphasis on stability. The entire Soviet elite grew older, as few members of the post-Brezhnev generation were added to its ranks. Soviet elites became entrenched in their respective institutions, organizations, and territories and defenders of their parochial interests. An atmosphere of corruption, fostered, in part, by the creation under Brezhnev of an extensive network of material privileges for the *nomenklatura* elite and, in part, by the growing insulation of these elites from external pressures, became pervasive. Privilege and immunity lent additional force to their commitment to the status quo.

By 1982, with Brezhnev aged and ill, the performance of the Soviet economy had gone into serious decline. The status quo could no longer be sustained.

FROM BREZHNEV TO GORBACHEV

The death of Brezhnev in November 1982 at the age of 76 was followed by the "election" of Andropov as general secretary. Andropov had been a party secretary and junior member of the oligarchy at the time of Khrushchev's ouster. In 1967, he was transferred from the party Secretariat to take over command of the KGB and was promoted to candidate member of the Politburo. He was then promoted to full member in April 1973 as part of Brezhnev's incorporation into the Politburo of the heads of the military, security, and foreign affairs bureaucracies. In May 1982, Andropov took control over the ideological sector, assuming the senior party secretaryship vacated by the death of Suslov in January. This move positioned him perfectly to assume the general secretaryship upon the death of Brezhnev.

Andropov immediately abandoned the commitment to "stability of cadres" that had characterized the Brezhnev period. He brought new faces to positions of authority at the center. For example, he brought in a provincial party secretary, Ligachev, to head the personnel department of the Secretariat and soon promoted him to party secretary. And he brought in a younger state planning official, Ryzhkov, to serve as party secretary for economic affairs. He redistributed power among the more capable of the remaining oligarchs. Gorbachev, for example, was assigned to oversee party personnel matters. Others were retired.

Outside the organs of oligarchic rule, Andropov began to remove and replace large numbers of central party *apparatchiks,* regional party officials and state administrators. He attempted to spur the society to more productive effort through a campaign emphasizing discipline and order. Most important of all, he subjected all aspects of the Soviet socioeconomic system to harsh, but informed, criticism. He called for a shift away from the Stalinist pattern of extensive development and toward a more intensive pattern of development. And he recognized that far-reaching changes would be required.

At the time of his appointment, Andropov was 68 years old and in poor health. He died after little more than 14 months in office. He was succeeded as general secretary by Brezhnev's former confidant, Chernenko. Over 72 years of age and in poor health, Chernenko achieved little more than to slow down the rate at which members of his generation were removed and replaced. Thirteen months later he, too, had died.

Chernenko was replaced immediately by Gorbachev, who, at 54 years of age, had already been functioning as second-in-command since Andropov gave him responsibility for overseeing party personnel and economic affairs in late 1982. Gorbachev moved rapidly to reconstruct the leadership. In the course of his first year in office, he managed to have three senior members of the Politburo, two less powerful candidate members, and two party secretaries removed from office. He also managed to promote four members of the leadership and introduce a dozen new faces into the ruling organs, many of them as party secretaries. This gave him a working majority within the Politburo and effective control over the Secretariat. By the end of 1988, all but one of the holdovers from the Brezhnev era had been removed from the leadership.

Widespread changes were also carried out in the central party apparatus, the central state administration, and the regional party leaderships. These changes were eased by the fact that so many of the individuals involved were of advanced age and could simply be retired without opposition. Not all of the new appointees can be assumed to be personal supporters of the general secretary, however.

Gorbachev's career experience was more limited in scope when he became general secretary than was Brezhnev's, for example. He had served in only one regional party apparatus before being picked in 1978 to serve as party secretary in charge of agriculture. After one year he was promoted to candidate membership in the Politburo, and after another year to full membership. He had thus been the most junior member of the oligarchy for only about four years when Andropov selected him to serve as second-in-command. This career pattern gave him only limited opportunities to build personal connections to other elite members of his generation or to generate support by exploiting the *nomenklatura.*

Gorbachev has also been constrained throughout this period by the more conservative views of other Politburo members, particularly Ligachev. Almost ten years senior to

Gorbachev, and with more career experience in the central party apparatus, Ligachev has advanced a more cautious, less radical view of the need for change in the Soviet Union than Gorbachev. Ligachev's conservatism has found broad support among Soviet elites, making him an influential member of the Politburo. That influence has also been enhanced by the continuing assertion of principles of collectivity by other members of the leadership, even those Gorbachev himself introduced into the Politburo. No member of the leadership wishes to see the oligarchic principles that have evolved since Stalin give way completely to one-man rule.

The rapidity with which Gorbachev was able to reconstruct the leading organs of the party and the state upon assuming the general secretaryship reflected the enormous political power that remains lodged in that office. The presence of another senior party leader who shares control over the exercise of that power is an important bulwark against the erosion of oligarchic rule and the reemergence of dictatorship. It is not surprising, therefore, that when Gorbachev shifted Ligachev to less influential responsibilities in the leadership in September 1988 (allegedly in response to efforts by Ligachev to organize a coup against him), and introduced organizational and other personnel changes in the party and the state that gave him more complete powers, concerns about the potential emergence of a dictator were heard.

In late 1988, Gorbachev carried out sweeping changes in the organization and staffing of the central party organs and initiated a constitutional reorganization of the central state organs. He removed 2 full members and 2 candidate members of the Politburo, all of them holdovers from the Brezhnev era. Included among them was the longtime foreign minister and later president of the Soviet Union, Gromyko, who was honorably retired at the age of 79. At the same time, Gorbachev promoted 1 of his own appointees to full membership and 3 to candidate membership. Of the 11 full members besides himself at the end of 1988, 9 were

his own appointees, although they included the 2 most conservative members, Ligachev and Chebrikov. The 2 other full members were Shcherbitskyi and Vorotnikov, the former a Brezhnev holdover and questionable supporter and the latter an Andropov appointee and probable supporter. Thus, Gorbachev commanded the support of at least 7, and as many as 9, of the 11 other voting members. All 8 candidates, or nonvoting members, were his own appointees and supporters.

Gorbachev also reorganized the central party apparatus. He created six "commissions" of the Central Committee, each headed by a party secretary: for agricultural policy (headed by Ligachev), for ideology (Medvedev), for international relations (Yakovlev), for legal affairs (Chebrikov), for party construction and personnel (Razumovskii), and for social and economic policy (Sliunkov). Nikonov, formerly the secretary for agricultural policy, remained a party secretary and was appointed vice chairman of the agricultural commission headed by Ligachev, possibly as a means of restraining the latter's freedom of action. Two former secretaries, Biryukova and Lukyanov, were both promoted to candidate membership and reassigned to positions in the state administration. The former secretary for international relations, Dobrynin, was retired. The most important members of the Soviet leadership, those with membership or candidate membership on the Politburo as of January 1989, are listed in Figure 4–1.

The fate of the 21 specialized departments of the Central Committee subordinated to the Secretariat remained unclear. They may be reorganized, consolidated, or even eliminated entirely. If eliminated, the changes outlined would constitute a reorganization of the Secretariat along functional lines, similar to the arrangements that existed prior to 1934. If not, the creation of these commissions may be an attempt to create alternatives to the party apparatus, through which Gorbachev might circumvent opposition to change.

Gorbachev also moved to assume direct

FIGURE 4-1 The Politburo, as of January, 1989

Full Members

Mikhail S. Gorbachev, general secretary; chairman of
the Presidium of the Supreme Soviet (president of
the USSR)
Viktor M. Chebrikov, party secretary; chairman of
commission on legal affairs
Yegor K. Ligachev, party secretary; chairman of com-
mission on agricultural policy
Vadim A. Medvedev, party secretary; chairman of
commission on ideology
Viktor P. Nikonov, party secretary; vice chair, commission on agricultural policy
Nikolai I. Ryzhkov, chairman of the USSR Council of
Ministers ("prime minister")
Vladimir V. Shcherbitskyi, first secretary of the Com-
munist Party of the Ukraine
Eduard A. Shevardnadze, foreign minister
Nikolai N. Sliunkov, party secretary; chairman of
commission on social and economic policy
Vitaly I. Vorotnikov, chairman of the Presidiium of
the Supreme Soviet (president) of the Russian Re-
public
Aleksandr N. Yakovlev, party secretary; chairman of
commission on international relations
Lev N. Zaikov, first secretary of the Moscow party or-
ganization

Candidate Members

Aleksandra P. Biriukova, deputy prime minister
Anatoly I. Lukianov, first vice president of the USSR
Iurii D. Masliukov, chairman of GOSPLAN
Georgi P. Razumovski, party secretary, chairman,
Commission on party construction and personnel
(cadres)
Iurii F. Soloviev, first secretary of the Leningrad party
organization
Nikolai V. Talyzin, deputy prime minister
Aleksandr V. Vlasov, prime minister of the Russian
republic
Dmitri T. Yazov, minister of defense

---

control over the state administration. After
reorganizing the party, he assumed the chairmanship of the Presidium of the Supreme
Soviet, making him the president of the Soviet Union. He also pushed through the
adoption of proposals to reorganize the legislative and executive organs.

By the end of 1988, Gorbachev had
achieved a position roughly equivalent to
that achieved by Khrushchev after his June
1957 victory over those attempting to oust
him: Gorbachev had completely recon-

structed the Politburo and Secretariat, staffing them almost completely with his own appointees, and he had extended his personal
power to the institutions of the state. Also
like Khrushchev, he had dedicated himself to
radical economic reform. But the tasks he
confronted were far more challenging than
those faced by Khrushchev.

THE STALINIST ECONOMY IN DECLINE

The German invasion of the USSR in June
1941, the occupation of vast portions of the
country, and the Soviet counterattack in
1943 and victorious campaign to repulse the
invaders, destroyed a large part of the Soviet
economy. Economic reconstruction of the
formerly occupied territories began as soon
as Soviet control over them was reestablished. The means employed to reconstruct
the economy were the same as those employed in the 1930s: the centrally controlled
mobilization of vast resources to re-create
the industrial base for autonomous, sustained growth, without much regard for the
efficiency with which those resources were
used. Once again, these methods proved
highly effective: By 1950, output exceeded
prewar levels in almost all categories.

Under the Stalinist command economy,
the state owns the means of production. Decision making is concentrated in the central
administrative bureaucracies of the state.
These bureaucracies determine the goods
and services to be produced, establish physical production quotas, control the formation and utilization of investment capital, set
prices as a means of enforcing already determined production plans, control the flow of
labor, and set individual income levels in the
form of wages and salaries. The entire economy is geared toward fulfillment of the physical production quotas established by the
central authorities.

Relatively high levels of economic growth
were sustained on this basis throughout the
1950s and 1960s. Organizational changes
carried out after the death of Stalin and in

the 1950s by Khrushchev did not alter the character of the Stalinist economy. Economic growth was based on the continuing mobilization of abundant natural and human resources. Both the total population and the labor supply increased at rates sufficient to keep pace with economic expansion during the 1950s and 1960s. Agricultural production was stimulated by bringing new lands under cultivation as part of Khrushchev's ambitious "virgin lands" program in Kazakhstan, Siberia, and other regions. And raw materials supplies could be increased by accelerating the exploitation of established sources and by opening up new ones. By increasing the available "inputs," Stalin, Krushchev, and for a limited period, even Brezhnev could make up for the inefficiencies of the command economy.

But the Stalinist economic model introduced certain deformations in the behavior of economic organizations and individuals that became increasingly costly over time. Because power over resources was concentrated at the center, producers were oriented toward fulfilling the demands of the central bureaucracies and ignored the demands of customers. In fact, in the absence of a market, producers had no "customers" in the Western, capitalist, market-oriented sense of that term. They had only assigned consumers, or delivery targets. Because success was measured in terms of the fulfillment of assigned quotas, all economic activity tended to become highly parochial. That is, it became focused on ensuring one's own ability to fulfill the quota, with little or no regard for the requirements of other actors.

Physical production quotas also encouraged producers to emphasize quantity over quality. Emphasis on quantity, in turn, encouraged producers simply to increase inputs with little regard for efficiency, resulting in excessively high costs of production. It also tended to make producers resistant to technological innovation for fear of short-term disruption of the production process.

For the general population, the greatest deformation of the Stalinist economy was its failure to produce consumer goods. This re-

sulted most of all from the long-standing priority of the regime's commitment to developing the heavy industrial sector and the ruinous effects of collectivization on agricultural production. But it also resulted from the continuing operation of the Stalinist principle of suppressing consumption to increase the capital available for industrial development. The Stalinist economy could not produce enough food and housing to satisfy demand and still meet its industrial production quotas. And the consumer goods it did produce were of such poor quality that consumers found much of them unacceptable even under conditions of extreme scarcity.

The absence of consumer goods on which to spend one's earnings produced an increasing imbalance between earnings and consumption. With little to buy, Soviet workers accumulated relatively high savings, and this reduced the incentive to work. Additional income had little meaning. By the 1970s and 1980s, a vicious cycle had set in: increased consumer goods could be produced only through increased effort, but increased effort was discouraged by the absence of consumer goods.

All these problems were well known even to Soviet planners. The regime counteracted them only in the military sector, where representatives of the military were assigned to factories to inspect products intended for use by the Red Army. These inspectors were empowered to, and did, reject those that failed to meet the military's standards. Military producers were thus forced to satisfy customers who had the option of rejecting their product or face severe financial penalties. This introduced at least some semblance of the discipline produced by market forces and may help to explain the ability of the Soviets to produce competitive military technologies and equipment.

Efforts to reform the broader economy in response to these problems in the late 1950s and early 1960s by Khrushchev, and by his successors in 1965, were either undone or sabotaged by the state bureaucracies, party apparatus, and other vested interests fearful of the loss of their power in a reformed

TABLE 4–1   Population Growth by Republic, 1950–1981 (in annual percent)

USSR	1950–60 1.8%	1960–70 1.3%	1970–80 0.9%	1980–81 0.8%
Slavic Republics				
Russian republic	1.6	0.9	0.6	0.6
Ukraine	1.5	1.1	0.6	0.4
Belorussia	1.3	1.0	0.7	0.7
Moldavia	2.6	1.9	1.1	0.7
Baltic Republics				
Estonia	1.0	1.2	0.8	0.8
Latvia	0.8	1.1	0.7	0.4
Lithuania	0.7	1.3	0.9	0.7
Transcaucasus				
Armenia	3.1	3.1	2.1	1.5
Azerbaidzhan	2.9	3.0	1.8	1.5
Georgia	2.7	1.3	0.7	0.6
Central Asia				
Kazakhstan	4.0	2.9	1.3	1.3
Kirgiziia	2.2	3.3	2.0	1.8
Tadzhikistan	2.9	3.7	3.0	2.7
Turkmenistan	2.7	3.3	2.7	2.5
Uzbekistan	3.0	3.5	2.9	2.5

Source: Murray Feshbach, "The Soviet Union: Population Trends and Dilemmas," *Population Bulletin,* Vol. 37, No. 3 (August 1982), pp. 10–11

economy. Khrushchev and his successors were compelled to resort to increasing inputs instead. By the 1970s, however, the ability of the regime to continue to increase inputs began to decline.

The population growth rate declined steadily throughout the 1960s and 1970s, so that by 1980 it was less than half the 1950s rate. The net annual increase in the size of the labor force began to drop off in the late 1970s, as the number of new workers declined and the number of retirements and deaths increased. Moreover, population growth and increments to the labor force became imbalanced. As the figures presented in Tables 4–1 and 4–2 reveal, growth was concentrated in the less developed southern republics, populated by Muslim and other

TABLE 4–2   Projected Increase in Labor Force: Selected Republics and Regions, 1980–2000 (1975–1980 increase = 100)

	1980	1985	1990	1995	2000
USSR	100	31	20	25	61
Slavic Republics					
Russian republic	100	−05	−22	−13	33
Ukraine	100	−02	−01	−14	10
Belorussia	100	30	06	05	50
Moldavia	100	45	43	52	76
Baltic republics	100	12	00	−18	05
Transcaucasus	100	69	45	43	75
Kazakhstan	100	67	58	59	78
Central Asia	100	92	93	112	143

Source: Murray Feshbach, "The Soviet Union: Population Trends and Dilemmas," *Population Bulletin,* vol. 37, no. 3 (August 1982), p 27.

TABLE 4–3 The Declining Soviet Economy: Selected Indicators, 1951–1985 (average annual increases, in percent)

	1951–55	*1956–60*	*1961–65*	*1966–70*	*1971–75*	*1976–80*	*1981–85*
Real GNP	—	—	5.0	5.3	3.4	2.3	1.9
Social product	—	—	6.5	7.4	6.3	4.2	3.5
National income produced	11.4	9.2	6.5	7.8	5.7	4.3	3.6
Industrial production	13.2	10.4	8.6	8.5	7.4	4.4	3.7
Agricultural production	—	—	2.2	3.9	2.5	1.7	1.0
Capital investment	—	—	5.4	7.3	6.7	3.7	3.7
Labor productivity	—	—	6.1	6.8	4.5	3.3	3.1
Real income per capita	7.3	5.7	3.6	5.9	4.4	3.4	2.1

Source: Real GNP data from Joint Economic Committee, Congress of the United States, Subcommittee on National Security Economics, *Allocation of Resources in the Soviet Union and China—1986* (Washington, DC: U.S. Government Printing Office, 1988), p. 12. All other data from Goskomstat, *NK SSSR za 70 let*, p. 51.

non-Russian peoples, while the Russian and other Slavic territories of the developed northwest experienced little overall growth and absolute declines in the size of the labor force.

At the same time, increasing material inputs became more costly. Energy in the form of West Siberian oil and natural gas, for example, became much more costly to produce, and the fall-off in world energy prices in the 1980s meant that their sale on world markets produced less capital. And, finally, the existing industrial infrastructure itself had grown obsolete. This meant that labor, capital, and equipment all became less productive. These factors contributed to a sharp decline in the 1970s and 1980s in annual growth rates in the Soviet real GNP, as measured by Western analysts, and in all of the Soviets' own indicators of growth. This economic decline is reflected in the figures presented in Tables 4–3 and 4–4.

TABLE 4–4 Declining Capital Returns, 1966–1985 (ruble increase in industrial production per ruble of capital investment)

1966–70	*1971–75*	*1976–80*	*1981–85*
0.92	0.84	0.53	0.45

Source: Goskomstat, *NK SSSR za 70 let*, p. 104.

MODERNIZATION AND SOCIAL CHANGE

The Soviet economic decline was driven by other, even more intractable factors as well. Social modernization, by itself an indicator of the success of the Stalinist system, produced changes that made large portions of the Soviet population less susceptible to physical dislocation and coercion. As the data in Tables 4–5, 4–6, and 4–7 suggest, by the 1980s the population had become more highly urbanized and more educated, and therefore more sophisticated and demanding with respect to its working conditions and other "quality-of-life" issues. Even the nature of work itself had changed. As shown in Table 4–8, the proportion of the labor force employed in white-collar and skilled

TABLE 4–5 Post-War Urbanization, 1940–1987 (urban population as a percent of total)

1940	32.5
1950	38.9
1959	47.9
1970	56.3
1979	62.3
1987	66.0

Source: Goskomstat, *NK SSSR za 70 let*, p. 373 and TsSU, *Narodnoe Khoziiastvo SSSR 1922–1972 gg* (Moskva: "Statistika", 1972), p. 9

TABLE 4-6   Educational Levels of the Population, 1959–1987
(number per 1,000 population aged 10+)

	1959	1970	1979	1987
Higher education	23	42	68	90
Incomplete higher	11	13	15	15
Specialized secondary	48	68	107	133
General secondary	61	119	207	282
Incomplete secondary	218	241	241	188
Total	361	483	638	708

Source: Goskomstat, *NK SSSR za 70 let*, p. 523.

jobs increased, while the proportion engaged in unskilled manual labor declined. In short, an urban, professional and semiprofessional middle class had emerged. This process of modernization unfolded even more rapidly in the formerly underdeveloped Muslim territories of Kazakhstan and Central Asia.

Popular satisfaction with the present and expectations for the future had long been based on comparisons with the dismal prewar Soviet past. By the 1980s, however, the new urban middle class and, to a great ex-

tent, the Soviet political elite itself, was coming to judge Soviet accomplishments, as well as their own personal condition, against higher standards. The present was coming to be measured against the performance standards established in the 1950s and 1960s. With the expanded international role and increased openness of the Soviet Union in the 1970s, knowledge of the vastly superior material standards of living in the developed West raised expectations still further and compounded popular dissatisfaction with the declining performance of the regime.

TABLE 4-7   Secondary and Higher Education by Republic, 1939–1986
(number per 1,000 population aged 10+)

	1939	1959	1970	1979	1986
USSR	108	361	483	638	701
Slavic Republics					
Russian republic	109	361	489	645	706
Ukraine	120	373	494	630	699
Belorussia	92	304	440	594	674
Moldavia	57	264	397	572	640
Baltic Republics					
Latvia	176	431	517	645	716
Lithuania	81	232	382	558	653
Estonia	161	386	506	630	701
Transcaucasus					
Armenia	128	445	516	713	751
Azerbaidzhan	113	400	471	652	741
Georgia	165	448	554	698	756
Central Asia					
Kazakhstan	83	347	468	633	688
Uzbekistan	55	354	458	639	698
Tadzhikistan	40	325	420	578	650
Turkmenistan	65	387	475	620	684
Kirgiziia	46	342	452	614	679

Source: Goskomstat, *NK SSSR za 70 let*, p. 525.

TABLE 4–8 Changing Soviet Social Structure, 1930s–1970s (occupational distribution of employed persons, by type and complexity of work, in percent)

Occupational Category	Late 1930s	late 1950s	Late 1960s	Late 1970s
Unskilled, simple physical labor	64	52	35	29
Semiskilled, complex physical labor	19	29	38	41
Simple mental (nonphysical) labor	8	4	4	5
Technical/professional	9	15	23	25

Source: L. A. Gordon and A. K. Nazimova, "The Socio-Occupational Structure of Contemporary Soviet Society," in Murray Yanowitch, editor, *The Social Structure of the USSR* (Armonk, N.Y.: M. E. Sharpe, 1986), p. 10.

Soviet sociological research revealed widespread aspirations for material affluence and social status. The growing demand for improved food supplies, better consumer goods, and higher-quality services, including medical care, was reflected in the expanding black market in goods and services, or the "second economy." Among the younger, more highly educated population, Soviet research revealed a growing impatience with the regimentation of state controls and a demand for greater personal freedom.

The frustration of these aspirations and demands contributed to the alienation of the Soviet populace. The most obvious manifestation of such alienation was the rise of alcoholism to unprecedented levels in the 1980s. Alcoholism contributed to a decline in male life expectancy, high levels of labor absenteeism and turnover, and family instability.

While the sociological composition and expectations of the population were changing, so was the nature of the economic tasks confronting the regime: the technological revolution that was sweeping the West, Japan, and such newly industrialized countries of the Far East as Taiwan and South Korea had bypassed the Soviet economy. Even if human, material, and capital inputs could once again be mobilized in quantities and at costs that would permit a dramatic increase in the production of existing goods and services, this would not stem the relative decline of the Soviet Union to the status of a third- or even fourth-rate world power. It was this sense of relative decline in technological competitiveness in comparison to the developed West, and especially Taiwan and South Korea, that imparted a sense of crisis to the task of reversing the decline.

The Soviet Union not only had to move from an extensive to an intensive strategy of development, it also had to move from obsolete to modern technologies. Some of the technology that would be required could be obtained in the West—legally, and through illegal means, including espionage and theft. But, without a domestic high-technology sector of its own, the Soviet Union would be condemned to eternal economic inferiority. And, as military capabilities were coming to depend heavily on advanced technologies, such economic inferiority promised to undermine even the military power on which the Soviet Union's claim to superpower status rested.

The technological revolution in the West was made possible by three antecedent conditions: (1) the creation of scientific and technical cadres capable of developing new technologies; (2) widespread research and development activities, carried out by entrepreneurial individuals and organizations; and (3) the information revolution, which created a virtually free flow of ideas. Entrepreneurial research and the information revolution fueled, and were themselves facilitated by, the revolution in personal computing.

Social modernization since World War II had already created the first condition in the Soviet Union by the time Gorbachev came to power. The number of highly trained scientific, technical, and professional workers, re-

TABLE 4–9 Scientific, Technical, and Professional Personnel, 1950–1985 (in thousands)

	1950	1960	1970	1980	1985
Doctors of science	8.3	10.9	23.6	37.7	44.3
Candidates of science	45.5	98.3	224.5	396.2	463.5
All scientific workers	162.5	354.2	927.7	1373.3	1491.3
Specialists with higher education	1,443	3,545	6,853	12,073	14,485

Source: Goskomstat, *NK SSSR za 70 let,* pp. 62, 418.

ported in Table 4–9, increased more than tenfold in the period 1950–1985, and the scientific sector as a whole was the most rapidly expanding sector of employment in the economy. That the second condition could be met was suggested by the highly successful research and development effort in the military sector and the space program. But this activity was neither widespread nor independent. And the information revolution characterized by the free flow of information, and especially the widespread distribution of personal computers in private hands, had not even begun.

No serious modernization of the Soviet Union could take place until the leadership accepted the necessity of introducing radical changes in the existing economic and political systems. When Gorbachev came to power in March 1985 he seemed intent on continuing the effort, begun by Andropov, to improve the performance of the economy without abandoning the central features of the command system. Hence, he called for *uskorenie,* or a "speeding up" of the existing system. However, during the summer of 1986, after little more than a year in office, he began to call for more comprehensive changes, for *perestroika,* or "restructuring." He appears to have undergone a dramatic learning process with respect to just how bad off the Soviet system really was in comparison to competing systems, and with respect to just how radically it would have to be changed to preserve the Soviet Union's status as a superpower. By July 1987, he was calling for a social, economic, and political "revolution."

5

The Gorbachev Reforms

PERESTROIKA

Gorbachev began to lay the foundations for restructuring while Chernenko was still general secretary. He started by calling for *glasnost* or "publicity" in discussions of the shortcomings of the old order. Usually translated in the West as "openness," the policy of *glasnost* appears at first to have been an attempt by Gorbachev to mobilize the support of those who wished to see rapid changes introduced within the framework of the existing order. *Glasnost* created opportunities for them to express their views publicly by loosening restrictions on the media. It constituted a more sophisticated example of a familiar Soviet leadership technique: the creation of a mass "campaign" to mobilize support for changes directed from above.

But *glasnost* was greeted most enthusiastically by the intelligentsia, who seized the opportunity to subject a broad spectrum of issues to critical reevaluation. The views which have come to be expressed in the Soviet media since Gorbachev assumed the general secretaryship in 1985 range from the most liberal to the most conservative and even reactionary and have included both expressions of support for *perestroika* and opposition to it. This diversity of opinion was acknowledged by Gorbachev when he spoke before the Central Committee in June 1987 about the diversity of interests in Soviet society, the conflicts among them, and the need to accommodate such interests in the political process. In February 1988, he legitimized the existence of a "socialist pluralism of opinions" in another speech before the Central Committee.

While Gorbachev may have initiated *glasnost* as a means of directing popular pressure against those elements of the old order he wished to change, it gave rise to an explosion of popular political activity. Hundreds, if not thousands, of groups based on concerns about particular social, economic, political, religious, environmental, and even ethnic issues and interests organized themselves, and began to produce scores of independent publications. These groups organized meetings, conferences, and even street demonstrations to advance their interests. In some cases, they even demanded and received meetings with prominent local and national leaders to present their grievances.

Glasnost has also contributed to a revitalization of other, officially sponsored groups. Within the academic professions, for example, it has prompted the publication of materials that had been suppressed or held back by their authors under earlier circumstances, new research and writing, and vigorous public discussion and debate. The mass media has become far more lively and open, treating even previously "taboo" themes and topics such as Stalinism, the terror, and the rehabilitation of its victims. Even culture and the arts have undergone a dramatic reinvigoration and diversification of creative activity.

Not only conservatives, but even Gorbachev has shown a certain degree of discomfort about these developments. In January 1988, for example, he reiterated his support for *glasnost,* but reminded his audience of leading figures in the mass media that he meant "*glasnost* in the interests of socialism." Because the definition of what constitutes "socialism" remains in the hands of the party leadership, Gorbachev in this way continues to reserve the right to suppress undesirable activity.

Nonetheless, the public expression of radical demands for change has aided Gorbachev by making his own calls for reform seem less threatening and by demonstrating the existence of an enormous reservoir of untapped creative energies in the Soviet people. He outlined the elements of "restructuring" at two key meetings of the party's Central Committee in January and June 1987. In the economic sphere, he advanced a series of changes, and proposals for further change, that reduce the level of detail subject to central planning; give economic en-

terprises increased control over their product mix, wages, investments, and, eventually, prices; require enterprises to finance themselves out of their own earnings; increase the role of workers in enterprise administration through a form of workers' self-management; permit private individual and cooperative economic activity; and even create opportunities for peasants to obtain long-term leases for control over the land, thereby reducing the role of the collective farm to service cooperatives among the leaseholders.

The success of these changes hinges on a shift toward marketization of the economy and the establishment of a market-based price structure. But there has been little evidence of a willingness on the part of Gorbachev and the Soviet political leadership to relinquish central control over the economy. The economic reforms outlined during 1987 and 1988 reflect an effort to encourage efficiency maximizing behavior at the enterprise level without introducing a true market. For to do so would shift substantial control over the economy from producers to consumers.

But even a limited economic restructuring cannot be achieved in the context of Stalinist authoritarian controls over individual thought and behavior. Enterprise managers and private entrepreneurs must be given substantial freedom of action. The media must be permitted to report critically on policies that don't work. Mechanisms must be created to compel enterprises and policymakers to respond to changing conditions. Popular enthusiasm and support, and especially creative energies, must be mobilized. Gorbachev has therefore also called for the "democratization" of political life.

To encourage popular participation and increase the accountability of public officials, he has advanced proposals to revitalize the network of local, regional, and central representative institutions of the state, the system of "soviets." He has called for multiple-candidate elections and expansion of the role of local soviets in the administration of society. He has suggested that positions of authority should be opened to nonparty members and has called for electoral reforms designed to increase the impact of popular sentiments on the choice of candidates by local party bodies. In many ways, Gorbachev's proposals for electoral reforms, greater state responsibility and accountability, and other changes in the way the Soviet state is organized and operates harken back to what might be called the "lost tradition" of *State and Revolution.* But the details of his plans remain uncertain, and the power of vested interests, such as the professional party apparatus, to undermine the effects of changes in the formal rules of the system remains considerable.

In late 1988, after completing his reconstruction of the political leadership, Gorbachev accelerated his drive to change the character of state institutions. He assumed the chairmanship of the Presidium of the Supreme Soviet, thereby making himself the president of the Soviet Union, and pushed through the adoption of proposals to create a new, constitutionally supreme representative body, the Congress of People's Deputies. Elections to the Congress were conducted in March 1989 and produced a stunning defeat for many key party figures. They also resulted in the election of many non-party, dissident, and even oppositional candidates. The Congress consists of 750 delegates elected from local districts of equal population, 750 delegates elected in equal numbers from the national territories, and 750 delegates elected by non-government, but party-controlled organizations such as the trade unions. The Congress first met in Spring 1989, and is scheduled to meet annually. By secret ballot, it elected Gorbachev president of the Soviet Union in May 1989. The president is limited to two five-year terms of office. The President enjoys broad domestic and foreign policy-making powers, and serves as Chairman of the Defense of Council, giving him command of the armed forces. The President of the Soviet Union serves as head of the Presidium of the Supreme Soviet, which serves as a coordinating body for the government. The day-to-day

functions of government are to be carried out by a streamlined Council of Ministers. Similar changes are slated for implementation at the regional and local levels.

The elections to the Congress of People's Deputies represented a dramatic opportunity for the expression of popular dissatisfaction with the *status quo.* One manifestation of this dissatisfaction was the political resurrection achieved through the electoral process by Boris Yeltsin. Yeltsin had been promoted by Gorbachev to a national party secretaryship, then to leadership of the Moscow party organization, and finally to candidate membership in the Politburo within a few short months in late 1985 and early 1986. But in the Fall of 1987, after having expressed impatience with the pace of political reform and after having attacked conservative opponents of change by name, he was suddenly removed from his Moscow post and, in February 1988, from the Politburo. He was consigned to a ministerial post and, it seemed then, to eventual obscurity. But in January 1989 Yeltsin sought and won nomination to the Congress of People's Deputies and, after a dramatic campaign that was opposed by the party but generated enormous popular support, won a landslide victory in the March 1989 elections. At the same time, Soviet voters rejected many prominent party officials who had been nominated to the Congress, including the Leningrad party chief, a candidate member of the Politburo.

Congress deliberations were characterized by sharp debates over such controversial issues as civilian control over the KGB, the size and burden of the heretofore secret military budget, the existence of a heretofore unacknowledged large annual budget deficit, the real depth of the economic crisis, and many other issues. It even saw the beginnings of an attempt by non-party delegates to the Congress to organize a political opposition. Yeltsin played a prominent role in the Congress debates, and was elected to membership in the Supreme Soviet—but only after a public outcry following his rejection by the party-controlled majority.

The Congress elected from among its own membership the 542-member Supreme Soviet that is to conduct the actual legislative business of the state. Although also composed of a comfortable party majority under the control of the leadership, the new Supreme Soviet also included many non-party delegates and therefore immediately assumed a more active role than its predecessor of the same name. Convening in June 1989, the new Supreme Soviet asserted its authority in the Soviet system by forcing the withdrawal of several candidates for ministerial positions in the new government, and the outright rejection of another.

These changes, in conjunction with electoral reform, have increased the role of popular opinion in the Soviet political process. They have moved the Soviet Union closer to a "presidential system" of government, in

Figure 5–1 Reorganization of the State, as of June 1989

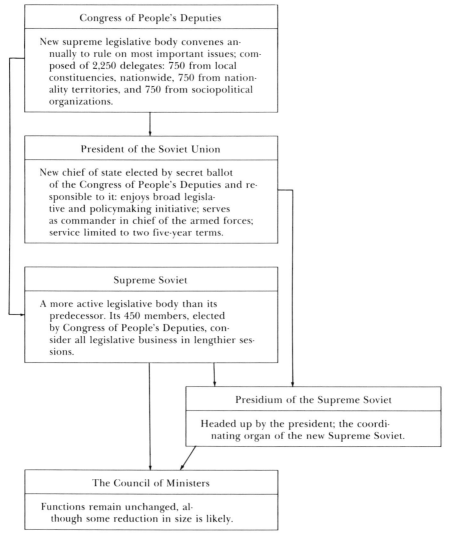

Congress of People's Deputies

New supreme legislative body convenes annually to rule on most important issues; composed of 2,250 delegates: 750 from local constituencies, nationwide, 750 from nationality territories, and 750 from sociopolitical organizations.

President of the Soviet Union

New chief of state elected by secret ballot of the Congress of People's Deputies and responsible to it: enjoys broad legislative and policymaking initiative; serves as commander in chief of the armed forces; service limited to two five-year terms.

Supreme Soviet

A more active legislative body than its predecessor. Its 450 members, elected by Congress of People's Deputies, consider all legislative business in lengthier sessions.

Presidium of the Supreme Soviet

Headed up by the president; the coordinating organ of the new Supreme Soviet.

The Council of Ministers

Functions remain unchanged, although some reduction in size is likely.

which the leader of the executive branch of government dominates a system in which power is divided, but must contend with powerful forces in the other branches of government. The changes introduced by Gorbachev make possible the emergence of genuine "interest group" politics, focused on the legislative organs at the local, regional, and national levels, as a potential counterbalancing force to the power of the president. Only time will tell to what extent such a politics is permitted to develop, for these changes have unfolded against the background of a simmering conflict between popular groups and forces attempting to break down all constraints on political activity and conservative forces growing increasingly uneasy about their activity. And this has made Gorbachev's position in the political middle more difficult to maintain.

GLASNOST AND POPULAR POLITICS

The loosening of restrictions on the mass media initiated by Gorbachev quickly produced a differentiation of the Soviet media. In the past, Soviet newspapers and journals were closely supervised by the party propaganda and other departments, and were subjected to careful censorship. As a result, they varied only marginally in content. Under Gorbachev, newspapers, journals, and the broadcast media have been granted greater autonomy. Individual editors have assumed greater control over the content of their respective organs. A wider variety of views are now being expressed. And no one view is necessarily "official."

Some editors, and their journals, are outspoken supporters of Gorbachev and the process of *perestroika*. Others are more conservative in their views. As a result, public discourse in the Soviet Union has become characterized by open debates and even polemical exchanges in the media. One example is the ongoing debate over the "Stalin question." The media have published criticisms of Stalin and the terror far more severe than any published during the de-Stalinization effort led by Khrushchev. These have included not only calls for the rehabilitation of Stalin's victims, but also direct questions about the implications of the Stalin experience for understanding the nature of the existing Soviet system. At the same time, arguments in defense of the developmental achievements of Stalin have also been published.

The limits on public discourse are as yet uncertain. The media have published numerous stories on such hitherto "taboo" subjects as sex, AIDS, drugs, and draft dodging. But the ability to "explore the unknown" still appears to depend on "protection" from above. And, in the event that the most tolerant members of the leadership are removed, these limits might very well be redefined very narrowly.

Glasnost was accompanied by a parallel easing of constraints on political activity, as well. Unofficial groups and intellectual movements of the pre-Gorbachev era became open and new ones arose. Political "dissidents" of the 1970s became political "activists" in the 1980s. Numerous groups founded their own journals, including one that attempted to serve as an umbrella publication for independent political activity throughout the Soviet Union, under the title *glasnost*. Environmentalist groups, cultural preservationists, groups seeking political rehabilitation for the victims of Stalin and more general de-Stalinization, Jews seeking the right to emigrate, and nationalist movements among the Russians and non-Russian peoples all became more active under conditions of *glasnost*.

PERESTROIKA AND THE NATIONAL QUESTION

The rise of nationalist movements has been the most destabilizing development in the era of *glasnost*. Up to now, Russian dominance in the Soviet Union has rested upon two foundations: the firm control exercised by Moscow over the party, the political system, and the economy, on the one hand, and the incumbency of Russians or other Slavs in positions of power and authority, on the other. Central decision-making institutions in Moscow and key positions of command and control throughout the Soviet system have been staffed and led primarily by Russians, and national policies have been determined largely on the basis of central priorities. This system of elite control from the center has ensured the subordination of local interests to national ones on issues of importance to the center.

With the onset of *glasnost,* however, local aspirations for increased autonomy have formed the basis for organized public protest across the Soviet Union. In the Baltic republics of Latvia, Lithuania, and especially Estonia, long-suppressed popular resentment of the Soviet annexation of these previously independent countries, and their subjection to culturally alien Russian rule, has given rise to mass movements seeking to establish cultural and economic autonomy from Moscow. These movements are able to mobilize tens of thousands of people for street demonstrations in support of their positions. They have become de facto opposition political parties, nominating and electing their own candidates to local and national political office and advancing their own platforms of political reform.

In the formerly underdeveloped regions of Kazakhstan and Central Asia, accelerated social modernization and material development created modern native elites with a large stake in the success of the Soviet system. Under Brezhnev, increasing numbers of them were promoted to leading positions in their home territories and began to play more prominent roles in Moscow. Local elites everywhere enjoyed expanded local autonomy. As part of the general effort to shake off the lethargy that had blanketed the system in the later Brezhnev years, Russian predominance was reasserted in Moscow and closer central control was reasserted over all local territories, including the non-Russian ones.

Not all the conscessions that had been made to local prerogatives under Brezhnev could be withdrawn, however. When the native party leader of Kazakhstan was replaced with an ethnic Russian in December 1986, Kazakh university students and would-be native elites engaged in a violent demonstration in Alma-Ata in defense of their claims to elite status and local autonomy.

The depth of popular support for local demands for autonomy appears to have produced a significant retreat by Gorbachev from the post-Brezhnev attempt to reduce that autonomy. A month after the Alma-Ata events, Gorbachev conceded in an address to the Central Committee that policy toward the nationalities required "special tact and care." He acknowledged the need to ensure the representation of all groups in leading positions in the party, state, and economy—a statement that stood in sharp contrast to the Russification of the leadership underway up to then. In another report to the Central Committee in June 1987, he included ethnic group interests among those he identified as interests that would have to be taken into account in the policymaking process. And in his report to the February 1988 plenum of the Central Committee, he elevated the national question to an issue of "vital" importance and called for increasing the role of the national republics in the Soviet state political system, including their representation in central political organs.

The February plenum took place against the background of rising ethnic tensions in the Caucasus, where relations between Christian Armenians and Muslim Azerbaidzhanis have long been characterized by conflict and even violence. In Armenia, local activists organized mass demonstrations in support of demands to reestablish Armenian sovereignty over their co-nationals in the Nagorno-Karabakh region of the neighboring Azerbaidzhani republic. Tensions between Armenians and Azerbaidzhanis in that region produced sporadic episodes of interethnic violence. But Azerbaidzhani resentment of Armenian demands exploded in mass violence in late February 1988, when Azerbaidzhanis indiscriminately attacked the Armenian residents of the Azerbaidzhani city of Sumgait, killing more than 30. The rapid escalation of the Armenian-Azerbaidzhani conflict into ethnic violence and rioting compelled Moscow to establish martial law in the region.

The continued festering of Armenian-Azerbaidzhani tensions, despite the direct military and political intervention of Moscow, reflects a tragic political dynamic characteristic of conflicts in many multiethnic societies. Additional episodes of ethnic violence in Uzbekistan and Kazakhistan, and demonstrations in Georgia in spring 1989 raise the direct threat of the disintegration of the Soviet political system, a threat that strengthens the position of conservative opponents to *perestroika*.

Nationalist unrest in the Baltic republics, the Causasus, and Central Asia has been accompanied by the rise of Russian nationalist sentiments in the central regions of the country, and especially in the large cities of European Russia. The views expressed by nationalist Russian literary and other cultural figures range from the most liberal to the most reactionary. The group that has drawn the most widespread popular support, however, has been the Russian nationalist organization *pamyat*, or "memory." "Memory" is both chauvinistic and anti-Semitic, and has adopted behaviors reminiscent of German and Italian fascism of the interwar period, including the adoption of a "uniform" of black shirts. The cultural, economic, and environmental issues it raises reflect the accumulated resentments of Russians who view the developmental benefits that have accrued to the non-Russian peoples and territories under Soviet rule as having come at the expense of Russia and the Russian people. And it unites the two most powerful sources of resistance to *perestroika:* cultural conservatism and political neo-Stalinism.

OPPOSITION TO CHANGE

Because of the closed nature of the Stalinist system, and the continuing level of censorship and control under Khrushchev and even Brezhnev, much of Western analysis of Soviet politics has tended to focus on the status and views of individuals in the Kremlin leadership, and their potential roles as sources of political opposition. Clearly, elite sponsorship continues to play a central role in contemporary Soviet politics, and careful study of leadership politics remains an important basis for understanding it. Indeed, the most dramatic outbreak of open opposition to *perestroika* has been attributed to the sponsorship of Ligachev. But *perestroika* represents a fundamental assault on the existing distribution of power and privilege throughout Soviet society, not just within the elite. Therefore, any effort to assess the chances of success for *perestroika* must place the day-to-day vagaries of elite politics, and especially Politburo politics, into a broader social, if not sociopolitical, context.

Changes in Soviet society, and in the level of tolerance for popular political activity, have increased the sensitivity of social groups to the potential consequences of reform, and have made it possible for them to act in suppport of, or opposition to them. Ultimately, it is the balance of popular opposition and support that will determine the fate of *perestroika* and its chief architect, for real change depends on changes in mass values and behavior. In the absence of such change, *perestroika* must fail. As such change takes hold, it will be increasingly difficult to oppose.

Up to now, the most pronounced resistance to change has come from social and political "conservatives" concerned about the loss of old values. Members of the vast network of ideological and educational workers trained under Stalinist conditions and socialized to Stalinist values, including the thousands of teachers of "Marxism-Leninism" courses at all levels of the educational system; members of the cultural and academic intelligentsias whose careers were established under the old system, and for whom the new conditions of openness and competition threaten to overturn the prestige of their past work and personal status; and members of the party and state apparatuses for whom *perestroika* means the loss of power and privileges all represent important sources of support for resistance to change.

The most dramatic expression of their resistance came in March 1988, in a "letter" ostensibly written by a Leningrad schoolteacher, Nina Andreeva, and published in the conservative Moscow newspaper, *Sovetskaia Rossiia*. The "letter" appears actually to have been drafted by members of Ligachev's staff and published as a call-to-arms for the conservative opposition in preparation for the party conference called by Gorbachev for June 1988. The Andreeva "letter" represented an attack on Gorbachev's attempt to open the Soviet past to full, critical reexamination. It was openly Stalinist, anti-intellectual, anti-Semitic, ethnocentric, and xenophobic in character. It became the centerpiece of a campaign by Ligachev and other conservatives to set such narrow intellectual and political limits on discussion of the past as to undermine *perestroika*. This campaign was defeated only by a determined effort by Gorbachev, beginning with a full-page counterattack in *Pravda* in early April.

Conservative opposition to *perestroika* did not end with the April counteroffensive, however. Even at the party conference called by Gorbachev as a means of mobilizing political support for reform and convened in June, prominent members of the political and cultural elite staked out positions far more conservative than those advanced by Gorbachev. And their positions were rein-

forced in later months by government actions to restrict the activities of private entrepreneurs, and a call for restrictions on the activities of independent political groups by the conservative Politburo member and party secretary, Chebrikov. The former chief of the KGB, Chebrikov reflected views already being expressed publicly by other security officials.

Underlying calls for such restrictions may be an increasing concern on the part of some members of the leadership about the growing potential for mass unrest among the Russian urban industrial work force. For the common citizen, *perestroika* has meant a perceptible worsening of material conditions, including simultaneous price increases and widening shortages of food and consumer goods. Moreover, economic reform has put an end to the job security heretofore enjoyed even by the least productive workers. For some Soviet workers, unemployment—long criticized by official propaganda as an evil of capitalist exploitation—has already become a reality. Such conditions contributed to the rise of worker unrest and the creation of the Solidarity movement in Poland. And, while Russian workers are very different from Polish workers, any outbreak of workers' strikes would represent a far more serious political challenge to the regime than the nationalist demonstrations it has faced up to now.

Paradoxically, some elements of *perestroika* have also met with resistance from some liberal intellectuals, who otherwise have been its strongest supporters. As Gorbachev accumulated increasing personal power and began to reconstruct the central organs of government, some intellectuals appear to have grown concerned about creating conditions for the potential reemergence of a dictator. Others, in the ethnic peripheries, appear to have grown wary of the centralization of decision-making power in Moscow inherent in proposals for constitutional reform. Still others appear to have grown impatient with the continuing refusal to permit the creation of opposition parties.

PROSPECTS AND DANGERS OF CHANGE

The 1980s have seen the gradual emergence of Soviet society as a partially autonomous force in Soviet politics. This process accelerated under conditions of *glasnost*. Gorbachev is attempting to mobilize the support of those forces seeking reform for a major reorganization and reduction in power of the party and state bureaucracies. However, Gorbachev continues to reserve to the Communist party alone the right to define the direction and parameters of change, and political opposition—especially competing political parties—remain forbidden. Thus, the changes Gorbachev has introduced do not add up to the "democratization" of the Soviet Union; at least, not in the sense that "democracy" is understood in the West. Rather, they appear to be aimed at "modernizing" the one-party system.

The accumulation of increasing personal power by Gorbachev appears to be part of a dual strategy for increasing popular support for changes that will make one-party rule economically more efficient and socially less repressive, increase its popular legitimacy, and thereby strengthen its ability to resist forces calling for its overthrow. On the one hand, he appears intent on accumulating sufficient personal power to reduce and reconstruct the party and state bureaucracies in Moscow and limit their power over the economy and society. On the other, he appears intent on mobilizing popular participation and channeling it into more active representative organs of government, while subordinating these organs to the relegitimated political authority of the party and its leader.

Pursuing the first strategy, however, brings him into direct conflict with the party apparatus and the state bureaucracies, and the use of his power to impose economic reform brings him into conflict with a whole stratum of managerial elites whose power and privileges are threatened by the prospect of worker's self-management and the imposition of objective, efficiency-based performance criteria. Soviet managers accustomed to dealing with central decision makers in the context of a planned economy will have to develop entirely new skills for dealing with labor, controlling costs, and marketing products to demanding consumers. For party *apparatchiks* and state bureaucrats, the transfer of even limited decision-making authority to autonomous enterprises represents a major loss of power. As reform proceeds, provincial party secretaries in particular will begin to lose power to successful enterprise managers and other entrepreneurial actors in their territories. Gorbachev's proposal to have these provincial secretaries assume leadership of revitalized provincial soviets offers little compensation, for it promises to subject them to even greater direct popular pressures.

Alienation of the party *apparatchiki* at the center and the party secretaries in the provinces is potentially very dangerous. These are the very groups most heavily represented in the Central Committee and whose discontent over similar threats to their positions contributed to the overthrow of Khrushchev in 1964.

At the same time, pursuing the second strategy requires Gorbachev to continue to support *glasnost* and the expanded opportunities for popular political action that that creates. Gorbachev appears to be gambling that popular demands can be accommodated within the framework of a reformed Soviet political system. If this turns out to be the case, increased opportunities for meaningful political participation over time will themselves strengthen support for the system. Such institutionalization of popular participation might strengthen the legitimacy of the Soviet system sufficiently to permit it to withstand higher levels of everyday political activity, including political conflict. In effect, Gorbachev is gambling on the emergence of a "civil society" in the Soviet Union.

However, Gorbachev's necessary insistence on preserving the party's political monopoly undermines the credibility of his political reforms. Moreover, increasing the opportunities for independent political activity in the short run, while the economic crisis confronting the regime remains unresolved, raises the prospects of worker unrest arising out of worsening material conditions, nationalist conflict arising out of ethnic competition for scarce resources or straightforward demands for political autonomy, oppositional activity by intellectuals seeking more radical changes, and other forms of behavior likely to prompt a conservative backlash. For Gorbachev to succeed, therefore, he must contain popular political activity within limits acceptable to conservatives.

Thus, Gorbachev is engaged in a political balancing act. He must create a new set of political forces, and institutionalize them in power, at a rate faster than he dismantles the old order. To institutionalize a new political order, however, he must reduce the power of the old one. Yet he cannot allow the old order to be weakened too rapidly, lest the new political forces slip out of control, for his goal is to save the Soviet system, not destroy it. This is the contradiction inherent in any effort to reform an authoritarian regime, noted more than 130 years ago by Alexis de Tocqueville in his study *The Old Regime and the French Revolution.* He observed

it is not always when things are going from bad to worse that revolutions break out. On the contrary, it oftener happens that when a people which has put up with an oppressive ruler over a long period without protest suddenly finds the government relaxing its pressure, it takes up arms against it. Thus the social order overthrown by a revolution is almost always better than the one immediately preceding it, and experience teaches us that, generally speaking, the most perilous moment for a bad government is one when its seeks to mend its ways. Only consummate statecraft can enable a King to save his throne when after a long spell of oppressive rule he sets to improving the lot of his subjects. Patiently endured so long as it seemed beyond redress, a grievance comes to appear intolerable once the possibility of removing it crosses men's minds.

For the mere fact that certain abuses have been remedied draws attention to the others and they now appear more galling.[1]

BIBLIOGRAPHY

AGANBEGYAN, ABEL. *The Economic Challenge of Perestoika.* Bloomington: Indiana University Press, 1988).

ALEXEYEVA, LUDMILLA. *Soviet Dissent.* Middletown, CT: Wesleyan University Press, 1985.

ANWEILER, OSKAR. *The Soviets.* New York: Pantheon, 1974.

AZRAEL, JEREMY R. *Managerial Power and Soviet Politics.* Cambridge, MA: Harvard University Press, 1966.

BIALER, SEWERYN, ed. *Inside Gorbachev's Russia.* Boulder, CO: Westview, 1989.

———. *Stalin's Successors.* Cambridge: Cambridge University Press, 1980.

BLACK, CYRIL E., ed. *The Transformation of Russian Society.* Cambridge, MA: Harvard University Press, 1960.

BORNSTEIN, MORRIS, ed. *The Soviet Economy: Continuity and Change.* Boulder, CO: Westview, 1981.

CARR, EDWARD H. *A History of Soviet Russia: The Bolshevik Revolution, 1917–1923,* 3 vols. New York: Macmillan, 1951–1953.

COHEN, STEPHEN F. *Rethinking the Soviet Experience.* New York: Oxford University Press, 1985.

———. *Bukharin and the Bolshevik Revolution.* New York: Alfred A. Knopf, 1973.

COLTON, TIMOTHY J. *The Dilemma of Reform in the Soviet Union,* rev. and expanded ed. New York: Council on Foreign Relations, 1986.

CONNER, WALTER D. *Deviance in Soviet Society: Crime Delinquency and Alcoholism.* New York: Columbia University Press, 1972.

CONQUEST, ROBERT. *The Great Terror.* Harmondsworth, England: Pelican Books, 1971.

DALLIN, ALEXANDER, and GEORGE BRESLAUER. *Political Terror in Communist Systems.* (Stanford, CA: Stanford University Press, 1972).

———, and BERTRAND PATENAUDE. *Knowledge, Power, and Truth.* (Stanford, CA: Stanford University Center for Russian and East European Studies, 1988.

DANIELS, ROBERT V. *Is Russia Reformable?* Boulder, CO: Westview, 1988.

---

[1]Alexis de Tocqueville, *The Old Regime and the French Revolution,* new translation by Stuart Gilbert (Garden City, NY: Doubleday/Anchor Books, 1955), pp. 176–177.

———. "Office Holding and Elite Status: The Central Committee of the CPSU." In Paul Cocks, Robert V. Daniels, and Nancy Whittier Heer, eds., *The Dynamics of Soviet Politics.* (Cambridge, MA: Harvard University Press, 1976).

———. *The Conscience of the Revolution.* New York: Simon & Schuster, 1969.

FAINSOD, MERLE. *Smolensk Under Soviet Rule.* New York: Vintage Book, n.d.

———. *How Russia is Ruled.* rev. edi. Cambridge; Harvard University Press, 1963).

GOLDMAN, MARSHALL I. *USSR in Crisis: The Failure of an Economic System.* (New York: W. W. Norton, 1983).

GORBACHEV, MIKHAIL. *Perestroika: New Thinking for Our Country and the World.* New York: Harper & Row, 1987.

GREGORY, PAUL R., and R. L. STUART. *Soviet Economic Structure and Performance,* 2nd ed. New York: Harper & Row, 1981.

GROSS, NATALIE. "Glasnost: Roots and Practice." *Problems of Communism,* vol. no. 36, 6 (November–December 1987), pp. 69–80.

HEWETT, ED A. *Reforming the Soviet Economy.* Washington, DC: The Brookings Institution, 1988.

HOLLANDER, GAYLE. *Soviet Political Indoctrination: Developments in Mass Media and Propaganda Since Stalin.* New York: Praeger, 1972.

HOUGH, JERRY F. "Gorbachev Consolidating Power." *Problems of Communism,* Vol. no. 36, 4 (July–August 1987), pp. 21–43.

———. *The Soviet Prefects.* Cambridge, MA: Harvard University Press, 1969.

KHRUSHCHEV, NIKITA S. *Khrushchev Remembers: The Last Testament,* trans. and ed. by Strobe Talbott. Boston: Little, Brown, 1974.

———. *Khrushchev Remembers,* trans. by Strobe Talbott. Boston: Little, Brown, 1970.

LAPIDUS, GAIL WARSHOFSKY. "Social Trends." In Robert F. Byrnes, ed., *After Brezhnev,* pp. 186–249. Bloomington: Indiana University Press, 1983.

LEWIN, MOSHE. *The Making of the Soviet System.* New York: Pantheon, 1985.

MCAULEY, ALASTAIR. *Economic Welfare in the Soviet Union.* Madison: The University of Wisconsin Press, 1979).

MCAULEY, MARTIN. *The Soviet Union Under Gorbachev.* London: Macmillan, 1987.

MEDVEDEV. ROY A. *Let History Judge,* trans. by Colleen Taylor, ed. by David Joravsky and Georges Haupt. New York: Vintage Books, 1973.

MILLAR, JAMES R., ed. *Politics, Work, and Daily Life in the USSR: A Survey of Former Soviet Citizens.* New York: Cambridge University Press, 1987.

MOORE, BARRINGTON, JR. *Terror and Progress— USSR.* New York: Harper & Row, 1966.

MOTYL, ALEXANDER J. *Will the Non-Russians Rebel?* Ithaca, NY: Cornell University Press, 1987.

NOVE, ALEC. *An Economic History of the USSR.* New York: Penguin Books, 1984.

ODOM, WILLIAM. "How Far Can Reform Go?" *Problems of Communism,* Vol. 36, no. 6 (November–December 1987), pp. 18–33.

OSBORNE, ROBERT J. *Soviet Welfare Policies.* Homewood, IL: Dorsey, 1970.

PIPES, RICHARD. *The Formation of the Soviet Union,* rev. ed. New York: Atheneum, 1968.

RIGBY, T. H. "Stalinism and the Mono-Organizational Society." In Robert C. Tucker, ed., *Stalinism,* pp. 53–76. New York: W. W. Norton, 1977.

———. *Communist Party Membership in the USSR 1917–1967.* Princeton, NJ: Princeton University Press, 1968.

ROSENFELDT, NIELS ERIK. *Knowledge and Power: The Role of Stalin's Secret Chancellery in the Soviet System of Government.* Copenhagen: Rosenkilde and Bagger, 1978.

SCHAPIRO, LEONARD. *The Communist Party of the Soviet Union,* new ed. rev. and enlarged. New York: Vintage Books, 1971.

SIMIS, KONSTANTIN. *USSR: The Corrupt Society.* New York: Simon & Schuster, 1982.

TATU, MICHEL. *Power in the Kremlin* New York: Viking Press, 1969.

TUCKER, ROBERT C. *Political Culture and Leadership in Soviet Russia: From Lenin to Gorbachev.* New York: W. W. Norton, 1987.

———. "Stalinism as Revolution from Above." In Robert C. Tucker, ed., *Stalinism,* pp. 77–108. New York: W. W. Norton, 1977.

ULAM, ADAM B. *Stalin.* New York: Viking Press, 1973.

VOSLENSKY, MICHAEL. *Nomenklatura.* Garden City, NY: Doubleday, 1984.

WOLFE, BERTRAM D. *Three Who Made a Revolution,* 4th rev. ed. New York: Dell, 1964.

Index